The Louisiana Purchase Bicentennial Series
in
Louisiana History

Glenn R. Conrad, General Editor

VOLUME I
THE FRENCH EXPERIENCE IN LOUISIANA

VOLUME II
THE SPANISH PRESENCE IN LOUISIANA, 1763 - 1803

VOLUME III
THE LOUISIANA PURCHASE
AND ITS AFTERMATH, 1800 - 1830

VOLUME IX
LOUISIANA SINCE THE LONGS
1960 TO CENTURY'S END

VOLUME X
A REFUGE FOR ALL AGES:
IMMIGRATION IN LOUISIANA HISTORY

VOLUME XI
THE AFRICAN AMERICAN EXPERIENCE IN LOUISIANA
PART A: FROM AFRICA TO THE CIVIL WAR
PART B: FROM THE CIVIL WAR TO JIM CROW

VOLUME XIII
AN UNCOMMON EXPERIENCE:
LAW AND JUDICIAL INSTITUTIONS
IN LOUISIANA, 1803 - 2003

VOLUME XV
VISIONS AND REVISIONS
PERSPECTIVES ON
LOUISIANA SOCIETY AND CULTURE

VOLUME XVI
AGRICULTURE AND
ECONOMIC DEVELOPMENT
IN LOUISIANA

VOLUME XVIII
EDUCATION IN
LOUISIANA

The Louisiana Purchase Bicentennial Series in Louisiana History

VOLUME XI

THE
AFRICIAN AMERICAN EXPERIENCE
IN LOUISIANA

Part B

From the Civil War
to
Jim Crow

EDITED BY

CHARLES VINCENT

CENTER FOR LOUISIANA STUDIES
UNIVERSITY OF LOUISIANA
AT LAFAYETTE

2000

Front Endsheets:

Courtesy of The Historic New Orleans Collection
Acc. No. 1974.25.9.326

Back Endsheets:

Photograph by Russell Lee
From the Farm Security Administration Collection, Library of Congress

Library of Congress Catalog Number: 96-84494
ISBN Number: 1-887366-37-7

Published by The Center for Louisiana Studies
P.O. Box 40831
University of Louisiana at Lafayette
Lafayette, LA   70504-0831

CONTENTS

SECTION III   POST RECONSTRUCTION: THE STRUGGLE FOR SURVIVAL
WITH HUMANITY

ABOUT THE EDITOR

Charles Vincent is a professor of History at Southern University and A & M College (Baton Rouge). He earned the Ph. D. in history from Louisiana State University. He is the author of *Black Legislators in Louisiana During Reconstruction*; and *A Centennial History of Southern University and A & M College, 1880-1980* and articles in professional journals. He has served as Eminent Scholar at Virginia State University, and is the recipient of the University Presidential Faculty Excellence Award, 1994, and 1996 Preservation Award of the Foundation for Historical Louisiana.

ACKNOWLEDGMENTS

A broader appreciation and awareness of the African American contribution to Louisiana's history and culture are my objectives. The scholarly works by numerous authors were instrumental in attempting to fulfill these goals. I am grateful to the vision of Glenn R. Conrad and his staff, especially Carl Brasseaux and Regina M. LaBiche, for this series and their confidence in permitting me to pursue this compilation as well as their strong support of my efforts. God has smiled on me and my family during this journey. My lovely wife Deloris and our children—Shari, Charles Lerone, and Shaun—have been extremely supportive. Indeed, my oldest son, Charles Lerone, was my principle typist, letting me infringe upon his college breaks as well as foregoing his development of some "basketball skills" to assist. Several students helped with bibliographical searches, exemplary are the efforts of Marva Spencer, Kitty B. Hollins, Candace Wright, LaShanda Nelson, Catherine LeBeouf and Stephanie Smith. The assistance of the Mwalimu Institute for the Study of People of African descent in Louisiana and the Western Hemisphere is greatly appreciated. The shortcomings and omissions are clearly my own.

ABOUT THE SERIES

It was in the spring of 1992 that first thought was given to the matter of how best the Center for Louisiana Studies might commemorate the bicentennial of the Louisiana Purchase in 2003. For the next few months the Center's staff and members of its Advisory Council intermittently discussed the possible project, but no consensus was forthcoming. Perhaps the reason being that the Purchase looms so monumentally in United States history there are seemingly few memorials of proper proportion to commemorate the event's bicentennial.

Nevertheless, as time passed the outlines of a project began to take shape. To properly mark the occasion the Center for Louisiana Studies should produce a lasting tribute not only to the people who crafted the Louisiana Purchase but also to the people who, during the last two hundred years, have had a role in transforming that vast wilderness into the heartland of America. But the Center's focus is not mid-America for all practical purposes, it is Louisiana, the state that took its name from the Purchase territory. Therefore, the Center's project would concentrate on a Purchase bicentennial memorial that embraced the full range of Louisiana history.

There was another reason for this decision. In March of 1999 the Gulf Coast and the Mississippi Valley would mark the tercentennial of the founding of the French colony of Louisiana and the beginning of the region's historical era. Thus, if the Center's endeavor for the Purchase bicentennial was to be a history of Louisiana, then it should tell not only about the American experience in the area but also the Native American, French, Spanish, African, British and other influences that helped to lay the foundations for the present-day state.

Questions arose: Will the Center's Purchase bicentennial memorial be yet another history of Louisiana? If so, should it be another survey or should it be a more detailed account? Who would write this account of our times and those of our forebears? What interpretation would emerge from such a monograph? Who was expert enough to incorporate a harmonious blend of the political, economic, and social ingredients of our society?

Another year slipped by while we pondered these and other questions concerning the Center's memorial to the Purchase bicentennial and the tercentennial of the founding of the colony. After more discussion, there began to emerge a collective concept that was at once imaginative, exciting, and, above all, challenging. As a fitting memorial for the Louisiana Purchase bicentennial, the Center would organize and direct the publication of a major historical series. Marking the anniversaries, however, should not be the only reason for such an endeavor.

As discussion of the nature of the series evolved, it became obvious that there was an overriding reason for it. The series, to be known as the LOUISIANA PURCHASE BICENTENNIAL SERIES IN LOUISIANA HISTORY, would be a fine sampling of twentieth-century scholarship, particularly the scholarship of the last half of the century which embraced new methodologies leading to broader interpretations of the state's history. Here, in a multi-volume series the student of Louisiana history would be exposed to a wide range of scholarship reflecting multiple interpretations of historical events.

Thus, the decision was made; the Series would bring together in one place the very best articles, essays, and book parts that have been published about Louisiana in the twentieth century, particularly the latter half of the century. Its focus would be to inform scholars, teachers, students, and laypersons on far-ranging topics of Louisiana history drawn from a great reservoir of scholarship found in media ranging from scholarly to popular to obscure.

Most important to the development of such a series, however, was the person or persons who would select the "very best" to incorporate into the Series. The answer came quickly, only widely recognized experts, acting as volume editors, would determine from the broad spectrum of sources those essays which reflect the best in research, writing, and interpretation on topics in Louisiana history.

Initially, twenty broad topics of Louisiana history were identified, and the Center plans to publish these twenty volumes between 1995 and 2003. There may be additional volumes, if they are warranted. It should be noted, however, proper presentation of some topics in Louisiana history cannot be confined to a single book; hence, some volumes may incorporate several parts in order to present the full spectrum of scholarship on the subject. Finally, the volumes will not be published in sequential order, although Volume I, *The French Experience in Louisiana* was the first to appear. Each volume will be announced upon publication.

THE LOUISIANA PURCHASE BICENTENNIAL SERIES IN LOUISIANA HISTORY presents a great source of information for anyone interested in the history of the colony and the state. It stands as an appropriate memorial to the men and women who shaped the colony and state down to the dawn of the twenty-first century.

Glenn R. Conrad, General Editor

INTRODUCTION

As indicated in the Introduction to Part A of this volume, people of African descent have had an enigmatic experience in Louisiana. Their presence and contributions have been major components in the state's history despite the fact that they have not been widely acknowledged. During the period of exploration, even before Columbus, and before the days of slavery, they went to many parts of the world in various capacities—shipmates, servants, laborers, and leaders.[1] Upon their arrival in Louisiana as slaves early in the eighteenth century, they brought more than muscle and brute strength. Their techniques in rice production, indigo processing, and farming were legendary among their skills. Sadly, recognition of their capabilities and its importance to Louisiana have yet to be fully appreciated.

In a sense, blacks have been the unsung heroes and heroines of Louisiana's history. Their lives have been characterized by such themes as the struggle for survival, resistance to oppression, advancement against odds, artistic and literary triumphs, unity and upward mobility. The task of demanding America to be "America for all of its citizens" has an endearing and solid history among blacks in Louisiana. In some respects, African Americans in the Pelican State are unique in this regard. Many of the most significant landmark events in race relations in the nation's history have occurred in Louisiana.

Part B of *The African American Experience in Louisiana* is presented in chronological arrangement and details events from the Civil War to the end of the nineteenth century. Confronting the most pivotal event in the country's history, the Civil War, blacks welcomed an end to slavery and a new beginning for the state and nation. Though no longer slaves, a more uncertain and precarious lifestyle would burden African Americans after the war, Reconstruction, and Redemption. The enigmatic experience of the African American in Louisiana during slavery, which I mentioned in the Introduction to Part A of this work, would continue throughout the remainder of the nineteenth century. Indeed, the nadir of their existence in the Pelican State occurred after all avenues to full citizenship were blocked by resurgent white supremacists.

This compilation of scholarly essays is necessarily selective owing to allotted space. The reader should be aware, therefore, that there are numerous scholarly essays which further enhance knowledge of the era from 1861 to 1900. Authors contributing to the historiography of the era, but whose work could not be included are Lawrence Lee Hewitt, Caryn Cossé Bell, Joseph Logsdon, Arnold Hirsch, Donald DeVore, Nell Irvin Painter, John Winters, Carolyn E. DeLatte, Donald Everett, Howard Westwood, Arthur Bergeron, Jr., James Haskins, Manoi K. Joshi, Joseph P. Reidy, Ira Berlin, Howard J. Jones, Germaine A. Reed, Riley E. Baker, C. Vann Woodward, Charles P. Roland, Lawrence N. Powell, Joe M. Richardson, Keith Wilson, Joseph Carlyle Sitterson, Roger W. Shugg, James D. Wilson, Michael Lanza, Jerry Purvis Sanson, David Rankin, Morgan Peoples, T. Harry Williams, William McFeely, Allen Trelease, Donald E. Reynolds, Paul A. Kunkel, Otto H. Oslen, Mark T. Carleton, and Geraldine McTigue. Moreover, several of the authors included in this work have other works which had to be omitted. A selective bibliography for further reading appears at the end of Part B.

Section I tells of the Civil War which was viewed by blacks as a fight for liberation that began in April, 1861, when Confederate forces fired on Fort Sumter, South Carolina. This struggle opened an era of deliverance from bondage for African Americans. From the outset, there were doubts among white Louisianians about black support for the Confederacy. The Confederate leadership had a difficult time controlling slaves but were willing to utilize their labor to release whites for military duty. Peter Ripley's "Confederate Slavery" documents how blacks left plantations at critical times, burned plantation buildings, shot at patrols, ran away, and in general conducted a slowdown of the work routine. These slaves "damaged the system," Ripley asserts "to the extent that anything short of abolition would have been cumbersome and nugatory."

Whites harbored constant fears and fantasies about black reaction to the war. Even Federal military officials, after arriving in southern Louisiana, instituted programs and policies to control blacks. Many slaves who ran away from plantation routines were forced to return to their masters. Federal generals who utilized blacks as soldiers "were on a collision course" with their commanders, according to William Messner's "Black Violence and White Response. . . . " The image of blacks that emerged was that of a docile individual after the "reimposition of order by the Union military signaled a reversion to the Sambo image of the Afro-American [sic]." Commanding officers still considered blacks as "a burden and desired to place the slaves under the control of their masters." Eventually, however, the value of utilizing black labor was confirmed during the campaign against Vicksburg in the summer of 1862, observes Messner in his article on the "Vicksburg Campaign." The "Union effort is historically interesting for it was a transitional phase in the Federal utilization of black labor in the Southwest." Prior to the campaign "Federal authorities had shown little interest in utilizing the manpower of the above population in Louisiana and had even attempted to buttress the peculiar institution in 'loyal' areas of the state." The value of the black man to the Union's cause would be reflected in the treatment they received after this ill-fated effort against Vicksburg.

Although black soldiers were not initially welcomed by the Federal authorities, once enlisted these men would write a new chapter in the annals of black history on the continent. The black military units that were eventually permitted to serve as Union soldiers—called Native Guards—and their struggle to participate offers another chapter in this history. The question of their willingness to fight as well as their bravery and valor in the attack on the Confederate fortress at Port Hudson are discussed by Mary Frances Berry in "Negro Troops in Blue and Grey" and by James G. Hollandsworth, Jr., in "I Regard It as an Experiment" and in "Unsuited for This Duty." Although first regarded as "an experiment" the black soldiers' conduct and courage in combat changed the nation's perception of African Americans resolve to make the war one of liberation. Berry writes that "the conduct of the Negro troops at Port Hudson was a milestone." They fought splendidly asserts Hollandsworth, yet they endured many indignities and their black officers were dismissed or forced out of service as "unsuited for their duty."

The sentiment and contribution of the Natchitoches *gens de couleur libre* of Isle Brevelle are discussed by Gary B. Mills in "Patriotism Frustrated: The Native Guards of Confederate Natchitoches." Obviously liberation had a different meaning for their participation. Mills observes: "shades of allegiance to the status quo, shades of militancy to the cause of freedom, and shades of brotherhood between the free man and the slaves, and the black man and part-black man were as diverse as were the shades of their skin and the economic and cultural opportunities that they enjoyed." For slaves, abandonment of the plantation, plans for insurrections, conspiracy, and hampering the Confederate war efforts were constantly on their agenda and of grave concern to the Confederate legislature and administration. Junius P. Rodriguez's "We'll Hang Jeff Davis on a Sour Apple Tree . . ." chronicles the numerous hangings of slaves for insurrectionist sentiment and activities.

Section I ends with Herman Belz's article, "Origins of Negro Suffrage during the Civil War." The liberation African Americans sought in fighting for the Union cause would be reflected in their quest for political participation. Belz finds the origins of black suffrage during the war in Louisiana because the state became a focal point for Presidential Reconstruction and because "the free Negro community in New Orleans, numbering about ten thousand blacks, most of whom owned property and were educated, demanded the right to vote."

No group as voters and participants in the political process has had its role more misrepresented by contemporaries and by posterity than black reconstructionists, according to John Hope Franklin.[2] Section II opens with Charles Vincent's articles on "Black Louisianians . . . ," "Antoine Dubuclet . . .," John W. Blassingame's "Land, Labor and Capital," and Robert Moran's "Local Black Elected Officials. . . ." These authors represent a more balanced revisionist view than earlier accounts of black officials. They indicate that black leaders were competent, compassionate, and offered beneficial programs and legislation for all citizens of the state. Black reconstructionist concerns for state supported schools, civil rights, and social legislation had a modern cast and formed an agenda that was appropriate for all citizens. In New Orleans, African Americans continued to work and held on to jobs, according to Blassingame and "this was their most important economic victory." In spite of the collapse of the Freedmen's Saving and Trust

Company in 1874, their distrust of banks did not halt their efforts to hold on to their "one-owner, service-oriented concerns and to establish commission houses and grocery stores."

Other issues confronting African Americans and their quest for full citizenship involved "The General Merchants and Crop Lien" observes Joe Gray Taylor. The "misfortune of Louisiana planters, farmers, and sharecroppers in Louisiana" was, asserts Taylor, "to live in an undeveloped agricultural economy which, because of its poverty and peculiar labor system had never developed adequate credit facilities and which had been further impoverished by war." Blacks faced unprecedented violence throughout Louisiana because the statewide efforts of the terrorist group Knights of the White Camelia "preempted the spread of the KKK," asserts James G. Dauphine. Gilles Vandal observes that this postwar violence in Caddo Parish was "closely linked to the redefinition of the black status and race relations. Whites particularly resented the assertiveness of the blacks who wanted to enjoy their new won freedom." The New Orleans violence as well as in other areas of the state was directed at black political participation and the opposition factions inability to gain black voters support, according to Melinda Meek Hennessey.

Blacks in the northern area of the state also faced many obstacles and harassment. Even Freedmen Bureau agent Marshall Twitchell who spent ten months as the Bureau's director in Bienville Parish witnessed "violent and contentious" environments asserts Ted Tunnell. The Bureau agent's duty was to acquaint planters and freedmen with "their changed relations from Master and slave to employer and employee giving them additional information that it was the order of the government that old master and old slave should remain where they had been (and) work as usual in the harvesting of the crop." Agents were "arbiters" in disputes concerning such issues as pay, working conditions or punishment, and education. The difficulties in the northwest area of Louisiana were compounded because of Freedmen's poverty, high water, poor cotton crops and white hostility.

Another great tragedy impeding African Americans was their inability to acquire confiscated and abandoned lands. Enacted in June 1866 by Congress the Southern Homestead Act "was designed to provide nearly forty-six million acres in five Southern states" but "proved relatively unsuccessful in Louisiana" argues Claude F. Oubre's "'Forty Acres and a Mule': Louisiana and the Homestead Act." Several factors facilitated this disappointment: assistant commissioners sympathetic to planters interest, inefficiency of the land officials, loyal whites favored railroad companies rather than aspirations of blacks to become landowners, and again white opposition and hostility. Even the expense and cost of traveling to New Orleans to file their affidavits "would be more that the value of the land under the graduation law" which set lower prices for public land at greater distance from railroad and navigable streams.

African Americans saw education as a vital instrument for upward mobility. Their enthusiasm according to Barry A. Crouch was singularly focused, involving building their own schools, communities, and churches. George T. Ruby of New York was an exemplary educator in the Freedmen's Bureau's desire to achieve what Howard Ashley

White labeled "Redeeming of the People from Ignorance." The racism and opposition to these efforts from conservatives were unrelenting. Efforts at integrated education was partially successful in New Orleans, writes Louis R. Harlan in "Desegregation in New Orleans Public Schools . . ." while in the rural or country schools "public school desegregation failed almost universally," asserts Roger A. Fischer. Similarly, African Americans desire to become landowners was hindered. "Plantations all over Louisiana," observe William E. Highsmith "remained in the hands of their antebellum owners or were transferred intact to banks, merchants, and other sources of credit."

Freedom to protest was one of the avenues that Reconstruction provided some blacks. Protest, boycotts, letter writing, and withholding funds would be utilized. "The New Orleans Car Controversy" was a pioneer protest inaugurated in 1867, observes Roger A. Fischer, and launched a challenge to the color line in public schools and places of public accommodation. Also, New Orleans experienced a degree of school desegregation according to Harlan. This benefitted black and white students in the Crescent City since there were "more white pupils in the public schools during desegregation than either before or after."

The post-Reconstruction years, outlined in Section III, witnessed a struggle for survival with dignity and humanity during the Bourbon regime. As the gains of Reconstruction slowly faded under a brutally repressive system, African Americans sought to consolidate gains and fought to retain some remnant of their civil rights. The retrenchment efforts of unfriendly forces as well as the war years and depression caused all elements of the black community to lose ground. The former free persons of color in antebellum Louisiana and their descendants owned less property and wealth in many areas of the state in 1900 than they did in 1860, argues Loren Schweninger. The "Loreauville Riot of 1884" is an excellent case study of the violence that accompanied many political elections before, during, and after Reconstruction. Gilles Vandal asserts that "the troubles that occurred in Iberia Parish during the summer and fall of 1884 show that politics under the Bourbons had degenerated into a moral cancer as political corruption, bribery, stuffing the ballot box, gross fraud, and intimidation became a means of governing and a part of the political culture of the state." Attempts to change the retrenchment tactics of the racist political leadership through strikes, union affiliation, and protest for higher wages and better working conditions were beaten back by white hegemony that eventually refused the populist inroads, asserts William Ivy Hair in "Black Protest and White Power." One avenue of last resort for relief was through the revolutionary action of migration, according to Joe Louis Caldwell in "Any Place But Here: Kansas Fever in Northeast Louisiana." Planters and landowners in the cotton areas of northeastern Louisiana were unwilling to implement a wage scale for laborers as had their counterparts in the sugar parishes. The Exodus when viewed from its original ideological perspective, asserts Caldwell, "was a black nationalist movement aimed at finding a permanent home for the dispossessed and despised black masses of the Lower Mississippi Valley."

Other revolutionary actions taken by a few African Americans involved armed retaliation and resistance. Robert Charles, an obscure black laborer drew national headlines when an encounter with New Orleans police caused a race riot in August 1900. He became an instant hero among some blacks. William Ivy Hair's "1208 Saratoga Street" details this gripping saga. On the other hand, the waterfront workers alliances on the New Orleans docks "challenged the strictures of white supremacy at the dawn of the Jim Crow era," asserts Eric Arnesen in "Biracial Unions in the Age of Segregation, 1893-1901."

Race relations in Louisiana continued to endure a roller-coaster existence until 1898, according to Henry C. Dethloff and Robert B. Jones in "Race Relations in Louisiana, 1877-1898" as well as Dale Somers's in "Black and White New Orleans. . . ." By 1898 Dethloff and Jones observe, segregation was "a permanent and thorough system of race relations." The great majority of white Louisianians, they observed, "believed in white supremacy and had never accepted as a means of racial adjustment a life in 'terms of quality' with the Negro." Thus Jim Crowism was "devised to maintain a white man's civilization." By the turn of the twentieth century, even in New Orleans, asserts Somers, "blacks in the city knew Jim Crow and racial intimidation as intimately as blacks in the countryside." The Robert Charles incident further established the pattern for "Negro-white relations for the next half century."

Part C of this volume will offer an account of the African American experience in Louisiana from the Jim Crow era to contemporary times.

Notes for "Introduction"

[1] Ivan Van Sertima, *They Came Before Columbus* (New York, 1976); Benjamin Brawley, *A Social History of the American Negro, Being a History of the Negro Problem in the United States, Including a History and Study of the Republic of Liberia* (New York, 1921), 2-3: Carter G. Woodson, *Negro in Our History* (Washington, 1922), 58; Leo Wiener, *Africa and the Discovery of America*, 3 vols. (Philadelphia, 1920-1922), vol. 1.

[2] John Hope Franklin, *Reconstruction After the Civil War* (Chicago, 1961), 133.

SECTION I
CIVIL WAR: THE FIGHT FOR LIBERATION

CONFEDERATE SLAVERY*

C. Peter Ripley

I Know why the caged bird sings, ah me,
When his wing is bruised and his bosom sore,—
When he beats his bars and he would be free;
It is not a carol of joy or glee,
But a prayer that he sends from his heart's deep core,
But a plea, that upward to Heaven he flings—
I know why the caged bird sings!
    —Paul Laurence Dunbar

When Edward Ruffin pulled the lanyard and sent a shot at Fort Sumter, he ultimately did more damage to the foundations of slavery than to the walls of that crumbling citadel. Only with quick, total victory could the South have saved her labor system. As the war continued from year to year, it brought de facto emancipation closer and closer. Institutional slavery was protected by state laws which legalized it and by court decisions which held slaves as sacrosanct as any private property. Yet historians generally acknowledge that more than laws and court decisions were necessary to sustain the peculiar institution. Rewards and incentives in any number of forms were common, as was corporal punishment from the perfunctory to the sadistic; the isolation of plantation life reinforced the system as did the monotony and routine of plantation labors; the threat of the auction block and the prospect of being owned by a new and possibly more severe master usually restrained slaves—as did some aspects of religion. But Eugene Genovese argues that a paternalistic master-slave relationship, more than any other feature or behavioral pattern, sustained slavery from within.[1]

---

*First published as Chapter 1 in C. Peter Ripley, *Slaves and Freedmen in Civil War Louisiana* (Baton Rouge: Louisiana State University Press, © 1976), 5-24. Reprinted with the kind permission of the author and the publisher.

The dominion of master over slaves was not absolute. Slaves maintained a considerable degree of conscious autonomy. John W. Blassingame concludes that within the slave community—away from the immediate supervision of the overseer or owner—slaves turned to their distinctive culture, their families, and their religion as buffers against harsher realities. Nevertheless, Blassingame sees slave behavior "bound up with" any number of influences, including such sustaining qualities as the "nature of the antebellum plantation [and] the behavior of masters."[2]

Slaves responded in a wide variety of ways to plantation life, to masters, and to the legal and sustaining features of slave society. Many tried to avoid contact with whites by working inconspicuously and by challenging the plantation regimen only occasionally. The other extreme was the violent slave. In the Louisiana State Penitentiary on the eve of the Civil War, 100 of 330 inmates were slaves, 79 of whom were convicted of violent crimes against whites—29 of those for murder and 4 for poisoning. Those figures only hint at the violent response of slaves, in that they do not include similar cases which never left the plantation or the parish. Somewhere between inconspicuous laborers and murderers were slaves who went on "strike" by fleeing. As described by Ulrich B. Phillips, they were usually prompted by an immediate and specific grievance; they hid nearby, returning after a tenuous agreement was reached with the master.[3] Temporary runaways were common and many no doubt were "strikers" as Phillips contends. Yet the voluntary return of most "strikers" was less a matter of believing that they had concluded successful labor-relation negotiations, as Phillips suggests, than of knowing that they had little chance of complete escape.

Running away was a less viable response to bondage than is often acknowledged, and slaves seem to have shown greater wisdom regarding it (and mass revolt, for that matter) than have many observers who question why there was not more of both. A major reason is that chances for success were virtually nonexistent in the Deep South states. And Louisiana was one of the deepest. There was the patrol, the pass system, the dogs, and the need for food. Many slaves would not leave their families behind, and fleeing with them appreciably lessened the already minute chance for success. In parts of Louisiana the only routes for even temporary escape led through bayous and swamps, which were hazardous because of deadly wildlife and bloodsucking insects, and because few bondsmen could swim; most slaves were deliberately prevented from acquiring that skill, and, because of that disadvantage, the dogs often found the runaways at the river's edge.

A more fundamental question is—where could a runaway slave go to reach freedom from Louisiana? There was no place close enough to offer reasonable hope.[4] Most slaves had seen the results of abortive escape attempts—a whipping or the stocks for the fortunate, maiming by the dogs or death for the unfortunate. Masters assembled slaves to watch the punishment, for it provided a gory lesson on the futility of running. The obstacles, the hazards, the concern for family, the lack of a relatively close free area, and the cost of failure discouraged those attempting to escape Louisiana slavery.

Essentially the same factors pertained to mass revolts and insurrections. The controls, the isolation, the lack of communication, and the cost of failure made the idea a desperate one. Even if initially successful, few escaped the better armed and better mounted white population, for freedom was too far away. Every region had its Nat Turner, either in reality or in folklore, and part of the traditional retelling included the ultimate failure—the hanging, the burning, the whipping, and the imprisonment of participants.[5] Knowledge of the past and an understanding of the system within which they lived convinced most slaves that revolt, like running, was usually futile.

The parish patrol, one of the more overt sustaining features of slave society, frequently served to enforce the master-slave relationship, particularly off the plantation. From the winter of the secession crisis through the outbreak of war, planters turned their attention to the patrols. Where the night riders were already operating, their size, frequency of rounds, and responsibility were increased. In many parishes they had to be revived; in others they were organized for the first time.[6] Whether new or old, patrols were needed, claimed one planter, because of "convulsive movements" in the country which "breed discontent and [which] will tend inevitably to open revolt in the absence of proper restraints."[7]

To provide the proper restraints, parishes were divided into wards and canvassed by patrols made up of at least five men drawn from the white population between the ages of fifteen and fifty. Participation was compulsory, and captains were authorized to call on all citizens if necessary. In some parishes directors or captains had to be slave owners or sons of slave owners. During each canvass all slave quarters in the ward were visited if not searched. Refusal by a master or overseer to allow access to the cabins was punishable by fines from fifty to five hundred dollars per offense. In Pointe Coupée Parish all slave cabins were numbered and the number of occupants posted in a conspicuous place to aid the patrol.[8]

While patrols also served as home militias, their major function was to control the "service population." In the weeks following the outbreak of war, police juries enhanced the patrols' authority by passing new local ordinances which supplemented the master and the *Code Noir* in controlling slaves. According to these laws slaves could not go out without a pass, assemble outside the plantation, hold balls or dances on the plantation unless supervised, gamble, watch gambling, loiter, drink alcohol, own or possess a horse "with or without . . . consent," tan leather or make shoes, "buy, sell or trade on [their] own account," or own a boat, dog, or weapon of any kind.[9] Whites and free blacks cooperating with a slave in any violation received fines or prison terms. Offending bondsmen received the lash. In theory and practice the entire black population was under the complete control of the patrols. Normally, only in capital cases did they need additional authority to inflict punishment.[10]

Despite stronger slave codes and revived parish patrols which supplemented the legal and sustaining features of slavery, the Civil War in Louisiana undermined the institution. The supportive influences could not offset the impact of Confederate hiring and impressment of slave laborers, of disruption and dislocation produced by refugee masters, of an increase in runaways and slave violence, of Federal raids, of Union capture of New Orleans, and of the presence of a blue-clad occupational army in southern Louisiana after April, 1862.

The Confederate government used slave labor as a means of releasing whites for military duty. For every black hired or impressed, a white could be armed and placed in uniform. Slaves built fortifications and worked on railroads, in salt works, coal mines, hospitals, saw mills, and in virtually every area of military and industrial activity.[11] The percentage of an owner's slaves eligible for impressment varied, but because of the early and continued Union threat in Louisiana, Confederate military authorities had wide discretionary powers in the matter. As early as the fall of 1862 the Confederate acting secretary of war wrote the commander at Port Hudson, Louisiana, that he should use all the resources at his command to defend his post. And even though planters were reluctant to furnish slaves to build fortifications, they could be called on "to contribute such a number of their slaves as may be needed for the purpose."[12] Two years later, in that part of Louisiana which was still Confederate all slaves and free blacks between eighteen and fifty years old were registered by the Bureau of Conscription and subject to call as laborers. Usually no more than one-seventh to one-fifth of the able-bodied hands were summoned, although state law provided that one-half the able-bodied males (ages eighteen through fifty) could be impressed.[13] Early in the war there were probably few states in the Confederacy where military hiring of slaves was used more widely than in Louisiana.

For slaves, working for the military was often a more difficult life than laboring on the plantation. Houses for impressed laborers at Fort Beauregard at Harrisburg, Louisiana, were sixty to seventy feet long, with no ventilation except one door. There were no sanitation facilities, no opportunities for bathing, no issuance of clean clothes, and no medical facilities. An irate surgeon wrote that "at present each negro had a space of *eleven inches wide and six feet long to his share*. If this state of things is continued half of these negroes will die of camp fever." And it does not appear that the surgeon was an alarmist, for a daily average of 10 percent of the slaves there were too ill to work.[14] The health situation at Harrisburg was not unusual, for "scores" of laborers returning from Port Hudson in early 1863 were described as mostly "sick and numbers of them have died of pnewmonia [*sic*]."[15]

Planters complained about the quality and quantity of the food, clothing, sanitary conditions and health treatment given their slaves in government employ. But they were even more concerned about physical abuse of their slaves hired by the army. Military authorities were repeatedly cautioned by superiors not to mistreat black laborers; soldiers were threatened with "severe penalties" for "maltreating, or beating . . . the slaves"—but with mixed success. In at least one instance planters refused to meet a call for one-third of their eligible laborers unless the military met certain conditions: planters would supply overseers to work the slaves and the military would assign a ward in the hospital for the slaves who would be attended by a planter-supplied doctor. Planters were demanding fair and humane treatment for their slaves, which, according to the planters, they had not been getting.[16] Shortly after this incident the Louisiana Legislature authorized owners whose slaves were impressed by the state or the Confederate States to provide overseers and "all things affecting their [slaves'] health and comfort." At the same time the legislature appropriated $500,000 "to pay for the hire or loss loss of slaves . . . by death or otherwise while employed . . . in the state."[17]

Civil authorities as well as the military hired slaves for building fortifications. Several parishes made a combined effort to defend the Red River area. The executive committee of that project was mindful of complaints against the military when it assured planters that their slaves would be well cared for. Transportation, food, shelter, medicine, and doctors were provided, and the committee personally guaranteed that "no slave shall be overtaxed or improperly treated." The civilians offered owners $25 per month per slave, $7 more than the army, and they, like the military, promised compensation for slaves lost through negligence.[18]

Throughout the war considerable competition existed for labor in Confederate Louisiana which added to the demands made of slaves. There was the normal, omnipresent plantation work. In addition, slaves were subject to call for labor on roads and levees in peacetime, and as the war dragged on and did more damage, that demand increased. But despite payment to planters of $1.50 and $2.00 a day per slave, levee and road inspectors had difficulty hiring a sufficient number of hands.[19] To these civilian needs were added the requests of various bureaus, agencies, and departments of the Confederacy. The Engineering Corps, the Quartermaster Department, the Transportation Department, the Ordinance Department, and the Cotton Bureau all wanted slave labor, and all made slave requisitions.[20]

Despite civilian and military needs, planters were reluctant to have their slave labor off the plantation. Even prior to the war many owners had to be threatened with fines before they would send bondsmen for levee or road work. The same was true during the war. But poor treatment and unfinished work on the plantation explain only part of the planters' reluctance. Planters realized the destructive effect that hiring and impressment practices had on the labor system. The sustaining qualities of isolation, dull routine, and monotonous plantation labors were threatened by moving about, changing jobs, and communication with other slaves. When sheriffs or squads of Confederate soldiers appeared on plantations and impressed workers, the effect was not lost on the slaves. Protests and objections by owners, when ultimately overruled, further eroded the master-slave relationship and the institution.

The disruptive influence of the war and Confederate policies on the stability of slavery are reflected by the increased acts of insubordination, resistance, and violence by slaves. For the most part those acts took the forms traditional to slavery: slowdowns became more common; runaways tended to offer greater resistance; house servants became "bolder," and many found themselves in the fields. Incidences of arson, murder, and insurrection rose also.[21] The state legislative appropriation for "paiement aux proprietaires d'esclaves convaincus de crimes"—including "crimes" such as murder, arson, or revolt, either successful or attempted—more than doubled the first year of the war.[22]

The arrival of a Federal army in southern Louisiana in April, 1862, accelerated the deterioration of institutional slavery and generated an increase in the number of runaways and in the amount of slave violence and insubordination in Confederate Louisiana. Securing the New Orleans area, Union forces made excursions into the interior of the state and extended their control. In order to escape the invaders many planters fled deeper into Louisiana, to Texas, or to Mississippi, abandoning homes, crops, and many times part of their labor force. They uprooted their families and left their way of life, in part, because they were aware that the presence of a hostile occupational army—even one dedicated to upholding slavery—would weaken the master-slave relationship and the institution. For those who fled when the military situation dictated, a single exodus was often not enough. One planter, perhaps typical, decided to leave the place and go to northern Louisiana "whenever it was apparent that the enemy are approaching," and planned that when northern Louisiana "becomes unsafe I will move further." Many who initially left Louisiana crossed into Mississippi, where they were forced to move again by a Federal threat there equal to the one in their own state. During one period the whole movement was described as a "panic," and for a time civilian traffic between the two states was stopped.[23] The movement of slaves to Texas was far more common than to Mississippi. A British traveler on the Louisiana-Texas border in the spring of 1863 wrote, "The road today was alive with negroes who are being run to Texas out of Banks' way. We must have seen hundreds of them." By early 1865, a resident of Bayou Boeuf, an area of large slaveholders, acknowledged that "most if not all of these families have removed their negroes to Texas."[24] The correspondence, diaries, and journals of those who either "ran" their slaves to Texas or offered hospitality to the refugees give an impression of a mass migration involving hundreds of whites and thousands of blacks. An even greater number made one or more moves to plantations of friends or relatives within the state.[25] The movement was so widespread that the already overtaxed Confederate forces in Louisiana were instructed "to render every assistance to planters removing their negroes, and to promote such action where negroes [are] at all liable to fall into the hands of the enemy."[26]

Yet, those masters who became refugees helped to undermine the master-slave relationship and the institution, for masters' and slaves' "running" was an experience which radically changed the determinants of that relationship. Planter paternalism often gave way to economic necessity as black wives and children were left behind and more valuable males went with masters. Isolation of slaves, much prized in the police jury regulations,[27] gave way to bondsmen mingling when traveling and when stopping at plantations. The dull routine of plantation life was replaced by dislocation and disruption in an exciting, if not panicked, wartime atmosphere. The master fleeing for his existence was not the same master who had ruled with whip and weapon when necessary. The aura of power and authority so central to his role in his slave system ebbed away as the plantation house was left behind; so too did the essence of the master-slave relationship.

Many planters did not flee; they remained at home in hopes of a Confederate victory, or awaited Federal occupation with cautious optimism. But they too witnessed the day-to-day destruction of their labor system and their way of life. This was true even in the parishes other than those initially controlled by Union forces, for Union lines provided a realistic destination for potential runaways. Although it is difficult to determine precise numbers, runaways apparently increased with the outbreak of war; after the fall of New Orleans they unquestionably increased. Once slaves had a destination, they left—singly, in groups and often as families—whenever they had the opportunity. A member of one of the larger planter families in Louisiana wrote in frustration: "I have feared for a long while that the negro would prove unreliable whenever an opportunity presented itself of their obtaining their freedom."[28]

Once Louisiana bondsmen had a realistic destination, such as Union-occupied parishes, not even the strict controls placed on black laborers in Confederate employment deterred them. In 1864, twenty slaves working on one rebel fortification left by boat; and although only seven managed to escape, the attempt by such a large number while under armed guard was a bold one. Others working in less well-supervised jobs had greater opportunity, though it is doubtful that any who wished to escape had better success than those assigned to the Cotton Bureau agent in Alexandria, Louisiana. On one occasion eight of the ten slaves assigned to the agent escaped. Two months later the same agent, after constant complaints of having insufficient help, was sent ten more black laborers; one escaped the first night and six more the next day.[29] Slaves no doubt understood that a flurry of activity to work on fortifications or to confiscate cotton meant the probable approach of a Federal army. Particularly in parts of Louisiana farthest from the occupied parishes, chances of escape were greater if Union troops could be met.

Newspapers and plantation journals increasingly mentioned runaways through 1861, but from the spring and summer of 1862 through the end of the war they were a constant matter of attention. The diary entries of a large slaveholder in the Lafourche area suggest the dislocation, disruption, and desertion which followed the occupation of New Orleans. There are seven references from the four-month period from July to November, 1862:

> July 7, 1862, "James Pugh's estate lost 10 Negroes last night."
> July 8, 1862, "There has been a perfect stampede of the negroes on some places in this vicinity."
> October 28, 1862, "The negroes are in a very bad way in the neighborhood and I fear will all go off."
> October 30, 1862, "Found our negroes completely demoralized some gone and some preparing to go. I fear we shall lose them all."
> October 31, 1862, "The negroes . . . run off. It looks probable that they will all go."
> November 2, 1862, "Our negroes . . . are still leaving, some every night. The plantation will probably be completely cleaned out in a weak."

November 5, 1862, "This morning there was a rebellion among the negroes at Mrs.
G. Pugh."[30]

This account is exceptional only for the frequency of its entries. Literally thousands of
bondsmen escaped from the interior and made their way to Union lines.

The mass escapes which took place in the Pelican State after April, 1862, provide
striking testimony about slavery and about the thinking of those in bondage. Clearly,
most slaves were realistically hesitant to make futile attempts for freedom; but given a
reasonable hope for success, they left in droves. Nor can their successful escapes be
credited to planter resignation or to a laxity of controls. Quite the contrary occurred.

With the arrival of Federal troops in southern Louisiana, the already oppressive
controls in the Confederate interior were supplemented and tightened. Patrols were
increased both in size and in the frequency of their rounds. Some parishes hired
permanent guards who worked from dark to sunrise daily; others created river patrols to
block that avenue of escape. At Baton Rouge skiffs were anchored on the Mississippi
River above and below the city, each manned by two men with shot guns to "prevent . . .
the absconding of the slave population." Towns responded with vigilance committees "to
act as guardians of the public safety," and owners allowing slaves to live in cities without
immediate white supervision were threatened with fines. Parishes appropriated funds to
hire managers for plantations lacking sufficient white males to maintain order, and
resourceful whites went to work as "Negro hunters" for the rewards. At Lake Washington
owners had insubordinate slaves sent to work under Confederate guards. The new controls
and the dislocation of the slave population necessitated the appointment of state agents to
handle captured runaways.[31]

The greater restraints were predictable responses to increased acts of black violence
(both real and imagined) after the spring of 1862. In the state capital "every sound in the
distance [was] translated into some message of slaughter and carnage." Slaves in Madison
Parish gave owners "a great deal of trouble" by killing several overseers and wounding
other whites (one resident claimed he could recall twenty such cases). In Tangipahoa
Parish slaves were discovered with a cache of horses and guns, thus prematurely starting
an abortive revolt in which several blacks were killed. Confederate soldiers were
dispatched to a plantation outside Cheneyville in southern Rapides Parish to take arms,
ammunition, and horses from blacks who had acquired them in the confusion following a
Federal raid. On Saint Louis Plantation in Iberville Parish a slave attacked the local
sheriff who reluctantly agreed to release the offender after lamenting the poor effect it
would have "at times like these." The sheriff added, "I cannot forbear telling you that
during my struggles [with the one slave] your other negroes (although they did not assist)
called on him to throw the white man in the ditch then kill him! If you wish come and
see my marks."[32] White apprehension of blacks increased as Federal troops approached,
and those fears explain, in part, the intensified controls, but it is clear that those fears
were founded in fact and experience.

Many slaves never attempted to depart for Union lines. The new wave of repression, or concern for their families, or loyalty kept them at home. But they had only to wait for the arrival of Federal troops in their locale for liberation. In 1863 and 1864 large-scale Union military movements cut across the state from New Orleans to within miles of Shreveport. Lesser excursions designed to bring undefended territory under Union control or to collect cotton, sugar, mules, horses, wagons, and slaves were numerous.

Wherever the troops went they disrupted the labor system by their presence. The "Teche Expedition" in the spring of 1863 was one of the most disruptive, with Federal troops crossing and recrossing no less than eight parishes, some of which were rich in sugar and cotton plantations previously untouched by the war.[33] Wherever they went, the soldiers were greeted by cheering slaves who materially aided the military effort. On countless occasions bondsmen furnished information about hidden horses, mules, sugar, cotton, or rebel strength and activities. Equal assistance was given to individual Union soldiers who were wounded, hungry, or ill.[34]

As the Teche Expedition progressed, slaves joined the advancing column. Many walked off the plantation as the army passed; others, hidden and restrained during the day, found their way to Federal camps at night; those who joined included "old men with canes, bare-headed and bare-footed, children, women in short dresses, with bandanas wrapped over wolly [*sic*] pates, and carrying infants in their arms. Big and little, black and yellow, old and young, cripple and infirm, all with bundles and all kinds of traps, come pouring in from every quarter, at every hour."[35]

The procession must have been an impressive sight. By the time the expedition turned homeward it stretched no less than five miles and included troops, horses, mules, cattle, fifty army wagons, over 400 plantation carts and wagons filled with household goods, and close to eight thousand slaves, who comprised an army of liberation by their example.[36] The black and white "Army of the Teche" was but one of many like it during the war. Even the militarily abortive Red River campaign returned with thousands of liberated blacks.[37]

Those slaves who for one reason or another could not or would not join the liberators were, to use a common planter term, "completely demoralized" after a visit by the Federals. Planters in contested or Confederate parishes complained after "those [who] did not go with the army remained at home to do *much worse*." For days following a Federal visit audacious slaves "had a perfect jubilee" and acted as if they were "practically free," even coming and going as they pleased. In one night the slaves on a large plantation killed thirty-five hogs to share with visiting bondsmen. On another they captured a rebel soldier and placed him in the stocks until he escaped. "The recent trying scenes through which we have passed," wrote one planter after a Federal raid, "have convinced me that *no dependence* is to be *placed* on the *negro*—and that they are the greatest hypocrites and liers [*sic*] that God ever made."[38]

Obviously Federal raids into Confederate or contested parishes went a long way in destroying slavery. They were a vehicle for freedom for thousands of bondsmen who wished to leave the plantation, and the freedmen in turn became an integral part of the forces of liberation. For those who did not leave, slavery would never again be the same. The features which sustained the institution—isolation, routine, paternalism, patrols, controls, and the master-slave relationship—could not survive the raids.[39]

Slavery in the Union-occupied parishes was similarly affected by the presence of the Federal army. But an important distinction must be made between the Union area and the Confederate interior. The Confiscation Act passed by the U. S. Congress in July, 1862, freed slaves of masters in the Confederate part of the state; but this act of Congress, like the Emancipation Proclamation which came six months later, exempted slaves in areas already under Federal control.[40] Thus slaves in the Confederate interior were liberated, but slavery in occupied Louisiana was bolstered by exemptions in the congressional legislation and in the Emancipation Proclamation. Planters and military officials were assured by Congress and the president that slavery in the Union parishes was safe, or so went the theory. But the theory worked poorly in practice; for the blacks, to judge from their actions, apparently no longer considered themselves slaves. They understood what the war was going to do to the labor system and took full advantage of the situation.

Masters and overseers in Federal Louisiana often found it difficult to control their labor force without compensation of some form. Slaves, using strikes and slowdowns, restructured the Old South labor system and altered the master-slave relationship until it more closely resembled employer-employee. In early September, 1862, the owner of Magnolia Plantation in Plaquemines Parish promised a "handsome present" for his slaves if they would end their slowdown and remain on the plantation. The slaves accepted the offer, but less than a month later some of the hands, in a "quite impudent" manner, demanded a month's pay which was refused. The slaves responded with another slowdown and occasionally worked only half days for the ensuing week and a half. When this produced no results, all the women went on strike and refused to return to the fields despite a visit by a Federal officer who encouraged them to be more cooperative. After a week the men of Magnolia joined the women in their strike; their idle time was spent erecting a gallows in the quarters. Only a visit by the absentee owner with a promise of compensation once the crop was harvested and sold ended the strike. After their initial and major success it took only "grumbling" on the part of the blacks to get more and better food and new clothes. The overseer's journal entry of December 25, 1862, graphically expresses the new order of things: "[The] negroes went to work [this] morning but came home at Breakfast saying that never having had a chance to keep [Christmas Day] before they would avail themselves of the privalege [*sic*] now."[41] The timing of the slaves on the Magnolia plantation is also significant. Although Federal troops had been in the area for some months, the hands waited until the busiest period of the year before acting. During the fall sugar cane is cut, hauled, and processed, and the entire crop can be lost if too much time elapses between cutting and processing.

The events on Magnolia were repeated throughout the area under Union control in the fall and winter of 1862. Many slaves left plantations and went to Union forts where they remained, contrary to Federal regulations. Occasionally more overt action was taken by blacks—plantations were burned, police and patrols were fired upon, and in Saint Martin Parish Federal troops were needed to control a roving band of blacks who were looting and terrorizing the parish.[42] Strikes, slowdowns, walkouts, confrontations, and armed violence were strange occurrences in an area where slavery was presumably protected by Federal legislation.

It must have been increasingly clear that laws and proclamations alone could not guarantee the survival of institutional slavery. That was particularly true when the sustaining features and behavioral patterns that reinforced slavery from within—routine, isolation, paternalism, the master-slave relationship among others—no longer functioned as they had in antebellum slave society. As the war progressed slavery crumbled throughout the state. In both Union and Confederate parishes, slaves, to varying degrees, confronted planters and overseers for wages and new freedoms and challenged old relationships. Runaways dotted the state and acts of insubordination and violence reached a new level. Except in the few northern parishes still under Confederate control at the end of the war, the traditional slave system in Louisiana had ceased being effective before the state legislature abolished the institution in 1864. Events of the war, actions by planters, policies of the Confederate States government, the presence of the Union army, and the actions of the slaves themselves altered and damaged the system to the extent that anything short of abolition would have been cumbersome and nugatory.

Notes for "Confederate Slavery"

[1]Kenneth Stampp, *The Peculiar Institution: Slavery in the Ante-Bellum South* (New York, 1956), 141-91; Eugene Genovese, *Roll, Jordan, Roll: The World the Slaves Made* (New York, 1974), 4-7.

[2]John W. Blassingame, *The Slave Community: Plantation Life in the Ante-Bellum South* (New York, 1972), 75-76, 103, 154.

[3]*Report of the Board of Control of the Louisiana Penitentiary to the General Assembly* [January, 1860] (Baton Rouge, 1859), 39-51; Ulrich Bonnell Phillips, *American Negro Slavery: A Survey of the Supply, Employment, and Control of Negro Labor as Determined by the Plantation Regime* (Baton Rouge, 1966), 303-4; see also Blassingame, *Slave Community*, 133-53, 184-216, for a complete discussion of slave responses and personalities.

[4]See, for example, Solomon Northup, *Twelve Years a Slave*, ed. Sue Eakin and Joseph Logsdon (Baton Rouge, 1968), 99-104, 182-85, for an intelligent discussion on this subject by a former slave from Louisiana.

[5]Ibid., 188-90.

[6]Iberville Parish Police Jury Minutes (PJM), July 23, 1859, January 14, September 2, 1861; Franklin Parish PJM, June 5, 1861; St. Charles Parish PJM, December 19, 1860, May 19, 1862; *Alexandria Constitutional*, May 25, 1861; *Greensburg Imperial*, February 16, 1861.

[7]Franklin Parish PJM, June 3, 1861; Clara Solomon Diary, Louisiana State University, Baton Rouge, Louisiana (hereafter cited LSU) July 5, 1861; A. Heise to Mr. Bowman, July 5, 1862, in Bowman Family Papers, LSU.

[8]Pointe Coupée PJM, May 1, 1861; *West Baton Rouge Sugar Planter*, July 6, 1861; Bienville Parish PJM, January 7, 1862; Caldwell Parish PJM, January 10, 1861; *Pointe Coupée Democrat*, June 8, 1861; *Opelousas Patriot*, June 15, 1861.

[9]See Joe Gray Taylor, *Negro Slavery in Louisiana* (Baton Rouge, 1963), Chapter 9; V. Alton Moody, *Slavery on Louisiana Sugar Plantations* (New Orleans, 1924), for information on the *Code Noir*; Lafayette Parish PJM, June 3, June 22, 1861; West Feliciana Parish PJM, June 5, 1860; Bienville Parish PJM, June 6, 1864; Caddo Parish PJM, June 4, 1861; Iberville Parish PJM, June 4, 1861; West Baton Rouge Parish PJM, April 26, 1861; Pass for Ceazar, April 9, 1863, in Ann E. Spears Papers, LSU.

[10]Resolutions of the Executive Committee of Trinity Vigillant Association [1861], in Moses and St. John Richardson Liddell Papers, LSU.

[11]E. Surget to George Logan, March 21, 1863, in George Logan Papers, Southern Historical Collection, University of North Carolina, Chapel Hill, North Carolina (hereafter cited UNC); George W. Deitzler to John A. Rawlins, February 3, 1861, *The War of the Rebellion: A Compilation of the Official Records of the Union and Confederate Armies* (Washington, D.C., 1880-1901), Series 1, Vol. 24, Pt. 1:15; hereinafter cited as *Official Records*. Unless otherwise indicated, all citations are to Series 1. Walter Guion to Bessie E. Guion, January 24, 1862, in Guion Family Papers, UNC; A. J. H. Duganne, *Camps and Prisons: Twenty Months in the Department of the Gulf* (New York, 1865), 183; *Shreveport News*, July 19, 1864; Receipt, undated in William Hale papers, LSU; see also Joe Gray Taylor, "Slavery in Louisiana During the Civil War," *Louisiana History*, 8 (1967): 27-33.

[12]J. A. Campbell to W. N. R. Beall, October 23, 1862, *Official Records*, 15:841-42.

[13]*Shreveport News*, August 2, 1864; *Acts Passed by the Twenty-Seventh Legislature of the State of Louisiana in Extra Session at Opelousas, December, 1862-January, 1863* (Natchitoches, 1864), 10-11.

[14]Payne Madison to George Logan, March 16, 1862, P. M. McKelvy to George Logan, January 23, 1863, Weekly Report of Soldiers, Men and Negroes Working on Fortification at Harrisburg, Louisiana, February 15, 1863, all in Logan Papers, UNC.

[15]Your Brother to Dear Albert, February 17, 1863, in Cummings-Black Family Papers, Howard-Tilton Memorial Library, Tulane University, New Orleans, Louisiana (hereafter cited TU).

[16]General Order No. 3, Fort Beauregard, December 25, 1862, Petition and Resolutions of Planters of Morehouse Parish, March 2, 1863, H. M. Polk to George Logan, March 11, 1863, all in Logan Papers, UNC.

[17]*Acts Passed by the Sixth Legislature of the State of Louisiana at Its Extra Session Held in the City of Shreveport on the 4th of May, 1863* (Shreveport, 1863), 17-19.

[18]*Natchitoches Union*, November 27, December 4,1862; Avoyelles Parish PJM, November 24, December 20, 1862; Caddo Parish PJM, May 5, 1862; Bienville Parish PJM, January [?], 1863.

[19]Franklin Parish PJM, June 4, 1861; Caldwell Parish PJM, January 10, 1861; Pointe Coupée Parish PJM, August 4, 1862; Avoyelles Parish PJM, September 1, 1862.

[20]See, for examples, Logan Papers, UNC; Thomas D. Miller Papers, LSU; *Shreveport News*, July 1, 1864, "Wanted—200 able-bodied men to work in Ordinance Department."

[21]See, for examples, John W. Meims to Major Liddell, June 8, 1861, in Liddell Papers, LSU; Kate Stone Diary (LSU), June 19, 29, 1861; *Alexandria Constitutional*, May 11, 1861; Alexander F. Pugh Diary (MS in Alexander F. Pugh Papers, LSU), August 26, 1861; Statement of 5th Judicial District, Parish of Iberville, December 21, 1861, in Letters Received, Provost Marshal, Iberville, Department of the Gulf Records (Union), Record Group 393, National Archives, Washington, D.C. [hereafter cited DGR (U)]; *Report of the Board of Control of the Louisiana Penitentiary to the General Assembly, November, 1861* (Baton Rouge, 1861), 21-23.

[22]*Annual Report of the Auditor of Public Accounts to the Legislature of the State of Louisiana, January, 1860* (Baton Rouge, 1860), 5; *Rapport Annuel de l'Auditeur des Comptes Publics, à le Legislature l'Etat de la Louisiane, Janvier, 1861* (Baton Rouge, 1861), 6; *Annual Report of the Auditor of Public Accounts to the General Assembly of the State of Louisiana [January, 1862]* (Baton Rouge, 1861), 6. Unfortunately no figures exist past January, 1862.

[23]Henry Miller to his sister, July 20, 1863, in William W. King Papers, LSU; Your bro[ther] to Albert, April 28, 1863, in Cummings-Black Family Papers, TU; Louise to Frank, May [5 or 6], 1863, in Benjamin F. Cheatham Papers, UNC; Sarah L. Wadley Diary (UNC), October 25, 1863.

[24]Arthur J. Fremantle, *Three Months in the Southern States* (New York, 1864), 85; George W. Guess to Mrs. S. H. Cockrell, February 9, 1865, in George W. Guess Papers, LSU.

[25]In addition to previous citations see also Louise Ellen Power Diary (UNC), December 29, 1862, May 24, 1863; Bayside Plantation Journal (UNC), November 2, December 24, 31, 1861; Mrs. M. C. Meade to Theodore Stark, May 25, 1863, in Theodore O. Stark Papers, UNC; S. Harding Diary (LSU), July 29, 1863; Wadley Diary (UNC), October 27, 1864; Thomas Miller to his sister, March 1, 1865, in King Papers, LSU; Plantation Journal (MS in Palfrey Family Papers, LSU), November 12, 1862, April 14, 1863; R. Taylor to J. C. Pemberton, November 10, 1862, *Official Records*, 15: 859; "History of Evan Plantation" (MS in Henry McCall Papers, TU), 13-14; D. E. Haynes, *A Thrilling Narrative of the Suffering of Union Refugees and the Massacre of the Martyrs of Liberty of Western Louisiana* (Washington, D.C., 1866), 12.

[26]E. Surget to S. S. Anderson, September 29, 1863, *Official Records*, Vol. 26, Pt. 2:286.

[27]See, for example, *Opelousas Patriot*, May 25, 1861, for an indication of how important isolation and noncommunication among slaves was considered. The paper reported that "a number of negroes have been seen gathering together to listen to the news which was read to them by one of their number." Readers were cautioned about letting newspapers fall into slaves' possession.

[28]William T. Gay to Ned, December 3, 1862, in Edward Gay Family Papers, LSU.

[29]Thomas D. Miller to R. W. Sanders, July 23, 1864, Miller to W. C. Black, July 27, 1864, Miller to G. Soule, September 27, September 29, 1864, all in Miller Papers, LSU.

[30]Alexander F. Pugh Diary (MS in Alexander F. Pugh Papers, LSU). See also, for examples, Plantation Journal (MS in August LeBlanc Family Papers, LSU); Plantation Journal, 1861-1863 (MS in Phanor Prudhomme Papers, UNC), "portes avec les yankees;" Bayside Plantation Journal (MS in Bayside Plantation Papers, UNC), May 1, 3, 4, 11, 1863; Plantation Journal, 1863 (MS in Andrew McCollam Papers, UNC), "Negroes that have left the place;" seventy-six of one hundred and one left as families. Okar to Gustave,

June 26, 1863, in Gustave Lauve Papers, LSU, "The negroes have all left their owners in this parish;" L. Martin to W. R. Beall, September 21, 1862, in DGR (C), "most of the slaves have fled to the Yankees."

[31]St. Charles Parish PJM, May 19, 1862; West Baton Rouge Parish PJM, June 21, 1862; *Natchitoches Union*, May 15, 29, 1862; Phelps to R. S. Davis, July 31, 1863, *Official Records*, 15: 535; Charles S. Crowe to C. L. Stevenson, March 31, 1863, *Official Records*, Vol. 24, Pt. 3:701; *Shreveport News*, September 13, 1864; Bienville Parish PJM, April 16, 1863; *Annual Message of Governor Henry Watkins Allen to the Legislature of the State of Louisiana, January, 1865* (Shreveport, 1865), 8; *Shreveport News*, July 19, August 23, 1864. On August 23, 1864, the state agent at Shreveport had 129 runaways under his care.

[32]*Baton Rouge Daily News*, August 7, 1862; Franklin Parish PJM, June 16, 1862; C. I. S. to John Perkins, September 12, 1862, in John Perkins Papers, UNC; T. D. C. to her husband, November 19, 1863, in R. J. Causey Papers, LSU; Special Order Number 162, June 23, 1862, Head Quarters, District of Western Louisiana, in H. D. Ogden Papers, TU; Jules Aucoir to Gay, April 27, 1862, in Gay Papers, LSU.

[33]The parishes included Lafourche, Lafayette, Assumption, St. Martin, St. Landry, St. Mary, Iberville, and Baton Rouge.

[34]See, for examples, Harris H. Beecher, *Records of the 114th Regiment N. Y. S. V.* (Norwich, 1866), 139-40; Edward H. Sentell Diary (NYHSL), May 7, 1863; George Gilbert Smith, *Leaves from a Soldier's Diary* (Putnam, Conn., 1906), April, 1863, 46-47; William B. Stevens, *History of the 50th Regiment of Infantry, Massachusetts Volunteers Militia in the Late War of the Rebellion* (Boston, 1907), 70; J. F. Moors, *History of the Fifty-Second Regiment Massachusetts Volunteers* (Boston, 1893), 156; George H. Hepworth, *The Whip, Hoe and Sword; or the Gulf Department in '63* (Boston, 1864), 140-42; Josephine Clare, *Narrative of the Adventures and Experiences of Mrs. Josephine Clare* (Lancaster, Pa., 1865), 4-5; Benjamin F. Stevenson, *Letters from the War* (Cincinnati, 1884), 274-75.

[35]Beecher, *Record of the 114th N.Y.*, 131.

[36]Thomas E. Chickering, *Diary of Forty-First Regiment Infantry Massachusetts Volunteers* (Baton, 1863), 10; Beecher, *Record of the 114th N. Y.*, 184-86; Alexander F. Pugh Diary (MS in Alexander F. Pugh Papers, LSU), May 25, 1863. Estimates of the number of slaves involved varies. One observer claimed 5,000 another 6,000, but both a military and a planter source offered 8,000.

[37]See, for example, Charles Barnard to Maggie, May 26, 182, in Charles Barnard Papers, Maine Historical Society Library, Portland, Maine (hereafter cited MHSL); [?] to Mide, July 28, 1862, in Louis A. Bringier Papers, LSU; Homer B. Sprague, *History of the 13th Infantry Regiment Connecticut Volunteers During the Great Rebellion* (Hartford, 1867), 79-80; Alexander F. Pugh Diary (MS in William F. Pugh Papers, LSU), October 26, 1862; Power Diary (UNC), May 25, 26, June 27, 1863; Kate to her brother, August 30, 1863, in Albert Batchelor Papers, LSU; G. A. Breaux Diary (TU), November 23, 1863; Wadley Diary (UNC), April 15, 1864.

[38]John H. Ransdell to Thomas O. Moore, May 29, 1863, in Thomas O. Moore Papers, LSU; William J. Minor Diary (LSU), January 3, 1863; [?] to Albert, September 21, 1864, in Batchelor Papers, LSU; John Ransdell to the governor, May 26, 1863, in Moore Papers, LSU; O. S. Acklen to Ade, August 23, 1863, in Acklen Family Papers, TU. In contrast, for slaves who remained loyal, see Clara Compton Raymond Memoirs (UNC), 12; "The Federal Raid on Ashland" (MS in Rosella Kenner Brent Papers, LSU), 19, 24-25; Pricilla Bond Diary (LSU), June 29, 1862.

[39]See, for example, Stevens, *History of the 50th Mass.*, 104; Smith, *Soldier's Diary*, 50, for the reaction of slaves seeing masters and rebel soldiers fleeing before an advancing Union army.

[40]See James G. Randall and David Donald, *The Civil War and Reconstruction* (Lexington, Mass., 1969), 372-373, for a discussion of the confiscation acts.

[41]Magnolia Plantation Journal (MS in Henry Clay Warmoth Papers, UNC), September 6, October 2, 4, 6, 7, 11, 14, 17, 18, 21, 22, 31, November 24, 26, December 25, 1862.

[42]See, for example, Plantation Journals, 1862-1863 (MS in Minor Papers, LSU); E. E. Kittridge to N. P. Banks, December 18, 1862, in Letters Received, Bureau of Civil Affairs, DGR(U); Munsul White to William Kennedy, September 7, 1862, in George F. Shepley Papers, MHSL; to Magnolia Plantation Journal, (MS in Warmoth Papers, UNC), August 12, 15-17, October 19, 21, 1862; Wadley Diary (UNC), May 26, 1863; Henry L. Wood to Colonel, April 28, 30, 1863, in Simon G. Jarrard Papers, LSU; S. W. Sawyer to James Bowen, June 3, 1863, in Letters Received, Provost Marshal General, DGR(U).

NEGRO TROOPS IN BLUE AND GRAY:
THE LOUISIANA NATIVE GUARDS, 1861-1863*

Mary F. Berry

The basic outline of the military history of Louisiana Negroes in the Civil War has been sketched by several historians, but the complete story long has remained untouched in the manuscript sources. Proper attention to the Louisiana Native Guards, Negro troops who served on both sides during the Civil War, is long overdue. Participation in the Civil War was not the first incident of military service for the free colored people of Louisiana. In 1727 armed slaves and free Negroes fought for the French against the Choctaw Indians and dug emplacements and garrisoned fortifications inside the city of New Orleans. In 1735 there were forty-five Negroes, commanded by free blacks, among the 589 colonial troops in New Orleans. Thus, after the Seven Years War, when France transferred Louisiana to Spain, Negroes were already performing military service in the colony. Spanish colonial officials continued the policy initiated by the French. There were over eighty free Negro volunteers among the forces of Don Bernardo de Gálvez when the Spanish captured the English forts at Natchez and Baton Rouge in September 1779. Even larger numbers of free black and mulatto militiamen and slaves joined Gálvez' army in the capture of Pensacola in March 1780. Negroes served continuously in the Louisiana militia and were still enrolled at the time of the Louisiana Purchase of 1803.[1]

After 1803 Louisiana was the only area under the jurisdiction of the United States government where Negroes were included in the militia. Elsewhere they were excluded by federal and state law.[2] The free colored men of New Orleans held fast to their military tradition. Despite protests from some members of the white population they remained organized and were present at almost all public ceremonies in the city. The free colored militia corps offered their services to the territorial government and helped to suppress a slave revolt in 1811. After Louisiana was admitted to the Union in 1812 the first legislature authorized the continued existence of a free colored militia corps. During the

*First published in *Louisiana History*, 8 (1967): 165-90. Reprinted with the kind permission of the author and the Louisiana Historical Association.

War of 1812 Andrew Jackson utilized two companies of colored militia at the Battle of New Orleans. There were some free Negro veterans of the War of 1812 who claimed service in the Mexican War in units of Louisiana volunteers.[3]

When the Civil War began there was wide speculation in Louisiana concerning the intentions of the free colored people. Almost as soon as secession was accomplished in January 1861, military companies were formed throughout the state, some with governmental aid and others through private philanthropy. After Fort Sumter, military organization was accelerated. The Negro population soon joined the enthusiasm for military service. On April 23, 1861, the *New Orleans True Delta* noted meetings of free colored men called to discuss possible participation in the Confederate war effort. The article closed with the observation that "these men whose ancestors distinguished themselves at the Battle of New Orleans are determined to give new evidence of their bravery."[4]

On April 27, Jordan Noble, drummer boy at Chalmette in 1815, inserted an advertisement asking all free colored persons who wished to offer their services to the Confederate government as Home Guards to attend a meeting at five o'clock that evening. Three days later it was reported that Gov. Thomas O. Moore was thinking of organizing a regiment of colored men. Such a regiment would teach the "Black Republicans of the North that they [Negroes] knew their false from their true friends." On May 1, the free colored nurses of the city offered their services to the Confederacy in case of attack. Their offer was accepted by Mayor John T. Monroe who praised their sense of duty and loyalty to the Confederate cause.[5]

On May 12, 1861, Governor Moore issued a proclamation providing for the enrollment of Negroes to form a free colored regiment, with colored officers, to aid in protecting New Orleans in case of Union attack. The organization was designated the First Native Guards, Louisiana Militia, Confederate States of America. By the end of May, a regiment containing 440 men with colored officers had been formed. Negroes were also recruited for militia units in other areas of the state so that by early 1862 there were more than 3,000 members of colored military organizations. This is a substantial figure since the entire free colored population of the state in 1860 was only 18,547, of whom nearly 11,000 lived in New Orleans.[6]

The colored officers of the First Native Guards Regiment were a representative section of the free Negro population of New Orleans. Many were skilled tradesmen and craftsmen; a few owned slaves. Capt. Noel J. Bacchus was a mulatto carpenter, forty years of age, who owned property valued at $800 in the Seventh Ward of the city. Capt. Michael Duphart, a shoemaker, was a mulatto, 62 years of age, who owned property valued at $1,200. Capt. Louis Rey was a 29-year-old mulatto clerk. First Lieut. André Cailloux, a cigar-maker and a fine horseman and boxer, was well known as "the blackest man in New Orleans." Capt. Alcide Lewis was a 34-year-old mulatto mason who owned $150 in real estate. Capt. Virgil Bonseigneur was a mulatto plasterer, 52 years old, who owned $2,000 in real estate and possessed $200 worth of personal property. Young First

Lieut. Arnold Bertonneau was a wine seller. The only drummer in the regiment was Armand Rey, the younger brother of Capt. Louis Rey. Capt. Ludgere Boguille appointed his brother Raoul as sergeant major of his company. Many of the companies contained all the male members of one family who were old enough to serve. For example, all of the male members of the Duphart family were enrolled, though not in the same company.[7]

Thus, six weeks after the outbreak of the war some members of the free colored population organized and joined the Confederate cause. Neither the state of Louisiana, the city of New Orleans, nor the Confederate government furnished the regiment with arms. Whatever equipment the men possessed was individually owned just as in other Confederate regiments. The regiment was ordered to engage in company drill and instruction in the rudiments of warfare at times specified by Maj. Gen. John Lewis, the militia commander. In September, 1861, it offered its services to the state militia as escorts for prisoners of war but was refused in a letter which Lewis' adjutant, Jonathan Devereux, sent to the New Orleans headquarters on September 29. Lewis indicated his appreciation of the offer but believed it unnecessary to use the regiment at that time and hoped that "it will be equally ready on a more important occasion."[8]

The disinclination of the state militia to use the colored regiment could be evidence of a continuing distrust of the free colored population by the white people of New Orleans, or evidence of acquiescence to the Confederate policy of excluding Negroes from the regular service, or it could be evidence that some coercion was used to force the free colored population to join the Confederacy. Many of the men were still without uniforms and equipment as late as January 10, 1862, as indicated by a note on the Morning Report of that date, stating that there was a high degree of absenteeism because of lack of uniforms and that one company had only ten muskets. There is no evidence to indicate that other Negroes supported the colored regiment in its action by contributing to the purchase of uniforms and equipment.[9]

The men in the regiment were called upon only to perform company drill for the entire time of their Confederate service. According to Joseph T. Wilson in his *Black Phalanx*, three free colored regiments were ordered to blow up the United States Mint building in New Orleans when the Union navy attacked the city; however, the official Confederate Records and the statements made by officers of the regiment to Gen. Benjamin Butler fail to indicate that such an order was given. When the Union naval bombardment ended in the withdrawal of the Confederate forces on April 28, 1862, the Native Guards refused to leave the city. It seems they did not want to leave their homes to fight with the Confederacy elsewhere. They waited to see what would result from the Union victory. Their action was in many respects similar to the typical Home Guard reaction to defeat and adversity. Many white Home Guards either remained in the city or went into camp with the retreating Confederate army, only to desert slowly, one by one, and return home.[10]

When General Butler ordered his troops to occupy New Orleans he was immediately beset with many apparently insoluble problems. Food was in short supply, sanitary measures were lacking, and hundreds of fugitive and abandoned slaves from the surrounding plantations daily straggled into the army camp and attached themselves to the various units. For example, by July 1, the Provost Marshal of the Twelfth Connecticut Infantry Regiment had seven hundred Negroes on his roll, all drawing rations and living about the camp. All regiments had "contrabands." The Twelfth and Thirteenth Connecticut had eighty washer-women and seventy men to clean and repair the customhouse which served as the regimental barracks. In addition, Negroes were utilized as nurses, hospital orderlies, and cooks. Bivouacked near the camp were 150 Negroes, "lately arrived from the other bank of the river." Their owner, in a rage, "ordered them off the plantation and bade them go to the devil." They went to the Union lines.[11]

The ubiquitous Negro was a continuing problem for Butler. Gen. John W. Phelps, the crusty old Vermonter in command at Camp Parapet outside New Orleans wished to form regiments composed of the wandering slaves who continually came into his lines. He even approached the officers of the Twelfth Connecticut Regiment about commanding Negro troops. By the middle of July a serious conflict developed between Phelps and Butler over Phelps' action in recruiting Negro regiments which he asked Butler to arm and equip. Butler refused, informing Phelps that under the Militia Act of July 17, only the president could authorize the use of Negroes as soldiers. Phelps, angered by Butler's refusal, tendered his resignation to Secretary of War Edwin M. Stanton, who did not accept the resignation immediately, but transferred Phelps out of the Department of the Gulf.

Butler, an opportunist, was unwilling to jeopardize his future by recruiting Negro slaves without support of the War Department. He also had information which led him to believe that the Department might soon change its policy. In June, Salmon P. Chase, secretary of the treasury, had written him that there was increasing support in the administration for abolitionist aims and that Butler should do everything possible to diminish any notion that he was pro-slavery. Butler, however, had told Phelps he preferred to wait until he received explicit orders from the War Department on the subject. Phelps, a strong abolitionist, was not willing to wait for the War Department to give orders on the disposition of Negroes. George Denison, a relative of Chase, assigned to manage confiscated property in New Orleans, thought Butler was jealous of Phelps. Denison wrote to Secretary Chase on August 25, 1862, explaining that the conflict between the two generals was not a matter of principle, but grew out of the fact that "General Phelps had the start on him, while Gen. B. [Butler] wanted the credit of doing the thing himself in his own way."[12]

As Butler set about to consolidate his occupation of the city one group of former rebels watched him with fearful eyes. The free colored regiment, formed and mustered in by the Confederacy, remained behind when the rebel army fled the city. They had not actually engaged the Union troops in battle, and they did not want to leave the city. The

War Department ordered Butler to hold New Orleans at all costs but offered him no additional troops. He was expected to obtain new recruits in Louisiana, and he succeeded in raising three regiments largely from among the "loyal" Irish and German populations. This was not nearly enough to satisfy his needs, and Butler began considering other alternatives. He knew from reading the New Orleans newspaper that the Confederacy had raised a free colored regiment. Charles St. Manat, a former officer of that regiment, was employed as a translator of Spanish, French, and German in the Union provost court. Butler discovered his presence and asked him to bring the captains of the regiments to see him. After discussion, a group of the mulatto captains responded to the invitation. Upon seeing them Butler remarked, "In color, nay also in conduct, they had much more the appearance of white gentlemen than some of those who have favored me with their presence claiming to be chivalry of the South."[13]

Butler indicated that when he asked the colored officers why they served with the Confederacy they said, "We were ordered out and dared not refuse, for those who did so were killed and their property confiscated." The testimony which Charles Gibson, a free colored citizen of New Orleans, gave before the Freedmen's Inquiry Committee lends partial support to the statement of the colored captains. Gibson said that he was taken from his home and forced to join the Confederate regiment as a private. Except for this testimony there was little evidence to substantiate the charge that fear of reprisal wholly induced the colored men to offer their services to the Confederacy. Their motives were no doubt complex and difficult to appraise. Their eagerness could have been due to their historically demonstrated loyalty to New Orleans and to the *de facto* government be it Spanish, French, or American. Perhaps they were influenced by the hope that service in the regiment would enhance the civil and political status of their race. Many of them were owners of considerable property including slaves. However, neither the number of Negro slaveholders nor the available evidence is sufficient to warrant the conclusion that the free Negro alliance with the Confederate cause was based largely on identical interest in slavery. Regardless of their motives, Butler was convinced of their loyalty and asked them to raise as many regiments as possible, which he would arm to serve the Union cause.[14]

In a letter to Secretary of War Stanton, August 14, 1862, Butler reported, "I am going to use the men of the free colored brigade of whom you have heard; they have been used by our enemies whose mouths are shut and they will be loyal." Two weeks later he wrote to Henry W. Halleck, general-in-chief of the Union army, that since military expediency dictated the use of all available forces, he had "called upon a free colored brigade which was in the Confederacy and was willing to take service." On September 1, 1862, Butler wrote to Stanton, "My Native Guards, 1,000 strong are to be filled up in the next 10 days, the darkest of whom is about the complexion of the late Mr. Webster."[15] Butler asked the War Department to sanction his recruitment of Negroes under the Militia Act of July 17, 1862. He received no reply for two months. In the interim, he went forward with his plans to form colored regiments and to supply his troops with weapons which he procured, in part, by confiscating the property of local rebel sympathizers. Finally, Stanton replied that the whole matter was left to Butler's discretion. For Butler, that was ratification enough.[16]

Recruitment for the regiments went forward rapidly. Jordan Noble, who had helped to raise the Confederate regiments, began recruiting for the Union forces in August. Additional colored officers were recruited among the free colored population of the city. In order to speed recruitment Butler applied the Confiscation Act of July 1862, which called for the confiscation of the property of Confederate officials or those persons giving aid to the rebellion; thereby former slaves were enlisted as free men. According to George Denison, when the Negroes enlisted, "no one asked whether slave or free," and some fugitives probably joined. Butler's order to expropriate the property of foreign nationals in New Orleans who favored the Confederacy, and to enlist their slaves into the Union army, was an additional stimulus to enlistment.[17]

Under General Order No. 63, Department of the Gulf, Butler assigned one of the assistants to the provost marshal, Col. Spencer Stafford, to organize the Native Guards. Stafford selected as a temporary barracks an almshouse built under the terms of the will of Judah Touro, a white citizen of considerable wealth. About 1,800 men enlisted and were organized into twenty companies. Ten of these were mustered into service as the First Louisiana Native Guard Infantry on September 27, 1862. The other ten companies formed the Second Louisiana Native Guards, mustered in on October 12, 1862. After additional recruiting, on November 24, 1862, a third regiment, designated the Third Louisiana Native Guard Infantry, was organized and mustered into service.[18]

The men were assigned to Camp Strong Station, near the Louisiana race course about four miles from New Orleans; there they were issued equipment and arms and began training. When the first new regiments arrived at Camp Strong, detached companies from the Eighth Vermont and the Twelfth Connecticut Regiments were on the field. The Native Guards and the companies of white troops were brigaded under the command of Colonel Stafford. Maj. Chauncey Bassett, formerly of the Eleventh Michigan, was assigned command of the First Regiment; Maj. Joseph Giddings, the Second Regiment, which had not yet arrived. Janson Payne, a twenty-eight-year-old white physician who had been assistant surgeon of the Twenty-first Massachusetts Volunteers, was assigned as surgeon for the First Regiment and remained in this capacity for the entire term of service. Asa Barnes, a young white Episcopalian minister who had formerly been first sergeant of the Thirty-first Massachusetts Volunteers, was assigned as chaplain for the First Regiment. The line officers of the First and Second Regiments were all Negroes. Their average age was thirty years; twenty-one-year-old Second Lieutenant Louis Snaer was the youngest. Captains Alcide Lewis, H. Louis Rey, William Barrett, and Andre Cailloux and Lieutenants Alfred Bourgeau and Eugene Rapp had been officers in the Confederate Native Guard Regiment. Pinckney B. S. Pinchback, later lieutenant governor and governor of Louisiana during Reconstruction, was appointed a captain in the Second Regiment.[19]

The officers of the Third Regiment were both white and Negro. The white officers, all attached to New England regiments serving in the Department of the Gulf and appointed to the Native Guard Regiments by General Butler, were Captains Charles Blake and Elias Carson and Lieutenants Charles Fallington, William Westover, James Aldrich, Rufus Clark, and Joseph Parker. The remaining company officers were Negroes, and the non-commissioned officers of all three regiments were Negroes.[20] The men of the first three regiments averaged twenty-eight years of age. Joseph Frick, forty-nine, was the eldest, and Aristide Desmange, nineteen, the youngest, Frick was a mulatto bricklayer, and Desmange was a waiter; both were from New Orleans. The average height of the men of the three regiments was five feet, six inches. The men in the First Regiment were described as having yellow complexions, grey or brown eyes, and black, brown, or light hair. Twenty percent of the men in the First Regiment were bricklayers; 15 percent, carpenters; 2 percent, plasterers; 6 percent, shoemakers; 12 percent, cigar makers; and the remaining 45 percent, laborers. The men of the Second and Third Regiments were described as having black complexions, brown or black-brown eyes, and black or red hair. Their occupations were either farmer or laborer, and they were recruited mostly in the sugar-growing Teche District of Louisiana. It seems that the Second and Third Regiments were composed largely of freedmen whereas the First Regiment had a large percentage of free Negroes.[21]

When the Native Guards began training at Camp Strong, their activities aroused a great deal of interest among the people of New Orleans. The streets and grounds around the camp were filled with visitors, especially from the free colored population, who viewed the afternoon dress parades with lively enjoyment. On October 24, 1862, Frank Barclay, editor-in-chief of *L'Union*, a daily French language newspaper published by the free people of color, went out to the camp to watch one the parades. He reported the good discipline, neatness of the camp, and knowledge of the use of arms and equipment exhibited by the Guards. The same issue of *L'Union* contained an advertisement calling for men to "rally to the Union flag" and volunteer to serve in the Third Regiment of Native Guards. Volunteers would receive one hundred dollars or 160 acres of land as a bounty for enlistment; pay of thirteen dollars a month and food for their families. The greatest demand was for volunteers who spoke both English and French to enlist as non-commissioned officers. Those who wished to join were asked to report to M. Louis N. Fouche at 96 Champs Elysees Street in the Third District.[22]

On October 25, 1862, the men of the First Regiment marched out of Camp Strong Station bound for Algiers, Louisiana, where they would receive orders from Col. Stephen Thomas of the Eighth Vermont Regiment. The men of the Second Regiment remained at the Touro Building until October 30, when they were ordered to Opelousas, about 130 miles from New Orleans. They journeyed to Opelousas partially by rail but marched most of the way. There they remained until December 31, guarding the railroads in the area. The Third Regiment filled up as rapidly as the first two and was mustered in on November 24, 1862. It was assigned to clear the sugarcane land in the Teche District for the next year's crop. Just three months after General Butler began to recruit Negro soldiers, three regiments totaling 2,700 men were in the field, and one infantry regiment and two artillery batteries were in training at Camp Strong.[23]

After one month of basic training, the men of the First Regiment began their service in the Union cause on October 25, 1862. They soon found that they were expected to aid in the dispersion of the Confederate forces in the Teche District. General Butler planned to move into western Louisiana and attack the rebel forces commanded by Gen. Richard Taylor. Butler organized the forces in the Teche District into a brigade consisting of two batteries of artillery, four companies of cavalry, and five regiments of infantry, which he ordered Gen. Godfrey Weitzel of the Corps of Engineers to command. Weitzel was one of Butler's principal military advisers during the successful attack on New Orleans and had demonstrated marked proficiency as a tactician and strategist. Butler planned to open Union railroad communications throughout western Louisiana in order to furnish a supply route and a means of transporting the sugar and cotton crops of local planters to New Orleans. Part of Weitzel's brigade would concentrate on repairing railroads while the remainder tried to engage the rebels in combat. In support of the army's action, Butler asked the navy to send light draught steamers, with iron coverings over their boilers, to attack the Confederate batteries at Berwick Bay. The ironclads would gain control of the waterways, thus cutting off Confederate supplies from Texas.[24]

On October 25, a portion of Weitzel's brigade successfully engaged the rebels in a light skirmish at Donaldsonville. Although the Native Guards did not engage in the fighting, they were already on the way to Algiers to begin the task of opening Union supply routes, and they arrived late that evening. Col. Sephen Thomas of the Eighth Vermont Infantry Regiment gave them their orders. The two regiments would be consolidated during the expedition, and Thomas was given the command. The combined forces marched from Algiers to Jefferson, a distance of twelve miles, carrying timber to be used for repair work. Jefferson was strategically located on the New Orleans, Opelousas, and Great Western Railroad. There they cleared away the grass between the rails and repaired the ties where necessary, thus restoring the line to service. On the morning of October 26, they marched to Bayou des Allemands where they were to repair the bridge which the retreating rebels had burned. They crossed the bayou in skiffs and set up camp on an abandoned plantation which was used as headquarters while the work was in progress. After rebuilding the bridge they moved to La Fourche where they established semi-permanent headquarters. In the six days since leaving Camp Strong, the First Native Guards and the Eighth Vermont Regiment opened fifty-two miles of railroad, built nine culverts, and rebuilt the bridge at Bayou des Allemands, which was 435 feet long.[25]

On November 3, the First Native Guards and the Eighth Vermont Regiment rejoined the rest of Weitzel's brigade. They were sent on numerous scouting and foraging expeditions in the La Fourche area. Supplies were confiscated from rebel sympathizers and sent to the New Orleans depot. On November 5, 1862, Weitzel wrote Butler that he could not continue to command colored troops since slaves outnumbered white persons in the area and he feared the possibility of a servile rebellion precipitated by his Native Guards. There were also, it seems, endless complaints of stealing, plundering, and other crimes perpetrated by the Negro soldiers. Butler ordered Weitzel to retain his command because "these colored regiments, raised by the authority of the President, and approved by him must be commanded by officers of the United States like any other regiment." Butler further reminded Weitzel that this removal would not necessarily prevent a servile rebellion, and he also pointed out that there had been no criticism of the troops for failure in their previously assigned tasks or for disobedience to their officers. Nor was there any official mention of outrages or pillaging by colored soldiers. It seemed to Butler that Weitzel should be more concerned with advancing Union war aims than with protecting local rebel sympathizers from a nebulous slave uprising. While Weitzel was worrying about the safety of the wife of General Bragg and other rebels in Louisiana, Bragg and other Confederates were fighting the Union army elsewhere. In deference to his repeated protestation, however, Weitzel was ordered to retain overall command of the brigade, and the colored troops remained unattached in a separate unit under Colonel Stafford until a few days before the Battle of Port Hudson.[26]

On November 30, 1862, the Third Native Guard Infantry, which had just finished clearing sugarcane land for the next year's crop in the Teche District, rejoined the First Regiment. During the month of December both regiments made two foraging expeditions within a radius of twenty miles from La Fourche during which they were viewed with anger, hostility, and fear by the white population. Most white persons were unaccustomed to the sight of armed and uniformed Negroes, and they hurled insults and curses at the men in the regiments. The expeditions were moderately successful. The Native Guards brought in fifty-one muskets abandoned by retreating rebels, along with some Confederate salt and the sloop in which it had been smuggled through the blockade.[27]

During the first three months of their active service there were only twenty-nine desertions from the First Native Guard Regiment, twelve from the Second Regiment, and ten from the Third Regiment. The men were harassed by the insulting attitude of the white civilian population, but they managed to withstand the pressure. The officers of the Native Guard Regiments were treated discourteously by the officers of white troops who refused to salute them or show them the respect normally accorded a fellow officer. Colonel Stafford was involved in an incident which was a factor in his dismissal from the service. On December 2, Stafford sent out teamsters and choppers from the Native Guards to gather wood. They had a pass permitting them to leave the company area. When they tried to return to camp, the guard at the gate, a member of the Thirteenth Louisiana Cavalry (which Butler had recruited from among the loyal white population of Louisiana) refused to allow them to pass. When the men tried to explain that they had a pass, the guard shook one of them roughly and called him a variety of insulting names. A Negro soldier, viewing the affair from inside the camp, reported the incident to Stafford who rode up to the gate on horseback and ordered the guard to allow the men to pass. Stafford then asked the commander of the Thirteenth Cavalry, Capt. Richard Barrett, who was drilling his troops at the time, to explain the conduct of the guard. When Barrett gave no satisfactory reply, "Stafford rode at him and knocked him to the ground."[28]

During these first two months there was a small flurry of accidents in the colored regiments caused by unfamiliarity with weapons and equipment. For example, Sergeant Eugene Francis was accidentally killed by a corporal who was practicing the firing of his weapon; Private Washington Lewis caught his foot in the crank of a railway handcart which required amputation of his great toe. The morale of the men remained generally high during those first months. On December 31, Colonel Stafford reported that, considering the growth of the regiment and the duty in which it was engaged, its drill and discipline were good. Stafford thought, however, that they had been saved from the demoralizing tendencies of segregation only by an earnest desire to prove the capabilities of their race.[29]

By January 3, 1863, Colonel Stafford felt that his men had shown they were capable of performing combat duty and requested that Gen. Nathaniel Banks, the new commander of the Department of the Gulf, allow his men to fight. If they were not fit to fight, they were equally unfit for the delicate and important job of guarding the New Orleans, Opelousas, and Great Western Railroad. He received no answer from Banks. On January 9, 1863, the Second Regiment received orders to proceed to Ship Island, where they were assigned to prison guard duty for most of the remainder of the war. On March 17, 1863, the First and Third Regiments finally received new assignments. They were ordered to march to New Brunswick and board the transport, *General Banks*, which took them to Baton Rouge. They arrived on March 19, 1863, and aided the Fourth Native Guard Infantry Regiment in rebuilding Fort Williams, which the Union forces had captured from the rebels. Colonel Stafford was soon in trouble again. He was charged by First Lieutenant E. D. Johnson of the Twenty-First Maine Volunteers with trying to cross a picket line without a pass. When he was not allowed to pass, he allegedly uttered "disrespectful or contemptuous language against President Lincoln," and called Captain Farland of the Twenty-First Maine Volunteers a "pusillanimous white livered coward." Stafford was jailed at Port Hudson on May 10, 1863, finally court-martialed and charged with conduct prejudicial to good military order and discipline. He was found guilty and dismissed from the service whereupon he returned to his home in Medlin, Delaware. Since he had shown a sincere interest in their welfare, the men in the regiment resented his dismissal. In January, 1871, he was accorded an honorable discharge which was retroactive to his dismissal.[30]

During the spring of 1863, the three regiments of Louisiana Native Guards got their first taste of real warfare. The Second Regiment had resigned itself to the boredom of garrison duty at Ship Island, but the men were happily relieved when they were assigned to a brief reconnaissance mission outside the fort. In April they marched up the Mississippi Sound to Pascagoula, recording enemy troop movements on the way. As they started back for the fort, they encountered a superior force of the enemy which they defeated; two members of the Second Regiment were killed and seven wounded.[31] They received no further opportunity to demonstrate their prowess in battle.

The First and Third Regiments had better luck. The persistent agitation of the War Department by their regimental commanders resulted in an opportunity to engage in a large-scale battle. The troops had grown tired of a constant round of guard, picket, and engineer duty. General Banks, who had relieved Butler as commander of the Department of the Gulf in December 1862, decided to include the two regiments in the Nineteenth Army Corps' campaign against the rebels at Port Hudson. Banks, hoping to pacify the white population without occasioning the enmity which Butler generated, retained the three Native Guard regiments but hesitated at first to enlist more Negro troops. However, he gradually responded to the changing attitude in Lincoln's administration as well as his own manpower needs by organizing more regiments of Negro troops with white officers, expecting to use them primarily for guard, engineer, and picket duty. Despite his lukewarm attitude, Banks decided to include the First and Third Native Guards in the Port Hudson campaign. He seemed to be influenced by the need for extra troops, by a desire to outshine Butler in the employment of Negroes, and by the efforts of George Denison, who continued to insist that Negroes be used for actual combat.[32]

From the time of his arrival in the Department of the Gulf, General Banks recognized the importance of the Mississippi River as a supply route. If the Union forces could control it, the Trans-Mississippi West would be effectively cut off from the rest of the South. Banks planned to drive the rebel forces from the area around New Orleans, and then group his own forces for an attack on Port Hudson. In January 1863, he sent General Weitzel's brigade to drive the rebels from the Teche District. Weitzel encountered Brig. Gen. Alfred Mouton's forces at the juncture of the Atchafalaya and the Teche and drove them out of this position; he smashed the Confederates' new iron-clad gunboat, *Cotton*, from offshore batteries, and returned to New Orleans. In March, Banks and Admiral David Farragut agreed upon a plan to station the Union forces upriver from Port Hudson in order to cut off rebel supplies by way of the Red River. This maneuver would also facilitate Union communication with Vicksburg and prevent construction of new rebel defenses between the two garrisons. On March 7, a major portion of the divisions of Maj. Gen. Thomas W. Sherman and C. C. Augur and Brigadier Generals William Emory and Cuvier Grover met in the area near Port Hudson and waited for a propitious time for the gunboats to sneak past the fort. Finally, at 8:00 P.M. on March 14, while the land forces exercised diversionary tactics, Admiral Farragut was able to steam upriver. The *Hartford* and *Albatross* passed successfully, but the *Mississippi* ran aground and was burned by her crew to prevent rebel capture. The *Richmond, Monongahela, Essex, Sachen*, and *Kineo* remained below Port Hudson. Banks felt that his forces were in a good position to attack the fort, but could get no reinforcements from Grant. On March 21, 1863, he returned to Baton Rouge. . . .[33]

The Union forces, including the First and Third Native Guards, remained at Baton Rouge during March. The entire group of Negro officers in the Third Native Guard resigned during this period. They signed a letter, written by Capt. Leon Forstall, which stated that they had met with nothing but scorn and contempt from both military and civilians. If they requested information of a white officer, they received only "abrupt and ungentlemanly" answers. The whites seemed to regard merely being spoken to by a colored officer as "an insult." On the assumption that they knew nothing of military discipline, even their commander abused them. Their position was thus insupportable, and there was no recourse except resignation from the service.[34]

In a letter to President Lincoln on August 17, 1863, Banks described the condition of the Negro regiments on his arrival in the Department of the Gulf as "demoralized from various causes." Their officers were constantly engaged in controversy with white troops so that the white officers of these regiments, as well as the colored men who were in commission, believed that it was impracticable for them to continue in service. The difficulty was caused, thought Banks, by the character of the Negro officer. They were unfit and were in arrest most of the time upon "charges of discreditable character."[35] Banks' explanations have some validity, but from available evidence, they do not apply to the Third Native Guards. In the First Native Guards, it seems that some of the officers were dismissed for cowardice after the Port Hudson campaign, but there was no evidence of cowardly behavior when Banks arrived in the Department of the Gulf. It is very likely, however, that the Negroes were not strict disciplinarians because of their lack of military knowledge. It was probably true also that they resented the white officers. In any case, when the two Negro regiments started for Port Hudson, the Third Regiment had white line officers.

General Banks planned to attack Port Hudson by way of the Teche District from the juncture of the Atchafalaya and the Red Rivers. He expected aid from General Grant, who was at Vicksburg, in the main assault on the fortress. The two men had communicated throughout the first two weeks of April. Grant had promised to send an army corps to Bayou Sara, just above Port Hudson. After taking the fort, Banks would send reinforcements to Grant. Banks, confident of receiving additional men, ordered most of his troops to move to Alexandria. They marched over land for most of the four hundred miles, because there was not sufficient rail and water transportation to move such a large army. Gen. Thomas W. Sherman started his division from New Orleans, and Generals Banks, Emory, and Grover started out from Opelousas. When Banks' forces arrived at Alexandria, a letter from Grant was received informing Banks that no reinforcements would be available. Grant wrote that he had met the enemy south of Port Gibson, and followed him to the Big Black River, and could not afford to retrace his steps. As Banks could not go to Vicksburg to aid Grant without endangering New Orleans, he marched his troops four hundred miles back to Baton Rouge to attack Port Hudson unaided.[36]

On the 14th of May, five days after their arrival at Alexandria, Banks' forces started back toward Port Hudson. They crossed the river in transports and marched to the bayou at the rear of the fort. On May 25, after marching overland from Baton Rouge, General Augur's brigade, containing the First and Third Native Guards, arrived at Port Hudson.

The commands were organized into four divisions commanded by General Augur, General Sherman, General Grover, and Colonel Paine. The First and Third Native Guards were retained in Augur's division. Paine took over Emory's division because Emory had become ill on the march from Alexandria and had returned to New Orleans. In each division there were three brigades of infantry and three field artillery batteries. There were 7,000 cavalrymen organized in two battalions and six troops. In addition, a regiment of heavy artillery, the First Indiana, was assigned the siege train. The white troops were drawn mainly from New England and New York regiments. Five regiments of Corps D'Afrique Engineers, recruited by Gen. Daniel Ullmann, were assigned to trench duty. Banks had a total of 20,000 effectives. There were approximately 12,000 rebel troops inside the garrison.[37]

The garrison at Port Hudson was well fortified. Earthworks along the sinuous brow of an elevated bluff served as formidable protection against the artillery of the Union army. There were twenty siege guns and thirty-one field pieces inside the garrison. The approaches to the fort were fairly well protected against assaulting columns by natural gullies alternating with abatis of felled trees. The Union army fought from a field position in a dense forest of magnolias, surrounded by heavy undergrowth and ravines choked with felled or fallen timbers.[38]

By May 26, the investment of the fort was completed and Banks ordered a general assault for the next morning at 5:00 A.M. Early the next day the artillery began bombarding the fort. At 10:00 A.M. Weitzel's brigade and two brigades from the Second Division, commanded by General William Dwight, moved to the attack in two lines. Dwight led, at first, driving the rebels in front through their fortifications. The Confederate artillery opened fire with grape and cannister, but the Union batteries soon took commanding positions within two hundred and three hundred yards of the works, which enabled them to keep down the enemy's fire. Grover began to move on the left of Weitzel, attacking at two points, but merely succeeded in gaining a position about two hundred yards from the works. General Dwight ordered the First and Third Native Guard Regiments, on the extreme right, to form for the attack. As soon as they started to advance, the Confederate line opened artillery and musketry fire. After suffering heavy casualties, the Native Guards were forced to retreat.

General Ullmann reported that the Louisiana Negro Regiment was on the extreme left of his own Engineers. The ground in that area was broken and covered with a very tangled abatis. The Native Guards made six or seven charges, but were "exposed to a terrible fire and were dreadfully slaughtered." Despite the unfortunate outcome, the assault of the regiment in the face of such terrible fire impressed those observers who had thought Negroes would not fight. On that day Ullmann saw a "marvellous change in the opinions of many former sneerers."[39]

In the first advance on May 27, both Capt. Andre Cailloux and Lieutenant John Crowder were killed. The diary of the Third Regiment indicates that the men advanced without difficulty until they were within pistol shot of the rebel fortifications. They were stopped, however, by the backflow of the creek in front of the garrison. The water was eight feet deep and some forty feet across. They tried to cross but were met with heavy fire. They advanced six times but were driven back on each attempt. The regiment lost 154 killed or wounded out of a total of 1,080 effectives. During the engagement they were commanded by Lieutenant Col. David Finegass. The regimental commander, Col. John Nelson, stayed on the Union side of the river and observed the proceedings.[40]

The Union failure in storming the garrison made it imperative that a siege be instituted. The men began the difficult task of constructing approaches, parallels, bombproof, and shelters for their artillery. Negro troops under General Ullmann performed most of the construction duty. Meanwhile, hoping to force a capitulation, the Union gunboats fired unceasingly at the Confederate garrison.[41]

On the 14th of June, Banks felt that it was time for another assault, and every available man was brought forward. Casualties and disease, however, had decimated the ranks. Banks asked for volunteers for a storming party, which would bear the brunt of the action. The entire First and Third Regiments of Native Guards volunteered for the mission. Only fifty-three men from the First Regiment and forty men from the Third Regiment were permitted to take part.[42] The attack began at daybreak on June 15, preceded by a general cannonade for one hour. The storming party attacked vigorously at the strongest point of the enemy's works. Sweeping enemy fire drove them back as they tried to cross the crest of the bluff, which was found later to be shaven bald, with every blade of grass cut down to the roots. The Union army lost hundreds of men in the two assaults. Colonel Paine himself was severely wounded, as he stayed at the front of the attacking party. The heat in the trenches, the foul odors resulting from inattention to sanitary measures, the dried-up brooks and creeks, and the pestilent river contributed to increasing illness and subsequent mortality. The effective Union strength at Port Hudson was hardly 9,000 at the end and would have been even less if all men who were sick had reported themselves.[43]

Meanwhile, the Confederate forces under Gen. Richard Taylor had reorganized, crossed the Atchafalaya, captured the garrisons at Brashear City and Donaldsonville, and were menacing New Orleans. On July 4, General Emory wrote Banks that he must choose between New Orleans and Port Hudson. On July 7, Banks decided to attack once more in a last desperate attempt to subdue the garrison. Just as the battle was about to begin, word came from General Grant that Vicksburg had surrendered. An aide threw a note containing the news over into the Confederate line, and at two o'clock the next morning, the Confederate garrison surrendered. The rebels capitulated because Vicksburg had fallen and because their forces were reduced to 3,000 half-starved men who were about to face another scorching attack. The Union army had 708 killed, 3,336 wounded, and 329 captured or missing. The official reports of the First Regiment of Louisiana Native Guards listed thirty-five killed, ninety-four wounded, and three missing or captured.[44] Colonel Stafford was imprisoned at Port Hudson on May 13 for insubordination; thus the First Regiment was commanded during the entire campaign by Maj. Chauncey Bassett, who had received a battlefield promotion to the rank of Colonel. The assault on May 27 was the first large scale encounter between white and Negro soldiers. One historian has stated that the regiments retreated in a "frightened and demoralized" condition after firing one volley. However, the men received lavish praise from Banks who was no Negrophile. In his official reports the general declared that no troops were more determined or daring. The Negro troops made three assaults on the enemy garrison, suffering heavy losses and consequently deserving the highest commendation.[45] But Banks soon forgot them; he even refused them permission to emblazon Port Hudson on their regimental banners.

The conduct of the Negro troops at Port Hudson was a milestone. Their behavior greatly heartened those who believed in the Negro soldier movement as a matter of principle. At a time when many whites thought that Negroes would not fight, the official reports clearly showed that they would. Just as conscription was getting under way in the North and a demand for increased manpower was being heard, attention was strongly focused on the possibilities of Negro troops. The efforts of Lorenzo Thomas and the Bureau of Colored Troops to obtain officers for Negro regiments were increasingly more successful. While few white men wanted to command regiments of stevedores, cotton pickers, and construction workers, those who yearned for commissions would be happy to command such valiant troops. The newspapers presented exciting accounts of the behavior of the Native Guards. On June 13, 1863, the *New York Times* editorialized on the abilities and willingness of Negro troops, and predicted that sneering at the military deficiencies of such persons was at an end.[46]

The colored people of New Orleans continued their long tradition of military organization during the Civil War. The Louisiana Native Guards served both in the Confederacy and in the Union army. It seems that they were the only Negro organization utilized by the Confederacy before the last-ditch attempt to enroll Negroes in the spring of 1865. The Native Guards performed only parade, drill, and guard duty during their period of service in the Confederacy, but they were utilized for combat and engineer purposes by the Union army. They repaired and reopened railroad communications with New Orleans in the fall of 1862. They guarded railroads, to prevent possible rebel attacks, and went on reconnaissance missions in the La Fourche District. Their heroic conduct at Port Hudson helped change public sentiment regarding the fighting capabilities of Negroes. At a time when the initiation of national conscription brought large numbers of Negroes into the service, the Native Guards clearly demonstrated the fitness of colored troops for more than guard and picket duty; Negroes could satisfactorily perform combat and fatigue functions as a large and valuable part of the Union war effort.

Notes for "Negro Troops in Blue and Gray:
The Louisiana Native Guards, 1861-1863"

[1]Joseph T. Wilson, *Black Phalanx, A History of the Negro Soldiers in the Wars of 1775, 1812, 1816-65* (Hartford, 1888); James McPherson, *The Negro's Civil War; How American Negroes Felt and Acted During the War for Union* (New York, 1965); Dudley Cornish, *The Sable Arm, Negro Troops in the Union Army, 1861-1865* (New York, 1956); Donald Everett, "Ben Butler and the Louisiana Native Guards 1861-1862," *Journal of Southern History*, 24 (1958): 202; John W. Caughey, *Bernardo de Galvez in Louisiana 1776-1783* (Berkeley, 1934), 41, 173-75.

[2]*U. S. Statutes at Large 1789-1869*, 15 vols. (Boston, 1845-73), 2:271-77, Militia Act of 1792. State laws were largely carbon copies of the federal statute except *Acts passed at the First Session of the First General Assembly of the State of Louisiana* (New Orleans, 1812), 72.

[3]William Cooper Nell, *Colored Patriots of the American Revolution* (Boston, 1855), 296, 313; *Messages of the President of the United States with the Correspondence therewith Communicated between the Secretary of War and other offices of the Government on the Subject of the Mexican War* (Washington, 1848), 935-37; The Negro in the Military Service . . . to 1888, a Compilation of Official Records . . . , Record Group, 94, MSS, National Archives, Vol. 3:397.

[4]*New Orleans Daily True Delta*, April 23, 1861; John D. Winters, *The Civil War in Louisiana* (Baton Rouge, 1963), 15, 21.

[5]*New Orleans Daily True Delta*, April 27, May 2, 1861; Everett, "Ben Butler and the Louisiana Native Guards," 203.

[6]*The War of the Rebellion: A Compilation of the Official Records of the Union and Confederate Armies*, 70 vols. in 128 (Washington, 1880-1901), Series 1, Vol. 15:555, hereinafter cited as *O.R.*; Muster rolls, First Native Guards Louisiana Militia, Confederate States of America, May 3, 1861, Record Group 109, War Department Collection of Confederate Group Records, MSS, National Archives, hereinafter cited as R. G. 109, C.G.R.; Winters, *Civil War in Louisiana*, 34-35, claims that the officers of the regiment were not Negroes.

[7]Eighth Census of Free Inhabitants of New Orleans (1860), Vols. 5-9, MSS, National Archives; Muster Rolls, First Native Guards, Confederate States of America, R.G. 109, C.G.R.

[8]*O.R.*, Series 1, Vol. 53, Supp. 746, Maj. Gen. John Lewis Commanding, Confederate Militia, State of Louisiana to New Orleans Militia Headquarters, Sept. 29, 1861.

[9]Morning Report, First Native Guards, Confederate States of America, January 10, 1862, R.G. 109, C.G.R.; Winters, *Civil War in Louisiana*, 35.

[10]*Report of the Joint Committee on the Conduct of the War*, pt. 3, 1863 (Washington, 1863), 364-65, Testimony of Maj. Gen. Benjamin F. Butler, February 2, 1863; James Parton, *General Butler in New Orleans* (Boston, 1864), 264; Wilson, *Black Phalanx*, 183.

[11]John William de Forest, *A Volunteer's Adventures, A Union Captain's Record of the Civil War*, ed. by James Croushore (New Haven, 1946), 26-27; Richard West, Jr., *Lincoln's Scapegoat General; A Life of Benjamin F. Butler 1818-1889* (Boston, 1965), 144-45; Hans L. Trefousse, *Ben Butler, The South Called Him Beast!* (New York, 1957), 107, 119-21; Parton, *Butler in New Orleans*, 301-22, 489-94.

[12]Benjamin F. Butler, *The Private and Official Correspondence of General Benjamin F. Butler During the Period of the Civil War*, 5 vols. (Norwood, Mass., 1917), 2:173-74, 229. For more information on the Phelps-Butler controversy see Parton, *Butler in New Orleans*, 496-516; Trefousse, *Ben Butler*, 130-31; West, *Scapegoat General*, 161; Everett, "Ben Butler and the Louisiana Native Guards," 208; Winters, *Civil War in Louisiana*, 143-45.

[13]*O. R.*, Series 1, 4:442-43; Everett, "Ben Butler and the Louisiana Native Guards," 205.

[14]*Report of the Joint Committee on the Conduct of the War*, pt. 3:367; Parton, *Butler in New Orleans*, 516-17.

[15]*O. R.*, Series 1, 4:549, 559; Everett, "Ben Butler and the Louisiana Native Guards," 208; Parton, *Ben Butler in New Orleans*, 516-17.

[16]The Negro in the Military Service, R.G. 94, 4:254.

[17]Butler, *Private and Official Correspondence,* 2:270-71; The Negro in the Military Service, R.G. 94, Vol. 4:554.

[18]Muster Rolls, First, Second and Third Louisiana Native Guard Infantry Regiments, R.G. 94, Adjutant General's office, MSS., National Archives, hereinafter referred to as A.G.O.

[19]Ibid.

[20]Muster rolls, Third Louisiana Native Guard Infantry Regiment, R.G. 94, A.G.O.

[21]Descriptive Books, First, Second and Third Louisiana Native Guards Infantry Regiments, R.G. 94, A.G.O.

[22]*New Orleans L'Union*, October 25, 1862.

[23]Carded Record of Events, First, Second, and Third Louisiana Native Guard Infantry Regiments, R.G. 94, A.G.O.

[24]*O. R.*, Series I, Vol. 15:158.

[25]Regimental Return, First Louisiana Native Guard Infantry Regiment, R.G. 94, A.G.O.

[26]*O. R.*, Series 1, 9:166-67; Winters, *Civil War in Louisiana*, 163; Everett, "Ben Butler and the Louisiana Native Guards," 213.

[27]Carded Record of Events, First, Second and Third Louisiana Native Guard Infantry Regiments, R.G. 94, A.G.O.

[28]Carded Military Service Record, Colonel Spencer H. Stafford, First Louisiana Native Guard Infantry Regiment, R.G. 94, Records and Pensions Office, MSS, National Archives.

[29]Regimental Return, 1862, First, Second, and Third Louisiana Native Guard Infantry Regiments, R.G. 94, A.G.O.

[30]Carded Military Service Record, Colonel Spencer H. Stafford, R.G. 94, Records and Pensions Office.

[31]Record of Events, Second Native Guard Infantry Regiment, March and April, 1863, R.G. 94, A.G.O.

[32]Letter Book, Third Native Guard Infantry Regiment, March 1863, R.G. 94, A.G.O.; Winters, *Civil War in Louisiana*, 208-209; Fred Harrington, *Fighting Politician, Major General N. P. Banks* (Philadelphia, 1948), 110-13.

[33]*O. R.*, Series 1, 19:255.

[34]Carded Military Service Record, Captain Leon Forstall, Third Louisiana Native Guard Infantry Regiment, R.G. 94, Records and Pensions Office.

[35]Wilson, *Black Phalanx*, 119; Harrington, *Banks*, 111.

[36]*O. R.*, Series 1, 26:315.

[37]Ibid., 321.

[38]*O. R.*, Series 1, 14:42. The figures for the Confederate army are estimated.

[39]Orders and Letters of Brigadier General Daniel Ullmann, General's Papers and Book, War Records Division, MSS, National Archives; Harrington, *Banks*, 121.

[40]Wilson, *Black Phalanx*, 525.

[41]Regimental Returns, 1863, First and Third Louisiana Native Guard Infantry Regiments, R.G. 94, A.G.O.

[42]The Negro in the Military Service, R.G. 94.

[43]De Forest, *Volunteer's Adventures*, 144.

[44]*O. R.*, Series 1, 26:44.

[45]Ibid., 47; Winters, *Civil War in Louisiana*, 253-55.

[46]*New York Times*, June 13, 1863; *Washington Daily National Intelligencer*, August 24, 1863.

BLACK VIOLENCE AND WHITE RESPONSE:
LOUISIANA, 1862*

William F. Messner

A curious duality marked antebellum thought regarding the black slave: the black image was a mixture of Sambo and Nat Turner, fawning simpleton and flaming revolutionary. White Americans explained this apparent anomaly in terms of the acculturation process which the plantation regimen imposed upon all slaves. By nature blacks were savage brutes, but through contact with the higher civilization of the white South the African had been domesticated. As long as the discipline of the white man was secure, the slave would remain a Sambo; but remove the authority of the master, and blacks would revert to type as bloodthirsty savages.[1] Although this pattern of thought was not peculiar to the South, in that region its influence was particularly pervasive, for the Southerner's belief in the black man's violent potential tended to reinforce the widely held opinion that a profitable production of staples could only be accomplished through the maintenance of a stable labor force. Slavery, therefore, had the complementary functions of ensuring white control over a potentially subversive minority population and of maximizing profits by the stabilization of labor.

The outbreak of civil war in 1861 sparked among whites a fear of imminent black violence, and in Southern war zones the exodus of slaves from plantations accompanied by sporadic acts of servile violence only sharpened in the white mind the image of the manic Afro-American. In Louisiana especially the racial stability secured by the slave system shattered beneath the weight of the Federal assault on New Orleans in the spring of 1862, and the resulting turmoil convinced both native whites and Federal military officials of the necessity for establishing mechanisms to check the black threat to law and order. While most Southerners favored a reinstitution of the slavery regime, Federal military officials during 1862 devised a series of contraband programs which stabilized the racial situation by placing blacks under white control and which also aided the Union war

*First published in *Journal of Southern History*, 41 (1975): 19-38. Copyright 1975 by the Southern Historical Association. Reprinted by permission of the Managing Editor.

effort. Prompted initially by the white fear of black violence, these programs served as precursors for future Federal efforts among the freedmen of the Southwest during the Civil War and Reconstruction.[2]

As soon as Federal warships appeared at the mouth of the Mississippi River early in 1862 plantation owners along the coast of Louisiana and Mississippi began to take precautions against the feared uprising of their slaves. Whites increased security measures, issued few passes for travel, and resorted more often to the whip. So fearful were planters of black violence that they refused to allow their slaves to congregate in large numbers even for such vital functions as repairing crevasses in the levee.[3] White fears were seemingly justified as blacks began to escape from their owners and to make their way by rowboat to the Federal staging area on Ship Island.[4] Other slaves bided their time until the Union assault on New Orleans was completed in May 1862. Believing the Union army had come to free them, slaves in the immediate vicinity of the city fled from their plantations and flocked into Union camps surrounding New Orleans. At Camp Parapet, just north of the city, 450 black refugees resided less than a month after the arrival of Union troops, and their number swelled to over a thousand by the end of the summer.[5]

Federal military officials were perplexed by the black exodus. "What shall I do with my niggers?" asked the hard-pressed commander at Fort Macomb.[6] "I am placed in an awkward dilemma," complained the commander at Fort Saint Philip; "I have no authority to feed them [the slaves] . . . or send them away. I cannot have them in the fort, and know not what to do."[7] A New Hampshire officer noted in his diary that the blacks were "coming into camp by the hundred and are a costly curse. They should be kept out or set at work, or freed or colonized or sunk or something."[8] The sentiments of an enlisted man were expressed in a letter from a private in the Fourth Wisconsin Volunteers. "Potatoes are knee high, & beans to the top of the poles," he wrote from Baton Rouge. "It is a nice country if it were not for the negroes [*sic*]."[9]

Accompanying the exodus of blacks from plantations were incidents of black violence which solidified in the white mind the image of the barbaric black man freed from the restraints of white discipline. During the summer reports abounded concerning black unrest in the parishes of southern Louisiana. ". . . there is an uneasy feeling among the slaves," reported a correspondent of the *New York Times* in late July; "they are undoubtedly becoming insubordinate, and I cannot think that another sixty days can pass away without some sort of demonstration."[10] Three weeks later the same reporter wrote that the slaves in two nearby parishes were in a state of "semi-insurrection."[11] The correspondent of the *New York Herald* concurred in these conditions. "There is no doubt that the negroes [*sic*], for more than fifty miles up the river, are in a state of insubordination," he reported from New Orleans. "The country is given to pillage and desolation. . . . The slaves refuse obedience and cannot be compelled to labor."[12] On a Plaquemines Parish estate the owner recorded the following disturbing scene: "We have a terrible state of affairs here negroes [*sic*] refusing to work and women all in their houses.

The negroes [*sic*] have erected a gallows in the quarters and give as an excuse for it that they are told they must drive their master . . . off the plantation . . . and that then they will be free."[13] On a neighboring plantation the slaves had already driven off the overseer and taken over the estate for their own use, and on another place blacks killed an overseer who had beaten slaves for refusing to work.[14] Frustrated in their own attempts at quelling the racial turmoil, slave owners turned to the Union army as the only means for restoring order in the parishes.[15]

The tide of racial turmoil extended even into New Orleans. On the outskirts of the city violent confrontations often occurred between police and black refugees attempting to enter Union lines. Disgusted with such militant actions, the *New Orleans Daily Picayune* declared in July 1862 that the slaves had "become impudent, disobedient and reckless. This morning fifteen, armed with clubs and cane knives, came up from a plantation below the city."[16] Two weeks later a New Orleans citizen noted in his diary that "late last night & early this morning there was a speck of servile war in the lower part of the city." Forty slaves had overpowered the police and were only routed when Federal troops arrived on the scene.[17] Once inside the city the behavior of blacks improved very little. Police reports for the Third District of New Orleans reflect the racial instability which gripped the city. Arrests of slaves accused of impudent and violent behavior were daily occurrences during the summer, and a constant stream of fugitive bondsmen flowed in and out of the city's jails.[18] Especially disturbing to whites was the frequency with which police arrested slaves for insulting and even assaulting their owners. One such incident was recorded by the *Picayune*: "A savage old nigger named Ben, forgetting all past benefits conferred upon him, was brought into court for insulting his mistress. Among other disloyal expressions the old rascal said that he wanted to get arrested, for then he could become a soldier, fight his mistress, and do what he pleased. He was sent to prison for three months."[19] Disturbances such as this confirmed the *Picayune's* opinion that "Recent events have made many of the negroes [*sic*] in this city and neighborhood almost unmanageable."[20]

The Union commander charged with the responsibility for restoring order to the Gulf Department was Maj. Gen. Benjamin Franklin Butler.[21] At first glance Butler appears to have been an unlikely choice for the command of the Union expedition against New Orleans. A professional politician, he had no military experience prior to 1861 save for the command of a brigade of Massachusetts militia. As a lifelong Democrat, the general had supported the Buchanan administration throughout its tumultuous term of office, and in 1860 he had campaigned for the election of John Cabell Breckinridge, the one Democratic candidate whom Butler believed had a chance of defeating Abraham Lincoln for the presidency. But with the secession of South Carolina the Massachusetts politician decided to divest himself of the robes of Hunker Democracy and took up the cause of the national government. In attempting to rid himself of the stigma of his Democratic past, Butler informed Massachusetts governor John Albion Andrew well before the outbreak of hostilities that he was ready to serve with the militia in case of an emergency. Eager to gain Democratic support for the Union war effort, Governor Andrew was only too glad to appoint the willing Butler commanding general of the state militia in the field. Only a month after Fort Sumter, Butler evoked the public's notice when, in response to severe criticism from the radical wing of the Massachusetts Republican party for having returned slaves to their master, he labeled three fugitive slaves who came into his lines at Fort Monroe, Virginia, contraband of war and refused to return them to their owners. Butler justified his politic maneuver on the basis of military necessity. The slaves had previously been aiding the Confederate war effort, and Butler's actions simply shifted their energies to support the cause of the Union.[22]

Despite having earned the reputation of a foe of slavery during his command at Fort Monroe, Butler was initially disinclined to tamper with the peculiar institution in southern Louisiana. His goal in the Gulf Department was to restore Louisiana to the Union by assuaging the fears of the planting and propertied interests who were "well-disposed toward the Union, only fearing lest their negroes [sic] should not be let alone. . . ."[23] Confiscation of slaves would have been, in Butler's opinion, an "injustice to the bona fide loyal creditor, whose interest the Government will doubtless consider."[24] Contributing to his determination to ensure that slaves remained under the control of their masters was his dread of the blacks' potential for violence. Deeply disturbed by the racial instability he met in New Orleans, Butler outlined his thoughts on slavery in a letter to Secretary of the Treasury Salmon Portland Chase:

> Be sure that I shall treat the negro [sic] with as much tenderness as possible but I assure you it is quite impossible to free him here and now without a San Domingo. A single whistle from me would cause every white mans throat to be cut in this city. Accumulated hate has been piled up here between master and servant, until it is fearful. . . . There is no doubt that an insurrection is only prevented by our *Bayonets*.[25]

Convinced of the necessity for maintaining civil order, Butler attempted to reassure the native white population that the Union army would not tolerate further racial unrest. During the first week of the Federal occupation he publicly declared that "All rights of property, of whatever kind, will be held inviolate, subject only to the laws of the United States." The object of the military in Louisiana was "to restore order out of chaos . . ." and "to have every species of disorder quelled." He also promised that all persons aiding this cause would not be disturbed in either their persons or property.[26] Determined to fulfill these promises, Butler directed his troops to confiscate only those slaves whose owners had committed an overtly treasonable act. All other black refugees who could not be employed by the army were to be excluded from Union lines.[27]

Butler delegated primary responsibility for implementing his slave-exclusion policy in New Orleans to the city police, for War Department orders prohibited military authorities from returning slaves to their owners. Throughout the summer of 1862 police officers gathered and imprisoned fugitive slaves from the streets of New Orleans and delivered them to their owners on demand.[28] Outside the confines of the city, however, the task of restraining blacks from leaving their owners belonged by default to the Federal army. Contrary to both national law and military orders, the army not only excluded slaves from its lines during the summer but also returned slaves to their owners and disciplined recalcitrant black workers.[29] Even the navy became involved in maintaining civil order. During the unsuccessful naval assault on Vicksburg in June blacks succeeded in boarding Union vessels despite the efforts of ship commanders to exclude them. Naval regulations required that these slaves be hired as laborers on the flotilla, but many were returned to owners who claimed loyalty to the Union.[30]

Although most officers in the Gulf Department agreed with Butler's contention regarding the slaves' potential for violence, not all concurred in his methods for controlling blacks. The most notable critic of the commanders' contraband policy was Brig. Gen. John Wolcott Phelps, a regular army officer who first articulated much of the thinking which would later shape Federal efforts among the freedmen of the Southwest. An outspoken proponent of the primacy of the Anglo-Saxon race and the efficacy of free labor, Phelps believed that the presence of the black slave thwarted the extension of Northern laborers and institutions throughout the South. He hoped the war would result in the abolition of slavery and the exportation of the slaves, but he believed special measures had to be taken during the war to care for blacks who, left to shift for themselves, would either initiate a race war or align with the rebels in response to native white promises of protection. In order to stabilize and control the black population Phelps proposed the organization of blacks into military units and the establishment of rigorous educational program for all slaves. At the end of hostilities he hoped to utilize his black troops as the vanguard of a black exodus to Africa for exploiting the "underdeveloped riches" of the Dark Continent.[31]

Immediately upon his arrival in the Gulf Department Phelps began implementing his antislavery beliefs despite General Butler's policy of buttressing the slave system. During the first weeks of Federal occupation slaveowners besieged the commander with complaints that their chattels were being given refuge at Camp Parapet, the headquarters of General Phelps. Butler attempted to cajole and then to scold his balky subordinate into submission, but all his efforts proved unavailing. Phelps believed that if the army continued to support slavery, "the danger of a violent revolution, over which we can have no control, must become more imminent every day," and therefore he continued to accept fugitive slaves into his camp and subsequently began a system of rudimentary black education and military training.[32]

Phelps's utilization of black troops placed him on a direct collision course with his commander. By writing department headquarters in late July and requesting provisions for his new troops, he precipitated the final confrontation with General Butler. As justification for the enlistment of slaves, Phelps argued that his program was "the best way of preventing the African from becoming instrumental in a general state of anarchy."[33] Butler reacted heatedly to this latest provocation. He wrote to his wife that Phelps was "mad as a March Hare on the 'nigger question.'"[34] Not even deigning to consider Phelps's proposal, Butler directed his subordinate to employ his "contrabands" in cutting down the trees around his camp. Regarding Butler's orders as an affront and unwilling to perform the functions of a "slave-driver," Phelps tendered his resignation.[35] By the end of the summer he had left the Gulf Department and the army, but his ideas lingered on. Through his efforts Phelps popularized the notion that programs could be established for transforming blacks into a positive element in the war effort and for eliminating the slaves' disruptive potential.[36] Even before his departure from the Gulf Department, Phelps's beliefs were beginning to replace the more conservative practices of General Butler.

The necessity for a basic alteration in the army's confiscation program was impressed upon Butler by a combination of local and national developments. Within the Gulf Department, despite the best efforts of the military, blacks continued to manifest their discontent with the institution of slavery, and black insubordination remained as the leitmotif of labor relations on sugar plantations. In Butler's opinion, the continuing racial instability threatened to make his department a "Sodom & Gomorrah," with the slaves acting as the "fire and brimstone" of God. At his wits' end concerning the unruly blacks, the commander exclaimed to his wife, "we shall have a negro [*sic*] insurrection here I fancy. If something is not done soon, God help us all. The negroes [*sic*] are getting saucy and troublesome, and who blames them?"[37]

At this juncture in the late summer of 1862, although Butler was still convinced of the necessity of maintaining control over the black population, he was no longer certain that this goal could be accomplished through the medium of slavery. Rather, over the last three months of the year Butler instituted programs which simultaneously signaled the demise of slavery in southern Louisiana and the reinstitution of white control over blacks. The final impetus for this change came from the national level. Administration spokesmen, such as Secretary of War Edwin McMasters Stanton and Secretary of the Treasury Salmon Chase, informed Butler during the late summer of a shift in national sentiment toward the abolition of slavery. They suggested that he place himself at the head of this movement by acting decisively against the peculiar institution in the Gulf Department.[38] Their opinion was confirmed by the passage of the Second Confiscation Act on July 17, which freed all slaves of rebel masters as soon as they came within Union lines.[39] Butler's politically astute wife analyzed the growth of antislavery sentiment for her husband in early August. She wrote: "Emancipation, and arming the negroes [*sic*] is held in check for a little . . . [as] soon as there is a plausible hope of success it will be brought forward again. . . . Phelps' policy prevails instead of yours. The abolitionists will have this a way to free the slaves at once if possible, nothing else is thought of. The Administration will assent to it just as fast and as far as the country will sustain it."[40] Ever responsive to shifts in the political winds, this information, coupled with the army's inability to control blacks as slaves, prodded Butler into a more radical direction regarding slavery.

The first action by General Butler which marked a movement away from his former policy of buttressing the institution of slavery was the enlistment of blacks into the Union army. Although he had been initially disinclined to utilize black soldiers, by the end of the summer Butler was faced with a dire need for more soldiers to bolster his increasingly diffused command. His need for additional troops, combined with his awareness of favorable administration sentiment and the necessity to discipline blacks, convinced him to "call on Africa to intervene . . ." in the war effort. On August 14 he informed Secretary of War Stanton that he was enlisting into the Union service a brigade of free black men raised the year before by the Confederates.[41] Butler's action was a reflection of his political astuteness. The Rebel regiment, entitled the Native Guards, was composed of New Orleans freemen and had originally been organized in May 1861 by Louisiana governor Thomas Overton Moore. Because of the Confederate origin of his new soldiers and their free status, Butler believed he had insulated himself from criticism. "I have kept clear of the vexed question of arming the slaves," he explained to Henry Wager Halleck, general-in-chief of the Union army. "I am fortified by precedents of a half century's standing, acted upon by the Confederate authorities within six months, and I believe I have done nothing of which the most fastidious member of Jefferson Davis' household political can rightfully complain. . . ."[42]

Butler's black military organization was an immediate success. Within two weeks after its founding over eighteen hundred black men had enlisted in the Native Guards, and by the end of the year Butler had formed three infantry regiments and two batteries of heavy artillery from his black recruits.[43] The reason for Butler's phenomenal success in locating recruits for his new organization was explained by a Native Guards officer: "Any negro [*sic*] who could swear that he was free, if physically good, was accepted. . . ."[44] Utilizing this tactic, the army was able to recruit slaves as well as free blacks for the Native Guards. Indeed, by the end of 1862 the overwhelming majority of enlisted men in the black organization were former slaves. For Butler to have followed any other practice would have been foolish, since the army desperately needed troops and fugitive slaves needed the discipline which only the military could provide. George S. Denison, customs collector for the port of New Orleans and Butler's political colleague, recognized this rationale for arming slaves: "One individual can control 50,000 disciplined men," he wrote Secretary Chase, "but cannot control a mob of fifty."[45] Blacks were not only utilized as enlisted men by Butler but were also given commissions in the Native Guards. Sixty-six black men, most of them "free men of color," received commissions as captains and lieutenants during 1862. The military's desire for racial stability also played a role in the decision to utilize free blacks as officers. Butler believed that the enthusiasm and intelligence of the freemen made them prime officer material and that their presence as Native Guards officers would have a stabilizing effect on the enlisted men. Racial hostility could be avoided if the slaves were treated fairly by being armed and given officers of their own color. Any other policy, according to Butler, would not only be unfair to the black man but would also be "an injustice which is pregnant with dangerous consequences."[46]

Butler's emphasis upon controlling the dangerous proclivities of African Americans and inculcating them with the essentials of military discipline was reflected by the use which the army made of its black auxiliaries. Very rarely were black troops in the Gulf Department permitted to assume combat roles. Rather, military efficiency and discipline, combined with the supposed immunity of blacks to climatic diseases, dictated that the Native Guards be placed in the role of a fatigue and garrison force. The army's utilization of the first three Native Guard regiments during 1862 was indicative of this pattern of thought. The First Regiment spent two weeks repairing railroad track and bridges and then devoted the rest of the year to foraging. The Second Regiment . . . [was] at Opelousas for the whole of 1862 and then traveled to desolate Ship Island, where it spent the next three years on prison guard duty. In late November the Third Regiment saw its first military duty clearing the sugar-cane fields in the Teche district for the next year's crop. After many weeks of this arduous labor the regiment closed out the year foraging the surrounding countryside.[47] The vaunted servility of the black man when placed firmly under white control made the Native Guards perfectly suited for these labor details, and Butler's utilization of black troops during 1862 established a pattern which would be uniformly followed in the Gulf Department for the remainder of the war.[48]

The second phase of General Butler's program for stabilizing the black population of the Gulf Department was the establishment of a wage-labor system on the sugar plantations of southern Louisiana. Sugar was the mainstay of Louisiana's economy, and the commander realized that the revitalization of this most important industry was an integral part of the reconstruction process in his department. But before any progress could be made in the restoration of the industry, sugar producers first had to acquire a reliable labor force. In the past slaves had assumed this role, but during the summer of 1862 blacks manifested an increasing reluctance to continue laboring as chattels. The situation was doubly irritating to planters because the sugar crop then reaching maturity was even more promising than it had been in record-setting 1861. Butler was aware of the planter's plight, if only because he was the unwelcome recipient of many slaves who had formerly composed the work force of the sugar plantations. On September 1 he reported to the War Department that his commissary was issuing twice as many rations to black refugees as it was to the troops of his command. "They are now coming in by the hundreds nay thousands almost daily," he lamented to General Halleck. "Many of the plantations are deserted along the 'coast'. . . . Crops of sugar cane are left standing to waste which would make millions of dollars worth of sugar."[49]

Prohibited by the Second Confiscation Act from excluding slaves any longer from his lines, Butler turned to wage labor as a means for placing blacks back on plantations, where they could aid in the development of the Gulf Department's agricultural resources. Secretary of the Treasury Chase had been urging the general throughout the summer to institute a wage-labor program, and Butler had received similar advice from Edward Lillie

Pierce, who had established a comparable program in the Sea Islands of South Carolina.[50] In addition, many planters had become convinced that wage labor was the only means by which blacks could be induced to work once again on sugar plantations. According to a *New York Times* correspondent, the planters of southern Louisiana were convinced that "so utterly disorganized have the slaves become, that the institution, under its old order, is forever destroyed and worthless, no matter what Mr. Lincoln or anyone else may say on the subject."[51] While this sentiment was by no means universal among sugar planters, there were many businessmen in the Gulf Department willing to utilize black wage labor if they could be reasonably assured of making a profit from sugar production.

By December the military in conjunction with sugar planters had developed the framework of a wage-labor program to be utilized on Gulf Department sugar plantations. The army's standard wage-labor contract provided a ten-dollar monthly wage for all black workers, with three dollars to be deducted for clothing. Employers also were required to provide their laborers with food and medicine as well as protection for the immediate relatives of workers incapacitated by sickness or old age. In return, the military required all blacks to return to plantations and to labor ten hours a day, twenty-six days a month. Butler forbade "cruel or corporal punishment" but promised to punish refusal to work or insubordination by "imprisonment in darkness on bread and water." The army guaranteed to provide each planter with an adequate supply of laborers as well as guards and patrols to "preserve order and prevent crime."[52] General supervision of the labor contract was placed in the hands of a three-man Sequestration Commission. This body was to supply laborers to planters and also to work for the government any plantations which had been abandoned by their owners. Because of the need for laborers and the army's desire to establish white control over black workers, the commissioners required that all black refugees return to the plantations under the stipulations of Butler's wage contract. The commission placed its workers under military guard and delivered them on request to planters and private businessmen leasing abandoned plantations from the army.[53]

Despite the seemingly liberal compensation called for in Butler's wage contract, few workers profited from the wage-labor program. Anxious to rid themselves of their black burden, many military commanders simply delivered blacks to planters with little or no regard for the wages promised to the laborers. Concurrently, many refugees, equally anxious to escape the drab and often unhealthy environs of the contraband camp, signed on with planters despite the meager recompense offered to them.[54] Even in those situations where workers were promised full wages, many employers simply turned off their employees after the harvest without paying them. On the Star Plantation, leased by Charles Weed from the army in the fall of 1862, the workers were still waiting for their first wages in July 1863.[55] The 330 workers on the David Pugh Plantation, hired at ten dollars a month, harvested a crop for their employer valued at $36,000, for which they received shoes and rations totaling $1,500. Sixty percent of the workers received no pay at all.[56] Cases such as these were by no means unique. In January 1863 Gen. William Helmsby Emory reported to department headquarters that "it appears that those who have been working for their own profit the abandoned plantations have in many cases turned off the hands without payment, food or clothing." As a result, blacks in a "wretched and destitute condition" were once again flocking into military posts and contraband camps.[57]

Although the army gave only perfunctory attention to the payment of workers, great care was taken to ensure the subordination of black laborers to white employers. General Butler had promised planters that the military would "preserve order" on sugar plantations by providing guards and patrols to "prevent abuse on one side and insubordination on the other." These military guards generally construed their role to be that of overseers for the plantation owner, and employers found it an easy matter to enlist the sympathy, and police powers, of Union soldiers on their behalf. Numerous incidents of plantation guards aiding planters in cheating workers were referred to Superintendent of Contrabands George H. Hanks, who reported to his commanded that he had "no doubt of their truth . . . and that many other cases of like injustices will be brought to light."[58] The military's emphasis on black subordination did not end with the termination of General Butler's command in the Gulf Department at the end of 1862. Although his successor, Gen. Nathaniel Prentiss Banks, eliminated some of the grosser inequities from the wage-labor program, the military continued to stress, in Banks's words, the need to "induce" blacks to return to plantations and the necessity of requiring them to "work diligently and maintain respectful deportment to their employers, and perfect subordination to their duties."[59] Under Banks the anomaly of a system of compulsory free labor reached its zenith in the Gulf Department, for only through such a program was the military confident that the "necessity of toil" could be impressed upon the black man.[60]

By the end of 1862 most Federal officers and Northern observers considered General Butler's wage-labor program an unqualified success. True, only one-third of the plantations within Federal lines had been worked and the harvest was only a fraction of the record total of the year before, but these debits were offset by the experiment's clear evidence that staples could be grown at a profit by free black labor. On plantations where the experiment was tried, "sugar was manufactured more rapidly than during any previous season," reported a correspondent for the *Times*, ". . . the same number of negroes [*sic*], with the same machinery, producing a hogshead and a half more of sugar each day than under the old system."[61] The wage-labor program successfully refuted the theories by which Southerners had justified slavery. "The labour necessary to the Working of Sugar Plantations can be done without the Aid of the Slave Drivers Whip," John Wilson Shaffer, Butler's chief quartermaster, reported to President Abraham Lincoln "Free labour on Sugar Plantations. Thank God, [it] is no longer an Experiment, it has been tried and found to be the better system."[62] The magnitude of the program's success was not lost on its founder. In late November Butler reported to the president that his program had proven that "Black labor can be as well governed, used, and made as profitable in a state of freedom as in slavery. . . ." Despite the opposition of some planters who refused to give up the use of the lash, Butler predicted the program would show enough profit to finance the department's relief measures for at least a half year. Although he believed that gradual emancipation was the most effective means for controlling blacks and restructuring the social institutions of the South, he thought it "quite feasible" for free blacks to be put to work immediately "with profit and safety to the white," but he asserted that it could "be best done when under military supervision."[63]

Two weeks after reporting the success of his wage-labor program to the president, Butler was relieved of his command and replaced by Gen. Nathaniel Banks, another Massachusetts political general. But the removal of Butler did not imply administration disapproval of his contraband programs.[64] Rather, the military utilized Butler's attempts at controlling blacks as the basis of its efforts among blacks in the Gulf Department during the remainder of the war and even into the period of Reconstruction. Specifically, the commander's emphasis upon "military supervision" was at the core of his successor's publicized efforts among the freedmen. Under Banks's leadership Gulf Department officials between 1863 and 1865 established an extensive series of contraband programs, including the institution of black wage labor throughout all of southern Louisiana, further black military enlistment, educational programs for the freedmen, and various relief measures for unemployed blacks. In all these programs the army stressed the necessity for maintaining firm control of its black wards. Soon after Banks's arrival in the Gulf Department the military developed the technique of the police dragnet, which it used with great success throughout the remainder of the war as a means of eliminating black vagrants from the towns and cities of southern Louisiana. Banks eliminated the black officer corps of the Native Guards because of white dissatisfaction with this administrative innovation. Compulsion became the watchword under the new commander in the army's efforts to recruit blacks for military and plantation labor. Even the efforts of the military to provide for black education and relief were utilized by Banks as a means of controlling the anarchic tendencies of the freedmen and of shaping them into productive farm workers.[65]

By the end of the war freedmen in the Gulf Department were the objects of a wide variety of contraband programs and were probably more secure physically than in any other area of the South. But the freedmen's security was purchased at a price. Under both Butler and Banks the fear of black violence played a role in shaping the army's contraband programs. Both commands considered strict white control to be essential in structuring freedmen's activities. Gulf Department officials considered independent thoughts and actions on the part of blacks as threatening to the reconstruction process, and the military's contraband programs therefore de-emphasized and even discouraged the growth of black economic and political autonomy.[66] The goal of Federal officials relative to the freedmen was the development of an efficient and stable plantation labor force, and within this framework there was little room for the uncurbed, and potentially subversive, gropings of black individuals.

A final result of the army's institution of contraband programs was a reshaping of the black image in the white mind. Just as the outbreak of war had given emphasis to the image of the black man as manic revolutionary, so had the reimposition of order by the

Union military signaled a reversion to the Sambo image of the African American. In explaining the success of blacks as wage laborers and soldiers, military officials in the Gulf Department never tired of emphasizing the innate docility of the black man. In the summer of 1863 General Banks appointed two former abolitionists to assess the progress made in the implementation of a wage-labor program in southern Louisiana.[67] The conclusion reached by these inspectors was that on those plantations where the army's experiment had been faithfully carried out the black workers were "docile, industrious, & quiet."[68] A year later Banks's superintendent of Negro labor reported that the blacks were "more willing to work, and more patient than any set of human beings I ever saw. . . . the negroes [sic] willingly accept the condition of labor for their own maintenance. . . ."[69] A similar line of thinking characterized white explanations of the freedmen's success as soldiers. A Massachusetts soldier characterized the suitability of the black man for the army in the following terms: "Their docility, their habits of unquestioning obedience, pre-eminently fit them for soldiers. To a negro [sic] an order means obedience in spirit as well as letter."[70] In the estimation of Gen. Daniel Ullmann, a commander of black troops in the Gulf Department, the freedman's outstanding qualification as a soldier was his "habit of subordination."[71] According to General Butler black soldiers were "more exact, inasmuch as they are more obedient."[72]

Even before the conclusion of the war, then, the black image in the white mind had come full circle, and blacks who in 1861 had been feared for their violent potential were now praised for their docile behavior. This development is of more than passing interest, for the reimposition of white control over blacks significantly diminished the need felt by whites for instituting new programs for Southern freedmen. Just as fear had been the catalyst for many of the military's contraband programs, so had the abatement of the white man's violent racial fantasies marked the end of the army's innovation in the field of freedmen's affairs. By 1865 the Union army had successfully reestablished racial order by putting young black males under military discipline and by placing the remainder of the Gulf Department's black population back on plantations as wage laborers under white control. These programs, first inaugurated under General Butler, checked the black threat to law and order and transformed the slave population into a positive element in the Union war effort. Having thus stabilized the racial situation in Louisiana, federal authorities during the period of Reconstruction felt little compulsion to move beyond the wartime experiences of the army in expanding upon the meaning of freedom for the former slave.

Notes for "Black Violence and White Response: Louisiana, 1862"

[1]See George M. Fredrickson, *The Black Image in the White Mind: The Debate on Afro-American Character and Destiny, 1817-1914* (New York and other cities, 1971) for a discussion of racial imagery in nineteenth-century America.

[2]Extended discussions of contraband programs in Louisiana can be found in Louis S. Gerteis, "From Contraband to Freedman: Federal Policy Toward Southern Blacks, 1861-1865" (Ph.D. dissertation, University of Wisconsin, 1969); J. Thomas May, "Continuity and Change in the Labor Program of the Union Army and the Freedmen's Bureau," *Civil War History*, 17 (1971): 245-54; and William F. Messner, "The Federal Army and Blacks in the Gulf Department, 1862-1865" (Ph.D. dissertation, University of Wisconsin, 1972). For a general treatment of black behavior during the war see Bell I. Wiley, *Southern Negroes, 1861-1865* (New Haven and London, 1938).

[3]George H. Hepworth, *The Whip, Hoe, and Sword, or, The Gulf-Department in '63* (Boston 1864), 151; Eliza McHatton-Ripley, *From Flag to Flag: A Woman's Adventures and Experiences in the South During the War, in Mexico, and in Cuba* (New York, 1889), 20-21.

[4]Neal Dow, *The Reminiscences of Neal Dow* (Portland, 1898), 668-69.

[5]Harrison Soule to his parents, May 8, 15, 1862, Harrison Soule Papers (Michigan Historical Collections, University of Michigan, Ann Arbor, Mich.); Frank D. Harding to his father, May 3, 1862, Eddy Harding Correspondence (State Historical Society of Wisconsin, Madison, Wis.); John W. De Forest, *A Volunteer's Adventures: A Union Captain's Record of the Civil War*, ed. James H. Croushore (New Haven and London, 1946), 17, 39-40; Dow, *Reminiscences*, 673-74.

[6]O. W. Lull to Benjamin Butler, May 11, 1862, Benjamin F. Butler Papers (Manuscript Division, Library of Congress, Washington, D. C.).

[7]*New York Times*, June 23, 1862.

[8]John M. Stanyan, *A History of the Eighth Regiment of New Hampshire Volunteers* (Concord, N. H., 1892), 105-7.

[9]De Have Norton to his parents, June 9, 1862. De Have Norton Correspondence (State Historical Society of Wisconsin).

[10]*New York Times*, August 1, 1862.

[11]Ibid., August 26, 1862.

[12]*New York Herald*, September 9, 1862.

[13]Quoted in J. Carlyle Sitterson, *Sugar Country: The Cane Sugar Industry in the South, 1753-1950* ([Lexington, Ky.], 1953), 209-10.

[14]Ibid., *New Orleans Daily Picayune*, October 11, 1862.

[15]Throughout the summer of 1862 military headquarters in New Orleans received a constant stream of requests from planters for aid in controlling their slaves. New York *Times*, August 26, 1862; W. Mitthoff to Benjamin Butler, May 29, 1862, Benjamin F. Butler, *Private and Official Correspondence of Gen. Benjamin F. Butler During the Period of the Civil War*, 5 vols. (Norwood, Mass., 1917), 1:525-27; Polycarpe Fortier to Butler, June 4, 1862, ibid., 553-54.

[16]*New Orleans Daily Picayune*, July 22, August 14, 1862.

[17]MS diary of "A Louisiana Rebel," entry for August 4, 1862 (New York Historical Society, New York City).

[18]Day and Night Police Reports, Third District, New Orleans Police Department (New Orleans Public Library, New Orleans, La.).

[19]*New Orleans Daily Picayune*, August 22, 1862.

[20]Ibid., July 22, 1862.

[21]Although the boundaries of the Gulf Department shifted during the war with the fortunes of the Union army, for the purposes of this study the Gulf Department is defined to include those parishes in southern Louisiana which President Lincoln excluded from the operation of the Emancipation Proclamation. These parishes are St. Bernard, Plaquemines, Jefferson, St. John, St. Charles, St. James, Ascension, Assumption, Terrebonne, Lafourche, St. Mary, St. Martin, and Orleans.

[22]Butler's contraband policy at Fort Monroe is discussed in Gerteis, "From Contraband to Freedman," 14-31.

[23]Butler to Edwin Stanton, June 29, 1862, Butler, *Private and Official Correspondence*, 2:13-16 (quotation on page 14).

[24]Butler to Stanton, May 25, 1862, Butler Papers.

[25]Butler to Chase, July 10, 1862, Salmon Portland Chase Papers (Historical Society of Pennsylvania, Philadelphia, Pa.).

[26]Proclamation, May 1, 1862, Butler, *Private and Official Correspondence*, 1:433-36.

[27]General Order No. 32, May 27, 1862; Special Order No. 45, May 27, 1862; General Order No. 44, June 21, 1862, *The War of the Rebellion: A Compilation of the Official Records of the Union and Confederate Armies*, 70 vols. in 128 (Washington, 1880-1901), Series 1, Vol. 15:445-46, 492; cited hereafter as *O. R.*

[28]*New York Tribune*, August 13, 1862; *New Orleans Daily Picayune*, June 4, August 2, 1862; Police Reports, Third District, New Orleans Police Department. During the summer over one hundred slaves were arrested as "runaways" in the Third District of New Orleans alone. In addition, city police jailed slaves for "safekeeping" on the request of their owners. Military authorities also permitted city jailers to whip insubordinate slaves and city newspapers to print notices of fugitive slaves. *New York Tribune*, August 5, 1862; *New Orleans Daily Picayune*, June 6, October 1, 1862; J. P. M. to Butler, July 18, 1862, Butler, *Private and Official Correspondence*, 2:84-86.

[29]*New Orleans Daily Picayune*, May 13, 24, 29, 1862; *New York Times*, August 18, 1862; *New York National Anti-Slavery Standard*, August 30, 1862; R. Smith to Butler, May 21, 1862, Butler Papers; Harrison Soule to his parents, May 8, 1862, Soule Papers.

[30]*New York Times*, August 6, 14, 1862; *New York Tribune*, August 2, 1862; *New York National Anti-Slavery Standard*, August 16, September 27, 1862; David D. Porter to Thomas T. Craven, June 24, 1862, *Official Records of the Union and Confederate Navies in the War of the Rebellion*, 30 vols. (Washington, 1894-1922), Series 1, Vol 18:571-72; Selim E. Woodworth to Porter, July 1, 1862, ibid., 664-66.

[31]Phelps's ideas must be pieced together from his correspondence, essays, and diaries, John Wolcott Phelps Papers (New York Public Library, New York City). His first recorded public statement on slavery was made in December 1861 shortly after his arrival at Ship Island. James Parton, *General Butler in New Orleans* (New York, 1864), 198-200.

[32]Phelps to R. S. Davis, June 16, 1862, *O. R.*, Series 1, 15:486-90 (quotation on page 487). For a complete discussion of the Phelps-Butler controversy see Messner, "The Federal Army and Blacks in the Gulf Department," 30-38.

[33]Phelps to R. S. Davis, July 30, 1862, *O. R.*, Series 1, 15:534-35.

[34]Butler to his wife, August 5, 1862, Butler, *Private and Official Correspondence*, 2:154.

[35]R. S. Davis to Phelps, July 31, 1862, Parton, *General Butler*, 506; Phelps to Davis, July 31, 1862. *O. R.*, Series 1, 15:535; Phelps to Lorenzo Thomas, August 2, 1862, Butler, *Private and Official Correspondence*, 2:146-47.

[36]To the end of his stay in the Gulf Department Phelps continued to stress the need for constructing new mechanisms for controlling the slaves. In August he informed Butler that Louisiana society was "on the verge of dissolution, and it is the true policy of the Government to seize upon the chief elements of disorder and anarchy, and empty them in favor of law and order." According to Phelps the black man threatened "to be a fearful element of ruin and disaster, and the best way to prevent it is to arm and organize him on the side of

the Government." Phelps to Butler, August [6], 1862, Butler, *Private and Official Correspondence*, 2:155-57 (quotation on page 157).

[37]Butler to his wife, July 28, 25, 1862, ibid., 115, 117, 109.

[38]Chase to Butler, July 31, 1862, Chase Papers; Stanton to Butler, August 7, 1862, *O. R.*, Series 1, Vol. 15:543.

[39]Butler was informed of the passage of the Second Confiscation Act in early August by Secretary Stanton. Stanton to Butler, August 7, 1862, *O. R.*, Series 1, Vol. 25:543. See James M. McPherson, *The Struggle For Equality: Abolitionists and the Negro in the Civil War and Reconstruction* (Princeton, 1964), 106-18, for a discussion of the growth of antislavery sentiment in the North during the summer of 1862.

[40]Mrs. Butler to her husband, August 8, 1862, Butler, *Private and Official Correspondence*, 2:164. See also Mrs. Butler's letter of September 28, 1862, to her husband regarding the political gains which could be made by arming the slaves. Ibid., 335-36.

[41]Butler to Stanton, August 14, 1862, *O. R.*, Series 1, 15:549.

[42]Butler to Halleck, August 27, 1862, ibid., 555-56. A discussion of the Rebel origins of the Native Guards can be found in Mary F. Berry, "Negro Troops in Blue and Gray: The Louisiana Native Guards, 1861-1863," *Louisiana History*, 8 (1967): 167-70.

[43]Berry, "Negro Troops," 174-76; *New York Times*, September 29, 1862.

[44]Joseph T. Wilson, *The Black Phalanx: A History of the Negro Soldiers of the United States in the Wars of 1775-1812, 1861-'65* (Hartford, 1888), 195, see also George Denison to Salmon Chase, September 24, 1862, Salmon P. Chase Correspondence (Manuscript Division, Library of Congress).

[45]Denison to Chase, October 8, 1862. Chase Correspondence.

[46]Berry, "Negro Troops," 174-76; Wilson, *Black Phalanx*, 169-70.

[47]Butler to Godfrey Weitzel, October 30, 1862, *O. R.*, Series 1, 15:587-88; Berry, "Negro Troops," 176-79; *Senate Reports*, 37 Cong., 3 Sess., No. 108; *Report of the Joint Committee on the Conduct of the War* (Serial 1154, Washington, 1863), Pt. 3:358-59.

[48]Even during the one major battle in which blacks assumed a combat role in the Gulf Department, the Battle of Port Hudson, the most important contribution of the Native Guards to the Union effort was the completion of extensive labor details. Messner, "The Federal Army and Blacks in the Gulf Department," 301-36; Dudley T. Cornish, *The Sable Arm: Negro Troops in the Union Army, 1861-1865* (New York, 1956), 142-44.

[49]Butler to Halleck, September 1, 1862, Butler Papers; *New York Times*, December 21, 1862.

[50]Chase to Butler, July 31, 1862, Butler, *Private and Official Correspondence*, 2:131-35; Pierce to Butler, August 20, 1862, Butler Papers; see also annual report of Secretary of War Stanton, December 1, 1862, *O. R.*, Series 3, 2:910-12, for a similar opinion concerning the institution of wage labor in the South.

[51]*New York Times*, November 3, 1862.

[52]Parton, *General Butler*, 523-24; G. Strong to G. Weitzel, November 2, 1862, *O. R.*, Series 1, 15:162-63.

[53]General Order No. 91, November 9, 1862, ibid., 592-94.

[54]F. S. Nickerson to William Hoffman, December 23, 1862, Records of United States Continental Army Commands, 1821-1920, Department of the Gulf, Box 5, Record Group 393 (National Archives, Washington, D. C.); cited hereinafter as RG 393, NA.

[55]Report of the Star Plantation, July 22, 1863, Records of Civil War Special Agencies of the Treasury Department, Third Special Agency of the Treasury Department, Vol. 71, Record Group 366 (National Archives).

[56]Benjamin Smith to Nathaniel Banks, March 7, 1863, Department of the Gulf, Box 3, RG 393, NA.

[57]Emory to William Hoffman, January 27, 1863, ibid.; see also John Clark to Richard B. Irwin, January 30, 1863, ibid.; *Second Annual Report of the New England Freedmen's Aid Society (Educational Commission)* (Boston, 1864), 46.

[58]Hanks to Banks, March 5, 1863; B. F. Smith to Banks, March 7, 1863, Department of the Gulf, Box 3, RG 393, NA; De Forest, *A Volunteer's Adventures*, 76; Edwin B. Lufkin, *History of the Thirteenth Maine Regiment . . . .* (Bridgeton, Maine, 1898), 42-43.

[59]*De Bow's Review*, Series 2, Vol. 3 (1867): 100-101.

[60]General Order No. 23, February 3, 1864, *O. R.*, Series 1, Vol. 34, Pt. 2:227-31. See Messner, "The Federal Army and Blacks in the Gulf Department," 106-200, for a description of Banks's free-labor program.

[61]*New York Times*, January 16, 1863.

[62]Shaffer to Lincoln, December (?), 1862, Robert Todd Lincoln Collection, Abraham Lincoln Papers (Manuscript Division, Library of Congress); see also George Denison to Chase, November 14, 1862, Chase Correspondence.

[63]Butler to Lincoln, November 28, 1862, Butler, *Private and Official Correspondence*, 2:447-50; quotations on page 450.

[64]Butler was removed from the command of the Gulf Department for political reasons. His controversial activities in Louisiana had alienated a good portion of the New Orleans diplomatic community, and his Democratic background and volatile behavior were considered detrimental to the delicate process of restoring Louisiana to the Union. Charles Sumner to Butler, January 8, 1863, *O. R.*, Series 1, 53:546. Banks, on the other hand, was a moderate Republican politician who had shown a genius for placing himself in the mainstream of national political movements. Fred H. Harrington, *Fighting Politician; Major General N. P. Banks* (Philadelphia and London, 1948).

[65]Messner, "The Federal Army and Blacks in the Gulf Department," Chapters 3-7.

[66]Although Banks gave lip service to the ideal of black proprietorship of farm land, during his administration the military made neither land nor credit available to aspiring black farmers. Rather, under both Butler and Banks the army placed sole emphasis upon compelling blacks to work on plantations as field laborers under white direction and control. Ibid., 242-57.

[67]Banks's inspectors were George Hughes Hepworth and Edwin Wheelock, both of whom were Unitarian ministers from Massachusetts and active members of the antislavery movement.

[68]Wheelock and Hepworth to Banks, April 9, 10, June 15, 28, 1863, Nathaniel P. Banks Papers (Manuscript Division, Library of Congress).

[69]George Hanks to James McKaye, March 28, 1864, quoted in J. McKaye, *The Mastership and Its Fruits: The Emancipated Slave Face to Face with His Old Master* (New York, 1864), 17.

[70]Quoted in Henry T. Johns, *Life with the Forty-ninth Massachusetts Volunteers* (Washington, 1890), 166-70; quotation on page 167.

[71]Ullmann to Henry Wilson, December 4, 1863, *O. R.*, Series 3, 3:1126-28; quotation on page 1126.

[72]Testimony of Benjamin Butler before the American Freedmen's Inquiry Commission, General Correspondence and Related Records, Records of the Adjutant General's Office, Record Group 94, National Archives Microfilm Series M-256, roll 200, frames 79-84. See Fredrickson, *The Black Image in the White Mind*, 168-71, for a discussion of the relationship between black Union soldiers and the Sambo image.

THE VICKSBURG CAMPAIGN OF 1862:
A CASE STUDY IN THE FEDERAL
UTILIZATION OF BLACK LABOR*

William F. Messner

Civil War scholars have generally relegated the Federal campaign against Vicksburg in the summer of 1862 to a position of minor importance in the history of the rebellion in the Southwest. Overshadowed by General Grant's successful assault against the rebel river city in the summer of 1863, the first Vicksburg campaign has gone relatively unnoticed by historians.[1] From a military perspective the historical neglect which this campaign has received is undoubtably justified, for the entire endeavor accomplished little besides inflicting heavy casualties on the Union army which labored through the hot Louisiana summer in a futile undertaking. But despite the paucity of military gains which this campaign produced, the Union effort is historically interesting for it was a transitional phase in the Federal utilization of black labor in the Southwest. Prior to the campaign Federal authorities had shown little interest in utilizing the manpower of the slave population in Louisiana and had even attempted to buttress the peculiar institution in "loyal" areas of the state. During the summer of 1862, however, the Federal government substantially altered its perception of the black man's value to the Union's cause, and nowhere was this change made more evident than in the treatment given to blacks by the Union army during the first campaign against Vicksburg. By the end of this ill-fated effort, all doubts had been dispelled from the minds of Federal military officials concerning the value of Louisiana's black population to the Union war effort.

The Vicksburg campaign of 1862 was part of a Union plan for gaining control of the Mississippi River during the second year of the Civil War. In early May of 1862 the first phase of this plan was successfully implemented with the capture of New Orleans by the Federal military under the combined commands of Com. David Farragut and Gen. Benjamin Butler. War Department strategy next called for Farragut to push his flotilla up

*First published in *Louisiana History*, 16 (1975): 371-81. Reprinted with the kind permission of the author and the Louisiana Historical Association.

the Mississippi River to Vicksburg, five hundred miles to the north, where he would join forces with the Western fleet sailing south from Cairo, Illinois. As a result of this joint effort the Federal government hoped to regain control of the Mississippi by the end of the summer and thus split the Confederacy in two. But Federal plans went awry as the Union forces in the Midwest became stalled in Tennessee and were unable to send a significant number of ships and men down the Mississippi River beyond Memphis. The planned assault against Vicksburg, therefore, became the exclusive responsibility of the Union forces in New Orleans. Commodore Farragut would have preferred to turn his fleet against the weakly defended city of Mobile, but the national administration was intent upon opening the entire Mississippi River to Federal navigation and ordered Farragut to proceed north against Vicksburg, accompanied by as many soldiers as General Butler could spare from his command in New Orleans.[2]

The Union expedition began propitiously enough with the capture of Baton Rouge, 135 miles upriver from New Orleans, in late May. Here, in the state capital, the army, under the command of Gen. Thomas Williams, first became acquainted with the "contraband problem."[3] The core of the problem was the tendency of slaves in the Baton Rouge area to quit their masters and flee to the camps of the Union army. Additional slaves became the wards of the army as a result of their confiscation along with other forms of rebel property by individual Union soldiers. The end result of this process was a flood of slaves into the Union camps at Baton Rouge which simultaneously perplexed and angered many soldiers who had never envisioned themselves as emancipators of Southern slaves.[4]

Among those soldiers for whom the black influx was a source of irritation was the Union commander, General Williams. No admirer of the black man, the general at Baton Rouge refused to be drawn into civil cases where even the most blatant types of discriminatory racial practices were clearly in evidence.[5] In concert with his superior, General Butler, Williams believed that the unsettled behavior of Louisiana slaves threatened an imminent racial Armageddon. He wrote to his wife in July the following disquieting prediction:

> If the war continues a year longer, I don't see how they're [the Confederates] to escape a servile war. the negroes are flying from their masters in all directions, and have become thoroughly impressed with the *idea* of being free. . . . The doom of slavery is already written, unless the South stops the rebellion. They began the rebellion to establish a great slave empire: they must stop the rebellion to save their country from destruction and servile war, and perhaps themselves from negro [*sic*] domination and Black Republic. What a terrible punishment![6]

Plagued by the specter of racial warfare, Williams was determined to rid himself of black burden and to place the slaves back under the control of their masters. His solution to the black influx was simple. On June 5, shortly after the capture of the state capital, he ordered the expulsion of all black fugitives from Union camps.[7] In addition, the general allegedly used his troops to return some of the blacks to their owners and also allowed slave-hunters to enter his lines.[8] Despite the fact that Williams's actions may have been in violation of Federal law, the general had ample precedent for his exclusion policy. Williams undoubtedly believed that his actions were in concert with the conservative racial policy of the national administration which had been recently reaffirmed by General Butler in New Orleans. During the first months of his command in southern Louisiana Butler had excluded blacks from his lines and even returned slaves to their owners, for he, like Williams, was disturbed by the slaves' unsettled behavior and convinced of the necessity for placing them firmly under white control.[9]

On June 20 General Williams, in command of a force of 3300 men, left Baton Rouge with Commodore Farragut's fleet and sailed north for Vicksburg. Upon his arrival in the parish of Madison below the rebel city, Williams, while waiting for reinforcements from Gen. Henry Halleck upriver, commenced work on a canal to divert the water of the Mississippi away from Vicksburg. The grandiose undertaking was the product of the fertile imagination of General Butler who had ordered the digging of a trench four feet deep and five feet wide which would hopefully serve as a new river bed for the Mississippi. "If the cut succeeds," explained General Williams, "the Mississippi will take the course of the cut off and Vicksburg becomes an inland town with a mere creek in front of it. So the batteries will be made useless, and Vicksburg will fall with the spade."[10]

Williams's formidable engineering task necessitated a large labor force, and the only source of workers were the cotton plantations which lined the Mississippi River. Despite his distaste for slaves, the general realized the success of his canal depended on their labor. Motivated by military necessity, Williams was transformed into an emancipator of rebel slaves. Details of troops traveled as far as one hundred miles above Vicksburg to requisition blacks from plantations. The slaves were generally quite willing to go with the Union army, for many were promised their freedom in return for their labor. By July 4 Williams had procured a force of 1200 laborers to work on his canal.[11]

Despite the acquisition of a large labor force, the Union offensive by mid-July was in desperate straits. The expected reinforcements from General Halleck at Corinth never appeared, and Williams was faced with the prospect of assaulting a city defended by fifteen thousand troops with a force of only 3300 soldiers.[12] Equally as disturbing was the realization that the construction of a canal to divert the waters of the Mississippi away from Vicksburg was a task of heroic proportions. On July 4 Williams reported to General Butler that "the labor of making this cut is far greater than estimated by anybody." The soil of the area was a hard clay, difficult to penetrate, especially with the crude tools used by the laborers.[13] Also, the level of the Mississippi was falling so rapidly that even if the cut were complete, it would probably be at a higher level than the river, making the flow of water through it impossible. Finally, work on the canal was begun in July, just at the height of the fever season. For the unacclimated troops of Williams's command, this factor proved debilitating. None of these difficulties, however, deterred General Williams. Declaring that "the project is a great one, and worthy of success," the general drove both soldiers and laborers in their work.[14]

Williams's enthusiasm was not shared by his troops who superintended the blacks working on the canal. The health of the soldiers, drilled every day in full gear beneath the hot sun, deteriorated quickly. Within two weeks of beginning work, the colonel of the Fifth Wisconsin Regiment reported that he had five hundred sick and not over fifty healthy men in his command.[15] In the Ninth Connecticut Regiment over 150 men died of disease.[16] Compounding the ravages of the climate was the shortage of staples needed to sustain life in the swamps. Food, medicine, and shelter were all in short supply. According to an army surgeon, "the accomodations [*sic*] for either sick or well while in this swamp were as poor as could be"[17] To all of this, General Williams was seemingly impervious. After the trench on which he had begun work collapsed, he commenced building a second structure, eight times the size of the original. By the end of July, out of a force of 3300 men which Williams had brought north to Vicksburg, only 800 remained fit for duty.[18]

While the white troops suffered in the swamps, the confiscated slaves labored on through the steamy month of July. Their condition was a matter of debate. According to Williams, the slaves "flourish and glisten and shine most when the sun's the hottest."[19] A correspondent of the *New York Tribune* painted an equally cheerful picture. The workers, he declared, "joyfully dig, with mirth and song," despite the oppressive heat.[20] A different account is given by other observers. According to a private who supervised the workers, "the Negroes died off like a disease infected flock of sheep."[21] A neighboring plantation owner reported that the slaves were "worked to death on the canal with no shelter at night and not much to eat."[22] According to an army surgeon, the incidence of disease among the workers was very high. An assistant surgeon was detailed to tend to the numerous sick among the blacks, but his medical supplies were scanty, as were suitable quarters to house and treat the ill. Most of the sick were laid on the bare floor of huts and fed a ration of hardtack.[23] What mirth and joy was evident among the laborers was not due to their good health, but rather to their belief that in payment for their labor they would be emancipated.

Freedom, however, was not to be theirs. Before beginning work on the canal Williams had decided that the workers would be freed only if the project was a success. By the end of July the situation had deteriorated to such an extent that it was no longer a question of a successful completion to the project, but one of survival. Finally realizing the futility of his venture, Williams ordered a halt to all work on July 21. He then placed the slaves taken from plantations below Vicksburg on board the steamer *Ceres* and returned them to their owners. Not having time to perform the same service for laborers taken from estates above the trench, the general gave them three days' rations and instructions to return to their masters. Realizing that their hopes for freedom were about to vanish a group of distraught workers attempted to force their way onto a troop ship, but were beaten off. The Union fleet then steamed off for Baton Rouge, leaving the slaves to the care of the rebels.[24]

The Vicksburg campaign was both the first wide-scale utilization of slave labor by the Union army in the Southwest and the final instance of the Union army engaging in the practice of systematically returning slaves to their owners. In this respect the campaign was a transitional phase in the Federal utilization of black labor. Although General Williams's abandonment of his black workers was sustained by his superiors, never again would the army tolerate such a squandering of black manpower. By the end of the summer General Butler was desperately in need of men to buttress his disease-ridden command in southern Louisiana, and blacks were the only possible source of aid.[25] Simultaneously, the commander was coming to the realization that the black agricultural workers of his department would no longer tolerate laboring on sugar and cotton plantations as slaves. Some alternate form of labor needed to be devised in order to insure the efficient cultivation of staples.[26] On the Federal level as well, sentiment was rapidly shifting toward a position favorable to the utilization of black manpower. This fact was made abundantly clear by the passage of the second Confiscation Act on July 21 in which Congress granted to the president the power to recruit black troops and also freed rebel-owned slaves giving service to the Union.[27] The day after the passage of this legislation President Lincoln ordered that the army utilize as laborers all slaves who could be "advantageously used for military and naval purposes."[28] Although Lincoln stopped short of publicly advocating the recruitment of blacks into the military, he privately favored the arming of slaves for purely defensive purposes.[29]

Nowhere in the Southwest was the military's expanded use of black labor made more evident than in the final phase of Farragut's and Williams's Mississippi expedition. On July 26 the remnants of General Williams's command arrived in Baton Rouge after a two-day trip from the Vicksburg region. Rumors abounded in the state capital concerning a threatened rebel attack to regain the weakly defended city. One week later these rumors were substantiated when two rebel divisions attacked the Union lines on the outskirts of the city. During the ensuing battle General Williams was killed, but despite the loss of their commander the Union soldiers were able to retain possession of Baton Rouge. For the next two weeks the Union troops, aided by the labor of hundreds of fugitive slaves who had escaped from neighboring plantations, prepared an elaborate series of breastworks and rifle pits in preparation for a second rebel attack.[30] By the end of August, however, Union officials in New Orleans had become greatly concerned over the vulnerability of their city to a rebel attack. On August 23, therefore, General Butler ordered the entire Union contingent at Baton Rouge to abandon the city and return to New Orleans to aid in its defense.

The evacuation of Baton Rouge stands in marked contrast to the Union retreat from Vicksburg one month earlier. Instead of leaving behind the black laborers who had aided the army, officials at Baton Rouge chose to take their workers with them to New Orleans. The flotilla's arrival in New Orleans was a scene which impressed itself on the minds of many Northern soldiers who had never before witnessed such a large congregation of black men and women. A Union private described the disembarkation in a letter to his fiancée: "The ther. is 120 and the river has fell fifty feet, but I am healthy and happy though the niggers is thick and musketeers Too. You ought to seen 1,500 niggers that come on Steamers from Baton Rouge. Some are white as any Girl and as pretty (except my sisters and *one more*) but most of them are vulgar and sloven."[31] A few of the blacks were lucky enough to acquire rude shelters of sugar cane or wooden rails, but most of the refugees simply squatted on the levee and waited for the meaning of their freedom to be clarified for them by their emancipators. Eventually the army provided tents and rations for the blacks, grouped them into contraband camps and even commenced drilling the likelier looking candidates for the army. By the fall of 1862, these black people, in conjunction with other refugees from the New Orleans and Lafourche areas, provided the army with a basis for establishing the first freedmen's programs instituted by the Federal government in the Southwest.[32]

Thus ended the ill-fated attempt by the Federal military to open the Mississippi River to Union navigation during 1862. That achievement would have to wait almost a year for the concurrent Union victories at Vicksburg and Port Hudson. But despite the absence of military gains, the campaign did highlight the marked change in Federal policy regarding the utilization of black labor. The travels of the army from New Orleans through Baton Rouge to Vicksburg and then back illuminate the progressive shift in military thinking regarding the value of black labor. From this perspective, if no other, the little noted Vicksburg campaign of 1862 deserves a place in the consciousness of the American historical community.

Notes for "The Vicksburg Campaign of 1862: A Case Study
in the Federal Utilization of Black Labor"

[1]The most extensive discussion of the first campaign against Vicksburg which this author has found is John D. Winters, *The Civil War in Louisiana* (Baton Rouge, 1963), 103-12. Winters devotes the bulk of his attention to the naval campaign against the rebel city. Peter F. Walker in *Vicksburg: A People at War, 1860-1865* (Chapel Hill, 1960), makes no mention of the Federal army's activities in the vicinity of Vicksburg in 1862.

[2]Winters, *Civil War in Louisiana*, 103-5.

[3]A native of New York, Williams was a professional soldier who had graduated from West Point in the late 1830s and amassed an impressive combat record in the Mexican War and on the frontier. Williams entered the war as a major in command of the Fifth United States Artillery and was commissioned a brigadier general of volunteers in September of 1861. From October, 1861, to March, 1862, he was in command at Hatteras Inlet and was then assigned to the command of a brigade in General Butler's Mississippi Expedition. G. M. Williams, ed., "Letters of General Thomas Williams, 1862," *American Historical Review*, 14 (1909): 304.

[4]James Bowman to A. Heise, July 11, 1862, James F. Bowman Papers, Louisiana State University; August LeBlanc Plantation Record Book, entries for June 2, 23, 1862, LeBlanc Family Papers, Louisiana State University; Charles Moulton to his wife, June 13, 1862, Charles H. Moulton Papers, Michigan Historical Collection, University of Michigan; *New York Tribune*, June 27, 1862; Report of Col. A. M. Dudley, June 7-9, 1862, *The War of the Rebellion: A Compilation of the Official Records of the Union and Confederate Armies*, 130 vols. (Washington, 1880-1902), Series 1, Vol. 15:19-21. Cited hereafter as *O. R.*

[5]According to a member of Williams's staff, the general at Baton Rouge refused to interfere in cases in which free blacks had been jailed by civil officials and charged with being runaway slaves. Williams's response to these cases was, "I wash my hands of niggers." James Biddle to his wife, June 19, 1862, James C. Biddle Papers, Historical Society of Pennsylvania.

[6]Thomas Williams to his wife, July 21, 1862, Williams, "Letters of General Williams," 325.

[7]Thomas Williams to Wickham Hoffman, n.d., Abraham Lincoln Papers, Robert Todd Lincoln Collection.

[8]Charges to this effect were drawn up against General Williams by Colonel Halbert E. Paine of the Fourth Wisconsin Volunteer Infantry on June 11 and can be found in the Abraham Lincoln Papers. See also Frank Boardman to Josiah Noonan, June 11, 1862, Josiah Noonan Papers, State Historical Society of Wisconsin. Paine and another officer refused to obey Williams's order excluding blacks from their camps and were arrested for their refusal by the general. N. H. Chittenden, *History and Catalogue of the Fourth Regiment Wisconsin Volunteers* (Baton Rouge, 1864), 9; *Army Correspondence, 1862-1863: Fourth Wisconsin Volunteer Infantry* (n.p., n.d.), 3.

[9]See William F. Messner, "The Federal Army and Blacks in the Gulf Department 1862-1865" (Ph.D. dissertation, University of Wisconsin, 1972), Chapter 1, for a discussion of Butler's contraband policy during the summer of 1862.

[10]T. Williams to his wife, June 28, 1862, G. M. Williams, "Letters of General Williams," 322; B. Butler to T. Williams, June 6, 1862, *O. R.*, Series 1, 15:25-26.

[11]John Q. Anderson, ed., *Brokenburn: The Journal of Kate Stone* (Baton Rouge, 1955), 125, 127; T. Williams to his wife, May 22, 1862, Williams, ed., "Letters of General Williams," 318; *New York Tribune*, July 18, 1862; F. Boardman to J. Noonan, July 5, 1862, Noonan Papers; Richard B. Irwin, *History of the Nineteenth Army Corps* (New York, 1892), 22-31.

[12]Instead of reinforcing Williams's troops at Vicksburg, Halleck chose to use the soldiers of his command to buttress Union armies in Tennessee and the Army of the Potomac in Virginia. Winters, *Civil War in Louisiana*, 107.

[13]Frank Moore, ed., *The Rebellion Record*, 8 vols. (New York, 1864), 5:Doc. 545-46.

[14]Ibid.

[15]Halbert Paine to Edward Salomon, July 21, 1862, R. T. Lincoln Collection; A H. Nostrand to E. Salomon, July 21, 1862, ibid.; F. Boardman to J. Noonan, July 14, 17, 1862, Noonan Papers.

[16]Thomas Murray, *History of the Ninth Regiment Connecticut Volunteer Infantry* (New Haven, 1903), 109-10. See also Charles Dimon to Sarah Dimon, July 21, 1862, Charles A. Dimon Papers, Southern Historical Collection, University of North Carolina.

[17]S. K. Towles to John Cleveland, Sept. 11, 1862, John P. Cleveland Papers, Essex Institute.

[18]T. Williams to B. Butler, July 17, 1862, *O. R.*, Series 1, 15:31-33; Chittenden, *Fourth Wisconsin Volunteers*, 10; Murray, *Ninth Connecticut volunteers*, 111-12; Morris Fyfe to his father, July 23, 1862, Fyfe Family Papers, State Historical Society of Wisconsin.

[19]T. Williams to his wife, July 2, 1862, Williams, ed., "Letters of General Williams," 323.

[20]*New York Tribune*, July 14, 1862.

[21]Newton H. Culver, "The Fourth Wisconsin at Vicksburg," typewritten copy at the State Historical Society of Wisconsin.

[22]Anderson, ed., *Brokenburn*, 128. See also Sarah L. Wadley Diary, entry for July 13, 1862, Southern Historical Collection, University of North Carolina.

[23]S. K. Towles to J. Cleveland, Sept. 11, 1862, Cleveland Papers; Paul Steiner, *Diseases in the Civil War* (Springfield, Ill., 1968), 186-98.

[24]T. Williams to his wife, July 2, 1862, Williams, ed., "Letters of General Williams," 323; *New York Times*, August 6, 1862; *New York Tribune*, August 2, 1862; *National Anti-Slavery Standard*, August 16, September 27, 1862; Anderson, ed., *Brokenburn*, 134; Edward Bacon, *Among the Cotton Thieves* (Detroit, 1867), 15-16.

[25]At the beginning of the Federal occupation of southern Louisiana General Butler was confident that a large number of native whites would enlist in the Union army. But Butler's hopes failed to materialize and the War Department was unable to send the general any of the 15,000 reinforcements which he requested in July. Messner, "The Federal Army and Blacks in the Gulf Department," 48, 59.

[26]Ibid., Chapter 3.

[27]General Orders, No. 91, July 29, 1862, *O. R.*, Series 3, Vol. 2:270-76, 281.

[28]General Orders, No. 109, August 16, 1862, Ibid., 397.

[29]Roy P. Basler, ed., *The Collected Works of Abraham Lincoln*, 8 vols. (New Brunswick, 1953), 5:338; Benjamin F. Thomas and Harold Hyman, *Stanton: The Life and Times of Lincoln's Secretary of War* (New York, 1962), 237-40.

[30]*Passages from the Life of Henry Warren Howe . . .* (Lowell, Mass., 1899), 125; John W. DeForest, *A Volunteer's Adventures: A Union Captain's Record of the Civil War,* ed. James H. Croushore (New Haven, 1946), 39-40; *Army Correspondence, Fourth Wisconsin Infantry*, 11.

[31]Quoted in John M. Stanyan, *A History of the Eighty Regiment of New Hampshire Volunteers* (Concord, N.H., 1892), 130. See also Eliza Ripley, *From Flag to Flag* (New York, 1868, 45-46; John Phelps Diary, entries for August 23, 25, 1862, John Phelps Papers, New York Public Library.

[32]DeForest, *Volunteer's Adventures*, 39-40. In August of 1862 Butler began the enlistment of blacks into the Federal army and in October the general instituted the beginnings of a wage labor program for the plantations of the Gulf Department. The blacks taken from Baton Rouge by the Union army were utilized in both of these programs which served as precursors for future efforts of the army and Freedmen's Bureau among Louisiana Negroes. Messner, "Federal Army and Blacks in the Gulf Department," Chapters 2 and 3.

"I REGARD IT AS AN EXPERIMENT"*
[THE NATIVE GUARDS AT THE SIEGE OF PORT HUDSON]

James G. Hollandsworth, Jr.

The major objective for the Union army in the Mississippi Valley in 1863 was to wrestle control of the Mississippi River from the Confederates. To that end, Ulysses S. Grant pushed his army slowly down the west bank of the Mississippi River, looking for a way to gain a foothold on dry ground below Vicksburg from which to launch an assault on the Rebel fortress. Nathaniel P. Banks was expected to make his way up the river from New Orleans to effect a juncture with Grant at Vicksburg, splitting the Confederacy in two.[1] The major obstacle confronting Banks was Port Hudson, a well-fortified Confederate stronghold clinging to high bluffs on a hairpin bend of the Mississippi River some fourteen miles north of Baton Rouge.

Banks tested the Rebel fortifications at Port Hudson on March 14 with a feeble diversionary attack while [David] Farragut attempted to run past the batteries covering the river. The whole affair was a disaster; Banks accomplished nothing, and Farragut's fleet was badly shot up. Nevertheless, the admiral did make it past Port Hudson with two ships and was able to establish contact with Grant's forces near Vicksburg. The Confederate stronghold at Port Hudson still held firm, however, and Banks fell back to Baton Rouge to reconsider his options.

By early April Banks decided to bypass Port Hudson. Moving up Bayou Teche to Vermilionville (now Lafayette) and on to Alexandria, Banks dispersed all Confederate attempts to resist his advance. Having accomplished his objective of opening a water route to the Mississippi River via the Atchafalaya Basin, Banks abandoned Alexandria and marched his army down the Red River toward the Confederate citadel at Port Hudson. By May 22 Banks had crossed the Mississippi River and invested Port Hudson from the north, while Union troops from Baton Rouge sealed off the fortress from the south. The seige of Port Hudson had begun.

*First published as Chapter 5 in James G. Hollandsworth, Jr., *The Louisiana Native Guards: The Black Military Experience During the Civil War* (Baton Rouge: Louisiana State University Press, © 1995), 48-58. Reprinted with the kind permission of the author and the publisher.

The 1st and 3rd Regiments of the Native Guards did not accompany Banks's army into central Louisiana but were left behind in Baton Rouge to fret over their inaction. As often happens when troops are frustrated by the dull routine of garrison duty, disciplinary infractions occurred. In late April, a local woman, who had nursed young Lieut. John Crowder back to health when he was sick with the fever, visited the 1st Regiment's camp, accompanied by a young girl. A private soldier, probably thinking to shock the lady, unbuttoned his trousers and exposed his penis. Capt. Alcide Lewis observed the incident but failed to discipline the man. When Crowder found out what had happened, he promptly had the soldier arrested, which made Lewis' inaction look like dereliction of duty. Lewis was incensed, but Crowder did not care. "My opinion of Capt. Lewis and Lieut. Moss has been reduced since my arrival in this city," he wrote his mother. "They are the most pucillanamous dirty Low life men that I ever seen. Like many others they have no respect for no one. they seem to think there is not a woman that they cannot sleep with. every woman seems to be a common woman with them. they have grown hateful in my sight."[2]

Two weeks later there was another incident, this one involving the 1st Regiment's colonel, Spencer H. Stafford.[3] On May 13, a woodcutting detail from the 1st Regiment was stopped at the picket line because the men did not have a pass. The detail went back to camp and told Colonel Stafford what had happened. Stafford returned with his men and rode up to the officer of the guard, Capt. J. P. Garland of the 21st Maine Infantry. "What in hell did you stop my teams for?" Stafford retorted, shaking his fist in the captain's face. "You stopped my men so that some of your Regt could steal my wood," Stafford charged. Garland responded that his orders came from Col. Edward P. Chapin, the brigade commander. "Yes," Stafford replied, "I have heard of that Brigade before and they are a set of God damn thieves." Garland held his tongue while Stafford continued his tirade but had the presence of mind to take out a notebook and record the colonel's remarks. Seeing what Garland was doing, Stafford slacked his anger and left with his men.[4]

Captain Garland immediately informed Colonel Chapin of what had happened. Chapin told Banks, and Banks ordered Stafford placed under arrest. In a letter protesting his detention, Stafford complained that the guard at the picket line had treated the black officer in charge of the detail roughly, calling him a "black son of a bitch." Stafford said that he was angered by the affront, for it was not the first time the men of his command had been so treated. "This excited my indignation unduly I confess, and I used expressions which I regretted as soon as I returned to camp and had time to reflect." Nonetheless, Stafford was charged with "conduct to the prejudice of good order and military discipline," found guilty, and dismissed from the service.[5]

The incident occurred just days before the 1st and 3rd Regiments of the Native Guards received orders to join Banks's army at Port Hudson.[6] They reached Port Hudson on May 23 and two days later found themselves posted on the far right of the Union line facing a heavily fortified Confederate position on high bluffs overlooking the Mississippi River.[7] Lieut. Colonel [Chauncey] Bassett commanded the 1st Regiment following Stafford's arrest. Lieut. Col. Henry Finnegass assumed command of the 3rd after its colonel, John A. Nelson, was given overall command of both regiments.[8] The black troops were in great spirits.[9] At least they were going to get the chance to prove themselves in battle.

On Tuesday, May 26, General Banks ordered an all-out assault on the Confederate works for the next day. The Native Guards' position straddled the Telegraph Road that ran along the Mississippi River between Port Hudson and Bayou Sara near St. Francisville. Across the front of their position lay Big Sandy Creek.[10] The Confederates had burned a bridge spanning the stream, but Federal engineers had constructed a light footbridge to take its place. A detachment from the Native Guards crossed the footbridge on Tuesday afternoon and pushed Rebel skirmishers back toward the Confederate lines so that troops from the 42nd Massachusetts Infantry could throw a pontoon bridge across the marshy bog. Despite an occasional shell from Confederate batteries mounted on the bluffs of Port Hudson less than half a mile away, work progressed, and the 280-foot span was completed by nightfall.[11]

The Union general in charge of the Native Guards was Brigadier General William Dwight, Jr. Dwight was thirty-one years old, the son of a Massachusetts family whose ancestors had arrived in America in 1635. Dwight had entered West Point in 1849 but had been allowed to resign just before graduation because of academic problems. It was rumored that he had been expelled "on account of his drunkenness and shameless association with obscene women." Dwight went into business following his resignation and pursued manufacturing interests until the Civil War, at which time he accepted the commission of lieutenant colonel in the 70th New York Infantry. Wounded during the Peninsula Campaign, Dwight was left for dead on the field of battle, captured, and eventually exchanged. Somewhat of a hero after his release, the pugnacious New Englander was given a brigadier's star and sent to Louisiana.[12]

Dwight's assignment at Port Hudson on the far right of the Union position was inconsequential given the plan of attack, but he saw in Banks's order an opportunity "to test the negro question," as Dwight put it. "I have had the negro Regts longest in the service assigned to me," he wrote to his mother on Tuesday evening, "and I am going to storm a detached work with them. You may look for hard fighting, or for a complete run away." Believing that this would be the first time black troops had been used in combat during the war, Dwight informed his mother that "the garrison will of course be incensed and fight defiantly. The negro will have the fate of his race on his conduct. I shall compromise nothing in making this attack," he added, "for I regard it as an experiment."[13]

Dwight prepared for the attack Wednesday morning by getting drunk before breakfast. He had not conducted a reconnaissance nor studied the maps; he knew nothing of the terrain over which the black troops would advance. When Colonel Nelson asked what the ground would be like, Dwight lied. The approach would be "the easiest way into Port Hudson," he told Nelson. The ground to the front of the Native Guards was anything but easy. In fact, the rugged terrain and tangle of trees made the Confederate position the Native Guards were about to assault the strongest at Port Hudson.[14]

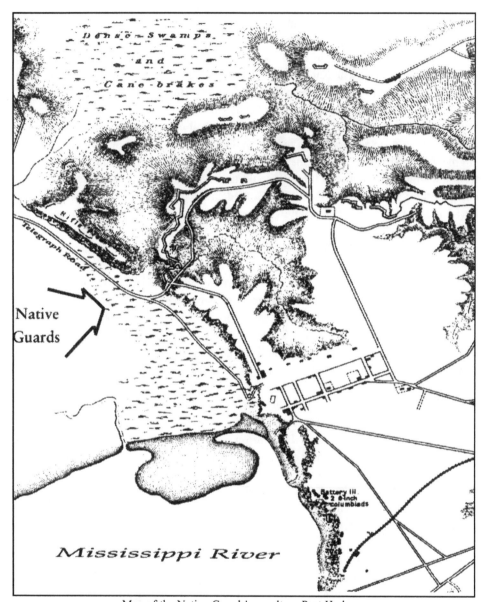

Map of the Native Guards' assault on Port Hudson.
Adapted from Plate XXXVIII of *Atlas to Accompany the Official Records of the Union and Confederate Armies* (Washington, D.C., 1891-95).

The main Confederate line was on a high bluff that dropped off abruptly to a flood-plain adjacent to the Mississippi River. The river was high, and much of the floodplain was under water. Jutting out from the main position was a jagged finger of land on top of which the Confederates had dug a series of rifle pits. The position was about four hundred yards in length and ran parallel to Telegraph Road, along which the Native Guards would have to advance. The outwork was manned by a detachment of forty-five men from the 39th Mississippi Infantry and fifteen men from the 9th Louisiana Cavalry Battalion. The main Confederate position was held by six companies of the 39th Mississippi supported by two batteries containing a total of six fieldpieces. Because of the floodplain, the black troops would have little room to maneuver once they left the protection of the woods behind Union lines. To make matters worse, two eight-inch Columbiads in a water battery on the river could rake the road as the troops advanced.[15] The Native Guards would thus be exposed to fire from three sides: the Mississippians in the rifle pits on the high ground to their left, the cannon in the main works to their front, and the Columbiads in the water battery to their right.

Early Wednesday morning, six companies from the 1st Regiment and nine companies from the 3rd crossed the pontoon bridge over the Big Sandy and filed to the right to form a line of battle in a grove of willow trees that covered the old riverbed south of the Telegraph Road. Initially, they were supported by two brass guns from the 6th Massachusetts Artillery and some dismounted troopers from the 1st Louisiana Union Calvary.[16] The artillerymen unlimbered in the road and engaged the Rebel guns on the bluffs ahead. They fired only one round, however, before the Confederate artillery responded with a vengeance. Two artillerymen went down in the fusillade, and three horses were killed. Quickly, the boys from Massachusetts limbered their cannon and withdrew, leaving the Native Guards to fend for themselves.[17]

At about ten o'clock, the Native Guards left the relative protection of the willow trees and started forward at a double-quick.[18] About six hundred yards separated the black soldiers from the main Confederate position. They covered about two hundred yards before all hell broke loose. As a newspaper report described it, the artillery opened fire with "shot and shells, and pieces of railroad iron twelve to eighteen inches long." The Mississippians in the rifle pits along the top of the outwork as well as infantry behind the breastworks commenced firing as soon as the black troops came within range.[19]

The color sergeant of the 1st Regiment, Anselmas Plancianois, was hit almost immediately, a shell taking off half of his head and splattering his brains on the men standing closest to him.[20] Two corporals on either side seized the colors before they hit the ground and tugged at the flagstaff between them, each wanting the honor of carrying it forward.[21] Capt. André Cailloux was out in front of his company, urging the men on. His left arm dangled uselessly by his side; a ball had shattered his elbow.[22] The Native Guards followed Cailloux across the open ground, only to see him cut down in a torrent of shot and shell.[23] Cailloux's death and the deadly fire from the Confederate position were too much for the Native Guards. After firing a single volley, they fell back in confusion.[24]

The Confederates continued to fire at the retreating troops. "We moad them down," one Louisiana artillerist recalled, "and made them disperse[,] leaving there dead and wounded on the field to stink."[25] A small contingent of black soldiers found that they could not retreat and hugged the ground under the lip of the hill between the Confederate rifle pits and the river. Although they were shielded from direct fire from the rifle pits above, these men were easy targets for the eight-inch Columbiads in the water battery.[26] Scarcely fifteen minutes had passed since the Native Guards had begun their assault. Although they left scores of dead and wounded behind them, the Native Guards had not inflicted a single casualty on the Confederate defenders.[27]

Nelson sent an aide to Dwight, informing the general of the failed assault and asking for orders. The aide found Dwight seated on the ground leaning against a tree. "Tell Colonel Nelson," Dwight told the aide, "I shall consider he has done nothing unless he carries the enemy's works."[28] The aide protested, pointing out that both regiments had been cut up badly and had lost half their men. "Charge again," Dwight commanded, "and let the impetuosity of the charge counterbalance the paucity of numbers." Apparently, Dwight was determined to press his experiment to its deadly conclusion.[29]

The aide recrossed the creek and relayed Dwight's orders. Nelson sent word to Bassett and Finnegass to prepare the men for another assault. But rather than start his men forward, Finnegass retreated to Nelson's command post behind the lines and asked the colonel for a chew of tobacco. Nelson ordered Finnegass to return to his regiment. Finnegass started back to the front, only to show up again a few minutes later. This time he wanted a drink of whiskey. And would the colonel have a match so he could light his pipe? Valuable time was being wasted. Return to your men and lead the advance, Nelson told the reluctant lieutenant colonel. It would be of no use to advance, Finnegass replied; the Rebel position was far too strong. Could he take his men to the rear to reform them? Nelson was flabbergasted. No, he said. A withdrawal under these conditions would demoralize the troops and encourage the Confederates on bluffs waiting for the attack. Finnegass said he would be damned if he would go and stoof off to the side as if that settled the matter.[30]

Finnegass' refusal to obey orders, the strength of the Confederate position, and the heavy casualties already sustained made it clear to Nelson that it would be suicidal for the Native Guards to charge again. He also realized that the drunken Dwight had no intention of leaving the safety of his headquarters to see whether his order was being obeyed. Consequently, Nelson ordered the men to continue firing from their position among the willows. Although they would not be able to hit any Confederates from there, at least they were not out in the open, and the sound of firing would make Dwight believe that his insane order was being carried out.

Throughout the afternoon, the Native Guards continued to shoot at the distant enemy. They were safe from rifle fire, but the Confederate guns shelled the thicket, shattering limbs and sending splinters from the fragmented trees slicing through the air.[31] Casualties would have been higher excerpt that the Rebel gunners could not depress their guns sufficiently to do further damage.[32] Nevertheless, the wounded continued to stream to the rear. One man, his arm shattered by a shell, walked along using his good arm to swing the broken one like a plumb weight. "Massa, guess I can't fight no more," he commented to an officer. Another wounded black soldier refused to leave the field. "I been shot bad in de leg, Captain, and dey want me to go to de hospital, but I guess I can gib'em some more yet." He then propped himself on a log and "Sat With his leg a swinging and bleeding and fierd thirty rounds of Ammunition" before allowing himself to be taken to the field hospital. He died a few days later.[33]

The Native Guards were not only the only soldiers in Banks's army to be repulsed that day. Every charge in every sector failed. The firing continued sporadically until 5:30 that evening, when someone had the good sense to raise a white flag and call a temporary cease-fire so that the wounded could be attended to. Union casualties on May 27 exceeded 450 dead and missing and over 1,500 wounded. Confederate losses numbered no more than several hundred.[34]

The Native Guards had gone into battle with fewer than 540 men in each regiment.[35] The 1st Regiment had lost two officers. One was Capt. André Cailloux. The other was Second Lieut. John H. Crowder, the young steamboat steward who had attempted to defend a lady's honor. Twenty-four enlisted men were also killed in action. Three officers and ninety-two men in the 1st Regiment were wounded. The 3rd Regiment lost a total of ten killed and thirty-eight wounded.[36]

Statistics alone belied the punishment these men had suffered. Capt. Thomas A. Prescott of the 8th New Hampshire Infantry appreciated how much the black soldiers had sacrificed when his company marched down Telegraph Road later that evening. "They suffered severe losses," he wrote, "and as we moved back at night to our quarters, we passed the little house on the road where a temporary hospital had been established for them, and at the back door of this house we saw a pile of considerable size of legs and arms which had been amputated from those poor fellows."[37]

Notes for "'I Regard It as an Experiment'"
[The Native Guards at the Siege of Port Hudson]

[1]C. Grover to Banks's AAG, December 17, 1862, *The War of the Rebellion: A Compilation of the Official Records of the Union and Confederate Armies*, 70 vols. in 127 (Washington, D.C., 1880-1901), 15:191 (hereafter cited as *OR* with volume and page numbers); also Special Orders No. 29, December 15, 1862, ibid., 609.

[2]Crowder to his mother, April 27, 1863, in Joseph T. Glatthaar, "The Civil War Through the Eyes of a Sixteen-Year-Old Black Officer: The Letters of Lieutenant John H. Crowder of the 1st Louisiana Native Guards," *Louisiana History*, 35 (1994): 213. It is not known whether Crowder's friend, identified only as Mrs. Marsh, was white or black. From Crowder's description, Mrs. Marsh was apparently well situated (Crowder to his mother, April 18, 1863, ibid., 211). The 1860 census recorded no Marshes in Baton Rouge, although an "M. Marsh" resided in Port Hudson, just up the road. M. Marsh was a thirty-eight-year-old white physician born in New York.

[3]Stafford quarreled frequently with officers in white units who he believed were treating his men unfairly. One such incident took place on December 2, 1862, at Camp Steven near Thibodaux when Stafford, apparently under the influence of liquor, ran his horse over Capt. Richard Barrett while Barrett was drilling Company B of the 1st Louisiana Cavalry (Charges and Specifications preferred against Col. S. H. Stafford of the first regiment of Louisiana Native Guards, in Stafford's Compiled Military Service Record, National Archives, Washington, D.C.). In "Negro Troops in Blue and Gray: The Louisiana Native Guards, 1861-1863," *Louisiana History*, 8 (1967): 180, Mary Berry confused this incident with the one on May 13 and treated the two as one. In addition, she misidentified the white unit in question as the 13th Louisiana Cavalry, possibly by reading the letter "B" of Company B as "13."

[4]Capt. J. P. Garland to Col. E. P. Chapin, May 14, 1863, in Stafford's Compiled Military Service Record, NA.

[5]Stafford to Banks, June 4, 1863, and Stafford to Maj. G. B. Halstead, May 19, 1863, both in Stafford's Compiled Service Record, NA. Gen. George L. Andrews recommended Stafford's dismissal on August 12, 1863. After the war, Stafford successfully appealed his case and was honorably discharged retroactive to the date of the original dismissal (Special Orders No. 1[extract], January 3, 1871, AGO, War Department, copy in Stafford's Compiled Military Service Record, NA).

[6]Special Orders No. 122, May 21, 1863, OR, 26, Part 1:498.

[7]Richard B. Irwin, *Nineteenth Army Corps* (1892; reprint ed., Baton Rouge, 1985), 166; Joseph T. Wilson, *The Black Phalanx: A History of the Negro Soldiers in the Wars of 1775, 1812, 1861-65* (1888; reprint ed., New York, 1968), 525.

[8]George W. Williams, *A History of the Negro Troops in the War of the Rebellion, 1861-1865* (New York, 1888), 216. Finnegass had been a first lieutenant in the 9th Connecticut Infantry and transferred to the 2nd Regiment of the Native Guards on January 1, 1862 (*Official Army Register*, 1:274).

[9]William H. Root, "The Experience of a Federal Soldier in Louisiana, 1863," ed. L. Carroll Root, *Louisiana Historical Quarterly*, 19 (1936): 658.

[10]The Big Sandy Creek was sometimes called Foster's Creek from the point of its confluence with the Little Sandy and the Mississippi River and is thus marked on some maps (David C. Edmonds, *The Guns of Port Hudson*, Vol. 2, *The Investment, Siege and Reduction* [Lafayette, La., 1984], 401, n4).

[11]Charles P. Bosson, *History of the Forty-second Regiment Infantry, Massachusetts Volunteers, 1862, 1863, 1864* (Boston, 1886), 364.

[12]Ezra J. Warner, *Generals in Blue: Lives of the Union Commanders* (Baton Rouge, 1964), 134-5; Edward Bacon, *Among the Cotton Thieves* (1867; reprint ed., Bossier City, La., 1989), 158.

[13]William Dwight, Jr., to his mother, May 26, 1863, in Dwight Family Papers, Massachusetts Historical Society, Boston, Massachusetts (hereafter cited MAHS). Dwight's request that the two black regiments be assigned to him is confirmed by Gen. Albert E. Paine in his diary on May 26, 1863, in William B. Stevens, *History of the Fiftieth Regiment of Infantry, Massachusetts Volunteer Militia, in the Late War of the Rebellion* (Boston, 1907), 144.

[14]Bacon, *Among the Cotton Thieves*, 159-60; Lawrence Lee Hewitt, *Port Hudson, Confederate Bastion on the Mississippi* (Baton Rouge, 1987), 148.

[15]Edward Cunningham, *The Port Hudson Campaign, 1862-1863* (Baton Rouge, 1963), 53; M. J. Smith and James Freret, "Fortification and Siege of Port Hudson," *Southern Historical Society Papers*, 14 (1886): 321-22; Hewitt, *Port Hudson*, 148; Irwin, *Nineteenth Army Corps*, 173.

[16]Hewitt, *Port Hudson*, 148.

[17]Bosson, *Forty-second Massachusetts*, 364; Smith and Freret, "Fortification and Siege of Port Hudson," 321. Smith and Freret reprinted a large portion of Colonel Shelby's afteraction report to Gardner (dated August 5, 1863, and addressed to Maj. S. F. Wilson, Gardner's AAG), which Shelby wrote from prison in New Orleans. The original is in the Louisiana Historical Association Collection, 55-B, Box 8, folder 5, Howard-Tilton Memorial Library, Tulane University, New Orleans, Louisiana (hereafter cited HTML). Also see Lieut. Fred M. Dabney's report on the siege of Port Hudson dated August 24, 1863, and found in the same folder as Shelby's report.

[18]Although the exact time the Native Guards began their assault is uncertain, it is known that they began to advance after Weitzel's attack had ended but before Augur's began (John C. Palfrey, "Port Hudson," in *The Mississippi Valley, Tennessee, Georgia, Alabama, 1861-1864*, vol. 8, *Papers of the Military Historical Society of Massachusetts* [Boston, 1910], 41). Banks placed their advance in conjunction with Weitzel's at 10 A.M. (Banks to Halleck, May 30, 1863), *OR*, 26, Part 1:43-44.

[19]Smith and Freret, "Fortification and Siege of Port Hudson," 322; *Chicago Daily Tribune*, June 10, 1863.

[20]Joseph E. Roy, "Our Indebtedness to the Negroes for Their Conduct During the War," *New Englander and Yale Review*, 41 (1889): 358; Williams, *History of Negro Troops*, 217.

[21]Wilson, *Black Phalanx*, 214.

[22]Brown, *The Negro in the American Rebellion*, 169, 171.

[23]*New York Times*, June 13, 1863.

[24]Hewitt, *Port Hudson*, 148-49; Irwin, *Nineteenth Army Corps*, 174; J. V. Frederick, ed., "War Diary of W. C. Porter," *Arkansas Historical Quarterly*, 11 (1952): 313-14. An account in Wilson's *Black Phalanx* (525-26) alleges that Capt. Quinn and thirty-five or forty men actually breached the backwater and scaled the Rebel parapets. This account also claims that the Native Guards made six separate assaults. There is no evidence from other sources to indicate that this account is accurate.

[25]Undated notes in Robert Hughes Papers, United States Military History Institute, Carlisle Barracks, Pa.

[26]Frederick, ed., "War Diary of Porter," 313-14.

[27]Smith and Freret, "Fortification and Siege of Port Hudson," 322.

[28]Johns, *Life with the Forty-ninth Massachusetts Volunteers*, 254-55.

[29]Stanyan, *Eighth New Hampshire Volunteers*, 229-30. Dwight's language was so bizarre that Stanyan took pains in his memoirs to assure the reader that the quotation was accurate. Also see the *New York Times*, June 13, 1863; Bacon, *Among the Cotton Thieves*, 159-61; Irwin, *Nineteenth Army Corps*, 174; Smith and Freret, "Fortification and Siege of Port Hudson," 321-22.

[30]John A. Nelson to Captain Dunham, June 1, 1863, and Charges and Specifications preferred against Lieut. Col. Henry Finnegass, 3rd Regt., Corps d'Afrique (no date), both in Finnegass' Compiled Military Record, NA. Finnegass was also absent from his regiment later that night when a false alarm caused the Native Guards to fall in under arms to repel a Confederate cavalry charge that did not materialize.

[31]Hewitt, *Port Hudson*, 150, 149.

[32]Bosson, *Forty-Second Massachusetts*, 365.

[33]*New York Times*, June 13, 1863; George R. Sanders to Mr. Burnham, July 15, 1863, in Civil War Miscellaneous Collection, YU. There are two accounts of this incident, which may refer to two different men or be two versions of the same event. I have chosen to treat them as two versions of the same event.

[34]Edmonds, *The Guns of Port Hudson*, 2:93; Banks to Halleck, June 29, 1863, *OR*, 26, Part 1:47, also 144, 147.

[35]The figure of 1,080 men in both regiments combined comes from the *New York Times*, June 13, 1863. Where the correspondent got his numbers is unknown, but it is the best estimate we have. The Union report of troop strength in *OR*, 26, Part 1:526, dated May 31, 1863, combines the 1st and 3rd Regiments with the 4th, which did not participate in the assault of May 27, for a total of 2,252 men present for duty. The 4th Regiment, which had been recruited just two months earlier, was probably somewhat larger than the 1st and 3rd. In addition, only six companies of the 1st and nine of the 3rd participated in the assault.

[36]*OR*, 26, Part 1:68. Two of the dead in the 1st Regiment, Louis Laville and Louis Fernandez, had served in the Louisiana militia.

[37]Stanyan, *Eighth New Hampshire*, 230.

UNSUITED FOR THIS DUTY*

James G. Hollandsworth, Jr.

After Port Hudson, Maj. Gen. Nathaniel P. Banks moved aggressively to increase the number of black soldiers in the Department of the Gulf. Using the Native Guards as a nucleus, he set out to organize an entire division of black troops, the Corps d'Afrique, he called it. Accordingly, the 1st and 3rd Regiments of the Native Guards became the 1st and 3rd Regiments of the Corps d'Afrique and were placed under the command of Brig. Gen. Daniel Ullmann.[1] The 2nd Regiment on Ship Island became the 2nd Regiment of the Corps d'Afrique.[2]

During July and August, 1863, these soldiers joined white units clearing the countryside around Port Hudson of remaining Confederate resistance. A detachment from the 1st Regiment was on one of these missions when Confederate cavalry swept down near Jackson, Louisiana. The Rebels captured twenty-one black enlisted men and their black officer, Lieutenant Oscar Orillion.[3] The next morning, Col. John L. Logan, the Rebel commander, ordered the 17th Arkansas Mounted Infantry to march the prisoners toward the Confederate lines. The guard set out several hours before the main body broke camp, took the wrong road, and eventually rejoined the main column minus the prisoners. Col. John Griffith of the 17th Arkansas reported to Logan that four of the black soldiers had attempted to escape, which "created some excitement and a general stampede among them, all attempting to effect their escape." Col. Frank Powers, Logan's cavalry commander, was more direct: "I ordered the guard to shoot them down. In the confusion, the other negroes [sic] attempted to escape likewise. I then ordered every one shot, and with my six shooter assisted in the execution of the order." Lieutenant James W. Shattuck of Scott's Louisiana Cavalry boasted later of having killed thirteen of the prisoners himself.[4]

The affair at Jackson gave evidence of the risk black men faced by serving in the Union army. This reality, coupled with their bravery before Port Hudson, should have increased the department commander's appreciation of their service. Instead, Banks chose

*First published as Chapter 7 in James G. Hollandsworth, Jr., *The Louisiana Native Guards: The Black Military Experience During the Civil War* (Baton Rouge: Louisiana State University Press, © 1995), 70-83. Reprinted with the kind permission of the author and publisher.

to reward their loyalty in a very curious way; he decided to get rid of all the black officers who remained in the Corps d'Afrique. Black officers were a source of "constant embarrassment and annoyance," Banks wrote, and their use "demoralizes both the white troops and the negroes [*sic*]." Furthermore, Banks argued, the "arrogance and self-assertion" of the black officers caused white soldiers to retaliate with violence. As far as their being officers, Banks informed Lincoln in August, 1863, black men were simply "unsuited for this duty."[5]

In reality, it was the reaction of the white troops rather than the qualifications of the black officers that goaded Banks into taking action. Some of Banks's white troops threatened to go home if reenlisting meant that they had to salute a black man. As one lieutenant told a newspaper correspondent, if a black man were to be allowed to hold a commission, "I must not only obey him, I must politely touch my cap when I approach him. I must stand while he sits, unless his captainship should condescendingly ask me to be seated. Negro soldiers are all very well," he continued, "but let us have white officers, whom we can receive and treat as equals everywhere, and whom we may treat as superiors without humiliation." A provost marshal under Banks agreed. "You should have a look here at these negro [*sic*] Captains, appointed by Gen. Butler," he wrote to a friend shortly after arriving in New Orleans. To him they looked "like dogs in full dress, ready to dance in the menagerie. Would *you* like to obey such a fool?" he asked. Colonel Paine of the 2nd Louisiana put it more succinctly: "They ought never to put a shoulder strap on a darkey."[6]

Bank planned to replace all of the black officers by filling vacancies in the Corps d'Afrique with white men.[7] The mass resignation from the 3rd Regiment in February had aided him greatly in attaining this goal, but getting rid of the black officers in the 1st and 2nd Regiments would not be as easy. All of the line officers in both regiments were black, and their pride of serving in the first black regiments in the Union army was great. It did not take long, however, for Banks to formulate a strategy to force these men out of the service. First, he set up an examining board to evaluate the black officers' proficiency in military matters. Second, Banks let it be known that he intended to pay black enlisted men and their white field officers but not the black line officers.[8]

Banks's examining board was expected to apply the highest standards to the officers who came before it.[9] In practice, this meant black officers, for their white counterparts were excused.[10] Three black officers from the 2nd Regiment were discharged from the service on February 24, 1863, for reasons of incompetence.[11] The other black officers on Ship Island reacted with anger and met on March 2 to formulate their grievances. Capt. P. B. S. Pinchback served as their spokesman and offered a series of resolutions for the department commander's consideration. First, the officers complained that they were kept busy "continually erecting Batteries, Magazines, and Fortifications, working both day and night." This constant fatigue duty prevented them from preparing for the board examination. They also protested Banks's decision to withhold their pay. But the main problem was the examining board. Noting that white officers charged that the examining board was a pretext for forcing them out of the service. "From the many rumors that have reached us," Pinchback wrote, "we are led to believe that it is the intention of the General to relieve us from our present command."[12]

Four of the petitioners anticipated Banks's reaction and did not wait for his reply. Ironically, all four had already been passed by the examining board.[13] The problem was prejudice. "When I joined the army I thought that I was fighting for the same cause, wishing only the success of my country would suffice to alter a prejudice which had long existed," Capt. Arnold Bertonneau wrote in his letter of resignation from Fort Pike. "But I regret to say," he continued, "that five months experience has proved the contrary."

Lieutenants Octave Rey, Ernest Morphy, and Robert H. Isabelle resigned at the same time for the same reasons.[14]

Most of the other officers in the 2nd Regiment waited to see what would happen. In May, Capt. William B. Barrett wrote General Ullmann directly to ask whether he planned to remove all black officers in the process of organizing the Corps d'Afrique. Ullmann responded that he had come "to no determination whatever" in regard to the disposition of black officers. He would wait until he assumed command before making that decision. Barrett decided to stick it out, but eight of his fellow officers saw the handwriting on the wall and decided to resign rather than risk dismissal.[15]

The next wave of resignations from the 2nd Regiment occurred in August, 1863, when the remaining black officers prepared for another round with Banks's examining board, composed of white officers from the same regiment. Incredibly, the white board members were all junior in rank to the black officers whose credentials they would examine. Any dismissals the white board members could effect would allow them to advance in rank, a clear conflict of interest. "A Board of Examination has been formed to investigate the Military Capacity of the *Colored Officers* of this Regiment," Capt. Samuel Ringgold protested. "The Officers detailed to compose said Board are in the Majority of inferior rank (Lieutenants of the same Regiment) whose promotion would be effected by our dismissal." Although Brig. Gen. William H. Emory explained that "when this board was appointed there were no officers of higher rank competent to sit on the board," six black officers in the 2nd Regiment, including Capt. [William B.] Barrett and Maj. [F. Ernest] Dumas, resigned rather than submit to this indignity.[16] Only seven black officers were left in the 2nd Regiment.

One of the seven who remained was Capt. P. B. S. Pinchback, whose company had been detached from the regiment and sent to garrison Fort Pike. Pinchback was the only black officer left at this isolated post, and by mid-September he too had had enough. "I find nearly all the officers inimical to me," he wrote to Banks on September 10, "and I can foresee nothing but dissatisfaction and discontent which will make my position very disagreeable indeed."[17]

Not all of the black officers who left the 2nd Regiment did so for reasons of prejudice. In December, 1863, Second Lieut. Frank L. Trask left his post as officer of the guard and was found asleep in his bunk. Charges were brought, and Trask was dismissed from the service in February, 1864. Second Lieut. Solomon Hayes also left the regiment under a cloud. In his letter of resignation dated February 11, 1864, he cited "the prejudice which exists in my Regiment, as well as the entire Service against Colored Officers." The 2nd Regiment's colonel, William M. Grosvenor, was pleased to see him go. "This officer is ignorant, unable to learn, & though a black has neither the respect or confidence of his men," Grosvenor penned in his endorsement.[18]

Hayes's resignation left four black officers in the 2nd Regiment. Capt. William Belley was the next to go. On March 31, 1864, he resigned without giving a reason. "After much patient endeavor I have despaired of ever instructing this officer in his duties," Grosvenor noted in his endorsement. "He is one of the original officers of the Regiment," he continued, "and yet, after fourteen months of service as a Captain, is not qualified for examination as second Lieutenant. His ignorance, however, does not so seriously disqualify him, as his mismanagement in the discipline of his company." Grosvenor did not stop there. "In every respect his resignation is, in my judgement[,] a fortunate thing for the Regiment." Regardless of the accuracy of Grosvenor's assessment of Belley's ability, it was getting harder and harder for a black officer in the 2nd Regiment to survive. Capt. Joseph Villeverde and First Lieut. Theodule Martin lasted until August, 1864, when they also resigned.[19]

Remarkably, the lone remaining black officer in the 2nd Regiment held on to his commission until the end of the war. He was Charles Sauvenet, the translator in the provost court whom Butler had approached in August, 1862, to discuss reorganizing the Native Guards. Sauvenet must have been an exceptional person, for he was recommended for promotion at a time when Banks was dismissing or forcing the resignations of blacks holding Butler's commissions. Just how Sauvenet survived is unknown. Clearly he was competent, and he served as the regiment's assistant quartermaster, a staff rather than line position. But it is also possible that Sauvenet's light complexion made his continuation in the service more acceptable to his white associates. Butler had described him as "hardly a mulatto."[20] Whatever the case, Sauvenet served three years, making him the black officer with the longest continuous service in the Union army.

The gradual elimination of black officers in the 1st Regiment at Port Hudson followed a similar path, although the first to go did not leave under the best of circumstances. In February, 1863, Capt. John De Pass resigned to return to England, his native country, planning to stop in Kingston, Jamaica, on the way to look after property he owned there. Apparently, De Pass was more interested in money than militancy, for Colonel Stafford noted in his endorsement that although De Pass "has sufficient capacity, his carelessness & volatility added to a decided want of principle render him unfit for his present position."[21]

By mid-August, 1863, six other black officers in the 1st Regiment had resigned their commissions for the honorable reasons of illness or physical disability.[22] Banks dismissed three in late August.[23] In early September, five black officers who were passed by the examining board were transferred to a new black regiment, the 20th Infantry, Corps d'Afrique.[24] Discouraged by having to leave the regiment in which they had fought and served for the past year and believing this to be a violation of the terms under which they had volunteered, four of the five resigned.[25] The fifth, Capt. Charles Sentmanat, held out for a month before resigning as well, citing poor health and the fact that he was the "only remaining colored officer" in the new unit.[26] During September and October, 1863, four more black officers in the 1st Regiment resigned for reasons of ill health or family hardship.[27]

Eight black officers in the 1st Regiment remained. They had been passed by the examining board so it was difficult for Union commanders to complain about their incompetence. Thus when Lieutenants James H. Ingraham and Alfred Bourgeau came up for promotion in October, 1863, Banks did not try to block their advancement. "They proved themselves thorough and efficient officers," their commander wrote in his recommendation, "and I consider them much better qualified than any we can get, to say nothing of their experience."[28] Nevertheless, the prejudicial treatment of black officers continued. "I respectfully tender my immediate and unconditional resignation," Capt. Joseph Follin wrote in February, 1864. "Daily events demonstrate that prejudices are so strong against Colored Officers, that no matter what would be their patriotism and their anxiety to fight for the flag of the native land, they cannot do it with honor to themselves."[29] One by one, the remaining black officers in the 1st Regiment, the first to volunteer, resigned, until only Captains James H. Ingraham and Louis A. Snaer remained.[30] Despite being promoted to captain in October, 1863, Ingraham finally called it quits without giving a reason on March 22, 1864. Like Sauvenet in the 2nd Regiment, Snaer retained his commission to the end of the war.[31]

Banks's policy of forcing black officers out of the army was shortsighted in several ways. He failed to use talent that was at his disposal. Banks's own Inspector General's Office reported in September, 1863, that the 1st Regiment was "partially officered by colored men, some of whom exhibited as much promptness and intelligence and knowledge of their duties, as a majority of the white officers of other regiments." Colonel John A. Nelson, commander of the 3rd Regiment, agreed with the inspector general's assessment. Responding to Capt. Joseph Oliver's resignation earlier that year, Nelson described the black man as an "excellent officer" whom I "can scarcely replace."[32]

Not all of the black officers in the Native Guards acquitted themselves with honor.[33] Capt. Emile Detiége's murder of an enlisted man near Terrebonne Bayou in December, 1862, Capt. Alcide Lewis' failure to discipline the exhibitionist at Baton Rouge, and Lieutenant Frank Trask's dismissal for leaving his post as officer of the guard on Ship Island gave evidence that some black officers were unsuited to hold commissions in the Union army. Nevertheless, many of the white officers who replaced them were no better.[34]

Competent white officers who could expect promotion and advancement in their own regiments generally refused assignment to black units.[35] Racism also played its part. "Any [white] man holding a commission in a negro [*sic*] regiment must feel degraded," a

Massachusetts soldier wrote home to his brother. Even the bravery of the black troops under fire at Port Hudson did not change these attitudes. "Who would not be a Niggadier General?" the *National Intelligencer* mocked in its report of the Native Guards' assault of May 27.[36] Consequently, many of those who did volunteer were incompetents dissatisfied with their current situation. Furthermore, it was widely known that white commanders unloaded their troublemakers on black companies.[37] Ullmann was disgusted by the hypocrisy of it all. "I well know that those prophets who declare that negroes never will make soldiers," he wrote to Sen. Henry Wilson of Massachusetts in December, 1863, "are striving to force their prophecies to work out their own fulfillment by appointing ignoramuses and boors to be officers over men who are as keen-sighted as any to notice the shortcomings of those placed over them. Men have been made field officers in this section who are not fit to be non-commissioned officers—men so ignorant that they cannot write three consecutive sentences without violating orthography and syntax."[38]

There were many examples of poor leadership among the white officers assigned to command the Native Guards.[39] The 1st Regiment's Colonel Stafford had been dismissed by court-martial in May, 1863, for "conduct to the prejudice of good order and military discipline."[40] Colonel Nathan W. Daniels of the 2nd Regiment was next. In August, 1863, Daniels and his adjutant, First Lieut. Elijah K. Prowty, encountered Lieut. Com. A. D. Perkins of the United States Navy and his wife riding in a carriage in New Orleans. "You say you are riding with a lady," Prowty smirked, "but you are riding with a damned whore." Apparently, Colonel Daniels did not order his adjutant to curb his tongue. "You are a damned shit ass," Prowty continued, "and I room at 122 St. Charles Hotel and will repeat the same thing tomorrow morning." Both Prowty and Daniels surrendered their commissions over this vulgar incident.[41]

Daniels' replacement, Col. William M. Grosvenor, who hastened the departure of several black officers with harsh evaluations of their competency, lasted until May, 1864, when a general court-martial charged him with "Conduct Unbecoming an Officer and a Gentleman." Grosvenor pleaded guilty to keeping "a woman, not his wife, by the name of 'Belle Fisher' " in his quarters on Ship Island.[42] But he pleaded not guilty to the charge of abusing Assistant Surgeon John H. Gihon of the 2nd Regiment after Gihon intervened when Grosvenor disciplined two black soldiers.[43] "Now mind, if you or any other Medical Officer ever again dare to interfere with any punishment that I may order to be inflicted," Grosvenor was charged with saying, "I will punish you or him in the same manner, and that within five minutes after, God damn you, Sir, I will let you know that I command this Post." The court found Grosvenor guilty of this charge as well and sentenced him to be dismissed from the service.[44]

Lieut. Col. Henry Finnegass of the 3rd Regiment, the coward of Port Hudson, was also dismissed from the service, although his court-martial for "disobedience of orders on the field of battle" hit a snag. Because Colonel Nelson had resigned in August, 1863, to go north, there were no witnesses to Finnegass' insubordination. On September 5, the judge advocate returned the court-martial papers to Brig. Gen. George L. Andrews, the commander at Port Hudson, stating that he could not bring the accused to trial. The judge advocate's opinion did not deter Andrews from getting rid of Finnegass, even if he could not be court-martialed. Andrews forwarded the paperwork with a strongly worded endorsement. "In my opinion Lieut. Col. Finnegass is in no wise qualified for the position he now holds," Andrews wrote. "His conduct as set forth by his commanding officer, Col. Nelson[,] and the present state of the regiment show clearly that his longer connection with the service will be detrimental thereto. I therefore respectfully recommend that Lieut. Col. Finnegass be discharged from the service of the United States." The War Department in Washington concurred and ordered that Finnegass be dishonorably dismissed from the service.[45]

Weak white officers and the purge of black officers played havoc with the morale among the black enlisted men.[46] After Capt. Emile Detiége resigned on September 25, 1863, a fourth of his company deserted. After the last black officer (except Snaer) left the 1st Regiment the following spring, some fifty men deserted. Observing the process of stripping black officers of their commissions from his home in Lowell, Massachusetts, Butler reacted in anger: "The negro [*sic*], whether the equal to the white man or not, knows when he is treated fairly, and appreciates an injustice quite as endearingly as if of a lighter color." Rhetorically Butler asked, "How can we expect the Black man to stand up against the White rebel when we allow him to be insulted by our own soldier because he [the Union soldier] is White?"[47]

The unfairness of the Union army's treatment of black soldiers was not lost on the men who had been forced to resign. At a mass meeting on November 5, 1863, in New Orleans, P. B. S. Pinchback, formerly a captain in the 2nd Regiment, declared that because black soldiers had fought and died for the Union, they should be allowed to vote. "They did not ask for social equality, and did not expect it," he told the large audience assembled at Economy Hall, "but they demanded political rights—they wanted to become men." Pinchback believed that if blacks were citizens, they should have the right to vote; if not, they should be exempted from the draft.[48]

Pinchback had a point. Conscription was in effect in Louisiana, and every man of military age was liable to be drafted into the Union army, regardless of his race. Among the exceptions were persons who had already served for two years.[49] The forced resignations of black officers meant that their term of service was less than two years, making them liable to be drafted into the army as privates. Late in the war, seventeen former officers in the Native Guards sought assurances from Banks that they would not be called up for additional service in the army. Banks forwarded their petition to Washington without comment. As expected, the superintendent of the draft refused the petition, citing the requirement for a full two years of service.[50] Fortunately for the black men who had come forward to serve their country in its greatest hour of need only to be discarded, the war was drawing to a close, and the subsequent demobilization of the Union army spared them the ultimate indignity of returning to the ranks of the men they had once commanded.

Notes for "Unsuited for this Duty"

[1]General Orders No. 40, May 1, 1863, U. S. War Department, *The War of the Rebellion: A Compilation of the Official Records of the Union and Confederate Armies*, 70 vols. in 127 Parts (Washington, D.C., 1865), 15:716-17; also Vol. 26, Part 1:726, 733; Vol. 53:561 (hereafter cited as *OR* with volume, part, and page numbers); Richard B. Irwin, *History of the Nineteenth Army Corps* (1892; reprint ed., Baton Rouge, 1985), 261. The change in designation from Native Guards to Corps d'Afrique was effective June 6, 1863 (General Orders No. 47, *OR*, Vol. 26, Part 1:539).

[2]Field and Staff Muster Roll, May and June, 1863, 74th U. S. Col'd Inf., in Compiled Military Service Records, National Archives (Washington, D.C.).

[3]George L. Andrews to Richard Irwin, August 6, 1863, *OR*, Vol. 26, Part 1:239. Orillion's race can be deduced from the date of his commission, September 27, 1862, which made him one of the original officers of the 1st Regiment, Native Guards.

[4]Frank Powers to John L. Logan, September 2, 1863, *OR*, Ser. 2, Vol. 6:258-59, also 244, 289, 960-61.

[5]Banks to L. Thomas, February 12, 1863, *OR*, Ser. 3, Vol. 3:46; *New York Herald*, February 4, 1863; Banks to Lincoln, August 16, 1863, *OR*, Vol. 26, Part 1:689.

[6]Charles Bennett to his father, February 18, 1863, in Charles Bennett Letters, Historic New Orleans Collection, New Orleans, Louisiana; *New York Herald*, February 4, 1863; see also report of *New York Tribune* correspondent reprinted in Joseph T. Wilson, *The Black Phalanx: A History of the Negro Soldiers in the Wars of 1775, 1812, 1861-65* (1888; reprint ed., New York, 1968), 527; Von Herrman to "My dear Captain," February 24, 1863, in Civil War Letters, 1862-63, Civil War Manuscripts Series, Howard-Tilton Memorial Library, Tulane University, New Orleans, Louisiana; Charles J. Paine to his father, in Charles J. Paine, Letters. Microfilm, Massachusetts Historical Society, Boston, Massachusetts, Microfilm P-382.

[7]Banks to L. Thomas, February 12, 1863, *OR*, Ser. 3, Vol. 3:46.

[8]Capt. P. B. S. Pinchback et al. to Banks, March 2, 1863, in Ira Berlin et al., eds., *Freedom: A Documentary History of Emancipation, 1861-1867*. Series 2, *The Black Military Experience* (New York, 1982), 322. Banks did not follow through with his threat to withhold pay. The black officers were paid along with the men in early May, 1863 (John H. Crowder to his mother, May 4, 1863, in Joseph T. Glatthaar, "The Civil War Through the Eyes of a Sixteen-Year-Old Black Officer: The Letters of Lieutenant John H. Crowder of the 1st Louisiana Native Guards," *Louisiana History*, 35 (1994): 214).

[9]*New York Times*, March 26, May 31, 1863; John W. Blassingame, "The Selection of Officers and Non-Commissioned Officers of Negro Troops in the Union Army, 1863-1863," *Negro History Bulletin*, 30 (1967): 8-12; Joseph T. Glatthaar, *Forged in Battle: The Civil War Alliance of Black Soldiers and White Officers* (New York, 1990), 35-59; Charles P. Ripley, *Slaves and Freedmen in Civil War Louisiana* (Baton Rouge, 1976), 116-17.

[10]The War Department in Washington established examining boards for white officers in black regiments on May 22, 1863 (General Orders No. 144, in *OR*, Ser. 3, Vol. 3:216), but the boards' standards for white officer candidates were described as "not to high" (Geo. B. Drake to Col. Sypher, October 2, 1864, in Elon A. Woodward, comp., *The Negro in the Military Service of the United States, 1639-1886: A Compilation*, 2796 [M-858, roll 3], National Archives, Washington, D.C.). For an account of a white officer in a black regiment who went before the board, see Levi Lindley Hawes, "Personal Experience of a Union Veteran," *Historic Leaves*, 4 (1905): 56-57.

[11]Special Orders No. 34, February 24, 1863, in Records of the U. S. Army Continental Command, Letters Received, Department of the Gulf, Record Group 393, National Archives, Washington, D.C., 166-67 (hereafter cited as Dept. of the Gulf, RG 393 with page numbers).

[12]Capt. P. B. S. Pinchback et al. to Maj. Gen. N. P. Banks, March 2, 1863, in Berlin et al., eds., *Freedom*, Ser. 2:321-23.

[13]The names of officers who survived their appearance before the board can be determined by comparing the list of officers ordered before the board published in Special Orders No. 34, February 3, 1863, with the dismissals noted in Special Orders No. 55, February 24, 1863, both in Dept. of the Gulf, RG 393, pp. 120-21 and 166-67, NA.

[14]Bertonneau to Capt. Wickham Hoffman, March 2, 1863, Morphy to Hoffman, March 3, 1863, and R. H. Isabelle to Hoffman, March 3, 1863, in their Compiled Military Service Records, Civil War, National Archives, Washington, D.C. (hereafter cited as Compiled Military Service Record) Octave Rey's resignation can be found in his pension file, also in NA. Both Bertonneau and Rey had served as officers in the Louisiana militia.

[15]W. B. Barrett to Ullmann, May 17, 1863, in Barrett's Compiled Military Service Record, NA, also in Berlin et al., eds., *Freedom*, Ser. 2:324; Moses C. Brown (Ullmann's AAG) to Barrett, May 26, 1863, in Barrett's Compiled Military Service Record, NA; *Official Army Register of the Volunteer Force of the United States Army for the Year 1861-1865*, 10 vols. (1865; reprint ed., Gaithersburg, Md., 1987), 8:248; Special Orders No. 126, May 30, 1863, RG 393, pp. 335-36; and Compiled Military Service Records for the eight officers in NA (see Appendix for names).

[16]S. W. Ringgold to Banks, July 7, 1863, in Ringgold's Compiled Military Service Record; also Samuel J. Wilkinson to Banks, July 6, 1863, in Wilkinson's Compiled Military Service Record, both in NA. See Compiled Military Service Records and Appendix.

[17]Pinchback to Banks, September 10, 1863, in Pinchback's Compiled Military Service Records, NA.

[18]Charges and Specifications preferred against Second Lieutenant Frank L. Trask, of Co. "C" 2d Infantry Corps d'Afrique, December 9, 1863, in Trask's Compiled Military Service Record, NA; Solomon Hayes to Major Drake, February 11, 1864, in Hayes's Compiled Military Service Record, NA, also in Berlin, et al., eds., *Freedom*, Ser. 2:326.

[19]Grosvenor's endorsement dated April 5, 1864, in Belley's Compiled Military Service Record, NA. Martin was discharged on August 15, 1864, citing illness (scurvy) as a reason. The reason for Villeverde's resignation is unknown, although he was found deficient in accounting for property for which he was responsible. Information from the officers' Compiled Military Service Records, NA.

[20]Sauvenet ended the war as a captain and assistant regimental quartermaster (*Official Army Register*, 8:248); Entry dated September 2, 1863, in Sauvenet's Compiled Military Service Record, NA. In May, 1864, Sauvenet's commissary sergeant, P. Flemming, committed suicide, which added to the difficulties of his position (Edwin C. Bearss, *Historic Research Study, Ship Island, Harrison County, Mississippi: Gulf Islands National Seashore, Florida/Mississippi*, National Parks Service, Technical Information Center, Denver, Colo., 221). An inspection report dated March 1, 1865, rated the 74th's arms and equipment as "in good condition," its quarters and barracks as "generally good," and the commissary-quartermaster storehouse as "very good" (ibid., 225). Testimony of Benjamin F. Butler before the American Freedmen's Inquiry Commission Report, M-619, roll 200, National Archives, Washington, D.C.

[21]De Pass to Colonel Stafford, February 19, 1863, with Stafford's endorsement of February 22, 1863, in De Pass's Compiled Military Service Record, NA.

[22]*Official Army Register*, 8:246; and Compiled Military Service Records, NA.

[23]Compiled Military Service Records for Hyppolite St. Louis, Louis A. Thibaut, and Alcide Lewis, NA. Lewis was dismissed for cowardice, although the record does not specify an incident. Lewis was the officer about whom Lieut. John Crowder had complained in a letter to his mother in April.

[24]*Official Army Register*, 8:246. Banks's organizational plan for the Corps d'Afrique called for regiments of five hundred men instead of the usual thousand (General Orders No. 40, May 1, 1863, *OR*, vol. 15:716-17). Because the three regiments comprising the Native Guards had been recruited to full strength, officers and men in excess of fifty per company were transferred to the 20th Regiment, Corps d'Afrique (Bearss, *Historic Resource Study*, 216).

[25]Compiled Military Service Records for Edgard Davis, Jules Mallett, Victor Lavinge, and Joseph L. Montieu, NA. Mallett's letter also appears in Berlin et al., eds., *Freedom*, Ser. 2:327.

[26]Eliot Bridgman to G. Norman Lieber, October 4, 1863, in Sentmanat's Compiled Military Service Record, NA.

[27]Compiled Military Service Records for Edward Carter, Emile Detiége, Morris W. Morris, and Eugene Rapp, NA. Emile Detiége had been charged with murder on December 12, 1862, for shooting one of his men to death.

[28]Lieut. Col. C. J. Bassett to Capt. G. B. Halstead, October 8, 1863, in Applications for Commissions, Ser. 1936, Part 1 [C-1053], NA.

[29]Follin to George B. Drake, February 18, 1864, in Follin's Compiled Service Record, NA, also in Berlin et al, eds., *Freedom*, Ser. 2:326.

[30]Lieut. Alfred Bourgeau resigned on March 7, 1863; Capt. James Lewis and Ehurd Moss both resigned a week later (Compiled Military Service Records, NA). Moss resigned to avoid dismissal.

[31]*Official Army Register*, 8:246; James H. Ingraham to Richard B. Irwin, March 10, 1864, in Ingraham's Compiled Military Service Record, NA.

[32]Inspection Report of 7 cos., 1st Regt. Corps d'Afrique, September 27, 1863, in Regimental Papers, U. S. Colored Troops, Record Group 94, Adjutant General's Office, National Archives, Washington, D.C., Box 44: 69th-75th U. S. C. Inf.; Capt. Joseph C. Oliver's Compiled Military Service Record, NA.

[33]Andrews' endorsement of Ehurd Moss's resignation read as follows: "This is a colored officer who is notoriously both incompetent and inefficient. His resignation is probably tendered to escape being discharged on the recommendation of the Board of Examiners" (Endorsement of First Lieut. Ehurd Moss to Lieut. Col. Richard B. Irwin, March 8, 1864, in Berlin et al., eds., *Freedom*, Ser. 2:328).

[34]Irwin, *Nineteenth Army Corps*, 49-50.

[35]For example, see Peter M. Yawyer to his brother, January 10, 1863, in Peter M. Yawyer Letters, Louisiana and Lower Mississippi Valley Collections, LSU Libraries, Louisiana State University, Baton Rouge, Louisiana; also John C. Palfrey, "Port Hudson," in *The Mississippi Valley, Tennessee, Georgia, Alabama, 1861-1864*, Vol. 8 of the *Papers of the Military Historical Society of Massachusetts* (Boston, 1910), 36. There were some exceptions, such as Capt. Hiram E. Perkins from the 8th Vermont, who resigned to become a major in the 1st Regiment of the Native Guards (Entry for April 11, 1863, in Rufus Kinsley, Diary, Vermont Historical Society, Montpelier, Vermont; and *Official Army Register*, 1:110; 8:246).

[36]Townsend to his brother, December 15, 1863, Townsend Letter, Manuscript 280, Historic New Orleans Collection, New Orleans, Louisiana; "Negro Troops," *National Intelligencer*, August 24, 1863.

[37]Glatthaar, *Forged in Battle*, 31-32, 39-41.

[38]Ullmann to Wilson, December 4, 1863, *OR*, Ser. 3, Vol. 8:1127.

[39]In January, 1865, Ullmann was relieved of command at Morganza because a fondness for the bottle made it difficult for him "to give highest attention to the duties devolving upon him." The officer who brought the order relieving Ullmann of his command reported that he "is full of whiskey all of the time—so much so tonight that he cannot walk steady" (*OR*, Vol. 47, Part 1:677, 984, 986).

[40]Stafford's Compiled Military Service Record, NA.

[41]The location of this incident must be implied from the letterhead of the stationery used to present the charges and specifications against Lieutenant Prowty, August 1, 1863, in Prowty's Compiled Military Service Record, NA. Daniels was charged with "conduct unbecoming an Officer and a gentleman" by "grossly insulting an Office of the Navy, while in the company of a lady." Their commissions were revoked in Special Orders No. 384, August 27, 1863, AGO, War Department, in both Daniels' and Prowty's Compiled Military Service Records, NA.

[42]General Orders No. 62, Department of the Gulf, May 28, 1864, in *War Record of Col.? W. M. Grosvenor, Editor of the Missouri Democrat* (N.p., n.d., copy in New York Public Library), 2-4. Grosvenor was also charged with keeping "a woman, not his wife, known by the name of 'Jennie Davis,'" in his quarters. Grosvenor pleaded guilty to this charge but attempted to make amends by marrying the woman (ibid., 3).

[43]*War Record of Col.? W. M. Grosvenor* spells the Surgeon's name "Gilson," but both Bearss (*Historic Resource Study*), who consulted the original transcript of the trial, and the *Official Army Register* (8:246) used the spelling "Gihon." The incident involved two black soldiers who were locked in the guardhouse for being drunk and disorderly. When they continued to create a disturbance, Grosvenor had them tied and gagged. About midnight, one of the two became very ill. The officer of the guard notified Colonel Grosvenor and sent for Surgeon Gihon. Without consulting Grosvenor, Gihon ordered that the bayonet used as a gag be removed.

When the second soldier responded with further ranting and raving, the officer of the guard had the gag replaced and informed Grosvenor of what had happened (Bearss, *Historic Resource Study*, 220).

[44]Grosvenor was also charged with abusing the 2nd Regiment's adjutant, Lieutenant F. Burchmore, by threatening him with the following language: "By Jesus Christ, I will put you under arrest; God damn you, Sir I will let you know that I command this post" (*War Record of Col.? W. M. Grosvenor*, 3). On August 3, 1864, President Lincoln abrogated the sentence "on the ground that the sentence appears not to be sustained by the evidence," but Grosvenor did not rejoin the regiment (Bearss, *Historic Resource Study*, 221-22). Grosvenor went on to an illustrious career following the Civil War. He served as economic editor of the *New York Tribune* from 1875 to 1900, wrote several books on business and finance, and developed an international reputation as America's foremost economist and statistician. He was also gifted in music, literature, mathematics, chess, tennis, and billiards (Walter Williams, "William Mason Grosvenor," in *Dictionary of American Biography*, 8 [1935]: 26-27).

[45]Capt. Charles B. Young to Andrews, September 5, 1863, Endorsement to Captain Young's letter of September 5, 1863, dated the same day, and Special Orders No. 122 (extract), March 19, 1864, AGO, War Department, all in Finnegass' Compiled Military Service Record, NA.

[46]For problems leading some men to desert, see Warren D. Hamilton to Hon. E. M. Stanton, May, 1865, in Berlin et al., eds., *Freedom*, Ser. 2:384-85.

[47]*Official Army Register*, 8:246; Regimental Books, Civil War, Descriptive Roll of Co. Co, 1st Regiment, Native Guards (73rd USCT), RG 94, AGO, NA; Monthly Returns for March and April, 1864, 73rd Inf., USCT, RG 94, NA; Butler to Chase, February 28, 1863, in Benjamin Franklin Butler, *Private and Official Correspondence of Gen. Benjamin F. Butler During a Period of the Civil War*, ed. by Jessie Ames Marshall, 5 vols. (Norwood, Mass., 1917), 3:24; see also Butler's comments regarding Banks's actions in his testimony before the American Freedmen's Inquiry Commission, November 28, 186[3], in Woodward, comp., *The Negro in the Military Service of the United States*, 2557-62 (M-858, roll 3), NA.

[48]"Mass Meeting at Economy Hall," *New Orleans Times*, November 6, 1863.

[49]*New Orleans Tribune*, October 25, December 7, 1864; "Revised Regulation for the Government of the Bureau of the Provost-Marshal-General of the United States," *OR*, Ser. 3, Vol. 4:658; Enrollment Order No. 1, Department of the Gulf, February 26, 1865, published in the *New Orleans Tribune*, March 12, 1865.

[50]"Gallant Officers to Be Put into the Ranks," *New Orleans Tribune*, May 14, 1865.

PATRIOTISM FRUSTRATED: THE NATIVE GUARDS OF CONFEDERATE NATCHITOCHES*

Gary B. Mills

The plastic patriotism of New Orleans' famed Native Guards has earned for them a definite, although ambiguous, role in history. Their services spurned by short-sighted Confederate leaders, the militarily organized *gens de couleur libre* of South Louisiana rebounded into the arms of the Northern troops who occupied New Orleans shortly thereafter.[1] Outside the Crescent City, in the backcountry of the state, other free men of color were imbued with a similar spirit of patriotism. Equally proficient in military tactics and equally enthusiastic, the two units of colored militia formed in Natchitoches Parish encountered the same ambivalent public sentiments as the Native Guards of New Orleans, but they responded in a totally different fashion. Yet the role and the response, of the rural, nonwhite home guards have yet to be assessed in any study of the Confederacy in Louisiana.

The *gens de couleur libre* of Natchitoches Parish—mainly centered on a fertile strip of alluvial land known as Isle Brevelle—had proven themselves worthy citizens long before the civil conflict divided friends and neighbors. Descended by and large from a family of slaves who had earned its freedom in the Spanish colonial period,[2] this colony of freedmen had accumulated some 15,000 acres of "the most productive cotton growing land in the State."[3] By 1860 they were, themselves, the owners of 379 slaves and held property that was conservatively estimated at $770,545.[4]

Stately homes graced the plantations of these rural *Creoles de couleur*, and private tutors educated their youth.[5] The first generation of the colony's freedmen had established its own Catholic chapel in an era when even the area whites had no convenient house of worship. Those whites—many of them possessing wealth and prominence—not only received the sacraments in the colony's church, but also took a back seat during services to the nonwhite family who built the chapel.[6] Area residents and visitors alike com-

---

*First published in *Louisiana History*, 18 (1977): 437-51. Reprinted with the kind permission of the author and the Louisiana Historical Association.

mented on the "gentlemanly manner" and "domestic and social happiness" of these free
people of color and described them as "honest, and industrious, and . . . good citizens, in
all respects."[7]

In the immediate prewar years, the position of all free people of color in Louisiana
became increasingly tenuous. As H. E. Sterkx explains, "free Negroes were physical
reminders to slaves that they too could and should be free."[8] Moreover, there existed a
fundamental doubt as to the allegiance of the free nonwhite: did his sympathies lie with
the whites who allowed his freedom or with the bondsmen who shared his former
oppression? The question of racial affinity undoubtedly caused inner conflict for many of
Louisiana's *gens de couleur libre.* As another authority points out: "Problems of racial
relations are exceedingly complex, but there can be no more intricate problem than that of
the relation of the mulatto to the two races whose blood, in varying proportions, united
in his veins." [9]

For the Isle Brevelle colony, as for many of their counterparts in Louisiana, the
conflict was not only one of race but of class as well. Occupation, income, education,
and even religion were crucial factors in each man's determination of personal allegiance.
These factors, for several generations, had served as effective barriers between the free
people of color on the isle and any ideological affiliation with blacks or slaves.[10]
Moreover, a Northern victory assuredly would eliminate their unique status as freedmen
and might well result in the destruction of their agricultural-based economy. For these
and similar reasons, the bulk of the Isle Brevelle colony fell into the general category of
"free blacks and mulattoes [who] showed little, if any, interest in abolition and . . . even
actively opposed the end of slavery."[11] Yet, on the other hand, these free people of color
were acutely aware of their relegation to second-class citizenship, and the Union promises
of social and political equality were enticing.[12]

Although the allegiance of a relatively small percentage of the isle's population was
later questioned, at a time when professed loyalty to the Northern cause presented a means
of economic survival, the colony publicly favored the Confederacy throughout the conflict
and provided no support, open or covert, to the Union cause. They deprived themselves
and their families to help maintain Confederate forces; indeed, their area of the parish was
frequently called upon to provide forage for Southern troops.[13] When the parish was
ordered to furnish three hundred male slaves to build defenses on Red River, 25 percent of
the known slave owners who volunteered hands were members of the Isle Brevelle
community. Four of the youths from the colony personally labored on these defenses.[14]

It was in the area of military service, however, that the *hommes de couleur libre*, of
Isle Brevelle responded most enthusiastically to the Confederate cause. Reverberations of
the shots fired at Fort Sumter had hardly subsided before the colony's men organized their
first militia unit, a squadron of cavalry called the Augustin's Guards,[15] in remembrance of
the revered patriarch of the colony, Augustin Metoyer. As did its counterpart in New
Orleans, this Isle Brevelle regiment supplied its own horses, uniforms, arms, and ammunition.[16] In compliance with the regulations of the Confederate government, officers

were selected from the ranks of whites, and the volunteers quietly accepted the prevailing opinion that nonwhites "were considered fit only to serve in the enlisted ranks. . . . Social delicacy alone foredoomed the commissioning of Negro officers."[17]

Shortly after the formation of the Augustin's Guards, still another regiment was formed on the isle. An infantry company, this second unit adopted the name Monet's Guards in recognition of another prominent family in their colony. This unit, likewise, was officered by whites,[18] but the volunteers in the enlisted ranks along with the volunteers of the Augustin's Guards were publicly recognized as members of a "people who are serving the country loyally and usefully," and they drew sincere praise for being "inspired with the same sentiments which aroused their forefathers in 1814 and 1815."[19]

The exact strength of the two contingents of nonwhite militia on the isle, and the identities of all the members of each, are not known. A news item early in 1862 indicated that the ranks of the newer company, the Monet's Guards, had been "completed" and its force totaled seventy-six men.[20] The older company presumably comprised a force of equal size, in which case their combined strength may be estimated at some 150 men. According to statistics provided by the 1860 federal census, this represents the entire male population of the colony that was fourteen or over when hostilities began.[21]

In December 1861 the *Natchitoches Union* reported its personal attendance at a drill conducted by the two units:[22]

> The squadron of cavalry, so skillfully trained by Dr. Burdin,[23] their uniformity and precision were admirable. [*sic*] The firm commands and good cadence of the captain, also that of the officers; the intelligent enthusiasm produced by all the soldiers; the excellent horsemanship by the squadron; all contributed to amaze the public who had come to attend these maneuvers. For us who have often attended cavalry drills in Europe,[24] we wonder how, in so little time, these men have been able to attain this degree of perfection.
>
> The company of infantry, newly formed, has need of practice, but we are convinced that having a little, their drills will be executed with as much precision as in the cavalry.

Earnestly endeavoring to achieve the standards expected of them, the infantry ordered a copy of one of the newest military manuals on the market, *Casey's Infantry Tactics for the Instruction, Exercise, and Manoeuvers,* compiled—ironically—by a general in the service of their enemy.[25]

Both units of the Isle Brevelle militia drilled regularly and thoroughly under Dr. Burdin. A "man target" was made by the drillmaster from old clothes stuffed with cotton; a hat was perched atop the effigy; and the pompous chest was labeled "ABE LINCOLN." Week after week, one of the cavalrymen later recalled, Burdin made them "pass by that thing on horseback and cut at it with our swords."[26]

Soon after the war began, the Augustin's Guards volunteered their aid to the Confederacy for field service against the United States. Their offer was refused, just as the services of the New Orleans Native Guards had been, "because the company was composed of free men of color.[27] Still the companies continued to drill. As the Federal occupation of New Orleans became imminent, hopes were revived in Natchitoches Parish that its organized *hommes de couleur libre* might be called to active service in the state's defense. The *Union,* in December 1861, editorialized: ". . . the cavalry and infantry will make excellent patrols at the coast, and contribute to maintaining the public tranquility. This article . . . congratulate[s] these two companies on their useful organization."[28]

Three months later the *Union* reported that the police jury of the parish had appropriated the sum of $600 to defray the expenses of the volunteers and families of the Isle Brevelle militia, whenever the companies should leave the parish for New Orleans to participate in the defense of that city. The appropriation was to be paid to their white officers who would expend or dole out the funds themselves after the volunteers were mustered into regular Confederate service. Moreover, a bounty of $25 (exactly half the amount of bounty established for white volunteers) would be paid by the president of the police jury to each nonwhite volunteer as he was mustered in as a "regular."[29]

Apparently, the Confederacy was still reluctant to accept the nonwhite patriots from Isle Brevelle. In May 1862 the *Union* again reported that the infantry still planned to go to New Orleans to help in its defense.[30] The city fell, however, before the two companies from the isle could gain acceptance.

The surrender of New Orleans to the enemy provided an alternate course of action for the state's Native Guards who had been spurned by Confederate leaders. Avowing that they had allied with the Confederacy only because they hoped "to advance nearer to equality with the whites" and that they "had longed to throw the weight of their class with the Union forces," the Native Guards of New Orleans readily accepted General Butler's invitation to join the Federal ranks.[31]

The three companies of Native Guards subsequently formed by Butler did not restrict their membership to the former Confederate guardsmen of New Orleans but recruited new volunteers statewide from the slave as well as free population. The promised bounty of one hundred dollars or 160 acres of land upon enlistment, the idea of regular wages of thirteen dollars a month, and the promise of food supplies for their families[32] were undoubtedly tempting to the war-impoverished families of Isle Brevelle.[33] Moreover, the ranks of the New Orleans Native Guards included a number of their kinsmen.[34] Yet, the muster rolls of these three nonwhite Union troops include some of the scorned guardsmen from Natchitoches Parish.[35]

Unwanted by the Confederacy, but still loyal to its cause, the Augustin's Guards and Monet's Guards continued to train regularly for another year and a half, through early 1864. There still remained the distinct possibility that their services might be needed in the defense of their home parish, especially after the disbandment of the white Natchitoches home guard, the Chasseurs à Pied, in 1863.[36]

During this period, Union sympathies rapidly mushroomed in central Louisiana. The fall of New Orleans and the other military reverses of 1862 "lowered the morale of the people and encouraged disaffection and disloyalty," and Natchitoches Parish soon achieved a reputation as one of the hotbeds of seditious activities.[37] Still the determination of the Isle Brevelle guardsmen to serve the Confederate cause did not dissolve, and there is no hint of their participation in any pro-Union activities.

In two and a half years of organization, the Guards of Isle Brevelle were allowed to perform one public duty, a brief and strictly "honorary" one. In March 1862 the body of their white neighbor, Felix Chaler, a regimental standard bearer who died of typhoid fever in service of the Confederacy, was returned home for burial. In company with the two white militia units of the parish, the Cloutierville Home Guards and the Natchitoches Chausseurs à Pied, the two "colored guard" units accompanied the body of their compatriot to the church, then to the adjacent cemetery. There the captain of each white unit fired his "farewell shot" into the grave of the dead soldier, and the "Colored Guards and infantry" fired above it, "thus paying the last sad tribute of respect to the memory of the . . . patriot and soldier."[38]

Early in 1864 death also claimed the white captain of the Isle Brevelle Guards. No qualified replacement was available among the diminished ranks of white men left in the parish. The units' drillmaster, Dr. Burdin—despite his fervor—was not accepted by the Guards as their officer. Subsequent events indicate that he enjoyed little rapport with his men, and that a lack of respect existed on both sides.[39] Unable to continue without white leadership, under Confederate regulations, the Guards then disbanded.[40]

The timing was inopportune. By March 1864 a Union force of some 45,000 men, representing all branches of service, had gathered at Alexandria, in the adjoining parish, with plans to ascend Red River as soon as spring rains swelled the river enough to make it navigable.[41] As the Union forces pushed northward into and through Natchitoches Parish in late March and early April, the army's line of march took them through the heart of Isle Brevelle.

Disorganized and unable to reorganize militarily without satisfactory, white leadership, the nonwhite residents of the isle had no defense. Nor could they expect any significant degree of military or moral support from their white neighbors. Countless area whites had fled before the Federal invaders.[42] The Natchitoches home guard was already defunct. And evidence indicates that the Cloutierville home guard—as well as that at Natchitoches—was composed of many Union sympathizers and foreign neutrals whose only purpose in organization was to provide police protection to the area and to satisfy the personal military obligation imposed on them by the Confederacy.[43]

Union forces camped in the midst of the isle on the night of March 31. For the Federals, the experience was an amusing one. For the *gens de couleur,* it represented disaster. One Union surgeon, recalling in his memoirs that he had spent that night "upon the fields of a wealthy planter," observed: ". . . it was difficult to draw them into conversation, for they were so thoroughly frightened at the advent of the Yankee savages, that they were almost speechless. The boys took great delight in witnessing the panic they had created among this ignorant people."[44]

If the *gens de couleur libre* entertained any hopes of receiving special treatment from the Union forces because of the slight color their skin possessed, they were disappointed. The invaders quickly recognized that "the inhabitants in this section [are] nearly all of French extraction,"[45] and inflicted upon them the same punitive measures that they imposed upon the white-owned plantations in the area. Livestock, food, crops, household furnishings, and especially arms, were appropriated or destroyed. In general, those valuables which were preserved by the colony were those that had been buried by its more foresighted or forewarned members.[46]

The worst blow to the Isle Brevelle community, and the death blow to the disorganized Guards, occurred upon the Federal retreat down Cane River after the Southern victories at the battles of Mansfield and Pleasant Hill. In vengeance, at least one battalion of retreating Union forces destroyed almost every plantation it passed.[47] With the onslaught approaching, a frenzied Dr. Burdin hastily conceived an ambush, and his attempt to execute it clearly illustrated the unsound judgment on his part which apparently had caused the guardsmen to reject him as their captain. The ardent drillmaster was not skilled as a military strategist nor as a leader of men.

Joseph E. Dupre, Jr., one of the younger guardsmen, was on his way to the Isle Brevelle church to attend the funeral of his aunt, the afternoon before the Federals' arrival, when he was approached by the doctor. Informing Dupre that there were "some jayhawkers a few miles above there and he wanted us to go and capture them," Burdin ordered Dupre to meet him at the church after dark. If anyone refused to go, the doctor warned, he would personally see to it that the coward's home was burned and his family killed.[48] Cavalryman Gassion Metoyer was at home that same afternoon when Burdin accosted him "with his rifle and forced him to march to the church."[49] Young Clemire Metoyer, Gassion's cousin, was similarly approached, but the alleged purpose of the meeting which Burdin related to Clemire was the urgency of "capturing a man he said was robbing people on the way."[50]

In one fashion or another the majority of the free men of color on Isle Brevelle, all members of the recently disorganized Guards, were summoned peremptorily by the doctor to meet with him at the church soon after dark. Each was ordered to bring with him "any weapons he had." Most of the guardsmen complied, many of them doing so only under duress, if later accounts by their spokesmen may be believed.

Reluctance, apparently, stemmed not so much from cowardice as from a keen awareness of the folly of Dr. Burdin's ill-timed and potentially suicidal plan. The families of Isle Brevelle had been left impotent by the earlier Union surge; almost all their weapons and horses had been confiscated. Voicing the feelings of his friends and family, Sévère Dupre inquired "with what we intended to defend ourselves, since the Yankees in passing up the River had deprived us of our arms." The retort from the agitated doctor was "Hush up, take axes, hoes, and sticks."[51]

With the apparent hope that their resident priest could reason with the disordered Burdin, the guardsmen insisted that the meeting be held that night in the rectory, rather than in the church itself. The little cottage adjacent to the church was filled; more guardsmen waited on the gallery; and many more spilled over into the yard. More than one of those present inside the house were able to recall vividly, decades later, the events that transpired that night, and stories of the incident were still being recounted by family descendants in the mid-twentieth century.[52]

According to all reports, the presence of the priest was ineffectual, and the "consultation" soon turned into a confrontation. Dr. Burdin ordered the men to march at once. Sévère Dupre repeated his reluctance to attack an army of many thousands with "axes, hoes, and sticks." Still another guardsman attempted to explain to Burdin that he had no authority or right to order them out.

Infuriated, the doctor announced that he would "make an example and thereupon fired at one of the members." The man took the ball in his shoulder. Burdin's fire was returned by others, and the doctor was killed, after which they "all dispersed and went to [their] homes." Burdin was interred in the cemetery behind the church, and his slayer left the area until "all blew over." Although the events surrounding the death of Dr. Burdin became open knowledge in the parish and were frankly admitted by those involved, no incriminations from authorities or citizens' action groups were suffered by any of the guardsmen.[53]

With Dr. Burdin were buried the last remnants of the fervent patriotism that had motivated these *hommes de couleur libre* to organize in support of the Confederacy. No further attempt was made by the Isle Brevelle men to reorganize or to offer their more-than-once-rebuffed services to the dying Rebel regime. Nor did they retaliate by joining the Union forces that invaded their parish as their New Orleans counterparts and cousins had done.[54]

Facing their prospects realistically, the people of Isle Brevelle recognized that their prewar economy was doomed, just as assuredly as was the Confederacy. The Red River Campaign had been as much a defeat for central Louisiana as it had been for the Union.[55] The blows rendered them by the Federal invaders and the Confederate pursuers had been fatal to the economy and the morale of Isle Brevelle. Rejected, dejected, exploited, and desperate, the *gens de couleur libre* of the isle turned within themselves, clinging to the little that was left in a last-ditch effort to survive in the changing society. With few exceptions they were to remain a "closed society" for a number of decades, asking little of the outside world and offering little to it.[56]

Three-quarters of a century of near-isolation nurtured the pride as well as the memories of the colony on Isle Brevelle. The former guardsmen, their children, and their grandchildren preserved with surprising accuracy of detail, the events of the Civil War as it affected their society. Invariably, in every account emphasis is placed on the fervor of patriotism that emerged among them after the secession of Louisiana from the Union and the desire of their forefathers to support the social and political regime that had allowed them to prosper. With pride they recall the support their men and women gave to the Confederacy. And, with occasional twinges of bitterness still evident, they recount the rejection of their volunteer guardsmen who assiduously prepared themselves to serve the Confederate cause.[57]

The role of the two guard units on Isle Brevelle and the sentiments that motivated them have not been so well remembered by historians. Alice Dunbar-Nelson's classic study of Louisiana's *gens de couleur libre* emphatically declares: "These men of New Orleans were the only organized body of [nonwhite] soldiery on the Confederate side during the Civil War," and her generalization was still being echoed as late as 1973 in Dorothea McCants' preface to her translation of Desdunes's noted study.[58] Neither source noted the existence of any similar units in the interior of the state. Likewise, Mary Berry's otherwise excellent analysis of the three native guard units in New Orleans observes: "It seems that they were the only [nonwhite] organization utilized by the Confederacy. . . ."[59] Only Sterkx has made reference to the existence of the Natchitoches Native Guards, but even this authority reported the organization of one company only the infantry identified as "Monette's Guards."[60] The older and more proficient cavalry has been overlooked entirely.

At least two separate and distinct Native Guard groups existed in Confederate Louisiana. Their origins were basically similar. Their members were related by blood as well as cultural ties. Both groups met the same public reaction. Yet each group responded differently. One group bartered its allegiance to the enemy in an effort to forcibly change the structure of the society that had slighted them. The other shunned the forces who promised liberty and equality and closed its ranks to the new breed of freedmen.

There has been a marked trend in more recent major studies of free nonwhites in the antebellum South to group all members of this class into a single ideological category. However, nonwhite culture was not so simplistic, and its solidarity was certainly not *de rigueur*. Shades of allegiance to the *status quo*, shades of militancy to the cause of "freedom," and shades of brotherhood between the free man and the slave and the black man and the part-black were as diverse as were the shades of their skin and the economic and cultural opportunities that they enjoyed. All nonwhites did not consider themselves Negro because of the small percentage of African blood which they possessed, nor did they all espouse a confraternity of black brothers in which all nonwhites were free and equal. The role of the Native Guards of Natchitoches and its general support of the "white Southern cause" is a clear case at point.

Notes for "Patriotism Frustrated: The Native Guards of Confederate Natchitoches"

[1]Mary F. Berry, "Negro Troops in Blue and Gray: The Louisiana Native Guards, 1861-1863," *Louisiana History*, 8 (1967): 165-90, provides an excellent study of the New Orleans Native Guards.

[2]For a study of the origins of this family see Gary B. Mills, "Coincoin: An Eighteenth Century Liberated Woman," *Journal of Southern History*, 62 (1976): 205-22, and Gary B. and Elizabeth S. Mills, *Melrose* (Natchitoches, 1973).

[3]Orton S. Clark, *The One Hundred and Sixteenth Regiment of New York State Volunteers* (Buffalo, 1868), 150. An estimate of the total landholdings of the colony is based upon an examination of all known public and private notarial documents dealing with the colony. The bulk of these records are to be found in the Office of the Clerk of Court, Natchitoches, Louisiana; the Natchitoches Parish Records Collection, 1734-1905 (Department of Archives, Louisiana State University, Baton Rouge); the Cammie C. Henry Collection (Eugene P. Watson Memorial Library, Northwestern State University, Natchitoches); and the Robert B. DeBlieux Collection of Cane River notarial documents (in private possession of Robert B. DeBlieux, Natchitoches).

[4]See Manuscript Census Returns, Eighth Census of the United States, Natchitoches Parish, Louisiana, Schedule One, Free Population, National Archives Microfilm Series No. M-653, Roll 414, and Schedule Two, Slave Population, Series No. M-653, Roll 429.

[5]Frederick Law Olmsted, A *Journey in the Seaboard Slave States in the Years 1853-1854 with Remarks on Their Economy* (1904; reprint ed., New York, 1968), 633; Succession of Pierre Metoyer, Succession No. 193, Office of the Clerk of Court, Natchitoches; J.J. Callahan and Others, *The History of St. Augustine's Parish; Isle Brevelle, Natchez, La..,1803-1953; 1829-1954; 1856-1956* (n.p., 1954), 31; interview with Mrs. Lee Etta Vaccarini Coutii, Isle Brevelle, March 24, 1974.

[6]Interview with Mrs. Coutii, ibid.; Rev. J. A. Baumgartner, "Isle Brevelle," quoted in Annie Lee West Stahl, "The Free Negro in Ante-Bellum Louisiana," *Louisiana Historical Quarterly*, 25 (1942): 362.

[7]Olmsted, *Journey in the Seaboard Slave States*, 634.

[8]H.E. Sterkx, *The Free Negro in Ante-Bellum Louisiana* (Rutherford, N.J., 1972), 304; Robert C. Reinders, "The Free Negro in the New Orleans Economy, 1850-1860," *Louisiana History*, 4 (1965): 285.

[9]James Hugo Johnston, *Race Relations in Virginia and Miscegenation in the South, 1776-1860* (Amherst, 1970), 298.

[10]Callahan, *History of St. Augustine's Parish,* 27; Mrs. Coutii to author, March 31, 1974; Sister Frances Jerome Woods, C.D.P., *Marginality and Identity; A Colored Creole Family through Ten Generations* (Baton Rouge, 1972), 46, 53-54.

[11]Carl N. Degler, *Neither Black nor White; Slavery and Race Relations in Brazil and the United States* (New York, 1971), 84.

[12]Remnants of formerly large libraries owned by the Isle Brevelle colony have been preserved by their descendants. Among these are a significant percentage of legal publications of the nineteenth century, which indicates a keen awareness by these *gens de couleur libre* of their civil status.

In later claims for damages inflicted upon them by Federal forces, six residents of the isle and their witnesses clearly stated their expectation that a Union victory would result in improved civil, social and economic rights, although they failed to prove that they had aided the Union cause. *See Suzette A. Morin, deceased, v. The United States,* Claim 13678; *Emilie Kirkland v. The United States,* Claim 41317; *Jean Conant v. The United States,* Claim 43565; *Jean Conant, Tutor, for Annie Metoyer and Others v. The United States,* Claim 43576; and *Jerome Sarpy v The United States,* Claim 43582, Records of the Southern Claims Commission (National Archives, Washington, D. C.).

[13]*War of the Rebellion . . .Official Records of the Union and Confederate Armies,* 130 volumes (Washington, 1880-1901), Series 1, 34:505, 561; Richard Taylor, *Destruction and Reconstruction, Personal Experiences of the Late War* (New York, 1890), 181; E. C. Bearss, ed., A *Louisiana Confederate: Diary of Felix Pierre Poché* (Natchitoches, 1972), 101.

[14]*Natchitoches Union,* November 27 and December 11, 1862; Claim 13678, Southern Claims Commission.

[15]Ibid., December 26, 1861.

[16]Interview with Mrs. Coutii, April 26, 1974; John D. Winters, *The Civil War in Louisiana* (Baton Rouge, 1973), 35. Mrs. Coutii today owns the sword of her great-grandfather Emanuel Dupre, a member of this cavalry unit.

[17]Winters, *Civil War in Louisiana*, 35.

[18]*Natchitoches Union*, December 26, 1862.

[19]Ibid., December 26, 1861, and May 1, 1862.

[20]Ibid..; May 1, 1862.

[21]Manuscript Census Returns, Eighth Census of the United States, Natchitoches Parish, Louisiana, Schedule One, Free Population, National Archives Microfilm Series No. M453, Roll 414.

[22] *Natchitoches Union*, December 26, 1861.

[23]Dr. Jean Napoleon Burdin was born 1812 at Dolaconafery, Department of Jura, France. In 1860 he settled in Isle Brevelle, one mile from the colony's church, where he farmed and practiced medicine until his death in 1864. *Adelaide Celeste Le Normand v. The United States,* Claim 209, Records of the French and American Claims Commission (National Archives, Washington, D.C.).

[24]The apparent author of this item, *Union* editor Ernest Le Gendre, was qualified indeed to assess the drill performance of the Guards. Le Gendre came to Louisiana as a political exile, a direct result of his active participation in the French Revolution of 1848. Obituary of Ernest Le Gendre, *Natchitoches Union,* February 20, 1862.

[25]Silas E. Casey, an 1826 graduate of the United States Military Academy, was the founder of a long line of distinguished military officers. The copy of *Casey's Manual* that was purchased in 1862 by the infantryman Sévère Dupre is now in the possession of his granddaughter, Mrs. Coutii.

[26]Testimony of Joseph E. Dupre, *Le Normand v. The United States.*

[27]Testimony of Clemire Metoyer and Joseph E. Dupre, ibid.

[28]*Natchitoches Union,* December 26, 1861. Still another editorial appraising the "Native Guards" of Natchitoches was presented in the *Union* by Le Gendre's successor on March 6, 1862.

[29]Ibid., March 27, 1862.

[30]Ibid., May 1, 1862.

[31]Charles H. Wesley, "The Employment of Negroes as Soldiers in the Confederate Army," *The Journal of Negro History,* 4 (1919): 243-44.

[32]Berry, "Negro Troops," 176.

[33]Sister Dorothea O. McCants, ed. and trans., *They Came to Louisiana: Letters of a Catholic Mission, 1854-1882* (Baton Rouge, 1970), 168-69, poignantly recounts the straitened circumstances of the formerly well-to-do planters in the Isle Brevelle colony.

[34]The *gens de couleur libre* of Isle Brevelle included several New Orleans natives who had migrated to the back country, taken wives on the isle, and settled in that community, i.e.; Jerome de Lisle Sarpy, Louis Amadée Morin, Oscar Dubreuil, Seraphin and Élisée Roques, and Emile Dupart. They and/or their sons all joined the two companies of nonwhite guards in Natchitoches Parish.

[35]"The Negro in the Military Service of the United States," Records of the Adjutant General's Office, National Archives Microfilm Series T-823.

[36]Testimony of Philippe Poeté, in *Philippe Poeté, Administrator, v. The United States,* Claim 399, French and American Claims Commission.

[37]Ethel Taylor, "Discontent in Confederate Louisiana," *Louisiana History,* 2 (1961): 411, 413; testimony of Clemire Metoyer, *Le Normand v. The United States.*

[38]*Natchitoches Union,* March 6, 1862; Gary B. Mills, "Cane River Country, 1860-1866," *Proceedings of the Seventeenth Annual Genealogical Institute, Louisiana Genealogical and Historical Society* (Baton Rouge, 1974), 2.

[39]Parish records, public and private, indicate that the Isle Brevelle *gens de couleur libre* were generally on excellent terms with their white Gallic neighbors. However, they also indicate that the colony exercised a considerable degree of selectivity in their social intercourse with whites, generally restricting their associations to planters and professional men of equal wealth and standing. Dr. Burdin was a chronically impoverished French emigré whose abilities and industriousness were held, apparently, in low esteem by both the white and nonwhite communities. His home, for example, was a rudely constructed cabin boasting no floor except the earth itself—falling far short of the housing standards observed by the isle's *gens de couleur libre* in that period. Testimony of Gervais Fontenot (white), Charles and Joseph E. Dupre, and Gassion and Clemire Metoyer, *Le Normand v. The United States,* Callahan, *History of St. Augustine's Parish,* 20-21.

[40]Testimony of Clemire Metoyer, *Le Normand v. The United States.*

[41]Harris H. Beeeher, *Record of the 114th Regiment, N.Y.S.V.* (Norwich, N.Y., 1866), 300.

[42]Henry A. Shorey, *The Story of the Maine Fifteenth* (Bridgton, Maine, 1890), 77; Robert A. Tyson Diary, 1863-1864 (Department of Archives, Louisiana State University, Baton Rouge). Tyson, a Union soldier, gleefully recorded in his day journal as he encamped in the white area of the isle: "Massa fund aha! Niggas staid at Home."

[43]Testimony of Philippe Poeté, *Poeté v. The United States*; testimony of Dr. Edward Royerson Bruwnell, *E. R. Brownell v. The United States,* Claim 43564, Southern Claims Commission.

[44]Beecher, *Record of the 114th Regiment,* 304.

[45]Ibid. In reviewing the treatment of free people of color by the Federals, Governor Henry W. Allen later reported that "in many instances [they] have been made the special objects of brutal treatment by the enemy." Sarah A. Dorsey, *Recollections of Henry Watkins Allen* (New York, 1866), 382.

It must also be noted that many of the free people of color along Cane River were so fair that race was not easily discernible. One Confederate soldier who passed through the isle during this Red River Campaign later uncertainly described Emanuel Dupre, one of the leading guardsmen, as "a Frenchman or colored man." Testimony of Green T. Morgan, *Poeti v. The United States.*

[46]Claims 13678, 41317, 43565, 43566, 43576, and 43582, Southern Claims Commission; Callahan, *History of St. Augustine's Parish,* 27; Hugh La Cour to author, Shreveport, Louisiana, February 19, 1974; Confidential Source to author, Isle Brevelle, March 24, 1974.

[47]Dorsey, *Recollections,* 279-80; Winters, *Civil War in Louisiana,* 365-66; Taylor, *Destruction and Reconstruction,* 193; Robert L. Kerby, *Kirby Smith's Confederacy: The Trans-Mississippi South, 1863-1865* (New York, 1972), 315, 318.

[48]Testimony of Joseph E. Dupre, *Le Normand v. The United States.*

[49]Testimony of Gassion Metoyer, ibid.

[50]Testimony of Clemire Metoyer, ibid.

[51]Testimony of Charles Dupre and Joseph E. Dupre, ibid.

[52]Ibid.; Testimony of Clemire Metoyer and Gassion Metoyer, ibid.; Callahan, *History of St. Augustine's Parish,* 20-21.

[53]Ibid.

[54]Hugh La Cour to author, March 4, 1974; Mrs. Coutii to author, April 15, 1974; Records of the Adjutant General's Office, National Archives Microfilm Series T-823.

[55]Maj. John M. Gould, *History of the First-Tenth-Twenty-Ninth Maine Regiment* (Portland, 1871), 434; Kerby, *Kirby Smith's Confederacy,* 318.

[56]For an overall view of the colony during this period, see J. E. Dunn, "Isle Brevelle" (Natchitoches) *Louisiana Populist,* February 26, 1897; Callahan, *History of St. Augustine's Parish,* 27-28, 32; and Calvin Dill Wilson, "Black Masters: A Side-Light on Slavery," *North American Review,* 181 (1905): 691-92.

[57]Hugh La Cour to author, February 19, 1974; interview with Mrs. Coutii, March 24, 1974; interview with Confidential Source, Isle Brevelle, April 26, 1974; interview with Mr. and Mrs. Tillman Chelettre, Sr., Isle Brevelle, October 12, 1974.

[58]Alice Dunbar-Nelson, "People of Color in Louisiana," *The Journal of Negro History,* 2 (1917): 67; Rodolphe Lucien Desdunes, *Our People and Our History,* Sister Dorothea O. McCants, trans, and ed. (Baton Rouge, 1973), xiii.

[59]Berry, "Negro Troops," 190.

[60]Sterkx, *Free Negro in Ante-Bellum Louisiana,* 213.

"WE'LL HANG JEFF DAVIS ON THE SOUR APPLE TREE": CIVIL WAR ERA SLAVE RESISTANCE IN LOUISIANA*

Junius P. Rodriguez

In a letter written shortly before the 1860 presidential election, Supreme Court Chief Justice Roger Brooke Taney speculated upon the South, its institution of slavery, and the grave prospects that Republican victory might have upon both. The aged jurist wrote, "I am old enough to remember the horrors of St. Domingo, and a few days will determine whether anything like it is to be visited upon any portion of our own southern countrymen." Stirred by the passionate intensity of painful remembrance, Taney mused, "I can only pray that it may be averted and that my fears will prove to be nothing more than the timidity of an old man."[1] Justice Taney's words, tinged with the grace of reflective eloquence, convey the weariness of an observer concerned that a generation, unacquainted with history, might precipitate actions that could invite servile war. Yet among those who experienced life amidst a black majority and lived in fear of slave unrest, the portent of Republican victory and the triumph of abolitionism were concomitant evils of the highest order. The "only wish" that one Baton Rouge resident mentioned in an October 1860 letter was that "black republican candidate Lincoln [sic] will be beat."[2]

Despite Southern efforts to avert the abolitionists' political assault and its anticipated social consequences, the Republican party triumphed by plurality and elected an avowed "free soiler" as president. For Southern states with black majorities, Abraham Lincoln's election on November 6, 1860, was the catalyst for secession. Prompted by South Carolina and Mississippi's decision to secede from the Union, Florida, Alabama, and Georgia, in rapid succession, also withdrew allegiance to the United States Constitution and laws. On January 26, 1861, Louisiana became the sixth state to secede, joining the other seceded states in forming the Confederate States of America on February 18, 1861.[3]

*First published in the *Gulf Coast Historical Review*, 10 (1995): 6-23. Reprinted with the kind permission of the author.

Louisiana Senator John Slidell shared concerns about secession, civil war, and the inherent danger of slave rebellion with President James Buchanan in hopes that reason and compassion might prevail. This conversation influenced the tone of Buchanan's annual message to Congress on December 3, 1860. The president said, "no political union . . . can long continue if the necessary consequence be to render the homes and the firesides of nearly half the parties to it habitually and hopelessly insecure."[4] In early January 1861, shortly before the state's decision to secede, Slidell addressed colleagues again cautioning against any invasion of the South for fear that it might induce a massive slave rebellion. The Northern press admonished Slidell for using such inflammatory rhetoric, but the senator recognized Louisiana's previous pattern of slave unrest and could easily speculate what the advance of an invading army might do to stir that rebellious tradition.[5] Mississippi Senator Jefferson Davis defended Slidell's stand, calling it courageous, and noting similarities between the French army's foray into Santo Domingo and a potential Northern invasion of Southern territory. Remarking that "history does not chronicle a case of negro [*sic*] insurrection," Davis argued that insurrection was not an act of spontaneous slave resistance, but rather, a response engendered by governments "sending troops among them [slaves]" to inspire unrest.[6]

Jefferson Davis's vision of slave rebellion did not correlate with views of Louisiana planters living in black-majority parishes. Understanding that war pressures would further dilute population by removing young white males for military service, residents suddenly realized that slave rebellion was a real and immediate danger. C. J. Mitchell, a Madison Parish cotton planter, wrote Davis to express common concerns about the domestic security crisis that civil war entailed. Mitchell informed the Confederate president that on the home front the threat of slave revolt "has produced a sense of insecurity here which has already brought men to think of their women and children." The planter speculated, "should even a John Brown raid occur, what with the sparse population and deep seated anxiety in regard to Negroes, such a panic would ensue as would be ruinous to our cause."[7]

While internal developments were alarming, the constant threat of importing slaves tainted with a rebellious spirit continued to plague the state. When Texas planters discovered dangerous conspiracies, many chose to sell their unmanageable slaves at New Orleans rather than "risk them in the scales of justice at home." Apparently the lure of compensation was greater than any ethical constraints for immediate justice since both sellers and buyers negotiated for the best bargains, regardless of social consequences in either state. An anonymous Texan, recognizing the dangers of *caveat emptor,* warned, "I would caution planters and others purchasing negroes [*sic*] not to touch any from the tainted district of this State at any price." The writer cautioned, "many of them have been so tampered with that it would be folly to place them in a position to contaminate others."[8] Yet the opportunity to purchase cheap slaves during an expensive market period convinced many to forego security considerations and bargain with the Texas traders.

The April 1861 attack upon Fort Sumter marked an epiphany of unrest across Louisiana as signs of servile disorder soon began to appear. Officially, the Southern attitude remained optimistic, focusing on a short war with no real problems of internal security. An editorial in the *New Orleans Daily Picayune* acknowledged, "The civilized world has not ceased shuddering at the recollection of the infernal massacre of St. Domingo. It will not allow the age to be disgraced by one in the Confederate States of America."[9] Yet, signs of tension manifested themselves as the specter of slave violence, both real and imaginary, emerged and white society responded.[10] In May 1861 New Orleans police arrested Dr. Thomas Jinnings, a free black physician who attended a charity bazaar sponsored by the local white Episcopal Church. Officials charged the doctor with "intrading [*sic*] himself among the white congregation . . . and conducting hisself [*sic*] in a manner unbecoming the free colored population of this city." The arrest report also mentioned the unforgivable transgression, that Jinning planned these actions "to create insubordination among the servile population."[11] Although such an incident appears trivial and almost amusing by modern standards, it was a serious affair in the emotionally charged wartime atmosphere of 1861.

The day of Dr. Jinning's arrest at New Orleans, a rural newspaper reported, "Our servile population remains perfectly quiet, happy, and contented, with plenty to eat, drink, and wear, and nothing to disturb their thought by day, or dreams by night."[12] Taken at face value, the report suggests an idyllic setting where contented servants labored happily in a land of plenty, but closer inspection, suggested by the revealing article title "Keep Your Eye on Your Neighbors," exposes a region fearing itself to be on the brink of massive slave insurrection. In June 1861 Louisiana's coastal residents in St. Mary and St. Martin parishes prepared to defend themselves against an expected invasion by abolitionist mercenaries. Public hysteria rose as the local press mentioned "rumored gatherings of slaves in considerable numbers on the banks of a certain bayou between sea marsh and main land, *soidisant* [it is said], to be drilled for unrighteous work." St. Martin Parish officials ordered Charley Miller, a German immigrant suspected of abolitionist leanings, to leave the community and warned that "Lincoln sympathisers" might become "a different flower" swinging from the boughs of local magnolia trees. Swift actions taken by the parish patrol prevented the spreading of the conspiracy, but the imprudent reporting of slaves' misdeeds to owners probably tempered the dispensation of justice. The *Attakapas Register* criticized the "improper step" that "to advise the owners of the slaves, of the deeds of the latter" meant "to put a man's interest in direct opposition to the course of legal proceedings in such cases."[13]

Despite suspicion of any moderating influences, local magistrates imparted punishment upon many slaves believed guilty of a role in a St. Martin Parish conspiracy. Those slave owners who felt financially victimized by the execution or imprisonment of their slaves submitted requests to the state's compensatory fund for monetary redress. Ten slave owners received a total of $8,500 in compensation for seventeen slaves implicated in the conspiracy. St. Martin Parish officials hanged six slaves on June 24, 1861, and the remaining eleven received sentences of imprisonment for life at hard labor.[14]

Residents of North Louisiana parishes were not immune to conspiracies and threats of slave rebellion like those that plague the state's southern parishes. In May 1861 Isaac Harrison, a Tensas Parish planter, hid in the crawl space beneath a slave cabin to overhear a conspiratorial meeting. Assuming the rapid advance of Federal forces, several slaves, supported by five local abolitionists, planned a revolt to begin on July 4, 1861, when they would "march up the River to meet Mr. Linkum" Early detection of the plot prevented any disturbance from occurring, but one observer noted "there are many who live in great fear."[15]

Tensas Parish officials used the heightened state of public anxiety as the perfect occasion to remedy an annoying problem. Having free persons of color living within a slave society was generally considered dangerous, since the presence of free blacks might encourage slaves to seek their own liberty. Many assumed that free blacks could provide a leadership role usually missing from most slave conspiracies and that this fact alone justified social separation of slaves from free blacks. Within weeks of the failed conspiracy, Tensas Parish officials arrested three free men of color on horse stealing and larceny charges and set excessive bonds to guarantee their lasting imprisonment. Since Tensas Parish recorded only eight persons of color in the Eighth Census, the imprisonment of Judson Hardin, Daniel Gaiter, and Frank Lockett, Tensas Parish's only free black males, eliminated them as a leadership source should other conspiracies arise.[16]

Both Concordia Parish, Louisiana, and Adams County, Mississippi experienced a coordinated slave disturbance in the summer of 1861.[17] Planters organized a patrol to capture the slave conspirators and then established an extralegal planter's court at Jacob Sugret's Ashley Plantation in Concordia Parish to try the accused.[18] As one planter who was serving as clerk transcribed the incident, those sitting in judgment allowed each slave to testify and confess involvement before sentencing the accused to death. The planters, sitting as judges, sentenced ten slaves from three plantations to death by hanging. They cited the authority of "orders of the committee." One Louisiana planter who witnessed the trial remarked, "from what I learned, I think the testimony was sufficient to justify the action of the committee."[19]

The testimony of the ten convicted slaves is quite revealing since their gallows confessions show no remorse, but rather, indicate a passionate, albeit convoluted, hatred of white society. Boasting "if the black folks were turned loose with hoes and axes they would whip the country," one participant's naiveté proved the insurrectionist's simple logic. The slave Harry Scott's testimony mentioned a threefold strategy among conspirators to "kill old master and take the ladies for wives and ride [with] the leaders" as the insurrection progressed. The slave Orange's statement suggested that conspirators also intended to steal their masters' money after killing them. The testimony of certain conspirators showed that sexual fantasy was a significant motivating factor in uniting the plotters. The slave George Bush predicted that "white women would run to the black men to hold them" once the rebellion began, and another slave's assertion, "Simon be damned if he don't have one too," reflects the societal taboo that sexual conquest epitomized the ultimate upheaval of white society.

Besides the stereotypical words and phrases that usually outraged Southern whites, the confessions included occasional germs of revolutionary rhetoric and suggested that slaves had rudimentary understanding of sectional politics. The plotters convinced a runaway slave with a double-barreled gun to join the conspiracy and this convert's fierce loyalty showed in a pledge to be "kicking ass" when the rebellion commenced. Unshaken by the terror of vigilante justice and inescapable death, the slave Simon exposed the fallacy of Southern manhood with the crude assertion that "Northerners make the South shit behind their asses." The testimony suggested a martial spirit among the plotters that encouraged the recognition of compatibility between goals of Northern armies and insurrectionists. Equating their conspiracy with formation of a strike force to "help old Lincoln out," the plotters predicted that joint operations between the regular army and slave rebels could speed the day when Gen. Winfield Scott "would eat his breakfast in New Orleans." Additionally, the conspirators mentioned that encouraging news from Kingston [Jamaica], where "the negroes [*sic*] had got up an army" set into motion the original plans for an armed insurrection in Louisiana.[20]

Under normal circumstances, blacks constituted 90.9 percent of the Concordia Parish population, but the exigencies of civil war, especially the insatiable demands for troops, would only exacerbate fears among the remaining white minority. White residents gloomily noticed the steady population decline and prayed that slaves would not seize the opportunity to rebel. Yet Bill Postlewaite, one of the convicted slave conspirators, mentioned the population differential during testimony and confided that insurrection was "an easy job now as so many men had gone away."[21] Southern governors understood this danger and purposefully withheld local troops to defend against possible internal slave violence. Historian Armstead L. Robinson noted that one-half of the Confederacy's forces were unavailable to commanders in July 1861 since local officials, preoccupied with preventing slave revolts, demanded their services at home.[22] For Southern field commanders, soldiers' preoccupation with maintaining domestic security at the homefront created a morale problem of immense proportions. News about incidents of slave unrest at home did little to encourage military order, but rather, made soldiers reconsider their commitment to states' rights when self-preservation and individual rights appeared endangered.[23]

Even the Northern press recognized that slave rebellion, either provoked or spontaneous, was a distinct possibility as the war progressed. A New York journalist wrote, "I see the Inevitable Horror—awful to me as to the South—creeping up sluggishly from the swampy poison-land—the dim devil-spectre of SERVILE REBELLION!" The knowledge that many slave owners in upper-South states like Virginia had sent slaves southward to avoid the financial loss that capture and liberation entailed, only heightened confidence and focused speculation among Northerners as to when and where the inevitable outbreak would occur. Although northern Virginia was the focus of battlefield action, many realized that "the devil is raising his head away down South in Dixie."[24]

In April 1862 as Federal gunboats steamed past the Forts Jackson and St. Philip guarding the Mississippi River's mouth, the impending capture of New Orleans excited servile passions to heretofore unparalleled heights. On several Louisiana plantations, anticipation of liberation prevailed as slave intransigence predated the arrival of Federal troops. Local commanders warned Confederate military headquarters of a "very marked sign of discontent" among Louisiana slaves and predicted inevitable disturbances of public security.[25] Describing a region burdened by "pillage and desolation," an observer echoed these apprehensions by acknowledging "the negroes, for more than fifty miles up the river, are in a state of insubordination."[26] At one plantation above New Orleans, slaves constructed a gallows and then issued the ominous warning that former masters and drivers would eventually swing from its gibbet. As these disturbing signs became manifest and the future appeared uncertain, one New Orleans diarist felt compelled to admit "there was a speck of servile war in the lower part of the city."[27]

Slaves abandoned the plantations and flocked to join their liberators so rapidly that Union forces, unaccustomed to detaining large numbers of refugees, were powerless to stop the exodus and ill-prepared to handle the growing crisis of the newly dispossessed. Unable to feed, clothe, house, or employ the multitude seeking succor at Union lines, Federal military commanders contemplated the vengeful fury that such an unruly mob might release upon former oppressors unless conditions improved immediately. This alarming prospect positioned Federal forces in a curious dilemma in which they found themselves protecting Louisiana's slave owners against the anticipated wrath of liberated slaves.

Gen. Benjamin F. Butler, Federal commander of occupied New Orleans, recognized the precipitous danger of servile war in Louisiana and used all commissioned powers to prevent racial hostilities from developing. Butler informed Secretary of the Treasury Salmon P. Chase that "a single whistle from me would cause every white mans [*sic*[throat to be cut in this city.[28] In a letter to his wife, the general stated that a risk of impending slave insurrection prevailed in Louisiana and that the uncertainty of time or place only exacerbated the anguish, making one unsure "whether he wished it more than he feared it.[29]

Butler, who had advanced active abolitionist sentiments before arriving at New Orleans, allowed the pressures of maintaining public order to direct military policy, thus modifying long-standing personal antislavery views. The general understood the military's twofold role in occupied Louisiana and recognized that "to have *every species of disorder quelled*" was not inconsistent with the other basic directive "to restore order out of chaos."[30] Butler's new conservative racial attitude often clashed with the active abolitionist sentiments championed by some Federal officers. Gen. John Wolcott Phelps, assigned to help Butler in the Gulf Department, was an early proponent of arming blacks as a preemptive measure to avoid the potential rebellion that idle, unemployed blacks might incite. Viewing labor as a redeeming social force, Phelps warned, "the danger of a violent revolution, over which we can have no control, must become more imminent every day," and asserted that the rigorous demands of military training, with its inculcated patriotic fervor, would prevent any manifestation of insurrection. He was decried as an "outlaw" by the Confederate Congress for "arming and training slaves for warfare against their masters." Phelp's ideas produced an expected chorus of criticism from Confederate circles, but also engendered reproach from General Butler. Calling Phelps "mad as a March Hare on the 'nigger question,'" Butler refused to adopt the "vexed question of arming the slaves," thereby giving tacit support to Louisiana's slaveholders who feared the consequences of such actions. This ideological rift produced no clear winners as Phelps resigned from the army on August 21, 1862, and on December 26, 1862, the War Department reassigned General Butler to other duties in Virginia.[31]

As civil war progress and Southern will stiffened, the exigencies of political reality forced Abraham Lincoln to redirect the war's aims by focusing the conflict as a liberating crusade to end slavery in the United States. With the Emancipation Proclamation's promulgation on September 22, 1862, Lincoln finally grasped the moral momentum of the abolitionist movement and tried to make that cause's fervor unify Northern resolve to continue the increasingly unpopular struggle. Yet, by declaring the intention to free all slaves in areas in rebellion on January 1, 1863, Lincoln inadvertently heightened Southern resistance by raising the ugly specter of slave rebellion.[32]

Gen. Daniel Ruggles, Confederate chief of staff, had warned political leaders that the unending demand for white males to fill Confederate armies produced situations where absence of "the ordinary and necessary control of the white man" created "pernicious influences" among slaves.[33] The Confederate Congress reacted swiftly to the threat that notions of emancipation might ignite a latent spirit of rebelliousness among slaves by passing a controversial measure to expand police protection on Southern plantations. On October 11, 1862, Confederate President Jefferson Davis signed "An Act to Exempt Certain Persons from Enrollment for Service in the Army of the Confederate States," ignominiously dubbed the "Twenty Nigger Law," enacted as a wartime measure designed to protect certain plantation districts against threatened slave insurrection by augmenting white population in those regions. The new military exemption act's most controversial aspect was a clause excusing masters and overseers who supervised twenty or more slaves from active service in the Confederate army, an indiscreet admission that many plantations faced great danger.[34]

Facing the related crises of conscription demands and insurrection anxieties, most people agreed that the pressures of impending emancipation would ignite servile war in certain parts of the Confederacy. The *Times* of London predicted that in places like Louisiana "where the negro [*sic*] race is numerous," slave insurrections "would extirpate the white population as completely as in St. Domingo."[35] The activities of Louisiana's delegates within the Confederate Congress suggest their understanding of the potential disaster to befall their state if massive slave unrest prevailed. Representatives Duncan F.

Kenner and Lucien J. Dupré, apparently recognizing the significance of their efforts to Louisiana, worked tirelessly to enact the military exemption bill that allowed greater policing of plantations. President Davis, immediately after signing this measure, responded negatively to a supplementary request by Confederate Congressman Dupré asking for special permission that some Louisiana regiments return to their home state to increase domestic defenses against possible disturbances.[36]

Within Louisiana, white residents at all levels of public and private life anticipated slave disturbances in the final months of 1862. Count Mejan, French consul at New Orleans, reported noticing "unmistakable signs" of upcoming slave unrest in Louisiana.[37] Confederate Gen. Daniel Ruggles raised the issue of war crimes by accusing Federal Gen. Benjamin F. Butler of encouraging "war on human nature" by "inaugurating, deliberately, servile war, by stimulating the half civilized African to raise his hand against . . . the Anglo-Saxon race."[38] Robert R. Barrow, a Terrebonne Parish planter, political leader, and prolific letter writer, attempted to rally fellow citizens to "expose and drive out from our country all sulking enemies who are here but to betray us."[39] New Orleans matron Julia LeGrand, acknowledging that "many are in great alarm," understood the immediate cause of public concern and admitted "it is scarcely human to be without fear." A neighbor named Mrs. Norton nervously awaited New Year's Day 1863, the announced arrival of emancipation, by waiting with "a hatchet, a tomahawk, and a vial of some kind of spirits" in dire expectation of an outbreak of hideous crimes against white residents.[40]

The uneventful passing of January 1, 1863, did not calm Louisiana residents' fears of slave insurrection. One resident commented that the tenuous and often indefensible position of white society's public safety generally required "Machiavellian diplomacy" toward Louisiana's blacks.[41] The promise of emancipation encouraged slaves to take a more active role in achieving their own liberation. One observer noticed that Louisiana slaves often gathered in canebreaks at night and "talked of the Yankees, and prayed for them and for the flag of the free."[42] Patrols prevented local conspiracies from expanding in Madison, Rapides, and Tangipahoa parishes, but brazen attempts at servile revolt only became more frequent.[43]

In April 1863, a force of forty armed blacks marched upon the town of St. Martinville. These insurrectionists battled sixty white residents near a bridge at the town's entrance in full view of the 52d Massachusetts Infantry. After killing four blacks and capturing several others, the victorious whites offered the captives to the Federal regiment's provost marshal who refused to accept the prisoners. Interpreting this refusal as an invitation for vigilante justice, local residents hanged the captured slaves from the Bayou Teche bridge in hopes of discouraging future slave unrest. Within a few days, the town again faced attack by insurrectionists, and a combined force of residents and Federal troops dispersed the motley army that disbanded and fled to nearby swamps.[44]

Unable to discount news of any conspiracy from the ridiculous to the substantive, Louisiana's white residents suffered a precarious existence in a world where anything could occur. Accordingly, citizens responded both to rumors and actual violent outbreaks by honing local defenses and remaining vigilant. The St. Landry Parish Police Jury, responding to an incident in nearby Cheneyville, revised its slave patrol ordinance to provide greater security against possible plantation restlessness.[45] In July 1863 James A. Seddon, Confederate secretary of war, alerted Louisiana Gov. Thomas O. Moore to recently discovered intelligence suggesting a massive federal scheme to foment slave revolt across the South on the night of August 1, 1863. Such a conspiracy seemed realistic to Governor Moore who received coincident details from Confederate commanders that Union advances in North Louisiana "turned the negroes [*sic*] crazy."[46] Evidence suggests that servile loyalty was a mere chimeric hope of white society since most slaves made "preparations for immediate skedaddling [*sic*]" when given an opportunity to escape.[47]

During the final months of the Civil War, thousands of Louisiana slaves abandoned their plantations and made the treacherous journey to the safety of Union lines. This final exodus, often misunderstood in the simplistic expression of the "jubilee spirit," represents the slaves' ultimate revolutionary sentiment, the manifestation of self-worth. Moved perhaps by religious fervor and imbibed with biblical notions of deliverance, these self-emancipated slaves were radicals—as evidenced by the lyrics "we'll hang Jeff Davis on the sour apple tree" sung to the tune of a Methodist anthem. Recognizing that the plantation South could not survive without their labor, these economic insurrectionists made the leap of faith necessary to achieve freedom and in so doing, hastened the fall of the Southern Confederacy.[48]

In *The Wretched of the Earth,* psychiatrist Frantz Fanon argued that "the oppressed, in order to prevent themselves becoming total victims, lashed out against their oppressors and in doing so, created their humanity.[49] The Civil War presented Louisiana slaves with the opportunity to employ their revolutionary tradition of insurrection, thereby proving their humanity. These slaves did not sit by as passive recipients of emancipation, but rather, they shared an active participatory role in gaining freedom. These men and women struggled together, planned work slowdowns together, conspired together, escaped together, revolted together, and fought and died together. They created their own humanity and recognized their own self-worth out of the formidable legacy of intolerance and subjugation that was their reward for misfortunate birth and they proved that a people ripe for revolt could endure in the social tinderbox of Louisiana.

Notes for "'We'll Hang Jeff Davis on the Sour Apple Tree':
Civil War Era Slave Resistance in Louisiana"

[1]Roger B. Taney to J. Mason Campbell, October 19, 1860, Benjamin C. Howard Papers, Maryland State Historical Society, Baltimore, Md; Don E. Fehrenbacher, "Roger B. Taney and the Sectional Crisis," *Journal of Southern History*, 43 (1977): 556-57.

[2]H. B. Jolly to Father, October 28, 1860, George H. S. Jordan Papers, Louisiana State Archives, Baton Rouge, Louisiana.

[3]Arthur M. Schlesinger, Jr., ed., *The Almanac of American History* (New York, 1983), 277-78.

[4]James D. Richardson, ed., *A Compilation of the Messages and Papers of the Presidents* (New York, 1897), 3158.

[5]James G. Blaine, *Twenty Years of Congress: From Lincoln to Garfield* (Norwich, Conn., 1884), 253.

[6]Jefferson Davis, *Jefferson Davis Constitutionalist: His Letters, Papers and Speeches,* ed. Dunbar Rowland (Jackson, Miss., 1923), 5:30.

[7]C. J. Mitchell to Jefferson Davis, April 27, 1861, Jefferson Davis Papers, Rice University, Houston, Texas; Armstead L. Robinson, "In the Shadow of Old John Brown: Insurrection Anxiety and Confederate Mobilization, 1861-1863," *Journal of Negro History*, 65 (1980): 279.

[8]*New Orleans Daily Picayune,* August 18, 1860; William W. White, "The Texas Slave Insurrection of 1860," *Southwestern Historical Quarterly,* 52 (1949): 279-80.

[9]*Daily Picayune,* May 8, 1861.

[10]Herbert Aptheker, "Maroons within the Present Limits of the United States," *Maroon Societies: Rebel Slave Communities in the Americas,* ed. Richard Price (Baltimore, 1979), 164.

[11]*Daily Picayune,* May 30, 1861; and Roger A. Fischer, "Racial Segregation in Ante Bellum New Orleans," *American Historical Review,* 74 (1969): 936.

[12]Franklin, La., *Attakapas Register.* May 30, 1861.

[13]Ibid., June 13, 20, 1861.

[14]State Auditor Journal G, January 1, 1860-December 31, 1861, Louisiana State Archives, Baton Rouge, La.; T. Lynn Smith and Homer Hitt, "The Composition of the Population of Louisiana State Penitentiary, 1859, 1860, and 1861," *Southwestern Social Science Quarterly,* 20 (1940): 372.

[15]Howard Hines to John Pettus, May 14, 1861; J. D. Davenport to John Pettus, May 14, 1861, Governor John J. Pettus Papers, Mississippi State Archives, Jackson, Miss.; Bell Irvin Wiley, *Southern Negroes, 1861-1865* (London, 1965), 82.

[16]1861 Grand Jury reports MSS, Clerk of Court's office, Tensas Parish Courthouse, St. Joseph, La.; United States Bureau of the Census, *Population of the United States in 1860; Compiled from the Original Returns of the Eighth Census, Under the Direction of the Secretary of the Interior* (1864; Reprint, New York, 1990), 1:188-97.

[17]For a complete investigation of these incidents see Winthrop D. Jordan's *Tumult and Silence at Second Creek: An Inquiry into a Civil War Slave Conspiracy* (Baton Rouge, 1993).

[18]Testimony from a vigilante trial is a rather suspect form of documentation. The testimony is included here because of supporting accounts by two eyewitnesses, but the information should still receive critical consideration.

[19]Lemuel P. Conner and Family Papers, 1861; William Minor Diary MS, September 25, 1861, Louisiana and Lower Mississippi Valley Collections, Louisiana State University Libraries, Baton Rouge, La.; Clement Eaton, *Freedom of Thought in the Old South* (Durham, N. C., 1940), 106-7.

[20]Ibid., Conner Papers.

[21]William Minor Diary MS, September 25, 1861.

[22]Robinson, "In the Shadow," 286.

[23]E. L. Roberts to Wife, December 18, 1861, Harrison-Roberts Family Papers, University of Virginia Libraries, Charlottesville, Va.

[24]Charles Godfrey Leland, "Servile Insurrection," *The Knickerbocker,* 58 (1861): 377-83.

[25]William N. R. Beall to Earl Van Dom, July 31, 1862, Earl Van Dom Papers, Library of Congress, Washington, D. C.

[26]*New York Herald,* September 9, 1862; William F. Messner, "Black Violence and White Response: Louisiana, 1862," *Journal of Southern History,* 41 (1975): 21.

[27]Messner, "Black Violence," 22; J. Carlyle Sitterson, *The Cane Sugar Industry in the South, 1753-1950* (Lexington, Ky., 1953), 209-10; "A Louisiana Rebel," MS, August 4, 1862, New York Historical Society Library, New York, N.Y.

[28]Benjamin F. Butler to Salmon P. Chase, July 10, 1862, Salmon P. Chase Papers, Pennsylvania Historical Society, Philadelphia, Penn.

[29]Joseph Cephas Carroll, *Slave Insurrections in the United States, 1800-1865* (New York, 1968), 207.

[30]Messner, "Black Violence," 24; James Parton, *General Butler in New Orleans: History of the Administration of the Department of the Gulf in the Year 1862* (New York, 1864), 518-19.

[31]Messner, "Black Violence," 26-29; Mark M. Boatner III, *The Civil War Dictionary* (New York, 1988), 109-10, 650; Jefferson Davis to CSA Congress, August 18, 1862, *The War of the Rebellion: A Compilation of the Official Records of the Union and Confederate Armies,* ser. 4, vol. 2 (Washington, 1900), 53.

[32]Stephen B. Oates, *With Malice Toward None: The Life of Abraham Lincoln* (New York, 1977), 317-23.

[33]Robinson, "Shadow of Old John Brown," 293; Daniel Ruggles to Samuel Cooper, October 8, 1862, *War of the Rebellion,* ser. 1, vol. 15:83.

[34]*Journal of the Congress of the Confederate States of America* (Washington, 1904), 2:268; Everette B. Long and Barbara Long, *The Civil War Day by Day: An Almanac, 1861-1865* (New York, 1971), 277-78.

[35]*Times* of London, September 19, 1862.

[36]Dunbar, *Jefferson Davis,* 5:352.

[37]Count Mejan to Godfrey Weitzel, August 12, 1862, *War of the Rbellion,* ser. 1, vol. 15:618-19.

[38]Daniel Ruggles to Benjamin F. Butler, July 15, 1862, Confederate Imprints.

[39]Robert R. Barrow, October 7, 1861, "Remarks on the Present War, the Objects of the Abolition Party," Confederate Imprints.

[40]Kate Mason Rowland and Mrs. Morris L. Croxall, eds., *The Journal of Julia LeGrand: New Orleans, 1862-1863* (Richmond, Va., 1911), 58-59; Harvey Wish, "Slave Disloyalty Under the Confederacy," *Journal of Negro History,* 23 (1938): 438-39; Eaton, *Freedom of Thought,* 106.

[41]Dan T. Carter, "The Anatomy of Fear: The Christmas Day Insurrection Scare of 1865," *Journal of Southern History,* 42 (1976): 359.

[42]George H. Hepworth, *The Whip, Hoe and Sword or, The Gulf-Department in '63,* ed. Joe Gray Taylor (Baton Rouge, La., 1979), 158-59.

[43]C. Peter Ripley, *Slaves and Freedmen in Civil War Louisiana* (Baton Rouge, La., 1976), 18-19.

[44]Ripley, *Slaves and Freedom,* 98-99; David C. Edmonds, *The Conduct of Federal Troops in Louisiana During the Invasions of 1863 and 1864* (Lafayette, La., 1988), 201.

[45]*An ordinance Organizing and Establishing Patrols for the Police of Slaves in the Parish of St. Landry* (Opelousas, La., 1863), 2-29.

[46]James A. Seddon to Thomas O. Moore, July 18, 1863, Lyon G. Tyler and S. A. Ashe, "Secession, Insurrection of the Negroes, and Northern Incendiarism," *Tyler's Quarterly Historical and Genealogical Magazine* (1933): 12-13; G. P. Whittington, "Concerning the Loyalty of Slaves in Northern Louisiana in 1863; Letters from John H. Ransdell to Governor Thomas O. Moore, dated 1863," *Louisiana Historical Quarterly,* 14 (1931): 491.

[47]Walter Lord, ed., *The Fremantle Diary—Being the Journal of Lieutenant Colonel James Arthur Lyon Fremantle, Coldstream Guards, on his Three Months in the Southern States* (Boston, 1954), 72.

[48]Nannie E. Case to Pet, April 1864, Albert A. Batchelor Papers, Louisiana and Lower Mississippi Valley Collections, Louisiana State University Libraries, Baton Rouge, La.; Wish, "Slave Disloyalty," 441, 444-45; C. L. R. James, *A History of Negro Revolt* (New York, 1938), 30-31.

[49]George P. Rawick, ed., *From Sunup to Sundown: The Making of the Black Community,* vol. 1 of *The American Slave: A Composite Autobiography* (Westport, Conn., 1972), 95; Frantz Fanon, *The Wretched of the Earth: The Handbook for the Black Revolution that is Changing the Shape of the World* (New York 1968), 52-53.

ORIGINS OF NEGRO SUFFRAGE DURING THE CIVIL WAR*

Herman Belz

Although no other aspect of Reconstruction became more controversial, the origins of Negro suffrage as a major political issue remain curiously obscure.[1] Republicans made black voting part of their Southern policy in the Military Reconstruction Act of March 1867 and approved the Fifteenth Amendment for the protection of Negro voting in 1869. Yet as early as 1865 Negro suffrage was the most prominent civil rights issue on the reconstruction agenda. After they passed the Thirteenth Amendment prohibiting slavery in January 1865, most Republicans looked beyond the problem of enforcing ordinary civil rights to the more politically explosive question of voting rights for freedmen. Radical Republican and abolitionist agitation was partly responsible for this situation, but the principal reason for it lay in the unusual circumstances of Louisiana politics.

Negro suffrage became a major issue even before the end of the war because the free Negro community in New Orleans, numbering about ten thousand blacks most of whom owned property and were educated, demanded the right to vote. Their demand placed the suffrage question in the forefront of reconstruction politics in Louisiana, and when the reorganized government of Louisiana sought readmission to the Union in the winter of 1864-65 the question of black voting rights became a decisive criterion in evaluating the new government. At the same time Negro suffrage formed a key part in a last-ditch attempt between the president and Congress to reach a compromise on reconstruction policy and thus heal the split that resulted from Lincoln's pocket-veto of the Wade-Davis plan of reconstruction in July 1864. These wartime developments, which thrust the issue of freedmen's political rights so abruptly and prematurely into national politics and defined it as an essential element in the problem of reconstruction, form the subject of this essay.

Negro suffrage, like the more general question of Negro citizenship, had long been a source of controversy in state politics. During the American Revolution suffrage laws in the states generally omitted racial restrictions, partly out of adherence to the principle of

*First published in *Southern Studies*, 17 (1978): 115-30. Reprinted with the kind permission of the author.

equality but mainly because free blacks were so few in number. Starting around 1800, however, a reaction set in which denied voting rights to free Negroes in many states where they had exercised the privilege. After Maine entered the Union in 1821, no state entered the Union which did not restrict voting to whites. As a result in 1860 only the New England states, with the exception of Connecticut, and New York, where they were required to own $250 worth of property, permitted free blacks to vote. Although antislavery reformers in the 1840s and 1850s tried to reverse this trend, their efforts brought no changes in state laws barring blacks from the polls.[2]

Basic to an understanding of the Negro suffrage issue was the fact that regulation of voting was a state rather than a federal responsibility. The Constitution provided that members of the House of Representatives should be elected by those who were qualified to vote for the most numerous branch of the state legislature. This meant that while the right of suffrage in national and state elections was lodged in the federal Constitution, it did not actually arise until after the franchise was conferred by the state.[3] Before the Civil War no conflict concerning suffrage regulation arose because a firm understanding existed that this subject belonged to the states.[4] During the war, however, there were obvious reasons to hold that in the reconstruction of loyal governments the federal government could regulate voting. Still, the weight of the antebellum constitutional tradition of state control of the suffrage was a formidable obstacle to congressional proposals for enfranchising Negroes.

The relationship between voting and citizenship as it existed in constitutional law also served to impede efforts to establish Negro suffrage. Popular thought generally assumed that the right to vote was an attribute of United States citizenship. This seemed a reasonable inference, for most voters were American citizens. Yet it was contradicted by two obvious facts that complicated the question of voting rights for freedmen. The first was that aliens were legal voters in some states; the second, that women and children, and paupers, criminals, and insane persons were not entitled to vote, although born or naturalized in the United States they were undoubtedly citizens of the United States.[5] Thus even if black citizenship were assumed—and that assumption could by no means be taken for granted—it would not necessarily follow that they should enjoy the privilege of voting.[6]

In the first two years of the war Negro suffrage was an impractical issue, even in the view of abolitionists who advocated it.[7] When reconstruction became a practical problem midway through the war, however, its relevance suddenly increased.

In December 1863 Lincoln announced a policy of reconstruction that excluded blacks from the reorganization of loyal governments in the rebel states. Yet three months later, after meeting with a delegation of free Negroes from Louisiana who petitioned for the right to vote, he recommended a qualified form of Negro suffrage to the reconstruction governor of the state. "I barely suggest for your private consideration," Lincoln wrote to Gov. Michael Hahn of Louisiana, "whether some of the colored people may not be let in was, for instance the very intelligent, and especially those who have fought gallantly in our ranks."[8] Thereafter Lincoln supported black suffrage in this limited form. When he learned that Frederick Douglass had criticized the administration for failing to protect blacks, Lincoln was concerned that Douglass knew he had recommended suffrage for certain classes of Louisiana Negroes. On one occasion Negro voting formed part of peace discussions. J.R. Gilmore, the businessman-author whom Lincoln allowed to conduct an unofficial mission in Richmond in 1864, recorded that the president thought representation in Congress might be based on the voting population in the states, as an inducement to the Southern states to extend suffrage to blacks. Finally at the end of the war Lincoln publicly endorsed suffrage for educated blacks and Negro soldiers.[9]

Despite Lincoln's acceptance of qualified Negro voting, many abolitionists attacked the administration for neglecting freedmen's rights. More than to legal remedies for securing ordinary civil rights, they looked to Negro enfranchisement as a fundamental solution to the problem of protecting Negro liberty.[10] Arguing further that only with the help of black votes could the Union restore loyal government in the South, abolitionists led by Wendell Phillips in 1864 tried to make Negro suffrage a new test of radicalism. Unable to gain support for this position within the Republican party, Phillips appealed to the radical Republicans, abolitionists, and War Democrats who met at Cleveland in May 1864 in an attempt to prevent Lincoln's reelection. Although the Cleveland platform did not expressly mention Negro suffrage, it advocated the absolute equality of all men before the law, and Phillips was satisfied that this included Negro voting rights.[11]

Other abolitionists and radicals refrained from joining Phillips's anti-administration campaign for Negro suffrage. Led by William Lloyd Garrison and Oliver Johnson, editor of the *National Anti. Slavery Standard,* they held that despite short-comings and injustices, Lincoln's policies toward the freedmen pointed in the direction of equal rights. Johnson believed an "immense change for the better" had taken place in freedmen's affairs, while Garrison asserted that the government by its enlistment policy had "recognized the manhood and citizenship of the colored population of the country." Garrisonian abolitionists noted with approval Lincoln's gradual movement toward Negro suffrage, but they strongly opposed making an issue of black voting rights.[12]

Although politically the question of Negro suffrage might resolve itself into simple dichotomy, in constitutional terms there were three basic approaches to the issue. The first held that all adult males should vote (universal suffrage); the second declared that the same criteria for suffrage should be applied to all persons irrespective of race (impartial suffrage); the third regarded blacks as a separate class, some of whom might be enfranchised by special qualifications that would not apply to whites (limited Negro suffrage).

To some extent universal suffrage was the position of radical critics of presidential reconstruction in 1864. Wendell Phillips and Frederick Douglass were the leading spokesmen for this view, and insofar as Phillips prevailed over William Lloyd Garrison in internal struggles involving Negro suffrage it represented the outlook of most abolitionists.[13] Nevertheless, many of Phillips's supporters had reservations about universal suffrage. Parker Pillsbury expressed the belief that voters should be able to read and write, while John Jay thought military service should be a qualification for Negro voting. The *Boston Commonwealth* disavowed universal suffrage and suggested an impartial literacy test for determining the electorate. Many abolitionists moreover saw the difficulty of insisting on voting rights for persons whose intellect, according to abolitionist teaching, had for years been deadened by slavery.[14]

Garrisonian abolitionists favored impartial suffrage as a way of preventing race from becoming the all-important test of voting. The *Independent* opposed enfranchisement of

Negro soldiers as tending to create a caste system among blacks, but endorsed educational criteria impartially applied to all citizens. Impartial suffrage also appealed to non-radicals. The conservative *Springfield Republican* argued that natural characteristics such as race should not be criteria for selecting voters. A literacy test or some other impartial device, the *Republican* declared in March 1865, appeared to be the only safe solution to the problem of recognizing the freedmen's political rights. In similar fashion the moderate Unionist I. N. Tarbox cautioned against making any distinction in voting rights on the ground merely of color.[15]

In substantive terms there was thus a good deal of uncertainty and variety in anti-slavery attitudes toward black suffrage. Among both radicals and non-radicals, however, a major reason for supporting some form of Negro voting was that it would enable the freedmen to protect themselves and promote their own interests without the necessity of permanent federal intervention in local affairs. Wendell Phillips reasoned that if blacks were given the ballot, politicians would respect their rights and seek their support. Suffrage would be a lever for securing social and economic advancement. Moderate Republicans, critical of plans to regulate emancipated slaves through a paternalistic government agency, believed the right to vote would protect blacks more effectively than an administrative bureau. "When a man can vote," asserted Sen. William Sprague of Rhode Island, "he needs no special legislation on his behalf."[16]

Besides serf-protection, Negro suffrage would avoid resumption of state power that might oppress blacks on the one hand, and permanent federal intervention that would encroach on local autonomy on the other. The nation must give the freedman the ballot, insisted the *Boston Commonwealth,* "unless [it] means either to abandon his cause when his services are no longer needed, or to retain him in swaddling clothes and keep a standing army to take care of him. . . ." Once the fence of state power was rebuilt, warned Wendell Phillips, blacks would be helpless without the right to vote. Yet the alternative which some radicals proposed—territorial government over the South—was also undesirable. That would tend toward despotism and undermine democratic principles, said Phillips. Non-radical Unionists could agree. Although federal intervention in local affairs was ordinarily to be opposed, the *Springfield Republican* observed, temporary intervention was necessary to determine who would reconstruct loyal governments in the South. The Union must create "voters there of some sort," the *Republican* argued, "for to govern that section solely by authority from without will not agree with our republican-ism. . . ."[17]

The security of the Union and of the Republican party were additional reasons to support some plan of Negro voting. Looking only at the expediency of the matter, Congressman Henry Winter Davis of Maryland said that abstract considerations of freedmen's rights were far less important than the adverse consequences that would ensue from allowing the former rebel states to organize on an all-white basis. Noting the defeat of a conservative Republican senator who had opposed the recognition of Negro political rights, the *Independent* pointed out the political value of black voting for non-radicals. Knowing that black votes could keep them in office, politicians might change their minds about Negro rights, the *Independent* suggested.[18]

Increasingly a matter of public debate, Negro suffrage became a concrete issue in national politics in 1864-65. That it assumed practical importance so rapidly, even before the defeat of the South was assured and emancipation confirmed, was owing to the fact that in Louisiana, the state in which reconstruction had advanced the farthest, a large free Negro population had forced the issue of black voting to the forefront of local politics.

Almost as soon as white Louisiana Unionists inaugurated a movement to organize a loyal state government, the free colored community of New Orleans demanded the franchise. Claiming American citizenship and pointing to their service to the Union and their position as property owners, a large number of free blacks petitioned Military Gov. George F. Shepley for voting rights in November 1863. Unsuccessful, they renewed their appeal with the support of a group of white radical Unionists after Gen. Nathaniel P. Banks assumed control of Louisiana reorganization and ordered an election of state officers under the pre-war constitution. Frustrated by Banks's evasiveness, Louisiana's Creole leaders then took their case to Washington and President Lincoln.[19] Although in the campaign preceding the election of state officers both the radical candidate, Benjamin F. Fianders, and the moderate candidate, Michael Hahn, opposed Negro suffrage, Lincoln and Banks were sufficiently impressed with the free colored argument to endorse limited Negro voting.[20]

The day after receiving the free blacks' petition, Lincoln, as noted earlier, advised the newly elected governor, Hahn, to consider extending voting rights to educated blacks and those with army service. The forum in which this step might be taken was the Louisiana constitutional convention, which Banks had called following the election of state officers and which met from April to July 1864.

At the outset the convention delegates were so opposed to Negro suffrage that they passed a resolution forever prohibiting the legislature from enfranchising colored citizens. Hahn and Banks disapproved this action, however, and forced its reconsideration and defeat. Under pressure especially from Banks, the convention went on to include in the new constitution a provision authorizing the legislature to enfranchise citizens of the United States who were judged qualified by military service, payment of taxes, or intellectual fitness.[21] While this measure disappointed free black leaders and their few white radical allies, it represented a significant tendency in the Lincoln-Banks reconstruction program that aimed at a moderate solution to the question of Negro suffrage. The prospective Negro voting provision may have been adopted reluctantly, but it is inaccurate to say, as a recent historian does, that it was a "hollow promise for the future."[22] It was not a promise, but an indication of the direction in which Lincoln and Banks were moving. And in the fluid political situation of 1864 some form of black suffrage seemed within the realm of possibility.[23]

Convinced that comprehensive Negro enfranchisement would never meet approval in Congress let alone in Louisiana, Banks conceived a plan for limited Negro voting that depended on the unique circumstances of the free colored community in New Orleans. Banks's idea was to declare that any person with a major part of white blood was white, and thus entitled to vote. Asserting that this action would give representation to several thousand Negroes and decisively break the color line in regard to the suffrage, Banks caused a measure aimed at this end to be introduced in the constitutional convention. When it was rejected 47 to 23, Banks devised a scheme whereby a judicial decision would accomplish the same result. Banks intended to have Judge Edward H. Durell of the Federal Circuit Court in Louisiana issue a decision stating that quadroons and octoroons were white and hence eligible to vote. For reasons that remain obscure, however, Banks was either unwilling or unable to arrange an appropriate case for this purpose. Banks's idea of redefining the status of colored citizens finally died when the state legislature rejected a quadroon voting bill in late 1864.[24]

Curious as this Negro suffrage plan seems in retrospect, it had a certain plausibility because judicial precedents existed for making the kind of legal distinction among blacks that Banks proposed, and because Louisiana law distinguished between Negroes and mulattoes in certain situations.[25] A more important basis for the plan was the division that existed in the free black community on the question of suffrage. Many Negro leaders, emphasizing the common interests shared by free blacks and emancipated slaves, argued for universal suffrage. Represented in public debate by the *New Orleans Tribune* and organized into a local branch of the National Equal Rights League, this faction rejected Banks's scheme as an attempt to create a caste system among blacks.[26] Yet other free blacks favored enfranchisement of certain classes of Negroes, and hoped to achieve this reform through the state legislature.[27] Indeed the delegates who petitioned Lincoln for the right to vote in March 1864 drafted their appeal on behalf of blacks "born free before the rebellion."[28] The fact moreover that the local chapter of the National Equal Rights League held a convention of all colored men in January 1865 in the hope of setting aside all differences and starting a new era marked by a spirit of unity, suggests that the recently defeated quadroon bill in the state legislature had provoked divisions within the black community.[29]

Despite the apparent reasonableness of a suffrage plan that rested on the obvious differences between free blacks and freed slaves, Banks's efforts failed. The major cause was the categorical opposition of white Southerners to any form of Negro suffrage.[30] But the opposition of white radicals, who excoriated Banks's free labor and reconstruction policy in general, and of free blacks, who denounced the voting plan as a scheme to divide Negroes, should also be taken into account.[31] Though his testimony was of course hardly objective, Banks himself blamed the failure of the suffrage plan on radicals who were impatient with any steps short of universal suffrage.[32] Besides political and ideological objections, there were practical difficulties associated with Banks's mulatto voting plan. Inquiries into ancestry would be necessary, yet these were often highly sensitive matters which led to violent controversy, including duels and murder.[33] Some supporters of the suffrage plan also feared that it would lead to an increase in prostitution among black women seeking white fathers for their children.[34]

Against the background of events in Louisiana that made black suffrage a major issue, Congress began to deal with the question in a practical way. The organization of Montana territory provided one occasion for national action. In March 1864 the House of Representatives passed a Montana territorial bill that authorized all white male inhabitants to vote for the territorial legislature. The Senate amended the bill to allow voting by all male citizens of the United States, and a conference committee composed largely of radicals reported the bill with the universal suffrage provision intact. The House, firmly opposed to Negro enfranchisement, rejected the report, however, and insisted on a bill that would confine voting to whites only.[35]

A second attempt to introduce Negro suffrage concerned the District of Columbia. In February 1864 Iowa Republican James Harlan proposed a bill for regulating elections in

Washington city which would have permitted blacks to vote. When the measure came up for consideration in May Negro suffrage had attracted much attention, and conservatives at once moved to restore the racial qualification of earlier legislation concerning city elections. Harlan acceded to this change, but other Republicans pressed the issue of black voting. Lot M. Morrill of Maine recommended a taxpaying and literacy test applied to both races, and Henry Wilson of Massachusetts favored a residential and property-owning requirement for blacks alone. Although several Republicans supported these proposals, the Senate took no action on the bill.[36]

With elections scheduled for June, Ben Wade of the District of Columbia committee proposed to conduct voter registration on the traditional racial basis. Fellow radical Charles Sumner objected, however, and moved to prohibit exclusion from voting on account of color. In subsequent maneuvering the Senate as a committee of the whole approved an amendment to enfranchise black soldiers in the District, but the main purpose of this action was to defeat Sumner's more radical measure. In the Senate proper the proposal for Negro soldier voting was defeated 18 to 20.[37]

To debate black voting in the territories and the federal district was to reconnoiter the issue in preparation for reconstruction, the context in which it was of crucial importance. In December 1863 radical Republican James M. Ashley of Ohio offered a reconstruction bill that enfranchised blacks, but the question of Negro suffrage was so premature as a national issue that it attracted no public notice.[38] Ashley could not even make his view prevail in the House Select Committee on the Rebellious States, which reported the Wade-Davis bill in February 1864. Like Lincoln's reconstruction plan of December 1863, this measure restricted voting to whites only. Although Senate radicals tried briefly to amend it to enfranchise blacks, Congress passed it in July 1864 with suffrage limited to white persons. Lincoln pocket-vetoed the bill because it threatened to interrupt the progress of executive reconstruction, not because of substantive differences over policy.

By the winter of 1864-65 the struggle for Negro suffrage in Louisiana and the imminent defeat of the South made the question of freedmen's political rights important enough to warrant more serious consideration in national reconstruction legislation. The Lincoln administration was eager to secure congressional approval of the reorganized Louisiana government, but radical Republicans were opposed to it because of the state's failure to enfranchise blacks. At the same time Congress and the executive branch were under pressure, now that the end of the war seemed near, to reach a compromise on reconstruction policy. In an attempt at accommodation that resulted Negro suffrage was a major bargaining point.

Senators and representatives from loyal Louisiana applied for seats in Congress in December 1864, thereby initiating a lengthy review of presidential reconstruction in the occupied South by both houses of Congress. Not for several weeks would the issue of Louisiana recognition be settled. Meanwhile the question of a compromise reconstruction bill in place of the pocket-vetoed Wade-Davis plan of the previous July occupied congressional attention. James Ashley started the accommodation process by introducing a bill that recognized Louisiana, as the administration desired, and organized the other seceded states according to the terms of the Wade-Davis plan, with the important addition of universal suffrage.[39] It was this provision for unlimited black voting that proved to be the sticking point. Lincoln was apparently willing to accept the congressional plan of reconstruction in the rest of the South in return for congressional recognition of Louisiana, but he balked at the idea of universal suffrage.[40]

Led by Ashley, the Select Committee on the Rebellious States amended the reconstruction bill to meet Lincoln's objection without abandoning the principle of Negro voting. According to the amendment, only whites could take part in the initial registration of citizens that would formally start reconstruction in a state, but blacks serving in the army who were residents of the state could also vote in the formation of a new constitution and government.[41]

Although Lincoln's opinion of the amended bill is not known, his earlier recommendation of suffrage for educated blacks and Negro soldiers suggests that he probably would have accepted it. There is evidence that several radicals also supported the compromise, including Sumner. Yet other radicals felt that admitting Louisiana without any form of Negro suffrage was giving too much, especially considering the importance of the precedent that Louisiana recognition would set on the one hand, and the small number of blacks who would be enfranchised on the other.[42]

Whether or not they took this view of the situation, Ashley in early January 1865 brought from the Committee on the Rebellious States yet another version of the reconstruction bill which for all practical purposes killed the idea of a compromise. The bill still provided for limited Negro suffrage, but now it proposed to recognize Louisiana only if the newly formed government, conducted a registry of all citizens, as the other states were required to do, and incorporated in its constitution the conditions imposed on the other seceded states.[43] Although the measure did not categorically repudiate presidential reconstruction in Louisiana, in effect it withdrew the offer to recognize the Banks-Hahn government by requiring terms that the administration could hardly accept, or that it did not need to accept. A large majority of Republicans promptly voted to postpone the reconstruction bill, thus demonstrating how badly the radicals had misjudged the situation, if indeed they thought they had the votes to win.[44]

The question of recognizing Louisiana by seating its senators—and representatives—elect remained to be dealt with, and in this issue too Negro suffrage played a conspicuous part. In the Senate, where the principal struggle took place, the judiciary committee and a majority of Republicans supported the readmission of the state. Conceding that the Louisiana constitution failed adequately to recognize Negro political rights, they nevertheless argued that it pointed in the right direction.[45] Charles Sumner and a handful of radicals, however, seizing on the denial of Negro suffrage, condemned the Louisiana government as undemocratic. Insisting that the state be kept out of Congress until it allowed blacks to vote, the radicals staged a filibuster to prevent a vote on the Louisiana question.[46] If they could not get their reconstruction plan approved with broader Negro suffrage than the compromise bill provided, they were determined to prevent approval of Louisiana reconstruction.[47]

Although the Thirteenth Amendment had not yet been ratified, there was a widespread belief at the end of the war, by no means confined to radicals, that federal reconstruction policy would insist on some form of Negro suffrage in the former rebel states. The conservative-tending *Springfield Republican* speculated that to secure loyal voters in the South "we may undoubtedly have to depend much upon the blacks. . . ." A Republican correspondent of the *Detroit Advertiser* and *Tribune* suggested that if representation in Congress were to be based on the number of qualified voters in a state, as many Republicans were proposing, Southerners themselves would extend suffrage to black citizens. Radicals were optimistic about securing political rights for blacks. "We have almost come up to the point of conceding this great, this all-important right of suffrage," the black leader Frederick Douglass declared." If abolitionists fail to persist now," he added, "we may not see, for centuries to come, the same disposition that exists at this moment. Hence I say, now is the time to press this right."[48]

Throughout 1865 Negro suffrage remained the chief focus of reconstruction thinking among Republicans.[49] As President Johnson's restoration policy went into effect, however, it became clear that the political status of the freedmen was a premature issue after all. The black codes that the former Confederate states passed defining the status and rights of emancipated slaves created a new form of oppression which made protection of Negro civil rights the government's first concern. Voting rights were necessarily deferred.

The history of reconstruction was profoundly affected by the failure of Congress to approve the moderate proposal for voting by Negro soldiers in the compromise reconstruction bill of December 1864. By 1867, after the South had rejected the Fourteenth Amendment for the protection of civil rights, nothing less than complete Negro suffrage seemed sufficient to give Republicans the political strength needed to form new governments in the South acceptable to Northern opinion. Accordingly the Military Reconstruction Act of March 1867 provided for universal suffrage. The apparent necessity of this step notwithstanding, complete Negro suffrage fell heavily on the South, especially because of its sectional nature,[50] Not the military character of radical rule, but the drastically expedient use of Negro suffrage imposed a heavy liability on the new state governments that were formed in the South.[51]

It seems plain in retrospect that the more circumspect approach to Negro suffrage proposed in the compromise reconstruction bill of December 1864 had advantages over the course eventually taken. It gave president and Congress a reasonable basis for agreement, and it would have weakened the force of the radicals' main objection that presidential reconstruction did not recognize black political rights. Most important, it would have broken the color line on voting without antagonizing white Southern opinion to the extent that the Reconstruction Act of 1867 did.

From the standpoint of both improved race relations and sound reconstruction policy the great need of the hour was not to enfranchise all black people, but to prevent color from becoming the test of political participation. The truth of this observation occurred more readily to foreign opinion than to the radical leaders in Congress. Thus the French visitor Agenor de Gasparin, sympathetic to radical purposes, wrote in 1865 that there was nothing humiliating in not voting, provided that the exclusion resulted from a condition that applied to all citizens impartially. To bar persons from political life on account of color, however, de Gasparin pointed out, was not an exclusion, "but an indignity." De Gasparin thought the number of Negroes who voted was not important, so long as voting did not follow racial lines.[52]

For this reason as well no doubt as for others, many Republicans, including President Lincoln, supported Negro suffrage at the end of the war. Together with Louisiana recognition, qualified Negro suffrage offered a way out of the impasse in reconstruction policy that existed in 1864-65. Radicals demanded more, however. Rejecting the view that events in Louisiana signified a movement towards the recognition of Negro political rights, they abandoned the compromise bill of December 1864 by refusing to accept Louisiana; even though the bill enfranchised black soldiers in the other rebel states. Either the radicals thought they could carry a majority, in which case they completely misjudged the situation and overreached themselves, or they gave up the issue, thinking that limited Negro suffrage in the other states would not counteract the damage that would be done by recognizing the one state that had been reconstructed, Louisiana, without any provision for Negro voting. Of course the radicals were not the only ones who could have produced a different and more satisfactory outcome of the issue of Negro suffrage and reconstruction. If Lincoln and Banks had applied greater pressure and insisted on limited black voting in Louisiana, the situation in Congress would have been very different. The radicals almost certainly would have had to accept less than universal suffrage, and the moral basis for their attack on Louisiana reconstruction would have been seriously weakened. For this result to have occurred it would have been necessary for some influential white Southern political leaders to support a moderate plan of Negro civil and political rights, but this never happened.[53] Even the radical Unionists in the Louisiana state elections of February 1864 refrained from endorsing black voting.

Given the racial attitudes of the day and the upheaval that accompanied emancipation at the local level, one can understand why local politicians avoided the issue of Negro suffrage. It is more difficult to understand why national lawmakers who were committed to Negro rights abandoned a compromise reconstruction plan that would have introduced limited black voting (plus other safeguards of Negro civil rights) in ten states, in return for recognition of Louisiana without Negro suffrage. If a national law establishing non-racial voting standards for the entire South save Louisiana had existed at the end of the war, the pressure to enfranchise Negroes in that one state would have been all the greater. Perhaps radicals like Ashley doubted that most congressmen would resist a determined effort by the administration to get presidential reconstruction accepted once Louisiana was readmitted, a national reconstruction law notwithstanding. Certainly Lincoln's reelection in November 1864 strengthened his hold on the party and enhanced his ability to proceed with a moderate reconstruction policy.

Universal suffrage, a minimal safeguard of Negro rights in the view of radicals in 1865 and almost all Republicans in 1867, appeared to white Southerners as the maximum evil. White Southerners would have opposed the limited Negro voting of the compromise reconstruction bill of December 1864, yet they were also prepared for the worst at the end of the war.[54] It seems likely that they would have accepted in a less hostile and more resigned spirit than they demonstrated two years later, a Negro suffrage plan that was manifestly less objectionable to them than the universal suffrage that eventually became the basis of radical reconstruction.

"Origins of Negro Suffrage During the Civil War"

[1]Cf. William Gillette, *The Right to Vote: Politics and the Passage of the Fifteenth Amendment* (Baltimore, 1965), Chapter 1.

[2]Charles H. Wesley, *Neglected History: Essays in Negro-American History* (Washington, 1969), 42-54; Leon F. Litwack, *North of Slavery: The Negro in the Free States, 1790-1860* (Chicago, 1961), 74-93; Emil Olbrich, *The Development of Sentiment on Negro Suffrage to 1860* (Madison, Wis., 1912), 127-28.

[3]Richard Claude, *The Supreme Court and the Electoral Process* (Baltimore, 1970), 24-25, 47-4.

[4]John Norton Pomeroy, *An Introduction to Municipal Law,* 2nd ed. (San Francisco, 1886), 426.

[5]Kirk H. Porter, *A History of Suffrage in the United States* (Chicago, 1918), 112-22; Opinion of Attorney General Bates on Citizenship, *Official Opinions of the Attorneys General of the United States,* 10 (1868): 388; Pomeroy, *An Introduction to Municipal Law,* 426; *Congressional Globe,* 37 Congress, session 2, 1638-39 (April 11, 1862), remarks of James Harlan.

[6]Negro citizenship was the first issue that had to be settled. Before the war the preponderance of evidence was against the proposition that Negroes were American citizens under the federal Constitution, the Dred Scott case epitomizing this point of view. During the Civil War Republicans moved toward recognition of Negro citizenship, for example, by enlisting blacks into the army. The attorney general also issued an opinion affirming that free Negroes were United States citizens. Nevertheless, the point remained constitutionally uncertain until the Fourteenth Amendment placed it beyond question.

[7]James M. McPherson, *The Struggle for Equality: Abolitionists and the Negro in the Civil War and Reconstruction* (Princeton, 1964), 239.

[8]Benjamin Quarles, *Lincoln and the Negro* (New York, 1962), 227-28; Lincoln to Michael Hahn, March 13, 1864, in Roy P. Basler et al., eds., *The Collected Works of Abraham Lincoln,* 9 vols. (New Brunswick, 1953-55), 7:243.

[9]John Eaton, *Grant, Lincoln and the Freedmen: Reminiscences of the Civil War* (New York, 1907), 173-75; James R. Gilmore, *Personal Recollections of Abraham Lin.coin and the Civil War* (Boston, 1898), 243-44; James G. Randall and Richard N. Current, *Lincoln the President: Last Full Measure,* 4 vols. (New York, 1945-55), 4:165-66; Harold M. Hyman, "Lincoln and Equal Rights for Negroes: The Irrelevancy of the 'Wadsworth Letter'," *Civil War History,* 12 (1966): 263-66.

[10]*Boston Commonwealth,* January 1, March 4, April 8, 1864; *Liberator,* March 11, 1864, letter by C.K.W.; *National Anti-Slavery Standard,* April 23, 1864, editorial.

[11]Ibid., May 21, 1864; *The Principia,* May 26, 1864; *Liberator,* June 10, July 15, 1864, correspondence between Wendell Phillips and Theodore Tilton; *National Anti-Slavery Standard,* July 9, 1864, letter of Wendell Phillips to the editor.

[12]Oliver Johnson to William Lloyd Garrison, May 4, 1864, William Lloyd Garrison Papers, Boston Public Library; *National Anti-Slavery Standard,* May 14, 1864, speech of Garrison; William D. Kelley to J, Miller McKim, May 1, 1864, J. Miller McKim to William Lloyd Garrison, May 5, 1864, Garrison Papers, Boston Public Library; *National Anti-Slavery Standard,* May 21, 1864, editorial, July 15, 16, 1864, correspondence between Wendell Phillips and Theodore Tilton; *Independent,* June 30, 1864; *Liberator,* June 3, 18, October 14, 1864, January 13, February 3, 1865, editorials; J. Miller McKim to William Lloyd Garrison, March 17, 1864, Garrison Papers, Boston Public Library, *National Anti-Slavery Standard,* February 4, 1865, editorial.

[13]The Massachusetts Anti-Slavery Society in January 1865 approved Phillips's resolution opposing Louisiana readmission and insisting on universal suffrage as a condition of reconstruction. *Liberator,* February 3, 1865; McPherson, *The Struggle for Equality,* 294-307.

[14]Parker Pillsbury to Charles Sumner, July 3, 1864, John Jay to Charles Sumner, January 5, 1863 [1864], Charles Sumner Papers, Harvard University Library; *Boston Commonwealth,* April 8, 1864; McPherson, *The Struggle for Equality,* 295.

[15]*Independent,* March 10, 1864, January 19, 1865; I.N. Tarbox, "Universal Suffrage," *New Englander,* 24 (1865): 165-66.

[16]*National Anti-Slavery Standard,* May 23, 1863; *Boston Commonwealth,* December 31, 1864, speeches of Wendell Phillips; *Cincinnati Gazette,* March 9, 1865; *Cong. Globe,* 38 Cong., I sess., 960 (February 21, 1864), remarks of William Sprague, 2104 (May 4, 1864), remarks of George S. Boutweil.

[17]*Boston Commonwealth,* April 15, 1865, December 31, 1864, February 18, 1865; *Liberator,* June 10, 1864; John Covode to Edwin M. Stanton, June 1865, Covode Papers, Library of Congress; E.P. Whipple, "Reconstruction and Negro Suffrage," *Atlantic Monthly,* 16 (1865): 238-47; *Springfield Weekly Republican,* March 11, 1865.

[18]Henry Winter Davis to Charles Sumner, June 20, 1865, Sumner Papers, Harvard University Library; Henry Winter Davis, *Speeches and Addresses* (New York, 1867), *559; Independent,* December 8, 1864, editorial.

[19]Joe Gray Taylor, *Louisiana Reconstructed, 1863-1877* (Baton Rouge, 1974), 26-27.

[20]Ibid., 40-41.

[21]W.E. Burghardt DuBois, *Black Reconstruction in America, 1860-1880* (Cleveland, 1964; Meridian ed.), 158; C. Peter Ripley, *Slaves and Freedmen in Civil War Louisiana* (Baton Rouge, 1976), 173.

[22]Ibid.

[23]Taylor, *Louisiana Reconstructed, 51.*

[24]Gerald M. Capers, *Occupied City: New Orleans under the Federals, 1862-1865* (Lexington, 1965), 230.

[25]Carl N. Degler, *Neither White Nor Black: Slavery and Race Relations in Brazil and the United States* (New York, 1971), 241-44; Charles S. Mangum, Jr., *The Legal Status of the Negro* (Chapel Hill, 1940), 3-4.

[26]Capers, *Occupied City,* 230; Charles Vincent, *Black Legislators in Louisiana During Reconstruction* (Baton Rouge, 1976), 29-30.

[27]Ripley, *Slaves and Freedmen,* 178, 180.

[28]James M. McPherson, *The Negro's Civil War* (New York, 1965), 279. Before submitting their petition to Lincoln, on the advice of white radicals, they added a statement urging suffrage for freed slaves, and "especially those who have vindicated their right to vote by bearing arms. . . ."

[29]Vincent, *Black Legislators in Louisiana,* 31-32.

[30]Taylor, *Louisiana Reconstructed,* 41.

[31]Vincent, *Black Legislators in Louisiana,* 29-30.

[32]*Weekly Republican,* March 11, 1865, letter of Nathaniel P. Banks to William Lloyd Garrison.

[33]DuBois, *Black Reconstruction,* 158.

[34]Capers, *Occupied City,* 230.

[35]*Cong. Globe,* 38 Cong., I sess., 1346 (March 30, 1864), 1361 (March 31, 1864), 1403 (April 4, 1864), 2348, 2351 (May 19, 1864), 2386 (May 20, 1864), 2347 (May 19, 1864).

[36]Ibid., 631 (February 13, 1864), 1162 (March 17, 1864), 2140 (May 6, 1864), 2239-44 (May 12, 1864).

[37]Ibid., 2486 (May 26, 1864), 2512 (May 27, 1864), *2545* (May 28, 1864).

[38]Herman Belz, *Reconstructing the Union: Theory and Policy during the Civil War* (Ithaca, 1969), 183, 185.

[39]Thirty-eighth Congress, H.R. No. 602, sec. 7-8, December 15, 1864, House of Representatives File of Printed Bills, National Archives.

[40]Tyler Dennett, ed., *Lincoln and the Civil War in the Diaries and Letters of John Hay* (New York, 1939), 244-45.

[41]H.R. No. 602, sec. 8, 10, December 20, 1864.

[42]*Boston Commonwealth,* January 14, 21, 1865, Washington letter; *Boston Journal,* January 12, 1865, Washington correspondence; *Cincinnati Gazette,* January 7, 1865, special dispatch on Louisiana, January 18, 1865, Washington correspondence.

[43]H.R. No. 602, January 7, 1865. The conditions required were prohibition of slavery and guarantees of freedom and equality of civil rights to all persons; exclusion of high ranking rebel officers from politics; and repudiation of the Confederate debt.

[44]*Cong. Globe,* 38 Cong., 2 sess., 301 (January 17, 1865).

[45]*Boston Commonwealth,* January 21, 1865, letter of B. Gratz Brown.

[46]*Cong. Globe,* 38 Cong., 2 sess., 1091 (February 25, 1865), 1101, 1104, 1111 (February 25, 1865), 1129 (February 27, 1865).

[47]In January Representative William D. Kelley of Pennsylvania, a radical Republican, proposed an amendment to the reconstruction bill that would have enfranchised all Negroes who could read the Constitution or who had served in the army. *Cong. Globe,* 38 Cong., 2 sess., 281-90 (January 16, 1865).

[48]*Springfield Weekly Republican,* March 11, 1865, editorial; *Detroit Advertiser and Tribune,* February 27, 1865; Charles W. Slack to Charles Sumner, February 28, 1865, Sumner Papers, Harvard University Library; *Boston Commonwealth,* February 25, 1865, speech of Frederick Douglass.

[49]David Donald. *Charles Sumner and the Rights of Man* (New York, 1970), 219-20; Joseph B. James, *The Framing of the Fourteenth Amendment* (Urbana, 1956), 3-33.

[50]Gillette, *The Right to Vote,* 31.

[51]William A. Dunning, *Essays on the Civil War and Reconstruction,* rev. ed. (New York, 1965), 192-93, notes the non-arbitrary, benevolent character of the military governments.

[52]Agenor de Gasparin, *A Letter to President Johnson,* 2nd ed. (New York, 1865), 26-32.

[53]DuBois, *Black Reconstruction,* 166.

[54]Eric L. McKitrick, *Andrew Johnson and Reconstruction* (Chicago, 1960), 151-58.

SECTION II

RECONSTRUCTION:
THE STRUGGLE FOR FULL CITIZENSHIP

BLACK LOUISIANIANS DURING THE CIVIL WAR AND RECONSTRUCTION: ASPECTS OF THEIR STRUGGLES AND ACHIEVEMENTS*

Charles Vincent

In the history of African Americans in Louisiana, no events made a greater impact than the Civil War and Reconstruction. The Civil War opened a bewildering era of uncertainty—but an era which allowed optimism. Blacks were eventually permitted to participate in the struggle which meant freedom and a new beginning. In the postwar era, Reconstruction, they would attempt to put the bitter four-year encounter behind and forge ahead with a more democratic society. As laborers and politicians, blacks continued to strive for the betterment of themselves and the entire citizenry during these turbulent years.

In the Civil War, blacks were not mere spectators, but in many instances, willing participants. Comprising almost 50 percent of the total Louisiana population in 1860,[1] white Louisianians were apprehensive about the black man's role in the war. Undoubtedly some blacks—the wealthy—sympathized with the Confederacy but the vast majority, the small landholders and slave, wanted to see slavery end and supported the Union army.[2] Whites apparently dictated that some blacks would serve the Southern cause. Many blacks were forced into service for the Confederacy. Those conscripted were not placed in the ranks and never engaged in any meaningful battle. But slaves in Louisiana, as throughout the South, served in such menial capacities for the Confederacy as building fortifications, bridges, forts, and helping with carrying artillery. Slave labor was used in order to release whites for military duty. In the fall of 1862, the Confederate commander at Port Hudson was instructed by the acting secretary of war to use all resources available to defend the post.[3] This policy became standard Southern procedure and was continued

*First published in Robert R. Macdonald et al., eds., *Louisiana's Black Heritage* (New Orleans: Louisiana State Museum, 1979), 85-106. Reprinted with the kind permission of the author and publisher.

throughout the war. By mid-1864, the Confederate Bureau of Conscription registered "all slaves and free blacks between eighteen and fifty years old" as possible laborers.[4]

The health and safety of conscripted blacks were of little concern to many Confederate officials in Louisiana. Often those forced into service by the Confederacy, such as the impressed laborers at Fort Beauregard in Harrisburg (Louisiana), were ill-clothed and ill-fed. No provision for hygienic care was given, and one frustrated medical doctor observed that if such conditions and situations were continued "half of these negroes (*sic*) will die of camp fever." The Harrisburg incident was not unusual and similar incidents were recorded at other forts and posts, and in planters' complaints to Confederate officials.[5]

In contrast to forced Southern support, blacks eagerly volunteered for the Union cause. Leaving the plantations in South Louisiana in almost epidemic proportions, especially after the capture of New Orleans in April, 1862, they flocked into the Union camps. They took their master's horses, mules, and joyfully followed the Yankee armies. Others had to escape from overseers, elude rebel pickets, and battle city policemen. Some were killed by planters and overseers in their attempts. By December, 1862, almost two hundred entered Union lines daily. Those reaching the Federal army provided useful service and brought military items.[6]

The free blacks in New Orleans also participated with and aided the Union and Confederacy during the war. Numbering almost 11,000 out of a total population of over 149,163, many served in regiments called the Native Guards, Louisiana Militia, Confederate States of America. These units had been designated and recognized as an organization by Gov. Thomas O. Moore in May 1861. Membership increased until early 1862, when there were more than 3,000 individuals in such military organizations.[7] Those units, armed at their own expense, made only ceremonial appearances in parades. The vast majority of these soldiers probably joined the Confederate ranks for their personal safety. When the Southern forces retreated from New Orleans, these men did not go with them. Evidently, they did not desire to fight for the South.[8]

Many of the black Confederate units met with the Union commander of New Orleans, Gen. Benjamin F. Butler, shortly after his arrival and volunteered their services. Butler at first was reluctant to accept their offer. At his previous command, he had surrendered slaves to slaveowners loyal to the Union. Since President Abraham Lincoln had indicated no specific policy regarding the use of black troops in the army, Butler acted cautiously. With pressure mounting to enlist blacks, and with subordinates threatening to resign,[9] Secretary of War Edwin M. Stanton told Butler to use his own discretion. Butler, who referred to the blacks earlier in the war as "contraband," saw the wisdom in enlisting blacks and issued his General Order No. 63, of August 22, 1862. The order recognized the legitimacy of black military units in Louisiana and called for volunteers. But this was done "not from the righteousness of their cause but from the tenacity of the Native Guards."[10] Thus, black soldiers were tentatively accepted by Butler primarily because there was no rejection by the government.

Blacks' enthusiasm for the fight was reflected in the courage of the soldier on the battlefield. But at first the general attitude of whites was that blacks would not fight. In Louisiana, this idea was laid to rest by the legendary performance and valiant efforts of black soldiers at Port Hudson, a Confederate fortress on the Mississippi River, and at Milliken's Bend, in northeast Louisiana. The new commander, Gen. Nathaniel P. Banks, was greatly impressed. In a letter to his wife, Banks stated that black soldiers "fought splendidly, splendidly!"[11] Two men often associated with the courageous charge at Port Hudson were Captains F. Ernest Dumas and André Cailloux. Dumas organized a company of his own slaves who served with him in the Second Regiment. Maj. Gen. Benjamin Butler said in reference to Dumas' knowledge of military affairs: "He has more capability as a major than I had as a Major General."[12] Of Cailloux, one black writer William Wells Brown said that Cailloux's bravery had lifted forever the racist prejudice that black soldiers would not fight.[13]

By the end of the war in April 1865, many blacks throughout America had actually helped the North win the war. Over 200,000 blacks fought in the Union army and navy. Many more blacks served in non-military capacities. "Without their help," observes historian James M. McPherson, "the North could not have won the war as soon as it did, and perhaps it could not have won at all." In Louisiana, over 24,000 blacks joined under the "Yankee" banner as soldiers—a significantly high number since much of Louisiana remained under Confederate control. Moreover, the black Louisianians' part in the Union effort takes on an even greater importance when it is noted that Louisiana furnished more black troops than any other Southern state.[14]

Blacks participated in the war because they saw it as a war of liberation. To most white Union soldiers this was a struggle solely to restore the Union, a tone set by Chief Executive Abraham Lincoln. Fearing that freed blacks would commit violent acts against whites in South Louisiana, Northern commanders urged a wage-labor system. Blacks were never viewed as capable of functioning in society as free men. The contraband education program was not fully supported, and many of these programs only reshaped in white minds the image of docile and humble blacks. Only lip service was given to their aspiration to become proprietors of farms, and land owners.[15]

Despite many unfilled promises blacks gained some advantages from the Civil War. First, it "wrought a revolution in the Negro's status, North and South." It brought freedom as the war helped dismantle the legal props of the "peculiar institution." The Emancipation Proclamation went into force on January 1, 1863. A Louisiana Supreme Court ruled in October, 1863, that blacks could no longer be held in slavery. In late December of that year, General Banks ordered the removal of all signs in New Orleans regarding the sale and imprisonment of bondsmen. By January 11, 1864, the state's constitutional provisions regarding slavery were suspended.[16]

Secondly, blacks gained educational opportunities. The new commander General Banks organized a system of education to teach reading and writing using the aid of the American Missionary Association. Chaplains in the regiments, and other volunteers were indispensable in this effort. The routine in one military camp included drills for four hours, and "one hour in school."[17] Around the campfires they studiously attended regimental night schools. They became better soldiers as a result and some returned to their home communities to become leaders during Reconstruction.

Thirdly, a sense of black pride developed during the war. They expected and began demanding their rights as men. The bravery exhibited by the soldiers at Port Hudson, Millikens' Bend, and other points in Louisiana were rallying symbols of accomplishment. Captain James H. Ingraham, first recognized at Port Hudson and later state senator, echoed the feeling of many in January, 1865, when he stated: "We must ask for our rights as men. If we are not citizens why make soldiers of us."[18]

Pride was reflected in different ways by blacks. Many blacks began formulating theories of how freedom could best serve the black mass. Their organ in articulating this program was the *New Orleans L'Union,* an uncompromising Republican newspaper that appeared tri-weekly in French, with a few issues in English. Initiated in September 1862, it was financed largely by Dr. Louis C. Roudanez, a pre-war free black physician trained in Paris, his brother, Jean Baptiste, teacher and freedom-fighter Paul Trevigne, and other friends. These men strove to shape the desires of blacks into a cohesive political force. The paper urged nationwide abolition of slavery and the unequivocal recognition of rights of blacks. Such objectives could be attained simply by upholding the ideas of the Declaration of Independence, and the enforcement of the United States Constitution.[19]

The newspaper also advocated other programs. In mid-1863 its writers announced, supported, and participated in "Union Meetings," that urged a more accommodating policy from the government. Petitions resulting from the meetings were sent to the U.S. military commander, Brig. Gen. George F. Shepley, asking for permission to register as voters—a right to which they considered themselves entitled.[20]

As the war drew to an end, and the national policy became more radical in outlook, blacks accelerated their demands for equal justice, President Lincoln saw Louisiana as a laboratory to test his lenient "ten-percent" Reconstruction policy. The groundwork for the state's readmission into the Union was laid with the seating of Benjamin F. Flanders and Michael Hahn in the Thirty-Seventh Congress. Opposing this faction in Louisiana was the radical movement spearheaded by blacks, and a white Northern-educated lawyer, Thomas Durant.[21]

The Union commander in New Orleans, General Banks, supported the conservative forces and the planters. His subordinate, Gen. George F. Shepley, was also opposed to mass enfranchisement. The radical movement continued to grow, however; petitions were sent to President Lincoln urging the extension of the franchise. The newly elected governor, Michael Hahn, who won in an election ordered by Banks, was also opposed to blacks receiving the right to vote. This was reflected in his influence at the Constitutional Convention of 1864. Although urged by Lincoln to extend the franchise to the wealthy free blacks, the convention did not follow his suggestion. It did, however, grudgingly include a provision which enabled the legislature to grant suffrage to persons who might be entitled to it because of military service, payment of taxes, or "intellectual fitness." "It was a safe assumption," wrote one historian, "that a legislature elected by white Louisianians would never do so."[22] This extravagant and corrupt assembly voted for segregated education and its provision abolishing slavery was more a result of the war instead of the convention's will. At the state's expense of $346,000, these sixty-three delegates consumed $9,400 worth of liquor and cigars, and "adjourned when there was nothing more to steal."[23]

Although the 1864 Constitution remained in effect for four years, it satisfied neither the conservatives nor the moderates in Louisiana. The demands by radicals for its repeal and a new convention in 1866, was facilitated by the constitutional provision that the president could call the old convention back into session. But at the time, the constitution had been ratified by over 10 percent of the population. Coupled with Lincoln's pocket veto of the Wade-Davis bill calling for stringent readmission guidelines, Louisiana went back into the Union or so it seemed to many ex-Confederates under Lincoln's provisions.[24]

The black community, and especially the press, watched the developments closely. Disappointed at not receiving the right to vote, the editors of the newly inaugurated successor to the *L'Union* the *New Orleans Tribune,* expressed dismay at the newly elected legislature's debate on the "quadroon bill." This measure was designed to permit persons having "one-fourth Negro blood" or less to be recognized as white. According to the newspaper's editorials, this move was "absurd." Instead of dividing blacks as the proponents of this measure hoped it gave more incentive for unity. "The sons of the land" should be linked together in "an unbroken column to front the common foe," asserted the *Tribune.* The editors also opposed a proposed literacy test for black voters.[25]

Similarly, Lincoln's election was not supported unanimously by the black press in New Orleans. During the presidential election of 1864, the newspaper cautioned blacks about political leaders at all levels. The editorial asserted that one factor that weakened Lincoln's chances for success in the bid for reelection was: *"He wants to maintain, if he can, Union and slavery."* This summation was correct; Lincoln probably never envisioned mass enfranchisement.[26]

Although the national administration did not favor the desires of blacks for total political rights, the elite blacks in New Orleans continued in the forefront of the movement to aid the freedmen and to win the franchise. Meeting at the so-called "School of Liberty," they formed local branches of the National Equal Rights League with James H. Ingraham as president. With members from Baton Rouge, Morganza, and other cities in the state, the local league called a Convention of Colored Men of Louisiana which met in January 1865. The former carpenter of Port Hudson fame, Army Captain Ingraham, then in his early thirties, was one of the main speakers. Many blacks took an active part in the meeting and were assigned to committees, served as secretaries, and acted as vice-presidents. The most noted were Captains William B. Barrett, Robert H. Isabelle, and Arnold Bertonneau, Lieut. C. C. Antoine, Emile Detiège, J. B. Jourdain, E. C. Morphy,

Thomas Isabelle, Oscar J. Dunn, and Dr. R. I. Cromwell. Most of these leaders, numbering more than 200, had been free before the war.[27] Whites were present and spoke, but the major portion of the proceedings was done by blacks. This type of experience served as another major step in training many for political careers during Reconstruction.

In the mid-1860s blacks joined and supported many political oriented organizations. They were members of the Equal Rights League, the Union Radical Association, and Friends of the Republican Party organization. Such clubs were ready to force the issue of universal suffrage and civil rights. When the executive board of the Equal Rights League called a mass meeting to announce the arrival of Chief Justice Salmon P. Chase in New Orleans, a large number of blacks attended. Chase advised the blacks in a few remarks that it was "both natural and right" that they should claim their rights.[28]

In addition to political clubs, there were organizations designed to aid blacks educationally and economically. The "Fair for the Benefit of the Orphans" held from late May until early June, 1865, was sponsored by the free women of color organization, Orphans Industrial and Educational Home for the Children of Freedmen. The treasurer of the organization was Mrs. Louis Charles Roudanez, and the president was Mrs. Louise DeMorie.[29] A branch of the Freedmen's Aid Association was established in New Orleans in April 1865. Similar efforts were recorded by such groups as the Board of Education for Freedmen in 1863, the American Missionary Association organized in 1865, and the Freedmen's Bureau. All societies were prominent in black education and readjustment to freedom activities. The degree of success registered by these organizations varied but all served a significant role in alleviating the early plight of the ex-bondsmen.[30]

Most blacks realized that no effective social or economic changes were forthcoming unless the political battle was won. In mid-June 1865, the National Equal Rights League sponsored a meeting for universal suffrage. The Friends of Universal Suffrage, a new political organization, was formed at the meeting, and the members proceeded to urge a "voluntary registration" of American citizens not recognized as voters. Blacks would vote although there was no national endorsement.

The new organization's actions were well timed as the changes in the national politics in the summer of 1865 had broad reaching ramifications. The Confederate army had been defeated on the battlefields; Lincoln had been assassinated; and President Andrew Johnson was rapidly granting amnesty to former Confederates. Gov. James M. Wells, who succeeded to the governorship after Hahn opted to become congressional representative, refused to recognize the petition of the Friends of Universal Suffrage calling for the vote. Disregarding the governor's actions as racist, the voluntary election resulted in the election of Henry C. Warmoth as a "delegate" from the territory of Louisiana. Born in Illinois in 1842, Warmoth had been a colonel under Gen. John McClernand in the Trans-Mississippi region. He remained in New Orleans at the end of the war engaging in the practice of law and politics.[31] The election was designed to demonstrate to Congress the views of Union men in Louisiana and to show the national party the support it could expect if universal suffrage were legalized.

The election encouraged the Republicans in the state as did developments in Washington the following year. Congress was considering the Fourteenth Amendment and had enacted the Civil Rights Act of 1866 (April).

Whites reacted quickly and violently to these new developments. The Wells-Democratic legislature enacted labor laws requiring "passes" for laborers leaving the plantation. Curfew laws followed such as the Opelousas Nine O'clock Rule, and vagrancy laws subjecting freedmen to conditions that closely resembled slavery.[32] Obviously, the Louisiana rebels had not repented.

Opposition reached a high point in 1866. Sensing a new mood in the nation, Governor Wells reluctantly issued the call for the Convention of 1864 to reconvene on July 30. Before the session opened, a mob of white policemen attacked the blacks who cheered the assembly from outside the convention hall. Fifty blacks were killed, a few whites, including radical A. P. Dostie, and scores injured in what historians call the New Orleans Riot of July 30, 1866. To the radical majority elected in the fall of 1866, the rebels had not submitted peacefully to the results of the war. Radicals in Congress devised a harsher plan of Reconstruction, which was embodied in the Reconstruction Acts of 1867, to settle the question of who won the war.

These new acts outlined a method of treating the South as a "conquered territory." One provision divided it into five districts governed by military commanders who were superior to state authority; black males twenty-one and over were registered as voters, while those disqualified under the proposed fourteenth amendment for supporting the Confederacy were excluded from voting. The governor and the legislature refused to take steps to implement the acts, or to repeal local municipal election laws.[33] Gen. Philip H. Sheridan, the military commander of the Louisiana and Texas District, acted decisively in supporting the measures. He dismissed state and local officials (including policemen) and the legislature. New local officials were appointed, and reorganization of authority instituted. Thomas Durant received the offer of the governorship but refused it. Benjamin F. Flanders thereafter was appointed.[34]

President Andrew Johnson was not pleased with Sheridan's action. Confronted with impeachment threats, the Tennessee Plebian wanted to soften the Reconstruction Acts. Thus, he dismissed Sheridan as commander of the district, and replaced him with Gen. Winfield Hancock. But the planned registration called for in the Acts had been inaugurated by Sheridan in August culminating in the election of delegates, on September 27 and 28, to a constitutional convention. At the New Orleans registration offices, blacks joyfully received another gain in their status as free men, their "voting papers." One correspondent of the *New Orleans Tribune,* J. Willis Menard, noted that "hundreds of colored men of all shades and ages waiting with joy-lit eyes for their turn to register. Yes, readers, they are there in City Hall." By the September voting day, 129,654 persons were registered, of which 84,436 or 65 percent were blacks.[35]

In New Orleans, blacks voted for delegates to the convention with intense eagerness. Throughout Louisiana the report was much the same. In Alexandria, one semi-hostile newspaper reported that blacks arose "long before day light" and the "steady tramp of the dark columns of the Radical Republican Clubs were heard marching into town from all streets leading into it, and soon our Town was filled, jammed and crammed with the impouring masses of the Nation's Wards marching to the music of the blue ticket and the promised land." They filed into the polls almost in military drill fashion, approached the commissioners' table and presented their registration papers. "This perfect system was kept up nearly all the time," observed the newspaper, "and the voting progressed quite fast—one hundred and forty votes to the hour being the average received." This was the scene on both days, as whites served as special policemen, attended to their private business, and looked on "with serene and cool indifference."[36] President David F. Boyd of the Louisiana State Seminary (later to become Louisiana State University) expressed the attitudes of many whites when he wrote to W. L. Sanford, vice president of the board of supervisors, that like the whole South "we have no control over politics and the nigger."[37]

Enthusiastically, blacks supported Republican candidates, black and white, with their votes. Throughout Reconstruction this was to be the norm; the Republican party was the ship, all else "was the sea." Black Democrats were often criticized, and one, Willis Rollins, was the object of threats from black Republicans.[38] Of the more than seventy-five thousand votes cast for the Constitutional Convention delegates, only four thousand were opposed. The ninety-eight delegates elected were evenly divided—forty-nine blacks and forty-nine whites—but almost all were Republicans.[39] Thus, these men so elected represented the first crop of black public officials in the history of Louisiana.

"The entrance of Negroes into the political arena was," wrote Professor John Hope Franklin, "the most revolutionary aspect of the Reconstruction program."[40] The background, and programs of the delegates were similar to the future black legislators. These men were, the early accounts maintained, a vicious ruling majority throughout the South. This is totally incorrect. Louisiana had an equal number of black and white delegates. Only South Carolina had more black delegates than whites. The other villains of Reconstruction, the carpetbaggers, were also a minority in every state except Mississippi.[41]

Not only have the number of delegates and legislators been severely questioned but their occupations and behavior as officials were made the center of controversy by historians. This criticism had little justification. All of the delegates and legislators shared similar attributes: education, native shrewdness, honorable military records, business ownership for some, and professional careers for others. Former slaves were among these elected officials, but their deportment was no reason for the hostile comments they received. They were "self-made men," wrote one source, "who through perseverance . . . and sometimes a little bit of luck, made their way up to positions of influence and importance."[42]

The first black elected officials were delegates to the Constitutional Convention of 1867-68. The majority of the delegates were in their late twenties or mid-thirties.

Captain Ingraham, from Caddo, was a thirty-five-year-old former carpenter. P. B. S. Pinchback was a former army captain, and at thirty-one, a polished politician. C. C. Antoine, an educated free man, was a grocer, barber, and a captain in the Seventh Louisiana State Militia. The thirty-seven-year-old Robert I. Cromwell, was a native of Virginia, and a medical doctor. Lieut. Jules A. Masicot had attended college for four years, and Ovide C. Blandin was a twenty-nine-year-old grocer in New Orleans. The Isabelle brothers, Thomas and Robert H., were businessmen in the city; Thomas operated a sewing machine store, and Robert was a clerk and dyer. Similarly, the Lange brothers, Robert and Victor M., were youthful businessmen from Baton Rouge. Although only Victor served in the convention, they were later elected to the 1868 legislature. The two delegates from Rapides Parish—George Y. Kelso and Samuel E. Cuney—were free men of color and property owners before the war. A native of Plaquemines Parish, twenty-five- year-old Charles T. Thibaut was one of that parish's delegates. Other black delegates were also competent: David Wilson, F.M.C., was a barber; Leopold Guichard was a young twenty-one-year-old clerk and Arnold Bertonneau was a former captain in one of Butler's regiments. The ex-slave Dennis Burrell was shrewd and a good speaker. Hy Bonseigneu was an owner of a cigar store; Fortune Riard was a lawyer, general commissioner, and later internal revenue agent.[43]

The next set of black officials were the legislators. Many of the above mentioned delegates would serve in the legislature. The background, numerical strength, performance, and property ownership of these men have been the source of much historical debate. One criticism questioned their background, supposedly, they were all illiterate ex-slaves. Contrary to these myths, the black Reconstructionists elected from 1868, after the constitution was adopted, until 1877 were capable, conscientious, and competent men. During the entire period in Louisiana only ninety-nine representatives and twenty-four black senators can be identified. In the years after Reconstruction, twenty-one additional representatives and nine black senators served.[44] Of the twenty-four senators who served, this writer has been able to identify only three who were ex-slaves. Similarly most of the black House members were free before the war. Moreover all of the senators and representatives were literate men.[45]

Other myths hold that they were without property, paid no taxes, and were contemptuous of property owners. Contrary to this view, one source indicated that "black legislators in the 1868-1870 legislature actually listed an average of $991.25 in assets in the 1870 census."[46]

Moreover, many of these delegates and black Reconstructionists in Louisiana were native-born, family men, masons, and civic leaders. Senator Pinchback, a mason, was married to Nina Hathorn and had three children.[47] Before his death in 1921, Senator Pierre Landry, a Donaldsonville native, fathered fourteen children by two marriages. All of his children received an education and entered various occupations including teachers, school founders, African Missionary worker, pharmacist, and medical doctor.[48] Henry Demas, of St. John the Baptist Parish, who served the longest term of any black in the Senate, was a family man with one child.[49] New Orleans-born Caesar C. Antoine was married and father of three children.[50] The ex-slave William Harper was married with one child, as was the ex-slave David Young.[51]

Black House members also had similar family responsibilities and civic obligations. Especially illustrative are the careers of Felix C. Antoine, Robert H. Isabelle, J. B. Jourdain, William Murrell, Octave Rey, and Moses Sterrett.[52]

Not only were these family men with children to educate, but they continued to prepare themselves by attending school. Many attended while the legislature was not in session, or after their tenures. Straight University Law School graduated P. B. S. Pinchback, Robert H. Isabelle, C. C. Antoine and L. A. Martinet. The class roll of 1874 listed other legislators who were in attendance: Joseph B. and Harry Lott, Victor Rochon, James H. Ingraham, John B. Lewis, and George Denezin.[53]

A profile of the political classification of the Reconstructionists indicate that they were either conservatives or radicals. The conservatives were mostly the white Democrats, while all blacks and a majority of the whites were radicals.[54]

Of the constitution and laws established by the Reconstruction constitutional convention and legislatures, W. E. B. DuBois wrote that they were "so wise and so well suited to the needs of the New South" that in spite of a retrogressive movement "following the removal of blacks from office much of this legislation still stands on the statute book." Although the Louisiana Constitution of 1868 lasted nine years, the constitution adopted after Reconstruction in 1879 retained some of its provisions.[55]

Beginning on November 23, 1867, the convention was in session until March 9, 1868. Some of the most sought after provisions were universal education, civil rights, a bill of rights, marriage laws, labor laws, and homestead provisions. These demands and programs indicate that the antebellum free blacks could speak for the ex-slaves. Delegate Victor Lange of East Baton Rouge favored the constitution and its universal education clause because it "secures to my child and all my children throughout the state the education for which their forefathers have been deprived of for two-hundred and fifty years."[56]

The constitution required that at least one free public school should be established in each parish, and that children from six to eighteen years of age should be eligible to attend regardless of race, color, or previous condition of servitude. A law to permit couples in common law marriage to "legalize their children" was proposed but not enacted until the legislature convened approximately a year later. Article Thirteen of the constitution embodied the notable civil rights law giving blacks equal rights and privileges upon "any conveyance of a public character."[57]

There were other provisions that affected the lives of blacks and whites in Louisiana. A rigid disfranchisement clause for ex-Confederates was opposed by several blacks. It set up state citizenship requirements and prescribed an oath, even for legislators, pledging that officeholders in the state accept the political and civil equality of all men. The legislature was given the power to adopt laws regulating the emancipation of children, divorce, and the adoption of children. Compensation by the state to slave owners for their emancipated slaves was prohibited; as well as a prohibition against the legislature enacting a property qualification for office. The Black Codes enacted by Democrats were eradicated and representation in the Assembly was based on total population. It was also the first constitution in the history of Louisiana with a formal bill of rights.[58]

The ratification of the constitution and election of state officials took place in the early spring 1868 (April 16 and 17). A recent congressional measure—that a majority of the votes cast would decide the election—applied because of the fear that many registered voters would not cast ballots. A number of tactics to prevent ratification was used by whites. A common way was to appeal to racial fears of whites. One newspaper asserted: "The issues before the people of the State in the coming election is a single one—Negro *equality.* Will all men, whigs, democrats, rebels, Americans and Union men, unite, on that one issue and VOTE DOWN THE CONSTITUTION!"[59] In spite of these sentiments the election passed off quietly, and a majority of blacks favored the constitution. It was ratified by a vote of 66,152 to 48,739. After a factional party struggle, Henry C. Warmoth was elected governor over James G. Taliaferro. Oscar J. Dunn, a black man, was elected lieutenant governor. Warmoth carried thirty so-called "black parishes" defeating Taliaferro by a vote of 64,270 to 38,118.[60]

This election resulted in blacks serving in national, state, and local offices. J. Willis Menard, Northern born and educated, was elected to Congress but was not admitted. He does hold the distinction of being the first black to speak in the House of Representatives. Charles E. Nash served in the Forty-Fourth Congress, 1874-76, from the Sixth District as the only black to represent Louisiana in Congress. A New Orleans native and former sergeant in the Union army, he was a bricklayer. The other black Louisianian to claim a seat in the 1872 Congress, P.B.S. Pinchback, was rejected. Pinchback did receive pay, totaling $16,666, for the time he would have served in the United States Senate.[61] Locally, blacks were elected to the state legislature, but did not dominate the legislature. Their membership during the entire period was roughly one-third of the total. One hostile visitor to the chambers in 1871 had to confess that the composition was "a few colored men sitting among a great majority of whites in the House of Representatives." Few blacks were chairmen, or indeed assigned, to key legislature committees.[62] The legislative laws urged and established closely parallel those set forth in the constitutional convention. In particular, black legislators unanimously supported universal education. Many wanted integrated schools but settled for segregated facilities as long as there were schools. An ex-slave, Dennis Burrell, of St. John the Baptist Parish, observed: "I want to see poor white and colored children admitted to all the blessings that flow from a perfect system of education."[63] Senator Pinchback supported integrated education because he felt that the black schools would suffer because of a lack of government support. On the whole, desegregation of New Orleans schools had some successes, but this rarely was the case in the rural parishes. Approximately 25 percent of the black children attended integrated schools in New Orleans; also, there were "more white pupils in the public schools during Reconstruction than either before or after."[64] Other educational interests of blacks included free passage to all school children on public ferries, roads and bridges. A more responsible state board of education was organized, and the newly restored state library was supported.[65]

Civil rights laws were strongly favored in the 1868 convention and the subsequent legislatures. Several were designed to enforce Article Thirteen. The black Reconstructionists, along with their white allies, enacted a total of *five* civil rights acts into the Louisiana statutory. The law of 1869 contained an *exemplary* clause: not only would the violators of the rights forfeit their business license but were subject to a fine.[66] These laws were necessary declared the *New Orleans Tribune,* maintaining that under the present "order of things, our manhood is sacrificed. The broad stamp of inferiority is put upon us."[67] Several court suits were filed, and isolated incidents of integration in theaters and taverns occurred, but blacks never tested these laws in mass protest. Senator Pinchback echoed the sentiment of most blacks on the question of forcing themselves upon whites by asserting in 1869: "I consider myself just as far above coming into an elevation with them. . . . I do not believe that any sensible colored man upon this floor would wish to be in a private part of a public place without the consent of the owners of it. It is false; it is wholesale falsehood to say that we wish to force ourselves upon white people."[68]

Other issues addressed by black legislators were rights of laborers on plantations, non-discrimination provision on rights given to railroad construction companies, incorporation of towns, relief appropriations, legislature funding for white and black institutions of higher learning, legitimizing children born of slave unions, a strict definition of vagrants, internal improvement measures, ferry privileges for themselves and others, tax measures, better oversight of charitable institutions, and larger funding for prisons, deaf, dumb and insane asylums.[69]

Blacks in executive offices did not dominate but those who served were qualified and efficiently carried out their responsibilities. No black was nominated by the entire party for governor, or held that office, although Pinchback served on an acting basis. Three blacks served as lieutenant governors, Oscar J. Dunn and Caesar C. Antoine were elected to the post, and Pinchback succeeded to the position. Northern-educated William G. Brown served as superintendent of education from 1872-76, and former Iberville Parish sugarcane planter Pierre G. Deslonde as secretary of state during these same years. The remarkable Antoine Dubuclet was state treasurer for ten years and after his records were closely scrutinized by the Democratic regime in the post-Reconstruction era, no funds were missing. This wealthy Iberville Parish sugarcane planter and family man was familiar with financing; he sent nine of his twelve children to France for their education and his plantation was valued at over $90,000 in 1864.[70] Moreover, Dubuclet's outstanding tenure takes on greater significance when one realizes that his successor, white Democrat E. A. Burke, stole $1,267,905.00 and escaped prosecution by leaving Louisiana.[71]

A small number of blacks served in other capacities during Reconstruction. More than nineteen or slightly over twenty black sheriffs were elected, the majority—seventeen—for only one term. Thirteen blacks can be identified as parish tax collectors, twelve as parish assessors, thirteen as parish coroners, two as parish judges, and four as town mayors. Although many were elected as justices of the peace, constables and police jurors, they never were elected in proportion to their number in the total population.[72]

The blacks who did serve were confronted with obstacles, overt and convert racism, hostile news reports and threats to themselves and their families. Caesar C. Antoine's son, Joseph was killed during a racial and political brawl amidst the presidential campaign of 1868.[73] Joseph L'Official was elected from East Baton Rouge Parish, but was killed by a mob on election night.[74] A Massachusetts-born and educated free black Monroe school teacher, Franklin St. Clair, was killed while returning from a speaking engagement in Morehouse Parish. He was a candidate for state representative. The man who killed him, J. T. Payne, went scot-free.[75] Black senator, Alexander Francois, was brutally murdered while serving in the legislature. In October 1875, John Gair was taken from sheriff's officers and killed while being transported from East Feliciana Parish to Baton Rouge. As his family helplessly watched, Claiborne Parish's former constitutional convention delegate, William R. Meadows, was murdered in his backyard in early 1869. Few individuals were apprehended, prosecuted, or punished for these lawless acts.[76] Although criticized and feared by white Southerners, the military occupation did not severely stop the law-breakers. Moreover, the confusion concerning the policy and role of the military added to its general inefficiency.[77] White racist organizations such as the White Camelias, White Leagues, and Ku Klux Klan were fairly rampant and received moral support from many white community leaders.[78]

Not all opposition to Republican, and especially black officeholders, was from the Democrats and white-supremacy groups. There existed deep, seated in-fighting within the Republican party. Republican Gov. Henry C. Warmoth, 1868-1872, received a great deal of criticism from fellow Republicans, black and white. Their disagreements with the governor included his corrupt deals, his veto of the civil rights acts of 1868 and 1870, his refusal to enforce the public education law, the unlimited autonomous power he possessed, and his appointment of Democrats to offices in the Customhouse. Many of these disputes culminated in the impeachment of Governor Warmoth during the latter part of his administration, called by some, "The Age of Warmoth."[79]

The other governor to serve during Reconstruction, William P. Kellogg (1872-1876), was "more hated than Warmoth had been."[80] A native of Vermont, Kellogg had lived in Illinois, and fought for a short time in the Civil War. He had been appointed by President Lincoln as collector of the port of New Orleans in 1865 and previously served as a judge in the Nebraska territory. Supported by President U. S. Grant the Kellogg era was less corrupt than Warmoth, and blacks enjoyed better relations with him. The struggle for control of the Republican party was not diminished, while bloody riots at Colfax, Coushatta, and Liberty Place (New Orleans) were applauded by the conservative press.

The ill-fated Unification Movement of 1873,—proposed by conservative business interests, and former free blacks of New Orleans—was not acceptable to the governor nor to most blacks, nor whites in the parishes roughly north of Baton Rouge. Opposed by many factors—dwindling Northern support after 1872, a divided party, the harsh depression of 1873, and ever-increasing hostility—caused the Kellogg regime to barely get underway and severely handicapped its effectiveness.[81]

These obstacles made many black efforts for progressive change uncertain. The political gains of blacks were perhaps the most tenuous and reflect their advances in other areas. Most blacks lived in the rural sections of Louisiana where their daily lives were bound to the land. They wanted to become not only voters but landowners as well. Most continued to work the land but few were permitted, or could afford to buy land, and in some cases fraud was used by the landowners and merchants to swindle them out of their hard earned wages and land. The plantation system in Louisiana, observes Roger W. Shugg, "not only survived but also expanded after the Civil War." The planters were aided in keeping their land by "cotton and sugar factors, merchants and banks of New Orleans" which extended credit and expanded "crop liens and blanket mortgages." At the same time, the planters and large landowners rejected blacks demands for higher wages, and land purchases by threatening to import Chinese and German laborers.[82] Even the Congress-enacted Southern Homestead Act of June, 1866, designed to set aside nearly forty-six million acres in five Southern states, "proved relatively unsuccessful in Louisiana." This was due to several factors: assistant commissioners sympathetic to the planter interest, loyal whites favored railroad companies rather than aspirations of blacks to become landowners, inefficiency of the land officials, and Southern white opposition.[83] Coupled with the continuation of the plantation system, the end of the Freedmen's Bureau,[84] the failure, in any respect, of the Homestead Act critically hindered landowners. Without land the blacks' economic security was uncertain.

Not all the aspirations and achievements of blacks were transitory. Freedom meant many things, and especially an opportunity to claim loved ones and families. Marriage among blacks became more the rule rather than the exception. Black legislators urged and passed laws legalizing children born of former slaves. Prof. John W. Blassingame asserts that by 1880 in New Orleans, the "average family in the black community, then, was patriarchal or male dominated. Of the 12,452 Negro families listed in the census, 9,776 (78.5 percent) were headed by males in 1880."[85] The family as an institution was under great strain due to poverty and unemployment causing many married women (30.5 percent) in New Orleans to be employed outside the home. Other stresses on the black family in New Orleans, as well as throughout the state, were high mortality rate, former system of slavery, and crime within the black communities. Despite these pressures, the black family in New Orleans, and probably throughout the state, was "remarkably strong by 1880."[86]

Educationally, black Louisianians exerted great efforts during Reconstruction. The gains were far fewer than were anticipated but they represented progress. Although slavery had stripped many blacks of personal drive, they were aware "that ignorance was the greatest threat to freedom." Historically, a small faction of the population, primarily the old free class, enjoyed some educational advantages during the antebellum period. With their aid, along with interested legislators, Northern groups, the Freedmen's Bureau, liberal minded whites, and sheer determination, blacks established many small one-room public schools, including twenty-six in New Orleans between 1868 and 1877. Three colleges were established—Straight, Leland, and New Orleans University—that offered little more than a high school education, but "probably had more impact on the community than the haphazardly public school." Supported by religious groups, especially the work of the American Missionary Association, these institutions had integrated facilities and offered a fairly broad range of courses such as law, journalism, theology, and pharmacy.[87]

Religious striving marked another high point of change for black Louisianians. Reconstruction marked the point of separation of black and white churches, for example, the division of the Methodist Church. Black membership in all denominations increased, with the Baptists having the greatest number, followed by the Methodists. Since the first Baptist doctrine in Louisiana was preached by a pioneer black evangelist, this probably had an impact on its popularity among blacks. Catholics and Presbyterians won black converts, while the Episcopalians gained the fewest members.[88]

Black intellectual expression during this era can also be noted. In antebellum New Orleans, free blacks enjoyed *Les Cenelles,* a volume of poetry, and other verses, drama, and literary publications. The popularity of the arts increased during Reconstruction, and these performers and their works reached a wider audience through the New Orleans black newspapers—*L'Union, Tribune, Louisianian* and the *Black Republican*—two of which were bilingual.[89] Other black newspapers were the *Concordia Eagle* (Vidalia), the *Grand Era* (Baton Rouge), *Lafourche Times, News Pioneer* (Iberville Parish) and the *Pointe Coupée Republican.* Although several were short-lived newspapers, and others would emerge after Reconstruction, they served as a cohesive and informative network within the black community.

Some writers contend that political Reconstruction was a failure in Louisiana, and in the South, primarily because blacks were freed and participants in the government. This negative view is incorrect. "Obviously," wrote Professor John Hope Franklin, "there are some men in both races who made their way to power through chicanery, duplicity and fraud."[90] But blacks did not commit most of the vices during the era. Undoubtedly, the odds were against blacks from the very outset of Reconstruction. Except for a few national radicals, most congressmen were never in favor of granting blacks the rights that were necessary to successfully operate as free men; indeed, many were reluctant to enforce the Constitution. Professor C. Vann Woodward reveals that many Northern radicals were more interested in keeping blacks in the South, than in protecting them and making their citizenship secure.[91] It appears then that blacks had to maximize their efforts toward gaining recognition of their rights which left little time for other activities.

Contrary to the views of early historians of the period, much of the credit for the achievements can be traced to the black membership in the legislature. First, the debates in the conventions, the legislature, and petitions in the newspapers indicate that blacks understood both the political and economic meaning of democracy; their presence made Louisiana's government more democratic. Blacks then attempted to persuade whites to accept their own doctrine of Christian brotherhood and to observe the Declaration of Independence. They spoke for universal education, civil rights, and humane treatment for the less fortunate—the blind, insane, and deaf—and within their hands and heart "the consciousness of a great and just cause" was awaken. Just as they fought willingly in the Civil War for and spoke in favor of the dignity of not only blacks but also oppressed people everywhere, they continued to do so during Reconstruction. They helped enact legislation covering property, the expanded functions of the state, and the punishment of crime which according to Dr. W.E.B. DuBois suited the needs of the New South.[92] Moreover, this era saw the nation enact the Reconstruction amendments—the Thirteenth, Fourteenth and Fifteenth—and outlaw repressive and conspiratorial acts. The participation of blacks was indispensable in completing this worthy experience called Reconstruction.[93]

Notes for "Black Louisianians During the Civil War and Reconstruction: Aspects of Their Struggles and Achievements"

[1]*Compendium of the Tenth Census* (June 1, 1880) (Washington, 1883), Part 1, 352-53.

[2]Mary F. Berry, "Negro Troops in Blue and Gray: The Louisiana Native Guards,1863," *Louisiana History,* 8 (1967): 167; Donald E. Everett, "Ben Butler and the Louisiana Native Guards, 1861-1862," *Journal of Southern History,* 24 (1958): 202.

[3]C. Peter Ripley, *Slaves and Freedmen in Civil War Louisiana* (Baton Rouge, 1976), 10; Jefferson Davis Bragg, *Louisiana in the Confederacy* (Baton Rouge, 1941), 208-10, 218-20.

[4]Ripley, *Slaves and Freedmen,* 10-12.

[5]Ibid., 12.

[6]John W. Blassingame, *Black New Orleans, 1860-1880* (Chicago, 1973), 27-28; W. Magruder Drake, "Notes and Documents," *Louisiana History,* 7 (1966): 71.

[7]Berry, "Negro Troops," 167; James M. McPherson, *The Negro's Civil War* (New York,1965), 164-65, 238.

[8]"New Orleans Riot: Report of the Select Committee," *House Reports,* 39th Cong., 2nd Sess., No. 16, pp. 12-23.

[9]Richard S. West, *Lincoln's Scapegoat General: A Life of Benjamin Butler* (Boston, 1965), 176; *New Orleans Daily Picayune,* August 27, 1862, May 29, 1863.

[10]Ripley, *Slaves and Freedmen,* 105; John D. Winters, *The Civil War in Louisiana* (Baton Rouge, 1963), 142-46.

[11]Ripley, *Slaves and Freedmen,* 122.

[12]John W. Blassingame, "The Selection of Officers and Non-Commissioned Officers of Negro Troops in the Union Army, 1863-1865," *Negro History Bulletin,* 30 (1967): 11.

[13]William Wells Brown, *The Black Man: His Antecedents, His Genius, and His Achievements* (Savannah, 1863), 301-2; Winters, *Civil War in Louisiana,* 253-54.

[14]George W. Williams, *A History of the Negro Troops in the War of Rebellion* (New York,1888), 140; Winters, *Civil War in Louisiana,* 209; Charles Dufour, *Ten Flags in the Wind* (New York, 1967), 238; McPherson, *Negro's Civil War,* 9-10.

[15]Ripley, *Slaves and Freedmen,* 25-27. This policy was followed despite the Confiscation Act of March which prohibited the return of runaways; William F. Messner, "Black Violence and White Response: Louisiana 1862," *Journal of Southern History,* 61 (1975): 30-31.

[16]Blassingame, *Black New Orleans,* 33; Many blacks in Confederate-controlled areas of the South, especially North Louisiana, did not learn of the Emancipation until June 19, 1865; blacks in these areas have celebrated June tenth as their date of liberation.

[17]Kenneth E. Shrewmaker and Andrew K. Printz, eds., "A Yankee in Louisiana: Selections from the Diary and Correspondence of Henry R. Gardner, 1862-1866," *Louisiana History,* 5 (1964): 278; John W. Blassingame, "Union Army as an Educational Institution for Negroes, *1862-1865,"Journal of Negro Education,* 34 (1965): 152-59.

[18]*New Orleans Tribune,* January 12, 14, 1865.

[19]*New Orleans L'Union,* September 27, 1862; F. Patrick Leavens, *"L'Union* and the *New Orleans Tribune* and Louisiana Reconstruction" (M.A. Thesis, Louisiana State University, 1966), 40-42.

[20]"Louisiana," *The American Annual Cyclopedia and Register of Important Events of the Year 1863* (New York, 1865), 591-92.

[21]Amos Simpson and Vaughan Baker, "Michael Hahn: Steady Patriot," *Louisiana History,* 13 (1972): 236-46.

[22]Joe Gray Taylor, *Louisiana Reconstructed, 1863-1877* (Baton Rouge, 1974), 47-49.

[23]Shrewmaker and Prinz, eds., "Yankee in Louisiana." 291-92; Roger W. Shrugg, *Origins of Class Struggle in Louisiana* (Baton Rouge, 1939), 201-10.

[24]John Ficklen, *Reconstruction in Louisiana: (Through 1868)* (Baltimore, 1910), 67-87.

[25]*New Orleans Tribune,* November 10, 12, 15, 16, 18, 22, 1864; the *Tribune* was described by one black as a "bold free-suffrage exponent, and never compromise principle for policy," see *New York Anti-Slavery Standard,* May 11, 1867. Initiated on July 21, 1864, the *Tribune* was the first black daily, with the exception on Monday, in America.

[26]*New Orleans Tribune,* September 22, October 11, 1864, George M. Fredrickson, "A Man but Not Brother: Abraham Lincoln and Racial Equality," *Journal of Southern History,* 61 (1975): 57-58; Lerone Bennett, "Was Abe Lincoln A White Supremacist," *Ebony Magazine, 23* (1968): 35-43.

[27]David Rankin, "The Origins of Black Leadership in New Orleans During Reconstruction," *Journal of Southern History,* 60 (1974): 420-21,436-40.

[28]"Louisiana," *The American Annual Cyclopedia and Register of Important Events of the Year 1865* (New York, 1866), 515-16; *New Orleans Tribune,* May 23, 24, June 6, 1865.

[29]*New Orleans Tribune,* June 6, 1865.

[30]Blassingame, *Black New Orleans,* 108-12; Broadside in the American Missionary Association Archives, Amistad Research Center, Louisiana Files, Dillard University.

[31]Henry C. Warmoth, *War, Politics and Reconstruction: Stormy Days in Louisiana* (New York, 1930), 24-25.

[32]"New Orleans Riot: Report of the Select Committee" *House Reports,* 39th Congress, 2nd Sess. No. 16. passim; Donald E. Reynolds, "The New Orleans Riot of 1866, Reconsidered," *Louisiana History* (1964), passim; James G. Randall and David Donald, *The Civil War and Reconstruction* (Lexington, Mass., 1969), 594-98.

[33]Warmoth, *War, Politics,* 273-78; *New Orleans Tribune,* July 19, 20, December 22, 1865.

[34]Roger A. Fischer, "A Pioneer Protest: The New Orleans Street Car Controversy of *1867,*" *Journal of Negro History,* 53 (1968): 228-29; *Personal Memoirs of P. H. Sheridan, General United States Army* (New York, 1888), 3, 253-54; 266-67, 274; *New Orleans Tribune,* June 4, 1867.

[35]Eric L. McKitrick, *Andrew Johnson and Reconstruction* (Chicago, 1960), 494-95; *New York Anti-Slavery Standard,* May 11, 1867; Fawn M. Brodie, *Thaddeus Stevens, Scourge of the South* (New York, 1959), 315-16.

[36]*Alexandria* (La.) *Democrat,* October 2, 1867.

[37]D. F. Boyd to W. L. Sandford, August 6, 1867 in David F. Boyd Letters, Fleming Collection, Box 5. Folder 33, Department of Archives, Louisiana State University.

[38]*New Orleans Daily Picayune,* July 23, 1868; *New Orleans Republican,* July 30, 31, August 4, 1868; October 17, 1871.

[39]*Daily Picayune,* June 23, 1871; Ficklen, *History of Reconstruction,* 193.

[40]John Hope Franklin, *Reconstruction: After the Civil War* (Chicago, 1961), 86.

[41]Ibid., 102-3.

[42]John Hope Franklin, "Reconstruction and the Negro" in *New Frontiers of the American Reconstruction,* ed. Harold M. Hyman (Chicago, 1966), 74.

[43]Charles Vincent, *Black Legislators in Louisiana During Reconstruction* (Baton Rouge, 1976), 49-58.

[44]Ibid., 221-22.

[45]Ibid., 224-25.

[46]Howard J. Jones, "The Members of the Louisiana Legislature of 1868: Images of Radical Reconstruction Leadership in the Deep South" (Ph.D. dissertation, Washington State University, 1975), 228.

[47]Civil War Pension Files, Records of the Veterans Administration Record Group 15, National Archives (hereinafter cited as Civil War Pension Files) James Haskins, *Pickney Benton Steward Pinchback* (New York, 1973).

[48]Interview, Lillian Landry Dunn, daughter of legislator Landry, August 7, 1974, New Orleans; *New Orleans Times Picayune,* December 24, 1921.

[49]Civil War Pension Files, RG 15, NA.

[50]Jones, "Members of the Legislature," 25.

[51]*U.S. Census* Population Schedule, 1870, Concordia Parish, Vidalia, Ward 4, 54; *Senate Report,* 46th Cong., 34d Sess., No. 855, xviii, 368-73.

[52]Civil War Pension Files, RG 15, NA.

[53]Rev. E. M. Cravath, D.D., field secretary of the American Missionary Association Class Roll for the Law Department of Straight University, June 1, 1874, Box 59, Amistad Research Center, Louisiana Files; Blassingame, *Black New Orleans,* 118-20.

[54]Jones, "Members of the Legislature," 147, 164, 182, 184, 191.

[55]W. E. B. DuBois, "Reconstruction and Its Benefits," *American Historical Review,* 15 (1910): 798-99.

[56]*Official Journal of the Proceedings of the Convention for Framing a Constitution for the State of Louisiana* (New Orleans, 1867-68), 201, 289.

[57]*Journal of the Proceedings,* 96-97, 121, 125, 242.

[58]*Constitution of the State of Louisiana with Amendments* (New Orleans, 1875).

[59]*Bossier Banner,* March 21, 28, 1868.

[60]Wyona Mills, "James G. Taliaferro (1798-1876): Louisiana Unionist and Scalawag" (M.A. thesis, Louisiana State University, 1968), 76-85.

[61]Edith Menard, "John Willis Menard, First Negro Elected to the U.S. Congress, First Negro to speak in the U.S. Congress: A Documentary," *Negro History Bulletin,* 27 (1964): 104-12; *Haskins, Pinchback,* 196-222.

[62]Robert Somers, *The Southern States Since the War, 1870-71* (University, Ala., 1965), 226-27; Vincent, *Black Legislators,* passim.

[63]*Debates of the Senate of the State of Louisiana* (1870) (New Orleans, 1870), 183-84.

[64]Louis R. Harlan, "Desegregation in New Orleans Public Schools during Reconstruction," *American Historical Review,* 67 (1962): 667-68; Blassingame, *Black New Orleans,* 121.

[65]*New Orleans Times,* June 21, 1870; Leon O. Beasley, "A History of Education in Louisiana During Reconstruction, 1862-1877" (Ph.D. dissertation, 1957), 45-95, 130-131; *Official Journal of the Proceedings of the House of Representatives of the State of Louisiana* (New Orleans, 1868), 217.

[66]*House Journal, 1869,* 20, 41, 55, 59; *Official Journal of the Proceedings of the Senate of the State of Louisiana, 1869* (New Orleans, 1869), 10, 67, 73, 91, 93, 95-96.

[67]*New Orleans Tribune,* February 7, 9, 12, 13, 18, 19, 21, 1869; the February 7 issue contains the above comment.

[68]Ella Lonn, *Reconstruction in Louisiana (After 1868)* (New York and London, 1918), 40-41.

[69]Vincent, *Black Legislators,* Chapters 4, 5, 6, 7, passim.

[70]William J. Hair, *Bourbonism and Agrarian Protest: Louisiana Politics, 1877-1900* (Baton Rouge, 1969); Tax Assessment Rolls, Iberville Parish, Comptroller's office, State Capitol, Baton Rouge, microfilm copy of original; H. E. Sterkx, *The Free Negro in Antebellum Louisiana* (Rutherford, N. J., 1972), 208.

[71]Hair, *Bourbonism,* 141.

[72]Vincent, *Black Legislators,* 220-22; the city of Baton Rouge remained largely under white Democratic control, see Terry L. Seip, "Municipal Politics and the Negro: Baton Rouge, 1865-1888" in Mark T. Carlton et al., *Readings in Louisiana Politics* (Baton Rouge, 1975), 242-66.

[73]Jones, "Members of the Legislature," 25.

[74]*Baton Rouge Weekly Advocate,* August 6, November 12, 1870; *House Journal, 1871,* 16, 18; *New Orleans Republican,* January 8, 1871.

[75]*Ouachita Telegraph,* April 22, 1868, quoted in the *New Orleans Times,* April 25, May 1, 1868.

[76]W.E.B. DuBois, *Black Reconstruction in America, 1860-1880* (New York, 1935), 672; James E. Sefton, *The United States Army and Reconstruction, 1865-1877* (Baton Rouge, 1967), 239-51; 261-63; *New Orleans Republican,* September 1, 3, 4, 5, 13, 1874 on White Leaguers; *Minden Democrat* quoted in September 5, 6, 1874 issues; *New Orleans Republican,* January 29, 1875.

[77]Sefton, *United States Army,* 252-54; 261-62.

[78]Allie B. Webb, "Organization and Activities of the Knights of the White Camellia in Louisiana, 1867-1869," *The Proceedings of the Louisiana Academy of Science,* 17 (1954): 110-18, *New Orleans Republican,* February 25, 28, March 1, 1876.

[79]Lonn, *Reconstruction,* 73-74; Althea D. Pitre, "The Collapse of the Warmoth Regime," *Louisiana History,* 6 (1965); Francis B. Harris, "Henry Clay Warmoth, Reconstruction Governor of Louisiana," *Louisiana Historical Quarterly,* 30 (1947): 622-23; F. Wayne Binning, "Henry C. Warmoth and Louisiana Reconstruction" (Ph.D. dissertation, University of North Carolina, 1969), passim.

[80]Taylor, *Louisiana Reconstructed,* 253.

[81]Ibid., 310-11; DuBois, *Black Reconstruction,* 684-85; Mamie Johnson, "The Colfax Riot of April, 1873," *Louisiana Historical Quarterly,* 8 (1930): 411-19; Stuart O. Landry, *The Battle of Liberty Place: The Overthrow of Carpetbag Rule in New Orleans, September 14, 1874* (New Orleans, 1955), passim.

[82]Roger W. Shrugg, "Survival of the Plantation System in *Louisiana,"Journal of Southern History,* 3 (1937): 313-15; 323-25; E. Russ Williams, Jr., "Louisiana's Public and Private Immigration Endeavors: 1866-1893," *Louisiana History,* 15 (1974): 153-73.

[83]Claude F. Oubre, "'Forty Acres and a Mule': Louisiana and the Homestead Act," *Louisiana History,* 17 (1976): 143, 157; Milfred C. Fierce, "Black Struggle for Land During Reconstruction," *Black Scholar,* 5 (1974): 13-18; Kenneth M. Stampp, *The Era of Reconstruction 1865-1877* (New York, 1965), 205-6, 214; *Alexandria Democrat,* November 20, 1867, for a convention of planters who refused to hire blacks; for the laborer-planter disputes in St. Mary and Terrebonne parishes over wages, see *New Orleans Republican,* January, 1874, passim; the March 16 issue has comments on the "Consolidation Association of the Planters of Louisiana"; see also the January 26, February 2, 9,16, 23, 25, 1876 issues.

[84]Howard A. White, *The Freedmen's Bureau in Louisiana* (Baton Rouge, 1970), 102; J. Thomas May "The Freedman's Bureau at the Local Level: A Study of a Louisiana Agent," *Louisiana History,* 9 (1968): 9-10, passim.

[85]Blassingame, *Black New Orleans,* 92; see tables 10, 11, 14.

[86]Ibid., 92, 102-5.

[87]Ibid., Chapter 5, passim, especially pages 108, 122, 124-26; Betty Porter "Negro Education in Louisiana, *Louisiana Historical Quarterly,* 25 (1942): 778-800; Jacquelyn S. Haywood, "The American Missionary Association in Louisiana during Reconstruction" (Ph.D. dissertation, University of California, Los Angeles, 1974), 50, 128-45; 162-64; William Hicks, *History of the Louisiana Negro Baptists, from 1804 to 1914* (Nashville, 1914), 29.

[88]Hicks, *Negro Baptists,* 17, 21, passim; Taylor, *Louisiana Reconstructed,* 430-54.

[89]Charles B. Rousseve, *The Negro in Louisiana* (New Orleans, 1937), 56-91; Rousseve, *The Negro in New Orleans,* 7-9; Rodolphe Lucien Desdunes, *Our People and Our History,* ed., Sister Dorothea Olga McCants (Baton Rouge, 1973), 10-45, passim.

[90]Franklin, "Reconstruction of the Negro," 74.

[91]C. Vann Woodward, "Seeds of Failure in Radical Race Policy" in *Frontiers. . . .,* ed. Hyman, 132-34.

[92]DuBois, "Reconstruction and Its Benefits," 798-99; Stampp, *Reconstruction,* 213-15.

[93]For critically reading this essay, the author wishes to thank Garland Millet, Thomas J. Davis, and E. Russ Williams.

LAND, LABOR, AND CAPITAL*

John W. Blassingame

The Negro in New Orleans quickly learned the responsibilities of free labor and managed to compete successfully against whites in many areas of economic life. This was especially true in certain occupations in which black workers initially garnered a disproportionate share of the jobs and managed to hold on to them until they were frozen out by white unions in the twentieth century. Although they did not compete as successfully against whites in the professions and industry, blacks obtained a significant share of the brokerage houses, retail groceries, cigar factories, and tailoring shops in the city. Negroes also began to learn more about the complexities of business organization and management and the nature and functions of labor unions; a number of the unions and businesses formed during this period were so strong that they lasted well into the twentieth century. Most of the economic failures of the Negro were due to forces outside the black community: racial discrimination, national and local depressions, and the indifference and criminal negligence of federal officials.

Often prohibited from obtaining loans and barred from jobs in even the most prosperous of times, the Negro began his economic venture into freedom in an unpropitious period. During Reconstruction New Orleans was still suffering from the long general depression in its economy which began in the early 1850s after the railroads began to tap the Mississippi Valley, upon which the commercial life of the city depended. The disruptions caused by the Civil War, the national depression of 1873, periodic yellow fever epidemics, riots, political crises, and by the blockage of the mouth of the Mississippi all exacerbated the situation. The rapid increase in the Negro population in the city between 1862 and 1880 simply added to the number of persons who were competing for the limited number of jobs which were available. Then, too, the initial

*First published as Chapter 3 in John W. Blassingame, *Black New Orleans, 1860-1880* (© 1973 by The University of Chicago), 49-77. Reprinted with the kind permission of the publisher.

attempts of Union officials to systematize labor in Louisiana were in many ways worse than the evils they sought to correct.[1]

The thousands of unemployed, ragged, penniless, and starving whites and Negroes in New Orleans in May 1862 posed a problem of massive proportions for Union officials. Even before the Union army occupied the city, thousands of hungry people were regularly receiving rations from the Confederate relief organization, the New Orleans Free Market. The situation was so serious that Benjamin Butler declared on September 1, 1862, that "the condition of the people here is a very alarming one. They have literally come down to starvation."[2] By the end of September 1862, Butler was issuing $50,000 worth of food per month to whites in New Orleans. Between January 1863 and March 1865 the number of white families receiving rations from the Union army varied from four to nine thousand.[3]

The ubiquitous refugee Negro added greatly to the relief problems Union officials faced. Often barefoot, half naked, and lame, sometimes old, feeble, and wracked with disease, the fugitives posed an immediate health problem and strained the ability of authorities to maintain law and order.[4] One officer reported in June 1862 that there arrived at his camp daily hundreds of fugitives who were "quite destitute of provisions, many having eaten nothing for days." On January 27, 1863, W. H. Emory asserted that there were continually arriving in the city Negroes who were "in a wretched and destitute condition, mostly unfit for labor or self support." As the number of fugitives escaping to New Orleans increased and Union officials brought thousands of blacks from the interior to the city, relief supplies were taxed to their utmost and life inside the refugee camps deteriorated rapidly. F. S. Nickerson, an army officer, described a typical camp:

> The Negro Quarters are wretchedly poor. But very few of any suitable materials have been provided of which to construct them. A few individuals might occupy them with some degree of comfort, but to crowd so many together in so small a compass is simply brutish. Nearly all of the huts are open and leaky—incapable of protecting either from rain or cold. Many of them are much more suitable for hog-pens than for human beings to inhabit.[5]

Union officials made several moves to alleviate the dangerous situation confronting them. First, they built more temporary shelters and issued rations to the fugitives; by September 1862 Butler was feeding about 10,000 black refugees. Secondly, in order to relieve overcrowding in the camps, army officers seized several abandoned buildings to house the blacks. The refugees' ignorance of sanitation defeated many of the efforts to protect their health. On March 17, 1864, for instance, the military mayor reported that "the colored population of this city are in many cases generating disease, by living in unsuitable tenements, habits of idleness and total disregard for the laws of health."[6]

With little work available for them, many blacks either lived in idleness or engaged in petty pilfering; others simply walked the streets aimlessly. In an effort to end vagrancy and to teach the fugitives that they had to support themselves, hundreds were put to work in the Quartermaster Corps, on the levees, and in constructing fortifications for which they received wages, clothes, and food. The army could not, of course, employ all of the black refugees. When Banks arrived in New Orleans he "found many thousand Negroes in idleness."[7] Banks tried to end this by strictly enforcing vagrancy laws against Negroes and increasing the number of plantations to which they could be sent. He insisted that the blacks were not forced onto these plantations, but that they were "encouraged" to go to them. The primary "encouragement" was undoubtedly Banks's coupling his January 1863 order that all able-bodied Negroes must work with his flat refusal to give rations to them. In January and March 1863 only 9 Negro families received rations; only 1,000 of the 10,286 families receiving rations in December 1863 were black. While Negroes constituted about 25 percent of the city's population during this period, they did not constitute as much as 20 percent of the total number of families on relief (1,284 our of 5,313) until March 1865.[8]

Realizing the importance of working the plantations in order to revive the commercial life of New Orleans and to add money to Union coffers, Banks met with several white planters and prominent Orleanians shortly after his arrival in the Crescent City. In January 1863 he inaugurated one of the earliest and most thorough systems to reconstruct labor and agriculture in the South. Asserting that able-bodied blacks had to work for their living, Banks had all those without visible means of support in New Orleans arrested and placed on plantations whey they signed annual contracts with planters who agreed to pay them from three to ten dollars per month.[9] The integrity of the laborer's family, his right to cultivate garden plots, to choose his employer, and to educate his children were guaranteed. While no corporal punishment was permitted, army officials were to promote the "subordination" of laborers and could punish them by fines, imprisonment in stocks, and expulsion from the plantation. Each laborer had to have a pass to leave the plantation and was liable for any damage to his employer's property.[10]

The linchpin of the labor system was the parish provost marshal. Ostensibly detailed to act as a referee between planters and freedmen and to make sure that both abided by the terms of the contract they had signed, the provost marshal soon replaced the slave patroller as a means of keeping laborers in subjection. The provost marshals, often young and inexperienced army officers, usually began their work conscientiously and fairly. They were soon seduced, however, by the hospitality, the wine, the dinners, and the flattery of the planters, and some of them caught blacks who ran away from the plantations, permitted floggings, and placed soldiers on the plantations to make sure the laborers worked. Frequently the provost marshals were unscrupulous and actively worked with the planters to keep the freedmen in thralldom.[11] Playing on the blacks' trust in Yankee blue, these men often disregarded Banks's regulations with impunity.[12]

Banks insisted that his system had "been established upon the basis of absolute emancipation, recognizing the entire freedom of the laborer, and securing to him a compensation at least equal to that paid labor of a like character in any part of the country." Three of Banks's officers, Chaplain T. W. Conway, B. Rush Plumly (chairman of the Department of the Gulf's Board of Education for Freedmen), and Chaplain George H. Hepworth, along with philanthropist Gerritt Smith, agreed with these views. On June 15, 1863, Hepworth, who had visited several of the plantations, claimed that "the Labor System as a whole is a decided success." In 1865 Conway wrote to Banks of "the wonderful benefits of your Louisiana policy."[13] A number of blacks also applauded the system because it gave the freedmen an opportunity to earn wages, protected their families, and provided education for them. Banks wrote his wife in February 1863 that "the better class of colored people are doing all they can to aid me as they think it is the first chance the Negro slave has had to try his hand."[14] Some proof of this appeared in March 1865 when the Cailloux Equal Rights League Number 9 passed resolutions thanking Banks for all he had done for blacks in Louisiana. When Banks returned to New Orleans after a brief absence in April 1865, hundreds of the city's Negroes greeted his boat, and the *Black Republican* published an original poem in his honor.[15]

The *Black Republican*, organized with the assistance of one of Banks's cohorts, Thomas W. Conway, was the general's most enthusiastic supporter. It insisted that only the old free Negroes opposed the labor system; the freedmen, its chief beneficiaries, realized that it was the best system in the country, that it had protected and nursed them in the first days of freedom. The freedmen, the *Black Republican* argued, lauded Banks because it was he "who gave them homes when they were homeless; wages and employment when they were in want; schools and teachers, books and Bibles, when they never had them before."[16] Banks's humane policy had saved the poor, defenseless blacks from starvation and ruin. The *Black Republican* summarized its views on May 18, 1865, when it asserted that

> the poor, who are nine-tenths of the whole colored population, are rising rapidly each day under the beneficent and humane policy instituted by him for their good. . . .
> There is no Department in the South where our poor brethren are so well cared for, or where they are so far advanced as they are in this. By another year we believe Gen. Banks will bring all labor systems to an end, because by his practical good sense, the freedmen will have risen to a point where they can take care of themselves, claiming and defending their own rights as other people do.

However, free Negroes, contrary to the claims made by Banks and the *Black Republican*, bitterly assailed his policy. Try as they could, they could see little difference between the system and antebellum slavery; laborers were restricted to the plantations, were bound by contract to work for a year, and had to retire at night at a certain hour. Forced to purchase provisions from their employers at ruinously high prices, the laborers obtained little benefit from the wages they received.[17] The wages were so low, according to the *Tribune*, that "the condition of the slave is not materially altered." Describing Banks's system as a "bastard regime" and semi-slavery which was "not complete liberty, but mitigated bondage," the *Tribune* compared the labor regulations with antebellum plantation rules published in *DeBow's Review*. The *Tribune* author was "unable to perceive any material difference [, with the exception of the lash,] between the two sets of regulations. All the important prohibitions imposed upon the slave, are also enforced against the freedman."[18]

Furthermore, the former slaveholder was one of the chief guardians of the Negro in Banks's labor system—another reason why most New Orleans Negroes rejected it. The planters were too interested in maintaining slavery under another name; they established wages without any reference to the laborer or market conditions and unilaterally determined the amount of clothing and provisions each family received. The lessees of abandoned plantations were even worse; they were so bent on making money that they took little interest in feeding and clothing the freedmen.[19] Henry Warner, a free Negro, begged Banks to revise his system in February 1863 because the "selfish and mean" planters were "only after to catch Negroes back which by Law and God they have no right to do." In 1864 George Hanks, the superintendent of the Bureau of Free Labor, asserted that the spirit of slavery was still alive among many planters who were "even more rampant to enslave the negro [*sic*] than ever before. They make great endeavors to recover *what they call their own negroes* [*sic*]. One planter offered me $5,000 to return his negroes [*sic*]. They have even hired men to steal them from my own camp."[20]

The *Tribune* opposed the idea of apprenticeship precisely because such attitudes were so pervasive in the white community in Louisiana. It cited the central problem of Banks's system on January 12, 1865, when it charges, "there is no white man in a slaveholding country fit to be a negro's [*sic*] guardian. The reason apprenticeship has failed is not because the blacks were not submissive, but because the whites were tyrants, as they always have been."

Despairing of modifying the labor system, the wealthy free Negroes, professing a deep sense of noblesse oblige and racial commitment, began in 1864 to organize to protect the freedmen. They argued that unless the wealthy and educated Negroes tried to educate, aid, and counsel the freedmen they would continue to be oppressed. At a meeting in December 1864 New Orleans Negroes organized the Louisiana Equal Rights League to promote the moral, educational, and industrial development of the black community. the league sent agents to the parishes to check on the condition of the freedmen, appealed to military officials for the redress of grievances, called for the establishment of more schools and asylums, and organized the Bureau of Industry to aid Negroes in New Orleans. In his first monthly report in March 1865, James H. Ingraham, superintendent of Bureau of Industry, declared that during February the bureau had received and spent $251 in obtaining rations for 190 of the 192 persons who applied for them, had written letters for 36 persons, had obtained employment for 32 of the 37 persons who applied for it, had obtained passes for 22 and been instrumental in getting 11 people out of jail, had obtained wood and coal for several people, and had given general assistant to 586 people.[21]

Members of the Equal Rights League, the *Tribune*, and several whites urged the wealthy free Negroes to help the freedmen to rent plantations. In 1864 the *Tribune* called upon the free Negroes to form a farmer's association to buy the abandoned plantations and lease them to the freedmen to be worked on shares. Not only would this be a good investment for the free Negroes, it would also bind their interest to those of the freedmen, give free Negroes an opportunity to break the power of the old planters, and help the freedmen learn to be self-reliant. Under the *Tribune's* plan the laborers would feed and clothe themselves, be free to move about, and receive monthly or weekly wages and a share of the crop.[22] The free Negroes had a golden opportunity: "We can give the freedmen under the influence of liberty, moral benefits and social enjoyment all he estimates and contend[s] for. Let us go to work, organize labor-colonies, and elevate our emancipated brethren, at the same time that we take our legitimate share in the cultivation of the country."[23]

The several groups trying to lease abandoned plantations for the freedmen formed the New Orleans Freedmen's Aid Association on February 27, 1865. The objectives of the association were to rent and lease plantations, to give loans, and to furnish supplies, education, and useful information to the freedmen. The members of the association also proposed the establishment of a bank, but they did not have enough capital to do so. In order to help finance its activities, each member of the association had to pay $20 in dues annually. Some of the wealthiest Negroes in New Orleans were among the sixty members of the association; they included J. B. Roudanez, coproprietor of the *Tribune*, grocer Victor Pessou, brokers Sidney Thezan, John Clay, and Aristide Mary, poet Camille Thierry, and Oscar J. Dunn, along with several others. Benjamin F. Flanders and Thomas J. Durant were the best-known white men who were members of the association.

The association appealed to Northerners and other freedmen's organizations for money, agricultural implements, and supplies, and sent agents into the parishes to investigate conditions. By August 1865 the association had rented several plantations, made loans to freedmen with a lien on their crops, furnished horses, seeds, and provisions to many laborers, and established prizes "to incite the industry and heighten the zeal of the Freedmen." Unfortunately, the rapid return of the plantations to their owners after the war effectively ended the work of the association.[24]

The Negroes in New Orleans clearly realized that their own economic position could not be secured without some fundamental changes in Louisiana's economy. It was obvious, for example, that too many Negroes were landless and that as such they were subject to every whim of the white planters. For instance, immediately after the war Louisiana planters combined to bar Negroes from renting or buying land. The *New Orleans Tribune* repeatedly called upon the legislature to break up these combinations because they were designed "to keep the colored people in subjection, so that their wages, their votes, their movements may be controlled by the whites. This is a kind of slavery to which our people will not submit."[25] In order to end such practices, the *Tribune* urged the Union to confiscate rebel property, and Negroes to settle on the public lands in Louisiana.

The economic philosophy of the Negroes in New Orleans centered on racial uplift, cooperation, and resistance to white exploitation of blacks. Blacks had to prove that they would work in freedom, support their families, churches, and schools, and end dependency and vagrancy in their community. The road to success, to respect from whites, to political and civil equality, and to self-respect, blacks felt, was through diligence, industry, frugality, self-denial, sobriety, and faithful and honest toil. In speeches and editorials Negro leaders in New Orleans tried to inculcate these virtues in the black community. It was only through consistent labor that Negroes could gain some measure of independence and obtain and maintain their rights.[26]

Although their efforts to find employment were often hampered by the periodic economic depressions in New Orleans, most blacks took advantage of the opportunities available to them. A few observers, however, complained that they were addicted to idleness. Friedrick Gerstäcker, a German traveler, found, he declared, thousands of "black idlers" drifting around the city in 1867. White-owned newspapers in New Orleans frequently repeated these charges, but the comments of disinterested observers disprove them. When Hilary Skinner arrived in New Orleans and saw the many Negro workers, he asked, "If the blacks will not work for wages, and work hard too, then are we gazing on sable phantoms of prodigious strength?" Maria Waterbury observed in 1869 that Negroes were "doing most of the work" in New Orleans.[27]

For the most part, statistical indices support the contentions of Skinner and Waterbury. Not only did blacks constitute a significant element in the New Orleans laboring population, they worked at several different kinds of skilled jobs during the Reconstruction period. A large percentage of the black artisans had learned their trades during the antebellum period, and most, undoubtedly, came from the free Negro class.[28] Discounting mortality, mobility, and other factors, if all the free Negro artisans listed in the 1860 census were still in New Orleans in 1870 they would have accounted for 60 percent of the Negro shoemakers, 52 percent of the printers, 51 percent of the tinners, 48 percent of the masons, 35 percent of the carpenters and joiners, and 100 percent of the tailors, while constituting only 13 percent of all black laborers.[29]

As a result of the training he received during the antebellum period, the New Orleans Negro was probably more highly skilled than black laborers in any other city in the United States. The black occupational structure was very complex. Negro males were engaged in 75 different occupations in 1860; 153 in 1870; and 156 in 1880. Many of them were skilled artisans: in 1880, 48 percent of them were engaged in skilled occupations. While most skilled blacks were heavily concentrated in the building trades, a few blacks were heavily concentrated in the building trades, a few blacks also worked as cabinetmakers, jewelers, engineers, bookkeepers, pilots, florists, photographers, and druggists.[30]

The Negro laborer had to fight against great obstacles in order to obtain and to hold his job. First of all, he was illiterate. In 1870 the illiteracy rate of Negro males over ten years of age in New Orleans was 57 percent. Secondly, the Negro laborer suffered more from periodic economic depressions than any other group: white employers were reluctant to hire him during boom periods, and fired him first during hard times. Because of this, he was often engaged in an unequal struggle against white workers. Negroes were excluded from some labor unions and sometimes were attacked when it appeared they were taking jobs from whites. For example, in 1880 white stevedores "forcibly drove the colored men away, by clubbing some, cutting others, and many had to take refuge in stores along the Levee."[31] Because of the violence and discrimination, the Negro male, while he represented only 25 and 23 percent of the labor force in 1870 and 1880, constituted 52 and 44 percent of the unskilled laborers, and 57 and 60 percent of the servants in those years.

In spite of discrimination, blacks were able to garner a disproportionate share of certain skilled jobs. While Negroes constituted only 25 percent of all jobs as steamboat-men, draymen, masons, bakers, carpenters, cigarmakers, plasterers, barbers, and gardeners in 1870. By 1880, though the percentages had changed, Negroes were still overre-presented in many of these occupations: constituting only 23 percent of the total labor force, Negroes held from 25 to 52 percent of the skilled jobs mentioned above.

Since foreign-born workers constituted 49 and 33 percent of the total number of laborers in New Orleans in 1870 and 1880, they represented the Negroes' chief competitors for jobs. The foreign-born workers were much more highly skilled than the Negro: in 1870, 86 percent of them were skilled. The differences in the occupational patterns of the two groups, however, enabled the Negro to hold on to some jobs. Negro workers tended to concentrate on a limited number of jobs, while foreign-born workers were spread almost evenly through the occupational ladder. For example, while 83 percent of all Negro workers were concentrated in thirteen occupations, only 31 percent of the foreign-born workers were represented in the eight occupations in which they were most heavily concentrated. Because of the differences in occupational patterns, Negroes held a larger percentage of the total number of jobs in 1870 and 1880 than did foreign-born workers in such occupations as steamboatmen, masons, cigarmakers, plasterers, coopers, and bakers.

As the number of foreign-born workers declined in the 1870s, the nature of the economic competition between them and Negroes changed. By 1880 both groups were being challenged in a number of occupations by native-born whites. The foreign-born were hardest hit by competition from native whites. Although there were seven occupations in 1870 and 1880 in which the percentage of the foreign-born workers exceeded their percentage of the total labor force, their representation in most occupations fell drastically. The percentage of all foreign-born workers had declined in 1880 by 12 to 50 percentage points from their share in 1870 in such occupations as butchers, shoemakers, fishermen, tinners, blacksmiths, barbers, wheelwrights, coopers, cabinet-makers, draymen, carpenters, and painters. In such occupations as steamboatmen, garden-ers, printers, cigarmakers, and masons their share declined by from 0.8 to 8 percentage points from 1870. In most of these occupations the Negro's percentage of the total number of workers declined from 1870 to 1880 by from 1 to 11 percentage points.

   While the percentage point decline of the Negro was smaller than that of the foreign-born worker in most occupations, the Negro's situation was frequently more serious. Negroes, for example, lost almost half of their share of the jobs as butchers, wheel-wrights, and printers. They were already seriously underrepresented in these occupations in 1870. Only in one occupation, fishing, did Negroes threaten foreign-born workers in the 1870s; they took over almost all the fishing jobs lost by the foreign-born workers. While the foreign-born workers' share of fishing jobs declined by 22 percentage points, the Negro's share increased by 22 percentage points between 1870 and 1880. Negroes also gained a larger share of the shoemaker, cabinetmaker, cooper, machinist, and blacksmith jobs, but the native-born white workers garnered the largest proportion of those jobs lost by the foreign-born. Even so, Negro artisans were able to maintain their supremacy in many jobs until the twentieth century. This was facilitated largely by the relative absence of white-union—controlled apprenticeship programs. Instead of having to struggle against the monolithic wall raised by omnipresent whites-only unions which existed in other cities, young Negroes in New Orleans could learn trades on an informal basis from their relatives or by becoming the apprentices of black artisans.[32]

   The occupational base which blacks established during Reconstruction served them well into the twentieth century. Because blacks held on to many jobs, for instance, they had to be included in some fashion in labor unions. Although there were relatively few blacks who served a formal apprenticeship, enough young men learned trades from their fathers, relatives, and friends during Reconstruction and afterwards for blacks to continue their strong representation in these trades. The connection between the Reconstruction patterns and the occupations of blacks in New Orleans in the twentieth century is obvious. In 1910, as in 1880, Negroes held a disproportionately high percentage of all jobs as boatmen, draymen, shoemakers, carpenters, coopers, masons, plasterers, and tobacco workers. The picture was generally the same in 1930. By that year a higher percentage of Negro men were engaged in a number of other occupations than their representation in the total labor force. These occupations included longshoremen, firemen (manufacturing), sawmill operatives, roofers and slaters, and mailmen. The economic successes of Negroes during Reconstruction were the most important factors in their ability to avoid complete strangulation by white unions, corrupt city officials, and anti-Negro employers in New Orleans in the twentieth century.[33]

   In spite of the opportunities he had to learn a skilled trade, the black worker faced many problems during Reconstruction. The cost of living was so high and unem-ployment so endemic in New Orleans that many blacks found it difficult to rise above the subsistence level. The economic security of the Negro worker varied with the differential in wages between different occupations. For instance, while 15 percent of all Negro carpenters, 14 percent of the Negro plasterers, painters, and bricklayers, 11 percent of all Negro shoemakers, and 10 percent of all Negro coopers held $200 or more in property, only 4 percent of all Negro unskilled laborers in 1870 held as much as $200 in property. The most serious problem the Negro worker faced, however, was chronic unemployment.

In 1880, for example, 18 percent of all Negro male workers were unemployed for at least one month. The highest rates of unemployment were among Negro laborers, painters, masons, carpenters, steamboatmen, plasterers, coopers, and cigarmakers. The average number of months Negro males were unemployed varied from 3.5 months for barbers to 5.7 months for cigarmakers.[34]

Unemployment, discrimination, and a desire for racial and economic uplift led Negro workers to form several rather weak quasiunions soon after the Civil War ended. The effort to unionize the blacks was seriously hampered, however, by the depressed economic conditions in the city, the lack of organizational skills among the workers, and the physical and political oppression of the blacks.[35] In spite of these problems, during 1865-80 blacks formed at least fifteen workingmen's clubs, benevolent associations, and unions among the longshoremen, steamboatmen, draymen, waiters, letter carriers, screwmen, cigarmakers, teamsters, and porters. A number of Negro workers also belonged to such integrated unions as the Cotton Yardmen's Beneficial Association and Teamsters' Association. By 1880 there were four Negro longshoremen unions, the largest of which was the Longshoremen's Protective Union, organized in 1873, with 450 members. The Teamsters and Loaders Association, organized in 1880, was one of the largest of the Negro unions, with 800 members. In their associations Negro workers set up funds to aid the sick and bury the dead, and provided social outlets for members and their families. Some of them were more ambitious. In 1875 one union established the short-lived Workingmen's Bank and another organization, the United Brotherhood Protective Association, established a grocery store.[36]

Although the black unions were more social than militant labor organizations, they often played prominent roles in the several strikes which occurred in New Orleans. For instance, one of the most serious strikes in the city began in May 1867 when about 500 Negro longshoremen struck because the contractors who hired them to unload the ships refused to pay them the wages they had agreed upon. On May 16, 1867, the longshoremen attacked one of these contractors and were about to lynch him when the police rescued him. The longshoremen then chased all of the other contractors off the docks, shouted down Mayor Heath when he tried to quiet them, and marched in a body to the Freedmen's Bureau office. Gen. Joseph A. Mower, state commissioner of the Freedmen's Bureau, addressed the men, counseled them to be law abiding and to stop their "rioting," and asserted that if they did not, "by the eternal God I will throw grape and canister into you." After a company of army troops was deployed on the docks, the longshoremen dispersed. They refused, however to go back to work. When the contractors hired scabs at $13.00 per day, the longshoremen chased them away from the ships. Mower ended the impasse by issuing an order that all captains and agents of vessels in New Orleans would be "held responsible for wages due freedmen."[37] On June 15 another dangerous situation arose on the docks. When a white engineer struck a Negro at the levee, the longshoremen chased him into a store and would not allow him to leave until the police arrived and dispersed the crowd.

The Negro longshoremen struck again in October 1872. During the strike they boarded a ship being loaded by scabs, and when the captain fired on them, they murdered him.[38]

There was an epidemic of strikes in New Orleans among both white and black workers in 1880. The first of these occurred in March when Negro longshoremen struck in Algiers. In July the 500 white and black members of the Cotton Yardmen's Association demanded higher wages. When the employers rejected the demand, the yardmen unilaterally set a wage scale to go into effect on September 1, 1880. This too, was rejected by the owners. The yardmen then went on strike and won acceptance of their demands. The integrated Teamsters Association went on strike on September 6, for a raise in wages to $3.00 per day. At about the same time black and white roustabouts, steamboatmen, and longshoremen struck for higher pay. This strike was broken with scabs from Mobile and Louisville. On October 15, the Negro waiters at the St. Charles Hotel struck for an increase from $15.00 (plus food and lodging) to $25.00 per month. The proprietors promptly fired all of the waiters and replaced them with white girls hired for $12.00 per month.[39]

The long and aggressive campaign of black workingmen to improve their lot in life was part of a multipronged drive to insure economic survival. The most consistent fight of blacks in New Orleans was their effort to promote thrift in the community. Negroes, their leaders asserted, spent far too much of their money for new fashions, whiskey, and pleasure, when they should have been saving to educate their children or to buy homes. Considering the ignorance and poverty in the community, the *Louisianian* was distressed by the Negroes' extravagance and pleaded with its readers to seek less pleasure and more wealth:

> Until we learn to become economical, we must ever be the dependent, helpless creatures that we are. Poverty is always to be deplored, and yet we as a people, don't seem to think it an inconvenience. We plead earnestly for more economy and less pleasure, much as we know we are thereby treading on the weakness of our people.[40]

Money, community leaders contended, was second only to education as a means of uplifting blacks and winning the respect of whites; it was the road to security, confidence, social standing, and self-reliance.[41] In an 1875 speech militia colonel James Lewis struck a refrain repeated by black leaders throughout the period when he insisted that the question of civil rights would be resolved by the Negro's industry and acquisition of wealth: "It is only interest which will drive out prejudice from the minds of whites. . . . Remember that the roads to prosperity are to be reached only through intelligence, and wealth and industry."[42]

Perhaps the most important impetus to the accumulation of wealth in the black community came from the Freedmen's Savings and Trust Company chartered by Congress in 1865. Drawing on the pronouncements of Benjamin Franklin about the advantages of savings, bank officials convinced many blacks that this was the road to true freedom.

Negro soldiers deposited their bounties (the bounty office was in the bank building), holders of the lucky lottery tickets their winnings, benevolent organizations and churches their dues, and hardworking laborers the few dollars left from their wages after providing for the necessities of life. By June 1867 more than $1,994,340 had been deposited. During the bank's seven-year existence, more than 10,000 individual deposits were made.[43]

After emancipation itself, the event which had the most far-reaching economic influence on the black community was the collapse of the Freedmen's Savings and Trust Company in 1874. Many Negro businessmen, already operating on a small margin, saw their small reserves disappear overnight. The simple laborers who had trusted in the United States government and had started saving money to buy homes or to gain some security were probably the hardest hit by the disaster. Having little understanding of bankruptcy proceedings, many of them quickly sold their deposit books to speculators for ten cents on the dollar. The treasuries of churches and philanthropic and benevolent societies either disappeared or were so sadly depleted by the crash that the organizations had to curtail activities. This was undoubtedly one of the reasons for the death of many clubs.

The baneful effects of the crash reverberated throughout the black community. Depositors bitterly assailed the Northern missionaries, philanthropists, and abolitionists who had, they felt, tricked them into putting their hard-earned money in the bank and then defrauded them. The most crippling and long-lasting effect of the crash was psychological: many Negroes would never again trust a bank. After all, if one could not safely deposit money in an institution chartered by the federal government, then no bank was sound. It was better, many blacks felt, to spend their money for immediate pleasure rather than to try to save for the future and be cheated out of it. The New Orleans *Louisianian*, which had been in the forefront of those urging Negroes to put their money in Freedman's Savings and Trust Company, almost despaired of ever convincing them to be frugal after the bank's crash.[44] The failure of the bank, it declared, "has caused on the part of our people, not only a feeling of distrust for other moneyed corporations, but has created a feeling of apathy in regard to saving and intensified the desire to spend in a round of pleasure, the earnings of a week, after the expenses of the household have been met."[45] Major responsibility for the lack of frugality among blacks in New Orleans in the 1870s rested squarely on the shoulders of the criminal incompetent officials of the bank and an indifferent United States Congress.

The failure of the bank and the general depreciation of property values in New Orleans in the 1860s and 1870s prevented the growth of a large black property-holding class. The total amount of personal property held by Negroes actually declined from $655,820 in 1860 to $560,143 in 1870. The overwhelming majority of the personal property holders held from only $20 to $500 worth of property; only 44 Negroes held more than $3000 worth of personal property in 1860, and only 9 in 1870. One Negro possessed $50,000 worth of personal property in 1860, while no one in the black community held more than $20,000 worth of personal property in 1870. However, Negroes made much more impressive gains in real estate between 1860 and 1870.

The number of Negroes who possessed real estate in New Orleans increased from 486 in 1860 to 933 in 1870, and the total value of real estate possessed by blacks increased from $1,488,500 in 1860 to $2,104,865 in 1870. While a majority of the Negro real estate owners in 1860 held property value at $3,000 or less, in 1870 a majority of the Negro landowners possessed property valued at $1,500 or less. There were, however, more Negroes who were large landowners in 1870 than in 1860. While only 17 Negro landowners held property worth more than $10,000 in 1860, there were 25 of them in 1870. Six Negroes in 1870 owned land worth more than $40,000; there had been none in 1860. The total value of property possessed by Negroes increased from $2,144,230 in 1860 to $2,664,828 in 1870.[46]

Since the 1880 census does not list property and the Orleans parish tax assessment rolls do not indicate race, it is practically impossible to do any more than estimate the total value of property Negroes possessed in 1880. This can be done by taking a sample of black property holders listed in the 1870 census and ascertaining how much taxable property they had in 1880. Forty-five of the Negro property holders listed in the 1870 census were also listed on the Orleans parish tax assessment rolls. In 1870 these blacks possessed $350,025 in property, 13 percent of all the property held by blacks in that year. Ten years later these same people held $241,830 worth of property. If their share of the total amount of property held by Negroes in 1880 was the same as it was in 1870, then blacks possessed at least $1,830,230 worth of property in 1880. They probably held considerably more than this, since the bias of the sample is toward an underestimate of property, for it does not in any way measure the new property holders. From 1860 to 1870 new property holders and the increase in wealth of the old ones led to an increase of $520,598 in the property held by Negroes. If there was the same total increase from 1870 to 1880, Negroes would have held $2,340,828 worth of property in 1880. Accepting this estimate as sound, the per capital wealth of Negroes in New Orleans was $40.58 in 1880.[47]

The largest black property holders in New Orleans during Reconstruction were the businessmen. While they were few in number, they exercised great influence in the black community: they were models to be emulated and were proof that the Negro could succeed in freedom. Successes in business, Negroes felt, represented the growth of the power they needed in order to obtain and to maintain their rights. Negro leaders urged their followers to enter all lines of business in order to keep the wealth they created in the black community.[48] Col. James Lewis spoke for many of them in 1875 when he said, "Our labor and our crops bring us money; we need banks wherein we have an interest in which to deposit. We like to insure our houses and our furniture, we then need insurance companies. The fact is we need to enter all the branches of trade." As Negroes were increasingly and violently driven out of politics in the mid-1870s, economic enterprise became the new panacea, and a number of prominent Negro politicians began to devote their full attention to business. The *Louisianian* expressed both the despair and the hope in the Negro community during this period when it declared, "Politics as a paying investment has had its days, we must now look for other avenues and pursuits to build up our fortunes, and to recover in a measure the ground lost in its avocation."[49]

Generally barred from intimate contact with white businessmen and, before the war, from buying stock or engaging in some enterprises, rarely able to borrow money from white-owned banks, and largely ignorant of business organization and practices, most Negro businessmen were concentrated in small, one-owner, service-oriented concerns. Of 169 Negro businesses listed in the 1870 city directory, all but three were one-owner concerns, and 42 percent of them were located in the home of the owner. These businesses included coffee-houses, restaurants, barbershops, rooming houses, cigarstores, ice houses, wood and coal shops, saloons, bakeries, shoe shops, and others. By 1880 many of these businesses had disappeared and more Negroes were concentrated in those requiring the smallest capital investment.[50]

The paucity of black-owned manufacturing concerns is indicative of many of the problems they faced. For instance, in 1875, after the *New Orleans Republican* called on the old wealthy abolitionists and blacks to organize cotton mills, several New Orleans Negroes met with the president of the New Orleans Chamber of Commerce to discuss the idea. Unfortunately, lack of capital and know-how, coupled with the hostile attitudes of the business community, prevented the establishment of this and any other large manufacturing concern by Negroes. There were, however, some manufacturing establishments run by Negroes; most of them were one-owner businesses employing a few workers and producing a small number of articles.[51]

The most important Negro establishments were those of cigarmakers and clothiers. Many of the plants were small; in 1870 three of the four Negro cigar manufacturers listed in the city directory had their plants located at their place of residence, and of the twenty-five property-holding cigarmakers listed in the 1870 census, fourteen owned $1,500 or less in property. Only three possessed more than $5,000 worth of property. The four Negroes listed among the cigarmakers in the 1880 census of manufacturing had an average of only $518 capital invested in their plants, employed an average of four workers, each of whom they paid an average of $503 annually in wages, and produced cigars valued at $1,699 annually.[52]

There were three Negro clothiers and tailors listed in the 1880 census of manufacturing in New Orleans. Etienne Dubois had the smallest business, with only $200 in capital invested and one worker whom he paid $2.00 for a ten-hour day and $625 annually. He operated his business all year, purchased $500 in raw material, and produced clothes valued at a total of $2,500 annually. Paul Bonseigneur had the largest business, with $1,000 in capital invested in his tailoring shop in 1880 and with five workers, each of whom he paid $1.00 to $2.50 for a ten-hour day and a total of $2,000 annually. He operated his shop only six months out of the year, purchased $900 worth of raw material, and produced clothing valued at $5,000 annually.[53]

While largely unsuccessful in manufacturing pursuits, blacks did organize a number of family partnerships and joint-stock companies. The New Orleans *Louisianian*, for example, was started in 1870 as a joint-stock company by Pinchback, Antoine, and several other Negro politicians. In December 1870, Antoine, Pinchback, Alexander E. Barber, P. G. Deslonde, George F. Kelso, J. J. Monette, and others incorporated the unsuccessful Mississippi River Packet Company, to be capitalized at $500,000 with shares to sell for $100.00. Several wealthy Negroes also organized the Metropolitan Loan, Savings and Pledge Bank Association in 1870. Although the wealthiest Negroes in the state, F. E. Dumas and L. T. Delassize, were on the board of directors, there is no indication that the bank did much business. Probably the most durable joint-stock company founded by the Economy Society, a benevolent organization. Another business which had some limited success was the Cosmopolitan Insurance Association, organized in 1882 with a capital stock of $25,000 and with C. C. Antoine as president, J. B. Gaudet as vice-president, William G. Brown as treasurer, and Aristide Dejoie as secretary.[54]

The existence of a relatively large number of wealthy planters in Louisiana encouraged a few Negroes in New Orleans to establish commission houses. Pinchback and Antoine opened one in New Orleans in 1869 with a branch in Shreveport; and J. F. Winston, a Negro bookseller, had established a similar business by 1870. C. C. Antoine and William G. Brown organized a commission house in 1877, and T. B. Stamps established one in 1878. Engaged in a highly competitive and risky business, the Negro commission merchants had to struggle against great odds. First of all, they had to win customers away from the houses with which they had been doing business for years. Secondly, they had to compete with rural merchants who obtained first liens on crops. While many of these same problems bedeviled white merchants, the Negro often fought a losing battle to win the confidence of his customers. Most of the Negro merchants conceded white planters to white merchants and appealed to Negro planters to support black business. The Negro merchants saw that they could build large businesses if they could only gain the patronage of the Negro planters—the Negro planters in Iberville, Natchitoches, and Plaquemines parishes alone could have supported several commission houses. T. T. Allain of Iberville parish, for instance, owned a 790-acre sugar plantation worth $15,000, employed 35 laborers on it, produced 7,000 hogsheads of sugar, 4,000 gallons of molasses, and other farm produce valued at $14,400 in 1870.[55]

Utilizing their prestige in the black community, appealing to racial pride and their political acquaintances, some of the Negro commission merchants built up sizable businesses.[56] The most successful and imaginative commission merchant during this period was the former legislator T. B. Stamps. When Stamps opened his house, he sent a circular to all of the Negro ministers to be read to their congregations urging Negro planters to support black merchants. He then took out a large ad in the *Louisianian* guaranteeing "prompt" sales, to purchase goods at the "lowest rates," and to give "liberal advances" to his customers. Stamps followed this up by sending an agent through the parishes in Louisiana and then by touring the state and parts of Mississippi and Arkansas himself to drum up business. The New Orleans *Louisianian*, praising Stamps for his "energy, determination and pluck," predicted in September 1879 that he would "receive nearly 6,000 bales of cotton this year, besides sugar and other produce. . . . In two years he estimates he will have employment for twenty men."[57] In November the *Louisianian* revised its estimate upward and predicted Stamps would handle 20,000 bales of cotton during the year. Apparently Stamps was successful in his endeavors: on March 6, 1880, the *Louisianian* reported that he was "rapidly building up a large business."

One of the largest groups of Negro businessmen was the grocers. Most of them ran small neighborhood concerns. Seven of the eight Negro-owned grocery stores listed in the 1870 city directory were located at the owner's residence. Twenty-two of the thirty-five Negro grocers listed in the 1870 census owned $3,000 or less in property, and only six owned more than $5,000 worth of property. The inventory of the small grocer was, of course, limited. The merchandise in a typical small Negro grocery store appeared in the inventory of the estate of thirty-year-old Murville Cheval; when he died in 1865 he had merchandise worth only $274.[58]

Several Negro grocers, however, owned sizable businesses. The contents of J. A. Lacroix's "well assorted" grocery store, for instance, were auctioned off for $4,500 after his death in 1868. Jean Baptiste Deterville Bonseigneur, a native of Haiti and veteran of the Battle of New Orleans, was one of the wealthiest of the Negro grocers. When he died in 1871 he had $2,111 in currency and an estate worth $19,669. Another larger grocer was J. J. Montford who owned $17,500 worth of property in 1860. The largest Negro grocer in New Orleans during the Reconstruction period was Victor Pessou, a wholesaler. He sold his products to small retail grocers, coffee houses, restaurants, plantations, and several prominent Orleanians. He had a thriving business; in 1871 there was a total of $60,678 due him from his customers, and the contents of his grocery store were valued at $15,818.[59]

The wealthiest Negro businessmen in New Orleans during Reconstruction were the brokers. By purchasing real estate, renting houses, managing the property of wealthy Negroes, making loans, and serving as executors of estates, a number of Negro brokers amassed a considerable amount of property. One of them, Myrtille Courcelle, made sizable loans to Negro businessmen and whites in New Orleans and charged them 8 percent annual interest. He loaned Dr. L. C. Roudanez $1,200 for his unsuccessful bid to save the *New Orleans Tribune*, Peter Caulfield $800 for his jewelry business, Gadane Casanave $300 for his funeral parlor, and J. J. Montford $2,350 to operate his grocery store. Between 1860 and 1872 Courcelle purchased $16,000 and sold $12,460 worth of real estate. When he died in 1872, he owned $15,000 in real estate and held 26 promissory notes worth $21,968.[60]

Another wealthy broker was Sidney Thezan. His "finely furnished" house on Esplanade Street was worth $5,000 and was run by his cook, gardener, and servant. In his brokerage business Thezan employed one clerk full-time and his son, Joseph, part-time.

Between 1860 and 1875 Thezan purchased $7,670 and sold $15,900 in real estate, but he actually made much of his money from the 6 percent annual interest he received on the short- and long-term loans he made, primarily to whites. At the time of his death in 1875, six people owed him a total of $4,205, and he owned $13,650 in real estate.

By 1870 Thezan had begun to manage the property of several wealthy Negroes in New Orleans, charging them from 2 to 5 percent interest on the income earned on their property. The largest of these accounts was that of Camille Thierry, a Negro poet who resided in France. Thierry's property, consisting of 55 shares of stock in the New Orleans Gas Light Company, 18 shares of the Citizens Bank of New Orleans, one U. S. Bond, and 6 houses, was worth $43,195. In his numerous letters to Thierry, Thezan kept him posted on commercial affairs in the city and advised him of the best times for buying and selling property. Thezan received a commission of 5 percent on the rent he collected for Thierry from 1872 to 1874 ($187 out of $3,735) and a commission of 2 percent on the stock and monies he managed for him ($226 out of $12,790).[61]

Probably the only successful Negro father-son brokerage team in the city was that of John Francis and John Racquet Clay. Beginning in 1860 John Francis Clay began to purchase several shares of stock. By 1864 he held 19 shares of the New Orleans Gas Light Company stock, 10 shares of stock in the Bank of Louisiana, and $270 worth of the New Orleans Mutual Insurance Company scrip. The total value of the stock at the time of his death was $3,248. Clay made most of his loans to whites, including Christian Roselius, C. Toledano, and James P. Freret. Most of these were relatively large loans at 8 percent annual interest; of the 23 promissory notes in Clay's possession at his death, only 4 were for less than $500, and one was for $3,187. The total amount of money due to John Francis Clay's estate from promissory notes, debts, and stock was $21,376. After his father's death, John Racquet Clay took over the business. Between 1871 and 1880 John R. Clay purchased $29,298 and sold $21,690 in real estate, and was more successful than his father in obtaining business as an executor of the estates of wealthy Negroes. For instance, when Myrtille Courcelle died, John R. Clay received a 2 1/2 percent commission as executor of his estate ($912 out of $36,482). In 1870 Clay possessed property valued at $21,500.[62]

The wealthiest Negro brokers in New Orleans were Aristide Mary, Drosin B. Macarthy, and Thomy Lafon; between them in 1870 they owned $253,800 in property. Aristide Mary, described as "wealthy, educated and refined," had inherited his money from his white father along with valuable real estate, including a whole block of Canal Street, the main thoroughfare in New Orleans. The most impressive of the trio was Thomy Lafon, who began life in relative poverty and died in 1893 with an estate worth almost half a million dollars. Although Drosin B. Macarthy already came from one of the wealthiest families in the state, he utilized his skill to increase his legacy from $35,000 in 1860 to $77,300 in 1870.[63]

For most of the period under review, Macarthy was the most successful of the Negro brokers. Between 1860 and 1870 he purchased more than $64,000 in real estate and sold more than $27,000 in property. After 1870 Macarthy retired from active trading and lived on the rent he collected. Thomy Lafon, the second leading broker until the 1870s, purchased more than $61,000 and sold more than $26,000 in real estate between 1860 and 1870. From 1871 to 1880, Lafon bought $41,000 and sold $22,000 in real estate. Unlike Lafon and Macarthy, Aristide Mary had inherited so many buildings on Canal Street that he rarely bought or sold land. Instead, he leased his buildings for $6,000 each every four years.[64]

The acquisition of sizable fortunes by a few blacks does not obscure the fact that most blacks were severely handicapped by the general depression in New Orleans' economy. Unemployment was endemic and ensured that the labor unions formed among Negro workers would be weak. At the same time, the general decline in property values (50 percent between 1870 and 1880) caused Negroes to hold property which was valued at only a little more in 1880 than in 1860. Apparently, however, there was an increase in the total amount of real estate that Negroes possessed in the city. Even so, in 1870 Negroes held only 1.4 percent of the total amount of property in Orleans parish and only 2.5 percent in 1880. For the most part, although there were some large Negro-owned businesses, the majority of them were small, one-owner concerns. In spite of the fact that there were few Negro apprentices during this period, Negro workers held on tenaciously to many of the jobs in the city. This was their most important economic victory. And although the criminal mismanagement of the Freedman's Savings and Trust Company deprived the Negro of thousands of dollars and encouraged extravagance in the black community, Negro workers maintained their dominant position in certain trades and gained a near monopoly of others.

Notes for "Land, Labor, and Capital"

[1]Janey Marks, "The Industrial Development of New Orleans Since 1805" (M.A. thesis, Tulane University, 1939), 1-20; *Commercial Reports Received at the Foreign Office from Her Majesty's Consuls, in 1867* (London, 1867), 260, 280.

[2]Benjamin Butler to Henry W. Halleck, September 1, 1862, Department of the Gulf, Letters Sent, Record Group 393, National Archives (hereafter cited DG, LS, RG (with number) NA).

[3]Willie Melvin Caskey, *Secession and Restoration of Louisiana* (University, La., 1938), 15-53; E. Whittemore to Nathaniel Banks, March 14(?), December 6, 1863, and E. G. Beckwith to George B. Drake, March 4, 1865, Department of the Gulf, Civil Affairs, Record Group 393, National Archives (hereafter cited DG, CA, RG [with number] NA).

[4]Caskey, *Secession and Restoration*, 50-54; Josephine Luke, "From Slavery to Freedom in Louisiana, 1862-1865" (M. A. thesis, Tulane University, 1939), 16-34; A. F. Puffer to John W. Phelps, September 2, 1862, DG, LS, RG 393, NA.

[5]Frank C. Peck to Benjamin Butler, June 15, 1862, W. H. Emory to Richard B. Irwin, January 27, 1862, F. S. Nickerson to J. S. Clark, January 27, 1863, Department of the Gulf, Letters Received, Record Group 393, National Archives (hereafter cited DG, LR, RG (with number) NA).

[6]Stephen Hoyt to V. F. Dannoy, DG, CA, RG, 393, NA; see also Kate M. Rowland, ed., *The Journal of Julie Le Grand* (Richmond, 1911), 60.

[7]Nathaniel Banks to W. H. Halleck, October 15, 1863, N. P. Banks Letterbooks, Louisiana State University, Department of Archives (hereafter LSU).

[8]Caskey, *Secession and Restoration*, 70-89; Luke, "From Slavery to Freedom," 21-58; George Hanks to Nathaniel Banks, March 28, 1864, N. P. Banks Papers, Library of Congress (hereafter LC); James K. Hosmer, *The Color-Guard: Being a Corporal's Notes of Military Service in the Nineteenth Army Corps* (Boston, 1864), 140; William R. Crane to Nathaniel Banks, March 26, 1863, and John Pickering to Colonel Chandler, April 2, 1864, DG, CA, RG 393, NA; Benjamin Butler to John W. Phelps, May 10, 1862, and Butler to Henry W. Halleck, September 1, 1862, DG, LS, RG 393, NA.

[9]John W. Blassingame, "The Union Army as an Educational Institution for Negroes, 1862-1865," *Journal of Negro Education*, 34 (1965): 154.

[10]Ibid.; *New Orleans Tribune*, August 23, 1864; Butler to Edwin Stanton, November 14, 1862, DG, LS, RG 393, NA; *Observations on the Present Conditions of Louisiana* (1865?, n.p.); Luke, "From Slavery to Freedom," 34-80.

[11]Albert O. Marshall, *Army Life: From A Soldier's Journal* (Joliet, 1864), 397; *New Orleans Tribune*, October 22, 1864; Homer B. Sprague, *History of the 13th Infantry Regiment of Connecticut Volunteers During the Great Rebellion* (Hartford, 1867), 183; Charles P. Bosson, *History of the Forty-second Regiment Infantry Massachusetts Volunteers, 1862, 1863, 1864* (New York, 1866), 337-42.

[12]George H. Hepworth, *The Whip, Hoe and Sword; or, The Gulf Department in '63* (Boston, 1864), 235.

[13]*Observations on the Present Conditions of Louisiana*, 5; George H. Hepworth to Nathaniel Banks, June 15, 1863, and T. W. Conway to Banks, March 17, 1865, Banks Papers, LC; *New Orleans Tribune*, October 12, 1864; *New Orleans Black Republican*, May 20, 1865; Hepworth, *Whip, Hoe and Sword*, 23-28.

[14]Banks to his wife, February 24, 1863, Banks Papers, LC.

[15]*New Orleans Tribune*, October 12, 1864; *New Orleans Black Republican*, April 22, 1865.

[16]*New Orleans Black Republican*, April 15, 22, May 13, 1865.

[17]*New Orleans Tribune*, August 13, September 1 and 24, November 17, December 8, 1864, January 12, February 7, March 14, April 9, 1865, December 31, 1867; A. J. H. Duganne, *Camps and Prisons: Two Months in the Department of the Gulf* (New York, 1865), 36.

[18]*New Orleans Tribune*, August 13, December 8, 1864.

[19]James McKaye, *The Mastership and Its Fruits: The Emancipated Slave Face to Face with His Old Master* (New York, 1864), 21-30; Hepworth, *Whip, Hoe and Sword*, 28; *New Orleans Black Republican*, April 15, 1865; *New Orleans Tribune*, December 4, 1864; Kenneth E. Shewmaker and Andrew K. Prinz, "A Yankee in Louisiana: Selections from the Diary and Correspondence of Henry R. Gardner, 1862-1866," *Louisiana History*, 5 (1964): 271-95.

[20]Henry Warner to Nathaniel Banks, February 10, 1863, DG, CA, RG 393, NA; McKaye, *The Mastership and Its Fruits*, 21.

[21]*New Orleans Tribune*, November 24, 30, December 27, 1864, and January 4, 7, 12, 14, February 4, March 7, 23, 28, 1865; James H. Ingraham to S. A. Hurlbut, February 11, 1865, DG, CA, RG 393, NA; S. A. Hurlbut to James H. Ingraham, March 23, 1865, Freedmen's Bureau, Commissioner, Record Group 105, National Archives (hereafter FB).

[22]*New Orleans Tribune*, January 28, 29, February 2, and March 31, 1865.

[23]Ibid., November 30, 1864.

[24]Ibid., February 23, 24, 28, March 7, 21, April 11, 13, and May 2, 16, 1865; *National Freedmen*, 1 (1865): 107-8; *New Orleans Black Republican*, April 15, 1865; Benjamin F. Flanders to Nathaniel Banks, May 17, 1865, W. R. Crane et al. to O. O. Howard, August 14, 1865, FB, Commissioner, RG 105, NA.

[25]*New Orleans Tribune*, January 20, 1869.

[26]New Orleans *Louisianian*, January 22, 1871, and June 27, 1874; *New Orleans Black Republican*, April 15, 1865; *New Orleans Republican*, November 20, 23, 1874; *New Orleans Tribune*, April 19, June 10, 1865, November 10, 1867, and January 8, 15, 20, February 2, 1869.

[27]Friedrick Gerstäcker, *Neue Reisen durch die Vereinigten Staaten, Mexiko, Ecuador, Westindien und Venezuela*, 2 vols. (Jena 1876), 1:365; John E. H. Skinner, *After the Storm; or, Jonathan an His Neighbors in 1865-1856*, 2 vols. (London, 1866), 2:69; M[aria] Waterbury, *Seven Years among the Freedmen* (Chicago, 1890), 59.

[28]New Orleans *Louisianian*, February 20, 1873.

[29]See tables 3-8.

[30]*New Orleans City Directory*, 1870; also see tables 3, 4, and 5. Unless otherwise indicated the source for all references to occupations in this chapter in tables 3-8.

[31]New Orleans *Louisianian*, July 3, 1880; *New Orleans Tribune*, June 21, 1867; *New Orleans Republican*, May 18, 27, 1867.

[32]Ambrose C. Fulton, *A Life's Voyage* (New York, 1898), 361.

[33]See table 10, Herbert R. Northrup, "The New Orleans Longshoremen," *Political Science*, 57 (1942): 526-44; Robert C. Francis, "Longshoremen in New Orleans," *Opportunity*, 14 (1936): 82-85, 93; Roger W. Shugg, *Origins of Class Struggle in Louisiana* (Baton Rouge, La., 1939).

[34]Mary S. Jones to Caroline Jones, March 14, 1865, Joseph Jones Collection, Tulane University; *New Orleans Crescent*, April 7, 1867; Census of Population, Orleans Parish, 1870, 1880, Record Group 329, National Archives.

[35]New Orleans *Louisianian*, October 18, 1879.

[36]Arthur Raymond Pearce, "The Rise and Decline of Labor in New Orleans" (M. A. thesis, Tulane University, 1938), 17-25; William Saunders, *Through the Light Continent; or, The United States in 1877-78* (London, 1879), 69; *New Orleans Crescent*, August 20, 1868; New Orleans *Louisianian*, December 18, 1870, November 30, 1871, January 21, 1872, April 3, 1875, November 17, 1877, and April 3, 1880; *Constitution and By-Laws of the Shoemakers Union of New Orleans* (New Orleans, 1879).

[37]*New Orleans Tribune*, May 19, 24, 1867.

[38]Ibid., May 16, 17, 18, 19, 24, June 16, 1867; *New Orleans Times*, May 17, 1867 and October 18, 1872; Saunders, *Through the Light Continent*, 69.

[39]New Orleans *Louisianian*, March 27, 1880; Pearce, "Rise and Decline of Labor," 17-25.

[40]New Orleans *Louisianian*, August 2, 1879.

[41]*New Orleans Times*, August 10, 1875; *New Orleans Tribune*, February 4, 1865, July 3, 1867, and February 21, 1869; New Orleans *Louisianian*, December 29, 1870, and January 12, May 18, June 1, June 8, 1871.

[42]New Orleans *Louisianian*, August 28, 1875.

[43]*New Orleans Tribune*, July 10, 25, October 26, December 17, 1867, and February 19, 1869; New Orleans *Louisianian*, April 2, June 15, July 20, October 26, 1871, and July 6, 1872; Walter L. Fleming, *The Freedmen's Savings Bank: A Chapter in the Economic History of the Negro Race* (Chapel Hill, 1927), 142-43; Record of the New Orleans Branch, Freedman's Savings and Trust Company, Record Group 101, National Archives.

[44]New Orleans *Louisianian*, June 26, August 28, 1875.

[45]Ibid., August 9, 1879.

[46]Census of Population, Orleans Parish, 1860-80, RG 329, NA.

[47]Tax Assessment Rolls, 1880, New Orleans, New Orleans Public Library; Census of Population, Orleans Parish, 1870, RG 329, NA. Two hundred seventy Negro men under the age of sixty who were listed in the 1870 census as possessing real property were checked against the tax assessment rolls of Orleans Parish for 1880. Although the sample included ten Negroes whose last names began with each letter of the alphabet, only forty-five of them appeared on the tax assessment rolls.

[48]*National Freedman*, 1 (1865): 266-67; New Orleans *Louisianian*, June 1, 1871, June 19, July 10, August 28, 1875, November 17, 1877, and January 11, September 20, 1879.

[49]New Orleans *Louisianian*, August 28, 1875, and September 20, 1879.

[50]*New Orleans City Directory*, 1870, tables 5, 6, and 7; *New Orleans Times*, September 19, 1867; Gerstäcker, *Neue Riesen*, 365-66; New Orleans *Louisianian*, May 25, 1871, August 3, 1872, and February 22, 1879; *New Orleans Tribune*, July 3, 1864, and September 4, December 3, 1867; *New Orleans Black Republican*, April 22, 1865.

[51]*New Orleans City Directory*, 1870.

[52]Census of Manufacturing, 1880, Census of Population, 1860, 1870, Orleans Parish, RG 329, NA; Tax Assessment Rolls, Orleans Parish, 1880; Rodolphe L. Desdunes, *Nos Hommes et notre histoire* (Montreal, 1911), 123-25; A. E. Perkins, ed., *Who's Who in Colored Louisiana, 1930* (Baton Rouge, 1930).

[53]Census of Manufacturing, 1880, Census of Population, 1860, 1870, Orleans Parish, RG 329, NA; Tax Assessment Rolls, Orleans Parish, 1880.

[54]New Orleans *Louisianian*, December 22, 29, 1870, February 26, 1871, and December 13, 1879; Succession Papers of Lucillia Tucker, Mary Jason, Madeline J. Roche, Oscar J. Dunn, and Octave Perrault, U. S. Court House, New Orleans; The Honorable C. C. Antoine, Scrapbook, pp. 71-81, Southern University Library.

[55]*New Orleans City Directory*, 1870; New Orleans *Louisianian*, March 16, 1871, and February 21, June 5, 1880; Antoine Scrapbook, 81; Census of Agriculture, Iberville, Natchitoches, and Plaquemines Parishes, 1870, 1880, RG 329, NA.

[56]New Orleans *Louisianian*, March 16, 1871.

[57]Ibid., May 3, September 20, November 22, December 25, 1879, and March 6, 1880.

[58]Succession Papers of Murville Cheval and Frederick Barthelmy, U. S. Court House, New Orleans.

[59]New Orleans *Louisianian*, May 3, June 21, 1879; Succession Papers of J. B. D. Bonseigneur, J. A. Lacroix, J. J. Montford and Victor Pessou, U. S. Court House, New Orleans; Census of Population, Orleans Parish, 1860, 1870, RG 329, NA.

[60]Succession Papers of Myrtille Courcelle, U. S. Court House, New Orleans; Conveyance Records, Orleans Parish, Orleans Parish Court House.

[61]Succession Papers of Sidney Thezan, U. S. Court House, New Orleans; Conveyance Records, Orleans Parish, Orleans Parish Court House.

[62]Succession Papers of John F. Clay, Myrtille Courcelle, and Pelagie Jacques, U. S. Court House, New Orleans; Conveyance Records, Orleans Parish, Orleans Parish Court House.

[63]New Orleans *Louisianian*, October 10, 1874, Desdunes, *Nos Hommes*, 125-29; Tax Assessments Rolls, Orleans Parish, 1880; J. M. Murphy, "Thomy Lafon," *Negro History Bulletin*, 7 (1943): 6, 20.

[64]Conveyance Records, Orleans Parish, Orleans Parish Court House.

LABOR, THE GENERAL MERCHANT,
AND THE CROP LIEN*

Joe Gray Taylor

SUGAR PLANTING was a semiindustrial operation. The capital investment required was much more than was needed for planting cotton. The fields had to be carefully ditched and drained, an item of considerable expense. The work force for a sugar plantation had to have a larger proportion of young and vigorous men, men who could demand and get higher wages than the blacks in the cotton fields. Another major factor in cane production was seed; between one fourth and one third of a year's crop had to be saved as seed for the next year.

More than this, a sugar plantation required far more equipment than a cotton plantation. A sugarhouse, where the juice was pressed from the cane, boiled down, then crystallized into brown sugar, was far more expensive than a cotton gin. In addition, wood had to be gathered to provide fuel for the sugarhouse. Also necessary were many carts to haul wood in the summer and cane to the sugarhouse during the harvest. Oxen, horses, and mules had to draw these carts and the plows used in cultivation. Because the soil in the sugar-producing regions was normally heavier than elsewhere, bigger and stronger work animals were needed. Finally, sugar was a crop which involved great risks. It was not so subject to insect damage as was cotton, but it was just as susceptible to flood. But the greatest danger came as harvest time approached. The longer the crop stood in the fields, the more sugar it would produce. But the longer the planter waited before cutting it, the more danger there was of a hard freeze which might ruin the crop completely.

After the Civil War it was exceedingly difficult to make money planting sugar. John Burnside remained the largest sugar planter, in terms of acres, for a decade after Appomattox. In 1869, which was a relatively good year for sugar, three of Burnside's seven plantations showed profits totaling $30,732.80 but the other four lost

*Excerpt first published in Chapter 9 in Joe Gray Taylor, *Louisiana Reconstructed, 1863-1877* (Baton Rouge: Louisiana State University Press, © 1976), 364-92. Reprinted with the kind permission of the publisher.

$161,964.89, for a net loss of $131,232.09. Two Northerners who bought Oakley Plantation in Iberville Parish found that expenses exceeded income by about $12,000 per year. In January, 1873, it was estimated that a third of the sugar plantations in the state were no longer planting cane. The 4,291 sugarhouses in Louisiana in 1861 had been reduced to 817 by 1869. It is obvious that sugar planting was unprofitable during Reconstruction, but one of the leading students of the sugar industry concluded that the inability of the planters to manage their enterprises efficiently was the single most important reason for failure.[1]

So difficult was it to resume sugar planting, and so unprofitable were operations which were undertaken, that many planters and, especially, smaller farmers in the sugar region turned to cotton or rice. South central Louisiana was not well adapted to cotton culture, especially in the years before insecticides, but cotton prices were high, and not nearly so much capital was required to put in a cotton crop. Plaquemines Parish had produced rice in some quantity before and during the Civil War, but afterward the cultivation of this grain was taken up temporarily in other parishes, especially Lafourche. Rice culture had not yet reached the prairies west of present-day Lafayette; that would come about after Reconstruction.[2]

Some people, including newspaper editors, hoped that the end of slavery would break up sugar plantations into smaller productive units worked by white men. A few sincere Radicals wanted them broken up into freeholds for former slaves. These hopes were not realized. Some of the already-present small farms in the sugar region began planting cane, but the plantations were not divided. The false impression given by the census of 1870, which listed sharecropper plots as separate farms, is now well known to historians. What really happened, as Roger Shugg has shown, was that the number of plantations in Louisiana increased almost 300 percent between 186o and 1890. In the same years, although the number of landholdings increased 89 percent, the number of small farms decreased by 14 percent. A reporter traveling from Thibodaux to New Orleans in 1869 noted that "The desire to hold on to large bodies of land is so great that the owners will never consent to part with any portion until under the sheriff's hammer."[3] Legislation which required foreclosed plantations to be broken up into smaller farms when sold had no lasting effect.

The fact that sugar plantations were not subdivided did not mean that they remained in the same hands as before the war. The pervading scarcity of capital forced more and more planters into voluntary or involuntary sales. Northerners began acquiring sugar plantations at war's end. They were joined by banks, corporations, country merchants and enterprising individuals. John N. Pharr, a steamboat operator in 1875, owned eight sugar plantations by 1903. Leon Godchaux, who had come to Louisiana as a peddler in the 1830s, purchased his first plantation in 1862 and by 1896 owned more than thirty thousand acres. One student estimated that one half of all the sugar plantations in the state had changed hands by 1869. This is probably a conservative estimate, because a check of planters who owned fifty or more slaves in 1860 against tax assessment rolls after the war shows that of thirty such planters in Ascension Parish in 1860, only thirteen still owned large tracts of land in 1871. Of ninety who had owned fifty or more slaves in St. Mary Parish in 1860, only twenty-five still held on in 1877. Thus the process of eliminating the prewar sugar-planting families was continuing throughout Reconstruction.[4]

One partial solution to the problem of lack of capital was some form of sharecropping, so that the worker would be obliged to wait for the harvest for part of his reward for a year's labor. On one place, blacks were cutting wood on shares in 1863, and that year on another sugar plantation the planter agreed to give his workers one twentieth of the crop—presumably in addition to food, clothing, and shelter. Some form of division of the crop became more common in 1864. In the sugar region the trend toward share-cropping was so pronounced by the end of 1865 that the Freedmen's Bureau encouraged this type of contract. After the sugar crop failed in 1866, the bureau advocated a return to monthly wages, but many of the freedmen preferred to stay with sharecropping.[5]

The early enthusiasm for sharecropping on the sugar plantations did not endure. The industrial nature of sugar production made centralized direction more essential than was the case on cotton lands. Reliable and thrifty croppers could benefit both themselves and the landowner, but most were just as careless with ditching, fences, stock, and tools as were wage workers, and they could not be supervised as closely. Another important obstacle to sharecropping in the cane fields was the difficulty of accurately separating the sugar made from one tenant's cane from that made from another's. Some sharecropping continued, especially when white tenants could be had, but by 1870 most plantations were firmly fixed on a system of contract labor for wages. The employees lived in what had been the slave quarter, and gang labor was the rule. Adventurous planters might experiment with various sharecropping arrangements, especially in Terrebonne Parish, but this type of tenure was not to become the rule in the sugar fields as it did in the cotton regions.[6]

If the vast majority of blacks in the sugar regions was fated to be contract laborers, they were also fated to be relatively well paid because scarcity of labor assured good wages. As the acreage under cultivation increased, additional imported laborers, estimated at about twenty thousand in five years, were absorbed, but pay did not go down. The Panic of 1873 did force wages down somewhat, but less than might have been expected. Planters held meetings at various times to seek agreement on wage ceilings; such agreements did not last. Some planters in dire need of labor would always offer more than the ceiling in order to save their crops.

It was reported in 1866 that freedmen in the sugar fields were receiving ten to twelve dollars per month on the average, some as much as eighteen dollars, plus shelter, food, fuel, medical care, and clothing. Those who provided their own clothing and food received twenty-five dollars. Wages seem to have reached their height in 1869. The average field hand in St. John the Baptist Parish earned ten to twelve dollars a month, food, clothing, shelter, and a plot of land on which to grow corn, vegetables, swine, and poultry of his own. In St. Mary Parish the same year the going wage for field hands was reported to be twenty dollars a month plus cabin, rations, and fuel. In 1870 a number of whites labored in the cane fields of West Baton Rouge Parish, and on the Teche, during grinding, white cotton farmers were said to have left their own crops in the fields in order to earn two or three dollars a day making sugar. Even after the panic occurred, wages of twenty-five dollars a month plus cabin and rations were not unheard of. Also, workers usually received a garden plot and time to work it. The most thorough student of sugar culture concludes that the freedman, working for wages, was as productive as the slave had been.[7]

In general the black laborers of the sugar region seem to have lived better lives in a material sense than sharecroppers on cotton plantations. Ordinarily, their wages were given in addition to housing and rations, and sometimes in addition to clothing. Thus they were not forced into debt as, too often, the freedmen on cotton plantations were. Probably they did not like living in the old slave quarter or having their rations passed out to them in the same fashion as under slavery, but the rations were at least as adequate as in the cotton fields, and the housing on sugar plantations was usually better. Furthermore, there was a plantation commissary, or a merchant nearby, where whiskey and modest luxuries could be bought at outrageous prices; there the worker could go into debt and, sometimes, be cheated. In general, life for the sugar plantation workman was better than life bad been under slavery. He had access to a church, and his children usually had access to a school. He could, with thrift and foresight, save money. Many did not go to church; most did not send their children to school; and few saved money; but the opportunities existed. Complaints that planters and merchants cheated their workmen were heard; no doubt some of these complaints were valid, but most of them were not.[8]

Probably the most important development in sugar during the Reconstruction period was the beginning of the separation of sugar cultivation and harvesting from the refining process. Before the Civil War a few planters may have processed the cane of neighbors who cultivated so few acres that they could not afford to build sugarhouses, but in general each production unit had its own refinery. This was inefficient, because as the machinery for refining was improved, one refinery would handle the cane from a number of plantations. In 1868, D. C. Avery agreed with one John Hayes to grind Hayes's cane "or as much as he can" for which Avery was to receive half the sugar produced, Hayes to get one barrel of molasses for each hogshead of sugar. Each man was to supply his own hogsheads and molasses barrels.[9] The immigration of small-scale white farmers to the sugar region gave impetus to the consolidation movement because the immigrants were forced, if they grew sugar, to depend upon some planter's sugarhouse for grinding. John Dymond of Plaquemines Parish began buying cane by the ton in 1871, and he was so successful that he sent boats up and down the river in 1872 to buy cane for his mill. The consolidation of sugar refining had only begun when Reconstruction ended, but it most definitely had begun.[10]

As may be seen from Table Two, the Civil War brought a drastic decline in sugar production. In only two years of Louisiana's antebellum history did production come within 100,000 hogsheads of the 1861 crop, and only the crop of 1858 came close to its value. The average crop of the 1850s was about 250,000 hogsheads, and the average price about sixty dollars. Production during Reconstruction never reached the average of the 1850s, but the total value of the crop of 1870 was greater than the total value of the very poor crops of 1850, 1851, and 1856. Furthermore, as the table shows, production was generally improving during Reconstruction. Although it was not until 1893 that the crop equaled that of 1861, from 1881 on the crop exceeded the average for the 1850s except in very bad years.[11]

TABLE TWO

Sugar Production During Civil War and Reconstruction[12]

Year	Hogsheads	Price	Value
1860	228,753	$ 63.25	$14,468,647
1861	459,610	84.62	25,097,271
1862	87,231	83.84	7,749,602
1863	76,801	179.70	13,801,139
1864	10,387	208.50	1,994,300
1865	18,079	157.50	2,847,442
1866	39,000	137.50	5,360,500
1867	37,647	154.00	5,797,638
1868	84,256	137.80	11,610,476
1869	87,090	140.00	12,442,251
1870	144,881	102.26	14,260,326
1871	128,461	97.16	12,487,020
1872	108,529	91.68	10,027,717
1873	89,496	86.50	8,122,575
1874	116,867	95.82	11,269,767
1875	114,146	95.90	11,265,000
1876	169,331	83.00	11,578,000
1878	149,469	72.00	9,007,000

Improved technology contributed to the gradual increase in sugar production. Louisiana sugar planters were aware of the potentialities of labor-saving machinery, but the machines which would help them overcome the postwar labor shortage did not have a great effect until after Reconstruction. The steam plow, which made use of two movable steam engines to draw a plow back and forth across a field, was the great hope of the immediate postwar years, and at least three were put into operation on Louisiana plantations. The most famous example was on Magnolia Plantation in Plaquemines Parish, partly owned by Henry Clay Warmoth. In the long run the steam plow was not successful. The initial cost was large, firm beds had to be established on which the two heavy engines could move the length of the field they were plowing, and shutdowns for repairs were frequent and expensive.[13]

Other failures were the use of the diffusion process for separating the sugar-bearing juices from the cane by dissolving them in water, and the use of coal as fuel for sugar mills. The real advances came in relatively simple horse-drawn tools such as cultivators and stubble diggers; such implements designed especially for use in cane cultivation were on the market by 1875. They were to have their greatest effect after Reconstruction, but the beginning of mechanizing what was to become one of the most highly mechanized crops in the nation was made before 1877.[14]

2

If wage labor was to prevail in the sugar industry, sharecropping was to triumph decisively in the cotton fields. Cotton lands were prepared for planting as early in the spring as rainfall and temperature permitted, and the seed was planted when the danger of cold weather was past. As cotton plants grew, they required much cultivation with plow and hoe, but ordinarily by July the crop could be "laid by." Then there was relatively little work to be done until late August or early September, when it was time to pick, that is to harvest the white cotton from the newly opened bolls. After being picked, the cotton was "ginned" to separate seed from lint, and then the lint was pressed into five-hundred-pound bales. After the harvest was complete, six weeks to two months might elapse before there was more work in the fields. This very routine of cotton cultivation, involving two fairly long periods when little besides "make work" tasks could be assigned to laborers, militated against the wage system. This was not, however, the only reason the wage system did not prosper.

Except in a few sanctuaries such as Bossier and Caddo parishes, the effect of contending armies on cotton plantations and their labor supply had been at least as harmful as in the sugar regions. But cotton continued to be king, the major source of income for Louisiana and all the South. High prices resulting from the scarcity during the war years gave hope that the old monarch would restore prosperity, but this was a short-lived hope. High prices did not last long, and the cotton grower was just as dependent as the cultivator of sugar upon Northern capital with which to produce his crop. Thus King Cotton was a figurehead, masking the real rule of Northern financial interests. But the scarcity of capital was not all. Labor was as scarce in the cotton fields of Concordia Parish as it was along the Teche, and cotton planters also had to learn from experience how to manage free labor. The costs of getting cotton to market were high, amounting to from 4 to 10 percent of the value of the crop. Just after the war the cotton planter feared, with considerable justification, that his crop might be seized by a Treasury agent as the property of the Confederate government. Even if not seized, it was subject to a punitive federal tax of three cents a pound. In general cotton planters and farmers were far from content with their lot. The Grange was popular in Louisiana in the 1870s, but the race question prevented its becoming effective politically. Such movements as the Knights of the White Camelia and the White League can be understood partly as expressions of the cotton farmer's discontent with his economic lot.[15]

The wage system was also tried in cotton cultivation. A few cotton planters, apparently very few, were able to raise enough capital to pay monthly wages. Even in these cases, however, the normal practice seems to have been to pay the workers only half the month's wages at the end of the month, and if the plantation had a store, purchases during the month were deducted from this half. The remainder of wages due, if any, was paid at the end of the year. Thus the workers were constrained to remain on the place and not go elsewhere when harvest time might have driven wages upward. Some planters worked as much of their land as they could with the laborers they could afford to hire; the remainder they left idle rather than subdivide it even into sharecropper plots. But most planters did not have the money to hire laborers; to survive economically they had to work their fields. At the same time, as most contemporary accounts agree, most freedmen preferred sharecropping to wages. Some planters sought to compromise by working their most fertile lands with wage labor and letting out poorer tracts to sharecroppers. But in the long run sharecropping was to prove the rule, wages the exception, on cotton farms and plantations.[16]

If the planter was constrained to sharecropping by scarcity of labor, scarcity of capital, and the rhythm of cotton culture, he quickly discovered that the system had some advantages. He could no longer rely upon the lash, and a share in the crop was a form of incentive. Furthermore, cotton farming was always a gamble, and in the alluvial regions after the war, protected hardly at all from overflow, the risks were greatly increased. From the planter's point of view sharecropping had the virtue of forcing the freedmen to share the risk.[17]

Sharecropping was being practiced across from Vicksburg to some extent in 1863, and in the Felicianas and East Baton Rouge and Concordia parishes in 1865. Some, perhaps all, of this early sharing was between the landowner on the one hand and the whole body of freedmen working the place on the other. Various forms of sharing were attempted in 1866, a year in which the crop was largely a failure. It has been asked whether sharecropping was voluntarily accepted by the freedmen or whether it was a device of the planters to exploit black labor.[18] Obviously the planters desired to exploit the workers to the extent that they hoped to profit from their labor, but it is equally obvious, insofar as Louisiana is concerned, that the black worker welcomed the new arrangement. He favored it more strongly after the crop failures of 1866 and 1867 than before. This may have been because be knew that the planter probably could not pay wages, but there is no evidence that Louisiana blacks were coerced or intimidated into sharecropping to any greater extent than were planters. The Freedmen's Bureau offered no opposition. Many planters, in fact, deplored the system even as they practiced it. There was much experiment and variation in sharecropping practices before a more or less common system came into use, but under the conditions that existed, some sort of sharecropping was inevitable. Vernon Wharton has suggested that whenever "a large class of landless laborers, a shortage of money or ready credit, and general dependency upon a cash crop which requires a long growing season" exist together, sharecropping "seems to develop naturally."[19]

In December, 1869, the *New Orleans Daily Picayune* could report that all farm hands in Richland Parish were working on shares, and that some had "got rich and quit," leaving cotton in the fields.[20] Middling cotton brought about thirty cents a pound much of the time in New Orleans during 1869, making it a prosperous year. The basic plan of sharecropping had now become fixed. The planter provided a cabin, as much land as the sharecropper and his family could work, teams, tools, seed, and supervision of varying degrees of intensity. The sharecropper provided the labor of himself and his family and assumed the responsibility for feeding and clothing himself and his family. Obviously the cropper had to have credit to obtain this food and clothing. This was provided by the planter or by a nearby merchant. Any extra expenses, such as fertilizer, or the cost of extra hands for hoeing or picking the crop, normally were divided equally between landlord and sharecropper.

When the crop was harvested, the proceeds were divided equally. There are some accounts of sharecroppers on very fertile land who received only a third or a fourth of the crop, but these reports are questionable. It seems probable that in such cases the landlord was providing rations for the tenant's family as part of the sharecrop agreement. In other instances, observers possibly confused share rent, described below, with sharecropping. Certainly in all but a fraction of agreements, the division was on a half-and-half basis. From his half the freedman had to pay at high prices increased by high interest for the food and clothing consumed by his family during the year. The planter had to repay the money he had borrowed to finance the crop. Both landlord and sharecropper might end the year in debt, and neither was likely to become rich. It should be emphasized that not all sharecroppers were black. As early as 1866 there were some white sharecroppers in the Red River Valley, and eventually, though not during Reconstruction, white croppers would outnumber black ones in the South as a whole.[21]

Some cotton lands in Louisiana were rented for cash, or for a promissory note, but these cash renters then normally became, in effect, landlords who let out the land to sharecroppers. The more prosperous landless farmers, white and black, usually made a share-rent agreement. This was a definite step above sharecropping, because the tenant provided his own work stock, animal feed, fertilizer, and tools as well as the labor of himself and his family. He probably bought on credit at the same general store or plantation commissary as the sharecropper, at the same high prices and high interest, but he had much greater control over what he planted and how he worked his crop. The agreement between landlord and tenant might be anything they could agree upon, but the general practice was for the share renter to pay in rent one fourth of the cotton and one third of the corn he produced. This system was used both for parts of plantations and for entire small farms. Evidence in newspapers and travel accounts, such as it is, indicates that from 1869 to 1872 a fairly large number of sharecroppers were managing in one way or another to become share renters. The depression which began in 1873 reversed this trend; sharecroppers who had advanced to share-renter status dropped back to become sharecroppers, and some white renters who had never before been sharecroppers descended to that economic level.[22]

Roger Shugg has shown that the myth that cotton plantations were broken up into small farms after the Civil War resulted from a misinterpretation of the inaccurate census of 1870. Shugg's findings have been reinforced by Floyd M. Clay, who clearly demonstrates the survival and in many cases the growth of plantations in the Felicianas. The superior economic resources, superior managerial skills, and perhaps the loyalty of some freedmen who had been their slaves before emancipation all gave an advantage to prewar planters. The fact that plantations had cotton gins and small farmers did not, gave the planters another advantage. Some "public" gins, owned by general merchants, were coming into operation during Reconstruction, but they did not advance the small farmer's ability to compete.

The tax assessment rolls, as demonstrated by Shugg, show that landholding was becoming more and more concentrated. Also, the prewar owners of cotton plantations were able to maintain possession to a greater degree than sugar plantation owners. In East Feliciana Parish, where fifty families owned fifty or more slaves in 1860, the same families owned thirty-seven large tracts of land in 1871, and seventeen plantations remained in the same name in 1880. Claiborne Parish, not a fertile area, had eight families with more than fifty slaves in 1860, but only one of these families, unless marriage had changed a female heir's name, still held on in 1876. In fertile Tensas Parish, 118 families owned fifty or more slaves in 1860, and sixty of these still held their lands in 1870. Overall, the actual percentage of plantations retained by prewar families is probably higher than the above would indicate, because there is no way of determining from tax assessment rolls whether a new name is that of a son-in-law or grandson of the 1860 owner.[23]

TABLE THREE
Cotton Production in Louisiana, 1866-1880[24]

Year	Acres Planted	Bales	Pounds per Acre
1866	1,020,00	131,000	57
1867	844,000	167,000	88
1868	652,000	248,000	169
1869	767,000	351,000	183
1870	932,000	567,000	269
1871	868,000	337,000	172
1872	980,000	503,000	228
1873	1,039,000	454,000	194

(Table three cont.)

Year	Acres Planted	Bales	Pounds per Acre
1874	975,000	536,000	242
1875	1,000,000	689,000	306
1876	899,000	564,000	276
1877	991,000	586,000	266
1878	961,000	462,000	215
1879	865,000	509,000	267
1880	920,000	274,000	187

As is evident from Table Three, the number of acres of cotton under cultivation followed no definite trend, but if an average is struck for three five-year periods, something more emerges. Despite the fact that more than a million acres were planted in cotton in 1866, the average of 1866-1870 is 129,000 acres less than the average for 1871-1875, and 84,000 less than the average for 1876-1880. The production figures for 1866-1870 are much lower than for the next two five-year periods, but it must be remembered that floods and cotton worms made disasters of the crops of 1866 and 1867. If production per acre was an indication of efficiency, then the trend was toward greater efficiency, because the average number of pounds per acre was increasing. However, it is doubtful that this measure of efficiency is particularly accurate. After the Civil War, as before, labor was expensive and land was cheap. Thus the desire of the planter was to obtain the greatest yield possible per laborer, and this could best be done by extensive rather than intensive farming. When this is borne in mind, it casts considerable doubt upon the many learned statements regarding the inefficiency of free labor. Furthermore, this may explain why sugar, which had been cultivated intensively before the war, was so much slower than cotton in recovering from the dislocation of the conflict.

TABLE FOUR
Cotton Production in Louisiana by Five-Year Periods, 1866-1880[25]

Years	Average Acres in Cultivation	Average Number of Bales Produced	Average Yield per Acre
1866-70	843,000	291,600	153.2
1871-75	972,000	503,800	226.4
1876-80	927,000	499,000	242.5

In 1875, the alluvial lands north of the mouth of the Red River, 16 percent of the state's area, produced 43.5 percent of the entire cotton crop. Alluvial lands south of that point had 12 percent of the total. Finally, the narrow alluvial valley of the Red River itself produced almost 8 percent of the crop. Thus the alluvial lands contributed over 63 percent of the total production. They averaged over 350 pounds to the acre. The loess soils of East Baton Rouge Parish and the Felicianas produced 5.6 percent of the state's cotton on less than 3 percent of the state's area. The oak uplands of northwestern Louisiana produced about 21 percent of the state's total. The prairies and pine lands contributed the small remainder. Production per acre was highest in the alluvial parishes along the Mississippi north of Red River. East Carroll averaged 425 pounds, Concordia 395 pounds. The average in the Felicianas, where the lands bad been long under cultivation, was only slightly more than two hundred pounds to the acre. The oak uplands averaged almost exactly two hundred pounds.[26]

The chart showing acres planted in cotton, yield in bales, and price per pound permits few significant conclusions. There was no real correlation, after 1865, between the price of cotton and the acreage planted. Indeed, there was little the farmers could do to adjust planting to the price they would receive, because when the spring crop was planted they could not know what the price would be in the fall. There is, after 1870, some rough correlation between decline in prices and decline in total production, but the number of acres planted did not decline, so the reduction in production was not intentional. Obviously, farmers, planters, and sharecroppers, as the price of cotton went down, attempted to cover their fixed costs by planting as many acres as they could, leading to lower production per acre. It also is evident that there was no significant decline in the efficiency of Louisiana labor or, if there was a decline, it cannot be proven, because the prewar practice of extensive cultivation persisted. The low production of 1866 and 1867, often used to demonstrate the inefficiency of free labor, was caused by floods and army worms.[27]

3

Most white people in Louisiana outside of New Orleans were neither planters nor sharecroppers, but rather yeoman farmers working their own land. In South Louisiana they might be Acadians or other gallicized peoples. In North Louisiana, Southwestern Louisiana, or the Florida Parishes they were more likely to be of "Anglo-Saxon" heritage Some of them had owned a slave or a few slaves. After the Civil War a few of them had one or two sharecropper families who worked lands they themselves could not work, but most of them worked their own acres. Surprisingly little is known about these people as individuals because they did not keep diaries, preserve the few letters they received, or attract the attention of travelers. Not all of them lived on the pine flats, in the hills, or on the prairies. Their small holdings were interspersed among the plantations both in the sugar parishes and farther north, but the planters' economic advantages, which had been slowly eliminating them from the better lands before the Civil War, continued after the war. In the oak hill regions of North Louisiana, however, their numbers increased during Reconstruction as a result of migration from worn-out lands of the Southeastern States.

This was the class which had suffered most during the Civil War. The replacement of lost, worn-out, or destroyed tools and livestock was more difficult for them than for the planters. They had never been subsistence farmers in the pure sense of the word. Before 1860 they had depended on cotton, sugar, rice, or in a few instances, tobacco, citrus fruit, or cattle as a source of ready money. Apparently this dependence was intensified after the war. To obtain the goods necessary to sustain life, they were as dependent upon the merchant as was the lowliest sharecropper. To guarantee the credit they received, they were forced to put more and more of their acres into a money crop, usually cotton, and into corn to feed their families and their animals.

Frederick Law Olmsted's prewar description of these people shows them to have been poor by national standards. After the war they were poorer than ever. The little recovery they experienced in the late 1860s and early 1870s was reversed by the Panic of 1873. Turning in blind anger to the White League, they provided the enlisted ranks for the war of intimidation waged against the Negro in the middle 1870s. Contrary to their economic interests, they allied themselves with the Bourbon Democrats, though it must be admitted that the Republicans probably would have done no more for them. There was a fairly strong Granger movement in the middle 1870s, going so far as to establish cooperative stores here and there, but the Grange was already declining in the North, and it was never a threat to the Louisiana planter-merchant oligarchy. Louisiana's yeoman farmers were destined to remain poor throughout the nineteenth and early twentieth centuries-so long as they remained yeoman farmers.[28]

Few Negroes succeeded in becoming landowners. As noted earlier they were seldom able to take advantage of the Homestead Act. In Concordia Parish one former slave was said to have bought three hundred acres from his onetime master and to have paid for it with one crop, but there were only two other freedmen in the parish who owned land. Poor as white farmers might be, they were more accustomed than blacks to independent farm operation, and generally they had better access to the capital needed even for small-scale cotton or subsistence production. Along the bayous in the south and in the hills to the north, the small farmers were almost entirely white. The black man who achieved independence, and few did outside of New Orleans, did so as an artisan or laborer in town.[29]

The black artisan in Louisiana has received little attention. Sterling D. Spero and Abram L. Harris estimate that in 1865 there were a hundred thousand black mechanics in the South as compared to twenty thousand white. One suspects that this was a conservative estimate insofar as blacks were concerned. Charles Wesley lists thirty occupations at which New Orleans blacks worked after the Civil War, but he sets the total number of such workers at 1,792. This is almost certainly too low for the decade following the Civil War. His count of 335 carpenters, 156 cigar-makers, 213 masons, and 82 tailors seems reasonable enough, but there were obviously more than seven stevedores. Such skilled men as draymen, barbers, and waiters, many of whom were

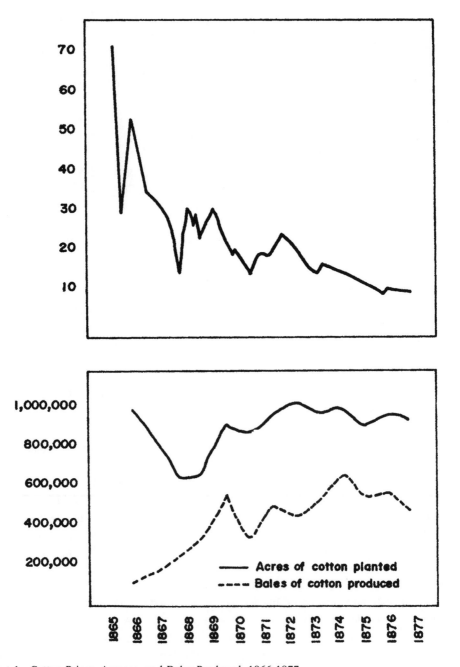

Chart 1. Cotton Prices, Acreage, and Bales Produced, 1866-1877

black, are not listed. In the smaller towns there were almost always a Negro blacksmith, a carpenter or two, and men in other trades. However, the white resentment of black artisans which had existed before the Civil War continued afterward, and white opposition was so effective that from the end of the Civil War to the mid-twentieth century the proportion of blacks engaged in skilled trades in Louisiana declined. Probably there was an absolute decline. There was also, however, a trend toward small business, black operated and catering to the black community. These were not numerous enough during Reconstruction to be important, but they were to grow in number.[30]

4

Class consciousness definitely existed among white and black workers in Louisiana during Reconstruction. As noted earlier, the constitutional convention of 1864 was dominated by the laboring class of New Orleans whites. Wages of skilled labor in New Orleans, $2.00 per day before the war, rose to $3.25 during the war. Some unions already existed, and others were formed, but the Federal authorities refused to permit strikes. In 1864 the legislature set daily wages for cartmen, mechanics, and foremen at $3.50 and wages for common laborers at $2.00. It must be emphasized, however, that this was action by and for white workers. These workers and their representatives were strongly opposed to black competition which they believed, correctly, could be used to force wages down.[31]

Thus Negro competition aligned the white workers of New Orleans with the Conservatives who flocked into the state legislature in 1865. From that time until the end of Reconstruction, the white working class of New Orleans was as reliable a group of Democratic voters as was to be found in the state. They continued their organizations and in a few instances engaged in strikes. The coopers, at least, organized their black competitors into a separate local union. But racism was stronger than whatever common economic interests existed between black and white workers. Indeed, except in a Marxist sense, black and white workers had few common interests. Not only did Negro artisans compete with whites; the hundreds of thousands of blacks on the plantations were potential competitors. White workers were well aware that blacks from the plantations could move to town, work for lower wages than whites received, and yet be better off than they were on the plantations.[32]

The blacks themselves, rural or urban, were not completely passive. As noted, wages were good during the early years of Reconstruction. As more lands were brought into production, more and more hands were needed. After the bad years of 1866 and 1867, the wages paid to field hands were high until 1874. Annual wage contracts were rare in the cotton parishes, but extra workers were frequently needed for cotton picking, and these laborers received what the traffic would bear. Pickers were paid by the pound, and the better pickers in Caddo and Bossier parishes were reported in 1869 to be earning four dollars a day. Probably the average adult picker was making two dollars a day at the same time, and this was the amount sugar planters were paying extra hands for grinding from 1869 through 1873. Wages fell some in 1874, but by 1877 they were as high as before.

Although most laborers worked in the cane or cotton fields, there were other opportunities for employment, such as levee and railroad construction. These opportunities continued despite the use of convict laborers. Some black workers had learned the uses of mobility. In spite of the constant importation of workers into Louisiana the demand for labor was never satisfied. Within the state workers migrated to areas where wages were highest or, if sharecroppers, to more fertile lands. Thus there was a rush from De Soto to Red River Parish in 1871, and throughout the 1870s there was a steady migration of blacks away from the impoverished Felicianas to the better lands west of the Mississippi. Some white commentators ridiculed the wagons loaded with pitifully sparse household belongings which crowded the roads in early January, but they were evidence that the freedmen were trying to improve their economic status. Probably most of them failed, but they made the effort.[33]

In January, 1874, planters in many of the sugar parishes held meetings and agreed among themselves to reduce wages. Generally they agreed to pay fifteen dollars a month, but in Terrebonne Parish the figure was set at thirteen dollars. This led to labor discontent everywhere, but the strongest reaction, naturally, came from Terrebonne. On January 14, 1874, the *Picayune* carried a headline of which yellow journalists twenty years later might have been proud:

WAR IN TERREBONNE
The Negroes Murdering, Outraging, and Burning
Gov. Kellogg and the Militia to the Rescue[34]

In fact a group of freedmen had decided to resist the reduction in wages and had formed an organization intended to halt work on sugar plantations in the parish. Most of them probably would have been happy to have obtained a restoration of wages, but the leaders demanded that each be allowed to rent a separate plot of ground and that the planter supervise the growing, grinding, and sale of their sugar crop. They were asking, in effect, for what cotton sharecroppers already had.

They got nothing. Radical Republicans were as horrified as Bourbon Democrats by a restive labor force. A posse of whites and blacks, led by the black sheriff of the parish, halted the strikers when they sought to persuade workers to leave the fields of the Henry W. Minor plantation near Houma. When state troops arrived Minor charged twelve of the labor leaders with violating his civil rights. Those charged were arrested and taken to New Orleans where, apparently, they were released soon afterward. It should be noted that the agreements on wage ceilings among planters did not last out the year. The demand for labor was too great.[35]

New Orleans workers, black and white, were more activist than rural laborers. Car drivers struck twice, coopers at least once, and cigar-makers once during the Reconstruction years. There were numerous strikes when wage reductions followed the Panic of 1873, and the discontent resulting from the depression was still manifest as Reconstruction ended. New Orleans labor seems to have been particularly outraged in 1877 when the city council decided to contract out city work rather than hiring directly, as had been the previous practice.

The most militant of all New Orleans workers were the black longshoremen. The loading and unloading of ships had been "white" work before the Civil War, but blacks took it over during the occupation. When white workers returned to the docks in 1865, they joined with the blacks in a strike for higher wages, but the effort was a failure. From this time on, there was little cooperation between whites and blacks on the docks, but black militance worked to the benefit of whites since black wages constituted a floor.

No significant labor trouble occurred on the docks in 1866, but short-lived disturbances broke out in May, 1867, with dissidents claiming that leaders showed favoritism in choosing workers out of the lineup. Longshoremen shared the general prosperity from 1868 to 1873, but there was a short strike in October, 1872, and another in May, 1873, when a group of armed Negroes refused to permit unloading at Algiers by workers who had agreed to accept less than the prevailing wage. When the panic struck in the autumn, white workers sought to persuade General Badger of the Metropolitan Police to arrest as vagrants "low, ignorant negroes [*sic*], who slept under tarpaulins and in barrel houses, and who . . . could afford to work at lower than regular rates."[36]

On September 14, 1873, black longshoremen met at Melpomene and White streets and adopted resolutions declaring that they were inadequately paid and demanding higher wages. They went out on strike on October 13, and they enjoyed some early successes. On October 25, however, General Badger announced that his Metropolitan Police would protect all who wished to work at the wages offered by employers. The Metropolitans were used, many blacks were arrested, and the strike was broken. Nonetheless, as late as October 29 the strikers could temporarily halt all work on the levee. Another walkout was reported on November 23.

The first full year of depression, 1874, saw much labor activity on the levee. Two black longshoremen were arrested in March for leading a group which sought to halt the unloading of a ship. That year the workers were successful in obtaining passage of a legislative act which forbade the employment of sailors in loading and unloading their ships. This act was described as a "monstrous absurdity," but the longshoremen enforced it and held their wages at three to four dollars per day. The same Radical legislature incorporated the Longshoremen's Protective Benevolent Association. In May, however, the state supreme court declared the law forbidding sailors to load and unload ships unconstitutional. The winning attorney in pleading the case was John A. Campbell, former associate justice of the United States Supreme Court, who had resigned when the South seceded.

The black longshoremen did not give up. In June, 1874, they attacked nonunion black workers in a coal yard in Algiers and were driven off by the Metropolitan Police after a number of them had been wounded. In July a meeting advocated the establishment of a central employment agency to serve all the unemployed. In September a "mob" of workers temporarily halted the loading of a steamer, and another ".iot" was reported from the levee in late January of 1875. On April 17 workers struck for $2.50 a day, but soon went back to work for the prevailing $2.00. In 1876 and 1877 the black longshoremen were once more struggling for higher wages. Labor militancy, white and black, continued in the Crescent City; it eventually culminated in a general strike of workers of both races in 1892.[37]

5

Negrophobia and the labor shortage led to much talk and some real effort to attract immigrants other than blacks to Louisiana during the Reconstruction years. In response to urging by Governor Wells and newspapers, the legislature in 1866 established a Bureau of Immigration and enacted a statute for the protection of immigrants. Carl Schurz recommended the continuation of Northern military occupation on the ground that the preservation of order would encourage immigration from the North and abroad, but the *Nation* had some doubt whether the Yankee race could settle in warm climates and retain its greatness![38]

Entrepreneurs were importing white immigrants into Louisiana before the end of 1865. Most of them were newly arrived from abroad, and Germans outnumbered other Europeans. European peasants had not been slaves in their homeland, however, and they refused to be treated as slaves in Louisiana. Also, they had an eye for economic opportunity, and many of them broke labor contracts before they left New Orleans or soon after arriving on plantations. On the other hand, German colonies in St. Landry and Acadia parishes, where the immigrants worked their own land, were successful, so much so that descendants of the original settlers live on the same lands today. The total number of Germans who moved to rural Louisiana during Reconstruction was probably less than a thousand, and some of these may have already been residents of New Orleans. None of them remained plantation workers long; quickly they made their way to New Orleans or the Middle West.[39]

From time to time other European immigrants arrived. Twenty-four Danes and Norwegians were reported at work in West Feliciana Parish in 1869, and a group of Swedes came in 1870. Some or all of these Swedes went to work on Oakley Plantation where they did well for a time but then became discontented. All of them departed except one who was too drunk to walk. Some Irishmen worked on the railroads and on the levees, but there is no record of them as field workers. In 1870 a St. Landry Parish planter contracted with a wealthy Canadian landlord for a hundred French-Canadian families. References are found to Portuguese workers, and in May of 1878 fifty Polish families, 277 persons, arrived on the Teche for work in the sugar fields at ten dollars a month for men, less for women and boys. Just as Reconstruction was coming to an end, planters turned to southern Italy as a source for labor. More Italians came to the sugar country than Europeans of any other nationality, but pride and industriousness prevented their staying long as plantation workers. Also, if the experience on Oakley was typical, they were prone to violence and were dangerous when crossed.

Despite editorials, immigration conventions, the State Bureau of Immigration, and numerous local immigration organizations, Louisiana attracted few European immigrants and the plantations kept almost none. Daniel Dennett could write that white labor was increasing and Negro labor decreasing every year in Louisiana, but saying so did not make it true. European immigrants did not come to America to be poverty-stricken and under-employed agricultural laborers; they were that in their homelands. They came to improve their economic lot, and the opportunities for the common man were far greater in the North and West than in the South.[40]

Throughout Reconstruction there was a trickle of immigration into Louisiana from the North and West and from other Southern states. This movement usually was one family at a time and therefore did attract attention from newspapers. It is known, as noted earlier, that many veterans of the Union army elected to stay in Louisiana when the war ended. Some of these, like the Twitchells in Red River Parish, were later joined by friends and relatives. A church paper in 1869 welcomed "immigration of intelligent and protestant families from Northern states"[41] to the Teche country; that same year four hundred white workers from the West arrived on the Teche to help with the sugar harvest. In 1871, twenty-five families from Kentucky arrived in St. Landry Parish on a steamboat they had chartered for the voyage. It was suggested after the Chicago fire that displaced laborers in that unfortunate city would be welcome in Louisiana, but none took advantage of the opportunity. Early in 1872 a number of white families from Alabama, bringing Negroes with them, settled in Richland Parish, and a group of farmers from Ohio established a "colony" near Mansfield in 1873. The Grange was active in promoting native white immigration to Louisiana and apparently enjoyed some success. Probably migration from the North would have been greater had it not been that Republicans were despised and ostracized in much of Louisiana, and if Louisiana had not had such a well-deserved reputation for lawlessness.[42]

Much attention was given to the possibility of using Chinese coolies in the fields; the pros and cons were debated from 1866 on. Proponents held that Chinese were hard working, docile, and accustomed to a low standard of living. Opposition was based first on racism. A writer from Plaquemines Parish said in 1866 that a state "with a black population of over three hundred thousand groveling in ignorance and darkness" would be indulging in the height of folly to bring in "another race of human beings more ignorant and degraded than we already possess in our midst."[43] Yet the shortage of labor and dissatisfaction with free black workers did encourage a number of Louisianians to experiment with Chinese laborers. Coolies were working on a plantation near Natchitoches in 1867, and a Dr. Kittridge in Assumption Parish was faced with about fifty Chinese employees who refused to work in September of the same year. Delegates from Louisiana attended a Chinese Labor Convention at Memphis in July, 1869, and returned enthused at the prospect of cheap Oriental labor. In 1870 Chinese on a sugar plantation received fourteen dollars a month, in gold, and daily rations of two pounds of meat, two pounds of rice, and an ounce of tea. For Chinese this was sumptuous fare, but these Cantonese workers were not so docile as had been expected; they insisted on the observance of the letter of their contracts. It is impossible to say how many Chinese came to Louisiana, but assuming that most arrivals were publicized, the total was probably under fifteen hundred from 1865 to 1877. Most planters seemed not to like the coolie, of whom one wrote: "He can't plow, he can't run a cultivator, he can't steer a mule, but otherwise his performances are admirable."[44] By 1890 only 372 Chinese were left in Louisiana.[45]

Thus the immigration movement was an abject failure. Louisiana was not to get Europeans, Northerners, or Orientals who would combine the industry of the Midwestern family farmer and the docility of the freedman. Louisiana plantation agriculture would depend almost entirely upon the Negro, and on a growing number of white sharecroppers who worked on the same terms and at the same pace as the Negro until the twentieth century brought mechanization. And even as the fourth quarter of the twentieth century draws near, practically every sugar or cotton plantation has its corps of black workers.

Notes for "Labor, The General Merchant, and the Crop Lien"

[1]John Burnside's Income Report, 1869, in James Amédée Gaudet Papers, Southern Historical Association, University of North Carolina (hereafter cited Gaudet Papers); Richard J. Amundson, "Oakley Plantation: A Post-Civil War Venture in Louisiana," *Louisiana History,* 9 (1968): 38; *New Orleans Daily Tribune,* September 24, 1864; Robert Somers, *The Southern States Since the War, 1870-71,* revised ed. (University, Ala., 1965), 198-99; *New Orleans Daily Picayune,* February 1, 1866, May 6, 1870, January 3, 1873; Howard Ashley White, *The Freedmen's Bureau in Louisiana* (Baton Rouge, 1970), 113; Ulrich B. Phillips, "Plantations with Slave Labor and Free," *Agricultural History,* 12 (1938): 92; William E. Highsmith, "Louisiana During Reconstruction" (Ph. D. Dissertation, Louisiana State University, 1953), 397; J. Carlyle Sitterson, *Sugar Country: The Cane Sugar Industry in the South, 1753-1950* (Lexington, Ky., 1953), 251, 259, 304-6, 313-14.

[2]Maurine Bergerie, "Economic and Social History of Iberia Parish, 1868-1900" (M. A. thesis, Louisiana State University, 1956), 30-33; *New Orleans Daily Picayune,* November 28, 1872; *Nation,* 2 (June 4, 1866): 706.

[3]*Baton Rouge Weekly Advocate,* June 12, 1869; see also *New Orleans Daily Picayune,* May 6, December 30, 1870, October 11, 1875, March 27, 1877; Roger W. Shugg, "Survival of the Plantation System in Louisiana," *Journal of Southern History,* 3 (1937): 313-15; Highsmith, "Louisiana During Reconstruction," 396-97; Bergerie, "Economic and Social History of Iberia Parish," 38; Sitterson, *Sugar Country,* 240.

[4]*New Orleans Daily Picayune,* May 6, 1870; Shugg, "Survival of the Plantation System in Louisiana," 319-20; Sitterson, *Sugar Country,* 312; Highsmith, "Louisiana During Reconstruction," 396-98; Joseph Karl Menn, *The Large Slaveholders of Louisiana, 1860* (New Orleans, 1964), 122-24, 327-36, 380-89; Ascension Parish Tax Assessment Rolls, 1870, Rapides Parish Tax Assessment Rolls, 1877, all on microfilm in Office of Comptroller, State of Louisiana.

[5]Bayside Plantation Records 2, May 6, 1875, Southern Historical Collection, University of North Carolina (hereafter cited Bayside Plantation Records); November 17, 1863; Andrew McCollam Papers, Southern Historical Collection, University of North Carolina, 7 (hereafter cited McCollam Papers) March, 1863; *Nation,* 1 (August 31, 1865): 259; *Baton Rouge Gazette and Comet,* November 30, 1865, cited in Roland Paul Constantin, "The Louisiana 'Black Code' Legislation of 1865" (M. A. thesis, Louisiana State University, 1956), 44-45; Theodore Saloutos, "Southern Agriculture and the Problems of Readjustment, 1865-1877," *Agricultural*

History, 30 (1956): 58-76; George A. Bentley, *A History of the Freedmen's Bureau* (Philadelphia, 1955), 85; J. Thomas May, "The Freedmen's Bureau at the Local Level: A Study of a Louisiana Agent," *Louisiana History*, 9 (1968): 13; White, *Freedmen's Bureau in Louisiana*, 121; Bergerie, "Economic and Social History of Iberia Parish," 36-37; Willie M. Caskey, *Secession and Restoration of Louisiana* (Baton Rouge, 1938), 142-43.

[6]*New Orleans Daily Picayune*, September 4, 1868, January 27, July 23, 1869, January 21, December 11, 1870, April 12, 1871, September 11, 1872, October 26, 1873, March 22, April 14, 1874, July 12, 1876, March 28, 1878; Charles Nordhoff, *The Cotton States in the Spring and Summer of 1865* (New York, 1876), 71; Sitterson, *Sugar Country*, 233-34, 239-41; J. Carlyle Sitterson, "The McCollams: A Planter Family of the Old and New South," *Journal of Southern History*, 6 (1940): 361-62; Bergerie, "Economic and Social History of Iberia Parish," 37-38; Highsmith, "Louisiana During Reconstruction," 438.

[7]Sitterson, *Sugar Country*, 237, 242-43; Shaffer Papers, Southern Historical Collection, University of North Carolina (hereafter cited Shaffer Papers), 7, 1876; Bayside Plantation Records 2, May 6, 1875, Southern Historical Collection, University of North Carolina (hereafter cited Bayside Plantation Records); Nordhoff, *The Cotton States*, 70; *Nation*, 2, (March 8, 1866): 334; Phillips, "Plantations with Slave Labor and Free," 92; Francis William Loring and C. F. Atkinson, *Cotton Culture and the South Considered with Reference to Immigration* (Boston, 1869), 5-6; *New Orleans Daily Picayune*, February 26, September 4, 1868, January 14, March 31, July 23, November 19, 1869, December 10, 1870, January 3, July 29, 1873, December 28, 1874; Roger W. Shugg, *Origins of Class Struggle in Louisiana: A Social History of White Farmers and Laborers During Slavery and After, 1840-1875* (Baton Rouge, 1939), 250-51; J. Carlyle Sitterson, "The Transition from Slave to Free Economy on the William J. Minor Plantation," *Agricultural History*, 17 (1943): 221.

[8]Shaffer Papers, 7, 1876; *Nation*, 2 (March 22, 1866), 365-66; *New Orleans Daily Picayune*, January, 1875; Loring and Atkinson, *Cotton Culture*, 26; Sitterson, *Sugar Country*, 323.

[9]Contract, December 19, 1868, in Avery Family Papers. Southern Historical Collection.

[10]*New Orleans Daily Picayune*, August 31, 1872, April 15, 1876; Edward King, *The Great South: A Record of Journeys in Louisiana, Texas, the Indian Territory, Missouri, Arkansas, Mississippi, Alabama, Georgia, Florida, South Carolina, North Carolina, Kentucky, Tennessee, Virginia, West Virginia, and Maryland* (Hartford, Conn., 1875), 80; Highsmith, "Louisiana During Reconstruction," 204; Sitterson, *Sugar Country*, 251, 257-59.

[11]*New Orleans Daily Picayune*, May 1, 1870, September 1, 1874, September 1, 1878; Highsmith, "Louisiana During Reconstruction," 203-4, 397-98; Somers, *The Southern States Since the War*, 230-31.

[12]*New Orleans Daily Picayune*, September 1, 1874—September 1, 1878. The *Picayune* published a commercial summary each September 1 during Reconstruction.

[13]*New Orleans Daily Picayune*, February 16, 1864, May 6, October 9, 16, 1870, January 14, 1872; Sitterson, *Sugar Country*, 274-75; King, *The Great South*, 81; Horace Greeley, *Mr. Greeley's Letters from Texas and the Lower Mississippi: To Which Are Added His Address to the Farmers of Texas and His Speech on His Return to New York, June 19, 1871* (New York, 1871), letter of May 17, 1871 (pages not numbered).

[14]*New Orleans Daily Picayune*, December 26, 1869, September 1, 1874, September 1, 1875; Sitterson, *Sugar Country*, 257, 275-76, 279-80.

[15]*New Orleans Daily Picayune*, December 5, 1872, July 13, 1873, January 8, 1874; Tax Notices, January, 1867, in Joseph Vidal Papers, Louisiana State University, Department of Archives (hereafter cited Vidal Papers); Somers, *The Southern States Since the War*, 206; Daniel Dennett, *Louisiana As It Is: Its Topography and Material Resources . . . Reliable Information for . . . Any Who May Desire to Settle or Purchase Lands in the Gulf States* (New Orleans, 1876), 50; James W. Garner, ed., *Studies in Southern History and Politics Inscribed to William A. Dunning . . . by His Former Pupils, the Authors* (Port Washington, N.Y., 1914), 294-95; Floyd M. Clay, "Economic Survival of the Plantation System within the Feliciana Parishes, 1865-1880" (M. A. thesis, Louisiana State University, 1962), 89; Harold D. Woodman, *King Cotton and His Retainers: Financing and Marketing the Cotton Crop of the South, 1800-1925* (Lexington, Ky., 1968), 359; Highsmith, "Louisiana During Reconstruction," 206-10; E. Merton Coulter, *The South During Reconstruction, 1865-1877* (Baton Rouge, 1947) 217-18 (vol. 8 of Wendell Holmes Stephenson and E. Merton Coulter, eds., *A History of the South* (Baton Rouge, 1947-); Fred A. Shannon, *The Farmer's Last Frontier: Agriculture, 1860-1897* (New York, 1945), 80 (vol. 5 of *The Economic History of the United States*); Saloutos, "Southern Agriculture, 1865-1877," 71; Theodore Saloutos, "The Grange in the South, 1870-1877," *Journal of Southern History*, 19 (1953): 473-87.

[16]*New Orleans Daily Picayune*, January 11, 1867, February 10, 20, June 5, 1869; Thomas W. Knox, "Beckoning Fields of Cotton," in William B. Hesseltine, ed., *The Tragic Conflict* (New York, 1962), 550; Senate Executive Documents, 39th Cong., 1st Session, No. 2, 28-29; Nordhoff, *The Cotton States*, 73; Woodman, *King Cotton and His Retainers*, 308-9; Clay, "Economic Survival of the Plantation," 97, 99; Bentley, *The Freedmen's Bureau*, 150; Shannon, *The Farmer's Last Frontier*, 87; Oscar Zeichner, "The Transition from Slave to Free Agricultural Labor in the Southern States," *Agricultural History*, 13 (1939): 29-30.

[17]Phillips, "Plantations with Slave Labor and Free," 90; Dorothy Lois Ellis, "The Transition from Slave Labor to Free Labor with Special Reference to Louisiana" (M. A. thesis, Louisiana State University, 1932), 30; Zeichner, "The Transition from Slave to Free Agricultural Labor," 31; Eugene M. Lerner, "Southern Output and Agricultural Income," *Agricultural History*, 33 (1959): 121.

[18]August Meier, "Comment on John Hope Franklin's Paper," in Harold M. Hyman, ed., *New Frontiers of the American Reconstruction* (Urbana, Ill., 1966), 80-81.

[19]Vernon Lane Wharton, *The Negro in Mississippi, 1865-1890* (New York, 1965), 68-69; see also *Nation*, 2 (March 22, 1865), 368; House Reports, 39th Cong., 1st Sess., No. 30, Part 4:141; *New Orleans Daily Picayune*, May 25, June 12, October 19, 1867; *Baton Rouge Weekly Advocate*, February 24, 1866; J. E. Hilary Skinner, *After the Storm: Or Jonathan and His Neighbors in 1865*, 2 vols. (London, 1866), 1:51-52; John William DeForest, *A Union Officer in the Reconstruction* (New Haven, 1948), 97; Clay, "Economic Survival of the Plantation," 46, 68-69, 75, 97-98; John Cornelius Engelsmen, "Freedsmen's Bureau in Louisiana," *Louisiana Historical Quarterly*, 32 (1949): 210; Carl N. Degler, *Out of Our Past: The Forces That Shaped Modern America* (New York, 1959), 198; Highsmith, "Louisiana During Reconstruction," 112.

[20]*New Orleans Daily Picayune*, December 5, 1869.

[21]Loring and Atkinson, *Cotton Culture and the South*, 25-26; *De Bow's Review, After the War Series*, 6 (February, 1869): 269-70; *New Orleans Daily Picayune*, August 2, 7, 1868; *Nation*, 2 (March 1, 1866), 269-70; *Natchitoches Times*, January 16, 1869, quoted in *Daily Picayune*, January 23, 1869; George Campbell, *White and Black: The Outcome of a Visit to the United States* (London, 1879), 149; Saloutos, "Southern Agriculture, 1865-1877," 67, 70-72; Rembert W. Patrick, *The Reconstruction of the Nation* (New York, 1967), 233; Shannon, *The Farmer's Last Frontier*, 88-89; Wharton, *The Negro in Mississippi*, 69-70.

[22]*New Orleans Daily Picayune*, April 14, 18, 1871, January 19, 1872; Loring and Atkinson, *Cotton Culture and the South*, 26; Clay, "Economic Survival of the Plantation," 76, 102-3.

[23]*Pointe Coupée Pelican*, quoted in *Daily Picayune*, September 4, 1878; Claiborne Parish Tax Assessment Rolls, 1871, 1876, East Feliciana Parish Tax Assessment Rolls, 1871-1880, Tensas Parish Tax Assessment Rolls, 1871, 1880, all on microfilm in Office of Comptroller, State of Louisiana; Shugg, "Survival of the Plantation System," 311-25; Clay, "Economic Survival of the Plantation," 106-7, 111-12, 129-30, 167-68; Menn, *The Large Slaveholders of Louisiana*, 194-95, 218-23, 399-412; Richard W. Griffin, "Problems of Southern Cotton Planters After the Civil War," *Georgia Historical Quarterly*, 39 (1955): 112.

[24]"Statistics on Cotton and Related Data," *Statistical Bulletin*, 99 (Washington, D.C., 1951), 51, 53, 55.

[25]Ibid.

[26]E. W. Hilgard, "Report on the Cotton Production of the State of Louisiana, with a General Discussion of the General Agricultural Features of the State," *U. S. Census, 1880, Report on Cotton Production* (Washington, D.C., 1883), 111-39.

[27]"Statistics on Cotton and Related Data," 51, 53, 55; Rosser H. Taylor, "Fertilizers and Farming in the Southeast, 1840-1950," *North Carolina Historical Review*, 30 (1953): 305-28; Loring and Atkinson, *Cotton Culture and the South*, 50-55; Clay, "Economic Survival of the Plantation," 1, 130-31; *Shreveport Times*, May 30, 1872.

[28]T. H. Harris, *The Memoirs of T. H. Harris, State Superintendent of Public Education in Louisiana, 1908-1940* (Baton Rouge, 1963), 1-19; Woodman, *King Cotton and His Retainers*, 317, 334-35; Nordhoff, *The Cotton States*, 73; *Shreveport Times*, July 7, 9, October 12, 1875; *Daily Picayune*, December 12, 1866, February 15, 1868, July 4, 1869, May 6, June 20, 1875, May 30, 1877; Acts of Louisiana, 1874, 102-3; Shannon, *The Farmer's Last Frontier*, 82-83; George Ruble Woolfolk, *The Cotton Regency: The Northern Merchants and Reconstruction, 1865-1880* (New York, 1958), 95-100; Coulter, *The South During Reconstruction*, 231; Shugg, *Origins of Class Struggle in Louisiana*, 266-73, 305-6; Samuel H. Lockett, *Louisiana As It Is: A Geographical and Topographical Description of the State*, ed. Lauren C. Post (Baton Rouge, 1970), passim.

[29]*House Executive Documents*, 41st Cong., 2nd Sess., No. 142, passim; *House Miscellaneous Documents*, 44th Cong., 2nd Sess., No. 34, 215-16; Coulter, *The South During Reconstruction*, 108; Ellis, "The Transition from Slave Labor to Free Labor," 62; Highsmith, "Louisiana During Reconstruction," 40-41; E. Franklin Frazier, *The Negro in the United States* (New York, 1957), 596-97.

[30]Sterling D. Spero and Abram L. Harris, *The Black Worker: The Negro and the Labor Movement* (Port Washington, N. Y., 1968), 16-17, 31-32; Charles H. Wesley, *Negro Labor in the United States, 1850-1925: A Study in American Economic History* (New York, 1927), 596; Meier, "Comment on John Hope Franklin's Paper," 81; *Baton Rouge Weekly Advocate*, October 6, 20, 1866; Nordhoff, *The Cotton States*, 72; Elaine Holmes Brister, "A History of Pineville, Louisiana" (M. A. thesis, Louisiana State University, 1948), 56-57; C. W. Tebeau, "Some Aspects of Planter-Freedman Relations, 1865-1880," *Journal of Negro History*, 21 (1936): 130-50.

[31]*Acts of Louisiana, 1864*, 6; *Debates of the Senate of Louisiana, 1864*, 94; Shugg, *Origins of Class Struggle in Louisiana*, 300-305; Gerald M. Capers, *Occupied City: New Orleans Under the Federals, 1862-1865* (Lexington, Ky., 1965), 152-53; Spero and Harris, *The Black Worker*, 15.

[32]*Daily Picayune*, March 26, 1874; Shugg, *Origins of Class Struggle in Louisiana*, 302-3; Spero and Harris, *The Black Worker*, 32.

[33]John F. Pollock to Thomas O. Moore, August 14, 1869, quoted in William E. Highsmith, "Social and Economic Conditions in Rapides Parish During Reconstruction" (M. A. thesis, Louisiana State University, 1947), 41; Wesley, *Negro Labor in the United States, 1850-1925*, 132; Martin Abbott, "Free Land, Free Labor, and the Freedmen's Bureau," *Agricultural History*, 30 (1956): 156; Loring and Atkinson, *Cotton Culture and the South*, 23; James P. Baughman, *Charles Morgan and the Development of Southern Transportation* (Nashville, 1968), 178-79.

[34]*Daily Picayune*, January 14, 1874.

[35]Ibid., January 14-21, 1874; Shugg, *Origins of Class Struggle in Louisiana*, 252-53; Sitterson, *Sugar Country*, 247-48.

[36]Shugg, *Origins of Class Struggle in Louisiana*, 302.

[37]*Daily Picayune*, July 15, December 28, 1865 (numerous other incidents are reported in 1873-1877); Shugg, *Origins of Class Struggle in Louisiana*, 301-4; *Acts of Louisiana*, 1874, 123-24, 131-32; C. Vann Woodward, *Origins of the New South, 1877-1913*. revised ed. (Baton Rouge, 1971), 231-32 (vol. 9 of Wendell Holmes Stephenson and E. Merton Coulter, eds., *A History of the South* (Baton Rouge, 1947-).

[38]Communication from His Excellency, J. Madison Wells, Governor of Louisiana, in Relation to Immigration, in *Legislative Documents, 1865-66*; *De Bow's Review, After the War Series*, 1 (1866): 10-13, 58-59; *Acts of Louisiana, 1866*, 198-202, 242-52; *Senate Executive Documents*, 39th Cong., 1st Sess., No. 2, 40-41; Woolfolk, *The Cotton Regency*, 95; *Nation*, 1 (August 3, 1865): 136.

[39]King to Caperton, January 1, 9, 13, 1866, March 4, 1867, in Thomas Butler King Papers, Southern Historical Collection, University of North Carolina (hereafter cited King Papers); *Daily Picayune*, January 7, 1866, February 5, April 2, 1871; *Weekly Advocate*, March 13, 1867; Sitterson, "The Transition from Slave to Free Economy," 223; Robert T. Clark, Jr., "Reconstruction and the New Orleans German Colony," *Louisiana Historical Quaterly*, 23 (1940): 513-14; Highsmith, "Louisiana During Reconstruction," 340-41.

[40]*Daily Picayune*, March 4, 1867, November 25, 1869, February 16, June 9, 1870, December 21, 1873, July 16, 1876, December 26, 1877, May 15, 1878; *Weekly Advocate*, February 4, 1871; Amundson, "Oakley Plantation," 27-32; Dennett, *Louisiana As It Is*, 161; Sitterson, *Sugar Country*, 238-39, 315; Coulter, *The South During Reconstruction*, 104; Shugg, *Origins of Class Struggle in Louisiana*, 258-59.

[41]*Southwestern Presbyterian*, April 22, 1869.

[42]Frederick B. Goddard, *Where to Emigrate and Why* (Philadelphia, 1869), 335-36; *Daily Picayune*, October 26, November 6, 1869, January 11, October 14, 1871, January 10, July 2, 1872, August 2, 1873, March 16, September 30, 1874, May 5, 1875; Woolfolk, *The Cotton Regency*, 104.

[43]*Daily Picayune*, November 13, 1866.

[44]Quoted in Sitterson, *Sugar Country*, 250.

[45]*Daily Picayune*, 1866-67; *Weekly Advocate*, June 5, 1869, October 29, 1870, May 13, 1871; *Southwestern Presbyterian*, July 14, August 5, 1869, January 20, 1870, July 1, 1875; Sitterson, *Sugar Country*, 236-38; Rowland T. Berthoff, "Southern Attitudes toward Immigration, 1865-1914," *Journal of Southern History*, 17 (1951):   329; Loring and Atkinson, *Cotton Culture and the South*, 93; Coulter, *The South During Reconstruction*, 105.

ASPECTS OF THE FAMILY AND PUBLIC LIFE OF ANTOINE DUBUCLET: LOUISIANA'S BLACK STATE TREASURER, 1868-1878*

Charles Vincent

Until recently, Reconstruction scholarship has treated with much severity the black Reconstructionist.[1] Black officeholders, such as in Claude Bower's *Tragic Era,* have most often been seen as the cause, in large part, as well as the effect of a time of gross mismanagement, misrule, and moral qualifications always consistently demeaned.[2] More current scholarship, however, has attempted to correct these unfortunate misconceptions. What follows—a brief review of the life and work of Antoine Dubuclet, a man of color highly praised for his work as state treasurer not only by his own Republican party, but by the Democratic opposition as well—is another endeavor in this very necessary task of revamping.

Corruption was certainly prevalent during the Reconstruction era. However, this was neither the first nor the last time rampant corruption was manifest in American politics, and at the time, it was by no means limited to the South. Furthermore, it had little, if anything at all, to do with the presence of blacks.

Antoine Dubuclet was the only black in the South to hold the office of state treasurer for more than one term, a fact few historians have mentioned,[3] and he was one of only two—the other man was Francis L. Cardozo of South Carolina[4]—to serve as state treasurer during Southern Reconstruction.

Dubuclet was born a free man of color in Iberville Parish in 1810, the son of a free man, Antoine Dubuclet, Sr. He was given part of his grandfather's name but carried his father's name since he was the eldest son. His father was originally from the Attakapas area of Southwest Louisiana, where he owned slightly over 406 acres of land. He was a prosperous and well-to-do free man of color.[5] How he obtained his freedom is not apparent in the records. Unlike other Deep South states, Louisiana's past political

*First published in *The Journal of Negro History*, 66 (1981): 26-36. Reprinted with the kind permission of the author and publisher.

heritage facilitated freedom for many blacks who possessed frugality and were hard workers. Perhaps the senior Dubuclet's parents—Joseph Antoine Dubuclet and Marie Felecite Gray—were by heredity free from the first appearance of the free Negroes in the Louisiana colony in 1724; or perhaps they had migrated to Louisiana during the Haitian Revolution of the 1790s; or perhaps they were the children of French or Spanish planters who manumitted them. Collectively, they were called *gens de coleur libre.* As a third caste, Louisiana's legal codes provided some flexibility for mobility, especially along economic lines.[6] Moreover, under the Spanish rule of Louisiana, 1769-1800, grants of lands were approved by the colonial governments with minor regulations—payment of surveyors' fees, clearance of the front of the tracts, and repair of roads—that an aggressive person could perform.[7]

The senior Dubuclet's economic base was agriculture, and he had slaves to cultivate his cane and other crops. According to the Catholic church records, his slaves were baptized, while he along with his wife, Rosie Belly, served as godparents.[8] His agricultural pursuits supported a large family of eleven children in 1828, ranging in ages from five into their twenties.[9] A man of moderate means, at his death in 1828, he was fifty-four years old and part owner of Cedar Grove plantation with twenty-two slaves, totaling in value $19,468.24.[10]

After his death, Widow Dubuclet and part of the family moved to New Orleans to "educate her children." Selling many of the movable items to finance her move, only the most necessary household furniture was left. The eldest son, young Antoine, probably remained in Iberville Parish to assist in managing the plantation. Having already received a "family education," and having had earlier experiences on the neighboring Poland plantation, he was intelligent and adept at operating a sugar plantation. One source indicated that he studied sugarmaking and "became an expert in the art."[11]

The plantation was successful for the next six years. In 1834, the land was partitioned and each child given a share. The economic crisis of the late 1830s hurt the financial stability of the plantation and a heavy mortgage was placed upon it. Widow Dubuclet mortgaged the property she acquired in New Orleans—totaling $10,000 in value—to lift the debt and to give the younger children an opportunity to share in the succession of their father.[12]

During this same period, the mid-1830s, Antoine met and married in a civil ceremony Claire Pollard, a wealthy free woman of color. They would later remarry in France in a church ceremony.[13] In addition to her properties, he acquired additional land, probably the adjacent lots. His land was located on the right bank (west side) of the Mississippi River, ninety-seven miles from New Orleans, with steam power in the sugar house.[14] By 1864, their combined real estate was valued at a record $94,700.00 and included over one hundred slaves.[15] One authority, H. E Sterkx, asserted that by 1860 Dubuclet was "not only the largest free Negro slave owner in Louisiana but the richest of his class as well."[16] Among the other free black slave owners, he was well respected and had a close personal relationship with the wealthy Cyprien Ricard and George Deslonde;

the latter owned a neighboring plantation. They were often godparents of each other's children and slaves.[17] Economically, there were no free Negroes who were as wealthy as Dubuclet and not many whites who were worth much more. For instance, a decade earlier, in 1850, only 1,479 planters in the entire South out of a total slaveholding population of 34,525 were in the same category. In another way he was unique because the total free Negro population in the South in 1860 was only 250,000; of the number, more than half of them were in Maryland and Virginia.[18] Statewide in 1860, Louisiana had nearly 21,000 white and free black slave owners, with only 275 people who owned from 101 to 200 slaves.[19] Within this third caste, Dubuclet enjoyed many social advantages, but within the larger Louisiana society the *gens de colleur libre* status was "just above the slave level." Although the treatment they received varied depending upon the location of families, there were always serious legal and social restrictions placed upon them. Many whites regarded social intercourse as a threat to the established social order.[20]

A product of a large, stable family, Dubuclet was married twice and father of twelve children. Before his first wife's death in 1852, they had nine children—Francois Louis, Sophie, Clarie, Eugenia (Regina), Eugene, Auguste, Pierre, Marie, and George. As was the custom of many free Negroes, in order to escape the oppressive society, he sent his four daughters to France for their education; later, his sons were sent. Three of his children—Eugenia, Clarie, and George—died in France, while his other daughters married Frenchmen. Their schooling generally cost $300 or slightly more per year and two of his sons received their medical degrees.[21] His second marriage was to Mary Ann Walsh in the early 1860s, and to this union three children were born, Rosaline D., Josephine, and Jean Oscar.[22]

The coming of the Civil War changed the lifestyle of practically everyone in Louisiana and in the nation. Slavery, which had been both an economic way of life and a system of racial adjustment,[23] was ended. Although Dubuclet was said to have been a kind master, to the slave a "master was a master," and the vast majority of slaves longed for freedom. The war brought freedom for slaves, as well as economic devastation to the southern area of Louisiana. The sugar industry was brought "to the brink of extinction,"[24] causing Dubuclet to suffer along with his fellow planters.[25]

There is no record of Dubuclet's serving in the Union or Confederate armies. However, his rapid political rise after the war under Congressional Reconstruction suggests that he offered little resistance to Union efforts.

Presidential Reconstruction actually began before the war ended, and Louisiana was one of the first states where these beginnings took place.[26] The political forces controlling the state at this time—largely conservative white planters—were inclined to grant black suffrage, as the Constitutional Convention of 1864 granted the legislature the power to extend suffrage. However, this was subsequently withdrawn through the Black Codes. It reappeared with the Reconstruction Acts of 1867, which were forced through

Congress by the "Radicals" in the Republican party, and which provided for universal male suffrage and a new Louisiana constitution.[27]

Although Dubuclet was not a member of the Constitutional Convention of 1867-68, he was a prominent figure within the state Republican party.[28] At the party's state committee nomination convention on January 14, 1868, he was nominated as the candidate for state treasurer. When Henry C. Warmoth, a 26-year-old carpetbagger, was elected along with the entire ticket, Dubuclet won an overwhelming victory. After congressional recognition of the new constitution and ratification of the Fourteenth Amendment, Louisiana was readmitted to the Union. The legislature convened on June 29, 1868, and unanimously approved Dubuclet as state treasurer.[29]

When Dubuclet took office, the treasury of Louisiana was bankrupt. According to Warmoth's account:

> Interest on the State and City (New Orleans) bonds had been in default for years; the assessed property taxable in the State had fallen in value from $470,164,963.00 in 1860 to $250,063,359.63 in 1870; taxes for the years 1860, 1861, 1862, 1863, 1864, 1865, 1866, and 1867 were in arrears. The city and state were flooded with state and city shin-plasters which had been issued to meet current expenses.[30]

Immediate legislative action was indeed necessary to stabilize the state economically. Moreover, the excess of expenditures over receipts for 1867 and 1868 totaled over $1,477,415.64. Dubuclet encouraged several acts in 1869 and 1870 as remedies. First, he proposed that the General Assembly guard against all unnecessary expenditures of the public monies and that it "put a stop to all extraordinary appropriations not absolutely necessary, so as to confine the expense" within the revenue. Secondly, he urged the Assembly to give special consideration to the manner and mode of collecting state revenue. Thirdly, he recommended "the passage of an act making greenbacks the only currency receivable hereafter for all public dues, all other laws upon the same subject matter to be repealed." These actions would restore the treasury to a "healthy condition."[31] His suggestions were not immediately enacted.

The following year (1870), he urged repeal of an act making taxes payable in warrants. He argued:

> It created perplexity and annoyance in this office and it so completely confounds the various funds that the Fund Book is thrown into inextricable chaos; one fund appears to have a large amount to its credit, when in reality it is overdrawn, from the simple fact that the state Treasurer is forced to pay or receive in payment warrants drawn against a fund out of money belonging to an entirely different fund.

If repeal was impossible, Dubuclet asked that it be amended to "authorize the tax collectors and treasurer to receive warrants in payment of taxes, *only* for the funds against which they are drawn." Tax collectors were further complicating the finances of the state by settling in warrants. Dubuclet wanted this practice stopped because these payments, "when compared with the Auditors' books, were found to have been artistically altered to larger denominations." A few such collectors had refused to clarify their records when approached. Although taxes were not high, Governor Warmoth and the legislature disagreed with the treasurer and continued to permit the collection of warrants as payment for taxes.[32]

Since Dubuclet's advice and recommendations fell on deaf ears, no programs or suggestions appeared in his 1871, 1872, 1873, 1874, and 1875 reports. However, he could find comfort in preventing the finances from further deterioration. It was rumored, with substantial validity, that the governor took bribes and was not above corruption. Apparently Dubuclet felt that he had lost the battle to modify collection procedures, but he was determined not to lose the war by stopping corrupt deals involving payments from the treasury. Such was the case with the 1869 levee bonds to repair levees along the Mississippi River. This involved the state selling the bonds through a levee board commission. The commission consisted of three whites—Governor Warmoth, Representative A. L. Lee of St. Bernard Parish, Senator Lynch—and Dubuclet. Lee and Lynch served as spokesmen in a trip to New York to sell the bonds. Although the commissioners sold portions of the bonds ($200,000 worth) for 68 percent, and 70 percent on the dollar for other portions ($120,000 worth), three members of the commission— Warmoth, Lee and Lynch—wanted to pay into the treasury the proceeds of the levee bonds at the rate of "forty-seven for a part and sixty cents for another portion" ($84,000). Thus they could pocket a large portion of the money. Dubuclet objected with vigorous protest,[33] and the commission adjourned. At another meeting of the board, of which Dubuclet was not notified, the proposition was adopted by Warmoth and Lee. Upon learning of this, Dubuclet took the matter to court. Since Lee had endorsed many of his warrants and received full payments, the state had to play host to this scandal.[34]

One fairly conservative newspaper, the *New Orleans Times* praised Dubuclet's action with these words:

> It is a noticeable incident that only white men were engaged in this nefarious transaction, whilst the only honest and faithful person who stood by the interest of the State, and held aloof from all the turpitude of the transaction, was a colored man.[35]

The *New Orleans Tribune,* a black-owned-and-operated newspaper, thanked the *Times* for complimenting Dubuclet in an editorial entitled "Character, Not Color." The paper further observed, "It gives us much pleasure to note these instances of reason triumphing over prejudices, and we trust that henceforth we may hear no more twaddle about this being a 'white-man's Government.'"[36]

The Constitution of 1868 stipulated the term for treasurer and auditor. Article 69 states that the treasurer would be elected for two years, and four years thereafter. Thus Dubuclet was reelected in 1870 to serve until 1874, and in the latter year he was reelected to serve until 1878. He won handily in the three elections in which he ran. In fact, one of the most conservative New Orleans newspapers supported him in 1874. When the

Republican party attempted to dump him in 1874 for a carpetbagger who would be more agreeable to corruption, the *Picayune* observed:

> Should Dubuclet be defeated, the Radical Government will not only lose its most reliable official but it will attest to the determination of a large class of voters that colored people must he put in the background and not encouraged to aspire to high offices.[37]

Dubuclet's statewide election[38] in 1874 meant that he was not only unbeatable but that he was serving under the third Republican governor, William P. Kellogg. (P. B.S. Pinchback, a black man, had served briefly as governor from December 9, 1872, until January 13, 1873, when Warmoth was impeached.) A native of Vermont, and a lawyer by training, Kellogg was less corrupt than Warmoth but was equally resented by white Democrats. His administration did confront the economic crisis. The funding bill—converting the whole bonded and floating debt of the state in consolidated bonds having forty years to run—aided in releasing some of the problem. By the end of his administration in 1876, Kellogg had reduced the bonded debt by over five million dollars.[39]

Governor Kellogg's administration faced much hostility. His tenure endured the greatest obstacle of the Reconstruction governors. The opposition formed tax resistance associations and an attempted *coup d'etat*. When dissenting militant White Leaguers seized control of the state house on September 14, 1874, in which over 50 persons died, they installed their man, D. B. Penn, as governor and replaced other officials. Treasurer Dubuclet was the only top official—along with his clerks, who were generally his well-educated sons[40]—allowed to carry on the affairs of his office without intrusion or interruption. On the next day, a new sentinel was placed at the state house by the militant White Leaguers. After the sentinel, not knowing Treasurer Dubuclet, refused him entry, Dubuclet went home. When the insurgent governor learned of this incident, one source observed, "He [Penn] ordered one of his aides to go to Dubuclet's residence in his, the Governor's carriage, and apologize to Mr. Dubuclet for the unintentional rudeness of the sentinel."[41] Within five days President U. S. Grant had ordered the lawlessness to cease and mobilized twenty-seven companies into New Orleans to suppress the insurrection. Kellogg was restored to the governorship.[42]

Other problems confronting Kellogg's regime and Reconstruction would involve Dubuclet. There was an attempted impeachment of the governor and treasurer in February, 1876, which fell short. Although the House passed an impeachment measure, the Senate adjourned before hearing charges. No question of personal dishonesty was involved. The complaint was that public funds in 1874 designated for interest payments were used to pay the police force. The impeachment effort was stillborn, but it was indicative of the coming election of 1876.[43]

This election was crucial to Southern Reconstruction. The "bargain" at the national election—the disputed electoral votes for Hayes—indicated that the Republican party was willing to forego its support of Southern blacks.[44] This did not, however, mean an immediate end to black participation. Blacks continued to serve in the Louisiana legislature until 1900. Moreover, Dubuclet was not up for reelection in 1876 and his tenure would end in 1878. He thus served under the Democratic Gov. Francis T. Nicholls. It was during this administration that the treasurer came under a detailed investigation by a five-man committee chaired by future Supreme Court Chief Justice Edward D. White. The majority report—White, James Hill, and Sam H. Buck—practically exonerated him. Although there were critical comments and criticism on irregularities, and minor illegalities, the committee reported that the "Treasurer certainly by comparison deserves commendation for having accounted for all money coming into his hand, being in this particular remarkable." The minority report—C. W. Ketting and T. T. Allain—completely exonerated him.[45] The investigation centered on two questions:

> 1. What was the condition of the accounts of Treasurer connected with the verification of the entries in such accounts, as well as ascertaining by such verification whether the receipts had been correctly entered and disbursed, and the cash properly and legally applied?
> 2. What mode of settlement had been established by the Treasurer in receiving revenue turned in by tax collectors?
> 3. What discrimination, if any, had been exercised in the payment of warrants?

On the first question, the committee discovered amounts illegally withdrawn but "all that should be on hand is accounted for." On the tax collector question, they found that the treasurer's office did receive several payments of taxes in warrants but all were made good. The committee suspiciously found that the holders of the larger warrants were paid but found no fraud. As stated above, the minority report submitted concluded:

> After an exhaustive examination made by the present committee in the books, papers, documents, moneys, etc., of the State Treasurer's department, the committee has ascertained that the State Treasurer has faithfully accounted to the State for every dollar paid into the treasury; that all the books, papers, vouchers and documents are in perfect order, and no one pretends that the State has any claim in the premises against that official.[46]

Dubuclet did not seek reelection in 1878. The divided Republican party met in Baton Rouge on September 19, 1878, and selected John Gardner of Baton Rouge as treasurer. An ex-Whig before the war, Gardner had served in the Louisiana legislature. When the state convention convened approximately three weeks later, it endorsed the ticket.[47]

The Democratic nominating convention also met and experienced dissension. It took fifty-seven ballots before E. A. Burke was selected.[48] Burke's place of origin is obscure. Some sources claim that he was born in Kentucky, but what is clearer is his employment with the Erie Railroad in Pennsylvania and later with railroads in Ohio. He appeared in Louisiana in 1870 and quickly joined the White League, but he is most remembered for his endeavors in the so-called "Wormley-House Bargain," placing him in the position of "Redeemer extraordinary." He would serve as state treasurer for over 10 years and rob Louisiana of over one million dollars.[49]

The election of 1878 was won by the Democrats. In the contest for treasurer, Burke defeated Gardner by a 43,128-vote majority. Even in Iberville, Dubuclet's home parish, Gardner received only 91 votes to Burke's 487.[50] The Democrats were back in control.

Dubuclet returned to his plantation home in Dorseyville (Iberville Parish) in 1879. There is no New Orleans residence address listed at 25 Robertson Street, where he had lived with his son, Dr. Eugene Dubuclet, from 1868 until 1875.[51] Other residential addresses were: 75 N. Rampart in 1875, 268 Canal in 1876, and 250 Canal in 1878. The treasurer's office was located on Royal Street at the corner of Conti until it was moved to the state house in 1875. In 1882, Dubuclet sold his large plantation, totaling over 14,000 acres, to his son, Francois.[52] Shortly after his return to Dorseyville, a Mrs. Felicite Roy came from New Orleans to live with him. Apparently they were never married but affectionately addressed one another as "my old man" and "my old woman" according to friends and neighbors. On Sunday, December 18, 1887, Antoine Dubuclet died in Iberville Parish. His remains were brought to New Orleans on Monday and were interred in the family tomb in the Claiborne Street cemetery.[53]

The lawful heirs to his property—real and personal totaling $1,130.70—were contested. His son, Dr. Eugene Dubuclet, successfully annulled a questionable will presented to the court on Mrs. Roy's behalf claiming that on May 13, 1882, he had left all his property to her. In the probate contest, Dubuclet's children were present, either in person or through lawyers. A summons to Mrs. Roy was not answered and after two days, the court returned a default against her. The property was divided among his nine children.[54]

Antoine Dubuclet's career as state treasurer of Louisiana was outstanding. His chief assistant and second assistant were his sons. In the "stormy days" of Reconstruction, he was untouched by scandals, and received bi-partisan praise. At his death in 1887, the conservative *Picayune* carried an extensive article, partially entitled, "Death of a Prominent Figure in the Republican Regime." Moreover, Dubuclet's service is more important when it is contrasted against his successor, Major E. A. Burke. Burke's irregularities cost the state $1,267,905.00. He fled the country, traveling in Europe before settling in Honduras, and engaged in various mining interests. He remained a fugitive from justice until his death in 1928.[55] One scholar of Bourbonism in Louisiana says of Burke's default: "No Reconstruction swindler had ever approached that figure."[56] The full story of these defaults was not uncovered until almost two years after Dubuclet's death. One can only venture to guess what Dubuclet's comments would have been, or indeed what the reactions were of those who knew of his scandal-free record.

The political career of Louisiana's treasurer during Reconstruction stands in sharp contrast to much of the criticism many earlier writers attributed to black officials. Perhaps Dubuclet was an exception, but the tenure of this intelligent and extremely sincere guardian of public funds for Louisiana was a challenge to the morality of the period. Along with many others of his race he contributed to the beneficial Reconstruction of Louisiana.

Notes for "Aspects of the Family and Public Life of Antoine Dubuclet: Louisiana's Black State Treasurer, 1868-1878"

[1]Howard K. Beale, "On Rewriting Reconstruction History," *American Historical Review,* 55 (1940): 807-10; Bernard A. Weisberger "The Dark and Bloody Ground of Reconstruction Historiography," *Journal of Southern History,* 25 (1959), passim; James T. Currie, "The Reconstruction Centennial: An Historiographical Commemoration," *Mississippi Quarterly,* 31 (1977), passim.

[2]Claude Bowers, *The Tragic Era: The Revolution After Lincoln* (Cambridge, Mass., 1929), passim.

[3]Several historians incorrectly say that he was treasurer from 1868-1869: see John Hope Franklin, *Reconstruction: After the Civil War* (Chicago, 1961), 134; although Dubois cites the correct years, on the same page he gives the above incorrect years, *Black Reconstruction in America, 1860—1880* (Cleveland, 1965), 470.

[4]Edward L. Sweat, "Francis L. Cardozo—Profile of Integrity in Reconstruction Politics," *Journal of Negro History,* 66 (1961): 217-32.

[5]Succession Papers, No. 378, Probate Court, Antoine Dubuclet, 1829. Iberville Parish Court House, Plaquemine, Louisiana (hereafter cited as Dubuclet, Sr., Succession papers). The certificate of his acquiring this land is dated May 29, 1811.

[6]Ibid., Gary Mills, *The Forgotten People: Cane River's Creoles of Color* (Baton Rouge, 1977), 105-8.

[7]"O'Reilly Ordinance of 1770," *Louisiana Historical Quarterly,* 11 (1928): 237-40.

[8]*Baptism-Marriage and Interment of Negroes, 1785-1858.* Saint Gabriel Archives, No. 10, The *SGA-IO.* Baptism of Agathe, Francois, Bernard, and Zachary are on pages 127, 128, 129, 145,147, 157. He was also the godfather of other slaves; see page 145.

[9]Dubuclet Sr., Succession Papers. Their ages varied: Felicite, Rose, and Solidele were of the "age of majority," indicating age 21; Rose was married; Petronille, age 20; Antoine, age 17; Uranic, age 15; Josephine, age 14; Hortense, age 12; Augustin, age 10; George, age 7; Euchina, age 5. This plantation in Iberville Parish had been acquired in May, 1815.

[10]*SGA-IO,* 328; *SGA-19,* Marriage, 62; *cf.,* Albert Grace, *The Heart of the Sugar Bowl: The Story of Iberville* (Plaquemeine, 1946), 72, which says he died in June, 1928. Neither the January nor June issue of the Parish's 1928 newspaper carried a notice.

[11]Dubuclet, Sr., Succession Papers; *New Orleans Daily Picayune,* December 21, 1887.

[12]Dubuclet Sr., Succession Papers.

[13]Grace, *The Sugar Bowl,* 72.

[14]P. A. Champomier, *Statement of the Sugar Crop Made in Louisiana in 1853-54 With an Appendix* (New Orleans, 1854), 11. The plantation was under the name, "Dubuclet and Durand." Production declined to 80 hogshead in 1855 but rose to 546 in 1859; earlier the production varied: 1856-57, 118 hogshead; 1857-58,450 hogshead, see Ibid., *1854-55,* 11; Ibid., *1858-59,* 10.

[15]The Tax Assessment Rolls, Iberville Parish, Comptroller's Office, State Capitol, Baton Rouge, microfilm copy of original. The values of his estate fluctuated: In 1864, he owned a lot valued at $5,000 on which he paid taxes totaling $97.40; but the same year, "Antoine and Co." owned 1,200 acres of land (cash valued at $94,700) and 100 horses, and paid $276.50 worth of state taxes. In 1866, "Dubuclet, Ant., f.m.c." possessed 150 acres, cash valued at $250.00, $2,000.00 loan on interest, $200.00 cash value of horses, $50.00 carriage, totaling $2,500.00. In 1870, his sugar plantation totaled $17,000.00; see *New Orleans Daily Picayune,* December 21, 1887.

[16]H. E. Sterkx, *The Free Negro in Ante-bellum Louisiana* (Rutherford, N.J., 1972), 208.

[17]Dubuclet Sr., Succession Papers.

[18]J. G. Randall and David Donald, *The Civil War and Reconstruction,* 2nd ed. (Lexington, Mass., 1969), 60, 67.

[19]Edwin Adams Davis, *Louisiana: The Pelican State* (Baton Rouge, 1975), 162.

[20]Sterkx, *Free Negro,* Chapter 4, passim.

[21]Succession Papers, No. 186, 6th District Court, Clarie Pollard Dubuclet tutorship), 1852, filed November 30, 1881, Iberville Parish Court House, Plaquemine (hereafter cited as Clarie P. Dubuclet, Succession Papers). *SGA-IO,* Baptism, 317, 319-20, 321, 326. The birth dates of the children were: Francois Louis, August 10, 1837; Sophie, February 26, 1839; Clarie, July 2, 1841; Eugenia (Regina) December 20, 1842; Eugene, July 8, 1845; the birth dates of the others were not listed; the dates of those who died in France were: Eugenia (Regina), February, 1859; Clarie, November, 1867; and George, October 1878. An interesting tradition within the family was the division of a deceased member's inheritance: Whenever a child died, his (her) inheritance was equally divided among the other family members, including their father.

[22]*SGA-19,* Baptism, card file; Succession Records, Iberville Parish Court House, Plaquemine. Upon Mary Ann Walsh Dubuclet's death, she had property in New Orleans totaling $7,793.30; see Clarie P. Dubuclet, Succession Papers; *New Orleans Daily Picayune,* December 21, 1887.

[23]Benjamin Quarles, *The Negro in the Making of America* (New York, 1969), 67.

[24]Charles P. Roland, *Louisiana Sugar Plantations During the American Civil War* (Leiden, Netherlands, 1957), 137; see also pages 66-74; J. Carlyle Sitterson, *Sugar Country: The Cane Sugar Industry in the South, 1753-1930* (Lexington, 1953), 203-27.

[25]A. Bouchereau, *Statement of the Sugar and Rice Crops Made in Louisiana in 1877-78, With an Appendix* (New Orleans, 1878), 17; Ibid., *1880-81* (New Orleans, 1881), 55. These sources reveal that Dubuclet's output for the first years of the war remained fairly high; for instance, he produced 473 hogsheads in 1861-62. Records for the postwar years are quite revealing. In 1877, the plantation was listed under "A. Dubuclet and Co.," and was renamed "Pollard." His "brick and shingle" roof sugarhouse contained both steam and kettle boilers, but his production was listed as 66. Four years later, 1881, his production increased only to 82 hogsheads.

[26]For comments on Lincoln's efforts see: John R. Ficklin, *History of Reconstruction in Louisiana* (Baltimore, 1910), 88-97; Willie M. Caskey, *Secession and Restoration of Louisiana* (Baton Rouge, 1938), 66-117; James P. McCrary, "Moderation in a Revolutionary World: Lincoln and the Failure of Reconstruction in Louisiana" (Ph. D. Dissertation, Princeton University, 1972), passim.

[27]Randall and Donald, *Civil War and Reconstruction,* 592-600.

[28]Charles Vincent, *Black Legislators in Louisiana During Reconstruction* (Baton Rouge, 1976), 41; *New Orleans Tribune,* September 2, 27, 28, 1865.

[29]Henry C. Warmoth, *War, Politics and Reconstruction: Stormy Days in Louisiana* (New York, 1930), 51; Joe Gray Taylor, *Louisiana Reconstructed, 1863-1877* (Baton Rouge, 1974), 178-79, 206; *Official Journal of the Proceedings of the Senate of the State of Louisiana 1868* (New Orleans, 1868), 4.

[30]Warmoth, *War, Politics and Reconstruction,* 79.

[31]Report of the State Treasurer for the Year 1868 to the General Assembly," *Louisiana Legislative Documents, 1869* (New Orleans, 1868), 3-4.

[32]Report . . . for the Year 1869. . . .," *Louisiana Legislative Documents 1870* (New Orleans, 1870), 3-5; Taylor, *Louisiana Reconstructed,* 207-8; No substantial personal papers of Antoine Dubuclet have been uncovered, or are known to exist. The Rene Grandjean Collection, Department of Archives and Manuscript, Earl K. Long Library, University of New Orleans, New Orleans, contains many volumes of Dubuclet's spiritualist worships, and are largely in French. Grandjean, a Frenchman, was married to one of Dubuclet's daughters.

[33]*New Orleans Times,* January 6, 23, 1869.

[34]Ibid., January 26, 1869.

[35]Ibid., January 28, 1869. This issue contains Dubuclet's full testimony.

[36]*New Orleans Tribune,* January 29, 1869. Court suits were often brought against Dubuclet for hasty payments but the Treasurer refused to be pressured into hurried questionable action. See *Reports of Cases Argued and Determined, in the Supreme Court of the Territory of Louisiana: Annotated Edition* (St. Paul, 1908); see 23 La. Ann. 267, 24 La. Ann. 16, 26 La. Ann. 80, 26 La. Ann. 127, 28 La. Ann. 932, 30 La. Ann. 662, and 33 La. Ann. 703.

[37]*New Orleans Picayune,* August 8, 11, 1874; The state's auditor, Charles Clinton, resigned under fire, *see* ibid., August 12, 15, 21, 1874.

[38]Dubuclet's Democratic opponent, John Moncure, brought suit in District Court alleging that he won. The Court decided against his claim. The *New Orleans Republican,* November 6, 7, 10, 1874; *New Orleans Picayune,* April 16, 30, 1875; *House Reports,* 43 Cong., 2nd Sess., No. 261, pp. 442-45.

[39]"Fourth Annual Message of His Excellency W. P. Kellog, Governor of Louisiana Delivered at Regular Session of the General Assembly, New Orleans, January 3, 1876," *Louisiana Legislative Documents* (New Orleans, 1876), 7-9; John E. Gonzales, "William Pitt Kellogg, Reconstruction Governor of Louisiana, 1873-1877," *Louisiana Historical Quarterly,* 29 (1946): 395, 466-70.

[40]The Gardner Directory lists his son Francois (Frank) as his chief clerk, and another son, Augusta D. as an assistant; see *Gardner's New Orleans Directory for 1869. . . .* (New Orleans, 1868), 140; *Edward's Annual Directory . . . 1870* (New Orleans, 1869), 188; *Edwards' Directory . . .1871-74,* passim; *Soard's Directory 1875* (New Orleans, 1875), 256; the same officers were listed for 1876, 1877, 1878.

[41]Stuart O. Landry, *The Battle of Liberty Place: The Overthrow of Carpetbag Rule in New Orleans, September 14, 1874* (New Orleans, 1955), 149. The conservatives claimed that the police had seized guns destined for private citizens (White Leaguers) as a reason for the coup.

[42]"Condition of the South," *House Reports,* 43 Cong., 3 Sess., No. 261, pp. 793-835; *New Orleans Republican,* September 15-20, 1874, passim.

[43]Ella Lonn, *Reconstruction in Louisiana After 1868* (New York, 1918), 393-98; *Senate Journal, Extra Session, 1876,* 283-87; *New Orleans Republican,* March 7, 9, 1876.

[44]Rayford W. Logan, *The Betrayal of the Negro* (London, 1969), 23-47; C. Vann Woodward, *Reunion and Reaction: The Compromise of 1877* (Boston, 1951), 208.

[45]*"Report* of Joint Committee to Investigate the Treasurer's Office, State of Louisiana, To the General Assembly," *Louisiana Legislative Documents, 1877* (New Orleans, 1878), 12, 15; Alice Dunbar Nelson, "People of Color in Louisiana, Part II," *Journal of Negro History,* 2 (1917): 76-77.

[46]"Report of the Joint Committee," 13.

[47]Marguerite T. Leach, "The Aftermath of Reconstruction in Louisiana" (M. A. thesis, Louisiana State University, 1933), 22-5; *New Orleans Democrat,* September 20, 1878; *New Orleans Weekly-Democrat,* September 21, 28, 1878.

[48]*New Orleans Daily Picayune,* August 4, 7, 8, 1878.

[49]C. Vann Woodward, *Origins of the New South, 1877-1913* (Baton Rouge, 1951), 70-71.

[50]*New Orleans Weekly-Democrat,* 9, 16, November 1878.

[51]*New Orleans City Directories,* passim.

[52]Tax Assessment Roll, 1881, Iberville Parish, p. 9; 1882, p. 8; Claire P. Dubuclet, Succession Papers.

[53]*New Orleans Daily Picayune,* December 21, 1887.

[54]Succession Papers, No. 371, 23rd District Court, Antoine Dubuclet, 1887, Iberville Parish Court, House, Plaquemine.

[55]James F. Vivian, "Major E. A. Burke: The Honduras Exile, 1889-1928," *Louisiana History,* 15 (1974): 175-81; Clarence H. Nichols, "Francis Tillou Nicholls, Bourbon Democrat" (M. A. thesis, Louisiana State University, 1959), 135-40.

[56]William I. Hair, *Bourbonism and Agrarian Protest: Louisiana Politics, 1877-1900* (Baton Rouge, 1969), 141.

LOCAL BLACK ELECTED OFFICIALS IN ASCENSION PARISH (1868-1878)*

Robert E. Moran

Many historians have described the period following the Civil War as a "tragic era," a time when illiterate, ignorant blacks dominated the governments of the South and threatened to destroy its civilization. Most of these historians have looked at state government to prove their case. In relatively recent years revisionist historians have taken a second look at the period and have come up with differing conclusions. One such historian, Vernon Wharton in his book, *The Negro in Mississippi, 1865-1890,* asserts that although blacks formed a majority in 30 counties, they almost never took advantage of their numbers to dominate politics in their locale. With the exceptions of Coffeeville and Greenville, no town had a black majority on its board of aldermen and only 12 men held the office of sheriff throughout the entire period.

While much has been written about the role of blacks in state government, little has been said about their role in county and city affairs. Some of these black leaders were literate and others, as has been suggested, were not. This illiteracy has been erroneously equated with ignorance, the inability to follow and understand debate, and the inability to learn from others. It is the contention of this article that in Louisiana, where allowed, blacks served as best they could on the local level and did not dominate local politics even where they were the majority.

Reconstruction in the South gave most blacks their first opportunity to participate in government. In Louisiana the freedmen and other blacks voted for the first time on September 27, 1867, in order to choose delegates to the state constitutional convention. On April 16, 17, 1868, an election was held for state officials and the ratification of the new constitution. The constitution was ratified by a vote of 66,152 to 48,739. At the same time, blacks were elected to both state administrative and legislative posts as well as to local positions, especially in those parishes where blacks were the majority.[1] All of

*First published in *Louisiana History*, 28 (1986): 273-80. Reprinted with the kind permission of the author and the Louisiana Historical Association.

197

the parishes of the sugar country were predominantly black and Republican, along with several parishes along the Red River and the Mississippi delta. The hill, prairie and pine-flat parishes were predominantly white and opposed to Republicanism throughout Reconstruction.[2]

Since many whites despised the idea of blacks voting and holding political office, they reacted with violence and threats of violence. Riots between 1866 and 1874 had a notable influence upon Reconstruction in the state. Chief among these were the New Orleans Riot of 1866, the Colfax Riot of 1873, and the Coushatta Massacre of 1874. In Ascension Parish, two days after the election of 1870, a bloody disturbance broke out in Donaldsonville. Whites fired on the militia who had come to quell the disturbance. Blacks in return shot to shreds a Republican judge and the newly appointed mayor. No attack on the city was made. Still some black leaders were arrested and imprisoned in New Orleans.

Besides the riots and murders, blacks were intimidated by arbitrary arrests, threats of discharge from their employment, and damage to personal property. Lt. General P. H. Sheridan, a military commander in Louisiana, in a letter to the secretary of war, W. E. Belknap, stated that between 1866 and 1875 nearly 3,500 persons, a great majority of whom were black, had been victims of violence.[3] Nevertheless, blacks continued to vote as Republicans or Democrats and to hold political offices throughout the 1870s.

One of the local political offices held by several blacks during this period was that of police juror, an office similar to that of county commissioner in other states. The police jury controlled the parish taxes, roads, bridges, and ferries. It provided for the upkeep of parish buildings, such as the courthouse and jail, and it dispensed small amounts of money to the poor. The juries at this time consisted of five persons usually elected at large, but sometimes by wards. When there was a vacancy on the jury as in other local offices, the governor had the authority to appoint a replacement. For example, Governor H. C. Warmoth appointed Pierre Landry, a Methodist minister and prominent leader from Ascension Parish, mayor of Donaldsonville in 1868 until another mayor was elected.

Ascension Parish, located among the sugar parishes of southern Louisiana, had a black majority in 1870; for the record shows there were 4,265 whites and 7,310 blacks. Prior to the election of 1872 there were 4,251 registered voters in the parish of which 1,061 were white and 3,192 were black.[4] The blacks of the parish almost to the man voted their tickets as they took their whiskey, straight, a straight Republican ticket and thus throughout Reconstruction carried the parish for the Radicals over Fusionists and Democrats.

During 1871 both Pierre Landry and Hillary Rice were members of the police jury. Rice was a 46-year-old blacksmith. Though illiterate, he was to be re-elected to several juries during the seventies. Pierre Landry who had served as mayor of Donaldsonville served also as a member of the school board and in 1872 was elected its president. While holding these local offices, he served from 1870-1874 as a member of the lower house of the legislature and from 1874-1878 as a member of the upper house.[5] In 1879 he represented Ascension Parish at the constitutional convention of that year and was defeated for the presidency of the convention by Lt. Gov. Louis A. Wiltz.

A general election throughout the state took place on November 9, 1872. Election day in Ascension Parish was a very quiet one. Each citizen seemed to vie with his neighbor in conducting himself decorously and contributing his share toward securing and maintaining the peace and good order that prevailed throughout the day in all parts of the parish. Notwithstanding the assurances of *The Chief*, the local newspaper, that the election in the parish would pass off without disturbances, some timid persons left town and remained away until after election day.[6] While only 17 percent of the voters went to the polls generally throughout the state, nearly 58 percent voted in the parish.

Winners in the election included the following blacks: Pierre Landry, state representative; Aaron Hill, sheriff; V. C. Cantrelle, coroner and an all-black police jury: Hillary Rice, Henry Johnson, Edward Cantey, William Kenner, and Allvidges Harrison. Commenting on the newly elected jurors, *The Chief* was to say:

> Our new police jury, composed entirely of colored men, will assemble the first day of January. . . . Our colored friends composing the new jury will have an excellent change to make enviable reputation in the community by adhering strictly to the path of rectitude in their new positions, and accomplishing all practicable reforms in parish government. We shall take great pleasure in according them their due need of praise whenever their official actions deserve commendation.[7]

On January 7, 1873, the all-black police jury was sworn in by order of the clerk of court. The jury went about its business by electing its own officers: William Kenner, president; F. A. Fobb, another black, secretary; Christian Kline, who had run for sheriff on the Fusion ticket, treasurer; and Dr. W. M. McGailliard, jail physician. As many had anticipated, the first session of the police jury was well attended by politicians, place hunters, and persons drawn there from mere curiosity at seeing the all-black jury at work. *The Chief* further commented that all business for which they had met was transacted with great promptness and dispatch.[8]

At its second meeting the jury elected a parish attorney, appointed a committee to make out a budget, a committee to call upon the former treasurer to turn over his books, and a committee on finance. The secretary, Frederick Fobb, who was also to be the "faithful and efficient" tax collector of Donaldsonville, was authorized to issue warrants for all accounts approved by the chairman and one other committeeman of the committee on claims. At the January 27 meeting the president appointed road commissioners for the eight wards of the parish and syndics for the wards. The police jury then heard the report of the committee to look at the books of the treasurer and the budget committee which estimated expenditures for the parish to be $20,790. "The police jury wisely recommends," said *The Chief*, "a strict enforcement of law relating to the collection of overdue taxes." One person named Hannah Carter was added to the pauper's list. She was to be paid $4.00 per month from the paupers' fund of $400.00.[9]

During the March 3 meeting the president appointed two physicians to vaccinate against smallpox all inhabitants of the parish. The physicians were to be paid $100 each. The jury then approved the payment of all bills and demanded that the tax collector turn over to the parish treasurer all taxes and licenses collected by him. If he did not, the president of the police jury would institute a suit against him. In May 1872, some citizens of Donaldsonville instituted a suit in district court against Charles F. Smith, the tax collector, who was white. The objective of this suit was to enjoin and prevent him from collecting parish taxes on property situated in the town of Donaldsonville. The district court dismissed the case whereupon the plaintiffs appealed to the Louisiana Supreme Court.

In the meantime, Pierre Landry introduced a bill in the legislature which would have exempted the propertyholders of Donaldsonville from parish taxes. The bill passed the house but failed in the senate. The state supreme court finally ruled that in this case there would be no such exemption. It also refused a rehearing of the case. The editor of *The Chief* was forced to conclude that the only incentive of the parties entering the suit was to delay the collection of parish taxes with the vain hope that the legislature would pass an act releasing them from payment altogether.[10]

For some time there had been trouble in the Ascension Parish Police Jury over finances and budgeting. The police jury on March 11, 1872, had brought in a budget in violation of State Law No. 42 of 1871, a budget in excess of the taxes for the year. This jury resigned and the new one commissioned in July repealed the March 11 budget.

While the controversy over finances continued, the all-black police jury, in a special session during May, 1873, authorized the sheriff to procure a building to be used as a hospital for smallpox patients and to employ a nurse. All persons who died there were to be buried at public expense. The president also appointed a superintendent for New River Lane who was to keep the land and bridges in good repair. The jury also established a ferry on Bayou Lafourche and appropriated $100 to defray the expenses of the parish attorney.

In spite of the expert assistance which this all-black police jury had, it fell upon hard times. A grand jury accused it of being extravagant in all its payment of claims and warned that it would take the necessary steps to check reckless and careless handling of the financial affairs of the parish. By June, 1873, Harrison and Johnson had been charged with extortion in office, and Kenner had been found guilty of extortion in office and sentenced to 80 days in jail or a fine of $80. *The Chief* commented that the police jury members had abdicated their positions, one compulsorily and the other two voluntarily.[11] The all-black jury was no more.

The collection of taxes, which had not taken place during the term of the all-black jury because of the suit, was still stymied until the governor filled the vacancies and the new jury organized. Gov. W. P. Kellogg appointed one black, Henry Heyman, and two whites, Henry Cook and Felix Reynaud, to replace the three blacks. The Republican editor of *The Chief* said: "The police jury as now constituted is a body that promises to inaugurate much needed reform and gain the confidence of the community which the preceding jury betrayed and lost."[12] Cook was never confirmed by the senate and Reynaud and Cantey resigned.

The vacancies left by Cook, Reynaud, and Cantey were filled by Pierre Landry who was elected president and two whites, J. B. Hebert and Louis LeBlanc. The jury continued to have a three-to-two black majority when William Diggs replaced Landry on the jury. Heyman and Rice served until the end of Reconstruction.

When wite Democrats in Louisiana felt that they could not overthrow Republican rule at the polls because of federal control, they then decided to circumvent Republican domination by subertfuge or extralegal action. In 1874 whites abandoned secret societies and organized the White League which openly vowed to overthrow the Republicans and re-establish "the white man's party."

During the election of 1876, there was very little violence in Ascension Parish, for intimidation there was more subtle but just as effective. In October, 1876, the Republicans attempted to hold a political meeting at Dutch Stores, but the "298", a mysterious local organization, objected. The editor of *The Chief* stated: "We trust that our friends were not deceived by appearances on Sunday; that the Democratic citizens intended to disturb our meeting; and that nothing further of this kind will occur to mar the fair reputation of Ascension as a parish where there is peace and comparative good feeling between the races and political parties.[13] After the election, the same Republican editor commented: "It would be hard to imagine a more peaceable election than that held in the parish." He also went on to say that he saw at and near the polls planters, merchants, and overseers who previously had not taken an active interest in elections, exhausting their powers of persuasion upon blacks in their efforts to get them to vote the Democratic ticket. He further stated that there were several instances of illegal means of persuasion, such as threats of discharge and bribery.[14]

After the election, Freeman Bell, a black Democrat, testified before a senate committee that he had been molested by colored Republicans. According to Bell, there were between two and three hundred colored men who belonged to his Democratic Club. This organization was a voluntary one where there was no attempt to persuade blacks to vote the Democratic ticket. Bell also reported that the election was perfectly quiet with no disorder.[15]

Again the parish voted the Republican ticket: S. B. Packard for governor and Rutherford B. Hayes for president. Statewide, the election was in dispute, for both Democrats and Republicans declared their candidate for governor the victor. From January 2 to April 2, 1877, Louisiana had two govenors, S. B. Packard and Francis T. Nicholls. meanwhile in the parish two blacks, Heyman and Rice, were re-elected to the police jury. Seven hundred registered voters failed to vote: some on faraway plantations stayed at home; others had lost their voting certificates, while still others failed to re-register. By April 1877, the election of 1876 had been compromised by giving Hayes the disputed electoral votes. As president he withdrew federal troops from the state; for the army had protected Republican government throughout the seventies. The Democratic nominee for governor, Nicholls, was recognized by Hayes as the legitimate governor of Louisiana, and Packard had to withdraw.

Governor Nicholls was given the power to re-appoint town officers and police jurors throughout the state, not to exceed five officials in each parish. In addition to the five elected jurors of Ascension Parish, Nichoills appointed five Democrats. This meant that there were two blacks and eight whites on the police jury, a definite attempt to dilute black and Republican influence in local government. Nicholls is supposed to have said: "I was determined that they [blacks] should feel that they were not proscribed and to this end I appointed a number of them to small offices sandwiching them on boards between white men where they were powerless to do harm."[16]

Later, the parish was divided into eight wards and Gov. Louis A. Wiltz, in 1880, appointed eight members of the police jury, none of whom were black. All of the general offices of the parish, such as the district judge, district atttorney, sheriff, clerk of court, recorder, coroner, representatives and senators were filled by competent white citizens elected by both white and black voters.[17]

Another local political office held by a black in Ascension Parish during the seventies was that of parish sheriff. Aaron Hill was elected sheriff in 1872 and re-elected in 1874. However, he was unable to finish his second term, for he was tried on June 3, 1876, before a parish judge for contempt of court and upon conviction was fined $100 and suspended from office. Thereupon Victor C. Cantrelle, the black coroner, became acting sheriff until the next election.

Immediately following the war, Ascension Parish, like the other parishes in the state, tried to provide education for the freedmen. One of the first such schools in Donaldsonville, the parish seat, was supported mainly by the Freedmen's Bureau and burned to the ground in January, 1865.[18] The responsibility for providing schools in the town of Donaldsonville lay with the board of school directors appointed by the state superintendent of education. The board in 1873 consisted of eight members, three of whom were black: Gloster Hill, Pierre Landry, president of the board, and Milton Morris. The state provided some funds for the schools in the parish, and the parish, through its tax collector, was authorized to collect 2 mills per tax dollar for the school fund. In its February 1, 1873, meeting, the all-black police jury budgeted $2,400 for the public schools of the parish. By the fall of 1873 there were eight public schools in the parish and two in the town of Donaldsonville.[19] One school in the predominantly black Fifth Ward was located in the Hopeful Baptist Church. Gloster Hill requested another so that Sixth Ward children might attend. By 1880 the Catholics had opened St. Augustine Parochial School for colored children. Thus, with the help of the Freedmen's Bureau, the police jurors, and the school board members, Ascension Parish had the beginnings of a system of public and parochial schools for black as well as white students in spite of having to overcome all sorts of obstacles.

By 1878, intimidation and violence had taken its toll on black voters. They would continue to vote until the end of the century, but they would hold fewer and fewer offices, local ones first and then the state ones, for blacks had never held many local positions throughout this period. Charles Vincent, in his study, has found between 1868 and 1877 19 black sheriffs, 13 parish tax collectors, 12 assessors, 13 coroners, 12 parish recorders, 4 mayors, 2 parish judges, and several justices of the peace, constables, and police jurors.[20] Some historians have over-emphasized black domination, the so-called corruption, ignorance, and illiteracy of black elected officials during Reconstruction. Further, they have called the turning over of the state to the intelligent, literate, capable leadership of the Redeemeres a blessing. But the fact of the matter is that blacks nowhere in the state were able to make decisions without help and assistance from whites, and blacks formed the majority on few decision-making bodies.

On the occasions where blacks were the majority, their tenure of office was short-lived, and instead of taking care of the business of the parish, it was necessary to spend much of their time justifying their legitimacy. In the end, their influence was either weakened by intimidation or was reduced to a minority in the police jury, town council, or school board. A look at other parishes where blacks were politically active, such as Iberville, West and East Feliciana, Orleans, Natchitoches, and Red River, shows the same picture of blacks being intimidated and discouraged from voting and holding political office, especially on the local level.

Notes for "Local Black Elected Officials in Ascension Parish, 1868-1878"

[1]Donald W. Davis, "Ratification of the Constitution of 1868—Record of Votes," *Louisiana History,* 6 (1965): 301-5.

[2]Joe Gray Taylor, *Louisiana Reconstructed, 1863-1877* (Baton Rouge, 1974), 159.

[3]*Appleton's Annual Cyclopedia* . . . (New York, 1876), 15:500; see also Taylor, *Louisiana Reconstructed,* 186.

[4]Sidney A. Marchand, *The Flight of a Century (1800-1900) in Ascension Parish* (Donaldsonville, La., 1916), 171.

[5]Charles Vincent, "Negro Legislators in Louisiana during Reconstruction" (Ph.D. dissertation, Louisiana State University, 1973), 170. See also *New Orleans Times-Picayune,* December 24, 1921.

[6]*Donaldsonville Chief,* November 9, 16, 1872.

[7]Ibid., December 28, 1872.

[8]Ibid., January 11, 1873.

[9]Ibid., January 27, 1871.

[10]Ibid., February 2, March 15, 1873.

[11]Ibid., May 31, June 7, 1873.

[12]Ibid., June 21, 1873.

[13]Marchand, *The Flight of a Century,* 183.

[14]*Chief,* November 11, 1876.

[15]*House Documents,* 44th Congress, 2nd Session, 108.

[16]Allie B. Webb, "A History of Negro Voting in Louisiana, 1877-1906" (Ph.D. dissertation, Louisiana State University, 1962), 32.

[17]H. Thompson Brown, *Ascension Parish, Louisiana: Her Resources, Advantages and Attractions . . .* (Donaldsonville, La., 1888), 12.

[18]Howard A. White, *The Freedmen's Bureau in Louisiana* (Baton Rouge, 1970), 184.

[19]*Chief,* October 11, 1873.

[20]Charles Vincent, *Black Legislators in Louisiana During Reconstruction* (Baton Rouge, 1976), 220-21.

THE POLICY OF VIOLENCE IN CADDO PARISH, 1865-1884*

Gilles Vandal

During the years immediately after the Civil War, sufficient time had not yet elapsed to efface the Southern whites' chagrin for having been defeated and conquered. The planter elite had fought for years to preserve the particularities of their culture and of their economic system, both based on slavery. With the end of war, they saw not only the end of their dreams, but also the end of the world as they knew it. The defeat brought extensive demoralization and the breakdown of confidence in the white community. To this social dislocation, the victors imposed new changes upon the Southern whites which transformed their way of life and redefined their relationship with their former slaves. These changes were not easily accepted, as whites continued to believe strongly in their racial superiority and in their right to govern and dominate other races as a law of nature. For many, violence became not only a means to oppose these changes, but also an instrument of self-preservation, a way to re-establish common values and a new sense of community.[1]

The situation was even more difficult in Caddo, a relatively young and prosperous parish located in the northwestern corner of Louisiana.[2] Indeed, Caddo was part of a region that had suffered comparatively little from the war. No rebuilding, no reconstruction needed to be done there. Further, the war had brought great prosperity to the area, as Shreveport became the capital of Confederate Louisiana after the fall of Baton Rouge. As the region escaped invasion and was occupied only after the surrender of the Southern armies, white people there did not feel they had been vanquished.[3] As a consequence, the white community in Caddo was periodically dominated by a class of daring and utterly reckless men who strongly resented the changes brought by the war and who did not shrink from anything, even from murder.[4]

*First published in *Louisiana History*, 32 (1991): 159-82. Reprinted with the kind permission of the author and the Louisiana Historical Association.

Violence and lawlessness were not new to Caddo, a parish that was already considered before the Civil War as one of the worst places in Louisiana.[5] But after the war, violence in Caddo reached a new high and the parish became infamous for its record of racial violence, earning the nickname of "Bloody Caddo."[6] Indeed, violence in Caddo Parish became part of a policy aimed at preserving the old order as much as possible and maintaining blacks in a state of subjugation. By asserting their new freedom and exercising their newly won political rights, blacks offended whites and became subject to chastisement.

1. Homicide Data

Collecting information on violent incidents and crimes has always represented a hazardous and difficult task. Police statistics and court records, particularly on petty crimes and on lesser forms of violence, are too often either unavailable or unreliable. For historians interested in examining post-Civil War racial violence in the South, the task is even more complicated. Indeed, many incidents were unrecorded by the court or were not even investigated by the authorities. It is possible, however, to make up for some of these deficiencies by basing this study on homicides. Historians are on sounder ground when dealing with homicides which characteristically produce quite a local sensation and were widely reported. For that reason, "homicides" in this article will be defined in its broader sense, including under that generic term all forms of violent death, with the exception of suicide and accident.

Fortunately, historical documentation on violence and race relations in Caddo is rich and diversified. During the years immediately after the war, the condition of affairs in Caddo was largely investigated by Federal army officers who served either as occupying forces or as agents of the Freedmen's Bureau. As a consequence, the general corres-pondence and documents of both the Gulf Department and the Freedmen's Bureau represent an important source for starting an investigation on violence and race relations in that parish.[7] Moreover, as violence broke out on a large scale during the presidential election of 1868, joint committees of the Louisiana State Assembly and a congressional com-mittee examined the situation in Louisiana and reported at length on the conditions in Caddo.[8] The general endemic character of lawlessness that underlined the years of 1868 to 1876 was also largely covered by five congressional reports.[9] The violence and the Caledonia riot that occurred during the congressional election of 1878 were also investigated by the congressional committee.[10] All these sources were complemented by a thorough examination of the local newspapers between 1865 and 1884.[11]

However, these sources contained often only limited information and must be cautiously used. Indeed, local newspapers and the congressional reports contained countless notices such as: "Last Saturday night a colored man name[d] Bryant Offort, who lived on Samuel McLean's plantation in this parish was taken from his home by some unknown persons and killed in the most brutal and atrocious manner."[12] Such sketchy information is not meaningless. Quite often the perpetrators of such murders were known by local people and even by the civil authorities. Too often law-enforcement officials made no attempt to find and arrest the murderers and when they did, they met with a wall of silence from local people.[13] In 1874, the number of people killed by unknown parties became so alarming that the parish coroner, afraid for his life, preferred to resign rather than carry out his duties in the countryside.[14] Moreover, in many instances of white assaults against blacks, the murderers were the only witnesses, and civil authorities were left with only a body. As a consequence, cases were often closed after a jury had been impaneled and had returned a verdict stating that the deceased had come to his death by gunshots at the hands of "a person or person[s] unknown."[15] Finally, military authorities were unable to compensate for this neglect and failure of the civil authorities to conduct proper investigations into each case of homicide.[16]

Cross-checking of individual cases from a variety of sources has made it possible to diminish the deficiencies of some lists and to establish quite an accurate data set that gives a comprehensive description of the level of racial violence in Caddo after the Civil War. It contains minimal information on date and place where the incidents occurred, on the sex, race, and age of both the victims and perpetrators of homicides and sketch information on the circumstances surrounding each homicide. The statistical breakdown of these homicides presents a panorama of the racial tension that troubled Caddo during those twenty years. Therefore, despite some shortcomings, this data set presents a fair view of the level of racial violence that prevailed in Caddo Parish. Information was compiled on 652 homicides[17] that occurred in Caddo Parish between 1865 and 1884 (Table 1). This homicide index represents a significant record of the real amount of physical violence that occurred in Caddo after the Civil War.[18]

Table 1

Caddo Homicides, 1865-1884

Year	Whites	Blacks	Unknown	Total	% of Blacks	Rates
1865	2	9	2	13	81.9	59.8
1866	6	11	1	18	64.6	82.8
1867	6	15	5	26	71.5	119.6
1868	5	154	26	185	96.9	851.0
1869	3	12	4	19	80.0	90.4
1870	6	50	10	66	89.3	303.6
1871	5	18	4	27	78.3	124.2
1872	6	33	7	46	84.7	211.6
1873	10	19	3	32	65.6	147.2
1874	12	74	19	105	85.8	483.0
1875	2	18	3	23	90.0	105.8
1876	2	3	1	6	60.0	27.6
subtotal	65	416	85	566	86.5	246.4

(table 1 cont.)

1877	1	6	3	10	85.7	37.0
1878	4	21	3	28	84.0	103.6
1879	1	4	0	5	80.0	18.5
1880	1	5	3	9	83.4	33.3
1881	2	7	2	11	77.8	40.7
1882	0	0	2	2	0.0	7.4
1883	2	3	3	8	60.0	29.6
1884	0	4	9	13	100.0	48.1
Total	76	466	110	652	86.0	140.6

N.B.: The annual homicide rates have been adjusted for a population of 100,000 inhabitants. The federal censuses of 1870 and 1880 had been successively used in calculating the rates for the years 1866 and 1876 and the years 1877 to 1884.

In Caddo, as in other parishes, blacks were charged by whites as being the main perpetrators of violence.[19] Repeatedly, the local newspapers printed statements such as: "We regret to notice that among the colored people human life is held in but light estimation in this parish;" or, "there seems to be 'blood in the moon' for the negroes [*sic*] in this section lately, and they are engaged in a war to exterminate their own species." Finally, even the Caddo grand jury concluded in 1875 that blacks were at the origin of most of the violence that occurred in the parish, that they were always quarreling and resorting to murder, attempting murder, and cutting and shooting to solve their quarrels.[20] The statistical breakdown of homicides in Caddo, however, tells a different story. (See Table 2.)

Table 2
Caddo Racial Distribution by Homicides

Race of Victims and Perpetrators	1865-1876	%	1877-1884	%	Number	%
unknown by unknown	44	7.8	20	23.2	64	9.8
unknown by whites	28	4.9	3	3.4	31	4.7
unknown by blacks	13	2.3	2	2.3	15	2.3
whites by unknown	12	2.1	1	1.1	13	2.0
blacks by unknown	66	11.7	3	3.4	69	10.5
whites by whites	41	7.2	9	10.4	50	7.7
whites by blacks	12	2.1	1	1.1	13	2.0
blacks by whites	295	52.1	22	25.5	317	48.6
blacks by blacks	55	9.7	2.5	29.0	80	12.2
Total	566	99.9	86	99.5	652	99.8

Significantly, blacks were victims of 86 percent of all the homicides that occurred in Caddo between 1865 and 1884, while whites were the presumed perpetrators of at least 80.4 percent of the blacks murdered.[21] Moreover, data on homicides in Caddo show that violence was primarily a male phenomenon. The quasi-absence of women either as victims or perpetrators of murders in Caddo is an important aspect that came out of this analysis.[22] The high rate of black men killed by white men is even more significant if one takes into account that violence in Caddo was directed towards a population of 3,300 black males between the ages of eighteen and forty-five.[23] This means that about 10 percent of black males in that age group were killed by whites during Reconstruction. Even more startling is the fact that about 40 percent of whites in Caddo between the age of eighteen and forty-five were involved in those homicides.[24] Evidence clearly shows that whites did not kill blacks at random, but that they resorted to a selective and deliberate policy aimed at eliminating black leadership and intimidating the black population. In numerous instance, black males were taken out of their cabins and shot by unknown white parties, while wives and children remained unmolested.[25]

Moreover, the index also confirms the conclusions of recent studies that much of the violence inflicted on the freedmen by whites had been well organized.[26] Indeed, 71 percent of blacks killed by whites during Reconstruction and 82 percent for the years 1877 to 1884 were by more than one person. (See Table 3.) These statistics stress that whites killed blacks not simply from personal quarrels but as a means of social control.[27] It also uncovers the problem for blacks to get justice in Caddo and tells much about the racial tensions and the difficulty of the white community to adjust to a new reality.

Table 3

Nature of White Homicides Against Blacks

	1865-1876	%	1877-1884	%	Total	%
Individual	79	29.5	4	18.1	83	29.0
Collective	188	70.5	18	81.9	206	71.0
Unknown	28	____	0	____	28	____
Total	295	100.0	22	100.0	317	100.0

Our data shows that whites in Caddo usually killed blacks in groups and also clearly indicates the determination of whites to keep their parish as a white-man's country. Indeed, the circumstances surrounding homicides in Caddo point out that whites murdered blacks mostly for political reasons. Moreover, the whites' efforts to maintain blacks in a state of subjugation were confirmed by most of the remaining motives. (See Table 4.)

And yet, data on surrounding circumstances and other statistical evidence on homicides alone fail to give a complete understanding of the racial tensions that underlined violence in Caddo. Let us now examine in more detail how violence worked in Caddo and how it was part of a policy of social and political control of the black masses.

2. Violence as a Means of Social Control

Before the war, whites in Caddo had been an essential part of the machinery aimed at maintaining plantation discipline. They regularly served on neighborhood patrols and were asked to apprehend and punish slaves who were away from plantations without a pass from their master. Moreover, they were asked to keep a close watch for any sign of a slave insurrection. Finally, they repeatedly joined vigilance committees established in periods of crisis by the Caddo police jury and were granted "power to arrest all suspicious persons and to take them to speedy trial."[28] After the war, the problem of controlling the black masses in Caddo was even greater.

Indeed, whites in Caddo not only resented the changes brought with the end of the war, but also found it more difficult to maintain their ascendancy over their former slaves who wanted to enjoy their newly won freedom and break away as much as possible from the plantation system. Moreover, this problem was made even more difficult in Caddo as blacks formed more than 70 percent of the parish population. The concentration of blacks in the parish countryside was even larger and reached a ratio of ten to one because more than half of the 7,000 white inhabitants of the parish lived in Shreveport.[29]

As a consequence, whites felt they could maintain their control over the rural areas only by resorting to violence and intimidation. Therefore, whites organized themselves in posses and paramilitary groups that scouted the countryside and kept a close watch on all black activities. Significantly, blacks who had previously been protected by their market value as slaves, felt the wrath of the whites after the war.[30]

As the war ended, whites in Caddo became "very actively engaged in cruelty and brutality" against blacks. Between May and August 1865, no less than 60 cases of white assaults on blacks were reported, including five murders. In December 1865, the *Shreveport News* reported: "Scarcely a day passed from the latter end of last week, but some negro had been drowned or killed. This is disgraceful and should receive investigation of the authorities." In 1866, ten to fifteen bodies of blacks were seen floating in the Red River, some hung by the neck alongside old logs, some with ropes around their neck, some shot and with throat cut. Many more murders were committed in Caddo in 1867 which were neglected by the civil authorities. Blacks in Caddo were indeed governed by the gun.[31]

Whites in Caddo became particularly inflamed as they saw black soldiers and black civilians wandering around armed. Indeed, blacks derived much personal pride and self-satisfaction from the possession of arms and tended to carry and display them ostentatiously. As blacks regularly carried arms, walked to the polls in military

Table 4
The Motives Underlying White Homicides of Blacks in Caddo

Motives	1865-1876	%	1877-1844	%	Total	%
Political	83	72.1	15	68.1	98	71.5
election	(56)		(0)		56	
riot	(5)		(13)		(18)	
being a witness	(2)		(2)		(4)	
fear of an insurrection	(15)		(0)		(15)	
others	(5)		(0)		(5)	
Economic	13	11.3	3	13.6	16	11.7
labor	(8)		(3)		(11)	
business	(2)		(0)		(2)	
others	(3)		(0)		(3)	
Social	11	9.5	1	4.5	12	8.7
laughing about a white woman	(2)		(0)		(2)	
live with a white	(3)		(0)		(3)	
protect his wife	(1)		(0)		(1)	
too arrogant	(3)		(1)		(4)	
trivial	(2)		(0)		(2)	
Criminal	8	6.9	3	13.6	11	8.0
robbery	(3)		(2)		(5)	
being a witness	(2)		(0)		(2)	
resist arrest	(3)		(1)		(4)	
Total	115	99.8	22	99.8	137	99.9

formation, and drilled during the night, they confirmed the worst white antebellum prophecies and gave root within the white community to numerous wild rumors.[32] Repeatedly, whites organized themselves in posse and scouted the parish in search of armed black men, as they felt it was their duty to crush any insurrection in its beginning.[33] In July 1874, a Spaniard, named Manuel Nunez who taught in a black school, was brutally murdered by four whites as he was allegedly charged with importing arms for blacks. The white community was then so aroused, that it became impossible for blacks to buy powder even for hunting.[34]

A significant part of the violence that occurred during the early years of Reconstruction originated in the difficult adjustment between blacks and whites to a new labor system. The transition to a free economy was not easy and was underlined by the strong opposition of planters who resisted the idea of abandoning the plantation discipline and of having to pay wages to their former slaves. Indeed, many whites in Caddo strongly endorsed the Louisiana Black Code of 1865, and considered that a black had no right to live idly, that he must work and that his labor and social activities needed to be controlled by whites. As a consequence, whites in Caddo, as elsewhere, prevented blacks from living outside of their former plantation, thereby denying them travel from one plantation to another.[35] Blacks in Caddo who conformed to the whites' demands, who kept their place, and who went to work, were treated kindly by their former masters.[36] But if a black refused to work or wanted to break away from the plantation system, intimidation, whipping, and beating became means to coerce him into complying with the planter's will.[37] In many instances, blacks were killed because they asked for a fair settlement for their crops.[38] The unwillingness of whites to see blacks renting land, living on their own, or refusing to live under white protection was shown in January 1869, when three blacks who had rented a land were shot and had their throats cut by unknown white parties.[39] It was not a rare occurrence that freedmen were killed by their former master, as happened to Isaac Friessen in 1868. Some were killed for such trivial reasons as taking and eating an onion from the garden of their former master.[40]

For whites in Caddo, emancipation could only be understood in a limited sense. The primary function of a black, they believed, was to work for a white man and to take care of his family. Not surprisingly, not all blacks conformed to the whites' desire. Many blacks reacted to white policies simply by refusing to work and began to live from the planters' stock, stealing mules, horses, cattle, hogs, and even corn.[41] This created much dissatisfaction among whites and provoked a near riot in August, 1868, as whites attempted to arrest thirty families of black squatters. By 1870, many white planters, dissatisfied with the new labor relations, made proposals to convert the parish into a stock and grain producing district, with a policy aimed at hiring as many whites and as few blacks as possible.[42]

Meanwhile, the development during the 1870s of the sharecropping system represented an attempt to accommodate the contradictory aspiration of both blacks and whites. Freedmen were reluctant to work under the new wage system implemented by the Freedmen's Bureau because they felt that the gang labor installed under that system too often resembled the old servile system. Therefore, the need for steady labor forced the planters to find a more suitable farming system. As planters refused to sell or even rent land to freedmen, the system which most appealed to both sides was sharecropping. Under this system, blacks were allowed to work in family units, and planters and store-owners furnished freedmen with supplies and lands for a share of the crops.[43] However, many planters and storeowners did not hesitate to defraud "the negroes [*sic*], not only in their settlement, but in advancing supplies, by charging them from two to four times the first cost." Whenever blacks or white Republicans protested too vehemently against white fraud, they were charged with stirring up violence.[44]

Evidence also reveals the social tensions related to breaches of racial etiquette. No less than eight blacks in Caddo were killed because they did not obey a white order quickly enough, they talked back, they refused to yield the road or sidewalk to a white, or they were "impolite" to a white woman.[45] In March 1875, a black man was killed in Shreveport by a storekeeper for not obeying an order to leave the store, when he became engaged in any angry discussion with a companion.[46] Others were killed because they protested too strongly while whites took away their wife or children.[47] Moreover, whites could become most brutal and sadistic in killing blacks, as in the mutilation and murder of Lucy Smith in 1868 near Shreveport. A group of white men who wanted to teach her a lesson cut off her breast, then disemboweled and decapitated her, afterward throwing her body onto the branches of trees.[48]

The burning of black churches and interference with black religious meetings are most revealing about the whites' intention to resist any encroachment or challenge on the part of blacks to white social control of black activities. As blacks found in their religious meetings a way to discuss their problems, to assert their new freedom, and to organize themselves, it is not surprising that black churches and religious meetings received preferential attention and became special targets of the whites' fury. The fact that this occurred more often in the countryside than in Shreveport would indicate that whites in Shreveport accepted in a paternalistic spirit a variety of organizational activities by blacks, while in the countryside whites responded violently to those activities which they saw more as a challenge to their domination.[49]

Evidences clearly indicate that whites in Caddo were not ready to accept any societal challenges or encroachments on the part of blacks. When a black had a dispute with a white man, the mere fact that he was sustained by another black instantly incited the whole white community. Calls were then made to put down a riot. For that reason, the leaders of the black community in Caddo cautiously advised other blacks not to make any demonstration of that kind.[50] Further, the breakdown of statistics shows that usually there was no danger of a black attack against whites. Indeed, a black would virtually never strike a white, and if he did, it was a desperate act done as a last resort. There were only thirteen cases of blacks killing whites for the whole period, and these homicides attracted much attention, being described by the local newspapers as outrageous assassinations.[51] In 1874, Jake Mcready, a black who had allegedly killed a white named George Simpson, was taken at night from his cabin by a group of armed white men led by the son of the victim. Both hands and feet of Mcready were tied and turpentine was poured on him. The whites then shot him several times and cut his throat before setting him on fire.[52] Indeed, the murder of a white by a black represented an unusual event and brought heavy retribution upon its perpetrator.

3. Violence as a Means of Political Control

Whites in Caddo did not really accept postwar changes and particularly objected to their political implications, knowing that in the long run political equality meant social equality. As whites did not retain enough power to preserve their once secure position of domination, they saw themselves confronted with unsolvable problems. They regarded their condition as particularly depressing, as they saw themselves at the mercy of corrupted Radical and black politicians from whom they could expect no justice. They asserted that they had been "deprived of their rights," that they had "no redress for the evils which afflicted them and impoverished them," and consequently that they had no other means but "to rely on their own arms to protect themselves and to avenge their wrong." Indeed, they perceived the situation to be worse than it was. As they saw their whole world threatened, a sentiment of suspicion and hatred arose and violence became, as a last resort, the ultimate response of whites to preserve their lands as a white-man's country.[53]

Not surprisingly, much of the white anger would be directed against blacks who began to engage in political activities, join Republican clubs, and assert their right to vote. Indeed, whites in Caddo particularly resented the Republican party's ascendancy over the black masses and its control of the parish and state governments. They felt that violence, as a last resort, was the only means to get rid of the "corrupt" Republican officials who manipulated and forced blacks to vote for them. If these politicians were overthrown, whites argued, there would no longer be disorders in Caddo and in Louisiana, and a war of the races would be prevented.[54]

In August, 1867, great excitement gripped Caddo because armed blacks were attending political meetings; they were parading and drilling like soldiers; and were organizing pickets and patrols to stop anyone found suspicious. This was too much for the whites and provided the rationale for the violent interference of more than one hundred armed white men on horseback who broke up a meeting of the Baptist society that was held on John Harrison's place on Black Bayou. All black men belonging to a Republican club were seized on the same occasion and brought away never to be seen again.[55] Similar incidents occurred again during the fall of 1867 as blacks attended political meetings fully armed in preparation for the election of delegates to the state constitutional convention.[56]

Rumors that a victory for Seymour and Blair in the presidential election would mean the overthrow of Reconstruction[57] brought violence into Caddo during the summer and fall of 1868. The eruption of a race riot in the neighboring parish of Bossier on September 30, 1868, created much excitement and transformed the parish into a hunting ground, a place where no law was enforced. Indeed, as white passions reached a paroxysm in October 1868, violence degenerated on several occasions into mass-murder. On October 1, nine blacks were taken to the bank of the Red River and told to swim for their lives. As they rose to the surface after having plunged into the river, the blacks were shot. Not one of them escaped.[58] On the same night, it was reported that thirty blacks had been taken from around Shreveport, marched to the bank of the Red River, tied together with ropes and shot in the back as they stood. During the following days, a raft of swollen bodies drifted down the turbid river until the bodies were eaten by alligators. On October 12, seven blacks were chained in an old abandoned building which was then burned to the ground.[59] Finally, a last mass-murder occurred during that month when a group of whites went to a brickyard and took five colored men away from their work. After tying their hands, they marched them down to the Red River and as these black men stood on the riverbank, they were riddled with bullets.[60]

It is difficult to ascertain the exact number of blacks killed during the "negro [*sic*] hunt" that struck Caddo in 1868. Whites took no prisoners and did not care for the wounded. There were many cases of murdered blacks who were impossible to identify. Official investigations, based on sketchy reports, put the number of blacks killed in Caddo that year at 300.[61] One witness asserted that as many as 400 to 500 blacks were murdered.[62] However, our data shows that 185 people, of which at least 154 were blacks, were killed in Caddo in 1868.

A second wave of violence struck Caddo during the summer and fall of 1874 as whites in large numbers joined the White League and engaged in overthrowing Radical rule. Then, frightful stories began to circulate about the deplorable condition that prevailed in Caddo as para-military groups began to scout the parish and terrorize blacks. Numerous bodies of unknown blacks were found, and the murders were reported to have been committed by unknown parties.[63] No less than thirty murders were reported having been committed in Caddo during the months of July and August 1874.[64] Moreover, as white Conservatives in Caddo were so determined to carry the parish in the November elections of 1874, they did not hesitate to resort to economic pressures. Individual calls were made on each planter of the parish demanding the discharge of all blacks who voted Republican.[65] Not surprisingly, they won the election only to have the results overturned by the state electoral board.[66]

Finally, a last wave of violence occurred in 1878 as local Democrats in Caddo were more determined than ever to carry the parish and to put an end to Radical rule. And for that, they needed either to get the black vote or to neutralize it.[67] Consequently, they proceeded with a pre-conceived plan. First, they asked Governor Francis Nicholls to appoint five extra members to the police jury in order to get a majority on that body. Since the police jury was entitled to fix the polling places and to choose the commissioners of election, whites saw their polling places fixed at center of the war, while only one polling station was designated for blacks, despite the fact that they formed 75 percent of the voting population, and it was put at the southern extremity of the parish. Secondly, they organized themselves in para-military groups and scouted the parish terrorizing blacks.[68]

The methods used by whites worked well except for a riot that broke out on election night at Caledonia, a small place twenty-five miles below Shreveport on the Red River. At first the fight involved seventy-five blacks and about twenty whites. But as only a few blacks were armed, they were rapidly driven to the swamps and other hiding places.[69] Then a "negro [sic] hunt" began as white reinforcements arrived from elsewhere.[70] No less than twenty blacks[71] were killed during the riot and the search for blacks that followed.[72] Thus ended Radical rule in Caddo Parish as the Democratic party carried the election overwhelmingly with a majority of 1,500 votes.[73]

The numerous murders and acts of violence committed during the weeks preceding the presidential election of 1868, during the summer and fall of 1874, and again during the congressional election of 1878, fully established the supremacy of the white race in the parish. The frightful lawlessness and terrorism that prevailed in Caddo created a great degree of fear within the black community. Moreover, when violence reached a peak, as it did in 1868, in 1874, and again in 1878, even the most moderate whites could not disagree with or oppose the conservative whites' policies of intimidation and violence.[74] It was indeed impossible to be Republican and to survive in Caddo during those tempestuous days.[75]

The Caddo cycle of violence came to an end with the Caledonia Riot of 1878. Local Democrats had finally achieved "the fixed and unalterable pourpose of our people, to redeem our parish and city, and place ourselves in line with other parishes."[76] It marked the political failure of Reconstruction policies at the sate and local levels. Caddo was indeed redeemed and white rule was restored within the parish. As our data shows, after 1878, whites in Caddo no longer needed to resort to large-scale violence, as they enjoyed control of the political apparatus in the parish. They were able to correct the past inequalities under which they had felt oppressed and to restore their social and political control over the blacks. Indeed, there was no longer any danger of turning back the clock and returning to the conditions that had prevailed during Reconstruction.

Conclusion

Post-Civil War violence has to be understood and analyzed from the point of view of the Southern thought and Southern values of the time. Whites in Caddo as elsewhere in the South, were afraid of losing their sense of identity and they were not ready to accept the changes that shattered the image they had of themselves and of blacks. Consequently, violence in Caddo has to be understood in a racist and white supremacist perspective, as a reactionary fear of a large segment of the white population, as a desperate attempt to regain the privileges they had once enjoyed over the land and over the black population.[77]

During the period immediately after the war, whites in Caddo felt they did not retain enough power to preserve their dominant position in society. Indeed, the majority of the white population was not ready to accept emancipation except in a very limited sense. Much of post-Civil War violence in Caddo, as shown by our data, was closely linked to the redefinition of the black status and race relations. Whites particularly resented the assertiveness of the blacks who wanted to enjoy their newly won freedom. Thus, violence reflected the growing white hostility toward changes in the black status brought in by the radical Republicans and imposed by the North.

As blacks in Caddo outnumbered whites three to one, the latter were afraid to lose control over the black masses. As a consequence, the hidden fear of a black revolt surfaced. Whites resorted to all means possible to prevent any black insurrection and to maintain their political predominance. Activities ranged from night raids to intimidation, whipping, rowdyism, and murder.

Periodically, as the political climate heated up, the wrath of the white community fell upon the blacks and the latter became terrorized and apprehensive for their lives. During the "negro [*sic*] hunts" of 1868, 1874, and 1878, many blacks chose to sleep in the woods or to take refuge in the swamps and other hiding places to escape the white fury.[78] Indeed, violence then became the ultimate means to coerce blacks to accept white supremacy.

After 1878, racial violence almost disappeared as whites were able to regain the rights they once enjoyed and reestablish their control over blacks under a system of law and social premises defined by them. Considering the deplorable conditions that prevailed in Caddo Parish, it is not surprising that the 1879 Black Exodus, the "Kansas Fever," originated in the area of Caddo and was largely organized by Henry Adams, a former slave from Georgia who had lived in Shreveport for many years after the Civil War.[79] The atmosphere of violence and lawlessness had long lasting effects in Caddo and Louisiana. "Shreveport guerrillas well versed in killing niggers" were reported to have come down to South Louisiana in 1887 to crush the sugar strike.[80]

Notes for "The Policy of Violence in Caddo Parish, 1865-1884"

[1] Eric Foner, *Reconstruction: America's Unfinished Revolution, 1863-1877* (New York, 1988), 31-32, 313-14, 341-42, 420-25, 441-42, 547-53. See also Richard Slotking, *Regeneration Through Violence: The Mythology of the American Frontier, 1600-1860* (Middletown, Conn., 1973).

[2] 44th Congress, 2nd sess., House Exec. Doc. 30, pp. 362, 383; J. Fair hardin, "An Outline of Shreveport and Caddo Parish History," *Louisiana Historical Quarterly,* 18 (1935): 785, 790-91, 805; Samuel A. Lockett, *Louisiana As it Is: A Geographical and Topographical Description of the State,* ed. Lauren C. Post (Baton Rouge, 1969), 58; Perry A. Snyder, "Shreveport Louisiana During the Civil War and Reconstruction" (Ph.D. dissertation, Florida State University, 1979), 23, 26-27, 32-33; Perry A. Snyder, "Shreveport Louisiana, 1861-1865: From Secession to Surrender," *Louisiana Studies,* 11 (1972): 52; George E. Warig and George W. Cable, *History and Present Conditions of New Orleans* (Washington, D. C., 1881), 297.

[3] 39th Congress, 1st sess., House Report 30, p. 160; Hardin, "Shreveport and Caddo Parish History," 859-61; Snyder "Shreveport, 1861-1865," 60, 65, 69-70; Snyder, "Shreveport During the Civil War and Reconstruction," 142. Edward Ayers shows that similar conditions prevailed in some of the unconquered regions of Georgia in *Vengeance and Justice: Crime and Punishment in the 19th Century American South* (New York, 1984), 159.

[4] 44th Congress, 2nd sess., House Exec. Doc. 30, pp. 194, 280, 383, 388; 43rd Congress, 2nd sess., House report 261, pp. 361, 367; 43rd Congress, 2nd sess., Senate Exec. Doc. 17, pp. 4-6; *New Orleans Times,* January 27, 1875; *Shreveport Times,* July 20, 1874; Joseph G. Dawson III, "The Long Ordeal: Army Generals and Reconstruction in Louisiana, 1862-1877" (Ph.D. dissertation, Louisiana State University, 1978), 364; Snyder, "Shreveport During the Civil War and Reconstruction," 196-97, 223-24; A. B. Windham, "Methods and Mechanism Used to Restore White Supremacy in Louisiana" (M. A. thesis, Louisiana State University, 1948), 54, 60.

[5]41st Congress, 2nd sess., House Misc. Doc. 154, p. 132; Snyder, "Shreveport During the Civil War and Reconstruction," 21-27, 32-33.

[6]*Donaldsonville Chief,* March 27, 1875; *Jefferson State Register,* July 23, 1870; 41st Congress, 2nd sess., House Misc. Doc 154, part 2, pp. 36, 161; 43rd Congress. 2nd sess., House Report 261, pp. 64, 379, 787; 44th Congress, 2nd sess., House Exec. Doc. 30, p. 362.

[7]The general correspondence of the Freedmen's Bureau and the Gulf Department were consulted in the National Archives in Washington. Two reports of the Freedmen's Bureau were particularly useful in our investigation. "Miscellaneous Reports, no. 1318, and Register of Murders and Outrages," no. 1322, Bureau of Freedmen, Refugees, and Abandoned Lands, Reg. 105, War Department, National Archives, Washington, D. C.; hereafter cited a BRFAL.

[8]41st Congress, 2nd sess., House Misc. Doc. 154 (2 parts); *Report of the Joint Committee of the General Assembly of Louisiana on the Conduct of the Late Election and on the Condition of Peace and Order in the State* (New Orleans, 1868); *Supplemental Report of the Joint Committee of the General Assembly of Louisiana on the Conduct of the Late Election and the Condition of Peace and Order in the State* (New Orleans, 1869), hereafter cited as *Supplemental Report*; *Report of the General Assembly of Louisiana on the Conduct of the Election of April 17 and 18, 1868, and the Condition of Peace and Order in the State,* (New Orleans, 1868).

[9]43rd Congress, 2nd sess., House Report 261; 44th Congress, 2nd sess., House Executive Document 30; 46th Congress, 2nd sess., Senate Report 693 (3 parts); 43rd Congress, 2nd sess., Senate Executive Documents, nos. 13, 17. House Executive Document no. 30 and Senate Report no. 693 were both particularly important as they furnished extensive lists and tables on homicides and violence in Caddo.

[10]45th Congress, 3rd sess., Senate Report, no. 855 (3 parts).

[11]*Shreveport South-Western,* 1865-1871; *Shreveport Daily Standard,* 1879-1884; *Shreveport Times,* 1870-1884.

[12]41st Congress, 2nd sess., House Misc. Doc. 154, part 2, p. 117; 43rd Congress, 2nd sess., House Report 261, p. 783; Supplemental Report 265; Shreveport *South-Western,* September 16, 1868; *New Orleans Republican,* August 20, 1874.

[13]Judge A. B. Levisse testified in 1875 before a congressional committee that there were many cases in Caddo of blacks who had been killed by white men under circumstances where the facts had never come to light. He further asserted that in Caddo it was not "an uncommon thing for a colored man to be found dead." When a black is found dead, he added, "a simple mention is made of it, perhaps orally or in print, and nothing is done. There is no investigation made. The coroner is sent for, perhaps to hold an inquest and we have him buried." This statement was further confirmed by Major Lewis Merrill of the U. S. Army who asserted that the killing of a black was not considered murder by the whites in Caddo and that no local grand jury would indict a white for such a murder. See 43rd Congress, 2nd sess., House Report 261, pp. 175, 366-67; 43rd Congress, 2nd sess., Senate Exec. Doc. 13, p. 4; 41st Congress, 2nd sess., House Misc. Doc. 154, p. 131; *New Orleans Bulletin,* January 29, 1875; Snyder, "Shreveport During the Civil War and Reconstruction," 232.

[14]43rd Congress, 2nd sess., House report 261, p. 783.

[15]43rd Congress, 2nd sess., House Report 261, p. 787-88. See also the *Opelousas Journal,* May 7, 1875; V. Redfield, *Homicide, North and South* (Philadelphia, 1880), 150.

[16]39th Congress, 1st sess., House Report 30, p. 153; 43 Congress, 2nd sess., House report 261, pp. 787-88; 44th Congress, 2nd sess., House Exec. Doc. 30, p. 77.

[17]In order to avoid any duplication or repetition of cases, we entered in our data set only cases for which existed clear information about the name of the victim, the date, place, and type of violence. Although it was asserted by different witnesses that more than 300 blacks were killed in Caddo in 1868, we retained only 185 cases for which we had information. We followed the same approach in entering data on the Caledonia riot of 1878, in spite of the fact that 50 to 75 people were reported killed then. Consequently, the level of homicides in Caddo was much higher than the 652 cases contained in our data set.

[18]With less than 3 percent of the state's population, Caddo Parish had 16.2 percent of the 3,494 homicides that were committed in Louisiana during Reconstruction, and 6.4 percent of the 1,335 homicides that occurred during the years 1877 to 1884.

[19]43rd Congress, 2nd sess., House Report 261, p. 7; *Louisiana Democrat,* February 23, 1875; *Opelousas Courier,* July 22, 1875; New Iberia *Louisiana Sugar Bowl,* April 21, 1873, November 24, 1874; April 3, 1877; *Thibodaux Sentinel,* May 22, 1877; Joe Gray Taylor also states that "for every black man killed by a white man, for political or other reasons, two were killed by other black men." Joe Gray Taylor, *Louisiana Reconstructed, 1863-1877* (Baton Rouge, 1974), 81, 421.

[20]*Shreveport South-Western,* August 8, 1871; *Shreveport Times,* January 24, 1875, June 19, 1880.

[21]We did not take into account here 146 homicides committed by unknow parties, although we could presume that most of them were committed by whites. Moreover, those rates were comparable to those for Louisiana where blacks represented 77.1 percent of the victims of homicides and whites 71.3 percent of the presumed perpetrators.

[22]Twenty women were killed in Caddo during Reconstruction and twelve for the years 1877 to 1844.

[23]The federal census of 1870 reveals that blacks formed 72 percent of the population of Caddo. Out of a total male population of 4,577 between the ages of eighteen and forty-five, there were approximately 3,300. Moreover, our data indicate that 82 percent of black victims were between the ages of eighteen and forty-five.

[24]White males in Caddo between the ages of eighteen and forty-five numbered about 1,300 (28 percent of 4,577). Moreover, our index reveals that at least 463 whites in Caddo were involved in these homicides and that 88 percent of them were between the ages of eighteen and forty-five.

[25]41st Congress, 2nd sess., House Misc. Doc. 154, part 2, p. 443; 44th Congress, 2nd sess., House Exec Doc. 30, p. 478.

[26]Leon F. Litwack, *Been in the Storm So Long: The Aftermath of Slavery* (New York, 1979), 278-79. See also Allen W. Trelease, *White Terror: The Ku Klux Clan Conspiracy and Southern Reconstruction* (New York, 1971), 127-36.

[27]These statistics are most significant when compared with those on homicides committed by whites against whites. In this last case, 67.2 percent of the homicides involved only one perpetrator.

[28]Minutes of the police jury of Caddo Parish, January and June 1861, Louisiana State University Archives; *Shreveport South-Western,* January 9, 1861; Snyder "Shreveport During the Civil War and Reconstruction," 57.

[29]43rd Congress, 2nd sess., House Report 261, p. 432; 44th Congress, 2nd sess., House Exec. Doc. 30, p. 362; *Shreveport Times,* November 7, 9, 13, 1878; *Louisiana Capitolian,* September 10, 1881; Snyder, "Shreveport, 1861-1865," 63; Ted Tunnel, *Crucible of Reconstruction: War, Radicalism and Race in Louisiana, 1862-1877* (Baton Rouge, 1984), 158; Warig and Cable, *History of New Orleans,* 296, 298.

[30]BRFAL, Letter of R. Wilkinson to General J. A. Mower, May 28, 1869, Caddo Parish, record 4501, box 4. See also the letters included in the report of General J. A. Moyer on Louisiana to the Secretary of War, October 15, 1869, Report of the secretary of War, 41st Congress, 2nd sess., House Exec. Doc. 1869-1870; 39th Congress, 1st sess., House report 30, p. 156; 39th Congress, 2nd session, Senate Exec. Doc. 6, p. 186; 44th Congress, 2nd sess., House Exec. Doc. 30, p. 415; *New Orleans Times,* September 30, 1867, July 17, 1870; *Shreveport South-Western,* March 10, 1869; *Shreveport Times,* August 27, 1874, May 8, 1875; Dawson, "The Long Ordeal," 61, 183; Taylor, *Louisiana Reconstructed,* 91, 317.

[31]BRFAL, letters received, 1866, microfilm 4495, report of Inspector Shuyler Crosby; 44th Congress, 2nd sess., House Exec. Doc. 30, pp. 77, 410; Dawson, "The Long Ordeal," 61; Foner, *Unfinished Revolution,* 119; Snyder, "Shreveport During the Civil War and Reconstruction," 166. The quote from the *Shreveport News* was taken from Taylor, *Louisiana Reconstructed,* 93-94.

[32]41st Congress, 2nd sess., House Misc. Doc. 154, part 1, pp. 340-41, 355, 474; Dawson, "The Long Ordeal," 117; Tunnell, *Crucible of Reconstruction,* 157.

[33]41st Congress, 2nd sess., House Misc. Doc. 154, part 1, pp. 340-41, 355, 361, 164, 474, part 2, pp. 118-19; *Shreveport South-Western,* August 12, 1868.

[34]43rd Congress, 2nd sess., House report 261, pp. 365 441, 765, 780-81, 787, 953; 44th Congreess, 2nd sess., House Exec Doc. 30, pp. 283, 384; *New Orleans Daily Picayune,* October 20, 1874; *New Orleans Republican,*

August 2, 1874; *Shreveport Times,* June 30, July 12, 19, 1874; January 31, 1875; Windham, "White Supremacy in Louisiana," 81.

[35]44th Congress, 2nd sess., House Exec. Doc. 30, pp. 418, 421-22, 425-26, 431, 445-47; Snyder, "Shreveport During the Civil War and Reconstruction," 166.

[36]41st Congress, 2nd sess., House Misc. Doc. 154, part 1, p. 80.

[37]44th Congress, 2nd sess., House Exec. Doc. 30, pp. 417-18, 421-22, 425-26, 430-31, 434, 444-47; Taylor, *Louisiana Reconstructed,* 93.

[38]44th Congress, 2nd sess., House Exec. Doc. 30, pp. 421-22, 426, 431, 444-47, 544.

[39]*New Orleans Republican,* February 5, 1869, quoted in the *Shreveport Caddo Gazette,* January 23, 1869.

[40]41 Congress, 2nd sess., House Misc. Doc. 154, part 1, 309, 440-43, 474-75; part 2, pp. 116, 119, 128-29, 132; 43rd Congress, 2nd sess., House Report 261, pp. 787-88; 44th Congress, 2nd sess., House Exec. Doc. 30, pp. 359, 379-80, 422.

[41]41st Congress, 2nd sess., House Misc. Doc. 154, part 2, pp. 119, 132; 43rd Congress, 2nd sess., House Report 261, pp. 143-441; Supplemental Report, 20; BFRAL, Nathaniel Burbank to Cunning Brown, letters sent, August 27, 1867, Micro 4498, box 3; *Shreveport South-Western,* August 12, 1868; *Shreveport Times,* October 19, 1875

[42]*Shreveport South-Western,* December 7, 1870.

[43]William Ivy Hair, *Bourbonism and Agrarian Protest: Louisiana Politics, 1877-1900* (Baton Rouge, 1969), 51-52; William E. Highsmith, "Louisiana Landholding During the Civil War and Reconstruction," *Louisiana Historical Quarterly,* 38 (1955): 45; Michael Wayne, *The Reshaping of Plantation Society: The Natchez District, 1860-1880* (Baton Rouge, 1983), 163.

[44]45th Congress, 3rd sess., Senate Report, no. 855, VI-VII; *Shreveport Times,* October 16, 29, November 3, 1878; Shreveport *Standard,* July 30, September 23, October 15, 29, 1878; Hair, *Bourbonism and Agrarian Protest,* 78; Morgan D. Peoples, "'Kansas Fever' in North Louisiana," *Louisiana History,* 11 (1970): 124.

[45]44th Congress, 2nd sess., House Exec. Doc. 30, pp. 418, 421-22, 425-26, 444-47.

[46]*Donaldsonville Chief,* March 27, 1875.

[47]44th Congress, 2nd sess., House Exec. Doc. 30, pp. 421-22, 435.

[48]41st Congress, 2nd sess., House Misc. Doc. 154, part 2, p. 443; 44th Congress, 2nd sess., House Exec. Doc. 30, p. 478.

[49]BFRAL, Thomas F. Monroe to L. O. Parker, Shreveport, August 20, 1867, letters sent, vol. 18, no. 1027, 4498, box 3; 43rd Congress, 2nd sess., House Report 261, p. 783; *New Orleans Daily Picayune,* August 24, 1874; *New Orleans Times,* September 30, 1867; Windham, "White Supremacy in Louisiana," 80.

[50]43rd Congress, 2nd sess., House Report 261, p. 366; *Shreveport Times,* July 23, 1874.

[51]43rd Congress, 2nd sess., House Report 261, pp. 149, 953; *Shreveport Times,* January 31, 1875.

[52]44th Congress, 2nd sess., House Exec. Doc. 30, p. 477.

[53]*Shreveport Times,* June 12, 30, October 27, 1874; January 31, December 24, 1875; Dawson, "The Long Ordeal," 315-16; Tunnell, *Crucible of Reconstruction,* 182.

[54]44th Congress, 2nd sess., House Exec. Doc. 30, p. 373; *Shreveport Times,* September 14, 1874.

[55]BFRAL, Thomas F. Monroe to L. O. Parker, Shreveport, August 20, 1867, letters sent, vol. 18, no. 1027, 4498, box 3; *New Orleans Times,* September 30, 1867. See also a petition of thirty white citizens from Bossier who protested the fact that blacks patrolled the parish fully armed. BFRAL, whites petition, August 10, 1867, vol 18, no. 1027, 4498, box 3.

[56]44th Congress, 2nd sess., House Exec. Doc. 30, part 1, pp. 340-41, 355, 474; 44th Congress, 2nd sess., House Exec. Doc. 30, p. 70.

[57]W. E. B. Dubois, *Black Reconstruction in America* (1935; reprint ed., New York, 1975), 474; Taylor, *Louisiana Reconstructed,* 164-73.

[58]41st Congress, 2nd sess., House Misc. Doc. 154, part 2, p. 126; 44th Congress, 2nd sess., House Exec. Doc. 30, p. 293; BFRAL, letters sent and report, T. F. Monroe to J. M. Lee, A. A. Inspector General, October 12, 1868, box 1, micro 4501; Supplemental Report, 265; Trelease, *White Terror,* 130; Tunnel, *Crucible of Reconstruction,* pp. 155-56.

[59]43 Congress, 2nd sess., House Report 261, p. 379.

[60]44th Congress, 2nd sess., House Exec. Doc. 30, p. 359, 392; Supplemental Report, p. 76.

[61]41st Congress, 2nd sess., House Misc. Doc. 154, part 2, p. 161; 43rd Congress, 2nd sess., House Report 261, pp. 64, 313, 362, 379; 44th Congress, 2nd sess., House Exec Doc. 30, pp. 168, 359; Supplemental Report, XVI-XVII, 75-76, 78; Tunnell, *Crucible of Reconstruction,* 155-56; Trelease, *White Terror,* 130.

[62]41st. Congress, 2nd sess., House Misc. Doc. 154, part 2, p. 443.

[63]43rd Congress, 2nd sess., House Report 261, p. 783; *New Orleans Republican,* August 20, 1874; Taylor, *Louisiana Reconstructed,* 299; Windham, "White Supremacy in Louisiana," 77.

[64]44th Congress, 2nd sess., House Exec. Doc. 30, p. 382; New Orleans *Weekly Louisiana,* August 9, 1874; *New Orleans Daily Picayune,* August 21, 1874; Snyder "Shreveport During the Civil War and Reconstruction," 215; Taylor, *Louisiana Reconstructed,* 399; Windham, "White Supremacy in Louisiana," 80, 88-92.

[65]Some 500 black families, making an aggregate of approximately 2,000 people, were reported as having been discharged in Caddo and were roaming around during the winter of 1875, creating great social chaos. 43rd Congress, 2nd sess., House report 261, p. 189; 43rd Congress 2nd sess., Senate Exec Doc. 17, p. 53; 46th Congress, 2nd sess., Senate Report 693, pp. 172-73, 182; *New Orleans Bulletin,* July 2, 1874; *New Orleans Bee,* January 20, 1875; *New Orleans Daily Picayune,* October 20, 1874; January 22, 1875; Dawson, "The Long Ordeal," 415-61; Snyder, "Shreveport During the Civil War and Reconstruction," 214, 221-22, 227; Tunnel, *Crucible of Reconstruction,* 203-4; Taylor, *Louisiana Reconstructed,* 299; Windham, "White Supremacy in Louisiana," 69-76; A. B. Webb-Windham, "A History of Negro Voting in Louisiana, 1877-1906" (Ph.D. dissertation, Louisiana State University, 1962), 16-18.

[66]Snyder, "Shreveport During the Civil War and Reconstruction," 225.

[67]*Shreveport Daily Standard,* November 3, 1878; *Shreveport Times,* October 19, November 3, 1878; Webb-Windham, "Negro Voting in Louisiana," 38; Hair, *Bourbonism and Agrarian Protest,* 76-78.

[68]45th Congress, 3rd sess., Senate Report 855, pp. 11-12; *Shreveport Daily Standard,* November 7, 1878; *Shreveport Times,* March 19, 1879; Monroe, La., *Ouachita Telegraph,* January 3, 1879; Singletary, "White Supremacy in Louisiana," 27-28; Webb-Windham, "Negro Voting in Louisiana," 74.

[69]45th Congress, 3rd sess., Senate Report 855, p. ix; *Shreveport Times,* November 7, 8, December 29, 1879; Webb-Windham, "Negro Voting in Louisiana," 75-76.

[70]Thirty young white men left Shreveport as the news of the riot arrived. Later, fifteen men arrived at Caledonia from Atkins's Landing, twenty from Bossier Parish, twenty from Riverdale, fifteen from DeSoto Parish and a large squad from Red River Parish. The following morning eighty more men arrived from Shreveport. 45th Congress, 3rd sess., Senate Report 855, IX; *Shreveport Times,* November 7, 1878.

[71]District Attorney A. H. Leonard, former editor of the *Shreveport Times* and leader of the Caddo White League in 1874, fixed the number of killed between fifty and seventy-five. However, the Democratic press fixed it at first at eight to twelve killed and increased it afterwards to fifteen. Meanwhile the Senate committee that investigated the riot asserted that no less than twenty people were killed. 45th Congress, 3rd sess., Senate Report 855, p. 44; Monroe, La., *Ouachita Telegraph,* January 3, 1879; *Shreveport Times,* November 7, 8, December 29, 1878; Hair, *Bourbonism and Agrarian Protest,* 78; Singletary, "White Supremacy in Louisiana," 29.

[72]45th Congress, 3rd sess., Senate Report 855, IX; *Shreveport Times,* November 7, 1878.

[73]45th Congress, 3rd sess., Senate Report 855, X; Webb-Windham, "Negro Voting in Louisiana," 75, 92.

[74]43rd Congress, 2nd Sess., House report 261, p. 361; 44th Congress, 2nd sess., House Exec. Doc. 30, p. 280.

[75]44th Congress, 2nd sess., House Exec. Doc. 30, p. 359; 41st Congress, 2nd sess., House Misc. Doc. 154, part 1, pp. 309, 440-43, 474-75; part 2, pp. 116, 128-29; 46th Congress, 2nd sess., Senate Report 693, XVIII; 41st Congress, 1st sess., House Report 27, pp. 251-52; Supplemental Report XVI-XVII, pp. 75, 78; New Orleans *Weekly Louisiana,* August 9, 1874; Monroe, La., *Ouachita Telegraph,* January 2, 1879; *Shreveport Times,* November 7, 8, December 29, 1878; Hair, *Bourbonism and Agrarian Protest,* 78; Taylor, *Louisiana Reconstructed,* 299; Trelease, *White Terror,* 130.

[76]*Shreveport Daily Standard,* November 3, 1878; *Shreveport Times,* October 19, November 3, 1878; Hair, *Bourbonism and Agrarian Protest,* 76-78; Webb-Windham, "Negro Voting in Louisiana," 38.

[77]Hair, *Boubonism and Agrarian protest,* 91; Taylor, *Louisiana Reconstructed,* 61; Webb-Windham, "Negro Voting in Louisiana," 54, 60.

[78]43rd Congress, 2nd sess., House Report 261, pp. 148, 175, 189, 953; 44th Congress, 2nd sess., House Exec. Doc. 30, pp. 193, 415; 43rd Congress, 2nd sess., Senate Exec. Doc. 17, pp.. 5, 50, 53; 45th Congress, 3rd sess., Senate Report, no. 855, IX; *New Orleans Daily Picayune,* August 21, 1874; January 28, 1875; *New Orleans Bee,* January 20, 1875; *New Orleans Republican,* August 9, 18, December 25, 1874; *Shreveport Times,* January 21, 1875, November 7, 8, December 29, 1878; Webb-Windham, "Negro Voting in Louisiana," 60, 80.

[79]46th Congress, 2nd sess., Senate Report, no. 693, part 2, p. 29; Hair, *Bourbonism and Agrarian Protest,* 83-106; Peoples, "Kansas Fever," 121-35; Webb-Windham, "Negro Voting in Louisiana," 95, 103, 109.

[80]Hair, *Bourbonism and Agrarian Protest,* 183.

THE KNIGHTS OF THE WHITE CAMELIA AND THE ELECTION OF 1868: LOUISIANA'S WHITE TERRORISTS; A BENIGHTING LEGACY*

James G. Dauphine

More than eighty years ago, Walter Lynwood Fleming described a general "Ku Klux movement" in the Southern states during the period of Reconstruction. Characterizing this movement was the formation of para-military organizations, such as the Pale Faces and the Ku Klux Klan, whose purpose was to oppose the implementation of Congressional Reconstruction following passage of the Reconstruction Acts of March-July 1867. Other para-military, or terrorist, groups would arise within the Southern states who patterned their activities after the widely advertised methods of the more famous Ku-Klux Klan, founded in 1866 in Pulaski, Tennessee.[1] In Louisiana, the Knights of the White Camelia, whose organization in southern Louisiana in May 1867 spread to the rest of the state during 1868, preempted the spread of the KKK.

As in Tennessee, Georgia, Alabama, and, indeed, nearly the entire unreconstructed South, Louisiana Democrats and Conservatives began to place their political hopes for the future in the outcome of the presidential election of 1868. Victory for the Democratic candidate Horatio Seymour over the Republican Ulysses S. Grant was considered not only possible, but a desired outcome to be attained at any cost.[2] Thus, political exigency served to justify the extra-legal means by which Southern Conservatives sought to wrest political control from the hated Republican "carpetbaggers" and "scalawags."

Reconstruction historians have elsewhere described the transformation of Tennessee's Ku-Klux Klan from the informal, secretive club which terrorized superstitious Negroes for sport in 1866, into the politically motivated terrorist organization which intimidated and murdered black and white Republicans during the 1868 election campaign.[3] In Georgia, where the organization spread during 1867 and 1868, the KKK was even more politically

---

*First published in *Louisiana History*, 30 (1989): 173-90. Reprinted with the kind permission of the author and the Louisiana Historical Association.

effective than in Tennessee. However, in Louisiana, the spread of the KKK was curtailed by the existence of other organizations with the same political motivation and tactics. Although opposition to Radical Reconstruction and the unwillingness of white Conservatives to share political power with Negroes characterized the entire South, the particular case of Louisiana, during the 1868 presidential campaign, stands out because of the political effectiveness of white terrorists there. Only the KKK organization in Georgia came near to matching the extent to which Louisiana Conservatives controlled the outcome of the November election in 1868.[4] As a consequence, the role of the Knights of the White Camelia in carrying Louisiana for Seymour in 1868 deserves closer description and analysis than it has received elsewhere.[5]

The organizational structures of terrorist groups, like the KKK and the KWC, differed in some respects, though the similarities outweighed the differences. In the case of the KWC, Councils intended to parallel the existing structure of state and parish governments were organized instead of Dens. Within a community or ward, the Council was composed of the leaders of individual Circles. Council Commanders and other leaders made up the the parish, or Eminent Council. In turn, these leaders represented their parishes on the state level, or Grand Council, headquartered in New Orleans. Provisions had been made for expansion into other states and the collective leadership would form the Supreme Council. However, despite reports of the existence of the KWC in Arkansas, Alabama, and even Philadelphia, Pennsylvania, no Supreme Council ever formed, and the extensive organization within Louisiana collapsed under the weight of members' apathy following Seymour's defeat in 1868. During its peak period of growth in the fall of 1868, however, the KWC managed to organize in nearly every parish in the state and appeared to have been more centrally organized and directed than Nathan Bedford Forrest's KKK.[6]

Council leaders selected targets in their parishes from among the prominent or politically active black and white Republicans. Warnings were issued to these men and failure on their part to leave or to become politically inactive resulted in harassment, floggings, and sometimes murder. Blacks not wanting to resist such intimidation joined Democratic clubs and were issued "protection papers," printed certifications of loyalty to the Democratic party. These were signed by T. L. Macon, president of the Democratic Party State Central Committee and also a member of the Knights of the White Camelia. Further, the KWC turned out at the polling places throughout much of the state, admitted only those with Democratic tickets, and then issued more protection papers to untrusted individuals to certify that they had indeed voted the Democratic ticket.[7] In twenty-nine of the state's forty-eight parishes, KWC intimidation and control of Republicans was so strong that Seymour outpolled Grant 64,097 to 6,118, which accounted for 91 percent of the vote. Thorough intimidation is the only explanation for such Democratic success, when it is remembered that nearly all Negro voters were Republicans and that they outnumbered white voters by about two to one over the entire state.[8]

In addition, it would be difficult to explain in any other way the unusual number of murders in Louisiana between April and November 1868. The Freedmen's Bureau reported that between September and November, 297 murders were committed in the state. A state legislative committee investigating the fall election put the figure at 784, while the more conservative Freedmen's Bureau reports show over one thousand in the twelve month period after November 1867—the bulk of these having been committed after the state elections of April 1868. Unquestionably, Democratic political fervor produced a reign of terror among the state's black population during the summer and fall of 1868.[9]

Prior to April 1868, the KWC had not yet expanded throughout the state, and the April election, in which a "carpetbagger" won the governor's seat, produced only the violence considered normal in such a state as Louisiana—where, in many localities, the social environment may still have been best described as frontier.[10] Some evidence indicates that, in southern Louisiana where the KWC had already extensively organized, Democratic leaders refrained from intimidation tactics by design during the spring, 1868 election campaign. H. N. Frisbie, a campaign stumper for Republican gubernatorial candidate James Taliaferro, reported that Democratic party leaders in the southern parishes of St. Mary, St. Landry, and Lafayette, conveyed to him plans for intimidation of Republicans in the upcoming presidential campaign. Frisbie claimed that the only reason intimidation was not used in these parishes in April was that Democrats feared possible repercussions from press sensationalism in the North and did not want to endanger Democratic chances for victory in the national election in November.[11]

Because of its clandestine nature, the Knights of the White Camelia left behind no records of the minutes or proceedings of any of the meetings of its various councils. However, there is a great deal of extant information bearing on the organization, purposes, and activities of the KWC in the published reports of investigating committees of Congress and of the Louisiana legislature, whose investigations were conducted during 1868 and 1869.[12] A primary purpose of these investigations was to discover why and how a state with as many registered Republican voters as Louisiana could have been carried by a Democrat by as large a margin as Louisiana gave Seymour in November 1868.[13]

During the state elections in April, in which Republican Henry Clay Warmoth was elected governor and a new state constitution was ratified, Republicans retained control of the majority of votes cast.[14] However, despite Republican expectations of a comparable victory for Grant in November, Grant outpolled Seymour in only sixteen of the state's forty-eight parishes. In seven parishes, Grant received no votes at all, totalled only eight votes in seven more parishes, and statewide, received only three of every ten votes cast.[15] Clearly, such unexpected Democratic strength required an explanation.

The preliminary report of a legislative committee in September 1868 gave the first indication of secret organizations attempting to control the outcome of the upcoming election. This committee's investigation came in response to a sudden outburst of complaints from Republicans in nearly every Louisiana parish, blaming "Ku-Klux Klans" for acts of violence and intimidation being committed against persons involved either in Republican campaigning or in expressing support for Grant and other Republican candidates. Numerous witnesses described to the committee how the "Ku-Klux" had been systematically involved in political intimidation ever since the April election.[16] Following the November election, the committee concluded its investigation, adding to its list of outrages committed, and this time specifically naming the Knights of the White Camelia as a secret organization responsible for much of the pre-election violence.[17]

As a result of the investigation, the Louisiana legislature petitioned Congress to appoint an investigating committee to look into the irregularity of the election. Quick to comply, the House committee sent a subcommittee of three congressmen to New Orleans in December 1868. Over a six-month period, the sub-committee's hearings took testimony from hundreds of witnesses from every parish in the state, eventually compiling a report over 1400 pages in length. Benefitting from the Louisiana legislature's prior investigation, the congressional sub-committee sought to uncover systematically as much information as possible concerning the activities of the mysterious Knights of the White Camelia.[18]

Despite the self-serving nature of much of the testimony taken, much factual information did emerge from the New Orleans hearings. KWC members generally did not attempt to hide their connection to the organization before the subcommittee. Although few witnesses admitted any connection between the KWC and the official Democratic political clubs and organizations, nearly all witnesses suspected of KWC membership answered directly and positively to questions about their involvement. In many cases, information about the organization's structure, oaths, secret signs, purposes, and activities were freely offered. Through such witnesses, the subcommittee compiled enough information about the KWC to make a rather extensive analysis of the organization possible. From the various testimonies of witnesses, a fairly clear picture has emerged concerning KWC strength, structure, methods, and intentions.[19]

The KWC originated in the town of Franklin in St. Mary Parish. It was founded here through collaboration between Alcibiades DeBlanc, an attorney from St. Martin Parish, and Daniel Dennett, editor of the *Franklin Planters' Banner*.[20] DeBlanc, the grand commander of the KWC, had been a colonel in the Confederate army. Before the Civil War he served as a state legislator and was a signatory at the Louisiana Secession Convention. He later became a justice of the Louisiana Supreme Court.[21] DeBlanc had prior experience in leading armed civilians in extra-legal activities through his connection with the St. Martin Vigilance Committee in 1859.[22] His experience with vigilantism, coupled with his social and political status as a war hero and civic leader, made DeBlanc an ideal choice for leadership in such an organization as the Knights of the White Camelia.

Daniel Dennett was a less conspicuous figure than DeBlanc, but apparently his views commanded respect from a wider area than his parish of St. Mary. Dennett came to St. Mary from Maine via Iowa to teach school in 1842, and began editing the *Planters' Banner* in 1848. Following a six-year tenure as operator of a stock farm in Texas, Dennett returned to St. Mary in 1858 and resumed editing the *Banner*. By his own admission, the paper became a widely respected agricultural journal. His reputation for agricultural knowledge, built during this time, was no doubt responsible for his position, after 1872, as agricultural columnist for the influential *New Orleans Daily Picayune.*[23] Something of the KWC's plans for the ideal social order emerges through the views of Dennett. During his later tenure at the *Daily Picayune,* Dennett became associated with various schemes for the introduction of Chinese and European immigrants to bolster the supply of farm labor, made less reliable by the freeing of the slaves and the intrusion of Radical Reconstruction politics. By 1872, Dennett had apparently become convinced that the traditional black farm labor supply was no longer sufficient for the improved agricultural production he thought essential for economic recovery in Louisiana and the South.[24] However, while editor of the *Planters' Banner* and propagandist for the KWC, it is clear that Dennett deemed the return of the Democratic party to control of state politics as necessary for the kind of antebellum social ordering he thought was needed for the restoration of agricultural production to pre-war levels.[25] In this connection, there was essential agreement between Dennett's views and those of DeBlanc.

At the conclusion of the war, DeBlanc was in command of Confederate troops in northern Louisiana. Unable to immediately occupy northern Louisiana following the Confederate surrender, Union Gen. Francis Herron delegated temporary responsibility for the maintenance of civil order to DeBlanc, as an existing authority already in the unoccupied territory. One of the first things DeBlanc did with his martial authority was to attempt revival of pre-war slave controls in order to prevent freedmen from leaving the plantations on which they worked.[26] Thus, through such actions and concerns of the KWC founders, it is clear that KWC strictures for the maintenance of racial purity and white superiority were motivated, not only by mindless racial prejudice, but also by a strong, conservative desire to promote social and economic stability along the lines of the traditional, antebellum Southern way of life.

This kind of social and economic outlook was, of course, shared by whites of all backgrounds in Louisiana and much of the South, but particularly and most earnestly by the old, established economic elite. With the assumption of control of Reconstruction policy by the Republican Congress after 1867, Louisiana Conservatives naturally placed all hopes for the restoration of traditional social and economic patterns in the success of the Democratic party—and subsequently in the defeat of the Radical Republican policies that would follow Seymour's election in 1868. Hence, amidst the confusion and turmoil of the Republican reordering of state government during the fall of 1867 and spring of 1868, Louisiana Conservatives began to plan for the fall election of 1868. Because of the mass block of Republican votes created by the institution of Negro suffrage, leaders of the Democratic party saw no hope of winning any election in Louisiana without some means of controlling Negro votes.[27] In the existence of the secret order of the Knights of the White Camelia, Louisiana Conservatives found the perfect means to their ends.

Despite the nearly unanimous denials by KWC members of a political connection between the KWC and the Democratic party, the connection between the two is too obvious to be dismissed. It is a striking fact that the leaders of the KWC, in every community and parish in Louisiana, were generally leaders of the Democratic party clubs and organizations and, in every case, were also men of economic and social stature in their communities. Such men were doctors, lawyers, politicians, judges, and planters with huge stakes in the preservation of their prominence. The ideas for social reform in the South, advanced by congressional leaders such as Charles Sumner and Thaddeus Stevens, moreover, posed a threat to the continuing dominance of Southern elites, stiffening their resolve to oppose Radical Reconstruction.[28]

The Knights of the White Camelia gave Louisiana Conservatives an opportunity to recruit a broad base of support for their views on the issue of race, and to enlist an army of vigilantes which would have the dual advantages of operation on the local level and centralized direction by an oligarchy of Democratic and KWC leaders in New Orleans. Through the testimony of witnesses before the subcommittee, the evidence is strong that the KWC expanded statewide during the spring and summer of 1868. Through contact with Democratic party officials, community and parish leaders became acquainted with the existence of the KWC and received authority and encouragement in organizing local councils of the KWC. For example, a Republican witness dated the appearance of the "Ku-Klux" in Morehouse Parish from the time that prominent Democratic leader Dr. Tom Jourdan returned from a trip to New Orleans, the headquarters of both the Democratic Party Central Committee and the KWC.[29] Numerous other witnesses all date the appearance of both the KWC and of the "Ku-Klux" outrages from about the same period of time, mostly between February and the end of summer in 1868. Without exception, moreover, witnesses who testified to membership, and even leadership, in the KWC denied the existence of the Ku-Klux Klan in their parishes, stating that the KWC was the only secret order they knew about. Such testimony from witnesses in every section of the state where "Ku-Klux" outrages occurred serves to dismiss the possibility of any co-existence between the KWC and the KKK in Louisiana in 1868.[30]

Articles concerning KKK activities in Tennessee, Virginia, Mississippi, and elsewhere were printed regularly in the Democratic press throughout 1868. Everyone knew about the "Ku-Klux" and anyone not engaged in active membership in the KWC naturally attributed the deeds of any secret organization to the KKK. As an illustration of this point, evidence pointing to activity by the KKK was strongest in Claiborne Parish, where KKK posters were tacked up around the town of Homer, and in Washington Parish, where an armed band of horsemen in white sheets were seen on parade in the town of Franklinton in the summer of 1868. However, every witness from these and surrounding parishes, suspected of "Ku-Klux" participation, while admitting membership in the KWC, had never heard of any organization of the KKK in these places.

Surviving evidence does indicate, however, that KWC councils adopted different methods of procedure in different places. In parishes in the Attakapas region of southern Louisiana, disguises were seldom worn, while the KWC in the Florida parishes wore such disguises as white sheets only at night. In northern Louisiana, disguises were sometimes worn in the parishes near Shreveport, but were more common in the parishes closer to

Monroe. In these latter places, Franklin Parish was the center of most of the "Ku-Klux" activity. Franklin Parish had been the scene of much violence by armed and disguised horsemen, known as the Black Horse Cavalry, as early as October 1866. These horsemen were distinguished by the simple technique of darkening their faces with lampblack. As the KWC expanded into Franklin, Ouachita, Caldwell, Union, and Morehouse parishes during the summer of 1868, incidences of violence perpetrated by armed horsemen with blackened faces began to be reported from across these parishes. Apparently, many KWC members saw no need for disguises, while others emulated the KKK, and still others drew inspiration from the Black Horse Cavalry.[32]

Most of Louisiana, in 1868, was rural and remote from the control of any civil or military agents of the state or federal governments. Even in such places as Bossier and Caddo parishes, where federal troops were stationed, the authority of state and federal governments was either non-existent, or ignored. Despite the presence of troops in nearby Shreveport, Bossier Parish residents refused to accept the authority of Republican officials elected in the April 1868 election. Instead, the officially deposed Democratic officials continued to run their offices beyond the expiration of their elected terms with the full knowledge and support of the white civilian population.[33] A freedman from Shreveport testified to the subcommittee that he had witnessed a multiple murder of freedmen by an armed band of whites, whose actions were known to a nearby detachment of U. S. Army troops. The troops, however, were infantry, as were most of the soldiers stationed in Louisiana, and could have taken no effective action in this instance even had they been so inclined, which, according to the witness, they were not.[34]

The only places in Louisiana, in fact, where the KWC did not openly intimidate white Republicans and Negroes, without fear of being arrested and brought to trial, were in parishes through which ran the state's major river systems.[35] Comparatively little pre-election violence occurred in the parishes along the Mississippi River, with the exception of Orleans, Jefferson, and St. Bernard parishes, near New Orleans. Grant received his largest majorities in the river parishes, especially in Carroll, Concordia, Madison, and Tensas parishes across the border from Mississippi. Farther south, along Bayou Lafourche and the Atchafalaya and Mississippi rivers, intimidation was more extensive than in the northern river parishes, but much less than in places requiring overland transportation to reach. Similarly, Rapides and Natchitoches parishes, along the Red River, witnessed less violence and gave majorities to Grant in November.[36]

Exceptions to the general rule of riparian tranquility were Bossier, Caddo, and Avoyelles parishes, along the Red River. These were areas of intense activity by the KWC and places where Seymour scored large majorities, despite a Democratic minority of registered voters. By way of explanation, it should be pointed out that Bossier and Caddo parishes were the scene of major racial rioting in the fall of 1868. Similarly, Avoyelles Parish is in close proximity to St. Landry Parish, where perhaps the worst racial rioting in Louisiana history took place in September 1868. The assumption of martial control of St. Landry by the KWC commanders, R. A. Littell and James M. Thompson, precipitated a great deal of violence and intimidation, which undoubtedly spilled over into surrounding parishes, such as Avoyelles, St. Martin, and Lafayette—where river transportation existed, but where no federal troops were stationed.[37]

Certainly, one reason why river parishes were comparatively free of violence and intimidation was that these were places where most of the federal troops were stationed. It was true that troops were few in number and generally inadequate to the task of protecting black Republicans throughout the state. However, in the places where troops were garrisoned, they were usually able to afford protection to Republicans casting ballots on election day.[38] But in places such as Bossier and Caddo, where sustained outbreaks of rioting occurred, no civil or military authorities proved adequate to the task of enforcing order, either on election day or before.

Another characteristic of the river parishes was that these were the locations of the best farm lands. Accordingly, these were areas of large plantations and heavy concentrations of the black population. Democratic planters in these locales, who formerly controlled local politics, may have logically preferred not to let politics interfere with the production of crops, partly explaining the comparative lack of violence in Black Belt areas. However, it is more likely that Democratic leaders doubted the ability of KWC bands to effectively intimidate large concentrations of black voters without causing general riots of the kind in Bossier, Caddo, and St. Landry.[39]

The other exception to the rule of comparative tranquility along rivers was the urban environment of New Orleans, Jefferson (Metairie), and Chalmette in Orleans, Jefferson, and St. Bernard parishes. In these places, all surrounding the city of New Orleans, the KWC attained a membership variously estimated at between fifteen and twenty thousand.[40] Considering that the Metropolitan Police Force of Governor Warmoth was under constant siege during the summer and fall of 1868, and the military commanders— Generals Robert Buchanan and Lovell Rousseau—never had available to them more than about five hundred soldiers, it is not surprising that the KWC and the various militant Democratic clubs openly practiced intimidation of Republicans around New Orleans.[41] As Michael Hahn, a former governor, remarked in 1868, Republicans came to the city to escape persecution in the country parishes only to find an equally repressive political environment.[42]

Governor Warmoth told the subcommittee that General Rousseau, commander of the Military District headquartered at New Orleans, was afraid to use troops in combatting the political violence in New Orleans. Referring to rioting in New Orleans in October, Warmoth claimed that General Buchanan, the former commander, had said Rousseau was justified in behaving as though he were retreating in battle before a superior force.[43] From this state of affairs, it is fair to conclude that a condition of open rebellion existed against both state and federal authority between April and November 1868. It is no exaggeration that a revolution had occurred, which was never forcibly put down, but which died of its own lack of momentum following the deflation of Democratic hopes in the wake of Grant's election to the presidency.[44]

In the thirty-two parishes carried by Seymour—twenty by majorities of ninety-four percent or more—membership in the KWC was nearly universal among the white, male, adult population. Moreover, as one leader of the KWC commented to a prospective recruit about the relationship between Democratic clubs and the KWC: ". . . out of one grew the other."[45] Within KWC councils, adherence to the doctrine of white superiority was essential, but it was conceivable that a white Republican could belong to the organization. However, it is clear by the election returns, that any Republican Knights found it prudent to register their votes for Seymour instead of Grant.[46] It is clear from testimony by KWC members that many of them considered the organization to have been a Democratic club.[47] However, it was a club which separated members and defined duties according to age. Where KWC councils determined it was necessary to intimidate Republicans from voting in November, it was up to the young men to "do the fighting," while the old men just acted as "good Democrats."[48] However, as asserted by the legislative committee investigating the election violence, the old men were just as responsible for the violence as were the younger men committing the actual deeds:

> . . . the state of lawlessness and unpunished crime prevalent in this State, is chargeable, not alone to the desperate and infamous characters who are its immediate agents, but to the apathy and silent connivance of that large and respectable class of the people of the State, who, while they would scorn personally to commit any of these violent acts, if they do not actually sympathize with their perpetrators, at least refrain studiously from any efforts to restrain or bring them to justice. . . .[49]

While preservation of status and of the antebellum social order were aspirations motivating the older, respected class of planters and professionals who were the leaders of the KWC, it is less clear what motivated the younger men who were faced with building their lives in the changed conditions of the postbellum South. It appears, however, that a form of mass nihilism, to use C. Vann Woodward's term, best describes the factors which motivated these young men.[50] One of the most perceptive observers of American society in the postbellum years, Carl Schurz, described the category of men who made up the rank and file of organizations like the KWC and the KKK as representing:

> The incorrigibles, who still indulge in the swagger which was so customary before and during the war, and still hope for a time when the southern confederacy will achieve its independence. This class consists mostly of young men, and comprises the loiterers of the towns and idlers of the country. They persecute Union men and negroes [*sic*] whenever they can do so with impunity; insist clamorously upon their 'rights,' and are extremely impatient of the presence of federal soldiers. . . . This element is by no means unimportant; it is strong in numbers, deals in brave talk, addresses itself directly and incessantly to the passions and prejudices of the masses, and commands the admiration of the women.[51]

In this way, Schurz described the largest group of progenitors of the KWC campaign of "Ku-Klux" intimidation. In the terminology of Eric Hoffer, however, what Schurz described was only one element of a larger mass movement, which involved the social aspirations of the white population in general.[52] As in other Southern states, this movement in Louisiana transcended the specific political and economic goals envisioned by KWC leaders. The movement reflected the beginnings of a Southern social quest for a lost collective identity, later romanticized by Thomas Dixon, in *The Clansman*.[53] Moreover, such passion as the movement inspired, died hard, and in later years the White League blossomed from the seeds of the fallen White Camelia, and Louisiana was "redeemed."[54] Tragically, through the movement, the antebellum past lived on to retard the progress of the "New South" and to warp the social and economic outlook of too many succeeding generations in both Louisiana and in the South. Interesting as they have been to historians, the Knights' real legacy is the racial hatred they helped engender in society. Moreover, it is this bequest of the Knights, and of the Klan, for which they should be remembered, and not for the romantic imagery too often associated with them in the past.

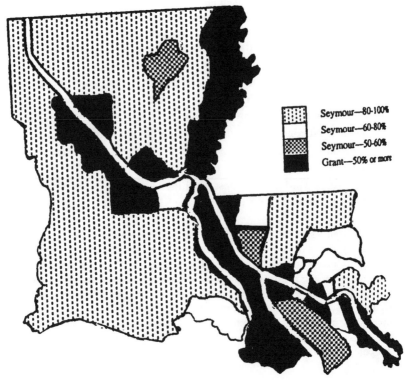

Louisiana Presidential Election, 1868
% by parishes

TABLE 1

The Presidential Election in Louisiana, 1868
The Vote by Parishes

Parish	Seymour	Grant
Ascension	1125	1491
Assumption	1375	1387
Avoyelles	1345	520
Bienville	1385	1
Bossier	1634	1
Caddo	2895	1
Calcasieu	782	9
Caldwell	503	28
Carroll	786	1392
Catahoula	809	150
Claiborne	2952	2
Concordia	201	1554
DeSoto	1260	0
E. Baton Rouge	1350	1247
E. Feliciana	1411	644
Franklin	1213	0
Iberville	704	2088
Jackson	1398	0
Jefferson	2222	672
Lafayette	1422	0
Lafourche	1796	1617
Livingston	670	149
Madison	163	1453
Morehouse	1525	1
Natchitoches	1375	1915
Orleans	24668	1178
Ouachita	1101	832
Plaquemine	273	1329
Pointe Coupée	896	1553
Rapides	1623	2176
Sabine	934	2
St. Bernard	473	1
St. Charles	264	1335
St. Helena	1094	136
St. James	775	2161
St. John	556	274
St. Landry	4787	0
St. Martin	1456	28
St. Mary	1819	1142
St. Tammany	704	470
Tensas	383	1018
Terrebonne	1296	1541

(Table 1 cont.)

Parish	Seymour	Grant
Union	1416	1
Vermilion	958	0
Washington	656	0
W. Baton Rouge	433	585
W. Feliciana	648	1136
Winn	711	43
Totals	80225	33263

Source: W. Dean Burnham, *Presidential Ballots, 1836-1892* (Baltimore, Md., 1955), 486-501.

Notes for "The Knights of the White Camelia and the Election of 1868: Louisiana's White Terrorists; a Benighting Legacy"

[1] Walter Lynwood Fleming, *Documentary History of Reconstruction: Political, Military, Social, Religious, Educational and Industrial, 1865 to the Present Time*, 2 vols. (Cleveland, 1906-1907), 2:327-29; Allen W. Trelease, *White Terror: The Ku Klux Klan Conspiracy and Southern Reconstruction* (New York, 1971), 3.

[2] Charles H. Coleman, *The Election of 1868: The Democratic Effort to Regain Control* (New York, 1933), 310-31, 368; Joe Gray Taylor, *Louisiana Reconstructed, 1863-1877* (Baton Rouge, 1974), 161.

[3] Trelease, *White Terror*, 3-27; Stanley F. Horn, *Invisible Empire: The Story of the Ku Klux Klan, 1866-1871*, 2nd ed. (Montclair, N.J., 1969), 7-20.

[4] W. Dean Burnham, *Presidential Ballots, 1836-1892* (Baltimore, 1955), 332-63. Seymour carried Georgia in 1868 with a majority of sixty-four per cent statewide; Trelease, *White Terror*, 117-19; Coleman, *The Election of 1868*, 384.

[5] The Knights of the White Camelia is the specific subject of only Allie Bayne Windham Webb, "Organization and Activities of the Knights of the White Camelia in Louisiana, 1867-1869," Louisiana Academy of Sciences *Proceedings*, 17 (1954): 110-18. Unfortunately, this source is too short in length and largely uninformative. Better sources of general information on the KWC are found in histories of the Ku Klux Klan and Louisiana Reconstruction: Trelease, *White Terror*, 92-98, 127-36; Taylor, *Louisiana Reconstructed*, 162-63; Horn, *Invisible Empire*, 285-92, 342-45; John Rose Ficklen, *A History of Reconstruction in Louisiana, Through 1868* (Gloucester, Mass., 1966), 215-20.

[6] Trelease, *White Terror*, 82, 94, 136, 173; U. S. *House Miscellaneous Documents*, 41st Congress, 2nd Session, Serial 1435, No. 154, Part 1 (Washington, D. C., 1870), 298, 555; hereafter cited as *Subcommittee*, Pt. 1; U. S. House, *House Miscellaneous Documents*, 41st Congress, 2nd Session, Serial 1435, No. 154, Part 2 (Washington, D. C., 1870), 235, 339; hereafter cited as *Subcommittee*, Part 2.

[7] U. S. House, House Miscellaneous Documents, 41st Congress, 1st Session, Serial 1402, No. 13 (Washington, D. C., 1870), 7, 9, 11, 22; hereafter cited as *Depositions*, No. 13; *Subcommittee*, Part 1:19, 110, 144, 335-37, 401, 608, 617, 654-66, 686-87; *Subcommittee*, Part 2:20, 156, 169, 191, 362; Louisiana General Assembly, *Report of the Joint Committee of the General Assembly of Louisiana on the Conduct of the Late Elections and the Condition of Peace and Order in the State*, Session of 1869 (New Orleans, 1869), 84; hereafter cited as *Legislature*, 1869; Trelease, *White Terror*, 128.

[8]Burnham, *Presidential Ballots,* 486-501; *New Orleans Daily Picayune,* March 21, 1868; *Subcommittee,* Part 1, appendix, xxix. Roger W. Shugg, *Origins of Class Struggle in Louisiana: A Social History of White Farmers and Laborers During Slavery and After, 1840-1875* (Baton Rouge, 1939), pointed out on pages 16-17 that whites outnumbered blacks in only fifteen of the state's forty-eight parishes in 1860.

[9]*Legislature,* 1869, 4; *Subcommittee,* Part 1:160-161; Records of the Bureau of Refugees, Freedmen, and Abandoned Lands, Records of the Assistant Commissioner for the State of Louisiana, 1865-1869, Washington, D. C., National Archives, Record Group 105, Microfilm 1027, roll 27, frames 16, 63, 262; roll 34, frames 206-308; hereafter cited as *Microfilm 1027.*

[10]Shugg, *Origins of Class Struggle,* 58-65.

[11]*Legislature,* 1869, 73; *Subcommittee,* Part 1:110, 287.

[12]Louisiana General Assembly, *Report of the Joint Committee of the General Assembly of Louisiana on the Conduct of the Late Elections and the Condition of Peace and Order in the State,* Session of 1868 (New Orleans, 1868); hereafter cited as *Legislature,* 1868; *Legislature,* 1869; U. S. House, *House Miscellaneous Documents,* 41st Congress, 1st Session, Serial 1402, No. 12 (Washington, D. C., 1870); hereafter cited as *Depositions,* No. 12; *Depositions,* No. 13; *Subcommittee,* Part 1; *Subcommittee,* Part 2.

[13]See Table 1.

[14]Warmoth polled just less than 65,000 votes, compared to just over 38,000 for his nearest rival, James Taliaferro, another Republican. The Republican constitution was ratified with 66,152 for, to 48,739 against. Taylor, *Louisiana Reconstructed,* 157-61.

[15]Burnham, *Presidential Ballots,* 486-501.

[16]*Legislature,* 1868.

[17]*Legislature,* 1869, 73.

[18]Congressional interest in the Knights of the White Camelia was evident from the questions about the KWC asked of witnesses throughout the investigation. See *Depositions,* No. 12; *Depositions,* No. 13; *Subcommittee,* Part 1; *Subcommittee,* Part 2. The subcommittee members were Job E. Stevenson of Ohio, S. S. Burdett of Missouri, and Michael C. Kerr of Indiana.

[19]*Subcommittee,* Part 1:19, 293-95, 300-308, 334, 348-50, 364, 369-70, 373, 375, 386, 483, 517, 565, 572, 577, 601, 678, 716-17; *Subcommittee,* Part 2:105-6, 111-14, 120, 146, 152, 222, 235, 364, 390, 397-400, 408, 414, 438.

[20]*Subcommittee.,* Part 1:554; *Subcommittee,* Part 2:339.

[21]Andrew B. Booth, comp., *Records of Louisiana Confederate Soldiers and Louisiana Confederate Commands,* 3 vols. in 4 parts (New Orleans, 1920), 572; *New Orleans Times-Democrat,* November 10, 1883; *St. Martinville L'Observateur,* November 10, 1883.

[22]Alexandre Barde, *The Vigilante Committees of the Attakapas: An Eyewitness Account of Banditry and Backlash in Southwestern Louisiana,* trans. by Henrietta Guilbeau Rogers, annot. and ed. by David C. Edmonds and Dennis Gibson (Lafayette, La., 1981), 274-75.

[23]*Subcommittee,* Part 1:541-63; *New York Times,* January 6, 1891; Shugg, *Origins of Class Struggle,* 253.

[24]Shugg, *Origins of Class Struggle*, 253-59.

[25]There are only five surviving issues of the *Franklin Planters' Banner*. However, Dennett's editorials in these issues leave no doubt as to his views on the place of Negroes in society. Dates of surviving issues are December 28, 1867, and January 8, April 11, June 27, and September 5 in 1868. These issues are contained on microfilm, available through the library services of Louisiana State University, Baton Rouge.

[26]Taylor, *Louisiana Reconstructed*, 62-63.

[27]The Democratic press admitted the futility of Democratic hopes for winning fair elections in Louisiana due to Republican voting strength. *New Orleans Daily Picayune*, March 21, 1868; Coleman, *The Election of 1868*, 318-19.

[28]Trelease, *White Terror*, 93; Taylor, *Louisiana Reconstructed*, 115, 122, 127-28; *Subcommittee*, Part 1:295, 307, 328-29, 348-50, 364, 369-70, 483, 518, 572, 591, 601, 754; *Subcommittee*, Part 2:76-98, 103, 146, 152, 191, 221, 273, 296, 396, 414, 451-54, 540.

[29]*Subcommittee*, Part 1:328-29; *Subcommittee*, Part 2:156, 230-45, 483, 572.

[30]Ibid., Part 1:19, 293, 295, 300-302, 307-8, 334, 348-50, 364, 369-70, 373, 375, 386, 483, 517, 565, 572, 577, 601, 678, 716-17; *Subcommittee*, Part 2:105-6, 111-14, 120, 146, 152, 222, 235, 364, 390, 397-400, 408, 414, 438.

[31]*Subcommittee*, Part 1:300, 483, 541-63; *Subcommittee*, Part 2:29-33, 105-6, 120, 385-405, 438.

[32]*Subcommittee*, Part 1:328-29, 335-37, 444, 608; *Subcommittee*, Part 2:105-6, 111-14; Trelease, *White Terror*, 128; *Microfilm 1027*, roll 27, frame 49; *Legislature*, 1868, 30; Horn, *Invisible Empire*, 288.

[33]*Legislature*, 1868, 13.

[34]*Subcommittee*, Part 2:444.

[35]See map.

[36]Burnham, *Presidential Ballots*, 486-501.

[37]*Legislature*, 1868, 18; *Subcommittee*, Part 1:666; Records of the Bureau of Refugees, Freedmen and Abandoned Lands, *Registers and Letters Received by the Commissioner of the Bureau of Refugees, Freedmen, and Abandoned Lands, 1865-1872*, Washington, D. C., National Archives, Record Group 105, Microfilm 752, roll 59, frames 366-72, 374-432, 436-37, 685-87; hereafter cited as *Microfilm 752*. For detailed treatment of the St. Landry riot, see Carolyn E. De Latte, "The St. Landry Riot: A Forgotten Incident of Reconstruction Violence," *Louisiana History*, 17 (1976): 41-49; and Claude F. Oubre, "The Opelousas Riot of 1868," *Attakapas Gazette*, 8 (1973): 139-52.

[38]In October 1868, 1,944 soldiers were stationed in twelve garrisons in Louisiana. This number represented more troops than in any other Southern state, except Texas and more than twice the number in Georgia in 1868. Troop locations identified in the sources were Shreveport, Natchitoches, Alexandria, Monroe, Vidalia, Amite, Baton Rouge, New Orleans, and unspecified locations in Carroll Parish and in the group of southern parishes including St. James, Iberville, Ascension, Assumption, St. Charles, Lafourche, and Terrebonne parishes. James E. Sefton, *The United States Army and Reconstruction, 1865-1877* (Baton Rouge, 1967), 262; Trelease, *White Terror*, 110; *Legislature*, 1868, 26-27; *Microfilm 1027*, roll 27, frame 2; *Microfilm 752*, roll 59, frames 439-41, 677-86; *Subcommittee*, Part 1:116-19, 225.

[39]Shugg, *Origins of Class Struggle*, 4-7; Trelease, *White Terror*, 64.

[40]In 1870, the adult, white male population in New Orleans was 32,000. Trelease, *White Terror,* 131; *Subcommittee,* Part 1:19; *Subcommittee,* Part 2:235.

[41]*Legislature,* 1869, 11, 12, 17; *Subcommittee,* Part 1:22, 119, 245-46; *Subcommittee,* Part 2:516-20; Trelease, *White Terror,* 135; Henry Clay Warmoth, *War, Politics, and Reconstruction: Stormy Days in Louisiana* (1930; reprint ed., New York, 1970), 76-78.

[42]Richard N. Current, *Three Carpetbag Governors* (Baton Rouge, 1967), 47-48.

[43]*Legislature,* 1869, 12; *Subcommittee,* Part 2:516-20.

[44]*Subcommittee,* Part 1:555; *Subcommittee,* Part 2:17, 360; Trelease, *White Terror,* 136.

[45]*Subcommittee,* Part 1:334; Burnham, *Presidential Ballots,* 486-501.

[46]*Subcommittee,* Part 2:39-45. John C. Tucker, the St. Landry Parish assessor of internal revenues, explained to the subcommittee that he joined the KWC and the Democratic party in order to avoid trouble and do his job without interference. Against his will, he voted for Seymour and also participated in the riot in Opelousas in September.

[47]*Subcommittee,* Part 1:334, 517; *Subcommittee,* Part 2:111-14.

[48]*Subcommittee,* Part 1:334-35.

[49]*Legislature,* 1868, 6.

[50]C. Vann Woodward, *Origins of the New South, 1877-1913* (Baton Rouge, 1951), 105-6. Woodward used the term "nihilism" in explaining the lack of reform spirit in the postbellum South, due to Redeemers' use of the issue of race to keep white voters in line.

[51]Fleming, *Documentary History of Reconstruction,* 54.

[52]Eric Hoffer, *The True Believer: Thoughts on the Nature of Mass Movements* (New York, 1951).

[53]Thomas Dixon, *The Clansman: An Historical Romance of the Ku Klux Klan* (New York, 1905).

[54]Taylor, *Louisiana Reconstructed,* 481-505.

RACE AND VIOLENCE IN RECONSTRUCTION
NEW ORLEANS: THE 1868 RIOT*

Melinda Meek Hennessey

New Orleans was as no other place in the South. A major port falling into Union hands early in the war, it was the most cosmopolitan and sophisticated city of the Confederate states. Although the Negro proportion of the population was not as high as in other places, 26 percent of the city's 191,000 residents, the blacks, too, were an uncommon group.[1] Among the 50,000 Negro residents of New Orleans were a substantial number of blacks who had been free before the war,[2] and a number of these free men of color enjoyed excellent, often European, educations and considerable wealth.[3] No other city in the South had blacks as capable of exerting real leadership as did New Orleans, yet the history of Reconstruction violence shows that the city suffered two major race riots, and in both the blacks, despite their antebellum opportunities, were unable to prevent the outbreaks or counter effectively the white onslaughts. The massacre of July 1866 had proved the vulnerability of the New Orleans black community, and it would be the largest, but not the only, Reconstruction race riot. In late October 1868 New Orleans again witnessed the races pitted one against the other, and black losses once more surpassed white casualties. But this time, blacks were better prepared and frequently fought back.

On September 4, 1868, P. B. S. Pinchback delivered a heated speech to the Louisiana senate in response to newspaper attacks on him. Blacks, he said, had reached the end of their patience. "The next outrage of the kind which they [the white Democrats] commit will be the signal for the dawn of retribution, of which they have not yet dreamed—a signal that will cause ten thousand torches to be applied to this city; for patience will then have ceased to be a virtue and this city will be reduced to ashes."[4] White suspicion of a black uprising, a deep fear left from slavery days, was heightened by Pinchback's words, and the speech would be remembered as a commencement of tension which

*First published in *Louisiana History*, 20 (1979): 77-91. Reprinted with the kind permission of the author and the Louisiana Historical Association.

deepened as the November 3 election neared.[5] Twice during that fall local Democrats invited Willis Rollins, a black Democrat given to drinking and heated speechmaking, to address Negroes. His presence so angered black Radicals that twice they attacked him as he tried to speak. A riot was avoided in the second incident only by the interference of Gov. Henry Clay Warmoth, who calmed the mob and enabled Rollins to escape safely.[6] The threat of violence hovered beneath the surface of New Orleans political activity.

On September 22, the first serious outbreak occurred. That night a number of Republican clubs, almost all chiefly black, held one of the frequent political processions through the streets of New Orleans. On the corner of Canal and Bourbon streets stood Dumontiel's confectionery, a restaurant and saloon, which was a popular gathering place for wealthy whites. Although some whites claimed the difficulty began when blacks entered and demanded service, most agreed that as the blacks came down Canal Street to the corner, a few whites gave a cheer for Seymour and Blair. Several blacks broke from the parade and gave chase, the whites ducking into Dumontiel's with the Negroes in pursuit. Lamps were thrown through the front windows of the store, and then a white stepped out on the upstairs gallery of the restaurant and began firing into the Republican clubs below. An exchange of shots followed between blacks and whites, which spread throughout the area and resulted in a large number of injuries to both sides and the death of one black man.[7] Fortunately for everyone, almost as quickly as it began, the violence ceased.

In searching for the causes of this and later tension between the races in the fall of 1868 in New Orleans, a number of factors emerge. Voter registration in the city favored the whites, but the advantage was not as great as the population differences indicated. The April 1868 election had gone poorly for the Democrats, and whites claimed one of the reasons was the importation of large numbers of illegal black voters who were brought by steamboat from the surrounding rural parishes. Democrats feared this importation, if repeated, would negate their numerical strength and swing the November election to Grant and Colfax.[8] The distasteful reminder that, legally or illegally, they must contend at the polls with large numbers of a race they believed inferior, barely removed from savagery, indeed their former slaves, was a bitter draught for New Orleans whites to swallow.

It did not help that blacks took so wholeheartedly to politics. From the early days of the Loyal League in other parts of the South, Republican leaders endeavored to make political action more than simply a matter of voting. One of the most popular methods of attracting blacks in New Orleans was through ward clubs, whose functions were social as well as political. The barbecues, speeches, and processions, enhanced by the attention paid them by white and upper-class Negro Republicans, offered a chance for lower-class blacks to express themselves and to feel needed, two luxuries not often enjoyed in their experience prior to emancipation. They joined with enthusiasm such Republican ward clubs as the Colfax Defenders, Warmoth Guards, Grant Invincibles, and Pinchback Zouaves.[9]

White political clubs were also popular for similar reasons. The white ward clubs provided the same social activities, but the most urgent reason for joining a white political organization was the perceived necessity of dealing with the frightening reality of black freedom and citizenship. The Constitutional Club, Jewell Guards, Seymour Sentinels, Workingmen's Club, Seymour *Infantas,* Swamp Fox Rangers, and Seymour Knights were among the most active of the seventy-eight separate Democratic clubs in New Orleans and its environs, clubs which numbered twelve to fifteen thousand members.[10] The largest and most feared of all the Democratic clubs was the Innocents, which had a maximum membership of twelve hundred according to its president, Pascalis Labarre.[11] Most residents believed the group to be composed chiefly of Sicilians, and the club did take its name from a Sicilian political organization, but while it contained a large number of Sicilians and Italians, the Innocents also included Americans, Spaniards, Portuguese, Maltese, and Latin Americans, and Labarre himself was a French Creole. The Innocents' garb of a red shirt and a cap bearing their name made them easily recognizable. They were further distinguishable by their banners, more explicit than those of other Democratic clubs, such as one which portrayed a black on the ground about to be stabbed with a knife. The belief was widespread among Democratic whites as well as blacks that the Sicilians were hotheaded, stealthy, and revengeful, and that they usually settled their duels and fights with knives.[12] This group would be pivotal in the coming difficulties.

Saturday night was a favorite time for political clubs of both parties to meet and parade, so the appearance of Democratic and Republican processions on Saturday, October 24, 1868, was not unusual. The Democratic Workingmen's Club stopped about 9:30 p.m. at the home of Thomas Hare on Poydras Street to serenade him. Also in the same vicinity were the Grant Guards, Colfax Guards, Tenth Ward Club, Eleventh Ward Club, and other Republican groups. Upon finishing, the Workingmen's Club continued their procession, marching down Canal Street. Just in front of them a procession of the Republican clubs turned off a side street onto Canal, and there was a lively exchange of cheers for their respective candidates between the two groups, but no violence. As the two parades marched down Canal, the blacks in front on the left side of the street and the Workingmen's Club about a hundred yards behind on the right, a small number of men and boys jumped from what was known as the neutral ground, the tree-lined center of the street, and fired into the Republican procession. Completely surprised, the paraders dropped their torches and began running, many meeting the advancing Democratic column, which also fired into them. Firing was general on Canal and through the lower part of New Orleans for several minutes as the black Republicans made their escape.[13] Blacks were unprepared for the violence, a panic seized them, and although a few did return the fire, most of the casualties and all of the deaths in this first stage of the riot were black. Seven blacks lost their lives in the short but deadly gunfire. Alfred Andrews, Nelson Dewey, Frank Hoskins, Edward Jones, and James Wilson all died from gunshot wounds suffered on Canal Street. The two other fatalities were an unidentified black, who died from a variety of wounds, and ten-year-old Joseph Antoine, the son of prominent

Louisiana State Senator C. C. Antoine, who was battered to death, probably trampled as the blacks ran to escape the shooting.[14]

Many blacks, infuriated by the attack, went home and gathered whatever weapons were available, from guns to knives and axes, and headed back into the streets. By 11:30 p.m. large numbers of Negroes were in the streets attacking every white man in sight. A streetcar was stopped on Dauphine Street and a white passenger, J. R. Small, was severely injured by a blow from an axe, and a number of other whites were shot or stabbed. Patrick Brady, a white carriage maker, was hacked to death by hatchets, and Cornelius Sullivan, a former Confederate officer who served as a member of the New Orleans Police Department until he resigned when blacks were first appointed to the force, was shot to death in the second fight that Saturday night. A detachment of United States soldiers finally brought an end to the fighting.[15] Although rioting was over for the time, New Orleans residents would see more violence in the following days.

On Sunday, October 25, there was no bloodshed in New Orleans, but excitement over the previous night's activities dominated street conversations and the thoughts of state and local officials. On Sunday afternoon a major riot began in St. Bernard Parish, just below New Orleans; and a minor disturbance in Jefferson Parish, west of Orleans, gave city residents the appearance of sitting in the middle of a sea of violence, an emotional assessment not really erroneous. The problem of preserving order was grave, and there was confusion over the duties, responsibilities, and capabilities of the various legitimate forces of restraint which were available in the city. The federal officer in direct command of New Orleans was Gen. Lovell H. Rousseau, a man whose Democratic leanings were known and who enjoyed the dubious honor of having a white Democratic ward club named for him.[16] General Rousseau had federal troops at his disposal, and he could request reinforcements if necessary. On the state level, Congress forbade state militias in the Southern states, so Governor Warmoth had no official state military body at his command.[17] But he and other Louisiana Republican leaders developed an ingenious way to bypass this impediment. Before adjourning on October 20 the Louisiana legislature passed the Metropolitan Police Bill, which established a five-man board of commissioners and created the Metropolitan Police District of Orleans, Jefferson, and St. Bernard Parishes. This armed force, financed by taxation on the municipalities within the district, superceded any local police organizations, and was under the control of the governor. In effect Warmoth had his state militia. The title Metropolitans, as the force was identified, quite naturally became as hated among white conservatives as other popular epithets of the day, such as Radicals and carpetbaggers. Democrats loathed the bill and refused to recognize its legality. While not unmindful of the possible political potential of the Metropolitans, the whites, on a more emotional level, reacted to the Negro presence on the force, for three of the five commissioners and about one-third of the policemen were black. Armed black men serving as legitimate forces of authority were anathema to Southern white men. J. A. Raynal and Oscar Dunn, the Louisiana lieutenant governor, were two of the black commissioners, and they both strongly believed that the wealthy, property-owning whites never accepted the force and refused to give it the backing of the community, support which was essential if the police were to be able to keep the peace.[18]

New Orleans Democratic newspapers were consistently critical of the performance of the black Metropolitans, and in fact, many of their reporters seemed unable to see any but the Negro members of the force. As a consequence, they almost gleefully rushed to criticize the performance of the Metropolitans in Saturday's violence. "The inefficiency of our negro [*sic*] guardians of the peace was thoroughly proved on Saturday night. They were not only worthless, but taking the place of better men they proved an impediment to the preservation of law and order," wrote the *New Orleans Times*.[19] The *New Orleans Daily Picayune* editorialized, "On Canal street, just after the riot on Saturday night, there was not to be seen a policeman, high or low. They must have disappeared as soon as the firing commenced."[20] The *New Orleans Commercial Bulletin* argued that if the "colored Metropolitans" had not turned and run at the first fire, there probably would have been no bloodshed at all that night.[21] The problem of the black Metropolitans and the police force in general would recur many times during the next few days, and there is little doubt that, as the violence continued, most Negro policemen did not report for duty. George L. Cain, who on November 1, 1868, accepted an appointment as chief of the embattled Metropolitan Police Force, believed that there was greater demoralization among the Negro policemen than among the whites but added, "The colored had most to fear," and claimed that three or four were killed during the riotous outbreaks.[22] Louisiana Freedmen's Bureau chief, Gen. Edward Hatch, agreed with Cain's assessment, as did a French reporter covering American politics for the Paris newspaper, *Temps*. From his vantage point in the North, Georges Clemenceau argued there was nothing strange in the Negro policemen's reluctance to report for duty, since no Negro could leave his home at that time without endangering his life.[23] Lazard A. Rodriguez, a French Creole mulatto and a rather conservative Republican, believed that the entire riot was premeditated by whites, not to intimidate blacks before the approaching election, but to attack and discredit the Metropolitans.[24]

On Monday, October 26, General Rousseau forwarded a communication he had received to Secretary of War J. M. Schofield. The communication was from Governor Warmoth, who admitted that the civil authorities in Orleans, Jefferson, and St. Bernard Parishes were unable to preserve order. Forbidden by Congress to organize a militia, Warmoth said he was turning to Rousseau to restore peace to these parishes, which was precisely what Secretary Schofield ordered General Rousseau to do in his response.[25] Despite these official efforts to keep the peace, Monday witnessed a reappearance of violence in New Orleans, and the fighting continued into Tuesday and Wednesday.

Sporadic fighting kept tension at a fever pitch throughout the day Monday, and rumors that Governor Warmoth, incapable of maintaining order, was resigning and fleeing the state did not assuage fears. About 2:00 p.m. a bipartisan conference including Governor Warmoth, A. L. Lee, editor of the *New Orleans Republican,* T. L. Macon, president of the Central Democratic Committee, Joseph Ellison, president of the

Democratic Central Parish Committee, and other prominent men called on General Rousseau. The leaders agreed to use their influence to persuade political clubs not to parade again before the November 3 election. To that end Governor Warmoth issued a proclamation later that day, requesting no public meetings or processions by either political party before the balloting.[26]

If white Democratic clubs received the message from their leaders, they ignored it. About 8:00 p.m. Monday white groups from all over the city began gathering and moving toward City Hall. Numbering about three thousand, the crowd offered their services to Mayor John R. Conway to help him patrol the city in place of the harried Metropolitans. It took little astuteness to realize the volatility of several thousand armed whites gathering together in the frustrated atmosphere New Orleans provided that night. Fortunately, five leaders stepped forward to address the crowd, and they spoke almost the same message. Gen. J. B. Steedman, a Democratic leader, Democratic Mayor Conway, former Confederate Gen. Harry T. Hayes, Democratic State Senator Robert Ogden, and Sheriff Thomas L. Maxwell all advised the men to return peaceably to their homes and expressed confidence that General Rousseau would keep the peace. Steedman and Ogden severely criticized Warmoth, and Ogden, not prone to understatement, observed, ". . . we have stood on the brink of a volcano—one of the greatest political convulsions that the world has ever witnessed."[27] Despite the rhetoric, the urgent and unanimous message was to disperse and the majority of those listening did. But not all.

The Innocents either did not receive the request to end processions or chose to ignore it, for about 10:00 p.m. they were again marching through the streets. Bearing trophies from the Saturday night fight, they paraded with a captured Negro Republican banner covered with caps belonging to black club members, which were garnered at the same time. It was not a display calculated to please already angry blacks, and twice the procession of three hundred Innocents was fired into from upper galleries as it passed. No one was hit by the shots fired on Common Street, but at the corner of Triton Walk and Dryades Street three shots rang out from a gallery and the Innocents returned the fire. Edward Malone, a thirty-six-year-old native of Ireland and a member of the Innocents, was killed in the exchange. His body, later picked up by the authorities, had six bullet wounds and a number of cleaver-inflicted cuts and slashes. The infuriated Innocents continued their retaliation much of the night; they were joined by scattered groups of whites, and shooting continued through the morning Tuesday. The efforts of the small and necessarily dispersed squads of U. S. troops were ineffective in ending the violence.[28]

On Monday night, the riot not only resumed, but also took a new form. Bands of whites began attacking the homes, establishments, and meeting rooms of blacks. P. M. Williams, a black Republican schoolteacher who had attended Dartmouth, suffered a twelve hundred dollar loss when a body of armed whites broke into his home, which also served as his school, carried off currency, watches and jewelry, and destroyed crockery and furniture.[29] Another target was the cigar store and factory which Armand Belot owned with his brother Octave, and in part of which Armand Belot resided with his family. The

Belots were wealthy French Creole mulattoes, active in the Republican party. Although the family escaped without injury, all the furniture was smashed with axes and practically every movable article in the house was thrown into the street. According to Lieutenant Governor Dunn, Belot recovered $20,000 in damages from the city for the destruction of his home and factory.[30] Prominent Negroes were not the only targets, and many ordinary black citizens of New Orleans were robbed and threatened at gunpoint that night by bellicose whites. Black barber shops, grocery stores, and churches were broken into, ransacked, and looted. Special targets of white anger indicated where many of their frustrations lay. The headquarters of the Colfax Legion, Second Ward Republican Club, Eighth Ward Radical Club, Seventh Ward Radical Club, and First Ward Republican Club were entered and their contents destroyed.[31]

As daylight came Tuesday morning, October 27, the situation in New Orleans was still grave. The shooting between the Innocents and other white groups and blacks continued unabated throughout Monday night and dawn Tuesday did not bring an end. The Metropolitan Police Force was completely demoralized, and General Rousseau's federal troops were not numerous enough to cover all areas of the city, so that they were only able to respond when violence occurred and not to prevent it. Casualties mounted on both sides Tuesday as fighting erupted in the French Market, on Canal Street, near the Trémé Market, and in other spots as far out as the levee. At the Innocents' headquarters lay the body of Malone, slain the night before, and rumors swirled throughout the city. At one point General Lee, the *Republican* editor, sought refuge for a few hours at General Rousseau's headquarters after hearing that the Innocents were marching to kill him. During the day additional United States troops arrived from Mississippi and were immediately distributed throughout the most troubled areas of New Orleans.[32] Following patterns similar to those of Monday night, on Tuesday evening white gangs ransacked and robbed Negro homes. There was one new offense, however, as many blacks reported their registration certificates, necessary for voting, were taken by the whites.[33]

At last the riot ebbed on Wednesday, October 28, and it was the last day in which there were several outbreaks, although isolated cases of violence continued until the election. As the city quieted General Rousseau announced the Metropolitan Board of Commissioners had elected Gen. James B. Steedman as chief of police and promised Steedman full support from the military in keeping the tenuous peace.[34] According to Oscar Dunn, the lieutenant governor and president of the Board of Commissioners, Steedman was selected by the board only because General Rousseau informed them that the only way he would continue to give military support to the police force was if Steedman were appointed. Steedman, a well-known Democrat, was quite acceptable to New Orleans whites. He already held the office of collector of internal revenue and did not want to give it up, so he agreed to take the post only temporarily. In fact he occupied the office but three days and resigned once in the middle of that period. Significantly, however, he was accepted by the Democrats, and his holding the position, if only symbolically, gave the Metropolitan Police Force a legitimacy in the eyes of white residents which it had never before enjoyed. This, along with the general waning of the riot, was sufficient to calm the passions enough for the violence to end, before George L. Cain received the job permanently on November 1. The period from Steedman's appointment on October 28 until Cain's assumption of the job on November 1 was quite chaotic and occupied much space in local papers. At one point Steedman did resign, and Mayor Conway appointed Thomas E. Adams, the notorious chief of police during the 1866 New Orleans riot. But Steedman was persuaded to withdraw his resignation, at least temporarily, and he held the job until peace was restored and Cain took over.[35]

The number of citizens who died during the New Orleans riot was high, although not as high as the estimate of sixty-three in the Louisiana legislative report. At least six and probably seven white men lost their lives in the violence between Saturday and Wednesday. Black casualties were higher, with a minimum of thirteen black men and one boy, young Antoine, perishing in the same period. The victims primarily suffered gunshot and stab wounds. Not especially bothered by the large death toll, the *Daily Picayune* commented, "We learn that our Northern cousins are greatly excited about the course of events in New Orleans. When they get the facts and find that all this terrible fuss and fury has resulted in the loss of no more lives than often happens from the turning over of an old fashioned stage coach, and that none but negroes, with hardly a name and certainly no position, even among negroes, have suffered on the Radical side, they will think it to have been 'great cry and little wool.'"[36] Also, the fact that at least four of the white men killed were born in Italy or Ireland may have lessened white concern over their loss.[37]

The result of the November 3 election was an overwhelming Democratic victory for Horatio Seymour and Frank Blair in Louisiana, as they carried the state 80,225 to 33,225 and New Orleans by a 23,897 to 276 vote.[38] Election day had no outbreaks, and explanations for the landslide Democratic victory and the calm of election day varied between and within the two parties. There were some complaints by blacks of harassment and forced voting for Democrats,[39] but there was no widespread attempt by whites either to keep blacks from the polls or to intimidate them when they voted, and yet the overwhelming majority of New Orleans Republicans failed to vote.

Heated disagreement characterized the two parties' explanations of this. Republicans agreed there was little trouble at the polling places and attributed it to the meager black turnout.[40] Democrats claimed that before the riot of late October, Governor Warmoth and other leading Republicans decided to advise blacks to stay away from the polls, because they believed that the Democrats were going to win and knew if the Negroes did not vote, they could claim intimidation and have the results overturned. This view was shared by Republican Lazard A. Rodriguez, a mulatto, who asserted the Republicans never canvassed for Grant and planned all along to contest the election.[41]

As expected, most Republicans disagreed. Governor Warmoth admitted he advised many Republicans not to vote because he did not feel it could be done safely, and he accused whites of terrorizing blacks to keep them from the polls. This argument was generally followed by Republicans. If Warmoth decided to try to get the election overturned by claiming violence, the actions of white Louisianians in the fall of 1868 certainly played into his hands. Blacks were terrorized by the very real violence that came their way at the hands of whites. Realizing that Republican cries of intimidation might appear valid, the Democrats canceled plans for a torchlight procession the Saturday night prior to the election and adopted resolutions between October 29 and November 3 calling for the preservation of peace at the polls. Republicans dismissed their actions, claiming the Democrats were just trying to undo the results of the riots because they realized the election results might be contested.[42]

The severe defeat in the April 1868 election must have greatly influenced Louisiana Democrats.[43] The political power of the community had shifted from their hands to those of carpetbaggers, scalawags, and Negroes. Surely it rankled and surely drastic steps were necessary to put that power back into white hands. The fall riots in 1868 in Louisiana, occurring not only in New Orleans but also in Bossier Parish, Opelousas, and St. Bernard Parish, had different tensions and precipitating incidents, the casualty figures varied although blacks always suffered in greater numbers, and yet the political results of intimidation and violence were everywhere the same—Democratic victory at the polls in November. As a political weapon, riots provided a successful method by which whites were able to wrest control away from Louisiana Republicans.

Notes for "Race and Violence in Reconstruction New Orleans: The 1868 Riot"

[1]U.S. Census Bureau, *A Compendium of the Ninth Census (June 1, 1870)* (Washington, 1872), 52-53.

[2]Ibid., 52-53.

[3]Two excellent studies of New Orleans blacks in this period are John W. Blassingame, *Black New Orleans, 1860-1880* (Chicago, 1973) and David C. Rankin, "The Origins of Black Leadership in New Orleans During Reconstruction," *Journal of Southern History*, 40 (1974): 417-40.

[4]*New York Times*, September 6, 1868.

[5]"Testimony Taken By the Sub-Committee of Elections in Louisiana," *House Miscellaneous Documents*, no. 154, 41st Cong., 2nd sess., part 1 (Washington, 1870), 383. Hereafter cited as "Elections in Louisiana."

[6]Joe Gray Taylor, *Louisiana Reconstructed, 1863-1877* (Baton Rouge, 1974), 167; "Elections in Louisiana," part 1:621-24, part 2:352-53; "Papers in the Case of *J. H. Sypher vs. Louis St. Martin*, from The First Congressional District of Louisiana," *House Miscellaneous Documents*, no. 13, 41st Cong., 1st sess., part I (Washington, 1869), 55. Hereafter cited as *Sypher vs. St. Martin*.

[7]"Elections in Louisiana," part 1:381, 747, part 2:278, 337, 500-502; *Sypher vs. St. Martin*, part 1:55; *New York Tribune*, September 24, 1868; Bureau of Refugees, Freedmen and Abandoned Lands, "Registers and Letters Received by the Bureau, 1865-1872," M752 (National Archives, Washington); Louisiana Legislature, *Supplemental Report of the Joint Committee of the General Assembly of Louisiana on the Conduct of the Late Elections, and the Condition of Peace and Good Order in the State* (New Orleans, 1869), 167-82, hereafter cited as *Louisiana Report;* "Use of the Army in Certain of the Southern States," *House Executive Documents*, no. 30, 44th Cong., 2nd sess. (Washington, 1877), 316-21, hereafter cited as "Use of the Army."

[8]"Elections in Louisiana," part 2:245, 355; John S. Kendall, *History of New Orleans*, Vol. 1 (Chicago, 1922), 318.

[9]*Louisiana Report,* 168-71.

[10]"Elections in Louisiana," part 1:379-80, 746, 754, part 2:76, 80.

[11]Ibid., part 2:331.

[12]Ibid., part 1:331, 334, 380, 624, 753, Part 2:279, 312, 447, 478. The only group more feared than the Innocents was the Knights of the White Camelia, and although they apparently did not participate in the New Orleans riot in any organized way, their presence surfaced nonetheless. Similar in every way to the Ku Klux Klan, the Knights of the White Camelia was founded in 1867 in Louisiana, probably by Judge Alcibiades DeBlanc, its first leader. Members of Democratic clubs vehemently insisted that they were separate from the Knights, primarily because they required no secret oath and because the Knights were not political but had as their purpose white supremacy. The division line was often fine and being a member of a political club did not preclude membership in the Knights, and in fact frequently went hand in hand. See Taylor, *Louisiana Reconstructed,* 162-63, and "Elections in Louisiana," part 1:379, 754-55, part 2:331-33, 338-42, 356, 360-61.

[13]*New Orleans Crescent,* October 25, 1868; *New Orleans Daily Picayune,* October 25, 1868; *New Orleans Times,* October 27, 1868; *Louisiana Report,* 182-88; "Elections in Louisiana," part 1:28-29, 745-47, part 2:357-58, 484-85; *New Orleans Republican,* October 26, 1868, as quoted in *New York Tribune,* November 2, 1868.

[14]*New Orleans Crescent,* October 27, 1868; *New Orleans Commercial Bulletin,* November 2, 1868; "Elections in Louisiana," part 1:1-6; BRFAL, "Registers and Letters," letter from General Edward Hatch to General O. O. Howard, November 10, 1868; *Daily* Picayune, October 27, 1868; *Louisiana Report,* 182-88; "Use of the Army," 526.

[15]*Daily Picayune,* October 25, 27, 1868; *New Orleans Crescent,* October 27, 1868; "Elections in Louisiana," part 1:29; *New Orleans Commercial Bulletin,* November 2, 1868; *New Orleans Times,* October 27, 1868.

[16]Taylor, *Louisiana Reconstructed,* 171; "Elections in Louisiana," part 1:749.

[17]Taylor, *Louisiana Reconstructed,* 170-71; *Daily Picayune,* October 28, 1868; "Elections in Louisiana," part 1:31.

[18]*Acts passed by the General Assembly of the State of Louisiana, at the First Session of the Legislature, Held and Begun in the City of New Orleans, June 29, 1868* (New Orleans, 1868), 85-98; Kendall, *History of New Orleans,* 1:330-31; John Rose Ficklin, *History of Reconstruction in Louisiana* (Baltimore, 1910), 208-9; Taylor, *Louisiana Reconstructed,* 177; "Elections in Louisiana," part 1:58-61, 176, 619-20; Francis B. Harris, "Henry Clay Warmoth, Reconstruction Governor of Louisiana," *Louisiana Historical Quarterly,* 30 (1947): 566.

[19]*New Orleans Times,* October 27, 1868.

[20]*Daily Picayune,* October 27, 1868.

[21]*New Orleans Commercial Bulletin,* October 27, 1868.

[22]"Elections in Louisiana," part 1:619-22.

[23]Ibid., 28-30; Georges Clemenceau, *American Reconstruction, 1865-1870* (New York, 1928), 258-59.

[24]"Elections in Louisiana," part 2:493-95.

[25]Ibid., part 1:31; *Daily Picayune,* October 28, 1868.

[26]*Daily Picayune,* October 27, 1868; *New Orleans Times,* October 27, 1868; "Elections in Louisiana," part 2:324, 329.

[27]"Elections in Louisiana," part 1:744, 751-53, part 2:352, 476-77; *New York Times,* October 27, 1868; *New York Tribune,* October 27, 1868; *Shreveport Daily South Western,* October 27, 1868.

[28]*New Orleans Bee,* October 27, 28, 1868; *New Orleans Times,* October 27, 1868; *New Orleans Crescent,* October 27, 1868; *Daily Picayune,* October 27, 1868; *New Orleans Commercial Bulletin,* November 2, 1868.

[29]*Louisiana Report,* 144; *New Orleans Bee,* October 28, 1868; *New Orleans Times,* October 28, 1868; "Elections in Louisiana," part 2:486; Rankin, "Origins of Black Leadership," 433.

[30]"Elections in Louisiana," part 1:178; Rankin, "Origins of Black Leadership," 427, 437; *New Orleans Republican,* October 28, 1868 as quoted in *New York Tribune,* November 4, 1868; *New Orleans Times,* October 28, 1868; *New Orleans Bee,* October 28, 1868.

[31]*New Orleans Times,* October 28, 1868; "Elections in Louisiana," part 2:482; *Louisiana Report,* 192-93.

[32]*New York Times,* November 2, 1868; *New Orleans Times,* October 28, 1868; *Daily Picayune,* October 28, 1868; "Elections in Louisiana," part 2:501-2.

[33]*Louisiana Report,* 199-201.

[34]*Daily Picayune,* October 29, 1868; *New York Times,* October 29, 1868; "Elections in Louisiana," part 1:31.

[35]"Elections in Louisiana," part 1:176-77, 743-48, 619; *New Orleans Crescent,* October 30, 1868; *New Orleans Bee,* October 31, 1868; *Daily Picayune,* October 29, 30, 31, 1868; *New York Tribune,* October 30, 1868; *New Orleans Commercial Bulletin,* October 30, 1868; Charles Gardner, comp. and pub., *Gardner's New Orleans Directory for 1868* (New Orleans, 1868).

[36]*Daily Picayune,* October 27, 28, 29, 30, 1868, quote is from October 30, 1868; *New Orleans Commercial Bulletin,* November 2, 1868; *Louisiana Report,* 13, 184; "Elections in Louisiana," part 1:6.

[37]*New Orleans Commercial Bulletin,* November 2, 1868.

[38]*Daily Picayune,* November 4, 1868; Taylor, *Louisiana Reconstructed,* 172; *Sypher vs. St. Martin,* part 2:22-23.

[39]*Louisiana Report,* 205-11; "Elections in Louisiana," part 2:487.

[40]"Elections in Louisiana," part 1:178, 620, part 2:463, 486.

[41]Ibid., part 2:326, 358, 493-95; *New Orleans Bee,* October 31, 1868; *Daily Picayune,* November 4, 1868.

[42]"Elections in Louisiana," part 1:633, part 2:313, 464, 521; Henry Clay Warmoth, *War, Politics, and Reconstruction: Stormy Days in Louisiana* (New York, 1930), 70, 78; *Daily Picayune,* October 31, November 3, 1868; *New York Tribune,* October 30, 1868; *Sypher vs. St. Martin,* part 1:32, 46-48.

[43]"Elections in Louisiana," part 1:764.

"FORTY ACRES AND A MULE":
LOUISIANA AND THE
SOUTHERN HOMESTEAD ACT*

Claude F. Oubre

Historians have generally agreed that one of the great tragedies of emancipation and Reconstruction was the failure to provide economic security for the ex-slaves, principally by failing to provide them with land, which their brawn and blood had helped clear and make productive. Perhaps this accounts for the belief that the benevolent government which emancipated the slaves should also have provided them with "forty acres and a mule."

In March 1865, Congress created the Bureau of Refugees, Freedmen and Abandoned Lands to assist freedmen in making the difficult transition from slavery to freedom. Congress instructed the Bureau to rent forty acres of confiscated or abandoned land to each freedman family.[1] By April 1866, however, most of the confiscated and abandoned lands had been restored to former owners or sold to Northern businessmen. Therefore, in order to make land available to the freedmen, Congress enacted the Southern Homestead Act in June 1866, restricting all remaining public lands in five Southern states (approximately forty-six million acres) to entry for homestead only. To assure that freedmen and loyal whites would have first choice of the public lands the Act restricted entry to these classes exclusively until January 1, 1867, and until June 1868, no entry could be made for more than forty acres of double minimum land, that is, land within six miles of a railroad or navigable stream, or eighty acres of minimum land. Moreover, the act provided that until June 1868 the homesteader would only pay a two dollar filing fee at the time of entry, and would not have to pay the five dollar registration fee until his patent was issued five years later.[2]

With this action Congress assumed that it had provided land for the freedmen as well as special provisions to assist them in homesteading. Oliver Otis Howard, commissioner

*First published in *Louisiana History*, 17 (1976): 143-57. Reprinted with the kind permission of the author and the Louisiana Historical Association.

of the Freedmen's Bureau, instructed the assistant commissioners of the various states to take all steps necessary to make the Bureau an efficient agent for homesteading freedmen on the public lands.[3] Despite all these special provisions relatively few freedmen actually succeeded in acquiring their "forty acres and a mule" on government land in Louisiana. Many factors contributed to this failure since none of the provisions took into account the ravages of war and nature, the depressed economic condition of the freedmen, the quality of the public land, the condition of the land offices in the Southern states, and the slow working of the government bureaucracy. Furthermore, any provisions intended for the exclusive benefit of blacks and loyal whites aggravated the existing racial and political tensions.

Probably one of the major deterrents to homesteading was the actual physical condition of the land. Throughout the Civil War neglect of the levee system resulted in flooded fields which prevented the state from recovering economically. Flooding in 1865 was so extensive that Gen. E. R. S. Canby, the military commander of the district, provided seed corn for replanting to those whose lands were affected by the flooding. Gen. Thomas Conway, Bureau assistant commissioner, provided 4,028 rations to refugees and 225,735 1/2 rations to freedmen in Louisiana in 1865. While Congress debated the Southern Homestead Act in late winter and early spring of 1866, the raging Mississippi again overflowed is banks, broke through the levee above Baton Rouge and rushed towards the Gulf of Mexico, flooding an area fifty miles wide by one hundred miles long. Everything east of the Teche near Barre's Landing and west of the Mississippi was inundated. The Red River, swollen by winter and spring rains, also over-flowed and flooded much of its valley. Approximately two-thirds of the state's alluvial land was under from ten to twelve feet of water and crops worth thirty million dollars were destroyed.[4]

Since the overflow of 1866 was more disastrous than that of 1865, Freedmen's Bureau Assistant Commissioner Absalom Baird and General Canby recommended that measures similar to those of 1865 be taken. They estimated that such action would cost approximately $400,000 for Louisiana. Although Congress, which was debating the bill extending the Bureau, provided no funds to replace seed and implements which had been destroyed by the flood, the Freedmen's Bureau did provide emergency rations to those dislocated by the disaster. Between January 1, 1865, and October 31, 1866, the Bureau in Louisiana issued 229,554 1/2 rations to freedmen and 153,463 rations to refugees at a cost of $71,760.57.[5] Obviously, because of the destitution caused by the flood, few settlers, either white or black, were able to take advantage of the Homestead Act in 1866.

The economic situation in Louisiana did not improve in 1867 as the state suffered still another flood. The new Bureau assistant commissioner, Gen. J. A. Mower, informed General Howard that whole parishes were submerged and that he would require rations for at least fifty thousand persons, most of whom were freedmen. Because there had been charges of graft and corruption against various Bureau agents, General Mower issued stringent regulations which specifically forbade the issuance of rations to those living on land which was still under cultivation. The *New Orleans Republican* reported that "There never was a time in the history of Louisiana when so many of the people were in peril of starvation." The *Republican* estimated in August 1867 that not one plantation in one hundred had met expenses that year. Conditions deteriorated to the point that by the end of August planters, who had provided subsistence for their workers as well as for 35,903 aged and helpless freedmen, were finally forced to call upon the Bureau for assistance just at a time when the Bureau received orders to discontinue issuing rations.[6] Although Louisiana experienced more flooding than some of the other Southern states in 1866 and 1867, economic conditions which prevailed in Louisiana also prevailed throughout most of the South.

Of the five Southern states involved in the Southern Homestead Act, Louisiana provides an excellent example of the chaotic conditions prevailing in the land offices. Considerable confusion had resulted from the sale of federal lands by Louisiana officers during the Civil War, and to compound that confusion the New Orleans land office burned in 1864. Following the war unionists in Louisiana complained that the land office in New Orleans, though rebuilt and reopened, had not been reorganized. They also complained that the register had resigned, and therefore, no business could be transacted since all official acts required the joint action of the register, who recorded the entry, and the receiver, who assessed and collected the fees. Finally, at the time Congress passed the Southern Homestead Act, many of the records lost in the New Orleans fire had not yet been duplicated. Consequently, the register and receiver had relatively little information concerning which lands were available in the Southeastern District of Louisiana.[7]

Even if the land office in New Orleans had been open for business, homesteaders would have had difficulty filing their entries since it was the only office open in the state. Prior to the war Louisiana had been served by five land offices: New Orleans, Greensburg, Opelousas, Monroe, and Natchitoches. After the war all five offices would have been required to facilitate homesteading freedmen on public lands. But President Johnson's decision to close the offices at Opelousas and Greensburg made it impossible for homesteaders to file entry before January 1, 1867, the deadline for exclusive entry for blacks and loyal whites.[8]

Against this background of chaos and confusion, the organized activities of the Freedmen's Bureau in Louisiana provides a contrast. In order to assist Congress in its deliberations concerning the Southern Homestead Act, General Howard requested that the assistant commissioners examine the remaining public land in their respective states and determine whether there was any land on which large groups of freedmen could be colonized in isolated settlements. Asst. Commissioner Absalom Baird sent Lieut. J. Cromie to examine the public lands of Louisiana. Lieutenant Cromie reported that although there were some excellent tracts of land along the proposed route of the New Orleans, Opelousas, and Great Western Railroad, there were few acres where the type of colonies envisioned by Howard could be established. Most of the best lands had already been taken by whites who were not anxious to have freedmen for neighbors.

Furthermore, the land was either swampy or heavily forested, or open prairie with few trees for building.[9]

When the Southern Homestead Act became law Assistant Commissioner Baird appointed J. J. Saville as locating agent for the Bureau. Advertising in the *New Orleans Tribune*, Saville encouraged freedmen to settle in companies of at least ten families to assist one another in cultivating their farms, establishing churches and schools, and protecting their investments. Since the Southern Homestead Act did not provide implements and seed, Saville discouraged freedmen from homesteading unless they had the equipment to cultivate the land and the means to support themselves until they produced a harvest. He urged that each company of ten families should have a horse or mule and implements to clear and cultivate the land.[10]

During the month of September 1866 Saville assisted forty-nine black families possessing cash totaling $6,260 in settling on land of their own. General [Philip] Sheridan, the new Bureau commissioner for Louisiana, doubted whether the blacks would be allowed to remain peaceably on the land selected for them. The Southern Homestead Act had only been in force one month when New Orleans erupted into a political riot with definite racial overtones. Throughout the remainder of 1866 there were numerous incidents of outrages against freed people and at least twenty-five authenticated cases of freedmen murdered by whites.

The assistant commissioner reported that many people were cutting and selling the best timber on the public lands. This action depreciated the value of the land and hindered freedmen from locating on those lands for fear of coming into contact with these lawless characters. The new settlers relied on the sale of the timber on their tracts until they had sufficient time to make a crop. Therefore, it was imperative that depredations on the public lands be halted. Without the assignment of a battalion of cavalry which could move rapidly to places distant from the military posts, it was impossible to protect the freedmen.[11]

By December 31, 1866, Saville settled a total of eighty-seven families of freedmen on homestead lands. Yet, a month later only seven of these families had filed their applications at the land office. The New Orleans land office finally opened for business on January 17, 1867, but the register and receiver apparently failed to understand the regulations established by the Southern Homestead Act which required an applicant to file an affidavit stating that he was twenty-one years of age, or the head of a family, and that he had not borne arms against the United States. The register and receiver contended that the affidavits had to be sworn in their presence so that those who settled in the western part of the state had to travel one or two hundred miles to file their affidavits, a trip costing from twenty to fifty dollars.

This presented a set of circumstances which were completely illogical to Saville. He pointed out that under the earlier public land laws, land once surveyed was offered for sale at a minimum price of $1.25 per acre if it was more than six miles from either a railroad or navigable stream. Lands within the six-mile limit—double minimum land—sold for

$2.50 per acre. After the land had been offered for a number of years, the price was reduced according to a scale established by the graduation law. By the time of the Civil War the price of most public lands in Louisiana had been reduced to twenty-five cents per acre. A purchaser could therefore secure eighty acres for twenty dollars plus a two dollar registration fee and receive title to his land immediately, Saville therefore contended that if the freedmen were forced to travel to New Orleans to file their affidavits, the cost of the trip would be more than the value of the land under the graduation law. It would be better to allow the freedmen to purchase and receive title immediately rather than homestead with the hope of receiving title after five years.[12]

Meanwhile, on March 29, 1867 (for some unexplained reason), the functions of register and receiver in the New Orleans office were suspended, and the officials ordered to close the office and await instructions. In April, they were instructed to execute new bonds and then reopen the office. The receiver resigned and President [Andrew] Johnson did not replace him until July 10, 1868. From January 17 to March 26, 1867, 259 entries were made and an additional 238 entries were made from July 17 to December 30, 1868. It is apparent that homesteading activity was delayed during the intervening fifteen months by the absence of a receiver.[13] Since appointments of registers and receivers were made by the president, he could subvert the intention of the Southern Homestead Act by simply refusing to appoint either one of these officers in a state, and, indeed homesteading actually was delayed in most Southern states because of the absence of the register or receiver. Therefore, one can only question the president's intention.

Since the register was no longer burdened with registering homestead claims, he was finally able to effect the transfer of records from his office to Natchitoches and from Opelousas and Greensburg to New Orleans. In May 1867, he completed an inventory of the records of his office and requested that the General Land Office supply him with sixty-five township plats for the Greensburg and Opelousas districts. A few months earlier he had requested the missing plats for the Southeastern District. He was informed that the entire drafting division of the General Land Office had been engaged for two years in duplicating the lost plats from the five states covered by the Southern Homestead Act and that it would be several months before the maps of the New Orleans consolidated district could be prepared. In August 1867, the General Land Office sent 126 plats for the Southeastern District and informed the register that the remainder of the missing plats would be forwarded as soon as possible. As late as November 1, 1869, the files at the New Orleans office were still incomplete.[14]

While the register reorganized his office, Saville continued his efforts to settle freedmen on the public lands of Louisiana. He noted the expiration, on June 3, 1866, of the grant of 621,266 acres of land to the New Orleans, Opelousas and Great Western Railroad, and, consulting a lawyer, was informed that the land was subject to entry. On the basis of this legal opinion, he settled several families of Negro ex-soldiers on lands covered by the railroad grant; however, when these veterans appeared at the land office in New Orleans, they were cautioned not to enter the land. They appealed the opinion only to learn that the land had been certified to the state on October 7, 1859, for railroad purposes and that this land could not be open to homestead unless Congress acted.[15]

In July 1867, Saville, now serving as Bureau agent as well as locating agent, reported that about one hundred families of freedmen were preparing to move to the homestead lands in September. Requesting congressional action on the expired grant of the New Orleans, Opelousas, and Great Western Railroad, he estimated that if these lands were subject to entry, no less than five hundred freedmen's families would settle on homesteads that fall and winter.[16]

Initially, resistance to establishing the freedmen on homesteads on the public lands came from Southern whites; however, as Saville pressed his recommendation that Congress declare the railroad lands forfeited, opposition intensified in a different quarter. The *New Orleans Republican* on April 17, 1867, recommended that the government renew the grant to the New Orleans, Opelousas, and Great Western Railroad. Saville charged that the *Republican* was interested in railroad speculation and was therefore opposed to giving the land to the freedmen. He determined that the most fertile land remaining in Louisiana was a stretch about twenty miles wide within the railroad grant from Opelousas to the Mermentau and Calcasieu rivers. He estimated that there were not more than one hundred thousand acres of government land fit for cultivation which lay outside the limits of the grant. Therefore, he recommended forfeiture of the grant as well as confiscation of all state lands. This would open approximately one million acres of fertile agricultural lands to settlement by the freedmen.[17]

Saville's arguments were acknowledged, for, in December 1867, Congressman George W. Julian initiated a two-and-a-half-year fight to declare forfeited to the United States approximately five million acres of land granted to aid in the construction of railroads in the states of Alabama, Mississippi, Louisiana, and Florida. The New Orleans *Republican* requested that the bill be amended to exempt the New Orleans, Opelousas, and Great Western Railroad, but Julian successfully resisted the attempt. Finally, by act of July 14, 1870, the lands granted to Louisiana in aid of the railroad were declared forfeited to the federal government. This land was opened for homesteading and the surveyor general for Louisiana indicated in 1871 that there was considerable interest in settling these lands. On March 15, 1873, due to increased efforts by railroad interests the land was restored to the state of Louisiana for railroad purposes, and on February 24, 1883, the governor conveyed the land to the New Orleans and Pacific Railroad.[18]

While Congress debated the railroad grant, freedmen continued their efforts to secure homes. Many squatted on government land north of Shreveport, which had not yet been surveyed. It was not open for entry, and since the Southern Homestead Act restricted entries to homestead for actual settlement, these squatters did not even have a preemption right to the land and its improvement once the land was surveyed.[19]

In some cases whites attempted to discourage freedmen from settling on homestead lands by telling them that the land had already been entered. When they threatened to drive them from the land, many freedmen, who were too poor to resort to court action, applied to the register for protection of their claims. The register was instructed to assure himself of the legality of the claim and then write the homesteader an official letter stating that he had the only legal claim to the land. This action would give the homesteader legal protection which he would present to the sheriff or to a court. However, should the interference continue and parties trespass upon his land, the homesteader must have recourse to the legal authority since the land office lacked jurisdiction in such matters.[20]

The political climate in Louisiana in 1867 and 1868 was certainly not conducive to homesteading. Radical Reconstruction began with the disfranchisement of white Democrats and the election of Republican delegates to the constitutional convention. Rumors were rampant that the convention would seize the estates of former rebels and parcel them into forty-acre tracts for distribution to ex-slaves. There was even an attempt to include in the constitution a section providing for the breakup of large plantations by limiting purchases at distress sales to 150 acres. Another provision would have imposed double taxation on uncultivated land thereby encouraging owners of such tracts to parcel them out and sell them to freedmen.[21] Neither of these provisions were approved by the convention, but as long as the convention remained in session freedmen apparently anticipated a division of the land. Obviously, few freedmen would risk settling on uncleared land or on open prairie far from the nearest timber when all they had to do was wait for the convention to give them the cleared land of their former masters.

Asst. Commissioner W. H. Wood reported in December 1867 that unless freedmen were provided with rations sufficient to sustain them until they could harvest their own crop, few indeed would risk homesteading. He therefore urged that such rations be guaranteed.[22] Unfortunately, Wood, who appeared to have a sincere concern for the freedmen, was replaced by Gen. Robert Buchanan who was more interested in assisting white planters to secure labor than he was in aiding freedmen to homestead.

Saville requested transportation and rations to assist those who were still willing to risk homesteading. When Buchanan refused his request Saville informed Congressman Julian that Buchanan issued rations to whites but refused to issue rations to the freedmen to assist them in homesteading. Apparently Saville misunderstood the conditions under which Congress authorized the issuance of rations. Rations were to be issued to the employers of freedmen who would sign a first lien on all crops and the equipment used to produce them. In other words, rations were not issued; employers were allowed to borrow from the Bureau only if the government was guaranteed that the loan would be repaid. Most planters could not employ laborers and produce a crop without borrowing the rations. Many, however, feared that the proffer of federal assistance was a scheme to deprive them of their land. Therefore, although $350,000 was allotted for loans in Louisiana, planters only borrowed $35,000.[23]

Apparently the freedmen continued to hope that either the state or the federal government would seize the land of their former masters. General Buchanan reported in April 1868 that less than half of the freedmen were working.[24] The remainder waited for the outcome of the election to determine whether the constitution was to be approved. Republicans and Democrats vied for the support of the freedmen in the April election, but the Republicans swept the state, adopting the constitution and gaining an absolute majority in all branches of state government, even though in several parishes the Democrats retained control of local offices. Republicans were determined to build their strength in those parishes in preparation for the presidential election. They organized the blacks in these parishes promising that if Grant was elected they would receive forty acres and a mule. They also warned the freedmen that if Seymour was elected slavery would be reinstituted. The Democrats also attempted to win the black vote by organizing black Democratic clubs and by holding barbecues and parades. Although some die-hard Confederates resorted to violence and night riding to intimidate the black voters, the majority of whites in the rural parishes preferred to work within the law. This should not be surprising when one realizes that most of the local officers were still conservative whites. As election day approached both parties increased their efforts to win the black vote. Incendiary remarks by leaders of both parties created a volatile situation which resulted in riots in New Orleans in August, in Bossier and St. Landry Parishes in September, and in St. Mary and St. Bernard Parishes in October.[25] Since most of the victims of the riots were black Republicans, this created an atmosphere of intimidation and fear which was not conducive to homesteading by freedmen. Yet, despite these impediments, some did attempt to secure homesteads.

When the New Orleans office finally reopened for business in July 1868, with both register and receiver in attendance, many homesteaders filed claims. Fifteen months were apparently insufficient time for the register to familiarize himself with the workings of his office. A survey of the letters of the commissioner of the General Land Office to the register and receiver of the New Orleans office indicates that the operations of that office were extremely inefficient. Many homestead entries were canceled, either because the affidavits were not in order or because either the applicant or the register forgot to sign the entry. Others were canceled because they were filed on lands which had been certified to the state as swampland. As previously stated, some entries which were made on the grant of the New Orleans, Opelousas, and Great Western Railroad were disallowed. Some conflicted with previous private entries and some conflicted with recent homestead entries. One can understand the register allowing entry on swampland or on a railroad grant, or even on private land because of the lack of adequate township plats. But it is difficult to understand how the register could enter conflicting homestead claims on entries which he alone could have processed. The tragedy of it all was that many freedmen had settled on the land at least one year before they could file their entry and had lived on the land for another year before the commissioner of the General Land Office disallowed their entries. In each case the register and receiver were instructed to "advise the respective parties that the cancellation is made without prejudice to their right to make other selections on tracts with which there are no interferences." Unfortunately, the freedmen lost two years labor and all their improvements.[26]

Despite the inefficiency of the land office and the many problems which beset those attempting to homestead, 1,932 families filed homestead entries from January 17, 1867, to December 31, 1870. In St. Landry Parish, the area Saville seemed most interested in, homesteaders filed 437 entries, or 22.62 percent of the total. Of that number, 34 or 7.7 percent were black. Approximately 24.48 percent or 107 applicants in St. Landry Parish received final homestead certificates. Ultimately, certificates were issued to six black families in the parish, representing 17.65 percent of the black applicants. The record for the entire state indicates that 34 percent of all homesteaders under the Southern Homestead Act completed their entries. Based on these figures one can safely estimate that in Louisiana approximately 200 black families actually filed homestead entries during this four-year period and that approximately fifty families carried their entries to completion.[27] None of these figures takes into account the many who settled on land and were unable to enter their claims.

As a means of providing land for the freedmen, homesteading proved relatively unsuccessful in Louisiana. This fact results from a variety of causes. As long as the assistant commissioner of the Bureau was in sympathy with the homestead effort, freedmen received assistance in locating and settling their land. When homesteading interfered with economic and party interests, loyal whites chose to aid railroad companies rather than press the cause of Negro land ownership. This loss of interest on the part of professed unionists, coupled with Southern white opposition precluded success in homesteading. Some success might have been achieved earlier, however, had it not been for the chaotic condition of the land records and the gross inefficiency of the land officers.

A study of the land records indicates that in general homesteading as a means of providing land to the poor of both races failed, not only in the South but throughout the nation. From 1862 to 1890 approximately 400,000 final homestead certificates were issued. However, if Louisiana can serve as an example of what transpired, the various local courthouse records indicate that many of those who received final homestead certificates either sold, abandoned, or lost their land for non-payment of taxes. It would therefore be impossible to determine how many homesteaders actually benefited from the Act either in Louisiana or in the nation. Nostrums which failed for whites who had never experienced slavery could hardly be expected to succeed for freedmen. The failure of the black masses to acquire land is the tragedy of Reconstruction in Louisiana. The newly freed slaves, under the leadership of Louisiana's *gens de couleur libre*, achieved some measure of political and civil rights; however, without the economic security provided by land ownership these gains proved to be transitory.

Notes for "'Forty Acres and a Mule': Louisiana and the Southern Homestead Act"

[1]U. S., *Statutes at Large,* XIII, 507.

[2]Ibid., 66-67.

[3]O. O. Howard to Assistant Commissioners for Alabama, Mississippi, Arkansas, Louisiana, and Florida, July 9, 1866, National Archives, Microcopy 742; Selected Series of Records Issued by the Commissioner of the Bureau of Refugees, Freedmen and Abandoned Lands, 1865-1872, Roll 2, p. 170; July 19, 1866, p. 176. This microcopy which contains part of Records Group 105 will hereafter be referred to as Microcopy 742.

[4]Samuel H. Lockett, *Louisiana As It Is: A Geographical and Topographical Description of the State,* Lauren C. Post, ed. (Baton Rouge, 1969), 20; O. O. Howard to E. M. Stanton, summary of rations issued in 1865, National Archives Microcopy 752: Registers and Letters Received by the Bureau of Refugees, Freedmen and Abandoned Lands, 1865-1872, Roll 49, p. 345. This microcopy which contains part of Records Group 105 will hereafter be referred to as Microcopy 752; Howard Ashley White, *The Freedmen's Bureau in Louisiana* (Baton Rouge, 1970), 67-68.

[5]White, *The Freedmen's Bureau in Louisiana,* 68-69.

[6]Ibid., 66-73; *New Orleans Republican,* April 25, 1867, August 28, 1867; Lockett, *Louisiana As It Is,* 20.

[7]*New Orleans Times,* May 23, 1866.

[8]J. M. Edmunds to Register and Receiver, June 28, 1866, Letters of the Commissioner of the General Land Office on file in the Louisiana State Land Office, Baton Rouge, La., J. Wilson to S. Jones, August 23, 1866, Letters of the Commissioner; *New Orleans Times,* November 17, 1866; *Opelousas Courier,* Nov. 24, 1866.

[9]M. Woodjull for Howard to D. Tillson, copies sent to W. Swayne, A. Baird, S. Thomas, and J. Sprague, January 18, 1866, Microcopy 742, Roll 2, p. 61; J. Cromie to A. Baird, March 7, 1866, Microcopy 752, Roll 28, p. 362. The lands Cromie inspected were alternate sections fifteen miles in depth on either side of the right of way of the proposed railroad.

[10]*New Orleans Tribune,* September 1, 5, 1866.

[11]U. S. Congress, Senate, Letter of the Secretary of War, Sen. Ex. Doc. 6, 39th Cong., 2nd Sess., 1866, pp. 2, 72; The *Nation,* 3 (October 25, 1866), 232; P. Sheridan to O. O. Howard, October 1, 1866, Microcopy 752, Roll 38, p. 371; October 17, 1866, p. 380; E. Whittlesey to O. O. Howard, January 24, 1867, Roll 45, p. 397; O. O. Howard to E. M. Stanton, November 1, 1866, Microcopy 742, Roll 2, p. 259.

[12]J. J. Saville to W. H. Sterling, January 28, 1867, Microcopy 752, Roll 45, p. 609.

[13]J. Wilson to Register and Receiver, March 29, 1867, Letters of the Commissioner, April 27, 1867, July 10, 1868; List of Homestead Entries in Louisiana found in Louisiana State Land Office.

[14]J. Wilson to Register and Receiver, April 12, 1867, Letters of the Commissioner; J. Wilson to J. Tully, May 7, 1867, May 13, 1867, May 17, 1867, August 14, 1867; J. Wilson to Register and Receiver, November 3, 1869.

[15]J. J. Saville to W. H. Sterling, January 28, 1867, Microcopy 752, Roll 45, p. 610; J. Wilson to J. Tully, March 19, 1867, Letters of the Commissioner; Endorsement on letter of O. McFadden to O. O. Howard, March 19, 1867, Microcopy 742, Roll 3, p. 440, endorsement sent on April 18, 1867, to General Land Office; Wilson to Register and Receiver, April 27, 1867, letters of the Commissioner, Wilson sent the lists of lands granted to the New Orleans, Opelousas, and Great Western Railroad. Of the total 571,391.75 acres fell within the lands formerly controlled by the Opelousas Land Office; J. Wilson to O. O. Howard, May 3, 1867, Microcopy 752, Roll 42, p. 1122. Wilson explained to Howard that the railroad grant encompassed all odd numbered sections falling within fifteen miles on either side of the route of the proposed railroad; J. J. Saville to G. W. Julian, *Congressional Globe,* 40th Cong., 2nd sess, p. 807, letter read in House of Representatives, January 28, 1868.

[16]J. J. Saville to W. H. Sterling, July 1, 1867, Microcopy 752, Roll 47, p. 344; F. D. Sewell to J. S. Mower, September 14, 1867, Microcopy 742, Roll 3, p. 319 refers to the appointment of Saville as Bureau agent on May 25, 1867.

[17]J. J. Saville to G. W. Julian, *Congressional Globe,* 40th Cong., 2nd sess., p. 807.

[18]*Congressional Globe,* 40th Cong., 2nd sess., pp. 95, 694, 806, 985; U. S. *Statutes at Large,* XVI, 277. The disposition of these lands is recorded in the various tract books for the townships and ranges involved. These tract books are located in duplicate sets in the state land offices and in the General Land Office; U. S. Congress, House, Report of the Government Land Office, H. Ex. Doc. 1, 42nd Cong., 2nd sess., 1871, p. 121. The New Orleans, Opelousas, and Great Western was the only Southern railroad to have its grant declared forfeited.

[19]White, *The Freedmen's Bureau in Louisiana,* 60-61; U. S. Congress, House, Report of the Government Land Office, H. Ex. Doc. 1, 42nd Cong., 2 sess., 1871. Throughout this report the commissioner indicated that preemption rights were not transferable to homestead entries but that since the Homestead Act was passed with the obvious intention of facilitating settlement of the public lands by the poor he was considering the possibility of permitting preemptors to transfer their rights to homestead.

[20]J. Wilson to Register, Sept. 27, 1867, Letters of the Commissioner.

[21]White, *The Freedmen's Bureau in Louisiana,* 58.

[22]W. H. Wood to E. Whittlesey, December 31, 1867, Microcopy 752, Roll 53, p. 977.

[23]White, *The Freedmen's Bureau in Loiuisiana,* 126-27; J. J. Saville to G. W. Julian, *Congressional Globe,* 40th Cong., 2nd sess., p. 807; O. O. Howard to G. W. Julian, February 25, 1868, Microcopy 742, Roll 4, p. 207; E. Whittlesey for O. O. Howard to J. J. Saville, February 25, 1868, Roll 4, p. 209.

[24]R. Buchanan to O. O. Howard, April 23, 1868, Microcopy 752, Roll 53, pp. 1265-67; April 30, 1868, Roll 59, p. 203.

[25]For a complete analysis of this aspect of the problem, see Claude Oubre, "The Opelousas Riot of 1868," *Attakapas Gazette,* 8 (1973): 139-52.

[26]J. Wilson to Register and Receiver, July 17, 1868, Letters of the Commissioner.

[27]Paul W. Gates, *History of Public Land Law Development* (Washington, D. C., 1969), 414. Gates provided the 34 percent figure for the state completion ratio. However, this figure is based on all entries made during the period from 1867 to 1876 while the Southern Homestead Act was in force. The total number of state entries are derived from the receipt books of the land office for the years 1867 through 1870. The homesteaders in St. Landry were derived from a section by section survey of the tract books. Black homsteaders were identified through the unpublished census schedules for St. Landry Parish in 1870. Unfortunately, those who either abandoned their claim or were driven from them do not appear in this census, therefore it is impossible to arrive at the exact number of black homesteaders. Furthermore, since no homsteaders by 1870 had received final certificates, the census taker did not identify them as landowners. The census schedules also contain many inaccuracies but they are the only records available which separate the population by race.

BLACK EDUCATION IN CIVIL WAR AND RECONSTRUCTION LOUISIANA: GEORGE T. RUBY, THE ARMY, AND THE FREEDMEN'S BUREAU*

Barry A. Crouch

During the Civil War and Reconstruction, George T. Ruby, a New York City-born mulatto, earned a reputation as an outstanding educator of Louisiana blacks.[1] Ruby's later political career in Texas has been extensively chronicled by historians, but confusion persists about his role during the three years he spent in Louisiana. Before moving to Texas in mid-1866, Ruby was involved in freedmen's education while also serving as a traveling agent for the Freedmen's Bureau. The foundation for his later entrance into politics was laid by his educational and Freedmen's Bureau activities in Louisiana.[2]

In March 1880, Ruby testified before a United States Senate select committee on the causes of black emigration to the North. Asked whether he had "given special attention to the condition and wants and treatment" of the slaves and freedmen during and after the war, Ruby stated he had worked closely with them as an educator and had become intimately acquainted with their social, civil, and political situations. Throughout his testimony, Ruby said little about his service as one of two black state senators in Texas's Reconstruction legislature, but he suggested that his prior educational experience with the United States Army and the Louisiana Freedmen's Bureau had been of inestimable value.[3]

Ruby was raised and educated in Maine, but little else is known about his early life or about his parents. Ruby became interested in writing, promoting black literacy, and advancing the economic status of African Americans when he moved to Boston in 1860. Taking a job with James Redpath's *Pine and Palm*, he traveled to Haiti to test his employer's thesis that blacks could compete effectively against whites if they had a sufficiently strong economic foundation. The Scottish reformer's scheme collapsed in

*First published in *Louisiana History*, 38 (1997): 287-308. Reprinted with the kind permission of the author and the Louisiana Historical Association.

1862, and Ruby returned to the United States. Ruby's whereabouts for the next two years are unknown, but he subsequently appeared in the Crescent City and began the business of educating former slaves.[4]

It is noteworthy that New Orleans had established public schools as early as the 1840s. Mostly for white children, they maintained their independence until the middle of the Civil War. At the time Union troops seized control, French was the language of instruction in schools below Canal Street, while English prevailed in the predominantly American districts. Most of the existing schools had excellent reputations. Under Union occupation directed by Gen. Benjamin P. "Beast" Butler, the Crescent City's educational systems were merged into a single system, and the students were taught in English. Teachers were required to take a loyalty oath and a board of visitors was established in each district to screen teaching applicants.[5]

Emancipation added more difficulties to an overburdened educational system. Small private schools for free people of color had existed in New Orleans since 1822. In 1862, a philanthropist opened a free school for former slaves. The freedmen were so insistent about becoming literate that they forced the army to consider their educational needs. In August 1863, the Department of the Gulf commander Nathaniel P. Banks created an Enrollment Commission which had within it the nucleus of an education section. Banks appointed W. B. Stickney, who served in the Eighth Vermont, to superintend the New Orleans system. By October the system boasted seven schools, sixteen teachers, and 576 students.[6]

Although the city produced an adequate supply of teachers for the black schools and Banks could sustain the educators for a time, Louisiana's military government could not expand the education system beyond New Orleans because of numerous roadblocks, particularly limited financial resources. The military, however, ultimately realized that the freedmen would not labor without assurances that schools would be established and staffed for the benefit of their children. The connection between work and education forced the army to seek ways to provide schooling for all black children in Louisiana, not just those residing in the metropolis. Banks consequently ordered that a tax be levied upon all property, which included crops to remove the educational system's financial burden from the Union army.[7]

Resolution of the financial problem did not solve all of the emerging system's difficulties. The establishment of new schools and a consistent educational policy was further hampered by a conflict between the American Missionary Association, the military, and the treasury department. Under Banks's guidance, the school system was revamped in 1864. A three-member board of education was instituted. Forty-eight-year-old B. Rush Plumly, who earlier served on the Enrollment Commission, chaired the body. Plumly was joined by Edwin M. Wheelock, the board secretary from Dover, New Hampshire. Wheelock was a Unitarian minister who had corresponded with radical abolitionist Theodore Parker before coming to Louisiana as a chaplain in the Corps d'Afrique. The third member, Isaac G. Hubbs, represented the AMA; he was later dismissed.[8]

What Ruby did between January and the latter part of June 1864 in New Orleans is not known. In 1880, Ruby recalled he had taught a night school for adult freedmen in the Reverend Hooker's Crescent City church. Beyond his teaching, there is no information of what else he did. The board employed Ruby during the last week of June 1864, for which he received wages of $12. Ruby remained on the board of education's payroll for July and August, receiving $60 a month, but sources fail to indicate whether he taught or performed administrative duties. By September he had been appointed an instructor in one of the schools in St. Bernard Parish. This began Ruby's two-year association with freedmen's education in Louisiana and Texas.[9]

By mid-1864, the education board had established fifty-one schools containing 93 teachers and 5,744 pupils in thirteen parishes. These statistics are misleading, however, for 30 percent of the schools, 40 percent of the teachers, and 50 percent of the students were concentrated in Orleans Parish. Throughout the remainder of the war, the board emphasized the necessity for expanding the system throughout the state. They partially succeeded, and although New Orleans remained a significant factor in the board's system, Crescent City schools, teachers, and students no longer comprised such high percentages. According to C. Peter Ripley, this drive to provide education for Louisiana blacks was the "greatest accomplishment during the wartime experiment."[10]

Along with the problems confronting expansion of the system, the freedmen faced a contentious educational future. The legislature of the state's Unionist government, which began meeting in 1864, was urged to establish a systematic and free school system for those recently "delivered from the lash." Despite long and acrimonious political debate, 55 percent of the estimated 20,000 black children residing within Union lines attended school in early 1865. Nor did this figure include those former slaves who frequented sixty Sunday schools and twenty night schools in southern Louisiana. The military's education program brought perhaps fifty thousand freedmen into contact with the "rudiments of an elementary education."[11]

Ruby taught in St. Bernard Parish for forty-one weeks (September 1864-June 1865). During this period he instructed a total of 3,018 students, with an average weekly attendance in his classes of 77 pupils. Ruby's impact as an educator was probably minimal because he had to perform numerous additional tasks besides teaching. In addition, teachers in the early freedmen's schools had to be versatile because of the wide disparity in the students background and abilities.[12] Some students were illiterate, while others were more advanced. The latter concentrated on spelling, reading, arithmetic, geography, and grammar.

Little else is known about Ruby's experience as a teacher in St. Bernard Parish. Circumstances which would influence his future were rapidly changing on the national and state scene. He would substitute one national employer for another. In March 1865, Congress created the Bureau of Refugees, Freedmen, and Abandoned Lands, which quickly became known as the Freedmen's Bureau, to supervise the emancipated slaves transition to freedom. The bureau assumed control of black education at a critical juncture, for the financing and administration of black schools became increasingly uncertain. The bureau had no separate congressional appropriation so a local solution had to be found in order to maintain schools for those recently freed.

According to conflicting reports, the Freedmen's Bureau administered 126 schools of varying quality. In these schools, 230 teachers of both races educated 19,000 pupils, including 1,000 federal soldiers stationed in the state, 4,000 adults, and 14,000 children. From the beginning, however, a shortage of funds for education plagued the bureau and the system entered a general decline. Black citizens petitioned the bureau chief to levy a tax to support education. Black schools throughout the state struggled to survive on necessarily limited funds.

In July 1865 as the Freedmen's Bureau began to assume responsibility for education in Louisiana, Ruby was transferred to the Frederick Douglass School in New Orleans.[13] The Fred Douglass school had the second largest student body in the New Orleans area.[14] The school's location at the corner of Esplanade and Moreau, "in the Old Slave Pen," had haunting memories for everyone at the school. From all indications it was one of the toughest teaching assignments in the city.

Ruby focused his attention upon teaching and administration.[15] Beginning as a first assistant, Ruby rapidly advanced to head teacher, and then after resigning, was appointed principal, undoubtedly because of his previous teaching experience.

When Ruby became principal, the Fred Douglass school had 793 pupils; 593 in the primary section; 93 in the intermediate and 107 attending evening classes. There were eleven faculty members. Over the Christmas 1865 holiday the enrollment declined to 670 pupils, probably because the bureau secured employment outside the city for the parents of these absentee students. The institution, although difficult to manage, was an excellent training ground for Ruby, who was then only twenty-three years of age. Ruby demonstrated organizational and supervisory abilities that would later benefit him. The school had a mixed group of students who needed to learn classroom decorum and teachers who required guidance. Professional evaluations indicate that Ruby steadily piloted the school through some murky waters.[16]

Ruby's first evaluation occurred in November 1865, shortly after he had become principal of the Fred Douglass School. The Board of Examiners inspectors found discipline lax, but they believed that the recent change in the school's administration would "improve the general order of the school." The report nevertheless described a troubled institution. The primary department was weak, and the teacher allowed "Negroisms to pass uncorrected."[17] The pupils in the Intermediate A classification— probably elementary students—were deficient in arithmetic, reading, and spelling. The Intermediate B students—probably at the middle school level, however performed at more acceptable levels and seemed to be making orderly progress.

The quality of education at the Fred Douglass School began to improve slowly under Ruby's leadership. When the examining committee visited the facility again in December, discipline at the school was found to have improved. Although the inspectors determined that high turnover among the teaching staff interferred with the school's educational mission, the committee concluded that the entire school demonstrated improvement. The inspectors also ascertained that the intermediate-level classes taught by Ruby were very good.[18] Indeed, the Fred Douglass School, which previously had a poor academic reputation among New Orleans city schools, attained an unprecedented level of excellence under Ruby's tutelage, according to City Superintendent Mortimer A. Warren. Warren contended that, because most of the pupils were ignorant and French-speaking, educators at the Douglass school were required to exercise greater patience and skill in educating their charges. Warren rated Ruby and his assistant as "excellent teachers of reading and articulation" who gave much attention to pronunciation. The superintendent did not know of any school "which considering the material to be wrought upon, shows better skill in management or more improvement."[19] Indeed, since passing under his management crowed the city superintendent, the school had improved "in almost every particular." Order had been restored in the yard and in the classroom. The students acted less like "cannibals," although they seemed to belong to "another race" of human beings. A mixture of creoles, French, plantation blacks, and wild men, their "'jumbo' talk" struck the superintendent as "abominable, and their actions correspond[ed] with their jargon," but Warren believed that Ruby was fast getting them civilized. Considering the composition and background of the student body, the educational advances at the Douglass school under Ruby's direction matched those of any other city school.[20]

In early 1866, the state school system, still directed by the Freedmen's Bureau, faced a financial crisis. The whole structure verged on collapse, and classes were suspended. In New Orleans, a tuition system was implemented, with costs ranging from $1.00 to $1.50 a month per pupil, depending upon family size. In the countryside, 5 percent of a laborer's monthly pay was set aside to support local teachers and schools. The freedmen, as well as planters, resisted this deduction, which was generally considered exorbitant. During this controversy, schools for the freedmen either languished or had to be discontinued. To end the impasse, the bureau ultimately paid the school debt.

Ruby continued to supervise and teach until March 1866, when he assumed a different role within the bureau.[21] Ruby's new responsibilities entailed travel and evaluation. Although the number of African American agents employed by the bureau is unknown, Ruby was certainly a rare individual who served the agency in two states and performed similar functions in both areas. The bureau has been castigated by historians for its lack of sensitivity regarding black aspirations, but the organization realized that its local agents faced daunting obstacles in their attempts to aid the freedmen. To ensure that agents actually attempted to assist the former slaves in Louisiana and Texas, the bureau used a black inspector to evaluate the performance of its white field agents.[22]

As a traveling inspector, Ruby had a tripartite job. First, he traveled and observed rural conditions. Second, he searched for potential school sites for the freedmen. Third, he evaluated the performance of the bureau field officers. In his travels throughout Louisiana, Ruby viewed the same phenomena that W. E. B. DuBois observed over three decades later. DuBois wrote that the men "which the Bureau could command varied all the way from unselfish philanthropists to narrow-minded busybodies and thieves." More often than not, DuBois declared, the "average was far better than the worst." Ruby discovered similar characteristics in the abilities of the agents he evaluated.[23]

In April and May, 1866, Ruby toured three sections of Louisiana to investigate the status of black education, to search for potential school sites, and to evaluate the performance of field agents. On such field missions, Ruby organized the black residents of rural communities to determine whether or not they could organize and maintain a school. He spoke to throngs of blacks, emphasizing that they had to take control of their educational destiny.

Ruby reported the results of his visits to towns and plantations and the reaction of blacks to his speeches. He also analyzed the freedmen's status, expectations, reactions to civil rights, legislation, and willingness to support financially educational institutions for their children. Ruby indicated that the former slaves believed that the federal government should subsidize education, but, from the tenor of his reports and letters, Ruby seems to have been somewhat overawed by the freedmen's obsession with education in almost every black community he visited.[24] Indeed, during Ruby's travels throughout Louisiana, he was continually amazed at the desire of both former free blacks and slaves to have their children educated. This was particularly true of St. Martin Parish's African American community. Ruby declared that these "people are alive here about their schools," and he had no doubt that "sacrifices of personal comforts will be made if need be to keep every child at school."[25]

According to Ruby's reports, the ensuing establishment of freedmen's schools followed a pattern. Upon his arrival at a community, Ruby generally spoke to a large assemblage about education, and the 1866 Civil Rights Bill was often read to the gathering. A local supervisory committee, either already selected or established during his visit, then assumed responsibility for establishing a local school system. The freedmen preferred to buy land upon which to erect schools, but if this was impossible, they resorted to renting or leasing properties. In Clinton, for example, the education com- mittee proposed the purchase of three lots—at a cost of $175—for use as the site of a multi-purpose structure that could accommodate 200 students and also serve as a religious and community center.[26]

Once the matter of a school site had been resolved, Ruby attempted either to identify prospective teachers or to bring established teachers under the auspices of the bureau. Ruby made concerted efforts to encourage the agency to employ teachers in impoverished communities. In East Feliciana Parish, he found a "public spirited freedman" named Harmon Morrison, "imbued with a desire for the education of his people." Morrison had received little education, but Ruby recommended his selection as an assistant teacher, because the freedman had begun to build a school upon land rented from freedman Robert Myers.[27] In Iberville Parish, Ruby encouraged the bureau to hire black educational pioneeer Edward F. Wilson because local freedmen could not pay his salary. At St. Martinville, Ruby persuaded the bureau to hire a woman as principal of a large African American school because the principal, Robert R. Igum, did not meet the inspector's educational standards for teachers. Igum was retained as an assistant.[28]

Ruby believed that organization was the key to a successful school system, but he also recognized the debilitating effect of inadequate funding. Due to the great diversity in the size and economic standing of the black communities he visited, there was no consistency in the ability of individual communities to fund schools and teachers' salaries.[29] The most common funding methods were tax levies and tuition fees. Tuition payments were often deferred. In cases where freedmen had difficulty operating established schools, Ruby offered the assistance of the bureau in the form of subsidies for teachers' salaries or schoolhouse rent, as in the case of a plantation school near Houma. Because the laborers worked on shares, they agreed to pay the school's only teacher $10 per year per student upon the sale of their crops. Ruby suggested, and the freedmen concurred, that the school, which was well conducted with some of the pupils being quite proficient in arithmetic, be brought under the aegis of the bureau.[30] Similar offers were made to the communities of freedmen on the Tucker[31] and Vick[32] plantations near Thibodaux.

Ruby could not provide much assistance, however, to those communities of freedmen that were unable to establish a school. In St. Mary Parish, parts of which had formerly been garrisoned by federal troops, the freedchildren had been able to attend the free government school. After the war many freedmen moved elsewhere, and those who remained were too poor to organize a school. As in other areas of Louisiana, the freedmen appreciated the advantages of education, but could not fund either a school or a teacher's salary until the the end of the harvest season. People had lost so much during the war that "ready money is an extremely scarce article" and the freedmen had little means.[33] "Meanwhile," Ruby lamented, "they toil hard to feed themselves and families." The same pattern prevailed in Patterson, where freedmen labored under the contract system and did not feel they could immediately provide the necessary 5 percent contribution to a school fund, preferring to wait until they had been paid for their harvest.[34] In Centerville, also in St. Mary Parish, Ruby encountered the same conditions.

Whenever possible in more diverse communities, African Americans with whom Ruby came into contact attempted to make provisions for those children whose parents were too poor to pay tuition. For example, in East Baton Rouge Parish the officers of the 65th United States Colored Troops donated $100 to purchase tuition tickets for children whose parents were too poor to pay the fee. The local pastor was chosen to select those needy children whose claims were most pressing. At Franklin, the local residents established a committee headed by a minister, "whose duty it shall be to see that every child of a suitable age is *kept* at school, impressing on parents a spirit of self sacrifice to this end."[35]

In Lafourche Parish the freedmen, who made every effort to keep their school open, selected a committee to "exert all their influence in keeping the children at school, and also assist those poor children in obtaining an education whose parents are unable to pay their tuition." The Lafourche freedmen also requested financial assistance from the bureau. Similar circumstances prevailed in Covington. The freedmen hired M. I. Hutchinson, a black woman, as a teacher, but the community asked that the school be placed under the aegis of the bureau. Because the local education committee had obtained a building and had collected money to pay the $3.00 monthly rental fee, Ruby persuaded the bureau to appoint Hutchinson as assistant teacher and that a principal be sent to the school.[36]

One of Ruby's educational objectives was to revive moribund schools that had been supported by the government during the war. At Madisonville, where forty students had once attended a black institution, Ruby discovered a small number of "old free colored" residents, who promised to maintain a school. The community's former slaves, however, were so poor that they could not raise enough money to pay a teacher. To demonstrate the bureau's commitment to the educaton of freedmen, Ruby gave the school slates, primers, school tablets, first readers, primary authors and charts of elementary sounds.

Ruby also persuaded the bureau to send teachers to a Port Hudson school established to educate black troops.[37] This school building, built through the efforts of the post commander, serviced 170 children, but only fifty parents could pay tuition. Ruby recommended that the bureau appoint a woman teacher who could negotiate room and board with a "well to do" local freedman named Tony Stewart. In St. Helena Parish, Ruby located two former government schools which had once accommodated over 140 pupils, but which had closed when the war ended. The local freedmen, who labored in sawmills and on farms, had meager resources and thus were unable to revive the school. With a former teacher residing in the area, Ruby believed the school could be reopened if the bureau paid a portion of her salary; the agency concurred.[38]

Although establishment and maintenance of freedmen schools commanded the lion's share of Ruby's attention, he was also required to ascertain the effectiveness of local bureau officials promoting education for blacks. Because it was difficult for the bureau's state headquarters to monitor field agents' performance, Ruby was periodically dispatched to the Louisiana countryside, to evaluate interaction between local agents and the black and white communities they served. Ruby's inspection tours are unusual only because this black inspector was evaluating white agents. It is presently unknown if other Southern state bureaus followed this policy, but Ruby served in this same capacity in both Louisiana and Texas.

Ruby did not hesitate to report field officers for shirking responsibilities. At Houma, teachers complained to Ruby that bureau agent Henry S. Wadsworth demonstrated no interest in their education, and one instructor stated that Wadsworth declared that he cared "nothing for the darkies and [was] heartily tired of them." Even the large planters asserted that as yet they had no bureau officer in their area, by which they meant "a *man* whom they could respect." From what Ruby surmised, Wadsworth spent most of his days loitering in coffee houses and billiard saloons. Ruby concluded that it was not surprising that the planters, the freedmen, and the "*solid* men" of the parish should be prejudiced against the bureau. Wadsworth was subsequently replaced.[39]

Disreputable agents such as Wadsworth were not the only threats to the bureau's educational mission. Ruby found among the freedmen a "disposition and intelligence" to maintain African American schools in Lafourche Parish, despite the local planters' open hostility. The bureau agent was compelled to use "firm and judicious measures" when freedmen complained that the local bureau agent was a pawn of the local elite. Speaking through "their representative men," the Lafourche freedmen complained "quite bitterly" of the parish agent's actions, and contended that he "caters and defers to the prejudices of planters too much, in fact assisting them to oppress" the former slaves. The parish's "intelligent planters," men who did all they could to assist the Confederacy, unwittingly confirmed the freedmen's contentions by confiding to Ruby that "they respect a *man* despite his opinion and that the Bureau errs in many cases in appointing officers as Agents who are mere boys in judgment."[40]

On the other hand, the Baton Rouge bureau agent M. J. Sheridan was anxious to establish freedmen schools, and he actively collected the education tax. But Sheridan had problems with the conduct of a male teacher and requested that Ruby investigate. Ruby found the man "guilty of conduct lascivious and degrading in its character." Although Ruby did not specify the charges against the instructor, he did request that the community take steps to resolve the dilemma. Concerned individuals subsequently met at the A. M. E. Bethel Church, where Sheridan summarized how the government would assist the community in procuring a new teacher. Ruby supported the agent's position, and the bureau eventually procured a new teacher.[41]

Ruby took an equally active role in resolving other educational problems in East Baton Rouge Parish. Even though Ruby attempted to be diplomatic with white planters because their cooperation was often essential, he did occasionally have to confront the local elite to promote black education. Ruby thought a black school could be sustained in East Baton Rouge Parish, but the freedmen had been unable to secure a suitable structure because the area planters refused to allow a building to be erected on their properties. Although Ruby was not able to locate a site himself, he promised the local black leaders that the bureau would assign a teacher to the school if they were to secure a suitable facility. Ruby subsequently honored his promise after M. J. Sheridan notified him and a school building had been secured.[42]

Ruby discovered that opposition to the Freedmen's Bureau also meant hostility to providing education for blacks. The "poor whites" in St. Helena Parish, "intensely rebel in sentiment, hating all Yankees most heartily," wrote Ruby, disliked the "trouble of education for themselves and children," but they also bitterly resented the idea of schools for the freedmen. They consequently did all they dared to intimidate and frighten local blacks. In April 1866, at one of the innumerable meetings Ruby initiated, two dozen of the hostile whites entered the building armed with cudgels. The freedmen were frightened, Ruby stated, and many a "stout fellow" became reluctant to attend the gathering.[43]

Ruby nevertheless spoke of the advantages of education and asserted that if the freedmen sustained a school "no person could molest them." When Ruby finished his short talk, other influential men urged the people to "avail themselves of the opportunity now offered and become men and women through the influences of education." The "Chivalry," except for an occasional mutter, generally remained quiet and finally slunk away leaving the meeting to the freedmen.

Ruby encountered similar hostility in Terrebonne Parish, where planters did not tolerate black education and wanted "as little to do with the Bureau as possible." Unless the local agent was firm in upholding his duties, Ruby emphasized, schools could not be maintained in the parish.[44]

Opposition to the freedmen schools was not confined to small demographic or geograhic enclaves. At Breaux Bridge, Ruby found the Cajuns utterly opposed to black schools. Even the Cajun small planters, characterized by Ruby as "ignorant and illiterate employers," resented efforts to educate the former slaves. The few large planters, whom Ruby characterized as "narrow-minded Creoles," were also "strongly prejudiced to any measure for the elevation of the freedmen." Schools in this section, Ruby insisted, could only be "maintained if *protected*. . . ."

Whites in New Iberia also opposed the education of blacks, and they hindered the bureau's efforts to establish a local school. The bureau investigator maintained that local whites were very misinformed, while the freedmen were "excessively ignorant." Ruby believed that New Iberia's bureau agent did all he could for education. He was "well spoken of" and regarded as an impartial officer.[45]

Ruby's encounters with whites in the plantation belt were not always confrontational. The bureau investigator often consulted local planters regarding educational issues. In Terrebonne Parish, he met with Houma-area landowners, along with the black residents, about establishing a school. Both blacks and whites in attendance unanimously decided to erect a building, but the students required primers, spelling books, slates, pencils, charts, and crayons from the bureau. A majority supported the appointment of a local black man, Edmund Thompson, who could "read and write fairly" well, as the teacher. Although the prospective instructor had a "good moral character" and was much respected by the local denizens, Ruby persuaded the local school supporters that Thompson "be taken on trial."[46]

Once appointed, teachers such as Thompson had to contend with threats of violence. Violence against teachers who taught in schools for blacks has been chronicled throughout the South, but vandalism of black-owned property was rare, according to Ruby. Although Ruby's reports do not mention attacks against black property owners, buildings owned by African Americans were damaged. In Lafourche Parish, a school building was broken into by some "malicious person who besides outraging decency" also "destroyed and stole books and other school property" which the freedmen did not have the means to replace. In Terrebonne, the miscreants peppered the school building with buckshot and other missiles to intimidate blacks into closing the facility.[47]

Upon completing his duties as a traveling agent for the bureau's educational department, Ruby returned to the classroom. In July 1866, Ruby was assigned to East Feliciana Parish, the area which he had initially visited the preceding April. The superintendent of education for the Louisiana Freedmen's Bureau requested that Ruby organize a school at Jackson, where considerable white opposition to black education persisted. Ruby seemed the perfect choice for this delicate assignment: He was familiar with the local situation, and he traveled extensively in the district when he had visited Port Hudson, Clinton, and Jackson.[48]

During his initial foray into East Feliciana Parish, Ruby experienced contrasting responses to his effort to promote the establishment of black schools in the communities of Clinton and Jackson. No school for blacks had ever existed in Clinton. When opposition to the freedmen school surfaced, Ruby had to inform local African Americans that they would be protected "in the education of themselves and children." As in other communities, local black leaders organized a school committee, armed with assurances from the local bureau representative that the agency would furnish a teacher once a schoolhouse was complete.[49] Ruby recommended Mary E. Cooke, a "free colored young lady," for the position of assistant teacher.

The best estimates suggested that 200 children would attend the school, which they planned to open later in the month. "Many of the freedmen here are good mechanics and farmers," Ruby observed, "and live despite disadvantages, extremely well." Outside the town, the educational situation was non-existent for blacks. In this particular parish, Ruby wrote, "it would be neither safe nor desirable to have schools on plantations." Those parents who worked on farms close to a town would have to send their children to the village school and pay tuition.[50]

In both Clinton and Jackson, Ruby claimed he was treated better by the freedmen than in any other locality he had visited. The people, he continued, were aware Ruby faced grave personal danger in order to assist them.

In Jackson, fourteen miles from Clinton, Ruby again encountered considerable excitement over the possibility of opening a local school. As in Clinton, no school had previously been available to these freedmen. But Jackson's whites, according to Ruby, were "more rebel in sentiment" than in Clinton and hated a "'Yankee,' [and] the Freedmen's Bureau," and did not "wish a colored school." The mayor possessed "tolerably right feelings" on black education, but he felt "'it would be better to have southern teachers.'"[51]

Despite the whites' hostility to educating Jackson's black community, Ruby believed he would be accepted by the community inasmuch as he had previously visited the area and both races knew him. When Ruby returned he discovered that as a visiting school agent he was "welcome enough, but as coming there for the purpose of establishing a school and remaining until the school could get a teacher, they would not stand it, and they commenced making threats." Ruby held classes at his boarding house. One day a group of whites appeared, seized Ruby and threw him in Thompson's Creek, but only after they "belabored" him "with the muzzles of their revolvers." They would not tolerate "any damned nigger school in that town."[52]

After this incident Ruby decided to relocate. Besides the attack, Ruby was influenced by other factors in his decision to move to Texas, where he could perform the now familiar functions of teacher and traveling agent for the Freedmen's Bureau. B. Rush Plumly and Edwin M. Wheelock had moved to Texas. Plumly had become deeply involved in Galveston politics, while Wheelock was employed by the bureau as superintendent of education. Ruby took up residence in Galveston, and his subsequent rise in Texas from teacher, local Union League organizer, and eventually president of the state organization, demonstrated how skillfully Ruby took advantage of his new opportunities.[53]

Throughout Ruby's sojourn in Louisiana, he advanced steadily upward in the organizational hierarchy of the Freedmen's Bureau. Although Ruby had certainly performed creditably as a teacher and supervisor, the Freedmen's Bureau required his abilities in a different area. As a principal he had been responsible for evaluating teachers who served under him and the bureau needed those skills to advance the cause of black education throughout Louisiana.

In Louisiana, and later in Texas, Ruby performed basically the same role for the state bureau; teacher and traveling agent. Certainly his Louisiana experiences had taught him much. He also simultaneously cultivated close ties with certain members of the educational bureaucracy (Plumly and Wheelock, among others), who would facilitate his rise in the Texas bureau and political circles. But it was in the Pelican State where Ruby first established his credentials. Throughout his Freedmen's Bureau career he served the agency well.

Ruby's career epitomizes the role of black carpetbaggers in Civil War and Reconstruction Louisiana. What originally drew him to the state remains a mystery, like so many aspects of his life, because so little personal correspondence remains. Nevertheless, Ruby saw an opportunity and seized it, serving his country while simultaneously advancing his own career. In this early stage in his development, Ruby was more concerned with assisting black Louisianians in the advancement of their educational dreams than in advancing his own political fortunes. His preoccupation with politics would come later. In Louisiana, Ruby was a competent and intelligent champion of literacy for his people.

Notes for "Black Education in Civil War and Reconstruction Louisiana:
George T. Ruby, the Army and the Freedmen's Bureau"

[1]Both as a teacher and as a principal.

[2]The leading account of Ruby's career is Carl M. Moneyhon, "George T. Ruby and the Politics of Expediency in Texas," in Howard N. Rabinowitz, ed., *Southern Black Leaders of the Reconstruction Era* (Urbana, 1982), 363-92. Other essays worth consulting are J. Mason Brewer, *Negro Legislators of Texas* (1935; reprint ed., Austin, Tex., [1970]), 20, 23-30, 53, 55-57, 61, 63, 75, 81, 115, 125-26; Randall B. Woods, "George T. Ruby: A Black Militant in the White Business Community," *Red River Valley Historical Review*, 1 (1974): 269-80; Barry A. Crouch, "Self-Determination and Local Black Leaders in Texas," *Phylon*, 39 (1978): 346-48, 354; James Smallwood, "G. T. Ruby: Galveston's Black Carpetbagger in Reconstruction Texas," *Houston Review*, 5 (1983): 24-33; Merline Pitre, "George T. Ruby: The Party Loyalist," in *Through Many Dangers, Toils and Snares: The Black Leadership of Texas, 1868-1900* (Austin, 1985), 166-73. A brief sketch is "G. T. Ruby," Walter P. Webb and Elden Stephen Branda, eds., *The Handbook of Texas*, 2 vols. (Austin, 1952), 2:513. The most recent and succinct information on Ruby is contained in Merline Pitre, "George Thompson Ruby," *New Handbook of Texas,* 6 vols. (Austin, Tex., 1996), 5:705-6; Eric Foner, *Freedom's Lawmakers: A Directory of Black Officeholders during Reconstruction* (Baton Rouge, 1993), 187. Eric Foner, in his magisterial *Reconstruction: America's Unfinished Revolution, 1863-1877* (New York, 1988), depicted Ruby as a "Northerner in his midtwenties who had organized schools for the Freedmen's Bureau and risen to head the [Texas] Union League," 319. There is no collection of Ruby papers.

[3]Senate, *Report and Testimony of the Select Committee of the United States Senate to Investigate the causes of the Removal of the Negroes From the Southern States to the Northern States*, 26th Cong., 2nd Sess., Report No. 693 [Serial 1899], 3 parts (Washington, 1880), Pt. 2, 37-38. Ruby's involvement in the Kansas exodus is briefly discussed in Nell Irvin Painter, *Exodusters: Black Migration to Kansas after Reconstruction* (New York, 1976), 213, 215-16, 245-46, 254. Ruby died from malaria on the last day of October in 1882, Moneyhon, "George T. Ruby," 389.

[4]George T. Ruby (Traveling Agent, Texas) to Charles Garretson (Acting Assistant Adjutant General [AAAG]), September 14, 1867, Assistant Commissioner (AC), Letters Received (LR), R-26, Texas, Records of the Bureau of Refugees, Freedmen, and Abandoned Lands (BRFAL), Record Group (RG) 105 (National Archives); *Austin Weekly State Journal*, July 28, 1870; Rodney P. Carlisle, *The Roots of Black Nationalism* (Port Washington, N.Y., 1975), 75-76. Hereafter Ruby will be abbreviated GTR. All citations are to the original assistant commissioner or superintendent of education records in RG 105 in the National Archives. Much of this material is now on microfilm. For Louisiana see *Records of the Assistant Commissioner for the State of Louisiana, Bureau of Refugees, Freedmen, and Abandoned Lands, 1865-1869* (36 Rolls); microcopy number M1027, and *Records of the Superintendent of Education for the State of Louisiana, BRFAL, 1864-1869* (12 Rolls); microcopy number M1026.

[5]Numerous publications have concentrated upon wartime black education in the Pelican State. Some overviews of the system, the military, politics, and how blacks interacted with all of this are Martha Mitchell Bigelow, "Freedmen of the Mississippi Valley, 1862-1865," *Civil War History*, 8 (1962): 38-47; Elisabeth Joan Doyle, "Nurseries of Treason: Schools in Occupied New Orleans," *Journal of Southern History*, 26 (1960): 161-64; Robert S. Bahney, "Generals and Negroes: Education of Negroes by the Union Army, 1861-1865" (Ph. D. dissertation, University of Michigan, 1965), 201-20; William F. Messner, "The Federal Army and Blacks in the Gulf Department, 1862-1865" (Ph. D. dissertation, University of Wisconsin, 1972), 108-30; Joe Gray Taylor, *Louisiana Reconstructed, 1863-1877* (Baton Rouge, 1974), 1-155; Peyton McCrary, *Abraham Lincoln and Reconstruction: The Louisiana Experiment* (Princeton, 1978), 186-211; Joseph G. Dawson, III, *Army Generals and Reconstruction: Louisiana, 1862-1877* (Baton Rouge, 1982), 5-23; Ted Tunnell, *Crucible of Reconstruction: War, Radicalism, and Race in Louisiana, 1862-1877* (Baton Rouge, 1984), 1-91, and the subsequent citations in the following notes.

[6]Fred Harvey Harrington, *Fighting Politician: Major General N. P. Banks* (Philadelphia, 1948), 108-10; William F. Messner, "Black Education in Louisiana, 1863-1865," *Civil War History*, 22 (1976): 45-46; C. Peter Ripley, *Slaves and Freedmen in Civil War Louisiana* (Baton Rouge, 1976), 128-29; Joe M. Richardson, *Christian Reconstruction: The American Missionary Association and Southern Blacks, 1861-1890* (Athens, Ga., 1986), 30-33; Howard A. White, *The Freedmen's Bureau in Louisiana* (Baton Rouge, 1970), 166-67; John W. Blassingame, "The Union Army as an Educational Institution for Negroes, 1862-1865," *Journal of Negro Education*, 34 (1965): 152-59; John W. Blassingame, *Black New Orleans, 1860-1880* (Chicago, 1973), 108; Roger A. Fischer, *The Segregation Struggle in Louisiana, 1862-77* (Urbana, 1974), 13-44. Stickney was considered a "practical teacher after the best model," Robert C. Morris, *Reading, 'Riting, and Reconstruction: The Education of Freedmen in the South, 1861-1870* (Chicago, 1981), 22-23. Older, and occasionally useful is Betty Porter, "The History of Negro Education in Louisiana," *Louisiana Historical Quarterly*, 25 (1942): 728-821. Messner, who has thoroughly studied the area, considers the Gulf Department those parishes in southern

Louisiana which Lincoln exempted from the emancipation proclamation. They included: St. Bernard, Plaquemines, Jefferson, St. John, St. Charles, St. James, Ascension, Assumption, Terrebonne, Lafourche, St. Mary, St. Martin, and Orleans. The slaves did not receive formal freedom until a year later, "Black Education," 42 n2, 43 n5.

[7]Messner, "Black Education," 44-49; William F. Messner, *Freedmen and the Ideology of Free Labor*: *Louisiana, 1862-1865* (Lafayette, La., 1978), 164-83. The education/work connection is ignored in J. Thomas May, "Continuity and Change in the Labor Program of the Union Army and the Freedmen's Bureau," *Civil War History*, 17 (1971): 245-54, which focuses upon Louisiana.

[8]Ripley, *Slaves and Freedmen*, 128-29, 131. Still the best source on the background of Plumly (whose surname is occasionally spelled Plumley) and Wheelock is Charles Kassel, "Educating the Slave—A Forgotten Chapter of Civil War History," *Open Court*, 31 (1927): 239-56; "Edwin Miller Wheelock," *Open Court,* 34 (1930): 564-69. Hubbs, superintendent of the AMA schools and financial officer of the Board, was charged with a variety of illegal acts, Dole, "Nurseries of Treason," 178; Messner, "Black Education," 48. Richardson wrote that Hubbs was "accused of selling books for profit, keeping faulty accounts, demanding money of some teachers as a condition of their employment, making false charges against other board members, and unbecoming conduct with a female teacher. The latter charge was almost certainly false." The other complaints are more difficult to refute, he contends. Hubbs denied everything. "Whatever the truth of the charges—and Hubbs at best was inefficient—they did not necessitate ousting the association," Richardson, *Christian Reconstruction*, 271 n39.

[9]Senate, *Report and Testimony* (Serial 1899), Pt. 2, 55; Journal of Accounts of the Board of Education, April 1864-June 1865, 8, 11, 15; Register of Weekly and Monthly Statistical Reports of Schools, September 1864-August 1865, Vol. 1:2; Register of Employees, Teachers in the City of New Orleans, 286, all in Louisiana, Superintendent of Education (SOE), BRFAL, RG 105. There are no Ruby letters in the Department of the Gulf, Office of Civil Affairs, Records of the United States Army Continental Commands, 1821-1920, RG 393 (National Archives) nor could Ruby's application for a teacher's position be located in RG 105. It is unknown if he had to take a qualifying examination. Reverend Hooker died in the 1866 New Orleans riot.

[10]Ripley, *Slaves and Freedmen*, 143-45.

[11]Messner, "Black Education," 55-56.

[12]Register of Weekly and Monthly Statistical Reports of Schools, September 1864-August 1865, Vol. 1; Record of School Districts, Vol. 49, Louisiana, SOE, BRFAL, RG 105. There is a great deal of debate about the type of education freedmen received during Reconstruction. For conflicting viewpoints over the schooling offered to black Louisianians, or their cohorts across the South, see Ronald E. Butchart, *Northern Schools, Southern Blacks, and Reconstruction*: *Freedmen's Education, 1862-1875* (Westport, Conn., 1980); Herbert G. Gutman, "Schools For Freedom: The Post-Emancipation Origins of Afro-American Education," in Ira Berlin, ed., *Power and Culture*: *Essays on the American Working Class* (New York, 1987), 260-97; James D. Anderson, *The Education of Blacks in the South, 1860-1935* (Chapel Hill, 1988), 7-10, 21-27, 69, 138-39, 170-71, 199, 211-21, 240; Richardson, *Christian Reconstruction*. A critique of this literature can be found in Morris, "Educational Reconstruction," in Eric Anderson and Alfred A. Moss, Jr., eds., *The Facts of Reconstruction*: *Essays in Honor of John Hope Franklin* (Baton Rouge, 1991), 141-66.

[13]Not Fort Douglas, as Ruby later recalled.

[14]Senate, *Report and Testimony* (Serial 1899), Pt. 2, 55; H. R. Pease (SOE), Report of Schools for the Parish of Orleans, August 1865; GTR to Pease, November 1, 1865; Roster of Employees, Vol. 44:260-61, 286; Receipt Roll of Hired Men, No. 161, October 1865; Mortimer A. Warren (City Superintendent of Schools), Monthly Report, November 30, 1865, all in Louisiana, SOE, BRFAL, RG 105.

[15]White, *The Freedmen's Bureau in Louisiana*, 152. See also William S. McFeely, *Yankee Stepfather*: *General O. O. Howard and the Freedmen* (New Haven, 1968), 166-89. Older works on the bureau are Honorine Ann Sherman, "The Freedmen's Bureau in Louisiana" (Master's thesis, Tulane University, 1949); John Cornelius Engelsman, "The Freedmen's Bureau in Louisiana" (Master's thesis, Louisiana State A & M, 1937), reprinted in *Louisiana Historical Quarterly*, 32 (1949): 145-224.

[16]Warren to Pease, January 1, 31, 1866, ibid.

[17]W. H. Pearce and Robert G. Seymour (Board of Examiners) to Pease, December 1, 1865, ibid. There is no evidence that the Board examined night schools.

[18]Examining Committee to Pease, December 28, 1865, ibid.

[19]Warren to Pease, January 1, 1866, ibid.

[20]Ibid.

[21]Pease, List of Teachers to be Retained in the Freedmen's Schools for the City of New Orleans, January 31, 1866; Receipt Roll of Hired Men, No. 164, March 1866, Louisiana, SOE; Absalom Baird (AC, Louisiana) to Oliver Otis Howard (Commissioner, BRFAL), October ?, 1866, Records of the Education Division, Commissioner's Office, all in BRFAL, RG 105. The planters also opposed the education tax because they thought it would be partially used to support the maintenance of the Republican party.

[22]For example, see Crouch, "Guardian of the Freedpeople: Texas Freedmen's Bureau Agents and the Black Community," *Southern Studies*, n. s., 3 (1992): 185-201, and, "A Political Education: George T. Ruby and the Texas Freedmen's Bureau," forthcoming *Houston Review*.

[23]W. E. Burghardt Du Bois, "The Freedmen's Bureau," *Atlantic Monthly*, 87 (1901): 360.

[24]On three separate occasions, Ruby visited the parishes of East and West Feliciana, St. Helena, East Baton Rouge, St. Tammany, Terrebonne, Lafourche, St. Mary, and St. Martin. The observations he made of local black communities, how they responded and assisted in their endeavor to promote education, and who might be available from the immediate area to either teach or assist in teaching a school are worth analyzing. Nor did Ruby neglect white society. He remarked about how receptive those in power were to black education, whether they assisted its progress, and also commented upon the views of poor whites.

[25]GTR to W. H. Cornelius (Agent, New Iberia), May 26, 1866, Louisiana, SOE, BRFAL, RG 105. For how one bureau official performed in this area see May, "The Freedmen's Bureau at the Local Level: A Study of a Louisiana Agent," *Louisiana History*, 9 (1968): 5-19. For comparisons sake, and conditions in a parish Ruby did not visit, see Tunnell, "Marshall Harvey Twitchell and the Freedmen's Bureau in Bienville Parish," *Louisiana History*, 33 (1992): 241-64.

[26]GTR to A. G. Studer (SOE), April 12, 1866; GTR to Cornelius, May 26, 1866, both in Louisiana, SOE, BRFAL, RG 105. Here, Ruby is describing Clinton and St. Martinsville, but it could have been any of the locations which he visited or the responses he received. The one unique feature about the Clinton blacks is that they seem to have been the only group which canvassed the opinion of their white neighbors concerning the education of blacks.

[27]Ibid.

[28]GTR to Studer, April 12, 1866, ibid.

[29]Terrebonne Parish serves as an example of how blacks funded education. The parish possessed some of the richest soil in the state with a larger number of cultivated plantations but the schools could not be sustained unless a teacher waited to be paid until after the crops were gathered. This was true whether the freedmen rented land or labored under the contract system. In St. Tammany and St. Helena Parishes, the freedmen had the money to maintain a building, which was also true in West Feliciana Parish (Bayou Sara), but the instructor would have to wait on the payment of tuition. In Greensburg, the community requested that the bureau send a teacher for their school because they could not afford the salary. GTR to Studer, April 12, May 1, 16, 1866, ibid.

[30]Ibid.

[31]GTR to Taggart, May 17, 1866, ibid.

[32]Ibid. Precisely what Ruby meant by "colored small planters" is unknown. He may have meant former free people of color.

[33]GTR to Studer, May 24, 1866, ibid.

[34]GTR to Charles E. Merrill (Agent, Franklin), May 23, 1866, ibid.

[35]GTR to Studer, April 12, 1866, ibid.

[36]GTR to C. P. M. Taggart (Agent, Thibodaux), May 17, 1866; GTR to Studer, May 1, 1866, both ibid. Ruby met a "Lawyer Hennen," formerly one of the wealthiest planters in the parish. He claimed that since emancipation "he was obliged to bid his people shift for themselves" as the land did not produce enough to feed them. A large plantation, it never paid expenses and Hennen used it as a summer retreat, relying on his

professional services for the "main support of himself, family and 'people.'" The Lafourche area has been characterized as those parishes immediately north of New Orleans and west of the Mississippi River, Ripley, *Slaves and Freedmen*, 36 n21.

[37]GTR to Studer, April 12, May 1, 1866, Louisiana, SOE, BRFAL, RG 105.

[38]GTR to Studer, April 12, 1866, ibid. For background on Port Hudson see James G. Hollandsworth, Jr., *The Louisiana Native Guards: The Black Military Experience During the Civil War* (Baton Rouge, 1995).

[39]Ibid.

[40]GTR to Studer, May 18, 1866, ibid. One of the teachers, a man named P. B. Randolph, had "acted in a very high handed manner" and attempted to overawe the other instructors and the agent. Ruby was not impressed.

[41]GTR to Studer, April 12, May 16, 24, 1866, ibid.

[42]GTR to Studer, April 12, 1866, ibid. The St. Mary Parish agent also performed creditably. Ruby characterized him as a "gentleman *well liked* and *respected* by *everybody*." In addition, there appeared to be a "kind feeling prevalent between employer and employed," GTR to Studer, May 16, 24, 1866, ibid.

[43]GTR to Henry S. Wadsworth (Agent, Houma), May 14, 1866, ibid.

[44]GTR to Studer, April 12, May 16, 1866; GTR to Taggart, May 17, 1866, all in ibid.

[45]GTR to Studer, May 26, 1866, ibid.

[46]GTR to Wadsworth, May 14, 1866, ibid.

[47]Ibid.; GTR to Taggart, May 17, 1866, ibid. For violence against schools and teachers see White, *The Freedmen's Bureau in Louisiana*, 184-85. The level of violence aimed at schools and teachers dramatically increased with the rise of the Ku Klux Klan; see Allen W. Trelease, *White Terror: The Ku Klux Klan Conspiracy and Southern Reconstruction* (New York, 1971), 127-36.

[48]Senate, *Report and Testimony* (Serial 1899), Pt. 2, 53. Ruby's last months in Louisiana are somewhat difficult to track because most of the Bureau records for 1866 have been lost or destroyed. There is also no information in the education commissioner's files in Commissioner Oliver Otis Howard's office.

[49]GTR to Studer, April 12, 1866, Louisiana, SOE, BRFAL, RG 105.

[50]Ibid. See also Jacqueline Jones, "Women Who Were More Than Men: Sex and Status in Freedmen's Teaching," *History of Education Quarterly*, 19 (1979): 47-59.

[51]GTR to Studer, April 12, 1866, Louisiana, SOE, BRFAL, RG 105.

[52]Senate, *Report and Testimony* (Serial 1899), Pt. 2, 53; James DeGray (Agent, Clinton) to AC, July 3, 1866; July 5, 1866; Studer to AC, July 5, 1866, Register of Letters Received, Vol. 2:129, 151, AC, LR, Louisiana; Endorsement, Studer, July 5, 1866, Endorsement Book, 83, in Louisiana, SOE, all in BRFAL, RG 105. Unfortunately, the above letters are only brief summaries of the attack upon Ruby. It is impossible to know the background of precisely what happened because the originals do not exist.

[53]For Ruby's Texas Bureau career see William L. Richter, *Overreached on All Sides: The Freedmen's Bureau Administrators in Texas, 1865-1868* (College Station, 1991), 158, 182, 212, 219; W. C. Nunn, *Texas Under the Carpetbaggers* (Austin, 1962), 23 n34; Crouch, "A Political Education."

MARSHALL HARVEY TWITCHELL
AND THE FREEDMEN'S BUREAU
IN BIENVILLE PARISH*

Ted Tunnell

Congress created the Bureau of Refugees, Freedmen, and Abandoned Lands, better known as the Freedmen's Bureau, near the end of the Civil War. In the late summer after Appomattox, a young captain in the 109th United States Colored Troops (USCT) visited the agency's branch headquarters in New Orleans, seeking a position. A native of Vermont, his name was Marshall Harvey Twitchell, and he stood on the threshold of a long and controversial career in Louisiana reconstruction. His reasons for wanting to be a bureau agent are unknown. Whatever they were, Thomas W. Conway, the Louisiana assistant commissioner, found them acceptable; he approved the application and offered the newcomer a posting in either Claiborne or Bienville parishes, in the northwestern part of the state. The captain's ten months as the Bienville agent, like his later career, were to be violent and contentious.[1]

The documentary record of Twitchell's bureau service is fragmentary. For the year 1866, the local agents' files in the National Archives are sadly incomplete. Little of Twitchell's correspondence after the first of the year is extant. Fortunately, he wrote an autobiography. His chapter on his bureau days is patchy, but it does contain information available nowhere else. Fortunately, too, the month that he reached Sparta, the parish seat, the *Bienville Messenger* began publication in the same place. The *Messenger* was anti-black and anti-bureau; even so, its news coverage was thorough for a country newspaper. It reported events that affected Twitchell and printed bureau circulars. The agent's official mishaps also aided the historical record, generating paper trails outside of normal bureau channels. In sum, despite the missing documents, a coherent picture emerges, although, in chiaroscuro.

*First published in *Louisiana History*, 33 (1992): 241-63. Reprinted with the kind permission of the author and the Louisiana Historical Association.

Bienville Parish was a large, irregular rectangle in the uplands of Northwest Louisiana. On its western boundary with Bossier Parish was twenty-mile-long Lake Bistineau. In the rainy spring the lake was two or three miles across, its turgid waters dotted with cypress stumps. In the low-water months of late summer and autumn, it was transformed into a large swampy bayou, lazily pumping its dark waters through Loggy Bayou into the Red River. About 6000 whites and 5000 blacks lived in the parish. Expanses of alluvial soil were scarce and so were big plantations. Before the war only eight planters had owned as many as fifty slaves, and none had owned a hundred. There were no cities, nor even any real towns, only villages. Cotton was the cash crop, but the inhabitants planted more corn than cotton. They also planted grain and potatoes and herded livestock. It was remote country, less than a generation removed from the frontier, and human life was cheap. It had belonged to the Southern Trans-Mississippi, the last part of the Confederacy to surrender.[2]

Sparta sat on a sandy, forested ridge in the center of the parish. In the late twentieth century only a small black church and cemetery remain of it, but from 1849 to 1892 it was a busy parish seat. In the fall of 1865, it boasted two or three hundred people, a wooden courthouse, hotel, school, newspaper office, churches, stores, saloons, houses, and lawyers in abundance. The village was laid out in blocks along a north-south thoroughfare with the courthouse square in the center.[3] When Twitchell rode in the last week of October, he found a provost marshal with a detachment of soldiers from the 61st USCT already on the scene. In addition to bureau credentials, Twitchell was also a provost marshal.[4] He relieved the officer and took command. He set up his headquarters in the jury room of the courthouse. His black troopers, about twenty in number, were quartered in a nearby house. His first reaction to his strange surroundings was a panicky sense of isolation. It was over forty miles to the regional military headquarters at Shreveport; bureau headquarters in New Orleans was a journey of several days. "In case of needing assistance, I was without telegraph, railway, or water connection. . . . I am free to confess that had I known beforehand what my position was to be, I should have remained with my regiment [in Texas]."[5]

Twitchell was the "symbol and substance" of the Union occupation. His was the responsibility of acquainting Bienville with the North's expectations of a free labor South. The "hearty co-operation of the Freedmen's employer is earnestly requested," read his first public statement.

> Their sincere aid will only serve to expedite the work of the Bureau. . . .
> While citizens are called upon to recognize in their former slaves free laborers, the employment of which the good of the parish demands, Freedmen are particularly warned from the erroneous belief that freedom from slavery implies freedom from work—a life of idleness and vagrancy must not be the result of their liberation.

A later announcement told freedmen to meet for "instruction at the time and places designated in this Circular."[6]

The agent received unexpected help from the brotherhood of Freemasons, of which he was a member. The fraternal order was strong in the region and helped him plan a speaking tour of the parish. The public buildings were too small for the crowds that turned out to hear him, and he usually spoke in the open or from the verandah of a well-placed house. As he interpreted his orders, his duty was to acquaint planters and freedmen with "their changed relations from master and slave to employer and employee, giving them the additional information that it was the order of the government that old master and old slave should remain where they had been [and] work as usual in the harvesting of the crop." The new free labor system was to be governed by yearly contracts negotiated under the bureau's watchful eye. If disputes arose over pay, working conditions, or punishment—the lash was prohibited—the agent would act as arbiter.[7]

Freedmen in the parish, it is safe to assume, had expected more from the bureau man. When the agency was first created, the possibility existed that some blacks might obtain homesteads on land seized by the government under the wartime confiscation and abandoned property acts. The government held 78,200 acres in Louisiana and 858,000 in the South. Commissioner Conway had already leased some 10,000 acres to freedmen and accepted applications for more.[8] The freedmen's grapevine telegraph transformed this lone ray of sunlight into the legend of "forty acres and a mule" for the Negro race. The reality, alas, did not even include the mule. Even as Twitchell entered the bureau, the hope of land was being quashed on orders from Washington. Conway was dismissed for being too radical, and Gen. Absalom Baird appointed in his place. Because Baird was not immediately available, Gen. James S. Fullerton—handpicked by the president—went to Louisiana as Conway's interim successor. A few days before Twitchell reached Sparta, Fullerton made a scornful "Address to the Freedmen of Louisiana."

> Slavery has passed away, and you are now placed on trial. . . . It is not the intention of the officers of this Bureau to nurse and pamper you. . . . Some of you have the mistaken notion that freedom means liberty to be idle. . . . You must not believe the idle and malicious stories that have been told you by bad men as to what the Government intends to do for you. . . . Neither rations, nor clothing, nor mules, nor working implements will be given to you hereafter. . . . *No land will be given to you.*

The address was published in the *Messenger*, and Twitchell spread the discouraging news by word of mouth.[9] The bureau's retreat on the land issue was a bitter blow to freedmen's hopes. In truth, only a small minority could have taken advantage of the original plan, probably none in Bienville Parish. Now even that faint hope was gone.

While Twitchell was powerless to affect the broad flow of events, some agency policies allowed him more discretion than others. Headquarters, for example, encouraged apprenticing black orphans and minor children to whites. "Bureau officials were careless about this phase of their work," writes the historian of the Louisiana bureau, and nothing in the Bienville records contradicts this verdict.[10] Twenty-eight child indentures bearing Twitchell's signature survive in the National Archives. Under slavery, bondsmen were commonly known by the names of their owners. In twenty-one of these documents, the surname of the child being bound is the same as the person defined as the "master" or "mistress." The names of certain "masters" also appear repeatedly. Nineteen of the youths mentioned were bound over to just five individuals. In January 1866, for instance, a planter named Hodge Raburn signed six black children, all named Raburn, to apprenticeships ranging from six to thirteen years. In all, Raburn contracted for fifty-four years of unpaid labor from children who, a year before, had almost certainly been his slaves. In the twenty-eight agreements, the average term of service was eight years. Such lengthy indentures might have been justified if the youths had been taught skilled trades that prepared them for productive adult lives. The only occupations mentioned in these papers, however, were "house servant," "farmer," and "field hand."[11] The inescapable conclusion is that apprenticeship, so defined, was merely a euphemism for child slavery.

Freedmen anticipating a messiah in blue no doubt found Twitchell a big disappointment. On the other hand, whites hoping for a pliant ally were to be discomforted, too. One of the agent's first actions in Sparta, for example, was to visit the parish jail. The only prisoner was a young black girl, a servant in the household of Ben Pearce, the town's most prominent citizen—lawyer, soldier, and ex-Confederate lieutenant governor. The young Negro was rumored to be Pearce's illegitimate daughter. In his absence, his wife Ann was wont to beat the girl and have her confined. Unable to find any formal charges against the youth, the agent took the bold step of visiting Ann Pearce. The lady declined to make a complaint, and he released the girl.[12] No matter how delicately he approached Mrs. Pearce, neither she, her husband (when he returned), nor other whites could have appreciated his intrusion in so sensitive an area.

In his November monthly report, the agent expressed misgivings about Gen. Fullerton's recent order—one of his last as interim director—closing bureau courts in the state—and transferring freedmen's cases to the civil courts. The order had appeared in the newspapers but had not officially crossed his Sparta desk. For that reason, he continued to try some cases himself, he wrote. In other instances, he turned matters over to justices of the peace, keeping an eye on the proceedings. He believed that Fullerton's order had increased black unrest in the parish. Even so, he wrote, "an equal number of free white laborers subjected to similar treatment, at work for the same pay, forced into a contract the contents of which in many cases were entirely concealed from or grossly misrepresented to them, would have given their employers and the authorities trouble much more serious than have the Freedmen." A number of planters had informed him of their intention to dismiss their "vicious and idle" workers. "I find without exception their vicious and idle are those who have the largest families of small children, for many of whom I can only see starvation without government aid." Black complaints also convinced him that all labor contracts "should be in writing and read by an agent of the Bureau to the Freedmen."[13] Clearly, this was not the report of a planters' today.

The daily life of a bureau agent was a hard regimen. Bienville Parish encompassed over a thousand square miles.[14] Even with an automobile and paved roads, Twitchell would have been hard pressed to cover his territory; on horseback it was impossible. Long days in the saddle were followed by long hours of red tape. "Everything must be recorded," a South Carolina agent wrote:

> the contracts must be entered alphabetically in the book of Contracts, with statement of employer's name, number of employees, date of signature, date of closure, and terms of agreement; letters forwarded must go in the book of Letters Sent, and letters received in the book of Letters Received; indorsements in the Indorsement Book; so with transportation; so with orders. If a document appeared in two books, each entry must be marked with reference numbers, so that the subject could be hunted from volume to volume. Along the margin there was a running index, by which every name might be traced from beginning to end. In short, the system of army bookkeeping is a laborious and complicated perfection.[15]

Another agent wrote: "My office is full from morning until night generally—I get nothing to eat from Breakfast until 5 or 6 o'clock P.M., and then comes camp duties—the outside duties of the office & these interminable Reports and Returns."[16]

Before the civil courts took over in December, arbitrating disputes consumed most of Twitchell's waking hours. "Everybody, guilty or innocent, ran with his or her griefs to the Bureau officer," a fellow agent recalled.[17] Twitchell's first memorable case concerned a planter who had hit his black foreman. The Negro filed a complaint, and the agent convened a bureau court, summoning the foreman, the planter, and two black witnesses. He instructed the planter to provide mules for the black men as they had a distance to travel. On the day of the hearing, the foreman (the plaintiff) appeared first, and he was afoot; his old master was in such a rage that he had feared to ask for a mule, he said. The witnesses arrived mounted, though. The facts, as presented by the landowner, the plaintiff, and the first witness, were simple enough. The planter had struck his foreman with a stick because he had repeatedly failed to keep the pigs out of the corn. The blow had injured the black man's dignity, but the physical hurt was momentary. The second witness, however, told a different story. "To my great surprise," the agent recalled, "he made out a case of such bad treatment that I think the plaintiff must have wondered that he was alive."[18]

An audience had gathered for the inquest, and blacks and whites alike eagerly awaited Twitchell's decision. "I told the plaintiff that the defendant had no right to strike him but that he had done him no injury, which was more than I could say of the corn crop." In the future, the agent advised him to follow his employer's instructions. Turning to the planter, Twitchell warned him against striking any of his workers again. Finally, the agent addressed the witness with the hyperactive imagination; he told him to "walk home and allow the plaintiff to ride his mule." The audience appreciated the humor in this. In another case, a planter whipped a black woman that had fought with his wife. Twitchell arrested the man and fined him twenty dollars.[19]

Physical abuse and disputes over wages headed the list of grievances but by no means exhausted it. Complaints often arose over small matters. "More than once have I been umpire in the case of a disputed jackknife or Petticoat," an agent wrote. Nor were all quarrels between whites and blacks; sometimes freedmen bickered among themselves. Like most agents, Twitchell considered the majority of complaints trivial, as indeed they were in the larger scheme of things.[20] To a black farmer with a hungry family, however, ownership of a pig, or even a side of bacon, was a legal issue of some importance. Nor could the planters, for their part, have appreciated the bureau's role in these affairs. When the Bienville agent balanced a landowner's word on the scales of truth against a freedman's, he transgressed a cardinal rule of white supremacy. Even if the agent decided in his favor, he was unlikely to be grateful.[21]

The South of Presidential Reconstruction was a troubled land. Dark clouds of fear and violence rumbled on the horizon; and in mid-December, they rolled over Bienville Parish. Since his arrival, Twitchell had fretted about the tension between whites and his black soldiers. In late November, the army recalled his 61st USCT men for mustering out. About seven soldiers from the 80th USCT in Shreveport replaced them. Among the new men was a thirty-five-year-old private named Wallace Harris. An ex-Virginia slave, Harris had enlisted at Baton Rouge in 1863 and made sergeant before being busted. He had a wife and new-born daughter living in New Orleans. The younger men called him Uncle, but his disposition was anything but avuncular.[22]

The soldiers' residence was opposite a grocery and saloon owned by Robert B. Love, a prominent citizen and, evidently, a law officer.[23] The trouble started innocently on a Sunday forenoon a week before Christmas, while Twitchell was away on business. Some black men were wrestling in the street in front of Love's place. Private Harris and other bystanders, mostly black, wagered on the contestants.[24]

An argument broke out. The black man holding the stakes called Harris a "damned liar." Harris cuffed and kicked the name-caller, saying no man talked to him that way. His victim did not hit back, but from the veranda of his store, Robert Love injected himself into the fracas, taunting Harris, according to one witness, "if you was a white man I would beat you and kick you till you got enough of it." Harris snapped back: "If you want to take this man's part come down and I will give it to you the same way." Love jumped down and grabbed him by the collar; the Negro knocked the storekeeper's hand away. Enraged, Love told a white onlooker to get his keys, that he was going to get his pistol and "shoot this nigger." Not the least bit intimidated, Harris pulled his own revolver and told the storekeeper to fetch his weapon. The white man refused to get Love's keys, telling him "he had no-business out there, with those colored boys." As he ushered Love away, the angry soldier, by some accounts, stomped after the pair, brandishing his cocked revolver and threatening Love's life.[25]

Private Narcisse Austin, in charge in Twitchell's absence, watched the altercation with alarm and quickly hurried Harris into the soldiers' house when it was over. After dark he and his companions saw armed whites milling about Love's store. A black informant warned that the townsmen were planning an attack. The frightened troopers slipped away and passed the night in a Negro farmer's corn crib.[26]

Twitchell returned about noon the next day to find peaceful Sparta a smoldering tinderbox. His soldiers were holed up in their quarters, rifles at the ready, and he could see nervous, gun-toting whites about town. Private Austin immediately appeared at his office and told him what had happened. While he was speaking, Love entered, took a seat, and listened, a double-barrel shotgun across his knees. The storekeeper later said that Harris "had threatened his life, and he was afraid to go unarmed."[27]

After the agent heard Austin's report, he immediately decided to put Harris under arrest. His intention was to send the soldier back to Shreveport and let the 80th USCT deal with him. Whether his purpose was ever clear to Harris—or whether Harris cared— was another matter.[28]

Love had the keys to the jail; he got them for Austin who then went to tell Harris of the captain's decision. Love also left. Austin returned soon with the news that Harris refused to be arrested. Twitchell strapped on his pistol and headed for the soldiers' quarters. As he passed the grocery, Love stepped out and proffered the loan of his shotgun, warning that Harris was dangerous. The agent declined the offer and walked on across the street into the men's house.[29]

He found Harris adamant, rifle in hand, and packed to leave. "If I must be arrested I will go to my company and be arrested," the soldier said. For Twitchell this was not good enough. "I told him," he was shortly to testify, "to take off his equipments, lay down his gun, and follow me. He refused. I told him I should have to shoot him if he did not obey. He replied that I would have to shoot then, as he was going to his Regt. I laid down my revolver, and commenced to unfasten his equipments, He struck down my hands and run out the door." Grabbing his pistol, Twitchell, with Austin, rushed out the door after him.

Harris was heading across the courthouse square. Austin saw Love's shotgun barrel protruding from the courthouse door. "Look out Captain he is going to shoot uncle Harris," he cried.

"No, he is not," Twitchell reportedly said.

"Yes he is!" Austin repeated.

"Halt! Stop right there!" Twitchell heard someone shout.

Smoke and flame belched from the courthouse doorway, and Harris slammed to the dirt, wounded in the head, the arm, and the lower body. The soldiers carried him back into their house.[30]

When Twitchell entered, Harris said, "Go out of here. I dont want you to come near me. You caused me to get shot." The agent left and returned ten or fifteen minutes later only to hear the soldier's bitter words repeated. He found a conveyance and rushed the wounded private to the regimental hospital at Shreveport, where he died at ten o'clock that night. Apart from his words to Twitchell, the only thing he said was "turn me over."[31]

The next morning, federal soldiers arrested Love in Sparta and took him to an army prison in Shreveport. Lt. Colonel Orrin McFadden investigated the shooting. The principal witnesses were Twitchell, Private Austin, and two other soldiers of the Sparta contingent. While the four men generally agreed on what happened, there were some discrepancies. On Sunday, when it all started, Austin denied that Harris had followed Love from the scene, waving his pistol and threatening him. Nor, the day after, had Austin heard a command for Harris to halt the instant before the fatal shot. Twitchell said that Harris appeared to be capping or cocking his rifle when he was shot. Austin and one of the other privates saw it differently. Harris carried his weapon "at a trail," and subsequent examination revealed that it was uncapped, they said. Understandably, the three privates identified with their fallen comrade and, like him, partly blamed Twitchell for the deadly outcome. Still, agreement was large, and witnesses to a killing rarely concur on every particular.[32]

Colonel McFadden concluded that the shooting was *"Premeditated Murder."* After seeing his report, Col. William S. Mudgett, the commanding officer of the 80th USCT, recommended that Love be held for trial before a military commission. The recommendation was rejected, and Love was released after a week or two in custody.[33] The record does not reveal the basis of the decision, or who made it, but the former can probably be deduced. To begin with, a strong suspicion of the storekeeper's guilt was insufficient for a murder or manslaughter conviction. The principal obstacle to prosecution was the victim. His behavior the last two days of his life parodied chip-on-the-shoulder machismo. He had struck a black man, drawn his pistol on Love, and physically resisted Twitchell. When he was shot, he had a rifle in his hands and was willfully disobeying orders. For his part, Love claimed to be aiding and defending Twitchell when he fired on Harris. There was just enough plausibility in this assertion to further muddy the waters.[34] Political considerations may also have influenced the army's decision. Putting a Confederate veteran on trial for killing a black soldier would have been bitterly resented in North Louisiana and that understates the matter. All things considered, however, Love would have had an excellent chance of going free even if Harris had been white.

Mudgett was also displeased with Twitchell. His "conduct in this case is highly culpable and demands a very close investigation if not his arrest and trial before a court martial," he wrote. This seems a harsh judgement. Without warning, the agent was thrust into a situation that threatened to turn Sparta into a battlefield. The circumstances allowed him no time for reflection. From the instant he dismounted his horse to the moment Harris was shot, no more than sixty minutes appear to have elapsed. Even so, his quick decision to arrest Harris was probably wise. The action was calculated to defuse the tense situation between the soldiery and the townspeople and, at the same time, get Harris safely out of harm's way.[35] Had the private not resisted, he almost certainly would have lived to see his wife and daughter again. Twitchell would have sent him to Shreveport under guard, probably that afternoon. There, in a fair hearing, he might have been let off with light punishment or possibly exonerated. Even if the 80th USCT had dealt severely with him, it would have been better than the sentence meted out from Love's gun barrel. In resisting arrest, Harris virtually signed his own death warrant. It is impossible to read into the mind of this man, but something appears to have been eating at him. Perhaps it was the loneliness and boredom of Sparta; perhaps it was the hostility of Bienville whites; or perhaps he was drinking heavily in Twitchell's absence. Whatever private griefs goaded him on, his behavior was almost suicidal. Whether such considerations influenced Shreveport, no action was taken against the Sparta agent.

Even as the events of the postwar Christmas season sputtered to their sad denouement, more trouble was budding in the Vermonter's vineyard. Education was a vital part of the Freedmen's Bureau mission in the South. Agency officials assumed that literacy was essential for uplifting black people from the degradation of slavery and preparing them for life in a free labor society. When Twitchell entered the bureau, the Louisiana Gen. Superintendent of Education, Capt. Henry R. Pease, managed 126 freedmen's schools employing 230 teachers. The superintendent's office was anxious to expand the bureau's schools. It was usually up to the local agents to get them started.[36]

In early December, Twitchell wrote Pease that there were 816 black children in Bienville Parish between the ages of five and sixteen. After the first of the year, he believed that a school could be established at Sparta and another at Mt. Lebanon, each accommodating about thirty-five children. He already had a teacher in mind for Sparta, a well-educated young man of good habits named Dubois, from "one of the first families of the town." Because of his social standing and knowledge of the people, he "would give the schools a popularity which a stranger though ever so good a teacher could not."[37] For reasons that we will come back to, the agent's initiative could not be acted upon at the time.

Two months slipped by; then, in February, 1866, Twitchell met the bureau's traveling education agent, Capt. Charles A. Meyers, in Shreveport. As Meyers recorded it, he asked for half a dozen teachers. A few weeks hence, Meyers hired Mrs. Mary E. Wardell and Mrs. Julia M. Thomas, with instructions to report to the Sparta agent.[38]

Mrs. Thomas was evidently from England while Mrs. Wardell was probably a Yankee "schoolmarm" or Southern Unionist.[39] Both were experienced teachers who had taught in the Department of the Gulf's freedmen's schools during the war. Their relations with their superiors had sometimes been strained. In April, 1865, Lieut. Edwin M. Wheelock, supervisor of the Gulf Board of Education, complained of lax discipline in Mrs. Thomas's classroom and of her habit of summoning the provost marshal to maintain order.[40] A month later he upbraided her again. The chaplain "reports that you punished a child in his presence by giving it only a gentle tap upon the head; a punishment so slight and insufficient as to induce only laughter on the part of the child."[41] Mrs. Wardell had also been the recipient of sharp missives from Lieut. Wheelock. After one such, she responded testily: "I felt no annoyance at any want of due respect from yourself, or other members of the Board, nor am I in the least 'fastidious' in regard to matters of 'etiquette' except when the departure therefrom affects the welfare of others. The idea that I wished to convey was *this*, that *I* know what books are required."[42]

For their part, the two women had grievances of their own: unruly students, frequent transfers, low pay and even no pay. "If it is convenient I should like to receive a little money," Mrs. Wardell wrote Wheelock in the spring of 1865. "When I came here in the autumn, I was, as I informed you, without funds. Since coming here, I have not received a dollar. As you may well imagine, I have suffered no little inconvenience during the winter for want of means."[43] Worries of a different kind are suggested by a letter Wheelock wrote Mrs. Thomas a month later: "You have no reason for alarm as to the rebels. Stand by your post of duty and do not lend an ear to idle rumors."[44] The impression is of two harried, overworked and underpaid matrons who were heartily sick of men in uniform peering over their shoulders and ordering them about.

In mid-March, Mrs. Thomas, with her child, and Mrs. Wardell reached Shreveport where they boarded the stage for Sparta. Exactly what befell them between Shreveport and Sparta is somewhat vague, but it was bad. They were set upon by thugs, insulted and roughed up. The ruffians evidently seized their baggage and then extorted their money from them as ransom for its return. Their treatment was politically inspired.[45] However noble in Northern eyes, Yankee teachers—whether literally Yankees or not—were held in low regard by white Southerners. In time, the likes of Julia Thomas and Mary Wardell would occupy a special niche in the dark legend of Reconstruction. The "Yankee schoolma'am," Wilbur Cash wrote venomously, was "generally horse-faced, bespectacled, and spare of frame, she was, of course, no proper intellectual, but at best a comic character, at worst a dangerous fool, playing with explosive forces which she did not understand."[46] In Albion W. Tourgée's classic Reconstruction novel, *A Fool's Errand*, whites describe such women as "nigger schoolmarms" or "free-love nigger-missionaries of the female persuasion." One of the book's characters sums up the point of view of postwar whites: "we can't help thinking that any one that comes from the north down here, and associates with niggers—can't—well—can't be of much account at home."[47]

By the time the stage rumbled into Sparta, the women were broke, angry, frightened, and weary. No one had written ahead, and Twitchell was not expecting them. More important, the political climate in the parish had taken an ugly turn since the agent's meeting with Meyers. On top of this, except for two orderlies, his soldiers had been recalled to their regiment. With only two men, he could not protect the women and was even afraid for his own safety. He had arranged accommodations for the teachers in private homes, but local thugs threatened to burn out anyone who let them stay, and the invitations were withdrawn. In short, schools were no longer feasible in Bienville, and they must leave, the agent said. The ladies' reaction to this unwelcome news was volcanic; their wrath welled up like boiling lava. What nerve! What impudence! After all they had endured! How dare this awful man treat them this way. One of the pair addressed him as "Gen." and then, over a three-day period, demoted him down through the ranks to plain "Mister." Their protests were unavailing, however. Twitchell gave them twenty-five dollars apiece and put them on the stage back to Shreveport. From there they made it to Natchitoches where the resident bureau agent took them in and gave them jobs.[48]

The matrons were not done with Twitchell, though. He hovered like a dark star, flickering malignantly, on their horizon. Mrs. Thomas's letters to bureau officials, recounting his beastly conduct, lost nothing in the telling. She demanded that his pay be garnished to reimburse herself and her companion for their losses. One of her letters was so vitriolic that the new superintendent of education, Maj. A. G. Studer, responded: "for the future letters couched in such language as your last from you or any other person in the employ . . . of the Freedmen's Bureau will receive no further notice except the summary dismissal of the writer." Despite his anger, Studer—and other bureau officials—believed the two women had a case. Why had Twitchell not canceled his request for teachers if schools were impossible? they asked. Why had he given the ladies only fifty dollars between them, a sum plainly insufficient for their return trip?[49] One agent even suggested that he was partly responsible for the women's mistreatment on the Sparta stage.[50] Accounts of the teachers' misadventures were virtually guaranteed to feature Twitchell as the heavy. Where the safety of women was concerned, the army expected its officers to adhere to a standard of honor harking back to medieval chivalry. The code stressed that women were chaste and delicate creatures that depended on gentlemen, especially in uniform, for protection.[51] It was impossible to reconcile events in Sparta with these archaic notions. Like Gen. Ben Butler with his "woman order," Twitchell was no knight in blue.

The Vermonter's version of these events has largely been lost. Except for a brief snatch, his official report is missing. The comments in his autobiography are brief and incomplete. The hullabaloo over his alleged want of gallantry, however, overlooked a vital element of the story: namely, that Julia Thomas and Mary Wardell were not the easiest people to get along with. Their record before Sparta shows this, and so does what they did afterward. Both women found employment as teachers in Natchitoches Parish. In August, Mrs. Thomas abruptly quit her job, forcing the closing of the Natchitoches town school. Mrs. Wardell resigned two months later. "During her period of service in the employ of this Office," the Natchitoches agent wrote, she "made herself extremely troublesome and her resignation was a great relief to all concerned."[52]

The personal issues aside, Twitchell's assessment of the situation in his district was assuredly correct. Even had it been possible to protect the schools, the problem of financing them would have remained. When Congress created the Freedmen's Bureau, it had neglected to appropriate any money for its operations. Thus, however important education was in theory, the bureau did not have the funds to carry out its goals. When Twitchell first proposed starting two schools in December, nothing was done because agency schools in Louisiana were in the act of closing down until spring, $80,000 in debt. For the bureau program to work, its schools had to be self-sufficient. The policy was for freedmen to pay 5 percent of their wages as a school tax. The program worked best in the towns where there was a semblance of a black middle class. There were no towns in Bienville, and most of its black farmers had not seen any wages since the war. If Twitchell had managed to get two schools started in the parish and keep them going, it would have been a tremendous achievement. Including himself, five men served as agents in Sparta after the war; when the bureau closed its doors in the village in late 1868, there were still no schools in the parish.[53]

The problems that plagued Twitchell also troubled his regional counterparts. The Shreveport office, for example, encompassed the entire northwestern corner of the state— Caddo, De Soto, and Bossier parishes. In November, 1866, the resident agent, Lt. Col. Martin Flood, reported that only one school was in operation and "that one was but a partial success." The difficulties included the freedmen's poverty, high water and a poor cotton crop, and white hostility. Flood laid particular stress on the last obstacle. The region bordering Texas and Arkansas was notorious for outlaws and marauders, he wrote. "Colored schools would have but furnished them with the opportunity for not only breaking up all such schools; but an excuse for commiting other depredations upon Freedmen." The planters were no help. They were generally opposed to Negro education and unwilling "to protect either school or teacher from insult or personal violence."[54] The truth was that the bureau's schools in Louisiana were in decline in 1866. At the beginning of the year, the agency had 150 schools, 265 teachers, and 19,000 students. Seven months later 66 schools, 76 teachers, and 2,239 students remained.[55]

Accounts of Twitchell's run-in with Mrs. Thomas and Mrs. Wardell took time to work their way up the chain of command to Assistant Commissioner Baird. "Capt. Twitchell has without doubt acted very badly," he wrote in May, "but under the circumstances, it will be impracticable to have him relieved."[56] In the meantime, by coincidence, the adjutant general's office in Washington had become concerned about Twitchell's continuance in office, because the 109th USCT—from which he was on detached duty while in the bureau—had been mustered out in February. In April Gen. Philip Sheridan, commander of the Gulf, cut a routine order for Twitchell's discharge after receiving an inquiry from the adjutant general. The order miscarried, however, and nearly three months slipped by before "Little Phil," somewhat irritated, issued it again.[57] Those three months were among the most important of Twitchell's life. Had he left the bureau in April or May, he probably would have returned to Vermont, his Louisiana career over.

Adele Coleman was a nineteen-year-old music teacher at Sparta Masonic Academy. Her home was in Brush Valley, eighteen miles to the southeast. The Colemans were originally from South Carolina and had moved to North Louisiana from Mississippi before the war. Her father Isaac Coleman had owned twenty-five slaves. As befitted a daughter of the gentry, Adele had been to finishing school in South Carolina.[58]

She lived at the Mays Hotel where Twitchell often dined. Exactly how they met is unknown, but by late spring the parish was buzzing with gossip. Adele's family was indignant, and for a time it looked as if Twitchell was as likely to win himself a headstone as a bride.[59]

Others shared the Coleman family's outrage. The comely Adele was one of the most eligible belle's in the parish. One of her admirers was newspaper editor J. M. C. Scanland. Like a young backcountry Horace Greeley, he came courting with bundles of the *Bienville Messenger* under his arm.[60] When Twitchell first arrived in the parish, a *Messenger* correspondent greeted him cordially: he "seems to be a gentleman in every particular, and I doubt not that he will do well by our citizens, if they will only receive him in the proper spirit." For about two months, favorable comments about the agent periodically graced the paper's columns, and bureau circulars were routinely printed over his signature.[61] Coverage stopped, however, in January, 1866, the same month Adele moved to town. Then, a month or so later, the journal ceased printing bureau circulars, too. From February on, as far as the *Messenger* was concerned, there was no bureau officer in Sparta.

Headstrong and rebellious, Adele overrode her family's opposition and ignored parish opinion, too. In the end, she had her way. She married her Yankee on July 24, two weeks before he left the army and the bureau.[62] Scanland's paper took no notice.

Twitchell was mustered out in New Orleans. His trip downriver coincided with the notorious July 30 massacre of blacks in the city, a major event of Presidential Reconstruction. In the ensuing weeks the Northern press was full of Louisiana stories. The *New York Tribune* printed a letter in mid-August from W. B. Stickney, a former bureau official, documenting the mistreatment of freedmen in the state. The letter contained an excerpt from Twitchell's report on the Julia Thomas-Mary Wardell affair, about the intimidation in Bienville Parish. When the *Bienville Messenger* picked up the piece in late September, it was chagrined. Predictably, it called Stickney an "unprincipled reprobate." As to ex-agent Twitchell, so long ignored, the column read: "there is some probability that Capt. Twitchell did not utter the above in his report, and that it is a vile fabrication of Stickney's; but if he did make these statements, he done so wilfully and maliciously—knowing the same to be false at the time. As Capt. Twitchell is, we believe, temporarily absent from the parish, we forbear further remarks." The newspaper was right about one thing: Twitchell was out of the parish. He and Adele's father were touring North Louisiana, Mississippi, and Arkansas, looking for plantation sites.[63]

For Twitchell, the bureau was a portal into the strange southern world so different from his native New England. "My duties," he later wrote, "led me into different sections of the country, giving me an acquaintance more thorough in one year than a person staying at home would acquire in a lifetime."[64] Had he never been the Bienville agent, he would not have become the parish's delegate to the constitutional convention of 1867-1868, nor parish judge, nor state senator, nor Republican boss of Red River Parish (carved out of Bienville and four other parishes).

After Twitchell, four men served as agents in Sparta—H. B. Blanton, Edward W. Devees, George Schayer, and Edward Newell Bean, respectively. The longest-tenured and most important of the group was Devees; the New Yorker was the agent from late 1866 to the spring of 1868. His surviving correspondence in the National Archives comprises an extensive record of his stewardship. Reading his reports, one is often reminded of Twitchell. In August 1867, for instance, Devees informed New Orleans that he had started the first schools in the parish. He conceded, however, that "the almost complete and entire failure of the Crops last and this year has rendered the freedmen to[o] poor to pay for the tuition of themselves and children." Three months later the schools were gone.[65] When Devees left the bureau, he became Twitchell's business and political partner.

The darkest moment of Twitchell's bureau days was the murder of Private Harris. The years rolled by but the soldier's dying words were etched in his memory. In the mid-1870s, after he entered the state senate, Mrs. Anna Harris, Harris's widow, applied for a federal pension as the widow of a Civil War veteran. Twitchell was crucial to her case, because his report on her husband's death would carry weight with the pension office. The ex-agent was in an awkward position. If he told the truth, her application would fail; the government would refuse a stipend in the case of a soldier killed fleeing military arrest. In a sworn statement, Twitchell wrote that he had ordered Harris back to his regiment in Shreveport—that the private was killed in the line of duty. It was untrue, of course, nor did it win Anna Harris her pension. After ruling in her favor, the pension bureau reversed itself. Still, Twitchell's mind probably rested easier for trying. Ironically, when he wrote his deposition, he was near his own rendezvous with a Southern assassin. On May 2, 1876, he was shot down on the Red River. Hit six times, he lived but lost both of his arms.[66]

Notes for "Marshall Harvey Twitchell and the Freedmen's Bureau in Bienville Parish"

[1]The Louisiana bureau needed agents when Twitchell applied. Circular No. 6, August 9, 1865, Bureau of Refugees, Freedmen, and Abandoned Lands, Louisiana, Record Group 105, National Archives Microfilm 1027, reel 26 (hereafter cited as BRFAL-LA, RG 105 [and the appropriate microfilm (M) and reel number]); Ted Tunnell, ed., *Carpetbagger from Vermont: The Autobiography of Marshall Harvey Twitchell* (Baton Rouge, 1989), 88-89. The basic study of the Freedmen's Bureau is George R. Bentley, *A History of the Freedmen's Bureau* (Philadelphia, 1955). The main work on the Louisiana bureau is Howard A. White, *The Freedmen's Bureau in Louisiana* (Baton Rouge, 1970); see also John Cornelius Engelsman, "The Freedmen's Bureau in Louisiana," *Louisiana Historical Quarterly*, 32 (1949): 145-224.

[2]Samuel H. Lockett, *Louisiana as It Is: A Geographical and Topographical Description of the State*, ed. Lauren C. Post (Baton Rouge, 1969); *United States Census, Population, 1860*, 194 (figures are estimates); *Biographical and Historical Memoirs of Northwest Louisiana* (Nashville and Chicago, 1890), 153-54; Philip C. Cook, "Antebellum Bienville Parish" (M. A. thesis, Louisiana Tech University, 1966), 110.

[3]J. Fair Hardin, *Northwestern Louisiana: A History of the Watershed of the Red River, 1714-1937*, 3 vols. (Louisville, Ky. and Shreveport, La., 1939), 2:126, 133-34; Cook, "Antebellum Bienville Parish," 79-86; *History of Bienville Parish* (Bienville, La., 1984), 30-33.

[4]Bureau agents that doubled as provost marshals frequently performed regular military tasks in addition to their bureau duties (Donald G. Nieman, *To Set the Law in Motion: The Freedmen's Bureau and the Legal Rights of Blacks, 1865-1868* (New York, 1979), 17). Twitchell's only military duties, as far as the record shows, pertained to supervising his contingent of black soldiers.

[5]Special Order No. 17, October 24, 1865, Regimental Papers, 61st USCT, Record Group 94, Box 41, National Archives; Tunnell, ed., *Carpetbagger from Vermont*, 89-91.

[6]John and LaWanda Cox, "General 0. 0. Howard and the Misrepresented Bureau," *Journal of Southern History*, 19 (1953): 428; *Bienville Messenger*, October 28, November 25, 1865.

[7]*Carpetbagger from Vermont*, 47, 91-92.

[8]LaWanda Cox, "The Promise of Land for the Freedmen," *Mississippi Valley Historical Review*, 45 (1958): 413-40; William McFeely, *Yankee Stepfather: General O. O. Howard and the Freedmen's Bureau* (New Haven, 1968), 91, 97-100; Nieman, *To Set the Law in Motion*, 45-53; Claude F. Oubre, *Forty Acres and a Mule: The Freedmen's Bureau and Black Land Ownership* (Baton Rouge, 1978), 32-37.

[9]McFeely, *Yankee Stepfather*, 174-79; Nieman, *To Set the Law in Motion*, 45-53; October 20, 1865, BRFAL-LA, RG 105, M-1027, reel 26; *Bienville Messenger*, November 11, 1865.

[10]Circular No. 25, October 31, 1865, BRFAL-LA, RG 105, M-1027, reel 26; White, *Freedmen's Bureau in Louisiana*, 82-83.

[11]BRFAL-LA, RG 105, Entry 1896.

[12]*Carpetbagger from Vermont*, 91; *Biographical and Historical Memoirs of Northwest Louisiana*, 193.

[13]Unfortunately, the agent's first full report is also the only one that has survived. Marshall Harvey Twitchell to Absalom Baird, December 1, 1865, BRFAL-LA, RG 105, M-1027, reel 13; Circular No. 24, October 30, 1865, ibid., reel 26; White, *Freedmen's Bureau in Louisiana*, 134-38.

[14]The parish was 856 square miles before the war, but its 1866 boundaries made it much larger than this. Cook, "Antebellum Bienville Parish," 164-65; *County-Parish Boundaries in Louisiana* (New Orleans, 1939), 81.

[15]John W. De Forest, *A Union Officer in the Reconstruction*, ed. James H. Croushore and David M. Potter (New Haven, 1948), 40.

[16]Quoted in Cox and Cox, "General 0. 0. Howard and the Misrepresented Bureau," 430. A good study of a local agent is J. Thomas May, "The Freedmen's Bureau at the Local Level: A Study of a Louisiana Agent," *Louisiana History*, 9 (1968): 5-19. See also James Smallwood, "The Freedmen's Bureau Reconsidered: Local Agents and the Black Community," *Texana*, 11 (1973): 309-20; and, by the same author, "Charles E. Culver, A Reconstruction Agent in Texas: The Work of Local Freedmen's Bureau Agents in the Black Community," *Civil War History*, 27 (1981): 350-61.

[17]De Forest, *Union Officer in the Reconstruction*, 30.

[18]*Carpetbagger from Vermont*, 92-93.

[19]Ibid., 92-93; Marshall Harvey Twitchell to Absalom Baird, December 1, 1865, BRFAL-LA, RG 105, M-1027, reel 13.

[20]De Forest, *Union Officer in the Reconstruction*, 29-30; *Carpetbagger from Vermont*, 93.

[21]*Carpetbagger from Vermont*, 92-93; Nieman, *To Set the Law in Motion*, 40-43.

[22]Marshall Harvey Twitchell to G. B. Furgeson, Military Division of Western Louisiana, Record Group 393, Entry No. 1918, National Archives; Wallace Harris Compiled Military Service Record, Record Group 94, National Archives; Wallace Harris Pension File, Record Group 15, National Archives.

[23]Love is listed as a constable before the war, a deputy sheriff in 1867, and sheriff in 1872. *Biographical and Historical Memoirs of Northwest Louisiana*, 154, 160; Hardin, *Northwestern Louisiana*, 2:140. The fact that he had the keys to the jail when his altercation with Harris occurred (Wallace Harris Compiled Military Service Record) suggests that he was a law officer at this time, too.

[24]Wallace Harris Compiled Military Service Record. This file contains the report of Lt. Col. Orrin McFadden upon which the following account is largely based.

[25]Ibid.; *Bienville Messenger*, December 23, 1865.

[26]Wallace Harris Compiled Military Service Record.

[27]Ibid.

[28]Ibid.; Wallace Harris Pension File; *Carpetbagger from Vermont*, 95-96.

[29]Wallace Harris Compiled Military Service Record.

[30]Ibid.

[31]Ibid.; Wallace Harris Pension File.

[32]*Bienville Messenger*, December 30, 1865; Wallace Harris Compiled Military Service Record.

[33]Contrary to Twitchell *(Carpetbagger from Vermont*, 96), some of the depositions filed by Harris's widow (Wallace Harris Pension File) claimed that Love escaped from the 80th USCT. This hardly seems possible. Love was soon back in his grocery and serving on the Bienville Parish Police Jury. That he broke out of prison and hid out in his store, in plain sight of Twitchell and his soldiers, is highly implausible. The depositions (dated 1876-1877) also claimed that Love's current whereabouts were unknown. The likely motivation for these assertions—if they were not simply a mistake—was that it made it more difficult for the pension office to locate the storekeeper and get his version of Harris's death, which would not have helped Anna Harris's claim (see the last page of this article).

[34]Wallace Harris Compiled Military Service Record.

[35]Ibid.; Wallace Harris Pension File; *Carpetbagger from Vermont*, 95.

[36]White, *Freedmen's Bureau in Louisiana*, 170-72.

[37]Marshall Harvey Twitchell to Henry R. Pease, December 2, 1865, BRFAL-LA, RG 105, M-1026, reel 2.

[38]A. G. Studer to A. F. Hayden, June 11, 1866, ibid., reel 1.

[39]The reason for believing that Julia Thomas was English is that her sister Agnes Maher arrived in New Orleans from England during the war. Agnes Maher to Board of Education, January 21, 1865 and Julia M. Thomas to Edwin M. Wheelock, April 2[?], 1865, ibid., reel 8.

[40]Edwin M. Wheelock to Julia M. Thomas, April [?], 1865, ibid., reel 1.

[41]Edwin M. Wheelock to Julia M. Thomas, May 5, 1865, ibid.

[42]Mary E. Wardell to Edwin M. Wheelock, January 20, 1865, ibid., reel 2.

[43]Mary E. Wardell to Edwin M. Wheelock, March 27, 1865, ibid.

[44]Edwin M. Wheelock to Julia M. Thomas, April 25, 1865, ibid., reel 1.

[45]A. G. Studer to A. F. Hayden, June 11, 1866, ibid., reel 1; A. G. Studer endorsement book letter, April 10, 1866, ibid., reel 2.

[46]Wilbur J. Cash, *The Mind of the South* (New York, 1941), 137. See Sandra E. Small, "The Yankee Schoolmarm in Freedmen's Schools: An Analysis of Attitudes," *Journal of Southern History*, 45 (1979): 381-402; and Robert C. Morris, *Reading, 'Riting,' and Reconstruction: The Education of Freedmen in the South, 1861-1870* (Chicago, 1981).

[47]Albion W. Tourgée, *A Fool's Errand*, ed. John Hope Franklin (Cambridge, Mass., 1961), 52-53.

[48]A. G. Studer endorsement book letter, April 10, 1866, BRFAL-LA, RG 105, M-1026, reel 2; Studer to Julia M. Thomas, May 19, 1866 and Studer to A. F. Hayden, June 11, 1866, ibid., reel 1; *New York Tribune*, August 15, 1866; *Carpetbagger from Vermont*, 97.

[49]The sum may have been inadequate, but it probably came from his own pocket. He may or may not have been reimbursed.

[50]A. G. Studer endorsement book letter, April 10, 1866, BRFAL-LA, RG 105, M-1026, reel 2; Studer to Julia M. Thomas, May 19, 1866, and Studer to A. F. Hayden, June 11, 1866, ibid., reel 1.

[51]Paul Andrew Hutton, *Phil Sheridan and His Army* (Lincoln, Neb., 1985), 142-43.

[52]Monthly School Reports, Natchitoches Parish, August 31 and October 31, 1866, BRFAL-LA, RG 105, Entry 1768.

[53]White, *Freedmen's Bureau in Louisiana*, 173-78, 181n.

[54]Martin Flood to A. F. Hayden, November 30, 1866, BRFAL-LA, RG 105, Entry No. 1873.

[55]White, *Freedmen's Bureau in Louisiana*, 177.

[56]A. G. Studer endorsement book letter, May 19, 1866, BRFAL-LA, RG 105, M-1026, reel 2.

[57]E. D. Townsend to Philip H. Sheridan, April 13, 1866, in Marshall Harvey Twitchell Compiled Military Service Record, Record Group 94, National Archives; Sheridan to Townsend, April 23, 1866, George Lee to Absalom Baird, July 5, 1866, Sheridan to Townsend, July 13, 1866, in Adjutant General's Office, Colored Troops Division, Entry No. 1864, Box 102, Record Group 94, National Archives.

[58]*Bienville Messenger,* January 6, 1866; *Biographical and Historical Memoirs of Northwest Louisiana*, 153; *Carpetbagger from Vermont*, 99-100.

[59]*Carpetbagger from Vermont*, 99-104.

[60]Adele Coleman Twitchell to Luella Coleman, November 4, 1866, Marshall Harvey Twitchell Papers, Prescott Memorial Library, Louisiana Tech University, Ruston; *House Miscellaneous Documents*, 41st Cong., 2d Sess., No. 154, Pt. 2:180.

[61]*Bienville Messenger*, October 28, November 25, December 16, 23, 1865.

[62]*Carpetbagger from Vermont*, 99-104.

[63]The excerpt included in Stickney's letter is the only part of the report extant. *New York Tribune*, August 15, 1866; *Bienville Messenger*, September 29, 1866; *Carpetbagger from Vermont*, 105-6.

[64]*Carpetbagger from Vermont*, 105.

[65]Personnel records, BRFAL-LA, RG 105, M-1027, reel 34; Edward W. Devees loyalty oath, May 13, 1867, ibid., reel 14; Devees Trimonthly reports, August 20 and November 20, 1867, ibid.

[66]Wallace Harris Pension File; *Carpetbagger from Vermont*, 170-74.

"REDEEMING OF THE PEOPLE FROM IGNORANCE"*

Howard Ashley White

At the outbreak of the Civil War, Louisiana had a superintendent of education who presided over a school system that was more a theory than a reality. While New Orleans boasted excellent public schools for white children, the rural areas of the state, like most of the South, were generally without free schools.[1] Since 1822, private schools had flourished in New Orleans for freeborn Negroes, but they were excluded from the city schools and other public schools in the state, except in a few cases of admission based on "fairness of complexion."[2] Slaves were denied access to any kind of schooling, for a state law of 1830 forbade teaching them to read or write on pain of imprisonment for one to twelve months.[3]

After Union forces occupied New Orleans in 1862, Mrs. Mary D. Brice, a teacher from Ohio, opened a free school for Negro children.[4] A federal Commission of Enrollment, organized under Lieut. William B. Stickney, encouraged other individuals to begin schools for the children of emancipated slaves, and by the beginning of 1864, eight such institutions had been established in New Orleans.[5] One of them was under the direction of P. M. Williams, a Negro graduate of Dartmouth College.[6]

On March 22, 1864, Gen. Nathaniel P. Banks issued General Order No. 38 to govern the organization and growth of Negro schools in the area he served as military commander. The directive established a board of education for the Department of the Gulf, with B. Rush Plumly as general chairman and Lieut. Edwin M. Wheelock as supervisor in Louisiana.[7] A few days after receiving his assignment, Wheelock, who was described by an associate as "a very efficient and popular officer,"[8] reported that his organization had employed ninety teachers to conduct forty-nine schools with an average daily attendance of 5,200 pupils. The effort to educate freedmen had spread to the country parishes, for fifty-two of the teachers were serving outside New Orleans, yet within Union

*First appeared as chapter 8 in Howard Ashley White, *The Freedmen's Bureau in Louisiana* (Baton Rouge: Louisiana State University Press, © 1970), 166-200. Reprinted with the kind permission of the author and publisher.

lines.[9] By the middle of September, 116 teachers served in seventy-four schools, fourteen of which were located in New Orleans.[10] On March 18, 1865, before the Freedmen's Bureau took over the schools, the *New Orleans Times* claimed that eleven thousand colored children were receiving instruction from 162 teachers.

General Banks intended that the expenses of the work should be borne by the people of the parishes where the schools were located. He instructed Col. T. E. Chickering, his assistant provost marshal general, to see that teachers were provided with living accommodations at the expense of each parish, and to make such tax assessments on property as might be needed.[11] Plumly received instruction to place "the burden of these schools . . ., upon the disloyal portion of our citizens."[12] The policy was hardly one to encourage a favorable attitude toward the schools on the part of the white people of Louisiana.

Union officials in high places praised the educational system established by the army. Plumly testified that in a conversation with Abraham Lincoln, the president said to him: "You shall foller the Flag with your Schools, Plumly; you'r doin' a big work." Salmon P. Chase, Chief Justice of the United States, visited New Orleans in June, 1865, and admired the schools.[13] Gen. Oliver Otis Howard, national head of the Freedmen's Bureau, considered the army's educational work excellent.[14] However, Banks's system received unfavorable criticism from a later bureau superintendent, E. W. Mason, who thought that Banks had deterred Northern agencies from assisting the work in Louisiana by informing them that he had created a self-supporting program.[15]

As the bureau prepared to take over the schools, General Howard made it clear that Northern aid associations would be asked to furnish teachers, books, and supplies, while the bureau would attempt to provide buildings, protection, and transportation for teachers. Howard proposed to raise funds for the bureau's part of the work by increased efforts to collect the tax that Banks had levied, and he stated that it was not the intention of the government to pay the cost of educating freedmen.[16]

On June 29, 1865, a telegram from Washington authorized Thomas W. Conway, then assistant commissioner, to take charge of the schools from Wheelock.[17] Plumly opposed the transfer and importuned Commissioner Howard to keep the educational work separate from other duties of his assistant commissioners. Plumly stated that Wheelock had worked hard to make a success of the schools, and that he had done so on the "beggarly pittance" of a lieutenant's pay. As for Conway, he would not only be too busy to run the schools, but was the Object of ecclesiastical jealousies that would interfere with his work.[18] Plumly's objections were unavailing, and Captain H. R. Pease of the 84th Colored Infantry was given Wheelock's place.[19] Aside from dismissing Wheelock and Plumly, Conway retained most of the officers and enlisted men who were engaged in educational work.[20]

Pease, who had served under Wheelock, had expressed his views on the subject of Negro education in June, 1864, when he called for teachers "of the 'right stamp,' actuated by pure philanthropic motives—working men—men who hated slavery— ABOLITIONISTS! dyed with the pure dyemen who dare face this *miserable, wheedling conservatism,* and do something to merit at least the prevalent epithet 'nigger on the brain.'"[21] After Conway, who doubtless shared Captain Pease's ideas, placed him in charge of schools, the new appointee installed a new organizational system. The state was divided into seven school districts, with a commissioned officer or civilian employee in charge of each. Serving under the officials were school directors for each parish and *"canvassers"* to collect the school tax in each district. Pease expected to employ two or three times the 250 teachers listed on the roster in September, and he was eager to collect the tax in order to pay them.[22] At the same time, he proposed to make radical reforms in the quality of instruction because he found a serious deficiency in the ability of some of the teachers. He immediately ordered a normal school to be held for them, and in September the Negro schools of New Orleans and vicinity were suspended while 139 teachers attended a normal school directed by Mortimer A. Warren, a graduate of the Normal School of New Britain, Connecticut. When an examination was held at the end of a month, 106 of the teachers passed, a number of whom were black.[23]

Negro teachers were in great demand because of the difficulty of securing boarding places for white instructors. After a call to the American Missionary Association of Chicago to supply Negro teachers, only six were sent to Louisiana. During 1867 and 1868 the number of black teachers ranged from 33 to 85, while the number of white teachers in the same period varied from 131 to 44.[24] White natives of the South, who had been employed on the basis of their antislavery sentiments, constituted the majority of teachers in freedmen's schools from 1865 through 1868.[25]

While Captain Pease was conducting a normal school to eliminate incapable teachers, his own performance was under scrutiny. Some of the white citizens demanded his removal on charges that he was wasting their tax money and stirring freedmen to sedition.[26] Conway rebuked him for failing to make proper reports, as well as for arresting Matthew Whildin, inspector of schools in New Orleans. Pease defended his action by charging Whildin with causing disturbances among teachers and employees of the bureau, committing forgeries, stealing government property, and circulating petitions for Pease's removal.[27] The captain was still having trouble with his superiors in December of that year when Gen. Absalom Baird, head of the bureau, stated that he ought to be removed for extravagance. Baird delayed action, however, pending the outcome of court-martial proceedings instituted by Gen. E. R. S. Canby against Pease. On March 2, 1866, Baird removed him from office and appointed Brevet Maj. A. G. Studer in his place.[28]

Officials of the bureau voiced great pride in the first few months of their educational efforts among freedmen. When the agency took over the Negro schools in July, 1865, there were 126 such institutions in the state, with 230 teachers and nineteen thousand pupils. One thousand soldiers, four thousand other adults, and fourteen thousand children were being taught.[29] Recognizing that the number of students assigned to each teacher was too large, Pease made an effort to employ additional instructors, and in New Orleans he succeeded in limiting the average teaching load to sixty pupils. One enthusiastic bureau agent then declared that the black schools of that city were superior to the white schools, but it is extremely doubtful that such outstanding results had been achieved in so short a time.[30] Conway was highly pleased with the progress in education under his direction, and Gen. Philip Sheridan reported in 1866 that schools had been established in most of the cities and parishes of the state. John W. Alvord, national superintendent of education for the Freedmen's Bureau, reported that the organization of colored schools in Louisiana was the largest and most excellent of any of the states. He boasted that more than fifty thousand freedmen had learned to read in New Orleans and vicinity.[31]

When freedmen learned to read and write, the major objective of bureau schools had been accomplished, since the curriculum emphasized only the most rudimentary approach to learning. While a few institutions in New Orleans gave courses in industrial arts for boys and cooking and sewing for girls, most of the teachers strove to acquaint their charges with the alphabet, spelling, reading, arithmetic, geography, and grammar. Copy books and slates aided the learning process, when there was money to buy them, and the texts included *McGuffey's Primer* and readers, *Monteith's National Geography, Spencer's English Grammar, and Price's English Speller.* Courses in oratory and religion were sometimes offered, depending on the tastes and views of the instructors. The blending of religious teaching with secular instruction produced considerable confusion and complaint, with bureau officials and teachers alike seeming to believe that government schools were legitimate areas of religious propagandizing.[32]

Problems of teachers and curricula were insignificant compared with the over-whelming difficulty of supporting the schools with the meager funds that were available. Little help was extended to Louisiana by Northern aid associations, since it was generally thought that the tax imposed by General Banks would pay all expenses.[33] That tax, however, failed to provide the necessary funds. In December, 1865, General Baird stated that teachers' salaries were three months in arrears in the amount of $57,000, and that an additional $19,000 would be required to pay full salaries for December.[34] The total cost of school operations for the last four months of 1865 was $87,283.79.[35]

The extreme financial difficulties facing the bureau's educational work provoked a controversy over the school tax that General Banks had authorized when he set up the system of army-supervised schools in March, 1864. At the end of October, 1865, [James S.] Fullerton estimated that if the tax had been collected, the amount accruing to the bureau would have been $228,000. At that time, however, the bureau had received only $52,000 from that source, and Fullerton wired Andrew Johnson that he would be unable to collect any more money without the use of military force.[36] The president's reply suggested that he suspend collection of the tax. On the following December 13, Baird urged his superiors to try to get the tax reinstated, on the ground that the money was badly needed and that "disloyal" men ought to pay the tax that had already been paid by "loyal" citizens. General Howard then ordered collection of the tax, and the matter of its continuance remained a source of confusion. In April the Louisiana house and senate passed a joint resolution, asking relief from the tax, to which Johnson replied that the levy had been suspended. Nevertheless, bureau records indicate that $50,749 was collected under the terms of Banks's order during the first nine months of 1866.[37]

The financial crisis toward the end of 1865 threatened to close the Negro schools. Realizing the gravity of the situation, certain black citizens petitioned General Canby to assess a tax against Negroes for the purpose of continuing the work. Among the petitions that poured in, mostly from the middle and lower income groups, was one thirty feet long with a thousand signatures. Not all Negroes favored the plan, however, for the *New Orleans Tribune* attacked special assessments against Negroes as taxation without representation. The opposition of that paper, combined with that of the wealthy Negroes of New Orleans, caused Canby to decide against that method of raising funds.[38]

A circular from Freedmen's Bureau headquarters, December 27, 1865, directed that all schools be suspended at the end of the following month. The Negro schools accordingly closed on January 31, 1865, with a debt of $80,000 hanging over them. The *New Orleans True Delta* lost little time in attempting to turn the situation against the bureau, inquiring as to what had become of the "heavy taxes recently collected . . . [and] the enormous receipts from abandoned lands?"[39] The funds which the *True Delta* mentioned were the subject of some friction within the army, with the quartermaster corps and the bureau each claiming jurisdiction. General Baird had continued the schools throughout January at the request of General Canby, under the impression that money would be forthcoming from resources created by selling confiscated property. At the time, Canby had about $900,000 of such money on hand, and at Baird's request, he agreed to transfer $50,000 to the bureau to pay teachers, but Gen. Philip Sheridan countermanded the order on the ground that the money could not legally be spent in that manner. Baird then urged Colonel Max Woodhull, acting adjutant general in Washington, to ask Commissioner Howard to use his influence to obtain funds for the bureau. In April sufficient funds were released from this source to relieve the financial strain of the bureau's school system, so far as indebtedness was concerned, but no regular system of support was established.[40]

Meanwhile, bureau officials were making desperate efforts to establish schools on a self-supporting basis. On February 5, 1866, Baird issued an order setting up a tuition plan. Tickets were to be sold in the towns at the rate of $1.50 per month for intermediate pupils and $1.00 for primary students, and in the country a tax of 5 percent was to be charged on the incomes of all Negroes. Strong objections on the part of some freedmen soon led to a modification of the provision, so that Negroes who had no children in school or groups unanimously opposed to the plan were not required to pay the tax.[41]

Many of the teachers who had worked under the former system attempted to continue under the new one, with extremely disappointing results. The new arrangement resulted in such drastic reductions in pay that some teachers received only $8.00 or $10.00 per month, and one by one the schools were discontinued. By March, 1866, the average monthly pay of teachers had declined to $31, less than half the amount they had received in January under the old system. Funds for their support were lacking because freedmen objected to paying the 5 percent tax or the tuition required in the towns. Even if freedmen had been willing and able to pay $1.50 per month, which was by no means the case, a teacher with sixty pupils would have received only $90, an amount insufficient to rent a schoolroom and support a teacher.[42]

The effect of the change was catastrophic. From an organization that was the largest of any state and that Alvord praised as unexcelled, Negro schools in Louisiana fell to a condition that the same official described as "paralyzed." A program that boasted 150 schools with 265 teachers and 19,000 pupils at the beginning of 1866 declined by July to 73 schools, 90 teachers, and 3,389 students, if the most generous report is to be received at face value. If, instead of Alvord's statistics, those of Frank Chase, state superintendent of education for the bureau, be accepted, the number enrolled in bureau schools at that time was only 2,239, with 76 teachers in 66 schools.[43]

To add to the chaos already prevailing, private schools for Negroes sprang up outside bureau control. Their teachers were mostly Negroes who could barely read and write, but their lower tuition rates attracted pupils who might otherwise have attended bureau institutions. Enrollment in such schools grew from 150 in February to nearly 3,000 in December, and actually exceeded the number registered in bureau schools. In that month private schools in New Orleans had 1,200 pupils, while only 396 were enrolled in schools directed by the bureau.[44]

Congress recognized to some extent that lack of funds was the chief hindrance in the way of Negro education, and on July 16, 1866, passed an act appropriating $521,000 for educational expenses in the South. Money from this source, together with funds obtained from the sale of confiscated property, was to be used for the purpose of renting or leasing buildings, while private benevolent groups were expected to pay teachers. The appropriation was of little benefit to the freedmen of Louisiana, for as late as October the bureau reported that not one dollar had been received from benevolent associations, although some of them had attempted to interfere in the schools. An additional $500,000 was then voted by Congress for support of freedmen's schools in the South on March 2, 1867.[45]

Even with the additional sum, total funds available to the bureau in 1866 and 1867 were insufficient to enable the agency to carry on an effective educational program. The cost of operating Negro schools in Louisiana during 1866 was $51,000. Of that amount, $26,000 had been raised from tuition tickets and the 5 percent tax. After January the bureau supplied only 97,500 toward maintaining the schools,[46] and the amount expended by the agency in 1867 was even less than the previous year. For the fiscal year ending September 30, 1867, the bureau listed expenditures from its own funds of only $10,000, and during the same period $23,000 was collected from freedmen, presumably to pay teachers.[47] In January, 1867, there were fifty-six bureau schools, employing sixty teachers, and enrolling 2,527 pupils. Sixty-five private schools brought the total number of pupils of both types of institutions for freedmen to 5,494. By October 11 the total had declined to 4,173, a figure much smaller than the number of working children among freedmen. The actual number of pupils in freedmen's schools in 1867 was less than half the number Commissioner Howard later reported in his *Autobiography.*[48]

As harassed bureau officials sought a solution to their financial problems in Negro education, they began to demand that state taxes paid by Negroes be used for the education of their children. Superintendent Chase estimated in March, 1867, that the Negroes of Louisiana had paid $84,000 in state or municipal taxes in 1866, but that the money had been used exclusively, so far as education was concerned, for white schools. Alvord took up the complaint in a report to Commissioner Howard, and by the end of the year agents of the bureau were urging state and local legislation looking coward the establishment of a public school system that would include freedmen.[49]

City authorities in New Orleans passed resolutions in May with a view of accepting public responsibility for educating freedmen. An education committee was appointed to make recommendations regarding needs and methods of meeting them. The *New Orleans Republican,* a Radical newspaper, sharply criticized what the committee seemed about to do, stating that schools were being planned for only five thousand black children, when there were twenty-one thousand in the city for whom facilities should be provided. The paper urged passing a school ordinance admitting all children of the parish to public schools without mention of color. In October the school board appropriated $70,000 for Negro education for the following year and made plans not only to segregate the races but to instruct males and females in separate schools. Thus the freedmen's schools of New Orleans were transferred to local authorities. Bureau officials believed that the facilities furnished by the city were insufficient to accommodate half of the colored children who needed to be in school. However, William O. Rogers, city superintendent, stated in reply that none of the Negro schools were crowded and that colored people were no longer attracted by the novelty of education.[50]

Although Negro schools in New Orleans were no longer the immediate responsibility of the bureau, the agency continued to maintain inspection of them. The new arrangement was much more successful than the old tuition plan. From twenty-one schools with 908 pupils in September, 1867, schools for freedmen in New Orleans increased to twenty-six in November, 1868, with 3,935 students enrolled. Although bureau officials commended the New Orleans school board for doing the best it could, the impoverished condition of the city treasury made it necessary to pay teachers in script that they could cash only at a heavy discount. In certain of the most needy and deserving cases, the bureau provided relief for unfortunate teachers by making a small monthly allotment to them.[51] Schools outside the city continued under the direct supervision of the bureau, and during 1868 they experienced further growth. At the beginning of the year there were 96 teachers in 117 schools, including 30 Sabbath schools. The figures represented an increase over the same month of the preceding year. In May, bureau schools reported an enrollment of 3,941 pupils in 132 schools with 108 teachers. At the same time, the public school enrollment for Negroes, presumably all located in New Orleans, was 3,857 pupils, and private institutions counted 2,179 on their instruction lists. Although there had been an increase over the previous year, the total of less than 10,000 pupils in colored schools of all kinds indicated that the educational program of the bureau failed, to reach many of the Negro children of the state.[52]

The plan of attempting to support school by means of the 5 percent tax or tuition system was, in most respects, a failure. Evidence in the records of the bureau overwhelmingly indicates that lack of financial support, rather than any other hindrances, prevented the greater growth of education in Louisiana. "The great drawback to education," Asst. Commissioner Robert C. Buchanan stated, "is not the opposition of the whites thereto, except in a few cases, but the want of means to support schools."[53] Most of Louisiana's white citizens were indifferent or antagonistic toward the establishment of schools for the former slaves. "A country lately in the throes of revolution," wrote Mayor Hugh Kennedy of New Orleans, was "not exactly in the mood for academical discussions."[54] A people who had seen their social and economic system overthrown were more interested in repairing their fortunes than in promoting education among their former slaves. Moreover, to the white people of Louisiana who had seen few free schools for their own children outside New Orleans, education for the Negro masses was a new and startling concept.

The racial prejudice of Southern whites was recalled by John W. Alvord, national superintendent of education for the Freedmen's Bureau. As Alvord walked the streets of New Orleans with a conservative legislator early in 1866, they approached a Negro school. The lawmaker asked, "Is this a school?"

"Yes," Alvord replied.

"What! of niggers?" the lawmaker exclaimed, " . . . this is the climax of absurdities!" Alvord considered the attitude typical of the majority of Louisiana's white citizens, despite the fact that the constitution of 1864 had provided for the establishment of colored schools.[55] Those who wished to keep Negroes in a menial status opposed such schools on the theory that freedmen would have to be kept ignorant if they were to remain dependable laborers.[56] Denouncing "wild theories of equality," the conservative *New Orleans Times* advocated industrial training for Negroes and predicted that most of them would be "hewers of wood and drawers of water for generations yet to come."[57] The *New Orleans Crescent,* organ of secessionist sentiment in prewar days, doubtless spoke for a large segment of the population when it said: "Rid the South of the 'freedmen's bureau,' the school marms and the peripatetic newsmongers from the East, and Sambo will occupy his normal position as a cultivator of the soil and a confiding dependent of his former friend and master."[58]

Additional causes of white hostility, to Negro schools were opposition to the tax that was levied for their support by General Banks; the inconvenience of the 5 percent payroll deduction plan established by the Freedmen's Bureau; fears that the schools would become political instruments of the Republican party; and religious convictions. Wherever they were dominant, Catholics opposed bureau schools because they believed such institutions tended to spread secular or even Protestant ideas.[59]

Intense opposition met the bureau's educational endeavors from their beginning. Thomas W. Conway, who launched the agency's program in Louisiana, said that the work faced hate and hostility. Ephraim Stoddard, supervisor in New Orleans, observed that former slaveholders "tried every means a hellish purpose could devise" to break up Negro schools. Alvord reported to Commissioner Howard that teachers faced ostracism wherever they went, and Assistant Commissioner Joseph Mower testified that their work was regarded as "odious and scandalous." Frank Chase, state superintendent of bureau schools, affirmed after two years in Louisiana that, in his opinion, only five of the forty-three parishes of the state would vote for Negro schools.[60]

Teachers in freedmen's schools found it difficult to obtain living quarters. Most planters refused to keep them in their homes. On one occasion, it was alleged, a planter who had been ordered by military authorities to board a teacher in his home sent his family away and converted his residence into a bawdy house.[61] Another teacher in a parish remote from New Orleans wrote of having to live with "dreadful people, dirty and vulgar . . . [with] nothing to eat but strong pork and sour bread," and being insulted as a "nigger teacher."[62]

Occasionally hostility toward colored schools went beyond taunts and insults to actual violence. In January, 1865, a school at Donaldsonville was burned, and, amid rumors of similar outbreaks, Conway ordered the arrest of any who interfered with educational institutions. Withdrawal of federal troops was sometimes the signal for the violent end of public schools. Minor annoyances, such as stones hurled by small boys, were considered by nervous teachers as portents of dreadful things to come. During the period of increased tension that followed the New Orleans riot of July, 1866, four school buildings in the city were burned. In 1868 a teacher's schoolroom was decorated with obscene pictures and language, and another teacher was murdered.[63] At Holmesville, Avoyelles Parish, a Negro teacher made the mistake, of voting Republican in 1868, and emissaries of the Ku Klux Klan visited the owner of the plantation where his school was located and informed him that they did not "want any d-d nigger School" there. The teacher was warned that some night he would "go up."[64]

Although sentiment against Negro schools was widespread and strong among most of the white people of Louisiana, a growing number of white citizens took a stand in favor of educating freedmen. The *Crescent* approved colored schools provided they were under Southern teachers who would save freedmen from the "mock philanthropists from Massachusetts."[65] *De Bow's Review* advocated education as a means of dissipating animosities and creating understanding between the races.[66] Planters increasingly came to believe that schooling made more efficient laborers of freedmen. In March, 1866, a traveling agent of the bureau reported that nine tenths of the planters in his district conceded the necessity of schools. By the first of the next year, some planters allowed teachers to board in their homes, and, in some cases, to give private instruction to their own children. Planters were known to maintain schools at their own expense and to donate land for the erection of school buildings, in order to obtain laborers more readily.[67]

Sentiment concerning schools for freedmen came to be divided somewhat along class lines. The division, however, was not that of the proletariat against greedy overlords, with poor whites making common cause with former slaves. Quite the reverse was true. The most intelligent and successful planters were usually the ones found supporting Negro education, while the bitterest opposition came from the lower classes.[68] All classes of Southern white people, however, opposed the Radical clamor to break down the barriers of segregation and enroll white and black children in the same schools. When the conservative legislature of Louisiana passed a law on February 15, 1865, forbidding such an arrangement, the *New Orleans Tribune* denounced the law and called for the elimination of all lines of distinction. The paper, edited by a Negro from Santo Domingo, replied to Gen. Stephen Hurlbut's plea that Negroes wait and work for advancement with a demand for a military order ending segregation.[69]

Freeborn Negroes joined white citizens in opposing nonsegregated schools. Although they did not enjoy a social status equal to that of white people, some of the Negroes who had been free before the war constituted an elite group among their color. Some were descended from refugees from the revolution in Haiti, while others were the offspring of white fathers and colored mothers. Many of them were referred to as "Creoles," a term usually applied to proud white citizens of French and Spanish descent. There were about two thousand such elite colored people in 1866 who had received a foreign education, and their number included merchants, bankers, and doctors.[70] Although members of this class allowed a few children of freedmen to attend one of their schools at St. Martinville, their usual policy was to exclude children of former slaves. Superintendent H. H. Pierce of the Freedmen's Bureau declared that white people of Louisiana would have sent their children to freedmen's schools more willingly than would these proud freeborn Negroes.[71]

Early attempts to break down segregation ended in failure. Franklin Institute opened in September, 1866, with the intention of admitting white and black students in New Orleans. About half of the one hundred pupils were of French or Italian descent and the other half colored. Fighting among the students soon ended the experiment, for they fought even after they were placed in separate rooms.[72]

The triumph of the Radicals in the congressional election of 1866 and the passing of the Reconstruction Acts of 1867 prepared the way for increased efforts in Louisiana toward ending segregation. A lively discussion of the issue dominated a meeting of the Louisiana Educational Association in New Orleans on September 21, 1867. The Reverend Mr. John Turner, presiding over the assembly, urged a spirit of moderation and tolerance. A Negro from Ohio, listed only as "Mr. Roxborough," spoke in favor of yielding to white demands for retaining segregation. He declared that only in that way would the work of education proceed without undue disturbance, and that something was better than nothing. Others, including P. M. Williams, a Negro teacher in the colored schools, were outspoken against segregation in all its forms and urged an immediate end to the practice.[73]

In November of that year, a convention largely elected by Negro voters met in New Orleans to draw up a new state constitution, and the document that was produced the following March provided for racial equality in public transportation, amusement centers, places of business, and schools.[74] The immediate result was not desegregation but a reaction that witnessed the decline of the number of white pupils in the schools that the Freedmen's Bureau had established. At no time were there more than fifty-four white students enrolled in freedmen's schools.[75] In November, 1868, not one white pupil was registered in such schools in New Orleans.[76] Apparently the *New Orleans Commercial Bulletin* had expressed white sentiment in asserting that the two colors would never be found in the same schoolroom unless the whites were "padlocked to the benches."[77]

During 1868 the bureau began a policy of withdrawal from responsibility for providing education for freedmen in Louisiana. In June Congress authorized the commissioner to sell school buildings to private organizations that would agree to maintain schools for freedmen. The response from Northern aid associations was so meager that bureau agents were still trying to erect buildings and pay teachers as late as November of that year.[78] Their efforts were largely unavailing, and Bureau schools were closed in nearly every parish of the state. The greatly diminished educational work of the bureau resulted in administrative changes that placed the ten northwest parishes of Louisiana under the same officer who supervised a large section of Texas. The remaining parishes of Louisiana were placed under E. W. Mason, who replaced H. H. Pierce as state superintendent for the bureau.[79]

With most of the bureau's work ended in Louisiana and the public schools generally closed to Negroes, Mason turned to Northern aid societies for help in extending education to freedmen. Public schools existed for only five thousand of the ninety thousand colored children of the state. White people were little better off, with only twelve schools outside New Orleans for ninety-four thousand educable children. The Crescent City had only fifty-three schools to serve approximately sixty-six thousand white pupils. Mason hoped, in view of these conditions, to enlist a greater degree of interest than Northern aid societies had previously shown in Louisiana.[80]

Mason offered financial assistance to religious organizations, chiefly the large Northern societies, in return for assurances that they would establish and maintain schools in Louisiana. Commissioner Howard had followed the policy for some time, and the practice had produced criticism of the government's support of sectarianism. Lyman Abbott, head of the nondenominational American Freedmen's Union Commission, objected to Howard's policy of matching funds with denominational agencies on the ground that church and state ought to remain separate in the United States. Abbott's objections were unavailing, however, and by July 1, 1867, the central office of his organization was closed, leaving the field largely to religious associations.[81]

J. W. Healy, Southern representative of the American Missionary Association, established headquarters in New Orleans in April, 1869, and rapidly extended the activities of that organization. In cooperation with the Freedmen's Bureau, his group supported thirty schools attended by about 3,000 pupils and was thus more active in educational work than all other such agencies combined.[82] In November of that year, the association opened Straight University in New Orleans in a building erected with the aid of $25,000 received from the Freedmen's Bureau. The institution was named in honor of Seymour Straight, a patron of the association, whose gifts helped to provide the land on which the university was located. In 1870 the institution had an enrollment of 900 students, but by 1872 the number was down to 413. The American Missionary Association also founded Baton Rouge College which was to serve as a normal school, and in 1870 it registered 250 students.[83]

The Northern Methodist Church became one of the chief educational agencies in Louisiana in 1869, and its efforts were also encouraged by the Freedmen's Bureau. In 1866 the Freedmen's Aid Society of that church had established a few schools in Louisiana that were, for the most part, maintained throughout the Reconstruction period.[84] The Methodist group expanded its efforts in 1869 mainly in the direction of higher education. Gen. Edward Hatch, then head of the Freedmen's Bureau, cooperated with John P. Newman, later to become Bishop Newman, in securing the coliseum in New Orleans for the purpose of establishing a normal school.[85] The bureau contributed $12,500 toward purchase of the property at the corner of Camp and Race streets, and the school opened on November 1. During the same year the Methodists opened Thomson University at Franklin, but because of small enrollments and financial burdens, the two schools were merged in 1873 and became known as New Orleans University. In 1888 only 228 students were enrolled in the school, and most of them were engaged in studies below the college level.[86]

Schools for Negroes grew to a remarkable extent through the bureau's cooperation with the American Missionary Association, the Methodist Freedmen's Aid Society, and the Free Mission Baptists. The bureau furnished small sums, usually about $500, toward construction of school buildings, and the societies established and maintained the schools.[87] In 1870 the religious groups increased their activities, and that year the bureau counted 686 colored schools with 41,160 pupils. Although the aid societies contributed significantly to the growth that had been achieved, perhaps the phenomenon is best explained by the fact that the legislature and school board pronounced against segregated schools that year, and, in effect, made Negro schools of many of the public schools of the state.[88]

Renewed efforts to desegregate the public institutions were made during the period when the bureau was relinquishing its control to the missionary organizations. In January, 1869, the *New Orleans Tribune,* the Negro newspaper that aspired to lead the freedmen, assailed Henry Clay Warmoth, carpetbag governor, for taking a stand against mixed schools, and called for legislation to render the constitution effective. Over Governor Warmoth's objections, the legislature passed laws affirming the right of all children between the ages of six and twenty-one, regardless of color, to attend schools supported by the state. The new legislation proved ineffective in ending segregation, however, largely because the lawmakers appropriated only enough money to pay officials and left nothing for extending the educational system.[89]

The following year, additional legislation looked toward abolishing racial discrimination in schools. Teachers refusing to admit any pupil would be subject to damage suits from offended parties, as well as fines and imprisonment. Authority was taken from local officials of New Orleans, and the schools of the city were placed under the state board.[90] The *New Orleans Picayune* declared that white people would resort to bloodshed before they would tolerate integrated schools. The paper voiced the fears of conservative white citizens in denouncing a Negro member of the legislature, one Isabelle, for saying he wished to see the races amalgamated. Commenting on Isabelle's proposal for a hotel where social equality would be practiced, the *Picayune* averred that only such persons as Governor Warmoth and "Parson" Conway, who was then state superintendent of education, would patronize it. The journal advised opponents of segregation to follow the examples of Philip Sheridan and Joseph Mower, who as former heads of the bureau had refused to tamper with Southern prejudice in that respect.[91]

After the legislation had been passed, Conway advised the people to be calm and accept his assurance that there would be far less trouble than some of them anticipated. The matter was soon put to a test, when colored students attempted to enroll in Fisk School in New Orleans. On the morning of May 8, 1870, eight Negroes applied for admission of their children, and even before the teacher could reply, the white pupils took their books and left the building. The incident produced great excitement in the crowd of black and white people who had gathered to watch the outcome. A similar scene occurred the following day at the Bienville Street School. E. W. Mason, bureau superintendent of education, reported the event to his superiors in Washington and predicted that after the excitement had died down, the schools would be conducted as before. Thus the bureau's superintendent aligned himself with his predecessors in refusing to work actively for nonsegregated schools.[92]

Conway and other Radicals, undaunted in their determination to desegregate the schools, gained a temporary victory in New Orleans from 1871 through most of 1874. Undeterred by legal fights and delaying tactics of segregationists, proponents of mixed schools persisted until they won a decisive court case in December, 1870, that enabled integration to begin in New Orleans public schools. Urban, cosmopolitan society combined with favorable political forces to make possible a notable, though temporary, success in desegregating at least five schools in the Crescent City.[93] Elsewhere in the state the effect of the school law was the establishment of private institutions for white children, inasmuch as state funds were largely expended on schools theoretically open to all, but actually attended by Negroes. This situation provoked a controversy between Conway and the administrators of the Peabody Fund, which aided some of the private white schools. Conway accused Robert Lusher, Louisiana agent for the fund, of racial prejudice in favor of the whites. Barnas Sears, general agent for the foundation, supported Lusher's practice on the ground that since the bulk of public money went to Negro schools, it was the business of his group to help those most in need. According to Conway, however, a scarcity of funds deprived the schools of significant aid from the state. He declared that state tax money would not support schools more than a month, and that local groups refused to vote levies for schools because of crop failures and fear of mixed institutions.[94]

The eager response of freedmen to the educational opportunities that were given them is no less than amazing when measured against the obstacles that stood in their way. Bureau officials bore witness to their enthusiasm. In a speech to a large audience at the New Orleans Theatre, November 5, 1865, General Howard said: "Whatever burdens you may be obliged to bear, whatever taxes you may be obliged to pay do not let the children's education be neglected." His hearers responded with cries of "Never!"[95] The following month, Mortimer A. Warren, bureau superintendent in New Orleans, noted that the continued attendance of nearly three fourths of the students, in spite of cold or smoke-filled buildings, proved the reality of their thirst for knowledge.[96] Numerous appeals described by Asst. Commissioner Absalom Baird as "most pathetic" reached the bureau for the establishment of schools in areas where they did not exist.[97] Superintendent Mason reported that two pupils had walked nine miles each way for six months to attend school.[98]

Notwithstanding the eagerness demonstrated by many freedmen, the majority of the Negro children of the state were never enrolled in any bureau school long enough to acquire even the most rudimentary knowledge of reading and writing; in fact, most of them were not enrolled at all. Never more than a fraction of the total colored population, the enrollment in Negro schools, as noted earlier, took a sudden and near catastrophic drop when financial difficulties forced the closing of free schools early in 1866.

When the free institutions were discontinued, many freedmen demonstrated their concern for education by accepting a heavy burden of taxation, and bore the major part of the cost of maintaining their schools from 1866 through 1868.[99] When the bureau made payment of the school tax optional, many of them elected to pay the assessment, although the majority chose ignorance for their children, a decision often based on deep poverty rather than lack of interest in education.[100] Among a people who subsisted at the lowest economic level, who needed their children to work, and whose meager incomes barely kept them alive, that some were willing to be taxed at all was a tribute to the immense potential for progress that was within them. Their determination to improve themselves was one of the most inspiring phases of a period of social chaos and uncertainty.

For those who remained in school, advancement was often more apparent than real. bureau officials boasted that great progress was made and that Negro schools were equal to white schools, which could, have been true and still have meant little.[101] Efforts to demonstrate the progress of the pupils often ended in ludicrous performances. On one occasion at a New Orleans school a thirteen-year-old girl made a verbose speech in praise of a Northern relief association, but the oratorical effort was obviously the work of the teacher.[102] In January, 1867, when nearly 5,000 pupils were registered in the freedmen's schools of New Orleans, 93 were able to read easy lessons and 299 were advanced readers.[103] A normal school for training teachers, praised by bureau officials in 1866 as a model institution, was described the next year by Ephraim Stoddard, a bureau teacher and superintendent, as "about played ot [out] entirely."[104] On January 5, 1869, the *New Orleans Tribune,* the Negro newspaper that had favored the bureau's educational efforts, pronounced the schools throughout the state a failure, except in the parishes of Orleans and Jefferson. Even in those parishes, said the *Tribune,* political mismanagement had hindered the progress of education, and ignorant school directors and teachers had been too often appointed for political reasons.

A lack of competent teachers was a constant problem in the freedmen's schools, and many of those who were employed were described in bureau records as "generally inefficient." In a period of distress and confusion, incompetent and disreputable people sought personal advantage wherever they could, and some of them found positions as teachers in the colored schools. Incompetent teachers "grievously imposed upon" freedmen in the northwestern part of the state, according to H. H. Pierce, bureau superintendent. In individual instances of unfit and unreliable teachers, one engaged in vitriolic denunciation of Roman Catholics in an area where that religion was dominant, while others dismissed school to go fishing, became involved in partisan politics, and violated accepted moral standards. Accusations of using harsh and abusive language toward their charges and generally fomenting strife were made against some instructors.[105]

On the other hand, some teachers received and clearly merited high praise from their superiors. Ephraim Stoddard, who rose from teacher in the New Orleans freedmen's schools to state superintendent of education, was often commended for his sincerity, zeal, and ability. Superintendent Chase stated in 1868 that most teachers in New Orleans were excellent. In the face of many obstacles, including taunts, social ostracism, and meager pay, many teachers carried on their work with a sincere sense of the mission they were fulfilling. Among them were such Negroes as P. M. Williams of New Orleans and Gertrude Velasco of St. Francisville, both of whom were outstanding examples of ability and devotion to duty.[106]

The most significant and outstanding failure of the bureau was apparent as early as 1866, when a growing and prosperous school system suddenly collapsed for lack of funds. It was unmistakably evident that the one obstacle that stood between the agency and a large measure of success was insufficient backing. After meager appropriations by Congress failed to remove the deficiency, it became customary for those who had been loud in lip service to the cause of Negro education to blame failures on white opposition. Undeniably such hostility did exist, but never to the point of disrupting the work in the state as a whole. To insist that the contrary is true is to set aside attendance figures and testimony of the bureau's highest officials.

The accomplishments of the Freedman's Bureau in education in Louisiana seemed at the time to be little more than lighting a weak candle in a dark night, but that it burned at all despite the gusty winds of the Reconstruction Era was a magnificent achievement. The precedents established by the bureau illuminated the actions of generations to come. The agency deserves high praise for beginning a system of public schools for freedmen in New Orleans and in the state. Its efforts stimulated interest in education not only among freedmen, but also among the white people. Its ministrations awakened the ruling classes to the wisdom and necessity of providing at least a minimum of education for all the poor and ignorant, both Negro and white. With prophetic vision Superintendent Mason wrote: "The fact cannot be denied that the elevation of the Freedmen has been the elevation of the white race, and the bureau will be recognized in coming times, as an important agent in redeeming of the people from ignorance and semi-barbarism."[107]

Notes for "'Redeeming of the People from Ignorance'"

[1]Clement Eaton, *A History of the Old South* (New York, 1949), 403, 476; *New Orleans Times,* September 12, 1865; Harvey Wish, *Society and Thought in America* (New York, 1950), 1, 440.

[2]Rush Plumly Report, *Report of the Board of Education for Freedmen, Department of the Gulf for the Year 1864* (New Orleans, 1865), 1. In 1850 there were one thousand Negro children in such schools in Orleans Parish. Donald E. Everett, "Free Persons of Color in New Orleans, 1803-1865" (Ph.D. dissertation, Tulane University, 1952), 260. There were between fifteen and twenty schools for free-born Negroes in New Orleans in 1866. One of them, founded in 1847, had 260 pupils and seven teachers in 1866. [Nathan Willey], "Education of the Colored Population of Louisiana," *Harpers Magazine,* 33 (1866): 246-47.

[3]Levi Peirce, Miles Taylor, William W. King, comps., *The Consolidation and Revision of the Statutes of a General Nature* (New Orleans, 1852), 552.

[4]Plumly Report, *Report of the Board of Education for Freedmen,* 4. In the period just prior to the Civil War, Northerners who attempted to organize Negro schools were not allowed to carry out their projects. John F. Cook, of St. Louis, was forced to abandon such a school in 1859. Everett, "Free Persons of Color in New Orleans, 1803-1865," 260; Honorine A. Sherman, "The Freedmen's Bureau in Louisiana" (M.A. Thesis, Tulane University, 1936), 21.

[5]*Second Annual Report of the New England Freedmen's Aid Society* (Boston, 1864), 47-49; *New Orleans Tribune,* September 20, 1864.

[6]Ford Report, June 16, 1864, RG 105, Box 277; Mason to Alvord, January 1, 1870, ibid., General Records, Box 1094.

[7]Mason Report, January-June, 1870, ibid., General Records, Box 1094; Plumly Report, *Report of the Board of Education for Freedmen,* 1; Ephraim Stoddard Scrapbook, Ephraim Stoddard Collection (Tulane University Archives), 11, 4 (hereafter cited Stoddard Scrapbook); *House Executive Documents* 39th Cong. 1st Sess., No. 70, p. 338; John W. Alvord, *Semi-Annual Reports of Schools and Finances for Freedmen,* 10 vols. (Washington, 1866-70), 1:8-9.

[8]Stoddard Scrapbook, 11, 4.

[9]Wheelock to Banks, April 1, 1864, RG 105, 38.

[10]The other schools were in the parishes of Iberville, Ascension, Baton Rouge, Assumption, Lafourche, St. Mary, Plaquemines, St. Bernard, Jefferson, St. Charles, St. John, and Terrebonne. Report of Schools, September 16, 1864, ibid., 46.

[11]Banks to Chickering, August 12, 1864, ibid., Box 277.

[12]Hurlbut to Plumly, October 20, 1864, ibid.

[13]Plumly to Howard, June 13, *1865,* ibid., General Records, Box 1094.

[14]Oliver Otis Howard, *Autobiography,* 2 vols. (New York, 1907), 2:302.

[15]Mason Report, January-June, 1870, RG 105, General Records, Box 1094.

[16]Howard to Wheelock, June 29, 1865, ibid., Box 276.

[17]Conway to Wheelock, June 29, 1865, ibid.

[18]Plumly to Howard, June 13, 1865, ibid., General Records, Box 1094.

[19]Stoddard Scrapbook, 9:4.

[20]Conway to Newman, August 3, 1865, RG 105, 15; Special Order No. 185, July 11, 1865, ibid., Box 262.

[21]*American Missionary,* 8 (1864): 150, quoted in Henry L. Swint, *The Northern Teacher in the South, 1862-1870* (Nashville, 1941), 51.

[22]Roster of Civilians, September, 1865, RG 105, Box 262; H. R. Pease Report, September 1865, ibid., General Records, Box 1094.

[23]H. R. Pease to Conway, October 11, 1865, ibid., Box 277.

[24]H. R. Pease Report, September 6, 1865, ibid., General Records, Box 1094; Mower Report, 1867, ibid., Box 263; Abstract of Reports, November, 1866—December, 1868, ibid., General Records, 46.

[25]*New Orleans Times,* March 18, 1865; Buchanan Report, May, 1868, RG 105, Box 263.

[26]*New Orleans True Delta,* quoted in *Flake's Daily Galveston Bulletin,* January 5, 1866.

[27]Conway to H. R. Pease, October 10, 1865, RG 105, Box 248.

[28]Baird to Woodhull, December 13, 1865, ibid., 27; Chase Report, October 21, 1866, ibid., General Records, Box 1094.

[29]*New York Tribune,* July 25, 1865.

[30]Stoddard Scrapbook, 11, 7, 8. The statement is contained in an unidentified newspaper clipping reporting on "Colored Schools in New Orleans" and signed "E. F. W." It is probable that "E. F. W." was E. F. Warren, who served in New Orleans as a director of Bureau schools. He was so listed in 1866. H. R. Pease Report, January 31, 1866, RG 105, Reports and Letters, Box 277.

[31]Telegram, Conway to Howard, July 5, 1865, RG 105, 15; Sheridan Report, 1866, ibid., General Records, Box 777; *House Executive Documents,* 39th Cong., 1st Sess., No. 70, pp. 338-39; Alvord, *Semi-Annual Reports on Schools and Finances for Freedmen,* 1:8-9.

[32]School Record, RG 105, 46; Parker Report, 1867, ibid., Microfilm; H. L. Irwin to Pierce, December 2, 1868, ibid., 349; O. D. Stillman to R. M. Lusher, September 8, 1866, Correspondence, Louisiana Department of Education, Box 20; Invoice, Barnes & Burr, September 16, 1864, RG 105, Box 277; Hanks to "Col. Frisbie," May 30, 1864, RG 105, General Records, 8; *New Orleans Crescent,* November 29, 1866; Dunwell to Sterling,

May 14, 1868, RG 105, 469; Industrial School Report, December 1, 1865, RG 105, 277; Stoddard Diary, January 24, 1867.

[33]Chase Report, October 21, 1866, RG 105, General Records, Box 1094; Jacob Shipherd to H. R. Pease, November 25, 1865, ibid., Box 276; Howard Report, *Senate Executive Documents,* 39th Cong., 2nd Sess., No. 6, p. 76. Exceptions to the general lack of Northern support were nine schools operated by the Freedmen's Aid Society of the Methodist Church, and six schools operated by the American Freedmen's Union Commission. *National Freedman,* 1 (1865), 270; ibid., 2 (1866), 157, 168; J. C. Hartzell, ed., *Reports of the Freedmen's Aid Society of the Methodist Episcopal Church, 1866-1875* (Cincinnati, 1893), First Annual Report, 10; *American Freedmen,* 1 (1866): 26.

[34]Telegram, Conway to Howard, July 5, 1865, KG 105, 15; telegram, Fullerton to Woodhull, October 18, 1865, ibid., Baird to Canby, December 6, 1865, ibid., 17.

[35]H. R. Pease Report, 1865, ibid., Box 248; Sheridan Report, 1866, ibid., General Records, 135.

[36]H. R. Pease to Fullerton, October 21, 1865, ibid., Box 277; telegram, Fullerton to Johnson, October 30, 1865, ibid., 15.

[37]Stoddard Scrapbook, 11, 4; Baird to Woodhull, December 13, 1865, RG 105, 27; Sheridan Report, 1866, ibid., General Records, Box 777; *New Orleans Crescent,* April 14, 1866.

[38]Alvord to Howard, January 1, 1866, RG 105, General Records, 8; Thomas Report, July 18, 1866, ibid., 17.

[39]Chase Report, October 21, 1866, ibid., General Records, Box 1094; Thomas Report, July 18, 1866, ibid., 17.

[40]Thomas Report, July 18, 1866, ibid., 17; Baird to Woodhull, March 9, 1866, ibid.

[41]Chase Report, 1866, ibid., General Records, Box 1094; Hayden to Brough, May 14, 1866, ibid., 17; Stoddard Scrapbook, 11, 4; Report to Howard, October, 1866, RG 105, Box 263.

[42]Report to Howard, October, 1866, ibid., Box 263; ibid., May 7, 1866, 17; Chase Reports, October 21, 1866, February 7, 1867, ibid., General Records, Box 1094.

[43]Alvord to Howard, January 1, July 1, 1866, ibid., General Records, 8; H. R. Pease Report, August 31, 1865, ibid., Box 248. According to Chase, the month with the highest enrollment after January was November, when 2,628 students were registered in 61 schools. Enrollment in private schools added 2,954 pupils to the total. Chase Report, February 7, 1867, ibid., General Records, Box 1094. Chase stated that drastic reductions in personnel after January 31, 1866, made it impossible to compile accurate records, ibid., October 21, 1866.

[44]Alvord to Howard, July 1, 1866, ibid., General Records, VII; Sheridan Report, October 31, 1866, ibid., General Records, 135; Financial and Statistical Report of Freedmen's Schools, October 1—December 31, 1866, ibid., Box 262; Chase Report, February 7, 1867, ibid., General Records, Box 1094.

[45]*Statutes at Large,* 19 (1868), 434.

[46]Chase Report, February 7, 1867, RG 105, General Records, Box 1094.

[47]School Report, 1867, ibid., General Records, Box 777; Reports of Expenditures, October 1, 1866-September 30, 1867, ibid., Microfilm.

[48]General Howard stated: "The number, however, was not large enough for that great State—only 246 schools with pupils 8,455." Howard, *Autobiography,* 2:342. For other figures see Chase Report, February 18, 1867, RG 105, General Records, Box 1094; Ward Reports, October 11, 1867, ibid., Microfilm.

[49]Chase Report, January, 1867, RG 105, General Records, Box 1094; ibid., March 18, 1867; Alvord to Howard, July 1, 1867, ibid., General Records, 8; Chase Circular Letter, December 30, 1867, ibid., 27.

[50]Mower Report, 1867, ibid., Box 263; ibid., May, 1867; *New Orleans Republican,* April 16, October 15, 25, 1867; *New Orleans Crescent,* September 22, October 3, 13, 18, 1867; Mower to Whittlesey, November 5, 1867, RG 105, 19; Wood Report, December, 1867, ibid., Box 263; Rogers to Mason, December 29, 1869, ibid., General Records, Box 1094.

[51]Statistical Report of Schools, 1867-1868, ibid., General Records, Box 1095; Pierce to Alvord, October 1, 1868, ibid.

[52]Chase Reports, February, June, 1865, ibid., General Records, Box 1059; Report of Schools, May, 1861, ibid., Box 263. In Natchitoches Parish there were three Negro schools when, in the opinion of the Bureau agent, there should have been thirty. Most parishes in the state had fewer than three Negro schools, and some of them had none. Those with no schools included St. Helena, Vermilion, Franklin, Caldwell, Tensas, Claiborne, and Bienville. In Bienville Parish, the state department of education reported that only 45 of 1,335 educable black children were in school. In that parish, on the other hand, a fairly high percentage of educable white children were in school, with 1,703 pupils out of a possible 2,043 enrolled. Hewlett to Pierce, October 14, 1868, ibid., 361; Alexander Hamilton Report, September 30, 1868, ibid., Dill; Edward Henderson Report, January 31, 1868, ibid.; Chase Report, June, 1868, ibid., General Records, Box 1095; Daniel Batchelor Report, February 22, 1866, Louisiana Department of Education Papers.

[53]Buchanan Report, April, 1868, RG 105, Box 263. Other testimony concerning the significant role of the lack of funds may be seen in Pierce Report, October 1, 1868, ibid., General Records, Box 1095; Chase Reports, February 18, March 25, 1868, ibid.; Garretty to L. H. Warren, January 31, February 29, 1868, ibid. 216; Buchanan Report, May 14, 1868, ibid., 469; Merrill to Pierce, September 3, 1868, ibid., 428; Francis Sternberg to Chase, March 26, 1868, ibid., 472.

[54]Kennedy to Johnson, September 12, 1865, Johnson Papers, 76, 6775-76.

[55]Alvord to Howard, January 1, 1866, RG 105, Educational Division, 8.

[56]Conway to Wheelock, July 17, 1865; ibid., 15; Masters Report, January 31, 1868, ibid., 503; Brough to Hayden, May 19, 1866, ibid., 307.

[57]June 25, 1864.

[58]September 5, 1866.

[59]*New Orleans Crescent,* April 14, 1866; Chase Report, July 14, RG 105, General Records, Box 1095; Mason Report, 1869, RG 105, Box 1094.

[60]Conway to Howard, July 6, 1865, RG 105, 15; Howard to Conway, July 15, 1865, ibid., Box 251; Alvord to Howard, January 1, 1866, ibid., General Records, 8; 392; Stoddard Scrapbook, 9, 4; Mower Report, August, 1867, RG 105, Box 263; Chase Report, June 16, 1868, RG 105, General Records, Box 1095.

[61]*New Orleans Tribune,* September 18, 1864. For additional evidence of difficulty in obtaining boarding places for teachers, see Plumly to Hurlbut, February 7, 1865, RG 105, 38; Alvord to Howard, July 1, 1867, ibid., General Records, 8; Mower Report, 1867, ibid., Box 263.

[62]Plumly Report, *Report of the Board of Education for Freedmen,* 8.

[63]Telegram, C. H. Newton to Wheelock, January 20, 1865, ibid., Box 276; *New Orleans Times,* July 17, 1865; Canby to Baird, November 17, 1865, RG 105, Box 249; J. Horace McGuire to Edward Henunivay, November 18, 1865, ibid., Hayden to De Grey, July 26, 1866, ibid., 18; Report to General Howard, October, 1866, ibid., Box 263; Sheridan Report, 1866, ibid., General Records, 135; unidentified newspaper clipping, Stoddard

Scrapbook, 11, 7, 8; Chase to L. H. Warren, June 8, 1868, RG 105, General Records, Box 769; Chase to Alvord, November 14, 1868, ibid., Box 1095.

[64]Chase Report, May 31, 1868, ibid., General Records, Box 1095.

[65]December 2, 1866.

[66]After the War Series, *DeBow's Review,* 1 (1866): 560; ibid., 3 (1867): 308.

[67]B. F. Burnham Report, March 13, 1866, RG 105, Box 277. Burnham traveled in Ouachita, Union, Morehouse, Winn, Caldwell, Franklin, Catahoula, and Concordia parishes. See also Chase Report, February 18, 1867, ibid., General Records, Box 1094; Alvord to Howard, January 1, 1867, ibid., 8; Mower Report, 1867, ibid., General Records, 136; Dunwell to L. H. Warren, January 31, 1868, ibid., 276; Mullen to L. H. Warren, February 20, 1868, ibid., 276; Webster Report, May, 1868, ibid., 275; John T. White to Pierce, September 13, 1868, ibid., 383; G. A. Hewlett to Pierce, October 14, 1868, ibid., 361; Mason to Alvord, January 1, 1871, ibid., General Records, 20.

[68]Alvord to Howard, July 1, 1866, RG 105, General Records, 8; W. H. Cornelius to Hayden, November 16, 1866, ibid., 447; Homer Report, February 18, 1868, ibid., 202; School Reports, November, 1868, ibid., Box 279; Chase Report, February, 1867, ibid., General Records, Box 1094.

[69]*New Orleans Tribune,* February 17, 23, March 29, 1865.

[70]Nathan Willey, "Education of the Colored Population of Louisiana," *Harper's Magazine,* 33 (1866): 246. See also Alvord to Howard, January 1, 1866, RG 105, General Records, 8.

[71]Cornelius to Hayden, November 16, 1866, RG 105, 447; O. H. Violet Report, January 31, 1868, ibid., 270; Pierce Report, 1868, ibid., General Records, Box 1095.

[72]*New Orleans Crescent,* September 15, 17, 1867.

[73]*New Orleans Republican,* September 21, 1867.

[74]John Rose Ficklen, *History of Reconstruction in Louisiana through 1888* (Baltimore, 1910), 198-99.

[75]Abstracts of Reports, October, 1866-December, 1868, RG 105, 46.

[76]School Reports, November, 1868, ibid., Box 279.

[77]October 9, 1867. The issues of September 13, October 4, 25, 1867, contain additional comment on the topic.

[78]*Statutes at Large,* 15 (1869): 83; RG 105, Circular Book, 7. Thomas W. DeKlyne, Circular Letter, November 10, 1868, ibid., 362.

[79]James McCleery to Conway, September 28, 1869, ibid., 440; Mason Report, July 13, 1869, ibid., General Records, 20.

[80]Mason Report, July 1, 1869, ibid., General Records, Box 1094; Chase Report, February, 1867, ibid., 18.

[81]Howard, *Autobiography,* 2:271; Ira V. Brown, *Lyman Abbott, Christian Evolutionist; A Study in Religious Liberalism* (Cambridge, 1953), 48, 49. Abbott's association maintained two schools in New Orleans and four in De Soto Parish in 1866. In 1867 the number had shrunk to three. *American Freedmen,* 1 (1866): 26; *American Freedman,* 2 (1867): 196; *National Freedman,* 2 (1866): 157, 168.

[82]A. D. Mayo, "The Work of Certain Northern Churches in the Education of the Freedmen, 1861-1900," *Report of the Commissioner of Education for the Year 1902* (Washington, 1903), 1, 288.

[83]Ibid.; Lucius Matlock to Mason, January 12, 1870, RG 105, General Records, Box 1094; *History of the American Missionary Association, with Facts and Anecdotes Illustrating its Work in the South* (New York, 1874), 36; Mason Report, January-June, 1870, RG 105, General Records, Box 1094.

[84]Methodists opened schools in 1866 at New Orleans, Baton Rouge, Thibodaux, Franklin, and Jefferson City. J. C. Hartzeli, *Reports of the Freedmen's Aid Society of the Methodist Episcopal Church, 1866-1875* (Cincinnati, 1893), First Annual Report, 10.

[85]Ibid., Third Annual Report, 10; Jay S. Stowell, *Methodist Adventures in Negro Education* (New York, 1922), 111.

[86]Matlock to Mason, January 12, 1870, RG 105, General Records, Box 1094; Hartzeli, *Reports of the Freedmen's Aid Society of the Methodist Episcopal Church, 1866-1875,* Third Annual Report, 10; Hartzell, Fourth Annual Report, 11; Hartzell, Sixth Annual Report, 21; J. C. Hartzell, ed., *Reports of the Freedmen's Aid and Southern Education Society of the Methodist Episcopal Church, 1888-1892* (Cincinnati, n.d.), Twenty-first Annual Report, 12, 31.

[87]Mason Reports, May-June, July 1, 1869, March 2, 1870, RG 105, General Records, Box 1094; List of Buildings, June 1-December 31, July 1-November 30, 1869, ibid.; Pierce Report, 1868, ibid., Box 1095; Report No. 21, *Index to House Reports of Committees,* 41st Cong., 2nd Sess., 30.

[88]Mason Report, January-June, 1870, RG 105, General Records, Box 1094. Few new schools were established in the northern part of the state. McCleery Report, June 30, 1870, ibid., 640; McCleery to Pempey Holmes, March 5, 1870, ibid.; McCleery to Whittlesey, n.d., 1870, ibid.; McCleery Report, March 15, 1870, ibid.; Mason to Alvord, January 1, 1871, ibid., General Records, Box 1094.

[89]*New Orleans Tribune,* January 1, 5, 12, 13, February 14, 1869; *New Orleans Republican,* January 25, 1870.

[90]Ella Lonn, *Reconstruction in Louisiana after 1868* (New York, 1918), 55-56; Myrtle H. Rey, "Robert M. Lusher and Education in Louisiana" (M.A. thesis, Tulane University, 1933), 12.

[91]February 9, 12, 13, 20, 1870.

[92]Mason Report, March 2, 1870, RG 105, General Records, Box 1094; *Annual Report, of the State Superintendent of Public Education for the Year 1870* (New Orleans, 1871), 28.

[93]For an extended discussion of desegregation in New Orleans, see Louis Harlan, "Desegregation in New Orleans Public Schools during Reconstruction," *American Historical Review,* 67 (1962): 663-75; for the political climate favorable to desegregation, see T. Harry Williams, "The Louisiana Unification Movement of 1873," *Journal of Southern History,* 11 (1945): 349-69.

[94]*Annual Report of the State Superintendent of Public Education for the Year 1870,* 41-42; Mason to Alvord, January 1, 1871, KG 105, General Records, Box 1094.

[95]Report of Howard Speech, ibid., Box 275.

[96]M. A. Warren Report, December, 1865, ibid., Box 278.

[97]Baird to Fournel, February 3, 1866, ibid., 17.

[98]Mason Report, January 1, 1871, ibid., General Records, 20.

[99]For additional evidence as to the willingness of many freedmen to pay the tax, see the report of B. F. Burnham, traveling agent of the educational department, March 13, 1866, ibid., Box 277, and the report of James Lewis, another traveling agent, March 11, 1866, ibid.

[100]One Bureau agent complained that thousands of freedmen spent more for balls and parties in a week than schooling for their children would have cost for a month. Report to Ketchurn, July 13, 1866, RG 105, 17. For other references to freedmen's attitudes toward payment of the tax, see Chase Report, January, 1867, ibid., General Records, Box 1094; ibid., February 18, 1868, Box 1095; Hayden to Brough, May 14, 1866, ibid., 17; Sheridan Report, October 31, 1866, ibid., General Records, 135; Cornelius to Chase, March 20, 1867, ibid., 447; Foiles Report, January, 1867, ibid., Box 342; Osbourne to Parker, September 10, 1867, ibid., 426; Randolph Report, April 12, 1866, ibid., Box 277; Thomas F. Monroe to Hastings, October 31, 1867, ibid., 439; Irwin to Pierce, December 1, 1868, ibid., 349; Dunwell to L. H. Warren, January 31, 1868, ibid., 276; Merrill to Pierce, September 3, 1868, ibid., 428; Hosner Report, February 13, 1868, ibid., 302.

[101]Report to General Howard, October, 1866, ibid., Box 263; Baird to Howard, May 7, 1866, ibid., 17; Stoddard Scrapbook, 11, 7; W. A. Brainerd to M. C. Cole, March 0, 1871, Correspondence, Louisiana Department of Education Papers, Box 20; Charles G. Austin, Jr., to Conway, July 11, 1870, ibid.; Garretty to L. H. Warren, April 30, 1868, RG 105, 216; Murphy Report, July 3, 1868, ibid., 299; Mower Report, 1867, ibid., Box 263.

[102]*New Orleans Republican,* June 7, 1867.

[103]School Report, October, 1866, KG 105, Box 342; Alvord to Howard, January 1, 1867, ibid., General Records, 8.

[104]Stoddard Diary, January 2, 1867.

[105]Pierce Report, 1868, RG 105, General Records, Box 1095; White to Pierce, September 12, 1868, ibid., 383; Benthien to Chase, July 31, 1868, ibid., 391; Finch to Chase, March 1, 1868, ibid., 468; Webster to Parker, August 31, 1867, ibid., 216; Mower Report, August, 1867, ibid., Box 263; Purchase Report, June, 1867, ibid., 274; H. R. Pease to Conway, October 10, 11, 1865, ibid., Boxes 248, 277; J. J. Moss to H. R. Pease, December 5, 1865, ibid., Box 278; Burnham Report, September 30, 1865, ibid.; Tyler Report, August 28, 1867, ibid., Box 277; A. E. Brown Report, September, 1865, ibid., Box 278; Edwin F. Warren to H. R. Pease, December 13, 1865, ibid., Box 277; M. A. Warren Report, January, 1866, ibid., Box 278; A. G. Studer to George Whipple, August 6, 1866, ibid., Box 277; Henry Savacool to Conway, August 29, 1865, ibid., Box 251; Report of Colored School Examinations, September 24, 1864, ibid., Box 277.

[106]Chase to Alvord, November 14, 1868, ibid., General Records, Box 1095; *New Orleans Republican,* June 28, 1867; Report to General Howard, October, 1866, RG 105, Box 263; Hill to Hutchins, October 31, 1868, ibid., 216; Dunwell to Sterling, May 14, 1868, ibid., 469; M. A. Warren Report, January, 1866, ibid., Box 278; Mason to Alvord, January 1, 1870, ibid., General Records, Box 1094; Alvord to Howard, January 1, 1866, ibid., 8; Stoddard Scrapbook, 10, n.p.

[107]Mason Report, June 30, 1869, RG 105, General Records, Box 1094.

DESEGREGATION IN NEW ORLEANS PUBLIC SCHOOLS DURING RECONSTRUCTION*

Louis R. Harlan

It is a fact not generally known even to historians that the New Orleans public schools during the Reconstruction period underwent substantial racial desegregation over a period of six and a half years, an experience shared by no other Southern community until after 1954 and by few Northern communities at the time. This essay is limited to a summary of the evidence that there was indeed desegregation in New Orleans in the 1870s and to an effort to explain it chiefly in terms of circumstances in New Orleans at the time. It is obvious that New Orleans, as the only real urban center in the overwhelmingly rural South, could not be an example from which any general conclusions can be drawn about Reconstruction in the region or even in Louisiana as a whole. The experience of one Southern urban community during Reconstruction, however, may hold interest for students of the rapidly urbanizing contemporary South.

For a generation of historians rather suddenly concerned with past struggles over civil rights, the interest of this study lies partly in the new crop that it makes in the much-plowed field of Reconstruction history. The historians both of Louisiana Reconstruction[1] and of Southern education[2] have pronounced the desegregation experiment of New Orleans an almost total failure. The conclusions of historians of the Dunning school may be explained by their preoccupation with political themes or their racialistic and sectional blind spots, but perhaps a better explanation is that they read in the partisan press the headlined stories of white walkouts and Negro evictions, but failed to note the undramatic evidence of the return of most of these pupils in the following days and months. Historians of Southern education seem to have relied too heavily on a secondary source by the Louisiana educational historian Thomas H. Harris, who in turn depended vaguely on the "testimony of men who lived through the period." Harris declared in 1924: "The

*First published in *American Historical Review*, 67 (1962): 663-75. Reprinted with the kind permission of the author and the publisher.

schools were never mixed. The law was evaded from the first, and the negroes were about as active in evading it as the whites."[3]

It is with some surprise, therefore, that we read the testimony in 1874 of Thomas W. Conway, the Radical state superintendent and prime mover of New Orleans desegregation:

> I had fully concluded to put the system of mixed schools to a thorough, practical test, and I did. The white pupils all left . . . and the school-house was virtually in the hands of the colored pupils. This was the picture one day. What will you think when I tell you that before I reached my office that day, the children of both races who, on the school question, seemed like deadly enemies, were, many of them, joined in a circle, playing on the green, under the shade of the wide spreading live oak. In a few days I went back to see how the school was progressing, and, to my surprise, found nearly all the former pupils returned to their places; and that the school, like all the schools in the city, reported at the close of the year a larger attendance than at any time since the close of the war. The children were simply kind to each other in the school-room as in the streets and elsewhere! A year ago I visited the same school and saw therein about as many colored children as whites, with not a single indication of any ill-feeling whatever.
>
> All that is wanted in this matter of civil rights is to let the foes of the measure simply understand that we mean it. Do this, and as in the case of the enemies of free schools in Louisiana, they will be quiet.[4]

The whole truth, of course, embraces both the historians' evidence of evasion and strident resistance and Conway's idyl of dancing on the green. Evasion lasted for three years, until the last legal recourse was exhausted, and then desegregation began. As desegregation spread slowly into more and more schools, as Conway said, there was indeed resistance, but it was fruitless, sporadic, separated by long periods of tacit acceptance, and successful in the end only because Reconstruction itself failed.

The forces of evasion were in effect even before the state constitution in 1867 prohibited the establishment of separate schools and required that no public schools should deny admission on account of race or color.[5] On the eve of the constitutional convention the city hastily established its first Negro schools to give credibility to its stand for "separate but equal" rather than desegregated schools,[6] and Freedmen's Bureau officials opposed to mixed schools[7] hastily transferred their local schools to the city board.[8] State Superintendent Robert M. Lusher resigned before the end of his term to become the state agent of the Peabody Education Fund, which spent more money in Louisiana than in any other state to aid in a system of private white schools.[9]

In New Orleans, where whites outnumbered Negroes nearly three to one, white Republicans in the city government cooperated with the city school board in efforts to thwart Superintendent Conway in his equally determined effort to give desegregation a thorough trial in that city. The city's newspapers meanwhile undertook to create an atmosphere of resistance and fear, advocating desertion of the schools en masse by the whites, establishment of private schools, and refusal to pay school taxes, and predicting the destruction of the public schools and race war.[10] The city school board resorted to a pupil replacement system[11] and all of the legal stratagems so familiar today. The loopholes of every school law were sought out, and a bewildering succession of suits and injunctions cluttered the courts. At one time five school cases were simultaneously on the dockets. Finally the sands of delay ran out; a court decision of December 1870 was acknowledged by all parties to be decisive, and desegregation began within a month.[12]

To overcome the forces of delay and evasion, the Radicals found it necessary to centralize and strengthen the school system. The city school board was replaced by another appointed by the state board of education, which in turn was appointed by the governor. The city board was allowed by state law to estimate its annual needs and require the city government to levy and collect a local tax sufficient to supply the amount. The high salaries that this arrangement made possible, though often tardily paid, attracted good local teachers and created a reasonably good *esprit de corps*.

The extent of desegregation cannot be measured precisely because the official reports made no separate accounting of the races and because the population of New Orleans was so peculiarly mixed, with so many very light colored persons and swarthy white ones, that observers often found it impossible to distinguish between them.[13] Nevertheless, there is considerable evidence of desegregation in official records and in newspapers, particularly in the reports of the annual examinations or closing exercises of the schools. From such sources it is possible to identify by name twenty-one desegregated schools and some others that may have been desegregated, about one-third of the city's public schools.[14] The school authorities at no time initiated desegregation, but simply required the admission of Negro children to white or mixed schools whenever they applied. Thus by choice or social pressure a majority of the city's school children attended either the separate Negro schools or white schools.[15] A surprising number of colored children, nevertheless, entered mixed schools under this arrangement. In 1877 the number was estimated at three hundred,[16] but that was some six months after the end of Reconstruction. Other evidence indicates that between five hundred and one thousand Negroes and several thousand whites attended mixed schools at the height of desegregation.[17] Light colored children, who could move about more easily in the white world, were usually the first to enter mixed schools and the last to leave them after Reconstruction, but children "as black as ebony" were reported "side by side with the fairest Caucasians" in the same classrooms.[18]

All of the five mixed schools with seventy-five or more Negroes enrolled were in the Second and Third Districts, below Canal Street, where descendants of the original French and Spanish inhabitants and the Irish, German, and Italian immigrants predominated. In this downtown area there was no rigid residential separation, and the houses of prostitution as well as school-houses were desegregated, though without causing as much public excitement. Since nearly all of the schools in these districts were desegregated,[19] one might assume that the character of the Latin or immigrant population explained everything. But this is not so. Negro residential areas were dispersed throughout the city, and some of the largest schools in the so-called American districts, the First and Fourth, contained Negro children.[20] One of these, the Fisk School, contained "a considerable number."[21] Below New Orleans proper, in the Fifth and Seventh Districts, the scattered settlements on both sides of the river contained some desegregated primary schools.[22] Of the city's three public high schools, two were desegregated. At the Lower Girls' High School, desegregation proceeded peacefully for years, about one-fifth of the students being colored.[23] At the Central Boys' High several Negro pupils attended after 1875,[24] and a Negro was professor of mathematics there for two years, until after the end of Reconstruction.[25]

Desegregation caused only a temporary decline of enrollment in the schools as a whole and in the mixed schools themselves. Enrollment dropped from 24, 892 to 19,091 in the first year of desegregation, but then rose steadily to 26,251 in 1875, which was higher than at any other time in the nineteenth century.[26] The report that 21,000 of these were white and 5,000 colored[27] indicates that there were actually more white pupils in the public schools during desegregation than either before or after.

In the desegregated schools the same trend was evident. The Fillmore Boys' School in the Third District, for example, was desegregated in 1871, when its enrollment as 377, and soon contained 100 colored pupils. In 1873 the conservative *New Orleans Times* reported 700 enrolled, "wonderful" attendance, and good discipline. Fillmore School was the largest in the city, crowded to capacity. In 1874 its enrollment reached 890, and the following year more of its graduates qualified for the high school, through competitive examinations, than those of any other boys' school.[28] Other mixed schools with large Negro enrollments had similar records of increasing enrollment and high academic standing. At the Bienville School, where attendance was cut in half in 1871 by desegregation and a river flood, both enrollment and average attendance by 1874 exceeded levels prior to desegregation. It sent more of its graduates to high school in 1873 than any other boys' schools.[29]

Why would desegregated schools be so crowded in a community as race conscious as New Orleans? The explanation seems to be that the quality of instruction was higher in those schools than in most of the others, because of the system of classification of elementary schools. Nearly all the mixed schools were classified as Grammar A schools, which had more teachers and a higher salary scale, and sent more graduates to the high schools than the Grammar B schools and Primary schools. Apparently this was why Negro schools were Grammar B, and, according to a report, "the mixed schools are the best in the city, and the colored schools the poorest—the poorest in quarters, furniture, text-books, and in every way."[30]

Desegregation of the public schools caused enrollment in private and parochial schools to increase, but not enough to damage the public schools. The most ambitious plan of the period, "an elaborate design for the establishment of schools by private enterprise," was presented to a mass meeting of citizens of the Second and Third Districts by former state superintendent Robert M. Lusher.[31] It temporarily evoked much enthusiasm, but Lusher later wrote: "The failure of the Canvassers appointed to raise means for making the plan effectual, to collect a sufficient amount, unfortunately caused the plan to be abandoned."[32] No coordination of private school efforts was ever developed.

Existing Catholic parochial schools, new Presbyterian and Episcopalian parochial schools, and the old and new private schools all expanded. Enrollment in these schools rose from about ten thousand in 1869 to seventeen thousand in 1873, but then declined to fourteen thousand the next year and subsequently even further.[33] "Parochial schools on the pay system are virtually a failure," confessed Father Abram J. Ryan, editor of the local Catholic weekly; the reason he gave was economic: "poor families who have three or four, sometimes eight or ten children . . . cannot possibly send them to the parochial schools at the rate of $2 or even $1 per month, each."[34] This consideration applied with even greater force to the private schools, where tuition was normally twice as high.[35]

Predicted racial violence and tax resistance did not materialize, and after experimenting with walkouts from mixed schools and with private schools, the people of New Orleans learned to live with the change. For three years, from the fall of 1871 until the fall of 1874, the tumult and the shouting diminished.[36] At the risk of oversimplification, two explanations may be suggested. First, desegregation was administered with such skill that the opposition was disarmed, but foremost, for reasons largely political, thousands of New Orleans whites and the leading newspapers actually sought to win the Negro's vote on a basis of recognizing his civil rights.

Though statesmanlike qualities are not generally attributed to Reconstruction leaders, and the school officials were certainly not plaster saints, they administered the New Orleans schools efficiently and without major scandal. "If an irrational prejudice is exhibited on one side of this question," said Superintendent Conway, "let it not be met by an equally irrational precipitancy on the other side. This great question of education for the people . . . should not be imperiled by injudicious action, even in behalf of a principle confessedly just and equitable."[37] Though rewarded with diatribes for their pains,[38] Conway, his Negro successor William G. Brown, and City Superintendent Charles W. Boothby pursued a "firm and yet moderate course" and conducted a school system good enough to win loyalty from the teachers and even occasional compliments from the opposition.[39]

The complex reasons why many New Orleans whites embraced or acquiesced in Negro civil rights between 1871 and 1874 have been treated elsewhere by T. Harry Williams[40] and can only be outlined here. The central fact was that Louisiana Negroes had a majority of the votes and were protected against intimidation be federal troops. As Reconstruction continued in Louisiana after its demise in other states, native whites realized that they had to win a substantial segment of the Negro vote if they hoped to oust the carpetbaggers. The Negroes were ably led, not so much by the white carpetbaggers as by their own well-educated New Orleans persons of color and Negro carpetbaggers. It was to these colored leaders that the white conservatives made overtures when the inevitable conflicts of interest developed between the white and colored wings of the Radical Republicans.

In 1871 and 1872 New Departure Democrats and new parties that abandoned the Democratic label partly because of its unpopularity among Negroes made bids for Negro votes by platform promises of recognition of civil rights and by parading a few Negro speakers at their rallies.[41] The vague commitments were insufficient to win the Negro vote in the election of 1872, and this failure led to the specific commitments of the unification movement of 1873. Simply stated, the unification movement proposed a fusion of the native white and Negro voters in which the Negroes would promise to assist in ousting the carpetbaggers and cutting the taxes and the whites would guarantee the Negroes full civil rights: suffrage, office holding, desegregated transportation and places of public resort, and mixed schools. Confederate Gen. P. G. T. Beauregard, the merchant Isaac N. Marks, and a thousand other New Orleans citizens of both races signed a unification manifesto endorsing desegregated schools in unmistakable terms and presented it for endorsement to cheering crowds. In this atmosphere it is understandable that the press and pulpits ceased to thunder against desegregation. After Marks had read the school clause of the manifesto to a mass meeting and a voice interrupted to ask, "Will you send your children to the public schools?" that is, to desegregated schools, the question was greeted with "hisses and other demonstrations" and an invitation to leave the hall.[42] The unification movement failed to achieve the interracial political alliance it sought, because of the reluctance of many whites, particularly in the rural areas, to concede so much to the Negroes, and because of Negro suspicion that the white unificationists would be unwilling or unable to make good their commitments. The movement did give desegregation a breathing spell, however, and its spirit continued to animate some New Orleans whites. Marks, stating his freedom of racial bias, took a seat on the city school board and helped to administer school desegregation.[43] In 1875 George W. Cable sent carefully reasoned arguments for mixed schools to a New Orleans paper,[44] and in the same year David F. Boyd, president of the state university, tried to publish a proposal to desegregate his school.[45]

To most New Orleans whites, however, the failure of unification was the signal for a change in policy and leadership. If Negroes could not be persuaded to vote with the whites, then enough Negroes had to be kept from the polls to ensure a white majority. The White League arose in 1874, spread quickly from the rural parishes to New Orleans, staged a three-day *coup d' état* in September until the arrival of federal troops, and installed a Conservative city government in December. In the same period the position of mixed schools was weakened by the removal from the congressional civil rights bill of the school desegregation clause.[46] The stage was set for the well-known school riots of December 1874, which reflected the momentary political climate of that period as clearly as the acquiescent mood of the previous three years reflected an opposite policy.

During three days of rioting, mobs often described as high school boys or "boy regulators" rudely ejected from mixed schools colored children who had been peacefully attending for years, insulted teachers, beat and threatened to hang the city superintendent.[47] What is not generally understood is that the White League and its newspaper supporters instigated and directed the mobs, which were composed mostly of men and adolescents not enrolled in the high schools, using a handful of high school rowdies as fronts.[48] Moreover, the riots failed to achieve their objective. Sober citizens persuaded the White League to call off "the boys," and the schools reopened after the holidays on a desegregated basis,[49] remaining so for another two and a half years, until after Reconstruction.

Even after the end of Reconstruction, it appeared at first that desegregation might survive the change. The schools remained mixed through the remainder of the term, and Negroes were appointed to the school boards.[50] But when the city school board voted to segregate the schools the following fall, the governor gave a Negro delegation neither aid nor comfort.[51] Resort to the state and federal courts proved equally futile. The Negroes lost three test cases despite the mandatory provisions of the state constitution,[52] and the constitution itself was rewritten in 1879 to permit separate schools and in 1898 to require them.

An obvious conclusion is that the Southern devices of evasion and resistance broke down, largely through their own internal weaknesses. On the other hand, New Orleans whites never really surrendered their concept of the public school as a sort of private club. The chief significance of the New Orleans experiment with desegregation, however, centers around the fact which was not merely incidental, that it occurred in a Deep Southern state with a large Negro population.

It was really universal suffrage—Negro suffrage protected by strong federal sanctions—that produced the mixed schools and sustained them through the years of trial. Negro votes in the constitutional convention secured the mixed school clause, and Negro votes elected school officers who would carry it out. Negro votes were the consideration for which whites were willing to bargain acquiescence in desegregation. And when the compromise of 1877 removed the federal sanctions for Negro suffrage, the mixed schools were an early casualty. Desegregation was only part of a broader social struggle in which the ballot was the primary lever of power.

New Orleans desegregation is not entirely explained by Negro votes, however, since the Negro majority was in rural Louisiana, where schools were only rarely desegregated.[53] In the adjacent rural state of Mississippi, the Negro majority permitted separate schools to be established by a local-option school law.[54] It would seem that any rural effort at mixed schools in the lower South was foredoomed by the weak economic position of Negro sharecroppers, the lack of demand for educated labor in the cotton fields, and the desire of white planters to maintain racial segregation as a means of social control. In Southern states outside of the cotton belt, of course, the Negro minority was too weak politically to win desegregation against almost unanimous white opposition.[55]

If the key to desegregation was to be found in the city, then why was the New Orleans experience so different than that of Charleston, South Carolina?[56] The South

Carolina constitution of 1868 also required desegregation, and that state also had a Negro majority of voters. Yet the state officials successfully opposed desegregation, and neither the Negro legislators nor the Charleston Negro community pressed the issue.[57] Explanation of the difference between these two urban centers involves consideration of such intangible but very real influences as the singular character of New Orleans and the structure of leadership in the New Orleans Negro community.

With a population of 200,000, New Orleans was metropolitan in size and in the radiating influence of its river trade and railroad connections. Linked with continental Europe by its Creole tradition, its large and diverse immigrant population, and the cultural ties of more recent French *émigrés*, and linked by trade with racially complex Latin America, it was in many respects the nation's most cosmopolitan city. Travelers, immigrants, and clients frequently reminded New Orleans citizens that Southern racial attitudes and practices were not widely accepted.[58]

In many other ways New Orleans was unique among Southern cities. Desegregated worship in the Catholic churches, which claimed about half of the city's population, possibly modified racial attitudes.[59] The colored population was residentially dispersed throughout the city and was only about one-fourth of the total population; it was not so large as to induce in whites the fear of being engulfed if racial barriers were lowered. The city had opposed secession and was part of the Confederacy less than two years, whereas it underwent Reconstruction for almost nine years prior to desegregation and for some fifteen years in all. The interest of many New Orleans leaders in sugar protection and in federal subsidies for river and harbor improvement and railroads made them ideologically more amenable to Whiggish Republicanism than the cotton planters of the Charleston area. The prominence of New Orleans merchants in the unification movement of 1873 suggests that many of them were more concerned with economic development than with social control. They were willing to compromise on racial issues in order to free themselves from a political regime on which they blamed the city's economic plight. Thus political polarization by race was incomplete and ephemeral.

The vigorous and ambitious leadership of the New Orleans Negro community was also a powerful stimulus to desegregation. The basis for the high quality of this leadership was laid during the slavery period, when the free Negroes of New Orleans enjoyed a status "probably unequaled in any other part of the South."[60] Whereas the Charleston free Negroes formed a truncated social pyramid in which artisans were the highest large class,[61] the New Orleans *gens de couleur* included a number of substantial merchants, cotton factors, caterers, doctors and lawyers, even newspaper editors and poets. Negroes also had much social freedom in cosmopolitan New Orleans. "The whole behavior of the Negro toward the whites," says Joseph G. Tregle, "was singularly free of that deference and circumspection which might have been expected in a slave community."[62] Though the social weather became stormier in the last years of slavery, the colored elite regained self-confidence during the Union occupation, serving as officers in the Union army and eventually as officeholders in the state government. Soon after the war they won a crucial struggle for desegregation of streetcars against almost the same arguments and dire predictions later used to obstruct school desegregation.[63]

The light-skinned New Orleans Negroes, abandoning an early effort to be classed legally as whites, merged their lot with that of the Negro masses and forged an impressive Negro solidarity on racial questions. Since New Orleans was the state capital in this period, they were able to incorporate the darker skinned rural political leaders into their upper-class circle.[64] There is little evidence in the Reconstruction period that the colored bourgeoisie of New Orleans was as isolated from the Negro masses as E. Franklin Frazier has found the same class in the mid-twentieth century.[65] Well educated in private schools, in the North, and in France, they maintained a highly articulate newspaper press and an efficient if opportunistic political organization. They held about half of the seats on the city school board and protected the desegregation experiment against occasional desertion and failure of nerve on the part of their white colleagues. Sharing with most professional men the belief that "knowledge is power," these Negro leaders pressed their own children steadily into desegregated schools in search of equal educational opportunities.

New Orleans desegregation, then, achieved its successes in the 1870s through a unique conjunction of circumstances. A political coalition was temporarily created between the rural Negro majority, the urban Negro minority, and Northern Republicans in control of federal and state governments. New Orleans was a metropolitan and cosmopolitan, not merely polygot, center, in which the Southern rural mores were challenged by other traditions, values, and interests. The prior development of a free Negro elite in New Orleans provided the leadership and steadfastness which outsiders could not furnish. Such a fortuitous convergence, however, depended too heavily on one *sine qua non*, the temporary sojourn of federal power in the South. Not until the whole region came more closely to resemble New Orleans, not until an urban South and a more strongly based Negro community emerged, could the experiment be renewed auspiciously.

Notes for "Desegregation in New Orleans Public Schools during Reconstruction"

[1]Alcée Fortier, *Louisiana Studies* (New Orleans, 1894), 267-68; John R. Ficklen, *History of Reconstruction in Louisiana* (Baltimore, 1910), 207-8; Ella Lonn, *Reconstruction in Louisiana after 1868* (New York, 1918), 54-55, 357; John S. Kendall, *History of New Orleans*, 3 vols. (Chicago, 1922), 1:331, 665; Roger W. Shugg, *Origins of Class Struggle in Louisiana* (University, La., 1939), 226; Garnie W. McGinty, *Louisiana Redeemed* (New Orleans, 1941), 24. George W. Cable, *Strange True Stories of Louisiana* (New York, 1889), 221-32, is more accurate, though limited to a single public school.

[2]Horace M. Bond, *The Education of the Negro in the American Social Order* (New York, 1934), 52; Charles W. Dabney, *Universal Education in the South*, 2 vols. (Chapel Hill, N. C., 1936), 1:368-71; Harry S. Ashmore, *The Negro and the Schools* (Chapel Hill, N. C., 1954), 7-8; John Hope Franklin, "Jim Crow Goes to School," *South Atlantic Quarterly*, 58 (1959): 225-35; Alfred H. Kelly, "The Congressional Controversy over School Segregation, 1867-1875," *American Historical Review*, 64 (1959): 537-63.

[3]Thomas H. Harris, *The Story of Public Education in Louisiana* (New Orleans, 1924), 30; an undocumented work.

[4]Conway to the editor of the *Washington National Republican*, in *Washington New National Era*, June 4, 1874.

[5]*New Orleans Tribune*, October 27, 1867 [all New Orleans newspapers hereafter cited without place name].

[6]*Tribune*, July 24, 1867; *Times*, July 31, September 19, October, 1, 9, 11, 15, 16, 20, 1867; *Crescent*, September 15, 17, 1867; Minutes of New Orleans City Board of School Directors [hereafter cited as Sch. Bd. Min.], September 16, October 2, 9, 1867 (7:203-14, 219-26), MSS volumes in Orleans Parish School Board Office, New Orleans.

[7]L. Jolissaint, parish of Orleans School Report, September 15, 1868, Tri-Monthly Report Book of Assistant and Sub-Assistant Commissioner, Parish of Orleans, Louisiana, Bureau of Refugees, Freedmen, and Abandoned Lands, National Archives; *Crescent*, September 17, 1867; *Picayune*, December 4, 1867.

[8]Sch. Bd. Min., November 6, December 4, 1867 (7:235-37, 251-53); *Times*, December 25, 1867.

[9]*Picayune*, April 14, 1868; Peabody Education Fund, *Proceedings of the Trustees*, 6 vols. (Boston, 1867-1914), 1, 91, 262-63, 408-12, 434-39 (July 1868, February 1871, October 1874).

[10]See, e.g., *Picayune*, October 22, 1867, August 13, 1868, November 24, 1870; *Commercial Bulletin*, February 7, 1870; *Times*, May 2, 1868, February 17, April 10, 1870.

[11]Sch. Bd. Min., May 21, 27, 1868 (7:323, 327-28). According to the *Picayune*, January 12, 1871, "everything worked smoothly, attempts at mixing the schools being frustrated by the plan adopted by Mr. Van Norden, the President of the Board, who issued permits on which alone admission could be gained, to applicants, and taking good care that no negroes [*sic*] were admitted into white schools."

[12]*Annual Report of the State Superintendent of Public Education for the Year 1870* [hereafter cited as *Annual Report*] (New Orleans, 1871), 17-28; *Picayune* and *Times* throughout 1869-1870, esp. *Times*, December 20, 1870; *Picayune*, January 12, 1871; *Commercial Bulletin*, January 11, 12, 1871. On earlier desegregation efforts, see ibid., April 27, 30, May 17, 18, June 30, 1870; Sch. Bd. Min., may 21, 27, June 3, 1868 (7:32-28, 336-37).

[13]*Times*, October 6, 1873; *Louisianian*, September 4, 1875.

[14]These were: Barracks, Bayou Bridge, Bayou Road, Beauregard, Bienville, Central Boys' High, Claiborne, Fillmore, Fisk, Franklin, Keller, Lower Girls' High, Madison, Paulding, Pontchartrain (Milneburg), Rampart, Robertson, St. Anne, St. Philip, Spain, Webster schools certainly desegregated, and Cut-off Road, Dunn, Gentilly, McDonoghville vaguely reported to be so. See *Bulletin*, January 11, February 1, 1871, December 11, 18, 19, 1874; *Republican*, April 12, 1873, December 12, 1874; *Picayune*, June 23, 1871, December 11, 12, 19, 1874, February 19, November 10, 1875, November 20, 1876, December 6, 1877; *Times*, April 10, June 7, October 6, December 13, 1873, December 18, 19, 1874, February 19, 1875, September 20, 22, 1876; *L'Abeille*, December 18, 1874; report on Claiborne Boys' School, March 10, 1873, Special Reports of Principals, Louisiana Department of Education Miscellaneous Papers, Department of Archives and Manuscripts, Louisiana State University; *Annual Report, 1872*, 242-43. Contemporaries estimated that between one-third and one-half of the schools were desegregated. *Annual Report, 1872*, 18; *Republican*, July 18, 1873, September 16, 1875; Edward Lawrence, "Color in the New Orleans Schools," *Harper's Weekly*, 19 (February 13, 1875): 147-48; *Louisianian*, February 13, 1875.

[15]*Annual Reports, 1869*, 13, *1871*, 308.

[16]City Superintendent William O. Rogers, in *Annual Report, 1877*, 303.

[17]The six leading desegregated schools alone were reported to have more than five hundred Negro pupils. *Picayune*, December 11, 1874; *Times*, June 7, December 13, 1873, December 18, 1874; *Bulletin*, December 19, 1874; *Republican*, April 12, 1873; report on Claiborne Boys' School, March 10, 1873, Education Archives, LSU.

[18]*Bulletin*, December 15, 1874.

[19]Ibid., October 22, 1874; *L'Abbeille*, April 16, 1876.

[20]Fisk, Franklin, Madison, Paulding, and Webster Schools in the First District and Keller School in the Fourth District.

[21]*Times*, December 18, 1874.

[22]Pontchartrain, Cut-off Road, Dunn, Gentilly, and McDonoghville.

[23]Cable, *Strange True Stories of Louisiana*, 219-32; Dora R. Miller to Cable, May 31, 1889, February 10, May 5, 1890, George W. Cable Papers, Howard-Tilton Memorial Library, Tulane University; *Republican*, April 12, 1873; *Times*, December 17, 18, 1874.

[24]Ibid., January 12, 13, February 4, 1875; *Bulletin*, January 13, 1875; *Picayune*, February 19, 1875; *Republican*, March 3, 1875.

[25]Harris, *Public Education in Louisiana*, 46; Sch. Bd. Min., September 11, 1875, December 6, 1876, November 7, 1877 (8:60, 200; 9:174, 177).

[26]*Annual Reports, 1871*, 321, 326, *1875*, 12, *1877*, 289, *1879*, 13; Robert M. Lusher, MSS autobiography, June 1890, Robert M. Lusher Papers, LSU. Kendall, *History of New Orleans*, 2:531, reported 23, 668 enrolled in 1899.

[27]*Picayune*, January 12, 1875, as reported in *Times-Picayune*, January 25, 1937, clipping in New Orleans Public Schools vertical file, Louisiana Room, LSU; *Times*, October 6, 1873; *Annual Report, 1877*, 303.

[28]*Picayune*, June 23, 1871, December 12, 1874; *Times*, December 13, 1873; *Annual Reports, 1874*, 183, *1875*, 208.

[29]*Commercial Bulletin*, January 12, 31, 1871; *Picayune*, June 23, December 11, 1871; *Republican*, June 23, 1871; *Times*, June 7, October 6, December 12, 1873; *Annual Reports, 1871*, 375, *1874*, 183, *1875*, 208-10.

[30]*Republican*, July 18, 1873; *Times*, June 18, 1870.

[31]*Commercial Bulletin*, May 25, June 8, 1870; *Times*, May 25, 1870; *Picayune*, June 8, 1870.

[32]Lusher, autobiographical MSS, May 31, 1889, Lusher Papers; Harris, *Public Education in Louisiana*, 56.

[33]*Annual Reports, 1869*, 27, 76, *1873*, 72, 284; *Morning Star and Catholic Messenger*, January 31, 1869, October 18, 1874. The figure for 1869 is a compromise between the state report, which estimated 1,200 in parochial schools, the Catholic press, which estimated 5,000 to 6,000 and the city superintendent, who estimated 15,000. Reports of the United States Commissioner of Education, 1873, 547, 1874, 535, 1877, 315 (Washington, D.C., 1874, 1875, 1879), estimate 13,779 enrolled in 1873, 14,235 in 1874, 12,000 in 1877.

[34]*Morning Star and Catholic Messenger*, May 22, 1870, July 4, 1875.

[35]*Picayune*, September 17, 1875.

[36]There were a few exceptions, such as editorials in *Picayune*, January 4, 1872; *Times*, April 10, 1873. Their news columns, however, reported favorably on desegregated schools. See *Times*, December 13, 1872, June 7, 1873; *Picayune*, September 29, December 11, 1872.

[37]*Annual Reports, 1869*, 12-13, *1871*, 47.

[38]*Times*, November 24, 1870; *Bulletin*, October 22, 1874; *L'Abeille*, February 21, 1875.

[39]The moderation was owing partly to opposition and occasional insubordination. M. C. Cole to Thomas W. Conway, September 9, 1871, William G. Brown to City Board of School Directors, June 1873, Department of Education Archives, LSU; Conway to Henry C. Warmoth, November 18, 1871, Henry C. Warmoth Papers, Southern Historical Collection, University of North Carolina; *Republican*, October 7, 1870; *Commercial Bulletin*, April 27, 28, 1870; *Times*, May 6, 1870, July 3, 1873.

[40]T. Harry Williams, "The Louisiana Unification Movement of 1873," *Journal of Southern History*, 11 (1945): 349-69.

[41]E. John Ellis to Thomas C. W. Ellis, February 29, 1872, E. John and Thomas C. W. Ellis Papers, LSU.

[42]*Times*, July 16, 1873; *Picayune*, July 16, 1873.

[43]Sch. Bd. Min., January 12, 1876 (8:125).

[44]These are in George W. Cable, *The Negro Question*, ed. Arlin Turner (Garden City, N. Y., 1958), 26-36.

[45]David F. Boyd, "Some Ideas on Education: The True Solution of the Question of 'Color' in Our Schools, Colleges & Universities, &c, &c," (December 12 or 13, 1875), Walter L. Fleming Collection, LSU.

[46]Kelly, "Congressional Controversy over School Segregation," 558; *Picayune*, December 18, 1874.

[47]*Times, Picayune, Bulletin, L'Abbeille, Republican, Louisianian*, for December 15-19, 1874; a convenient summary is *Annual Report, 1874*, liii-lxxxvi.

[48]"Notes on Mixed School Embroglio Dec. 1874," at end of Ephriam S. Stoddard diary for 1874-75, Ephriam S. Stoddard Collection, Tulane University; Dora R. Miller to Cable, February 10, May 5, 1890, Cable Papers; Lawrence, "Color in the New Orleans Schools," 147-48; Cable, *Strange True Stories of Louisiana*, 223-32; *Times*, December 19, 20, 1874, January 3, 1875; *Republican*, December 19, 1874; *Picayune*, December 20, 1874; *Louisianian*, December 26, 1874.

[49]*Bulletin*, January 13, 1875; *Times*, February 4, 19, 1875; *Republican*, March 3, 1875; *L'Abbeille*, April 16, 1876.

[50]Lusher Diary, March 31, 1877, Lusher Papers; Barnes F. Lathrop, ed., "An Autobiography of Francis T. Nicholls, 1834-1881," *Louisiana Historical Quarterly*, 17 (1934): 257, 261.

[51]Sch. Bd. Min., June 22, July 3, 1877 (9:56-60, 63-64); *Picayune*, June 27, 1877; *Democrat*, June 27, 28, 1877.

[52]See *Times*, September 27, 28, 30, October 3, 24, 31, November 29, 1877, May 22, 1878; *Picayune*, October 6, 24, 1877; *Louisianian*, September 29, 1877, November 29, 1879.

[53]*Annual Report, 1871*, 120, 189; *Louisianian*, March 13, 1875.

[54]Governor James L. Acorn defended this policy in *Washington New Era*, June 2, 1870; *Congressional Globe*, 42 Cong., 2 sess., 3258 (May 9, 1872). Some Negro dissatisfaction is indicated in Vernon L. Wharton, *The Negro in Mississippi, 1865-1890* (Chapel Hill, N. C., 1947), 243-46; correspondence from Mississippi in *Washington New National Era*, April 4, May 2, June 6, 1872, April 10, 1873, July 2, 1874.

[55]See William G. Brownlow in *Congressional Record*, 43 Cong., 1 sess., 4144 (May 27, 1874). Only in Louisiana, Mississippi, and South Carolina, states with Negro majorities, did the Reconstruction constitutions contain school desegregation clauses.

[56]This was suggested by Professor August Meier, Morgan State College, in floor discussion of this paper at the Southern Historical Association meeting, Tulsa, Oklahoma, November 11, 1960.

[57]Francis B. Simkins and Robert H. Woody, *South Carolina during Reconstruction* (Chapel Hill, N. C., 1932), 434-39; Dabney, *Universal Education in the South*, 1:234-35; Richard H. Cain in *Congressional Record*, 43 Cong., 1 sess., 565 (January 10, 1874); ibid., 43 Cong., 2 sess., 957,960, 981 (February 3, 4, 1875). South Carolina did experiment with desegregating its state university.

[58]See "A Frenchman" to the editor, *Times*, July 1, 1877.

[59]George Rose, *The Great Country* (London, 1868), 191.

[60]Joseph G. Tregle, Jr., "Early New Orleans Society: A Reappraisal," *Journal of Southern History*, 18 (1952): 34.

[61]E. Horace Fitchett, "The Traditions of the Free Negro in Charleston, South Carolina," *Journal of Negro History*, 25 (1940): 142-43; George B. Tindall, *South Carolina Negroes, 1877-1900* (Columbia, S. C., 1952): 129-52; Simkins and Woody, *South Carolina*, 26, 91; E. Franklin Frazier, *Black Bourgeoisie* (Glencoe, Ill., 1957), 32.

[62]Tregle, "Early New Orleans Society," 33; Donald E. Everett, "Free Persons of Color in New Orleans, 1803-1865" (Ph. D. dissertation, Tulane University, 1953); Annie L. W. Stahl, "The Free Negro in Ante-Bellum Louisiana," *Louisiana Historical Quarterly*, 25 (1942): 301-96.

[63]*Tribune*, June 25, 1865, May 4, 7, 9, 12, 1867.

[64]Donald E. Everett, "Demands of the New Orleans Free Colored Population for Political Equality, 1862-1865," *Louisiana Historical Quarterly*, 38 (1955): 55-64; Germaine A. Memelo [Reed], "The Development of State Laws Concerning the Negro in Louisiana 1864-1900" (M. A. thesis, Louisiana State University, 1956), 72-82; unanimous petition of Louisiana Negro legislators for passage of the civil rights bill, in *Congressional Globe*, 42 Cong., 2 sess., 815 (February 5, 1872).

[65]Frazier, *Black Bourgeoisie*, 24-26.

A PIONEER PROTEST: THE NEW ORLEANS STREET-CAR CONTROVERSY OF 1867[*]

Roger A. Fischer

Civil rights demonstrations are generally considered part and parcel of the mid-twentieth-century Negro rebellion against racial discrimination. In its many forms—marches, mass meetings, boycotts, sit-ins, picket lines, rallies, even riots—the demonstration has become the symbol of the colored crusade to Americans of both races. But like the movement itself, the demonstration as an instrument of protest was not born in our time at a Tennessee lunch counter or on an Alabama highway. Its origins go back at least a century, perhaps to the May weekend in 1867 when the Negroes of New Orleans declared war upon streetcar segregation.

The streetcars had been a source of irritation for New Orleans Negroes since they were first placed in service on the streets of the city in the 1820s. A few of the street railroad companies operated special cars for colored passengers. Other lines excluded them altogether. In rare instances Negroes were permitted to ride on the regular cars, much to the disgust of many of the white passengers. The sight of two "overdressed negro wenches" riding on a Dryades Street vehicle in 1861 prompted an outraged white woman to ask of the *New Orleans Daily Crescent*, "If the omnibusses are for negroes [*sic*], why not say so? If for white people, it is important that it should be known."[1] But with few exceptions, the New Orleans streetcars remained strictly segregated throughout the antebellum period.

The Negroes resented this practice bitterly, for it caused them considerable inconvenience and afforded them a constant reminder of their inferior station in society. Uncommonly free from the deferential demeanor exhibited by most antebellum Negroes south of the Ohio,[2] the New Orleans colored community made no secret of its discontent. In July, 1833, several Negroes on their way to Lake Pontchartrain were refused passage on a car reserved for white traffic. They forced their way onto the car and a furious battle

[*]First published in the *Journal of Negro History*, 53 (1968): 219-33. Reprinted with the kind permission of the author and the publisher.

broke out between the Negroes and the white passengers, carmen, and bystanders. The colored intruders were finally driven from the car, but they soon returned with pistols and threatened the life of the driver.[3] But the New Orleans Negroes lacked the power to change the rules and regulations of a society built upon slavery, and manifestations of their discontent were largely limited to such sporadic eruptions of violence.

Negro hopes were raised when New Orleans fell to the Union invaders in April, 1862. A delegation of prominent free people of color called upon occupational commander Benjamin F. Butler and asked him to desegregate the city's streetcars. General Butler, the "Beast" of local legendry, ordered the omnibus lines to accommodate colored passengers, but the directive was challenged by the car companies and set aside by a local court.[4] Butler was removed in December, 1862, and his successor, Major Gen. Nathaniel P. Banks was able to persuade the street railroads to allow Negro soldiers to ride on the white cars, but colored civilians remained restricted in their car travel.[5]

The cars operating on Baronne Street allowed whites and Negroes to ride on the same cars, but segregated the races by providing separate inner compartments. Although whites complained of indiscriminate mingling on the upper deck, this method apparently satisfied most travelers and removed the necessity of car duplication.[6] But most of the omnibus lines operated totally separate cars for whites and Negroes. To eliminate possible confusion, they embellished the front, rear, and sides of each car designated for colored passengers with large stars. The cars operated for white travelers were left unmarked.[7] Negro cars were almost always referred to as "star cars," and the term "star" soon became a local label for all varieties of segregated Negro facilities, much as the term "Jim Crow" would be adopted by a later generation throughout the country.

Negro leaders intensified their struggle against streetcar segregation in January, 1865. The *New Orleans Tribune*, founded by brothers Louis and J. B. Roudanez in 1864 as the first Negro daily newspaper in the United States, began to give the streetcar issue saturation coverage. Charles E. Logan and Dr. R. W. Rogers urged the formation of a committee to draft a memorial to military authorities to protest "the restrictions imposed upon the colored people, preventing them from riding in the city cars."[8] One Negro spokesman thought it "a shame that a colored soldier be received in the cars, and his mother be expelled." Capt. W. B. Barrett demanded "that no distinction be made between citizens and soldiers." The colored Union officer urged Negroes, "We must claim the right of riding for every one of us, and claim it unconditionally."[9]

Negro demands met with temporary success in August, 1865, when Gen. E. R. S. Canby, Banks' superior since the disastrous Union defeat at Mansfield in 1864, issued an order that "the attempt to enforce police laws or regulations that discriminate against the negroes by reason of color, or their former condition of slavery . . . will not be permitted."[10] The *Tribune* exultantly informed its readers that "the distinction between 'star cars' and 'no star' is no longer of any value" and reported that colored passengers were being admitted "with little or no difficulty" on all of the omnibus lines in the city.[11] The hosannas proved premature, however, for once again the car companies took the matter to the courts. Only two weeks after the Canby order had been put into effect, it was invalidated by United States Provost Judge Benedict, who ruled that the edict infringed upon the basic right of private corporation to refuse service to any group or individual it so desired.[12] Once again one third of the cars were decorated with stars and segregation prevailed.

The "star" system worked to the disadvantage of colored travelers, for while they were severely limited by their exclusion from two thirds of the cars in the city, their own "star" cars were often taken over by impatient whites. Taking note of this situation in November, 1864, the *New Orleans Daily Picayune* warned, "White persons can ride in the 'star' cars if they choose, but they have no right to object to the presence of darkeys there."[13] In September, 1865, "A Citizen" reported to the *New Orleans Times* that on Sundays the cars operating on Canal Street—white and "star"—were often taken over completely by white travelers, thus excluding the Negroes.[14] This condition was not alleviated, for the *New Orleans Crescent*, certainly no advocate of equality between the races, pointed out in May, 1867, that "It constantly occurs that white men, women and children fill the star cars, to the exclusion of colored persons, and it is a spectacle frequently seen, that white people occupy the seats in these cars, while colored persons of both sexes are compelled to ride standing in the aisles."[15]

The streetcar segregation controversy was finally settled in the spring of 1867, after it had become the focal point for racial unrest that threatened to set off city-wide rioting between the races. In April the *Tribune* intensified its militant campaign against the "star car" system.[16] Chiding the segregationists for their backwardness, the *Tribune* declared, "All these discriminations that had slavery at the bottom have become nonsense. It behooves those who feel bold enough to shake off the old prejudice and to confront their prejudiced associates, to show their hands."[17] Radical Republican orators and organizers, eager to channel black discontent into a massive bloc vote, found streetcar discrimination an excellent topic for inflaming the passions of their colored audiences.[18]

On Sunday, April 28, words gave way to actions. William Nichols, a Negro, tried to force his way onto a white streetcar and was forcibly removed by starter Edward Cox. Nichols was arrested for a breach of the peace, but two days later City Recorder Gastinel, hoping to avert widespread trouble, dismissed the charges against the Negro on the grounds of insufficient evidence. But Nichols, who apparently incited the fracas to bring streetcar policies into the courts,[19] was unwilling to let the matter rest. He promptly countersued Cox for assault and battery.[20]

The Cox-Nichols incident triggered a chain reaction of Negro attempts to challenge the color line on the white streetcars. This presented the car companies with a delicate dilemma, for they wanted to retain segregation without running the risk of violence or lawsuits. Omnibus authorities tried to resolve the problem by a policy of "passive resistance." Streetcar personnel were ordered not to assault colored intruders, whatever the provocation, but they were instructed not to start the car on its destination until the Negro tired of the game and voluntarily departed.[21] This strategy was put to a practical test on

Friday, May 3, when Negro P. Ducloslange boarded a white streetcar on St. Charles Avenue. Ducloslange was not ejected, but the car remained stationary. Some of the white passengers departed when the Negro boarded, others left during the filibuster, and it then became a contest of endurance between Ducloslange and the driver. After a considerable delay, the Negro departed and the car proceeded on its route, empty but victorious.[22]

The weekend of May 4-5 brought New Orleans to the brink of race warfare. On Saturday a bellicose crowd of colored men and boys gathered on Love Street, in the Third Municipal District and began harassing the passing white cars by shouting curses, blocking the street, and showering the cars with a variety of projectiles. One of the leaders of the mob, a Negro named Joseph Guillaume, jumped aboard a white car and defiantly refused to leave. When the enraged driver forgot his instructions and tried to eject the Negro bodily, Guillaume overpowered him, seized the reins, and began to make off with the streetcar as a trophy of war while the terrified passengers evacuated as best they could. Guillaume was finally cornered by Third District police after a spirited chase and taken into custody.[23]

The mob grew uglier, and the arrival of the police only seemed to make matters worse. Sergeant Strong of the Third District Station reported to Chief of Police Thomas E. Adams that "squads of colored men, fifteen or twenty in a gang, armed with clubs, are gathering on Love Street, jumping on the cars and making threats toward the drivers."[24] A short time later Officer Kiernan, desk clerk at the Treme Station, described the disturbance to Adams as "a large crowd of colored men in open riot."[25] City police units from neighboring stations reinforced the beleaguered Third District lawmen, contained the mob, and prevented the violence from spreading. But tensions remained intense. A *Crescent* reporter thought the "public mind" to be "in a very feverish condition during the day, apprehensions having possessed people that a serious, perhaps calamitous disturbance might come upon the city, as a result of the continued agitation of this car question."[26]

On Sunday, May 5, the unrest reached its climax. Early in the morning D. M. Reid, superintendent of P. G. T. Beauregard's New Orleans and Carrollton Railroad Company, relayed reports he had received from way-station personnel to Mayor Edward Heath that "threats have been made by coloured persons that they intended to force themselves on the cars reserved for white persons . . . and that should the driver resist or refuse them passage, they would compel him to leave the car and take forcible possession themselves." Convinced by events the day before that this threat would lead to "much danger of riotous conduct," Reid urged the mayor to take all possible precautions to "insure the preservation of the public peace."[27]

Despite the strong possibility of violence and destruction, Reid and other omnibus officials decided to keep their cars running and to maintain their strategy of passive resistance. That policy was put to the test early in the morning when two colored women boarded a white streetcar and adamantly refused to leave, causing the white passengers to disembark in disgust. The driver, faithfully executing company procedure, refused to continue on his route and the increasingly familiar battle of patiences began. But this confrontation went to the Negroes. After some delay, the driver succumbed to his impatience and drove the two triumphant women to their destination.[28] A few more Negroes tried to ride in the white cars with less success, but by and large the morning passed with surprising tranquility.

That afternoon the smouldering resentments of generations of second-class status flamed into open violence throughout the city. A band of colored men tried to force their way on to a white streetcar on Canal Street, but they were driven off by an equally determined group of white passengers after a savage struggle. A gang of twenty Negroes jumped aboard a white Rampart Street car, overpowered the white travelers, and forced the terrified driver to parade them past wildly cheering throngs of their fellow protesters. A lone Negro vaulted onto another white omnibus, encouraged by choruses of "stay on, stay on" from the colored onlookers lining the sidewalks. Another gang of Negroes tried to take possession of a white car, but were turned back by a single white Union solder, who reportedly told the Negroes that he had a mother and sister and would not tolerate this insult to the white ladies on the car. Throughout the city, scattered fights broke out between roving bands of whites and Negroes.[29]

As the news of the disturbances traveled, inevitable transformations took place in the throngs of people, white and black, who ventured forth onto the streets. The less bellicose white New Orleanians stayed away from the likely battle-grounds, particularly the streetcars. Angry gangs of white men and boys roamed about in search of colored cadres on which to vent their wrath. A number of them armed themselves and boarded cars, riding in wait for a Negro attack. The colored mobs grew correspondingly larger and bolder, their mood uglier. Their sorties against the white cars were now carried out by small armies, wielding such weapons as clubs, bottles, knives, and occasional pistols.

The most massive of the colored crowds gathered together on Rampart Street near Congo Square, the traditional assembly ground for Sunday slave dances during the antebellum period. Earlier in the afternoon some twenty Negroes had taken possession of a white streetcar after a pitched battle and had coerced the driver to chauffeur them back and forth in front of a cheering crowd. The excitement brought other Negroes to the scene and still more were called from passing "star cars" to join their rapidly swelling ranks. Soon an estimated five hundred colored protesters were milling angrily in Congo Square, laying siege to every unfortunate white streetcar in their way. A number of the Negroes boarded the cars, rode triumphantly for a few blocks, then returned to rejoin the Congo Square festivities. Impromptu orators rose up wherever they could attract an audience, shrieking a gospel of hate and violence that the mob was only too willing to listen to and act upon.[30]

At this point Mayor Edward Heath decided that the time had come to intervene. Awakened that morning by a note from railroad executive D. M. Reid urging him to take all measures to "insure the preservation of the public peace,"[31] Heath had kept a careful watch over the disturbances that now threatened to get out of control. Now a decision had to be made. He might have done nothing, hoping that the riot would burn itself out. But Negro emotions seemed to be intensifying, not diminishing, and the less reputable white elements might soon step in if the officials did nothing. He could have called in more policemen, but he realized that his local lawmen lacked the manpower to crush the disturbance and their presence might only further inflame the Negroes.[32] His ultimate resort was the Federal forces garrisoned in New Orleans under his good friend Gen. Philip Sheridan, commander of the Fifth Military District. The troops certainly had the power to quell the riot, but Heath, a moderate Republican, evidently feared the political repercussions from the powerful Radical faction in Washington, who were certain to be displeased at his use of Federal soldiers against the Negroes.[33] Rejecting all of these alternatives, the mayor courageously decided to go to Congo Square and reason with the mob personally. If words failed, then and only then would force be summoned.

Since his appointment to the mayoralty by Sheridan a few months earlier, Heath had won a well-earned reputation for fair play among the Negroes of New Orleans. It now served him well. He pleaded with the multitudes to disperse and return to their homes before a bloodbath similar to the disastrous disturbance of July 30, 1866, was touched off.[34] He promised the Negroes that the proper authorities would re-examine streetcar policies immediately and that their case would be given full consideration. Heath's pledges were greeted by a few grumbles from the group, but its martial spirit had been broken. Soon Congo Square was empty. The peace had been preserved.[35]

On the following day Mayor Heath, General Sheridan, and railroad representatives met to settle the matter. Car company spokesmen asked Sheridan to support the "star" system on their lines with Federal soldiers, but the hero of Cedar Creek flatly refused their request. The executives then withdrew and met by themselves to forge a common racial policy. They stood to lose a considerable volume of white business if they mixed the races, but they ran the greater risk of losing their property and even more traffic if the Negro disorders were to continue. Finally they took the line of least resistance and abandoned the "star" system altogether. That evening, omnibus drivers and starters were instructed to permit travelers of all colors to ride the cars.[36] To prevent further fracases on the cars between the races, Chief of Police Adams warned sternly, "No passenger has the right to eject any other passenger, no matter what his color. If he does so, he is liable to arrest for assault, or breach of the peace."[37]

The actual death of streetcar segregation came more slowly. On May 8 the *Daily Crescent* reported "very little change" in Negro riding habits. According to the *Crescent*, "Nearly all of the colored travelers still go in the star cars, and even wait for them though a car for whites may be passing or present."[38] Two days later the same newspaper informed its readers that colored passengers, "of their own volition, still take the star cars. The cases of negroes [*sic*] entering the cars hitherto assigned to whites are exceptional."[39] But gradually the exceptions became the rule, as the meeker Negroes followed their more adventurous cohorts onto the mixed cars as soon as they realized that havoc would not ensue. After a few weeks the stars formerly designating Negro cars were painted over.

The white New Orleanians accepted streetcar desegregation remarkably well. On May 10 a relieved company spokesman informed a *Crescent* reporter that the omnibus lines were experiencing "little difference in the amount of travel on the city railroads since the distinction between cars has been abolished."[40] On the night of May 20, a gang of white men armed with pistols and clubs forced their way aboard several mixed cars in the vicinity of the levee and ousted the colored passengers, injuring one rather seriously.[41] Then the turmoil abated.

Explanations of the causes of the confrontation were varied. The Democratic press did not overlook the splendid opportunity to reap a political harvest, and accordingly laid the blame at the feet of the Republicans. As the *Daily Picayune* saw it, "the more impetuous of our colored population" had been prodded into actions so unbecoming their lowly station by "the few Radicals in our midst, who would move heaven and earth, if possible, to revolutionize society for their own personal aggrandizement."[42] Striking the same chord, the *Times* inveighed against "vindictive and avaricious adventurers" who "have poured the leprous distilment of dissatisfaction" into the ears of "the ruder and more reckless portion of our negro population."[43]

These accusations were not without their germ of truth. Radical Republican organizers had descended in large numbers upon New Orleans in the spring of 1867 to capture Negro allegiance and they soon found the streetcar issue a ripe topic for their purposes. But these evangelists of the Stevens-Sumner gospel were more likely catalysts than creators, for the Negro resentments had been there a long time before there was a Republican party. The moderate *Crescent*, which placed the brunt of the blame on those inconsiderate whites who usurped Negro seats on the "star cars," may have come closer to the truth.[44] But the fundamental cause was most probably the basic conflict between Negro status and Negro aspirations. The "star car" system had symbolized white supremacy itself, the traditional order of things in an age when many whites had been masters and most Negroes had been slaves. That era had been buried at Appomattox, and New Orleans Negroes saw the Union triumph as their chance to elevate themselves to full equality with all the prerogatives of first-class citizenship. As the *Tribune* explained during another struggle against segregation two years later, "under the present order of things, *our manhood is sacrificed*. The broad stamp of inferiority is put upon us. So far as the present custom goes, we are treated as pariahs of the country."[45] Thus the colored crusade against the "star cars" was at bottom a broader and deeper quest for human dignity itself.

Contemporaries disagreed on the importance of the controversy they had just witnessed. The *Daily Crescent*, giving too much attention to the tumult and too little to the underlying issues, reported with relief that the matter had been put to rest "and the probability of a collision of races averted."[46] The *Times*, noting that the "star cars" had been identical to the white ones, disgustedly dismissed the whole incident as "a clamor for shadows."[47] Even the *Tribune*, the Negro newspaper which had led the agitation against the "star" system, dismissed its downfall as "minor" and began to campaign against segregation in the public schools.[48] But the militantly white supremacist *Daily Picayune* saw more clearly than its competitors that the car controversy was "simply the introductory step to more radical innovations, which must materially alter our whole social fabric." Darkly hinting of a "covert design in the whole movement," the *Picayune* ominously predicted that the "sudden change . . . promises to assume a serious aspect as far as social tranquility and good order is concerned."[49]

During the decade of Radical Reconstruction that followed, the *Picayune* prophecy was borne out, for the streetcar struggle proved to be precisely that "introductory step to more radical innovations." Through the voter resignation provisions of the First Reconstruction Act,[50] the Radical Republicans came to power in Louisiana in the autumn of 1867, and New Orleans Negroes played powerful roles in the formulation of Republican policies. Some of them sat in the "black and tan" constitutional convention of 1867-68, and prodded that assembly into prohibiting racial segregation in the public schools, places of public business, and common carriers.[51] Other New Orleans Negroes guided through the legislature the enforcement bills that extended the constitutional bans on racial separation to the common law.[52]

In rural Louisiana, where Radical authority was illusory and white shotgun sovereignty remained the law of the land, segregation survived without serious challenge. But in New Orleans the situation was altogether different. Under the protective aegis of a friendly Republican regime, city Negroes mounted determined campaigns against the color line in the public schools and places of public accommodation. They enjoyed little success in their drive to desegregate theatres, restaurants, and saloons, although a few of the more persistent pioneers did win the right to sit in empty galleries, eat salted food, and quaff drinks doctored with liberal doses of Cayenne pepper.[53] A fairly substantial number of their sons and daughters attended the white public schools from 1870 to 1877.[54] Segregation was eventually secured again by the Democratic restoration of 1877, but not before the "radical innovations" prophesied by the *Picayune* had come to pass.

Negroes and whites continued to ride together in the same streetcars throughout the nineteenth century. While the white Orleanians defied school and saloon desegregation with every means at their disposal, they were strangely indifferent to the mixed omnibuses. Perhaps the *New Orleans Republican* was correct when it observed that it demanded "a great strain of the imagination to make a mule car appear a place of social resort."[55] More probably, white opposition was allayed by the general adherence of the colored riders to the unwritten rule that they take seats in the rear of the car.[56] Whatever the explanation, the mixed cars caused little controversy. In December, 1874, at the peak of a white effort to resegregate the public schools by mob force, rumors circulated that the streetcars were to be the next target.[57] The negrophobic *New Orleans Bulletin* exhorted its readers, "We have now but one more duty to perform, and that is to secure a return to the system of star cars on our street railways."[58] But despite the frenzy of white emotions, nothing was done and the cars remained integrated.

When the city streetcars were finally resegregated by state law in 1902,[59] most white New Orleanians were altogether apathetic and a few even voiced their opposition to the measure. Bills demanding separate cars for white and colored passengers had been defeated in 1894 and 1900, after arousing strong protests from the railroad companies and some of New Orleans newspapers.[60] Profits, not philosophical egalitarianism, apparently motivated the railroad opposition. As the *Republican* had pointed out in 1874, the companies would not enjoy "the soothing custom of sending two cars six miles to take home one colored and one white man late at night, when one car could do the service as well."[61] The 1902 bill won passage only after its separate car provision was dropped in favor of one that separated the races by portable screens within the same car. Even so, the powerful *Daily Picayune* branded the bill "a nuisance"[62] and a number of white Orleanians expressed the opinion that the measure merely echoed local custom and threatened to incite antipathy between the races.[63] But supported overwhelmingly by the rural representatives, the bill became law. Thirty-five years after the Congo Square demonstrations, streetcar desegregation became the final casualty of the Negro crusade against the color line in New Orleans.

Notes for "A Pioneer Protest: The New Orleans Street-Car Controversy of 1867"

[1]*New Orleans Daily Crescent*, September 24, 1861.

[2]Joseph G. Tregle, Jr., "Early New Orleans Society: A Reappraisal," *Journal of Southern History*, 18 (1952): 33; *New Orleans Daily Picayune*, January 27, 1859; *New Orleans Bee*, September 30, 1835; June 22, 1855.

[3]*New Orleans Argus*, August 1, 1833, as quoted in *Niles Register*, August 24, 1833.

[4]*New Orleans Tribune*, January 13, 1865.

[5]Ibid.

[6]*New Orleans Times*, October 12, 1865.

[7]*New Orleans Daily Picayune*, November 9, 1864.

[8]*New Orleans Tribune*, January 13, 1865.

[9]Ibid.

[10]Quoted in ibid., August 20, 1865.

[11]Ibid.

[12]*New Orleans Times*, September 3, 1865.

[13]*New Orleans Daily Picayune*, November 9, 1864.

[14]*New Orleans Times*, September 3, 1865.

[15]*New Orleans Daily Crescent*, May 7, 1867.

[16]*New Orleans Tribune*, April 9, 21, 1867.

[17]Ibid., April 21, 1867.

[18]*New Orleans Times*, May 1, 1867.

[19]When the case came up for final disposition after the car question had been resolved, Nichols dropped the charges he had filed against Cox, claiming that his sole objective had been to bring streetcar segregation before the courts. *New Orleans Daily Crescent*, May 9, 1867.

[20]*New Orleans Times*, May 1, 1867.

[21]*New Orleans Tribune*, May 4, 1867.

[22]Ibid.

[23]*New Orleans Times*, May 5, 1867.

[24]Quoted in ibid.

[25]Ibid.

[26]*New Orleans Daily Crescent*, May 7, 1867.

[27]D. M. Reid to Edward Heath, May 5, 1867, in the G. T. Beauregard Papers, Louisiana State University Archives.

[28]*New Orleans Daily Picayune*, May 7, 1867.

[29]Ibid.; *New Orleans Daily Crescent*, May 7, 1867; *New Orleans Times*, May 7, 1867.

[30]Ibid.

[31]Reid to Heath, Beauregard Papers.

[32]Relations between the city police and the Negro community were less than cordial, particularly after the fighting on Love Street the day before.

[33]Congressional Radicals had reacted very strongly against the brutal tactics used by New Orleans police against the Negroes in the tragic massacre of July 30, 1866, and it would have been easy for Heath's Radical enemies to draw a parallel. See Donald E. Reynolds, "The New Orleans Riot of 1866, Reconsidered," *Louisiana History*, 5 (1964): 5-27.

[34]On that occasion, provoked by the ill-fated attempt to re-convene the constitutional convention of 1864 with a Radical majority, thirty-four Negroes had been killed and 119 wounded. See ibid., 13.

[35]*New Orleans Daily Picayune*, May 7, 1867.

[36]Ibid., May 7, 8, 1867; *New Orleans Tribune*, May 7, 1867; *New Orleans Daily Crescent*, May 7, 8, 1867.

[37]Thomas E. Adams to Lieutenant Ramel, May 6, 1867, as quoted in the *New Orleans Daily Crescent*, May 7, 1867.

[38]*New Orleans Daily Crescent*, May 8, 1867.

[39]Ibid., May 10, 1867.

[40]Ibid.

[41]*New Orleans Tribune*, May 22, 1867.

[42]*New Orleans Daily Picayune*, May 7, 1867.

[43]*New Orleans Times*, May 7, 1867.

[44]*New Orleans Daily Crescent*, May 7, 1867.

[45]*New Orleans Tribune*, February 7, 1869.

[46]*New Orleans Daily Crescent*, May 7, 1867.

[47]*New Orleans Times*, May 7, 1867.

[48]*New Orleans Daily Crescent*, May 8, 1867.

[49]*New Orleans Daily Picayune*, May 7, 1867.

[50]After all adult Negro men had been registered and some white men disfranchised for disloyal activities, the registration rolls contained 82,907 Negroes and 44,732 whites.

[51]Particularly prominent New Orleans Negroes there were G. M. Wickliffe, R. I. Cromwell, and P. B. S. Pinchback. Wickliffe wrote the anti-segregation clause into the school article. Cromwell and Pinchback were responsible for the segregation ban in places of public accommodation.

[52]*Acts of Louisiana, 1869*, No. 38, p. 37; ibid., *2d Session, 1869*, No. 121, pp. 175-189; ibid., *1870*, No. 6, pp. 12-30; ibid., *1873*, No. 84, pp. 156-157.

[53]Such incidents were frequent after the federal Civil Rights Act became law on March 1, 1875. See the *New Orleans Daily Picayune*, March 10, 23, 1875; *New Orleans Bulletin*, March 10, 1875; *New Orleans Bee*, March 10, 1875; *New Orleans Times*, March 23, 1875.

[54]At the height of the "great experiment" just before the disturbances of December, 1874, more than 500 colored children were enrolled in at least nineteen formerly white public schools. For an excellent but slightly over enthusiastic treatment, see Louis R. Harlan, "Desegregation in New Orleans Public Schools During Reconstruction," *American Historical Review*, 67 (1962): 663-75.

[55]*New Orleans Republican*, December 24, 1874.

[56]A. R. Holcombe, "The Separate Street-Car Law in New Orleans," *Outlook*, 72 (1902): 747.

[57]*New Orleans Republican*, December 22, 1874.

[58]*New Orleans Bulletin*, December 23, 1874.

[59]*Acts, 1902* No. 64, pp. 89-90.

[60]*New Orleans Times-Democrat*, July 2, 3, 5, 1900; Germaine A. Memelo, "The Development of the State Laws Concerning the Negro in the State of Louisiana, 1864-1900" (M.A. thesis, Louisiana State University, 1956), 137-40.

[61]*New Orleans Republican*, December 24, 1874.

[62]*New Orleans Daily Picayune*, June 3, 1902.

[63]Holcombe, "Separate Street-Car Law," 747.

COUNTRY PARISH SCHOOLS, 1868-1877*

Roger A. Fischer

The "black and tan" constitution [of 1868] that prohibited segregated places of public accommodation also decreed that every public school in Louisiana be open to all eligible children, white and black alike. In the country parishes this proviso presented a more serious challenge to the color line than did the mandate for mixed accommodations. The schools were state property, under the control of a centralized state agency, so desegregation would not have to be initiated by private lawsuits. Unlike the campaign for desegregated steamboats and saloons, which attracted strong support from only urban, well-to-do Negroes, the struggle for a single system of integrated public schools appealed to blacks of every station throughout Louisiana, for nearly all Negroes regarded a quality education as an essential rung in the ladder to real freedom.

Thomas W. Conway, elected state superintendent of public education in April, 1868, sympathized fully with the constitutional mandate for mixed schools. A Baptist minister from New York, Conway came to New Orleans after the Union conquest as a chaplain to a regiment of Massachusetts Negro soldiers, and he soon became active in early black welfare work. Appointed by General [Nathaniel P.] Banks in 1864 to head the army's Bureau of Free Labor, he was selected in 1866 to direct Freedmen's Bureau activities in Louisiana. An excellent choice on ideological grounds, Conway proved somewhat less than adept at public relations. His unabashed enthusiasm for racial equality enraged many whites, and Conway returned their antipathy in full measure. In the autumn of 1866 he warned that the "southern rebels, when the power is in their hands, will stop at nothing short of extermination. . . . They are looking anxiously to the extermination of the whole negro [sic] race from the country."[1] A few weeks later he was abruptly replaced by the more pliable Gen. J. S. Fullerton as part of an apparent "understanding" between

*First appeared as Chapter in 5 Roger A. Fischer, *The Segregation Struggle in Louisiana, 1862-77.* Copyright 1974 by the Board of Trustees of the University of Illinois. Used with the permission of the University of Illinois Press.

President Andrew Johnson and Provisional Governor J. Madison Wells to emasculate the bureau in the state.[2]

Conway went to work for the Union League and soon became one of the organization's most successful orators. Throughout Louisiana and Mississippi he told black audiences of the many virtues of the Republican party. One of his favorite themes was free, universal, desegregated public education.[3] His partisan zeal and popularity among Negroes attracted the attention of leading Louisiana Republicans, including Henry Clay Warmoth. Despite their differences on segregation, the two became close friends. When Warmoth won the gubernatorial nomination in 1868, he secured Conway's place on the ticket as superintendent of public education. During the campaign Conway's views were vilified by the conservative press. According to the *New Orleans Times*, "If he had been born a woman he would have been the queen of scandal; if a monkey or gorilla, the disgrace of the menagerie; but being only a man, he is simply a slanderer, an apostate, and a carpetbagger."[4]

Once in office, Conway confirmed the worst fears of his white supremacist critics. Unlike his friend Warmoth, the new superintendent placed precious little faith in the "good sense . . . and inherent love of justice" of native whites and no confidence that such latent traits would result in the "gradual wearing-away" of their racism. During the summer of 1868, while the governor was grandly promoting his "moderate and discreet" approach to race relations, Conway was quietly preparing a public school bill designed to bring about mandatory school desegregation by requiring compulsory attendance. The bill stipulated that all children between the ages of eight and fourteen were to attend school for at least six months a year. If the parents or guardians, after one warning, refused to enroll their children, a justice of the peace could fine them twenty-five dollars for the first offense and fifty dollars for each subsequent infraction. If the parents ignored three admonitions, the bill required the state board of education to place the children in a school of its choice for at least five months a year, at the expense of the parents if they could afford it.[5]

This plan was altogether unrealistic. It must be remembered that public education was still in its infancy in Louisiana. Apart from New Orleans, which had operated a municipal school system before the war, public schools were virtually nonexistent in antebellum Louisiana.[6] The very idea of free public education financed by taxation was opposed by many Roman Catholics with parochial school systems of their own, by wealthy families who could afford academies or private tutors, and by many poor but proud Louisianians who still equated public education with "pauper schools."[7] Moreover, the sheer physical problem of building a system of public schools throughout the state was monumental. In nearly every community the work had to start from scratch. Funds for construction, supplies, and salaries had to come from the taxation of a citizenry impoverished by a military defeat and the consequent economic dislocation. Without the resources to educate a fraction of the children of Louisiana, a law requiring the compulsory education of all of them was patently ridiculous.

Moreover, the constitutional ban on "separate schools. . . established exclusively for any race" compounded the difficulties enormously. Without the support of the native whites, such necessities as adequate buildings, literate instructors and administrators, and local financial aid were simply not available in many communities. Abhorred by the whites as "chambers of amalgamation," the public schools in many areas became totally dependent upon the meager economic resources and limited training of local Negroes. Conway's proposal added the possibility of danger to the certainty of inadequacy. Compulsory attendance would force white parents to choose between racial integration and physical resistance. The *New Orleans Daily Picayune* predicted that passage of the bill "will stir up civil war, if nothing else will."[8] But fainter hearts than Conway's prevailed in the legislature, for the measure was quietly buried in committee.

An act setting up the state system of public education was finally passed in 1869, minus the compulsory attendance feature. Section eighty-one prohibited all parishes, municipalities, school officials, and teachers from turning away any child between the ages of six and twenty-one who was entitled to admission by state law and local school board regulations. Violation was classified a misdemeanor, punishable by a fine of not less than one hundred dollars nor more than five hundred dollars and by imprisonment in the parish jail for a period of not less than one month nor longer than six months. To expedite prosecution, the law decreed that "all such causes shall have preference before other criminal cases upon the docket of the court before which it [*sic*] shall be brought." In addition to these rather severe penalties, the law stated that "such persons so offending shall also be liable to an action for damages by the parent or guardian of the child so refused."[9]

Determination to uphold the law and remold the schools marked Conway's first year in office. In his annual report to the legislature for 1869 he declared that "the right of any child to admission into any school of the district in which he resides, and to which he is by law entitled, is one that must be enforced." A "republican State," according to Conway, "can make no distinction between those who are equally citizens, nor can any humiliating conditions be made in the bestowment of benefits to which all have an equal claim." But a year's experience led him to inject a note of caution. "The removal of prejudices, however irrational," he noted, "is rarely the work of a day. . . . In all great changes . . . time is needed for the public mind to adjust itself to the change. . . . At such times a too precipitate attempt to force desirable reforms might delay their secure establishment."[10]

Conway's second thoughts were well founded, for the initial attempts to bring about school desegregation encountered uncompromising white resistance. In Algiers, where a predominantly white electorate had voted in a Democratic school administration, four public schools were in operation in 1869: two for whites and two for blacks. When a Republican executive committee in New Orleans brought this to the attention of the state board of education, Conway wrote to M. M. Lowe, secretary of the Algiers board, demanding an explanation of this breach of the law. In his reply, Lowe told Conway that when the board was formed two black schools run by the American Missionary Association were already in operation in the community. According to Lowe, the schools remained segregated solely out of consideration for Negro parents, who wanted to keep their children in the same schools under the same teachers. Despite angry protests from local Negroes active in Republican politics, the schools in Algiers remained segregated.[11] This incident was altogether typical of many successful local efforts in blocking school desegregation.

White opposition to mixed schooling was virtually universal throughout rural Louisiana. Some white supremacists condemned the very idea of educating Negroes. For example, the *Livingston Herald* complained bitterly in 1870: "It is worse than throwing money away to give it to the education of niggers. . . . To the devil with the present school system."[12] But most whites could tolerate it as long as the races were strictly segregated. The Benton *Bossier Banner* reported that it was "glad to see the education of the blacks growing in favor with our people," but it warned that "Conway's plan of having both races educated together cannot be carried out."[13] Claiming "no ill will to the colored people as a class," the editor of the *Clinton Patriot-Democrat* added, "I say emphatically that the white race is superior to them socially, intellectually, and morally, and any movement or attempt to place them on a footing with us, or us with them, socially must fail."[14]

The stigma of racial integration virtually ruled out any possible cooperation from rural whites. Those who had the education and standing in the community to assist measurably the program usually refused to accept positions as teachers or directors. Sympathetic whites who might have been willing to serve, according to Conway, "have, in many instances, been deterred from accepting the trust by the apprehension of persecution, and even social ostracism, on the part of the opponents of the law."[15] When Second District Superintendent Ephraim S. Stoddard was introduced to a prominent citizen in one of the parishes in his division, the man told him, "I wish you success, sir, but I can inform you, beforehand, that you will be the most unpopular man in the parish."[16]

Throughout the country parishes, the desegregation decree was almost always disobeyed or circumvented. Evasion of the law took different forms in different areas, depending upon local conditions. In the Florida parishes of southeastern Louisiana no attempt was made to mix the schools. In early 1869 Dr. R. C. Richardson, district superintendent of education, called upon the editor of the Clinton *East Feliciana Democrat* and informed him "that in arranging the public schools of this district, they will not be mixed, the whites and blacks being entirely separate."[17] Although official reports did not classify students by race, private correspondence from southeastern Louisiana attested to the total, unchallenged racial separation practiced there. Elizabeth C. Booth, in a letter to Conway pleading for back salary, referred to herself as "a teacher in the public school for colored children" in Ponchatoula, and Thomas Garahy, writing for the same reason, identified himself as the former principal of the "white school" in the town. Herman C. Collins, a resident of rural Tangipahoa Parish, wrote Conway in 1871 to protest the absence of a school near his home. According to Collins there were "thirty five children within two miles—half of them are white but the school director here won't have a school because the black and white children would be together."[18]

In the northern parishes of the state the racial character of the schools often depended upon the political persuasion of the school board. Where white Democrats held power, Negroes were not only kept out of the white schools but were also frequently denied facilities of their own. M. H. Twitchell complained to Conway in 1870 that the Democratic school board in De Soto Parish had given all of the public schools to white children, excluding the Negroes altogether. In a letter to William G. Brown, a Negro who succeeded Conway as state superintendent in 1873, a black Bossier Parish director complained that he was scorned as a "damned nigger teacher" but noted that if he resigned the board would be dominated totally by the Democrats and then "goodbye to colored education in Bossier." James Brewster reported in 1874 that the Democratic board in Bienville Parish had allocated seven of the ten public schools to white children, despite the huge numerical majority of Negroes in the parish.[19]

The white prejudice against school integration was so strong in northern Louisiana that many communities would not tolerate white teachers in the Negro schools. Bowson Holmes of Bossier Parish wrote Conway in 1871 requesting "a lady teacher in the city (colored) who desires to teach a school of females." W. Jasper Blackburn, editor of the *Homer Iliad* and prominent conservative Republican, asked Conway in 1872 "to send us a colored teacher, to teach a colored school." Edwin Sherwood, a northern-born teacher who had lived in the South for many years, complained to Conway that he was unable to secure an appointment in the Bienville schools "because I agree to teach black children. They have the same right to a good teacher as if they were white. I propose doing and taking the same pains to educate or learn them as if white."[20]

In other northern Louisiana districts whites and Negroes apparently quietly agreed to ignore official directives and maintain separate schools. In many of these communities a measure of white support was achieved, and the systems operated with little friction. Samuel J. Powell, a school director in Bayou Sara, reported to divisional superintendent James McCleery in 1870, "I have excited in the minds of our good citizens an interest in this school question—and with an assurance from you to me . . . that there will be no attempt to mix the schools, I have induced some of our best men, in their respective wards, to accept the appointments." W. O. Davis, a school director in Athens, explained to Conway in 1871 that the Claiborne Parish board had set up two schools for whites and one for blacks, "the Freedmen refusing to send their children with the whites." The public schools in Ouachita Parish were originally boycotted by wary white parents, but in 1874 director James Brewster reported record enrollments in the schools in western Ouachita, "both white and colored." Three months later Brewster observed proudly that Morehouse Parish now had twenty-two public schools in operation, explaining that "the colored people have had their full share of the benefits."[21]

Segregation was maintained with similar success in the public schools of rural southern Louisiana, particularly where the great strength of the Roman Catholic church provided a choice between the state system and the parochial schools. Attempting to justify the small number of white students in the St. Martinville public schools in 1873, the secretary of the St. Martin Parish board reported, "This is a Catholic community, and the clergy of that church are not friendly to free public instruction." The treasurer of the Jefferson Parish school board reported that Catholic clergymen in the parish were leading the opposition against the public schools and "are doing all in their power to establish schools of their own, which are, strictly speaking, anti-Republican, and dangerous to free government." A similar frustration led J. L. Belden, treasurer of the Terrebonne Parish board, to note, "My observation has convinced me that the colored race manifest a far deeper interest in education than the whites."[22]

Coupled with religious misgivings, hostility toward racial equality resulted in white indifference toward the public schools throughout Catholic Louisiana. George W. Combs, board treasurer in St. John the Baptist Parish, reported in 1871 that local whites were maintaining a number of private schools but observed that "out of the five public schools now in operation in this parish, four of them are taught in churches belonging to the colored people." George E. Bovee, secretary of state from 1868 to 1872 and later treasurer of the St. James Parish school board, reported in 1874 that none of the fifteen public schools in the parish was patronized by the whites except "one located in a district where there are few colored children." A report from Jefferson Parish in 1871 indicated that of the five public schools on the left bank of the Mississippi River, "four of them are attended exclusively by colored children, and the fifth by whites."[23]

Public school officials in southern Louisiana made no effort to hide their beliefs that fears of racial integration were responsible for the white hostility to the state schools. Treasurer McKay of Jefferson reported, "The whites will not mix in the schools with the blacks, and any attempt to mix them will prove disastrous to the public school system." In St. James Parish, according to Bovee, "All attempts to establish mixed schools seemed to have proved failures, and will continue so until the existing prejudices against color are removed." Voicing a nearly universal complaint among rural school officials, Bovee reported that "the intelligent white people of the parish take little or no interest in the public schools" and advised his superiors that "the work of public education would be much easier, and would advance far more rapidly, without engendering ill-feeling between the races, if the schools were separate."[24]

In those southern Louisiana communities where Bovee's advice was accepted by local Negroes and school officials, a measure of white support was usually achieved. Many white parents enrolled their children, interracial controversies were kept to a minimum, and the public school systems often prospered. By 1871 Iberville Parish was operating thirteen public schools, five for whites and eight for blacks, with a total enrollment of nearly one thousand students. Reporting similar results in Iberia Parish in 1871, the *New Iberia Times* explained, "We have it from a good source that the colored people of our parish do not want mixed schools, and . . . they are not going to apply for admission into the white schools when they have houses prepared for them."[25]

The best contemporary commentary on the problems of public education in rural southern Louisiana is found in the diary, correspondence, and official reports of Ephraim S. Stoddard, superintendent of the second division throughout Reconstruction. Born in Vermont in 1837, Stoddard migrated to Illinois, served during the war as a sergeant in the Seventy-seventh Illinois Volunteers, was captured in the vicinity of Mansfield, Louisiana, and spent the last thirteen months of the conflict in a Confederate prison camp. After Appomattox he remained in Louisiana, labored for two years as a school administrator for the Freedmen's Bureau, worked briefly as secretary of the state board of education, and served as a divisional superintendent in the sugar parishes from 1869 to 1877.[26]

Even more than his friend and superior Conway, Stoddard exemplified the visionary spirit of Northern egalitarianism. In a letter to his brother, he prophesied that the "*Typical American*" was being created by "the blending and fusing of every nation and every race created by God," proclaiming, "*A unified race*—what a thought! The idea excites the power of my mind to follow. When its completion has been wrought—then is the millennium."[27] According to Stoddard, the Negro would be "swallowed up, not by extermination but by absorption." He dismissed white revulsion over racial amalgamation by pointing out, "You have saved me the trouble, my Southern friend, of advocating that doctrine . . . for there is not a family to the manor born south of 'Mason and Dixon's line' whose blood does not course freely in the veins of Africa."[28]

Stoddard's unfettered optimism was buffeted considerably in the sugar parishes. In his annual report to Conway for 1871, he offered a rather harsh but nevertheless realistic appraisal of the difficulties confronting public school desegregation. Describing the upper-class whites as "never friendly to public education at all," he pointed out that they generally chose to send their children to "private institutions, sometimes at home, but more commonly abroad." He portrayed the poorer whites as victims of a dilemma, unable to afford private schooling but "reared as they have been in superstition and ignorance . . . they will be the last to patronize a school that admits a colored child to a seat therein. . . . Uneducated themselves, their appreciation of learning is not equal to their prejudice deeply rooted in superstitious ignorance."[29] Stoddard's experiences frequently confirmed these observations. In a diary entry in 1875, he recorded that a teacher in Roseland had reported to him that "white people will not permit her to teach a mixed school and there are not children enough for two schools."[30]

In a few extremely rare instances, desegregated schools were operated in the back settlements of the sugar parishes. J. W. Burke informed Conway in July, 1870, that he was teaching a small school with eleven white children and fifteen Negroes at Bayou Mangoin in the remote wilderness of the Atchafalaya marshes. According to Burke's enthusiastic report, "Most of them did not know their alphabets now they can spell well, as well as read."[31] Another racially integrated public school was maintained with evident success in rural Lafourche Parish. It was taught by Colonel A. Laforest, described by

Stoddard as "an old planter of the parish, and . . . a highly educated gentleman," on his own plantation. Stoddard reported in 1875 that the school was "about equally attended by white and colored children" and reiterated Laforest's assurance that "there was not the least difficulty on that account."[32] The success of this arrangement was probably less attributable to the new doctrines of racial equality than to the old patterns of plantation life. Laforest apparently taught the children of his former slaves and those of a few white neighbors, secure from criticism by his social position and by the tacit understanding that plantation children of both races had always associated with each other without confusing caste priorities.

There may have been other public schools in rural southern Louisiana in which white and black children studied together, but references are vague. S. C. Mollere, secretary of the Assumption Parish school board, reported in 1871 that in certain unnamed communities "children of both colors have attended schools in common, and in such schools the improvement of the pupils was astonishing . . . accounted for, I suppose, by the constant emulation between the two races."[33] Third Division Superintendent R. K. Diossy reported in 1871 that virtually all of the public schools in the southwestern parishes were segregated "by the choice of both children and parents of all classes," but alluded vaguely to schools in isolated settlements attended by white and black children together.[34] These mixed schools most likely resulted from longstanding familiarity between local whites and Negroes, not from any discernible commitment to the Republican doctrine of racial equality. Whatever the explanation, integrated schools remained oddities throughout the country parishes.

Displeasure over public school policies led many white parents to support secular and parochial private schools in the country parishes. In many Catholic communities systems of parochial schools begun before the Civil War were greatly expanded during Reconstruction. Although whites and blacks still worshiped together at this time in most Catholic churches, schools operated by the denomination were strictly segregated. Such orders as the Sisters of St. Joseph, Sisters of the Holy Family, and Sisters of the Sacred Heart began Negro schools in Baton Rouge, Opelousas, and Grand Coteau during the 1870s, but the vast majority of Catholic schools were supported for and by white parents alarmed over the twin dangers of secularism and egalitarianism in the public schools.[35]

Most country parish private schools, however, were nondenominational institutions established by individual entrepreneurs and educators. Remarkably diverse, these private schools varied in quality from truly excellent academics to pathetic operations run by functional illiterates. Physical plants ranged from elegant mansions to abandoned sheds. In many communities the great majority of white schoolchildren attended such institutions. Negroes totally monopolized the Alexandria public schools until 1873, and as late as December, 1875, the *Alexandria Louisiana Democrat* could complain that the only white public school in town was held in an "old fly-specked shanty."[36] Official reports for 1875 indicated that the twenty-two public schools in Rapides Parish were nearly all for Negroes and that nine private schools were educating 905 white students.[37] This situation was by no means unique. In 1874 in the second division, Stoddard estimated that 2,301 white children were enrolled in private schools and only 805 in the public system.[38] Often poorly financed and frequently short-lived, these independent private schools nevertheless gave the rudiments of an education to a large number of white boys and girls whose parents feared the racial policies of the public schools.

One attempt was made during Reconstruction to establish a statewide system of white schools. In February, 1867, philanthropist George Peabody, a New England financier and merchant, endowed a fund to be used to help develop education in the South.[39] A year later the Peabody trustees appointed former State Superintendent Robert Mills Lusher to administer the fund's aid to schools in Louisiana. An outspoken racist who viewed education as a means to "vindicate the honor and supremacy of the Caucasian race," Lusher used the Peabody grants and local contributions in an attempt to build an exclusively white school system similar to the one he had established as state superintendent from 1865 to 1868. In August, 1869, the Peabody trustees allocated $11,000 for Louisiana. Lusher used it to supplement $35,000 raised in the state to support white schools in Arcadia, Natchitoches, Bastrop, Homer, Shreveport, Pleasant Hill, Plaquemine, Amite City, Alexandria, Donaldsonville, Franklin, Tangipahoa, Bayou Sara, Clinton, Baton Rouge, Greensburg, Eureka, Franklinton, Algiers, and Gretna.[40]

At its meeting of May 1, 1869, the state board of education had already declared itself the "proper medium for the care and disbursement" of Peabody funds in Louisiana, but the trustees ignored the contention. In October, 1870, Superintendent Conway wrote Peabody General Agent Barnas Sears an attack on Lusher for building a system "antagonistic to that of the State," fomenting a rebellion against the public schools, and placing the Peabody trustees "in the false position of establishing a caste system of education . . . at variance with the declarations put forth by them." Conway suggested that all future Peabody allocations be distributed through his agency to bring about greater efficiency, economy, and democracy. Sears replied that he would like to cooperate with the public school authorities, but that he had been informed that white boycotts over desegregation had created a public school system monopolized by Negroes, thus depriving the poorer white children of Louisiana of the chance to obtain an education. Denying that he or the trustees were in any way passing judgment on the idea of racial integration, Sears justified Lusher's policies on the grounds that "we are helping the white children in Louisiana, as being the more destitute, from the fact of their unwillingness to attend mixed schools."[41]

Peabody grants, under Lusher's supervision, continued to finance white private schools and anger Radicals throughout the Reconstruction period. In September, 1873, tile *New Orleans Republican* complained that Sears was being misled by "a pensioner on the bounty of his trust" to believe "that the destitute children of Louisiana are confined to a class of children known as whites."[42] Lusher's refusal to report enrollment figures and other statistics to State Superintendent William G. Brown on the grounds that Brown was elected by "fraud and actual usurpation" prompted the public school officials to renew demands for Lusher's ouster.[43] But Sears and the Peabody trustees, actively assisting Negro education in Southern states where segregation was official policy, retained Lusher as their director in Louisiana and kept limiting grants to white schools in the state throughout the period.

In 1871 the fund allocated $13,800 to supplement $41,445 raised locally to assist six schools in New Orleans and individual schools in Amite City, Arcadia, Bastrop, Baton Rouge, Bayou Sara, Clinton, Columbia, Fairview, Franklinton, Gretna, Harrisonburg, Homer, Livonia, Minden, Monroe, Natchitoches, Plaquemine, Pleasant Hill, Shreveport, Thibodaux, Terre aux Boeufs, and Winnfield. This marked the zenith of Peabody assistance to Louisiana education. In 1872 it disbursed only $7,550 to be used with $36,229 in local contributions to aid schools in Amite City, Arcadia, Columbia, Bayou Sara, Gretna, Clinton, Homer, Montgomery, Pickneyville, Thibodaux, Trenton, and Terre aux Boeufs. By 1873 the Peabody allotments were decreased to $5,940 for sixteen schools, and the 1874 allocation amounted to only $3,250 for schools in Amite City, Minden, New Orleans, Jackson, and Montgomery.[44] Since Peabody funds were given in ratio to local contributions, the declining grants reflected an obvious flagging of local white support as the spectre of integration failed to materialize in the country parish public schools.

The struggle over segregation involved one country parish institution of higher learning, the Louisiana State Seminary, located four miles from Alexandria until 1869, when a fire forced it to move to Baton Rouge. The racial ideology prevalent at the seminary was summed up by Trustee G. Mason Graham, a former Confederate general, when he confided to a professorial candidate, "frankly, we are a white man's party, and negrophilists, or those in sympathy with them, can find no favor in our eyes."[45] Its quasi public status, Confederate heritage, and unreconstructed demeanor made the seminary an inviting target for Republican integrationists. An article requiring the school to accept all students "without distinction of race, color, or previous condition" was dropped from the final version of the Constitution of 1868, but the issue was not forgotten by such egalitarians as State Superintendent Conway and many powerful black Radicals.

Governor Warmoth, whose distaste for compulsory desegregation was by no means limited to public accommodations legislation, was instrumental in shielding the school from a confrontation over its admission policies during his term in office. In July, 1868, Seminary President David French Boyd informed former President William Tecumseh Sherman of widespread fears that Warmoth would seize control of the school, but noted, "I do not think so. I had several talks with his Excellency while in N.O., and believe that he will not interfere with us, unless *party pressure* becomes much greater."[46] His prediction proved correct. Warmoth supported the conservative board of supervisors of the seminary throughout his term and, without exception, followed Boyd's recommendations in naming new trustees to that board. The student body remained lily-white, yet state funds were appropriated annually. When the seminary was destroyed by fire in 1869,

Warmoth personally found temporary quarters for the school in a building belonging to the state deaf and dumb asylum in Baton Rouge.[47]

The crux of the controversy between the integrationists and the school was the "beneficiary" system, a program whereby the police jury of each parish selected two young men to attend the seminary at public expense. General Graham and others feared that Radical police juries would nominate black beneficiaries, thus forcing the school to desegregate or face a virtually certain curtailment of state appropriations.[48] A plan engineered by Superintendent Conway to coerce the seminary to integrate its beneficiary program was thwarted by a compromise, worked out by Warmoth, Boyd, and State Senator J. C. Egan, which extended the beneficiary system to Straight University, a black college in New Orleans.[49]

Despite Warmoth's protection, the seminary, which was renamed Louisiana State University in 1870, remained a choice target for Republican egalitarians. Conway, in particular, continued to entertain hopes of bringing the college under his personal control. Boyd's failure to provide enrollment statistics for 1870 prompted Conway to suggest in his report for that year "the propriety to bringing the University into such a relation to the State Board of Education as will insure possession of the information."[50] In response to a Boyd proposal for free tuition financed by state appropriations, Conway suggested in his 1871 report that "the ends sought by Colonel Boyd would be attained more satisfactorily by an ordinance making the State University a part of the state system of public schools." Noting that he considered free tuition a fine idea, he added pointedly that he looked forward to working with Boyd "on the ground of making it absolutely within the reach of the young men of Louisiana, irrespective of race or color."[51]

Hostility between the university board and the Radicals often flared up over trivial incidents. When some of the students removed an annoying bell from the deaf and dumb asylum, the *New Orleans Republican* exaggerated the prank into a scandal and demanded an official investigation, prompting Boyd to call the *Republican* editor a "miserable cur."[52] Another incident nearly developed into a more serious controversy. Commandant of Cadets Edward Cunningham, egged on by some of his students, refused to shake hands with two black legislators touring the campus. The outraged representatives threatened retaliatory measures. Cunningham offered his resignation to protect the school, but Boyd rejected it, secured written apologies from the guilty cadets, and advised trustee W. L. Sanford, "I think it best to let it die, as it seems to be doing."[53] Boyd's prognosis seemed correct at the time, for the offended legislators could not garner enough support from their colleagues to force Warmoth to take a stand on the matter, and the uproar gradually subsided.

Eventually, however, the university was forced to pay an enormous price for its arrogant elitism and white supremacist admissions policies. Relations between the school and the state government deteriorated rapidly after Warmoth's fall from power. Unlike his predecessor, William Pitt Kellogg had little sympathy for racial segregation and even less for a college run by men diametrically opposed to his political persuasion.

As soon as the 1873 legislative session began, integrationists revived their campaign to force the university to admit black cadets. When Boyd and the trustees refused to do this, the legislature abruptly withdrew all financial support, including funds for the beneficiary cadets.[54]

This gambit placed university officials in a decidedly precarious position. As Boyd complained to Sanford, "Now the legislature won't support us, because we have no negroes [*sic*] here; and the whites are afraid to send us their sons, because the negro [*sic*] may come here."[55] Forced to make the final choice between integration and poverty, Boyd decided to try to keep the school alive without state appropriations "till right, & reason, & enlightenment again have their due might in our Legislature."[56] On March 8, 1873, he discharged the beneficiary cadets, praising them as "our brightest and best boys" and advising them to think of their dismissal "in the light of an indefinite furlough."[57] The session of 1873/74 closed with only 24 cadets, compared with 131 four years earlier. The 1874/75 term began with 10 students and ended with only 4. The university somehow endured for two more years with a handful of cadets; a faculty of Boyd, his brother Thomas, and a cadet-tutor; and seemingly limitless credit from local merchants, until the Democrats regained control of the state government in 1877 and restored financial aid to the school.[58]

In a sense the conflict between the Kellogg administration and the university symbolized the larger struggle between the white citizens of the country parishes and the Republicans over the racial composition of the public schools. In October, 1867, nearly six months before the voters made school integration a part of Louisiana law, the *New Orleans Tribune* predicted that economic inevitabilities would guarantee the success of the arrangement. Arguing that a "father of four or five children will not pay three dollars a month, for each of them, for private schools, when he can get them educated freely in the public schools—be it even along side colored children," the *Tribune* observed, "Prejudices are not allowed to affect the pocket as they affect the brain."[59] Ten years of subsequent controversy proved that the *Tribune* was wrong and that rural white Louisianians valued their racial supremacy far more than economic self-interest, political tranquility, or even education itself.

Throughout the country parishes, public school desegregation failed almost universally. In rare instances white and black children studied in the same classrooms in remote back settlements in rural southern Louisiana, but these mixed schools were examples of the survival of plantation hegemony, not manifestations of a new spirit of racial brotherhood. In nearly every community where whites and Negroes did not reach tacit agreements to maintain separate schools, public education was monopolized by one race or the other. In the parishes where public schools were segregated by common consent, they were often attended and supported by whites and blacks alike. On the whole, the cause of public education made substantial advances in rural Louisiana during Reconstruction, but this progress came only after segregation, the *sine qua non* of country parish race relations, had been firmly established.

Notes for "Country Parish Schools, 1868-1877"

[1]Quoted in Walter Lynwood Fleming, *Documentary History of Reconstruction: Political, Military, Social, Religious, Educational and Industrial, 1865 to the Present Time*, 2 vols. (Cleveland, Ohio, 1906), 1:362-63.

[2]J. Thomas May, "The Politics of Social Welfare: The Decline of the Freedman's Bureau in Louisiana," unpublished paper delivered at the Missouri Valley History Conference in Omaha, Nebraska, March 12, 1971, 1-14.

[3]*New Orleans Tribune*, June 5, 1867.

[4]*New Orleans Times*, March 24, 1868.

[5]*New Orleans Daily Picayune*, August 11, 1868.

[6]A state public school system was established by the constitution of 1845, and some schools were operated in rural Louisiana, but the system broke down before the Civil War. See Roger W. Shugg, *Origins of Class Struggle in Louisiana: A Social History of White Farmers and Laborers During Slavery and After, 1840-1875* (University, La., 1939), 69-75.

[7]Thomas H. Harris, *The Story of Public Education in Louisiana* (New Orleans, 1924), 4; *Report of the Superintendent of Public Education, to the General Assembly of the State of Louisiana, 1871*, 119, 132; 1873, 223; hereaftercited *Report of the Superintendent* with year.

[8]*New Orleans Daily Picayune*, August 11, 1868.

[9]*Acts of Louisiana*, 1869, no. 121, 175-89.

[10]*Reports of the Superintendent*, 1869, 12-13.

[11]Louisiana State Board of Education, *Proceedings and Minutes, 1869-1909* (microfilm copy, Louisiana State University), December 23, 1869, cited hereafter as *Proceedings and Minutes*; Conway to Lowe, January 4, 1870, and Lowe to Conway, January 11, 1870, in Louisiana State Department of Education Correspondence, Orleans Parish, Louisiana State University Archives, cited hereafter as Education Correspondence, by parish.

[12]*Livingston Herald*, February 16, 1870.

[13]Benton *Bossier Banner*, April 2, 1870.

[14]*Clinton Patriot-Democrat*, July 10, 1875.

[15]*Report of the Superintendent*, 1870, 28.

[16]Ibid., 61.

[17]Clinton *East Feliciana Democrat*, February 27, 1869.

[18]Booth to Conway, April 14, 1870; Garahy to Conway, May 5, 1870; Collins to Conway, February 1, 1871, all in Education Correspondence, Tangipahoa Parish.

[19]Twitchell to Conway, May 25, 1870, in Education Correspondence, DeSoto Parish; Bossier Parish school board member to Brown, December 8, 1875, in Education Correspondence, Bossier Parish; Brewster to M. C. Cole, August 27, 1874, in Education Correspondence, Ouachita Parish.

[20]Holmes to Conway, May 6, 1871, in Education Correspondence, Bossier Parish; Blackburn to Conway, February 10, 1872, in Education Correspondence, Claiborne Parish; Sherwood to Conway, January 28, 1872, in Education Correspondence, Bienville Parish.

[21]Powell to McCleery, June 25, 1870, in Education Correspondence, Caddo Parish; Davis to Conway, February 15, 1871, in Education Correspondence, Claiborne Parish; Charles G. Austin, Jr., to Thomas W. Conway, June 11, 1870, and Brewster to M. C. Cole, July 30, October 11, 1874, in Education Correspondence, Ouachita Parish.

[22]*Report of the Superintendent*, 1873, p. 223; 1871, 130, 132.

[23]Ibid., 1871, 132, 136; 1874, 136.

[24]Ibid., 1871, 132; 1874, 136.

[25]Quoted in ibid., 1871, 205.

[26]Ephraim S. Stoddard Papers, Tulane University Archives.

[27]Ephraim S. Stoddard to H. R. Stoddard, January 12, 1875, Ephraim S. Stoddard Papers, Tulane University Archives.

[28]Ibid., January 12, 18, 1875.

[29]Quoted in *Report of the Superintendent*, 1871, 119-20.

[30]Ephraim S. Stoddard Diary, May 26, 1875, Tulane University Archives.

[31]Burke to Conway, July 28, 1870, in Education Correspondence, Iberville Parish.

[32]*Report of the Superintendent*, 1875, 142.

[33]Ibid., 1871, 199.

[34]Ibid., 189.

[35]Sister Mary David Young, "A History of the Development of Catholic Education for the Negro in Louisiana" (M. A. thesis, Louisiana State University, 1944), 29, 37, 59-62, 67-68.

[36]*Alexandria Louisiana Democrat*, December 15, 1875; William Edward Highsmith, "Social and Economic Conditions in Rapides Parish during Reconstruction" (M. A. thesis, Louisiana State University, 1947), 122; William David Mckay, "History of Education in Rapides Parish, 1805-1915" (M. A. thesis, Louisiana State University, 1936), 45.

[37]Report of the Superintendent, 1875, 234, 292.

[38]Ibid., 1874, 270.

[39]R. Freeman Butts and Lawrence A. Kremin, *A History of Education in American Culture* (New York, 1953), 411-12.

[40]Myrtle H. Rey, "Robert Mills Lusher, Louisiana Educator" (M.A. thesis, Tulane University, 1933), 39.

[41]Proceedings and Minutes, May 1, 1869; Conway to Sears, October 28, 1870, and Sears to Conway, November 8, 1870, both reprinted in *Report of the Superintendent*, 1870, 40-42.

[42]*New Orleans Republican*, September 28, 1873.

[43]*Report of the Superintendent*, 1873, 31-32.

[44]Rey, "Robert Mills Lusher," 41-45, 50.

[45]Graham to Fred V. Hopkins, August 4, 1868, in the Walter L. Fleming Collection, G. Mason Graham Papers, Louisiana State University Archives.

[46]Boyd to Sherman, July 27, 1868, in the David F. Boyd Letter Book I, 1865-1868, Louisiana State University Archives.

[47]Walter L. Fleming, *Louisiana State University, 1860-1896* (Baton Rouge, 1936), 153-59.

[48]Boyd to Warmoth, December 15, 1868, in the Walter L. Fleming Collection, Louisiana State University Official Papers, Louisiana State University Archives.

[49]Fleming, *Louisiana State University*, 153-59.

[50]*Report of the Superintendent*, 1870, 43.

[51]Ibid., 1871, 26-29.

[52]Boyd to W. L. Sanford, December 23, 1871, in the David F. Boyd Letters, Louisiana State University Archives.

[53]Boyd to Sanford, March 7, 1871, in ibid., Fleming, *Louisiana State University*, 195.

[54]Fleming, *Louisiana State University*, 200.

[55]Boyd to Sanford, April 11, 1874, in the David F. Boyd Letters.

[56]David F. Boyd Diary, 1874-1875, I, July 23, 1874, Louisiana State University Archives.

[57]General Order No. 2, March 8, 1873, in the Walter L. Fleming Collection.

[58]Boyd to Sanford, July 27, October 26, 1874, in the David F. Boyd Letters; "Commencement Remarks of D. F. Boyd, Superintendent, to the Cadets of Louisiana State University, June 30, 1875," typescript, Walter L. Fleming Collection.

[59]*New Orleans Tribune*, October 29, 1867.

LOUISIANA LANDHOLDING
DURING WAR AND RECONSTRUCTION*

William E. Highsmith

The economic system which emerged in Louisiana during the decades before the Civil War was based on large landholdings in areas where the soil was fertile, and where waterways provided transportation to New Orleans. City merchants presided over the flow of agricultural produce from the great valley of the Mississippi River, and also supervised the importation of goods from all over the world. They realized that much of their enviable wealth depended on the production of cotton and sugar in large quantities on the Louisiana plantations. Owners of estates in the fertile areas knew that their way of life depended on the commercial people who disposed of their crops and imported the numerous items which were not produced locally. The planter-merchant alliance was important in Louisiana because it brought producer and distributor together in an understanding which included the basic aspects of society, economics, and politics.

The great bulk of Louisiana's poor, white, rural population lived outside of the wealth-laden valleys. The small farmers' land was usually in sections of the state where the soil was thin and sandy or where it was difficult to use the steamboats which carried agricultural produce to New Orleans and returned with imported supplies. It is true that there were some small farms in the alluvial valleys, but their aggregate value and production was negligible when compared with that of the neighboring plantations. Louisiana's farmers on the eve of the Civil War concentrated on subsistence crops rather than the cotton and sugar which was so important in the trade between city and plantation.

Economic conditions such as existed in antebellum Louisiana have frequently resulted in demands for agrarian reform. In the Bayou State, however, the presence of Negro slaves complicated the issue. The rural population of Louisiana, that is, the population outside the city of New Orleans, was Negroid by a ratio of slightly more than three to two. In thirty-three of the state's forty-seven rural parishes there were more slaves than

*First published in the *Louisiana Historical Quarterly*, 38 (1955): 39-54.

whites.[1] Although slaves were scattered throughout the state, their heaviest concentration was in areas where the soil was rich and where there were only a small number of whites. For example, in the seven parishes on the west bank of the Mississippi from the Arkansas boundary southward to Iberville Parish there were 18,231 white people and 82,442 slaves.[2]

The existence of slavery as a system of controlled labor was not of paramount importance to many of the yeomen farmers, who might have been expected to offer serious resistance to a system which guaranteed to them a depressed condition. They accepted slavery as the best way of keeping Negroes in a subordinate position.[3] It was a high price to pay for white supremacy, but they paid it.

In analyzing the important developments in Louisiana during Civil War and Reconstruction, notice must be taken of the distribution of land ownership because the system of landholding was basic to the social and economic superstructure. The unpublished census returns are valuable sources of information on this subject, as they contain material which is not available in the published summaries. The manuscript schedules for agriculture show the names of occupants of each farm, and indicate the amount of land and other data pertaining to their agricultural holdings.[4] This study is based primarily on an examination of the unpublished census returns, and a comparison of that material with other sources of Louisiana's history.

The 1860 census demonstrated the importance of the plantation system. In Concordia and Madison parishes, for example, approximately 90 percent of the population were slaves, 95 percent of the total value of land was in plantations worth more than $25,000 each, and almost 90 percent of the cotton crop of 1859 was in units of more than 200 bales. These two parishes, located on the west bank of the Mississippi River, were areas of great fertility and were extreme examples of large-scale landholding.

In Rapides, which in 1860 extended from the Red River to the Sabine, the soil was thin and sandy except for a narrow valley created by the Red River. The way in which plantations could dominate the economic picture was well demonstrated in this parish. Of the 830 farms listed in the 1860 document, 120 of them, all in the Red River valley, contained nine-tenths of the land value of the parish. Slave property was also concentrated in the valley, with 11,000 of the 15,000 in the parish being held in groups of fifty or more. Furthermore, 83 percent of the 1859 cotton crop was produced by planters whose yield was more than 200 bales.

Winn, located north of Rapides, had similar thin soil and was one of the piney-woods parishes. Unlike Rapides, however, it had no large stream creating a valley and providing a waterway upon which steamboats might operate. As a result, there were no extensive plantations or large farms. The land in that area simply would not support capitalistic agriculture on the large scale. Ninety-six percent of the farms in Winn Parish had fewer than 200 improved acres and were worth less than $4,000 each. There were only three farms in the parish evaluated at more than $10,000.

Sugar planting areas of South Louisiana had systems which were similar to the cotton parishes in the northern part of the state. Where the land was fertile and near a navigable stream there were large plantations and many slaves. In Iberville, which had frontage on the Mississippi, sugar plantations evaluated by the census at more than $25,000 constituted 92 percent of the total value of farm land in the parish. Sugar planting required large investments because of the expensive sugar houses which were considered a necessary part of each plantation.[5]

Before secession and war, people in the plantation sections, called collectively the Black Belt, produced cotton or sugar, sent their crops to New Orleans, and used the proceeds to pay for items consumed during the year. The Federal blockade of the Mississippi, which began in the summer of 1861, demonstrated what happens to one-crop economies when sources of supply are imperiled. Prices of clothing materials, soap, coffee, and especially foodstuffs increased rapidly.[6] There was little demand for sugar, and the widespread belief that the withholding of cotton from the market would aid Confederate diplomacy in Europe kept the fleecy staple from the New Orleans market.[7]

The Federal capture of New Orleans in the spring of 1862 and subsequent campaigns in the sugar parishes and the Red River valley brought the ravages of war to much of the state's best farm land. As the war went on its dreary course, many of the areas which had been centers of productivity suffered from the destructiveness of military campaigning and from gross neglect. The state presented a sad picture in the early summer of 1865 when planters and soldiers began returning to their homes. The task was obvious; they must rebuild the desolate plantations and farms. Yet in the simple matter of resurrecting the agricultural economy lay one of the key problems of Reconstruction—who would do the work?

Plantations in the valleys had always grown the cotton and sugar for the New Orleans market, and in those areas the laborers were the former slaves. Both planters and merchants believed that unless the Negroes returned to the fields there would be little produce to send to New Orleans, no purchasing power for imported goods, and small chance of attracting capital from the North or from Europe. The *New Orleans Price Current,* journal of the city's mercantile interests, summarized the issue when it commented that "The ability of the Southern planter to pay for Western produce must ever depend upon the degree of his success in the culture of cotton and sugar."[8]

In the fall of 1865, a special election placed control of public affairs in the hands of many of the antebellum leaders, who believed that the state's immediate problem was regaining productivity on the plantations. The small farm regions, where most of the rural whites lived, were not the sources of the staples which were so vital to trade. Hence, their agricultural productivity was not held to have much bearing on the return of prosperity. The legislation of the new assembly indicated the economic thinking of its members. Among the acts passed by the new legislature were a series of laws aimed at forcing the Negroes to work by using the police powers of the state.[9] The legislators in 1865, representing chiefly the ideas of planters and merchants, believed that the freedmen must return to the fields *en masse* if the antebellum type economy was to be restored. An article in *De Bow's Review* expressed the attitude of many of the state's leaders when it demanded that the state government "compel [Negroes] to engage in coarse, manual labor . . . punish them for dereliction of duty or non-fulfillment of contract."[10] The *Price Current* thought it could "see no other sure resort than a new labor system to be prescribed and enforced by the State."[11]

The *Price Current* expressed a widely held grievance when it stated: "It is not lands we want, it is labor."[12] For, in spite of all efforts to regain a supply of controlled cheap labor, there was a labor shortage for several years after the war.[13] The lack of available field hands was a result of the Negroes' desire to move around before settling down and their reluctance to sign contracts of a year's duration. Moreover, the majority of Negro women refused to return to the fields under any circumstance.[14] Although there were many ideas about how to make the former slaves work without actually restoring slavery, the labor supply continued to trouble the planters.

One of the ideas hit upon as a means of solving the labor problem was immigration. There were two schools of thought, however, as to the ultimate purpose of bringing in people from Europe or Asia. Planters wanted them to take the place of freedmen in the fields. After immigration had been discussed and publicized for several years, a planter writing to the *New Orleans Picayune* said, "Immigration should be encouraged rather with the view of supplying the place of the present farm laborers than in the hope they will embark to any extent in farming on their own account."[15] On the other hand, there was a lively and vocal group of agrarian reformers who wanted frugal, conscientious immigrants to come into Louisiana with the idea of eventually becoming land owners. The leading spokesman of this group was Daniel Dennett, a newspaperman who edited the *Franklin Planters' Banner* and also wrote for several New Orleans papers. Dennett was a Jeffersonian who believed that "the most public spirited, sociable, and happy communities, are those made up of small farmers."[16] The essence of Dennett's writing and speaking, and there was plenty of both, was that planters should disgorge their excess land. Dennett wanted the Louisiana plantations to be replaced by a diversified agricultural economy which would be based on small farms operated by owners. In Dennett's scheme of things, there was no place for the Negro, either as landowner or agricultural laborer.[17]

The planters' reluctance to sell land to small purchasers was an important factor in keeping down the number of people coming into the plantation regions of Louisiana. Immigrants into the United States went elsewhere because they could look forward to the prospect of owning land. J. C. Kathman, director of the state's immigration bureau, accused the planters of wanting to treat immigrants "like cattle on an unsettled labor market."[18] Agrarian reformers, who increased in numbers as post-war years witnessed continued depression, incessantly denounced one-crop agriculture as a principal cause of general distress. George McCranie of Monroe, an editor and once candidate for Congress, thought that "Cotton has nearly been the ruin of the South."[19] E. R. Biossat, editor of the Alexandria *Louisiana Democrat,* was enraged at the number of steamboats unloading foodstuffs at the village landing. "Will the planters of Rapides never learn a lesson?" he asked. If they "stick to cotton and buy corn . . . the place will go to H———."[20] Rural newspapers throughout the state led the attack on one-crop planting by analyzing the system which drained regions of money which was being spent for items which could easily be produced at home. A Baton Rouge newspaper wanted livestock and orchards as a balance to cotton and cane.[21] McCranie's paper, the Monroe *Ouachita Telegraph,* publicized for several years the ills of a one-crop economy and how they could be combated by growing livestock, orchard produce, and vegetables rather than importing them. The *Opelousas Journal,* finding one man who had spurned cotton to grow vegetables, said, "We are glad to see that one at least is so far cured of the cotton mania . . . to produce . . . without buying from producers in other states."[22]

Analyses of one-crop planting led logically to criticism of the plantation system of landholding. As discussion went on, reformers started arguing that a balanced economy could not emerge while land in alluvial areas was held by a few people. Daniel Dennett told how St. Mary, the leading sugar parish before the war, "had 14,000 slaves, and but little over 3,000 white people. . . . The American planters, as they became the proprietors of more acres and more negroes [*sic*], gradually absorbed the small farms, crowded out the white people of the parish, and almost annihilated white society in neighborhoods eight to ten miles in extent. . . ."[23] Dennett feared that whether the planters used Negroes or imported Chinese as laborers, eventually a few white planters would own everything and there would be no place for white laborers or farmers.

The *New Orleans Tribune* expressed the feelings of another landless group, the Negroes, when it proclaimed: "We may be free, but we are a landless people." The *Tribune* published the most trenchant and coherent demands for recognition of the rights of the freedmen. This paper pointed out that without land the Negroes would be a wandering people, drawn hither and thither by caprice and promise of wages. It prophesied that "They cannot rise, except in extraordinary cases. They cannot be independent freemen. They cannot, in most cases, accumulate property. They must be servants to others, with no hope of bettering their condition . . . without homes, without any rights in the soil, what freedom our people have, must gradually be reduced."[24]

Although there were few demands for expropriating land, reformers often suggested that all would be benefited if the planters would sell acreage not actually in cultivation to white farmers. The *Opelousas Journal,* for example, called attention to the many planters who were leaving fields untilled because they hated to part with any of their land.[25] Planters ordinarily shrugged off the demands of critics, or replied that the latter were trying to be generous with other peoples' property. Occasionally, however, a planter would write to a newspaper to protest against the demands for land distribution. The *New Orleans Picayune* published many of these letters, usually unsigned. One sugar planter, for instance, thought it would be impossible to break up sugar plantations because they centered around the sugar houses and the expensive machinery. He insisted that land could be distributed among several owners, but not a mill.[26] Another sugar planter maintained that small farms could not replace plantations, as good land in South Louisiana could only grow sugar profitably.[27] One important objection to land distribution in alluvial areas, especially in the sugar parishes, was that small owners could not bear the cost of maintaining the levee and drainage systems which were vital to the entire area and which had been financed by planters.[28]

The position of the people demanding agrarian reform was often contradictory and inconsistent. Most of the reformers mingled their attacks on the plantation system with bitter denunciations of the Negroes. Demands that white yeomen farmers replace white planters in the alluvial Black Belt areas made no provisions for the thousands of former slaves who were concentrated in fertile valleys all over the state. The closest Dennett ever came to answering the question of how to bring white yeomen farmers into areas occupied by planters and their former slaves was when he remarked, "The Negroes are nearly a failure. They are dying out and passing away."[29] Had the plantations been divided into small farms, to suit the economic ideas of the reformers, ownership would have gone to Negroes who were already there, or the people would have been faced with the ponderous task of moving Negroes out of the Black Belt land and white farmers into it. Such people as Dennett and McCranie, who were among the severest critics of the Negroes, certainly did not believe that, for the sake of a balanced economy, Negroes should replace planters as owners of the best land in the state. Neither were they prepared to offer a plan whereby white farmers could move into the valleys in the wake of a Negro exodus. What actually happened was that while Dennett and the other critics were talking about the evils of the landowning and labor systems, planters were importing Negro laborers by the thousands.[30] Moreover, there was no widely demonstrated desire on the part of white people to move into valleys where there were Negro majorities. Dennett himself asserted that he "would rather live in the piney woods than in an Africanized parish."[31] In such a situation, with a Negro majority remaining in the Black Belt, and with no prospect of owning land, the old systems would continue. It is important to note that the Republican regime of 1868-1877, which was based on popular support by Negroes, made no important gesture towards obtaining for the freedmen economic independence from their former masters.

During Reconstruction one of the most important economic developments was the rise of sharecropping in the cotton-producing parishes of North Louisiana. The widespread use of the sharecropping techniques affected seriously the economy of the region and also complicated the gathering of statistics pertaining to Louisiana's rural economy. The lack of understanding about sharecropping, plus the indolence of many of the enumerators, made the census of 1870 a document which must be handled with circumspection. Census takers usually listed each sharecropped unit separately, with distinguishing the occupant as owner, renter, or sharecropper. Moreover, statistics published for crops, land values, and values of implements and improvements were too small to present an accurate summary. Where there were many sharecroppers, the schedules, in the handwriting of the enumerators, show page after page of occupants' names and number of acres tilled, but no figures for crops, land values, livestock, or implements. The few census takers who took the trouble to object complained that the sharecroppers believed that there was a connection between census and taxes, and refused to give the desired information. On the sheets turned in by the enumerators there were comments about the accuracy of the figures. The following note was written on the reverse side of the last sheet of the Madison Parish return:

> I feel assured that the officers of the Census Department can understand the difficulty [*sic*] that have to be met by those who labor with the Negro Population in making enumerations for Statistical purposes. Taxation is a new thing with them, and in spite of all protestations to the contrary, they could not be made to believe but what this work has something to do with Taxes. Consequently their Report of Production, I fully believe to be at least 25 per cent below, what it should have been.

Viewed as an indication of trends rather than as an accurate statistical summary, the 1870 census can be a document of some usefulness. For one thing, it showed how much sharecropping had taken over in some of the cotton areas, although it did not designate sharecropped farms. In Madison Parish there were four farms with fewer than fifty improved acres in 1860, and 1,435 of that size in 1870. If one assumes that practically all of the farms in the smallest category were in reality sharecropped sections of much larger units, as later censuses demonstrate, the land ownership pattern appears to be as it was in 1860. Concordia was one of the few cotton parishes where the census shows plantations as units. Although there was no change in the total improved acreage in the parish, the percentage of land in units of more than 1,000 improved acres increased from thirty-two in 1860 to forty-two in 1870. In the sugar planting regions of South Louisiana the concentration of ownership remained at about the same level; in some instances it increased slightly. In Terrebonne, a sugar parish in the extreme south, the percentage of land in plantations with more than 500 improved acres increased from 45 percent in 1860 to 50 percent ten years later. The concentration of land values became more pronounced. Terrebonne plantations worth more than $10,000 in 1860 constituted 91 percent of all land values; in 1870 the figure was 87 percent, but that was after a severe depression in the general value of land.

Sharecropping in the cotton fields started making important changes in the internal trade. Before the war, planters bought supplies in bulk for their own use and for their slaves. When they shipped their crops to New Orleans the cotton or sugar was ordinarily handled by the merchant who had furnished supplies during the year. With the emergence of sharecropping, planters lost much of their centralized control over purchasing. Many of the sharecroppers did not depend on the planters for supplies because country store-keepers were anxious to advance the needed items on credit. To be sure that the freedmen took advantage of their credit, wagons went through the countryside bringing loads of necessities and attractive gadgets to the front doors. Country storekeepers knew when each man would pick his crop; and when a sharecropper weighed his cotton, both planter and storekeeper were waiting to collect their portions. Frequently the laborer had to contract for another year, as his share did not often pay for the year's purchases. One rural editor, seeing the effective tapping of new sources of income, commented that "The country storekeeper has risen to the dignity of country merchant."[32]

Loans for planting both cotton and sugar caused constant bickering between city and country. The *Opelousas Journal*, a critic of the one-crop system, published an editorial entitled "Where the Money Goes—the Credit Business," which asserted that there could never be a general rural prosperity so long as New Orleans banks and merchants loaned money to planters at ruinous rates of interest.[33] The *Journal* had already prophesied that "the old population will be sold out to pay their board to commission merchants, and a new class of people will own and grow rich on the lands of the former lords of the soil."[34] Daniel Dennett editorialized that "There is no money in circulation in this State, and never will be, so long as those who make crops borrow millions from New Orleans merchants at high rates of interest. . . ."[35] The rate of interest to which Dennett objected was 2 percent per month. Rural people all over the state echoed the sentiment, but went on borrowing. The *Price Current,* nevertheless, took the position that "As long as cotton is a more profitable crop, planters will endeavor to extend its cultivation and neglect grain."[36] Frequently the *Price Current* replied to rural critics by pointing out that city capital played an important part in the economy and that if loans were not forthcoming there would be no production for anyone to enjoy.[37]

Neither planters nor merchants considered seriously the possibility of developing a more balanced and diversified economy. Planters wanted to continue large-scale production of sugar and cotton, and they had to accept large-scale financing. New Orleans capital preserved the plantations, even if it did not preserve some of the individual planters.[38]

The persistence of concentrated ownership of valuable land is demonstrated by the census of 1880. It is true that there was an increase in the number of farms operated by owners during the 1860-1880 period, but most of the increase was in areas where the soil was poor or where there were transportation problems. The increased number of owner-operated farms was largely the result of an increase in rural population of about 200,000. In spite of its great improvement over the 1870 census, the 1880 document does not have all the information necessary for a mathematical analysis of landholding. The manuscript schedules list the occupants of farms by name, and state if they are owners, renters, or sharecroppers. What is missing, and it is an important omission, is the name of the owner of the land listed as rented or sharecropped. The 1880 returns help in locating land that was not owned by the person working it, but it would be of great value to know who did own such land. If such information were available, it would be possible to develop a complete statistical analysis from the unpublished census returns. One can, nevertheless, see the over-all picture of continued concentration of ownership in the alluvial areas.

Concordia Parish, where almost all of the land was alluvial and which was one of the principal cotton parishes, had 200 farming units listed in 1860, and 1,499 in 1880; and

1,382 of them were operated by tenants. Moreover, the number of places with more than 1,000 improved acres, being cultivated as a unit, went up from twenty-five in 1860 to forty-three in 1880. If one takes the amount of land in tenantry and adds it to the land of the eighty-two owners of more than 100 improved acres, the aggregate shows a concentration similar to that of 1860.

Comparing 1880 land ownership with that of 1860 is comparatively simple in sugar areas, where there was only a small amount of sharecropping. In Iberville Parish, where there were only five sharecroppers in 1880, the number of plantations with more than 500 improved acres rose from forty-nine to sixty-eight during the years under review. In 1860 Iberville's most valuable 100 plantations were worth 92 percent of the land value of the parish. Twenty years later the most valuable ninety-four plantations were worth 89 percent of the total. Similar developments may be observed in other non-sharecropping areas. In Terrebonne and Plaquemines, for example, the number of places with more than 500 improved acres doubled between 1860 and 1880.

Plantations all over Louisiana remained in the hands of their antebellum owners, or were transferred intact to banks, merchants, and other sources of credit. The end of the Reconstruction era found Negroes in the same fields they had tilled as slaves. They had about the same standard of living and social status. White farmers still struggled to wrest a living from land which was usually their own, for what it was worth. Masters of the plantations had frequently left, but the plantations remained. The antebellum system and landholding, based on controlled labor in the plantation regions, directly financed by New Orleans capital and indirectly supported by race-conscious yeomen farmers, survived a decade and a half of war and feeble attempts at reconstruction.

Notes for "Louisiana Landholding During War and Reconstruction"

[1]*Population of the United States in 1860,* The Eighth Census (Washington, 1864), 188-93.

[2]Ibid.

[3]For an excellent analysis of this aspect of antebellum life, see Roger W. Shugg, *Origins of Class Struggle in Louisiana* (Baton Rouge, 1939), passim.

[4]Unless otherwise cited, all agricultural statistics in this study were derived from the Manuscript Census Returns of the United States for 1860 (Schedule II, Slaves; Schedule IV, Agriculture), 1870 (Schedule II, Agriculture), and 1880 (Schedule II, Agriculture). The Louisiana documents are deposited at the Duke University Library, Durham, North Carolina.

[5]E. J. Forstall, a New Orleans expert on the sugar industry, estimated that in 1860 Louisiana's sugar planters had $82,000,000 invested in land and sugar houses and $105,000,000 invested n slaves. He thought that the total investment in the state's sugar industry was $199,000,000. See article by Forstall in *De Bow's Review* (New Orleans, 1846-1880), After the war Series, 1 (1866): 305.

[6]The *New Orleans Daily Picayune, Crescent,* and other papers were full of comments about the supply situation. The *Daily Crescent* of October 2, 1861, for instance, suggested that dried sweet potatoes be tried as a substitute for New Orleans' famous coffee.

[7]Jefferson Davis Bragg, *Louisiana in the Confederacy* (Baton Rouge, 1941), 76 ff.

[8]*New Orleans Price Current,* September 1, 1865.

[9]*Acts of the Louisiana Legislature,* Extra Session, 1865 (New Orleans, 1866), 14-24.

[10]*De Bow's Review,* After the War Series, 2 (1866): 578.

[11]*New Orleans Price Current,* September 1, 1865.

[12]Ibid.

[13]For an example of the planters' frantic efforts to hire laborers, see letters of former Governor Thomas O. Moore and former Confederate General St. John R. Liddell. They are in Thomas Overton Moore Papers and Moses and St. John R. Liddell Papers, Department of Archives and Manuscripts, Louisiana State University.

[14]L Bouchereau, *Statement of the Sugar and Rice Crop Made in Louisiana in 1871-1872* (New Orleans, 1872), ix.

[15]*New Orleans Daily Picayune,* August 4, 1873.

[16]*Franklin Planters' Banner,* May 26, 1869.

[17]See numerous editorials in *Franklin Planters' Banner* during the 1865-1875 period.

[18]*New Orleans Crescent,* October 26, 1867.

[19]*Monroe Ouachita Telegraph,* March 14, 1867.

[20]Alexandria *Louisiana Democrat,* February 19, 1869.

[21]*Baton Rouge Tri-Weekly Gazette and Comet,* August 19 and September 5, 1865.

[22]*Opelousas Journal,* March 28, 1868.

[23]*Franklin Planters' Banner,* September 15, 1869.

[24]*New Orleans Tribune,* January 8, 1869.

[25]*Opelousas Journal,* January 4, 1873.

[26]*New Orleans Picayune,* September 4, 1873.

[27]Ibid., September 2, 1873.

[28]Walter Prichard, "The Effects of the Civil War on the Louisiana Sugar Industry," *Journal of Southern History,* 5 (1939): 331.

[29]Quoted in *New Orleans Times,* April 5, 1866.

[30]For glimpses into the planters' problems in getting laborers from other states, see letters of Thomas O. Moore in Moore Papers.

[31]*Franklin Planters' Banner,* May 26, 1869.

[32]*Opelousas Journal,* November 14, 1873.

[33]Ibid.

[34]Ibid., February 18, 1871.

[35]*Franklin Planters' Banner,* March 1, 1871; cf. Roger W. Shugg, "Survival of the Plantation System in Louisiana," *Journal of Southern History,* 3 (1937): 324-25.

[36]*New Orleans Price Current,* September 1, 1870.

[37]Ibid., August 31, 1872, and September 1, 1873.

[38]Shugg, *Origins of Class Struggle in Louisiana,* passim.

SECTION III
POST RECONSTRUCTION:
THE STRUGGLE FOR SURVIVAL WITH HUMANITY

ANTEBELLUM FREE PERSONS OF COLOR IN POSTBELLUM LOUISIANA*

Loren Schweninger

It all seemed as if it were a dream, the arrival of the sheriff, the gathering of friends and neighbors, the high pitched voice of the auctioneer, the shouts and greedy excitement of the bidders. But for Josephine Decuir it was not a dream, but a harsh reality. Only a decade before she and her husband, Antoine Decuir, Jr., had been among the wealthiest free people of color in the South. They had owned more than a thousand acres of fertile land along a river in Pointe Coupée Parish, raised sugarcane, corn, and rice, and produced wool and molasses. Their total estate, including real property, machinery, livestock, and 112 slaves, had been worth in excess of $150,000.[1] After Antoine had died during the last year of the Civil War, Josephine had taken over as mistress of this once great plantation. But now, at dusk on the second day of spring in 1871, she listened as the final bids were recorded for her plantation house, stables, cabins, machinery, sugarhouse, and the remaining 840 acres of her plantation. In a single day the accumulations of a lifetime had disappeared before the auctioneer's gavel. When the final tally was made, she received only $25,752 for her land and other holdings, an amount which failed even to cover the estate's outstanding debts.[2]

The difficulties experienced by Josephine Decuir were by no means unique. During the first fifteen years after the Civil War the landholdings of former free persons of color in Louisiana virtually disappeared. While historians have long shown an interest in the economic activities of Louisiana's free people of color during the prewar era, they have been less concerned with the fate of this group during the postwar period. Nor have they compared this decline to the changes in black wealth-holding patterns in other Southern states. This is perhaps understandable, since tracing a small group of fewer than 4,000

*First published in *Louisiana History*, 30 (1989): 345-64. Reprinted with the kind permission of the author and the Louisiana Historical Association.

families following the emancipation of more than 330,000 slaves presents unique problems. Yet in some ways an analysis of the difficulties they confronted after the Civil War shows more clearly their unique and privileged prewar status than does an examination of the antebellum period. This essay seeks to examine the remarkable economic ascent of Louisiana's free people of color, the problems they confronted before and during the war, and their precipitous decline during the postwar era. It does so by focusing on property ownership, a key variable to understanding relative economic condition, and by comparing the wealth holdings of free blacks and former free blacks with whites. It also attempts to unravel the complex social and cultural changes which occurred as a result of emancipation and connect them with the economic changes which took place.[3]

The origin of the state's free colored population dated back to the colonial era when some French and Spanish settlers took black women as their wives and mistresses. Despite the strictures of the Catholic church against whites marrying slaves, many men lived openly with Negro women, often recognizing their mulatto children as their own and providing them with land and financial assistance. In addition, the free Negro population was augmented by a stream of emigres from the Caribbean, first from Saint-Domingue following the Haitian Revolution in the 1790s, then from Cuba, following the Spanish persecution of the French during the early 1800s. By the time of statehood in 1812, the free black population in the state had swelled to 7,585, with nearly one out of five blacks claiming the status of freeman. Often literate, possessing skills as artisans and farmers, they had already established themselves as part of the economic life of the state.[4]

One of the most important traditions emerging from the colonial to the American periods was the ability of free persons of color to enjoy the same rights and privileges as whites with regard to ownership of property. In their possession of real estate and slaves, one law stated, they could not be molested, injured, or ill-treated "under the penalties provided by laws for the safety and security of the property of white persons." In addition, free blacks could petition the government for redress of grievances, sue and be sued, testify in court against whites, be baptized, married, and buried with the sacraments of the Roman Catholic church, secure an education, and enter any occupation or business. While these privileges came under attack during the post-1820 period, the state's unusual customs with regard to free people of color contrasted sharply with the proscriptive laws, mores, and institutions confronting blacks in other regions of the South.[5]

As a result, Louisiana's free persons of color emerged as the most prosperous group of blacks in the South. By the 1830s, in New Orleans and smaller towns and cities, they owned mercantile stores, grocery stores, and tailoring shops. They also worked as brick-masons, carpenters, coopers, stonemasons, mechanics, shoemakers, cigar makers, and in other capacities as skilled artisans. In rural parishes, Creoles of color[6] managed produc-tive farms and plantations, raising cotton, sugar, rice, and corn, and owning herds of cattle, sheep, and horses. One of the most successful planters was Jean-Baptiste Meullion of St. Landry Parish, who farmed 1,240 acres along Bayou Teche, but in each of a half-dozen other parishes prosperous planters and farmers had emerged: Plaquemines Parish sugar planters Andrew Durnford, Louise Oliver, and Adolphe Reggio; St. John the Baptist Parish slaveowner Louisa Ponis; Pointe Coupée Parish cotton planter Zacharie Honoré; Iberville Parish plantation owners George Deslonde, Antoine Dubuclet, and Cyprien Ricard; and Natchitoches slave masters Nicholas Augustin Metoyer, Marie Suzanne Metoyer, and Dominique Metoyer.[7]

To maintain their businesses and agricultural enterprises free persons of color purchased increasing numbers of slave laborers. By 1830 slave ownership had become widespread among free blacks in Louisiana. In New Orleans, 753 free persons of color were members of the slaveholding class, including twenty-five who owned at least ten bondsmen and women, and 126 who owned between five and ten slaves. Business woman Eulalie de Mandeville Macarty, who owned a wholesale mercantile and dry goods store, distributed her commodities to retail outlets with a large slave labor force. She owned a total of thirty-two blacks. In eight rural Louisiana sugar and cotton parishes, forty-three Creoles of color (1.2 percent of the total number of free black masters in the country) owned a total of 1,327 blacks, or nearly one out of nine slaves owned by Negroes in the United States. In St. John the Baptist Parish, three plantation owners held 139 blacks in bondage—an average of 46 slaves each; in Pointe Coupée Parish, eight planters owned 297 slaves, an average of 37 slaves each; and in Iberville Parish, six planters owned 184 bondsmen and women—an average of 31 slaves each. In all, in 1830, 965 Negro slaveowners owned 4,206 bondspeople. These were the highest totals in the South; nearly one of three free Negro families in the state was a slaveholder.[8]

Like their white neighbors, some were benevolent masters, granting their blacks special privileges, emancipating especially loyal servants, respecting the sanctity of slave families. But most considered their blacks as chattel property. They bought, sold, mortgaged, willed, traded, and transferred fellow Negroes, demanded long hours in the fields, and severely disciplined recalcitrant blacks. A few seemed as callous as the most profit-minded whites, selling children away from parents, mothers away from husbands, and brutally whipping slaves who ignored plantation rules. On sugar estates, where the harvesting and pressing of the cane demanded, as it did in the Caribbean, sixteen- and eighteen-hour workdays, mulatto owners pushed their slaves incessantly; and, when women were unable to work such long hours, they stocked their plantations with young men. Among the twenty-eight field hands on Louise Oliver's estate, the men outnumbered the women three to one; in the age group fifteen to thirty-six, the ratio was four to one; only two women had any children.[9] "You might think, master, dat day would be good to dar own nation," one anonymous slave told a white traveller, "but dey is not. I will tell you de truth, massa; I know I'se got to answer; and it's a fact, dey is very bad masters, sar." He would rather "be a servant to any man in de world, dan to a brack man." "Dey was a big diff'ence mek between de slave niggers and de owner niggers," one freeborn black said describing St. Mary Parish planter Romaine Verdun, "as much diff'rence between dem as between de white folks and culled folks."[10]

During the 1840s and 1850s, as in other states, free blacks came under increasing attacks from dominant whites. One 1843 law allowed New Orleans police to arrest "alien" (those not born in Louisiana) free black residents and incarcerate them until it could be determined whether or not they posed any threat to peace. As several observers pointed out some of those arrested were long-time residents who had owned property for many years. Nine years later the state legislature adopted a "passport" system which authorized the mayor to issue documents of temporary residency for "out-of-state" free blacks. At the same time, several anti-free Negro delegates to the Constitutional Convention of 1852 attempted, unsuccessfully, to introduce a proposition to prohibit free blacks from acquiring real estate by inheritance or purchase, and in 1859, a group of St. Landry Parish planters, also without success, urged the legislature to forbid free persons of color from owning "beings of their own color, flesh and blood," a practice, they said, which was "repugnant to the laws of good society, good government, Nature and Nature's God."[11]

Despite these laws and the increasingly hostile racial climate, free people of color generally maintained their high economic standing during the late antebellum period. The pre-1840 expansion rate, however, slowed considerably, and the 1840s and 1850s could best be described as a levelling off period. Although precise statistics on slave ownership are not available for these two decades the decline among free black slave owners in the Crescent City was probably offset by an increase in some rural parishes, at least as reflected in a rise in the total estates (real and personal property holdings) of some planters and large farmers. Similarly, the 1850s drop among relatively prosperous real-estate owners (those with at least $2,000 in realty) in some parishes—in New Orleans from 311 to 263; in Jefferson Parish from 25 to 8; in Natchitoches from 41 to 27; and in St. John the Baptist from six to four—was offset to some extent by rises in St. Landry Parish from 8 to 25, in St. Mary Parish from 8 to 13, in St. Martin Parish from 4 to 15, and in East Baton Rouge from 6 to 13. While it was true that some "literate and respectable free colored people," as one newspaper called them, emigrated from New Orleans in 1859 and early 1860 bound for the Negro republic of Haiti, between 1850 and 1860 the number of prosperous free blacks in the state declined only slightly, from 504 to 472, and the value of their real-estate holdings, while not keeping pace with rising land values, increased from $3,992,500 to $4,867,000.[12]

Thus, while some free people of color experienced losses, others purchased new lands, acquired additional slaves, or started new businesses. If whites made inroads into some skilled occupations, blacks still maintained profitable businesses, especially as tailors, dry goods merchants, and cotton brokers. During the pre-Civil War decade, Louisiana's free people of color remained, by far, the most prosperous group of African descent in the United States, controlling substantially more property than free Negroes in any other state. In fact, in 1850, with 7 percent of the South's free black population, they controlled 59 percent of the region's free black real-estate holdings. A decade later, with the same proportion of the population, they still controlled 43 percent of the real estate, nearly five times the total of the next highest state. The proportional drop from 59 percent to 43 percent was more a reflection of the significant rise of free black property ownership in the Upper South than any precipitous decline in Louisiana.

Several of the state's Creoles of color substantially expanded their wealth during the decade of the 1850s. Pierre Casenave, a New Orleans undertaker who invented a secret embalming process, increased his annual income from $10,000 to $40,000; merchant and real-estate broker Bernard Soulié doubled the estimated value of his real-estate poss-essions, from $50,000 to $100,000; tailor François Lacroix, who speculated in city properties, acquired an estate of $242,600 (one of the largest for a free Negro in the South); and Iberville plantation owners Madame and Pierre Ricard increased their holdings from $80,000 to $200,000 during the 1850s. In 1859, one observer described the Ricard family as "doubtless the richest black family in this or any other country."[13]

In all, despite a brief recession in 1857-1858, fluctuations in the price of cotton and sugar, and political turmoil, the number of property owners in the state between 1850 and 1860 remained almost exactly the same (1,244 compared with 1,262), while the total value of their landholdings went from $4,535,900 to $5,514,500, and their mean holdings form $3,646 to $4,370. Some of the real estate valuations included "slave property," which was listed in some parishes under "real" rather than "personal" property. Never-theless, the average real-estate holdings of $1,479 (including propertyless family heads) compared favorably with the average of $1,492 for white males in the nation as a whole. Though they were less likely to own at least some real estate than whites in the nation (34 percent to 43 percent), and though they owned less realty on average than other Southerners, free colored people in the state were slightly better off in economic terms than whites in the Northeast (mean real estate = $1,461) and the Northwest ($1,284) and nearly twice as well off as foreign-born Americans ($833). Thus, by the eve of the Civil War, the small group of free blacks in the state, now representing only 5 percent of the black population, had made substantial economic progress.[14]

They had achieved their high economic standing in part by adopting a unique set of social and cultural values. To maintain their property holdings, they formed small, tightly knit communities. They lived on the same streets, or nearby plantations, socialized with one another, attended church together, provided an education for one another's children, and arranged for the marriage of their children with children of free blacks of the same relative economic standing. Among prosperous Creoles of color in Louisiana, endogamous marriages were almost universal. Antoine Decuir and Antoine Dubuclet, the richest blacks in Pointe Coupée Parish, signed formal contracts concerning their children. In the case of Decuir's son, Antoine, Jr., and Dubuclet's daughter, Josephine, they drew up a four-page document (in French) specifying the date of the wedding, the size of the dowry, and arrangements for the distribution of property. Decuir contracted for his second son Augustin to marry the granddaughter of Iberville Parish planter Cyprien Ricard, at the time the wealthiest free person of color in Louisiana. Similar arrangements were made by the Donato, Meullion, Simien, Guillory, and Lemelle families in St. Landry; the Conant, Metoyer, Rocques, and Llorens families in Natchitoches; the Reggio, Oliver, and Leonard families in Plaquemines; the Bienville, Ricard, Turpin families in East Baton Rouge; and the Honoré and Decuir families in West Baton Rouge. By forming these family networks free persons of color sought to separate themselves from the dominant whites as well as from the masses of their brethren in bondage.[15]

At the outbreak of the Civil War, most free persons of color in Louisiana supported the Confederacy. In 1861, they organized two splendidly equipped battalions, modeled after the French *Chasseurs d'Afrique,* to fight for the South. In all, more than three thousand Louisiana free Negroes—three out of four adult free men of color in the state— joined colored military or militia units. Some of them, one observer recalled, were as strongly in favor of the rebellion "as the veriest fire-eater [from] South Carolina." As slave owners and property owners, they looked with "sorrow and sadness" at the intrusion of Union gunboats and the occupation of New Orleans early in the war, and even as some of them were adjusting to the presence of Northern soldiers, a few others, including St. Landry Parish's Charles Lutz, Jean-Baptiste Pierre-Auguste, and Leufroy Pierre-Auguste, were fighting as regulars in the Confederate army, seeing action at Shiloh, Fredericks- burg, and Vicksburg. Still others supported the Southern cause by donating slave laborers to work on fortifications, purchasing Confederate bonds, or providing food and supplies for the army.[16]

When it became clear that a Union victory was imminent, however, they quickly changed their stance. Those who had served in the home guard or professed loyalty to Jefferson Davis now asserted that they had acted out of fear of retaliation. How could any black, one of them queried, support a government set up for the distinctly avowed purpose of keeping his brethren and kindred in eternal slavery. Louis Roudanez, owner of the first black daily newspaper in America, the *New Orleans Tribune,* urged freemen and freedmen to work together for "the common cause of black equality." This avowed support of the Union by those who had previously been willing to shed their blood in defense of their native land was vividly revealed by a postwar claims investigator in Pointe Coupée Parish. Taking testimony from those who said they had lost property during the war but had been loyal Unionists and deserved to receive compensation from the government under an act passed by Congress, agent C. B. Hauk explained that he had closely compared the list of postwar claimants with "the [antebellum] Muster Roll of a Company of free colored persons who served as Home Guard & offered their services to the Rebel Government." He found "a great many" of the names were identical.[17]

Despite their professed willingness to join in a "common cause" with their black brethren, the war and its aftermath spelled disaster for the great majority of the state's property owning free persons of color. "When war commence it purty hard on folks," a free Negro in St. Mary Parish recalled. First came the Confederates who swept up the slaves, including those owned by blacks, and took them away to build fortifications. "Dey line my daddy up with de others, but a white man from town say, 'Dat a good old man. He part Indian and he free.' . . . So dey didn't take him." Then Yankee raiding parties rode through, burning, pillaging, and looting. "Dey take a whole year crop of sugar and corn and hosses." Everywhere the Union army advanced free blacks told of death and destruction. "The road all the way to Natchitoches," one observer said, describing the region where some of the wealthiest free persons of color in America owned their plantations, "was a solid flame." His heart was "filled with sadness" at the sight of those lovely plantations being burned to the ground. In St. Landry Parish, despite declarations of loyalty to the United States, Antoine Meullion lost 30 head of cattle, 150 sheep, 26 hogs, and 5,000 fence rails to a band of Union soldiers under the command of Nathaniel Banks. Pierre and Cyprien Ricard, descendants of the wealthiest free person of color in the state, lost virtually everything during the war. In 1868, a final 161 acres was seized by the Iberville Parish sheriff for non-payment of debts and sold at public auction. Similarly, the Ponis family in St. John the Baptist Parish, the Verdun family in St. Mary Parish, the Deslonde family in Iberville Parish, and the Porche family in Pointe Coupée Parish witnessed the disintegration of their antebellum fortunes during the war.[18]

Those who somehow sustained themselves, and, still possessing large tracts of fertile soil, hoped to rebuild, discovered that the wartime destruction was only a harbinger of things to come. The problems in securing farmhands, the flooding and crop failures in 1866 and 1867, the difficulties in obtaining credit, forced many black landholders off the land, while pushing others to the brink of disaster. Within a few years after the war the vast majority of the wealthiest rural Negroes in antebellum America—Louisiana's Creoles of color—had not only lost their slaves, farm machinery, livestock, buildings, and personal possessions, but their land as well. During the war, Antoine and Josephine Decuir were forced to mortgage their house, the adjoining land, even their crops. The Metoyer family in Natchitoches Parish, declining since the 1850s, experienced a final economic disaster during the depression of the 1870s. In the first year of the depression, 1873, forty-four members of the family were listed as having had their land sold at "tax sales." Often these sales were conducted for non-payment of assessments amounting to only a few dollars. Following the death of their mother in 1866, Andrew Durnford, Jr., and his sister Rosema Durnford struggled desperately to regain the antebellum production of sugar that had made their father one of the richest free Negroes in the United States, but in 1874, besieged by creditors, they were forced to sell St. Rosalie Plantation for a few thousand dollars. In St. Mary Parish, once affluent mulattoes eked out a subsistence on small plots of their old plantations. During the 1860s the mean value of real estate held by black planters in the state dropped from nearly $10,000 to under $2,000, a decline greater than the general depreciation in postwar property values.[19]

The decline of antebellum free persons of color during the postwar era was also apparent in the decreased value of the holdings among blacks in skilled occupations.

Between 1860 and 1870, the mean value of real-estate owning black bricklayers dropped from $2,888 to $1,022; among carpenters from $1,406 to $948; among merchants from $10,925 to $6,925; among grocers from $10,480 to $3,067; among shoemakers from $1,972 to $804; among cigar makers from $1,780 to $1,403; and among boardinghouse keepers from $2,794 to $2,243. Part of this decline was due to small numbers of former slaves entering these occupations, and the depreciation in some urban property values, though the latter was far less precipitous than in rural areas. The drops in the average wealth holdings generally reflected an economic decline among former free Negroes. So too did the drop in the proportion of free women of color who owned real estate, from 28.4 percent in 1860 to 13.5 a decade later. In addition, at least as roughly gauged by the United States census, only about one out of five former free Negroes survived the war as property owners. Some, like Antoine Decuir, died during the 1860s; others left the state; some of the women married and took new surnames. While little is known about the "persistence rate" among white property owners in Louisiana during the Civil War period, compared to other sections of the South where fighting occurred this was a relatively low persistence.[20]

Only a few former free persons of color escaped the war years unscathed. Those who did had usually invested heavily in urban real estate (rather than slaves) and maintained profitable businesses. In New Orleans, land speculator Thomy Lafon, who became a large contributor to various black charities, increased his wealth from $10,000 to $55,000 by speculating in swamplands during the Union occupation. Money broker John Racquet Clay added $16,500 to his estate during the 1860s, and another broker, Drauzin Barthélemy Macarty, increased his fortune from $45,000 to $77,300 during the same period. Between 1860 and 1870, real-estate dealer Aristide Mary acquired $70,000 worth of property, while antebellum plasterer Oscar James Dunn, builder Jean-Baptiste Roudanez, and tailor Sidney Thezan entered various professional and business fields to enhance their wealth holdings. Several other prosperous free persons of color in the city, while not increasing their wealth, maintained their high prewar economic standing: merchant Bernard Soulié, who had loaned the Confederate government $10,000, kept the bulk of his $100,000 estate, as did landlord Edmond Dupuy, whose $200,000 worth of real estate in 1870 made him the second wealthiest Negro in the South.[21]

But those who survived the war in such a manner represented only a small proportion of prewar wealthholders. A close study of Creoles of color in the Fourth, Fifth, and Sixth wards, the heart of the free mulatto community, reveals a marked decline. Among the 98 free persons of color listed in the 1860 and 1870 census returns, nearly half experienced losses, only one of four kept their holdings intact, and only 23 expanded their wealth. Musician Nicholas Dabron saw his real estate drop from $11,000 to $4,150, grocer Felix Roberts from $5,600 to $1,000, and carpenter Casimir Labat, from $3,000 to no wealth at all in 1870. Labat was joined by 31 other propertied antebellum men and women in the three wards who had lost everything.[22]

But the war caused more than economic decline among former free persons of color. Having lost their unique standing, they were now forced to compete with ex-slaves. While some attempted to maintain their separate family and social values this became increasingly difficult during a period of rapid social and political change. Most looked back longingly and nostalgically on the antebellum period. Several former free persons of color who had survived the war with their estates intact found it impossible to adjust to the rapid changes occurring in the wake of emancipation. Saddened by the passing of the old regime, disheartened by their loss of status, and angered at being mistaken for ex-bondsmen, they ignored their business obligations and allowed their real-estate holdings to evaporate. François Lacroix seemed not to care about the disintegration of his fortune. Even after the war, Lacroix, a tailor and realtor, maintained control over 198 separate pieces of real estate in the Crescent City and surrounding areas. Nor was he without funds to pay the taxes which he ignored until the sheriff confiscated his property. In 1874, the once vibrant Lacroix, wearing a vacant smile, stood silently as the "splendid creation of his industry" crumbled before the auctioneer's gavel. According to one witness, Lacroix seemed "forlorn and sorrowful." Two years later he was dead. Three other rich Creoles of color, Aristide Mary, John Racquet Clay, and Jean-Baptiste Jourdain, men who had not only distinguished themselves in various business ventures but also had gained stature as the most "intelligent and well educated" colored Creoles in the Crescent City, suffered similar financial reversals. Depressed and unable to cope, one by one each of them ended his own life, Clay by putting a pistol to his temple and pulling the trigger.[23]

Such extreme responses were rare, but few free persons of color escaped the postwar years unscathed. Within a generation they were truly "a forgotten people." By the dawn of the twentieth century there were only 124 landowning Negro farmers in Pointe Coupée Parish, compared to 1,145 black cash tenants and 1,566 share tenants. The total value of black-owned property in the parish was substantially below what it had been on the eve of the Civil War, despite the huge population increases. In Natchitoches, Plaquemines, and Iberville parishes, where once prosperous families controlled thriving farms and vast plantations, black tenant farmers and sharecroppers toiled on small plots averaging fewer than twenty-five acres. The total black-wealth holdings in rural areas of the state did not rise above the 1860 figure until 1901-1903, and even at a high watermark in 1907, despite nearly a hundredfold increase in the free rural black population (from approximately 5,441 in 1860 to 553,029 in 1910) the total wealth of former slaves and their children had not yet doubled the 1860 wealth holdings of free persons of color.[24]

An analysis of the plight of antebellum free persons of color during the postwar era reveals a great deal about the unique and privileged position of free blacks before the war. However much historians have focused on the anti-free Negro laws and attitudes during the 1840s and 1850s, the economic standing of the group remained strong. This was due in some measure to their significant property accumulations, but it was also due to their skills, business acumen, industrious work habits, and their social and cultural values.

Moreover, even in the midst of the political turmoil on the eve of secession, they were defended by some whites. "They are an industrious and honest people, respected generally by the white population," one white planter in St. Landry Parish noted during the postwar era, describing the "free born colored population." Before the war they had owned land, livestock, and slaves. Even during 1858-1859, he and others had defended them and voted down anti-free Negro legislation. During the postwar era, however, former free people of color were unable to adjust to new conditions. The war not only diminished much of their property holdings but also destroyed their privileged position. "The war levelled the old barriers," one late nineteenth-century observer explained, and former free Creoles of color "lost their individuality." Thrown together with the masses of their brethren, they quickly discovered that they had little in common with freedmen.[25]

Illustrating their loss of prestige, self-esteem, and economic standing was the career of Adolphe Donato (Donatto), a member of one of the richest black slave-owning families in the South. In 1883, Donato was working as a body servant to a white man. Accompanying his employer on a trip to the nation's capital, he saw streets "as smooth as glass" and buildings "more magnificent than I ever dreamed of." "My room is small but I have a good bed and a stove and, what is better than any thing else, a servant comes in every morning to make my fire." Just think, he explained to a friend in Opelousas, how much of a luxury it was to be waited on "but then you Know 'folks of fashion are bound to put on airs.'" Dressing in the latest styles, strolling along Pennsylvania Avenue, window-shopping at the downtown stores, he feigned being a "distinguished colored gentleman." Each morning, however, he was expected to serve his employer coffee and then wash the cups and saucers. "But I do this so quietly," he noted, "that the servant never supposes for a moment that I am other than a 'gentleman of leisure.'"[26]

Like the seizure and sale of Josephine Decuir's plantation, the confession of Adolphe Donato symbolized the end of an era. The economic rise of free people of color in the state had been a gradual process. With each passing decade prior to 1840 they had substantially expanded their wealth holdings. Even during the late antebellum period they had been able to maintain their high economic standing. On the eve of the war, Louisiana's free Creoles of color were the richest group of blacks in the country. They had risen to an economic level equal to that of the average white American. But they had done so like their white Southern counterparts with the labor of slaves. And like the white slave-owning class they discovered conditions during the postwar period were much different. With their unique and privileged status now gone they struggled to maintain their old ways and regain their former economic standing. In the end, they failed. Looking longingly toward the past they had to content themselves with memories of their former wealth and prestige. Within a generation even those memories seemed like a long forgotten dream.

Appendices

In the wealth estimates for 1850-1870, I have relied primarily on the United States Population Census. During these decades, census takers were instructed to inquire of each household head the estimated true value of his or her real (1850-1870) and personal (1860-1870) property. While this type of inquiry has its limitations, respondents were generally fairly accurate in their estimates. According to Louisiana law, however, slaves were supposed to be listed as real, rather than personal property. This rule was ignored as much as it was applied. In 1860, in thirty-four of fifty-three parishes, census takers included the value of slaves under personal holdings. For some property owners this inconsistency will inflate the estimated value of their realty holdings. Nevertheless, I have decided to leave the original census estimates for real property.[27] Census takers were also instructed to include only property owners with at least $100 in real and/or personal holdings. I have excluded those listed with less than $100. In citing individual property owners, I have used the numbers in the upper right-hand corner of the right-hand page. These were often handwritten, but when printed I have cited the printed page number for both the page on which the printed number appears and the facing page. I have also made a determination with regard to family heads, or what might be termed independent property owners, excluding children listed with small amounts of property under their names, spouses in the same category, or free women of color living with white male property owners. Several other criteria were followed with regard to determining black wealth: those listed as being born in Ireland, Spain, Italy, France, Hanover and other German states were most often excluded unless other indications pointed to state of birth being in error; those listed as white in one census and free Negro in another were most often included when other indications pointed to their being Negro; and property estimates were rounded off to the nearest hundredth (*i. e.,* $775 = $800). A few property owners were listed as mulatto but were actually white. Thus, I have excluded, among others, Pierre LaCour of Natchitoches Parish, who was incorrectly listed in 1850 as a free person of color with real estate worth $50,000.[28] To complete my data lists for 1850, 1860, and 1870, I have checked the names of black property owners cited in various primary and secondary sources. Thus, in 1860, among the 1,262 realty owners, I have included 53 property owners found in local parish records (4), H. E. Sterkx's *The Free Negro in Ante-Bellum Louisiana* (1), Mary Berry's "Negro Troops" (1), David Rankin's "Black Leadership" (40), and the Louisiana Papers at the Moorland-Spingarn Research Center at Howard University (7).[29] For property owners in 1870 who owned less than $1,000 in total property, I have drawn a sample from every twentieth printed page of the manuscript census and considered them to be 5 percent of the property owers. I have checked this sample against the findings of Lee Soltow, who used a random sampling technique, and found them generally compatible, but the 1870 data as cited in Appendix 3 are rough estimates and for individual parishes could be as much as 15 percent more or less than the actual total value of property owned by blacks. Even so, the obvious precipitous downward trend in most parishes is obvious.

The post-1893 total black wealth-holding estimates frcm the Louisiana tax assessment lists in Appendix 3 are probably more precise than the census estimates. But in the post-1893 assessments there is no racial breakdown for Orleans Parish. The earlier assessments for the Crescent City are so uneven as to be virtually useless except for certain individual assessments. In 1856, the assessments listed 179 free persons of color who owned property; the next year, the number jumped 100 percent to 357, at a time when the emigration movement was gaining strength in the Crescent City.[30] There were also some parish boundary changes and the formation of new parishes which make comparisons more difficult. Despite these problems, the statistical evidence presented in the following appendices strongly supports the general thesis set forth in this essay.

Appendix 1
Black Real Estate Owners in Louisiana, 1850

Parish	total value	average value	owners
Avoyelles	$2,900	$967	3
Bienville	2,300	767	3
Caddo	1,200	1,200	1
Calcasieu	3,300	825	4
Catahoula	3,000	3,000	1
East Baton Rouge	40,400	1,554	26
East Feliciana	700	350	2
Franklin	1,000	500	2
Iberville	271,900	30,311	9
Jefferson	166,200	1,955	85
Lafayette	5,700	407	14
Lafourche	6,000	6,000	1
Livingston	8,400	8,400	1
Natchitoches	386,200	4,291	90
Orleans	2,465,000	3,840	642
Ouachita	1,900	950	2
Plaquemines	305,600	5,992	51
Pointe Coupée	428,700	6,213	69
Rapides	4,100	820	5
St. Bernard	26,800	5,360	5
St. Charles	4,000	4,000	1
St. Helena	500	500	1
St. James	1500	750	2
St. John the Baptist	132,600	13,260	10
St. Landry	87,800	915	96
St. Martin	34,100	1,066	32

(Appendix 1 cont.)

Parish	total value	average value	owners
St. Mary	64,700	1,961	33
St. Tammany	48,500	1,865	26
Terrebonne	4,800	1,600	3
Vermilion	300	300	1
Washington	200	200	1
West Baton Rouge	18,600	1,240	15
West Feliciana	7,000	1,000	7
Total	$4,535,900	$3,646	1,244

Appendix 2
Black Real Estate Owners in Louisiana, 1860

Parish	total value	average value	owners
Ascension	$1,400	$1,400	1
Assumption	3,300	825	4
Avoyelles	6,000	1,200	5
Caddo	8,500	2,833	3
Calcasieu	13,700	806	17
Carroll	400	400	1
Catahoula	3,600	720	5
East Baton Rouge	100,800	2,016	50
Iberville	651,800	46,557	14
Jefferson	80,900	3,677	22
Lafayette	10,500	618	17
Lafourche	16,900	939	18
Natchitoches	253,700	2,371	107
Orleans	2,628,200	4,524	581
Plaquemines	181,500	3,490	52
Pointe Coupée	770,000	9,390	82
Rapides	90,600	3,485	26
St. Bernard	600	600	1
St. Charles	41,500	8,300	5
St. John the Baptist	77,000	6,417	12
St. Landry	170,400	1,852	92
St. Martin	150,000	2,542	59
St. Mary	118,900	5,170	23
St. Tammany	28,700	844	34
Terrebonne	17,800	2,967	6

(Appendix 2 cont.)

Parish	total value	average value	owners
Vermilion	1,300	650	2
Washington	900	450	2
West Baton Rouge	77,100	6,425	12
West Feliciana	7,200	1,029	7
Winn	1,300	650	2
total	$5,514,500	$4,370	1,262

Appendix 3

Total Black Property Holding in Selected Rural Parishes, 1860-1913

	1860	1870	1901/ 1893	1903	1907	1913
Bienville		$65,200	$79,470	$198,800[a]	$278,610	$162,570
Bossier		175,500	233,143	344,530	348,854	272,530
Caddo	$13,200	229,900	n.d.	505,960	696,520	889,000
Claiborne	300	115,100	159,296	206,375	342,195	291,870
Concordia	100	68,000	109,581	196,746	251,869	80,695
De Soto		62,000	225,455	297,690	n.d.	448,700
East Carroll[b]			96,835	155,080	267,020	223,980
East Feliciana		118,000	124,975	187,735	364,460	181,905
Iberia		162,700	207,482	320,080	491,740	411,670
Iberville	665,100	104,600	196,315	158,910	193,325	169,490
Jefferson	129,400	129,000	130,190	118,725	133,870	107,700
Lafayette	33,400	93,400	129,005	169,898	307,478	325,796
Natchitoches	739,700	370,800	397,480	455,160	534,287	437,670[c]
Ouachita		68,800	n.d.	220,570	288,180	277,066
Plaquemines	379,700	341,000	173,545	n.d.	168,770[d]	144,208[e]
Pointe Coupée	796,000	259,600	173,005	133,765	327,465	122,327
Rapides	113,200	101,300	62,060	101,415	192,150	309,710
St. John	214,100	49,700	49,880	54,395[f]	120,170[g]	121,045
St. Landry	609,900	236,200	n.d.	371,960[h]	734,470	530,870
St. Martin	188,700	140,900	197,670	310,320	335,580	332,270
St. Mary	228,700	83,100	240,296	315,046[i]	390,050[j]	434,630
St. Tammany	85,800	29,000	82,804	101,902	88,304	137,628
Tensas	100	205,600	161,840	179,770	237,560	177,810
Webster[k]			110,070	138,685	229,570	216,780
W. B. Rouge	88,500	20,800	89,080	103,430	133,922	82,028
W. Feliciana	15,200	22,900	177,864	216,733	227,620	132,700[l]

(Source: Computed from USMSPC, 1850, 1860, 1870; Assessment Rolls, Louisiana parishes, 1893-1916, Louisiana State Archives, Baton Rouge, Louisiana. Assessors were instructed to list the actual value of land and personal holdings. Postwar land values in the state dropped 70 percent. See U. S. Department of Agriculture, *Report of the Commissioner of Agriculture for the Year 1867,* 12 vols. (Washington, D. C., 1867), 102-19; Roger L. Ransom and Richard Sutch, O*ne Kind of Freedom: The Economic Consequences of Emancipation* (London, 1977), 51.)

aThe data for Bienville are for 1892.
bEast Carroll was formed out of Carroll Parish in 1877.
cThe data for Natchitoches are for 1911.
dThe data for Plaquemines are for 1911.
eThe data for Plaquemines are for 1916.
fThe data for St. John are for 1899.
gThe data for St. John are for 1908.
hThe data for St. Landry are for 1900.
iThe data for St. Mary are for 1902.
jThe data for St. Mary are for 1905.
kWebster Parish was created from portions of Bienville, Bossier, and Claiborne parishes in 1871.
lThe data for West Feliciana are for 1915.

Notes for "Antebellum Free Persons of Color in Postbellum Louisiana"

[1]Records of the Parish Probate Court (hereafter RPPC), Pointe Coupée Parish, La., Successions, #203, July 11, 1865. In this and subsequent succession citations, I have used the filing date, although packets pertaining to an estate usually contain documents post-dating the original probate entry date.

[2]United States Manuscript Agricultural Census (hereafter USMSAC), Pointe Coupée Parish, La., 1850, 579; Joseph Karl Menn, *The Large Slaveholders of Louisiana, 1860* (New Orleans, 1964), 316; United States Manuscript Population Census (hereafter USMSPC), Pointe Coupée Parish, La., 1850, 40; ibid., 1860, p. 796; ibid., 1870, p. 324. See Appendixes for page number citation procedure for USMSPC.

[3]David Rankin, "The Impact of the Civil War on the Free Colored Community of New Orleans," *Perspectives in American History,* 11 (1977-1978): 379-416; David Rankin, "The Origins of Black Leadership in New Orleans During Reconstruction," *Journal of Southern History,* 40 (1974): 417-40. See also David O. Whitten, *Andrew Durnford: A Black Sugar Planter in Antebellum Louisiana* (Natchitoches, La., 1981); Herbert E. Sterkx, *The Free Negro in Ante-bellum Louisiana* (Rutherford, N. J., 1972); Donald Everett, "Free Persons of Color in Colonial Louisiana," *Louisiana History,* 7 (1966): 38, 45, 48-49; Gary Mills, *The Forgotten People: Cane River's Creoles of Color* (Baton Rouge, 1977); Robert Reinders, "The Decline of the New Orleans Free Negro in the Decade Before the Civil War," *Journal of Mississippi History,* 24 (1962): 88-98; and Robert Reinders, "The Free Negro in the New Orleans Economy, 1850-1860," *Louisiana History,* 6 (1965): 273-85.

[4]Laura Foner, "The Free People of Color in Louisiana and St. Domingue: A Comparative Portrait of Two Three-Caste Slave Societies," *Journal of Social History,* 3 (1970), 408-11; James Robertson, ed., *Louisiana Under the Rule of Spain, France, and the United States, 1785-1807; Social, Economic, and Political Conditions of the Territory Represented in the Louisiana Purchase,* 2 vols. (1910-1911; reprint ed., Freeport, N. Y., 1969), 1:218-19; P. M. Bertin, comp., *General Index of All Successions, Opened in the Parish of*

Orleans, From the Year 1805, to the Year 1846 (New Orleans, 1849), passim; Sterkx, *Free Negro,* 91-92, 204; Donald Everett, "Emigres and Militiamen: Free Persons of Color in New Orleans, 1803-1815," *Journal of Negro History,* 38 (1953): 377-80.

[5]Everett, "Free Persons of Color," 49.

[6]Creoles of color were persons of French or Spanish and Negro descent born in the Americas. In Louisiana, the term "Creole" was also applied to whites culturally related to the original French settlers. See Ira Berlin, "Time, Space, and the Evolution of Afro-American Society on British Mainland North America," *American Historical Review,* 85 (1980): 45.

[7]RPPC, Plaquemines Parish, La., Inventories, vol. 1846-1858 (May 6, 1857), 404-9; ibid., Pointe Coupée Parish, La., Successions, #176, April 5, 1839; ibid., Pointe Coupée Parish, La., Conveyances, #1192, October 22, 1822; and #4312, January 23, 1832; ibid., St. Landry Parish, La., Successions, #1544, February 1, 1851; and #1700, February 28, 1853; ibid., Wills, bk. L-1 (September 2, 1847), 75-76; ibid., Natchitoches Parish, La., Successions, #375, July 26, 1839; ibid., #362, December 15, 1838; ibid., #193-1, July 6, 1833; ibid., #355, September 7, 1838; ibid., #606, October 14, 1847; Sterkx, *Free Negro,* 204-7; Mills, *Forgotten People,* 74-76.

[8]Helen Catterall, ed., *Judicial Cases Concerning American Slavery and the Negro,* 5 vols. (Washington, D. C., 1932), 3:392, 589, 611; Carter G. Woodson, ed., *Free Negro Owners of Slaves in the United States in 1830* (Washington, D. C., 1924), 11, *passim.* The general statistics are calculated from Woodson's listing. While most of the forty-three large slave owners mentioned have been verified in parish records, Woodson's list contains a few free blacks who did not own the slaves listed in their households. See R. Halliburton, Jr., "Free Black Owners of Slaves: A Reappraisal of the Woodson Thesis," *South Carolina Historical Magazine,* 76 (1976): 129-42.

[9]RPPC, Natchitoches Parish, La., Successions, #375, July 26, 1839; ibid., Plaquemines Parish, La., Inventories, vol. 1846-1858 (May 6, 1857), 404-9; ibid., St. Landry Parish, La., Successions, #2256, September 9, 1859; ibid., Pointe Coupée Parish, La., Successions, #176, April 5, 1839, and #355, January 31, 1844.

[10]Frederick Law Olmsted, *The Cotton Kingdom: A Traveller's Observations on Cotton and Slavery in the American Slave States,* ed. Arthur M. Schlesinger (New York, 1953), 262; George Rawick, ed., *The American Slave: A Composite Autobiography,* 19 vols. (Westport, Conn,, 1972), 5, pt. 4, 4838.

[11]Richard Tansey, "Out-of-State Free Blacks in Late Antebellum New Orleans," *Louisiana History,* 22 (1981): 373, 378; Sterkx, *Free Negro,* 172-73, 197.

[12]Computed from USMSPC, Louisiana, 1850, 1860. Wealth estimates for nine property owners were taken from the USMSAC, 1850; Reinders, "The Free Negro in the New Orleans Economy," 273-85; Rankin, "The Origins of Black Leadership," 417-40; and Sterkx, *Free Negro,* 216. See also USMSPC, New Orleans, La., 1st Mun., 7th Ward, 1850, pp. 376, 396; Reinders, "The Decline of the New Orleans Free Negro," 95-96.

[13]Comparative data computed from USMSPC, 1850, 1860; Juliet E. K. Walker, "Racism, Slavery, and Free Enterprise: Black Entrepreneurship in the United States Before the Civil War," *Business History Review,* 60 (1986): 354, 361-62; USMSPC, New Orleans, La., 1st Mun., 7th Ward, 1850, p. 396; ibid., New Orleans, 3rd Ward, 1860, p. 257; ibid., 4th Ward, p. 82; ibid., 5th Ward, p. 729; RPPC, New Orleans, La., Successions, #38,677, May 27, 1876, in New Orleans Public Library (hereafter NOPL); Leonard Curry, *The Free Black in Urban America, 1800-1850: The Shadow of the Dream* (Chicago, 1981), 42; Rankin, "The Impact of the Civil War," 396, 402; USMSPC, New Orleans, La., 1st Mun., 4th Ward, 1850, p. 150; ibid., 1st Mun., 7th Ward, 1850, p. 376; RRPC, New Orleans, La., Successions, #41,626, November 19, 1879, in NOPL; Tax Receipts, no. C-530, 1845-1847, in ibid.; USMSPC, New Orleans, La., 3rd Mun., 2nd Ward, 1850, p. 119; USMSAC,

Natchitoches Parish, La., 1850, p. 425; ibid., Plaquemines Parish, La., 1850, pp. 485, 549; ibid., Pointe Coupée Parish, La., 1850, p. 569; ibid., St. John the Baptist Parish, La., p. 661; ibid., St. Landry Parish, La., 1850, p. 695; ibid., St. Mary Parish, La., 1850, pp. 727-29; ibid., Iberville Parish, La., 1850, p. 81; USMSPC, Iberville Parish, La., 1850, p. 329; David O. Whitten, "Rural Life Along the Mississippi: Plaquemines Parish, Louisiana, 1830-1850," *Agricultural History,* 58 (1984): 484; James Freeman Clarke, *Present Condition of Free Colored People of the United States* (New York, 1859), 13.

[14]Lee Soltow, *Men and Wealth in the United States, 1850-1870* (New Haven, 1975), 64, 76, 81, 186. These, of course, are rough estimates based on an estimated 3,729 free Negro families (approximately one-fifth of the total 18,647 free black population). See Ira Berlin, *Slaves Without Masters: The Free Negro in the Antebellum South* (New York, 1974), 136.

[15]"A Contract of Marriage Between Joseph Metoyer and Marie Lodoiska Llorens," January 28, 1840, Cane River Collection, The Historic New Orleans Collection; RPPC, Pointe Coupée Parish, La., Marriage Contract, February 26, 1835. In 1860, in St. Landry Parish census takers often included the maiden name of women listed as "keeping house" in each household. Partners were usually members of either one or another among seventeen families. USMSPC, St. Landry Parish, La., 1860, passim; RPPC, St. Landry Parish, La., Successions, #1544-1545, February 1, 1851; RPPC, Natchitoches Parish, La., Successions, #344, September 7, 1838; ibid., Successions, #375, July 27, 1839; ibid., Successions, #606, October 14, 1847; ibid., Plaquemines Parish, La., Successions, #167, May 12, 1840 ibid., East Baton Rouge Parish, La., Successions, #640, August 14, 1855; ibid., West Baton Rouge Parish, La., Successions, #176, July 18, 1829; ibid., New Orleans, La., Successions, #361, April 19, 1879, in NOPL.

[16]Nathan Willey, "Education of the Colored Population of Louisiana," *Harper's New Monthly Magazine,* 33 (1866): 247; U. S., War Department, *The War of the Rebellion: A Compilation of the Official Records of the Union and Confederate Armies,* 70 vols. (Washington, D. C., 1880-1901), ser. 1, 15:556; Mary Berry, "Negro Troops in Blue and Gray: The Louisiana Native Guards, 1861-1863," *Louisiana History,* 8 (1967): 167; Arthur W. Bergeron, Jr., "Free Men of Color in Grey," *Civil War History,* 32 (1986): 248; John D. Winters, *The Civil War in Louisiana* (Baton Rouge, 1963), 21; Rodolphe Desdunes, *Our People and Our History,* trans. Dorothea McCants (Baton Rouge, 1973), 22; George S. Denison to Salmon P. Chase, August 26, 1862, in *Annual Report of the American Historical Association for the Year 1902,* 2 vols. (Washington, D. C., 1903), 2:311; Joseph T. Wilson, *The Black Phalanx: A History of the Negro Soldiers of the United States in the Wars of 1775-1812, 1861-'65* (Hartford, Conn., 1897), 481-83.

[17]G. B. Hauk to Charles F. Benjamin, February 28, 1874, Records of the Claims Commission, Records, of the Treasury Department, Record Group 56, reel 11, National Archives; George Tucker to Charles F. Benjamin, February 28, 1874, in ibid.; Whitelaw Reid, *After the War: A Tour of the Southern States, 1865-1866,* ed. by C. Vann Woodward (1866; reprint ed., New York, 1965), 244; Rankin, "The Origins of Black Leadership in New Orleans," 433.

[18]Rawick, ed., *The American Slave,* 5, pt. 4, p. 158; quoted in Mills, *Forgotten People,* 237; Petition for Relief of Antoine Meullion, December 1889, #8090, in Meullion Family Papers, Louisiana State University; RPPC, St. Landry Parish, La., Successions, #5040, October 14, 1890; USMSPC, St. Landry Parish, La., 1860, pp. 886-887; RPPC, Iberville Parish, La., Deeds, bk. 9 (July 15, 1868), 221-23; J. Ward Gurley, Jr., to Charles Benjamin, May 18, 1875, Records of the Claims Commission, Records of the Treasury Department, Record Group 56, reel 6, National Archives; Joseph Tournoir to J. Ward Gurley, Jr., September 5, 1874, in ibid.; USMSPC, Pointe Coupée Parish, La., 1870, 324, 333, 396, 398.

[19]Computed form USMSPC, 1860, 1870.

[20]RPPC, Pointe Coupée Parish, La., Successions, #203, July 11, 1865; USMSPC, Pointe Coupée Parish, La., 1860, p. 796; RPPC, Natchitoches Parish, La., Conveyances, vol. 69 (December 20, 1873), 601-4, 637-39;

Mills, *Forgotten People,* 218-19; RPPC, Plaquemines Parish, La., Successions, #252, April 27, 1867; ibid., Conveyances, bk. K (May 5, 1874), 791-93; USMSPC, St. Mary Parish, La., 1870, p. 574. See Jonathan M. Wiener, *Social Origins of the New South: Alabama, 1860-1885* (Baton Rouge, 1978).

[21]USMSPC, New Orleans, La., 1st Mun., 7th Ward, 1850, p. 396; ibid., 1870, 5th Ward, pp. 73, 216; ibid., 1870, 7th Ward, p. 549; RPPC, New Orleans, La., Successions, #35,055, December 2, 1871, NOPL; ibid., New Orleans, La., Successions, #41,616, November 19, 1879, NOPL; ibid., New Orleans, La., Successions, #37, 326, July 28, 1874, in Louisiana Papers, 65-2, Moorland-Spingarn Research Center, Howard University, Washington, D. C.; ibid., New Orleans, La., Successions, #37,326, July 28, 1874, in ibid.; Rankin, "The Origins of Black Leadership in New Orleans," 431-32; Charles E. Wynes, "Thomy Lafon: Black Philanthropist," *Midwest Quarterly,* 22 (1981): 105-9; John Blassingame, *Black New Orleans, 1860-1880* (Chicago, 1973), 57, 144, 213; Curry, *The Free Black in Urban America,* 42.

[22]USMSPC, New Orleans, La., 6th Ward, 1860, p. 170; ibid., 1870, p. 235; Rankin, "The Impact of the Civil War," 396-98.

[23]*New Orleans Daily Picayune,* September 9, 1874; RPPC, New Orleans, La., Successions, #38,677, May 27, 1876; Rankin, "The Impact of the Civil War," 403-6.

[24]U. S. Bureau of the Census, *Twelfth Census of the United States, Taken in the Year 1900,* part 1, *Agriculture,* Vol. 1:88-89; *Population of the United States in 1860; Compiled from the Original Returns of the Eighth Census* (Washington, D. C., 1864), 195; *Negro Population 1790-1915* (Washington, D. C., 1918), 92.

[25]Adolphe Garrigues to Charles F. Benjamin, January 28, 1876, Records of the Claims Commission, Records of the Treasury Department, Record Group 56, National Archives; P. F. de Gournay, "The F. M. C.'s of Louisiana," *Lippincott's Monthly Magazine,* 53 (1894): 517.

[26]Adolphe Donato to Jules Perrodin, December 16, 1883, Miscellaneous Letters, #2946, Louisiana State University.

[27]See Menn, *Large Slaveholders of Louisiana,* 79, 92-93.

[28]See Mills, *Forgotten People,* 213.

[29]See footnotes above for complete citations.

[30]Tansey, "Out-of-State Free Blacks," 384.

POLITICS AND VIOLENCE IN BOURBON LOUISIANA: THE LOREAUVILLE RIOT OF 1884 AS A CASE STUDY*

Gilles Vandal

On November 1, 1884, three days before the presidential election that put Grover Cleveland into the White House, the small town of Loreauville in Iberia Parish was struck by a riot that took the lives of no less than eighteen people, and left a larger number of wounded. The incident was small compared with the numerous and larger riots that had perturbed the political scene of Louisiana during Reconstruction. The Loreauville tragedy was one of the largest political disturbances during Bourbon rule in Louisiana.[1] And yet, the Loreauville riot attracted little attention at the time in a nation tired of hearing of violence occurring in the South. Since then it has been largely ignored by historians.[2]

For several days following the event, the New Orleans and rural press sought to explain what had transpired at Loreauville. Most newspapers agreed with the *Bossier Banner* when it described the riot as "the most deplorable and bloody affray ever perpetrated" in Iberia Parish. The press also acknowledged that the riot grew out of the political difficulties that had been troubling the parish for several months. The *Pioneer* of Assumption, which was not a Republican paper, blamed the riot on Democratic adventurers hungry for office, while most of the other papers charged the Republicans with having provoked the riot by conducting a bitter campaign.[3] Since no paper attempted to present the riot in a larger perspective and since no inquiry was conducted into the causes or the origins of the riot, the incident sank quickly into oblivion in a state and in a nation more preoccupied with industrial growth and economic development than with civil rights.

The historical significance of the Loreauville riot does not arise from the number of lives lost nor even from the fact that it sealed the fate of Republican rule in Iberia Parish.

*First published in *Louisiana History*, 30 (1989): 23-42. Reprinted with the kind permission of the author and the Louisiana Historical Association.

As a matter of fact, this riot did not differ markedly from the numerous incidents of violence that underlined politics during Reconstruction and early Bourbon rule in Louisiana. Nevertheless, the Loreauville incident does leave its mark in Louisiana history as the last major political riot of the nineteenth century and the end of Republican rule even at the local level. More importantly, however, the Loreauville riot revealed much about the nature of politics under the Bourbons.

Iberia had been established as a parish in 1868 from portions of St. Mary and St. Martin parishes. It was the result of long-festering grievances of the local population which felt it did not receive its share of the parishes' spending for road maintenance and ferry privileges. A first attempt to create a new parish aborted in 1838, but the efforts culminated in success in 1868 under the leadership of Alfred Duperier. Duperier was a well-known and respected doctor and planter of southern Louisiana. As was the case with many former Whigs, Duperier joined the Republican party after the war and subsequently became a friend of Reconstruction governor Henry Clay Warmoth. In 1868, Duperier convinced Senator John Ray of Ouachita Parish, who was also a former Whig, to push a bill through the senate for the creation of Iberia Parish. Supported by the conservative elements of the Republican party in Iberia and assured by Governor Warmoth of control over the patronage in the new parish, Duperier emerged as the main Republican leader in Iberia during its early days.[4]

Iberia was created amidst the political and social turmoil that troubled all Louisiana during Reconstruction. The first years of the new parish were underlined by a high level of criminality and personal violence. Indeed, depredations caused by gangs of robbers, numerous acts of individual violence, including murder, created a climate of insecurity in the parish that prevailed for most of the period. The problem was considered so serious in 1873, in 1874, and again in 1876 that on each occasion the local population organized vigilance committees to fight this scourge.[5] Robberies by roving gangs of highwaymen lasted until the 1880s in Iberia. In 1883, the *New Orleans Times-Democrat* reported that Iberia was still infested by a gang of daring burglars who plundered country stores and rich plantations. As it was almost impossible to detect the thieves in their nefarious projects, the authorities of the parish were largely accused of lack of efforts in bringing the criminals to justice.[6]

A review of congressional reports and local and state newspapers brings to light the troubled conditions that prevailed in Iberia Parish between 1868 and 1883.[7] There were no less than 81 murders during this period (Table 1). While violence in Iberia Parish was well above the state level (42.5) during Reconstruction (1868 to 1876) with an average of 71.5 per 100,000 inhabitants, it dropped during the post-Reconstruction years (1877 to 1883) to the state level (17.3) with an annual average of 18.2.[8] Politics seems to be the main cause of violence in Iberia as it was elsewhere in Louisiana. Indeed, out of the 81 killings that occurred in Iberia between 1868 and 1883, 23 had political causes, while 13 were related to family quarrels, 8 to robberies, 7 to labor conflicts, 5 to marital disputes,

3 to black insubordination, 1 to gambling, 1 to heavy drinking, 1 to rape, and the remaining 20 originated form trivial causes or unspecified arguments.[9]

Reconstruction in Iberia as elsewhere in Louisiana was underlined by political violence. Tensions and ill feelings between Republicans and Democrats were present at the establishment of the parish and persisted during the whole period. Although the black voters represented the backbone of the Republican party in Iberia as well as elsewhere in Louisiana, an important segment of the white population, composed mainly of former Whigs, supported the Republican party at the outset.[10] The Iberia Democrats who were well aware of the strength of the Republican party in Iberia, tried to divide local issues and politics on racial lines by appealing to white solidarity and resorting to violence. The Democrat strategy was only partially successful because the strength of the Republican party in Iberia remained after 1876 in the hands of a small group of less than 50 white Radicals who organized and controlled the black vote.[11]

TABLE 1
Number of killings in Iberia

Years	Whites	Blacks	Unknown	Total
1868	1	2	1	4
1869		2		2
1870	6	6		12
1871	2	3		5
1872	2	4	1	7
1873	2	6		8
1874		6		6
1875	2	6		8
1876	3	2	2	7
1877	2			2
1878	1	1		2
1879	1			1
1880	4			4
1881		2	3	5
1882	1	2		3
1883		4	1	5
Total	27	46	8	81

Political violence erupted in 1874 when a White League was organized within the parish. The strategy of the White League at the local and at the state level was aimed not only at intimidating blacks but also at the expulsion of white Republicans from the parish.[12] As a result of the League's actions, the Republican members of the police jury were compelled to resign, some 1200 blacks did not register to vote and some 150 of those who did register were compelled to vote for the Democratic ticket for fear of losing their employment.[13] Moreover, following the 1874 election, many black Republicans in Iberia Parish lost their jobs as bands of whites rode through the countryside compelling planters to discharge blacks who had voted Republican. Only blacks who had voted Democratic were able to secure a job.[14] In January 1875, Iberia Parish was in a particularly troubled condition since some 160 black families were on the verge of starvation after having been discharged by planters.[15]

Elections in Iberia Parish and throughout Louisiana during Reconstruction were frequently characterized by intimidation of blacks to prevent them from voting. The election of 1876 marked, however, a shift in the Conservative strategy as whites resorted to violence, not to prevent blacks from voting, but in order to coerce them to vote for the Democratic ticket.[16] By 1878, the strategy of the white Conservatives consisted in turning the vote of the parishes of North Louisiana, which had a large black population, into a Democratic majority. Riots broke out in Natchitoches and Caddo parishes, while general intimidation became the rule in Madison, Concordia, and Tensas parishes.[17] The level of violence even shocked Gov. Francis T. Nicholls, a moderate Democrat who opposed the use of violence.[18] Meanwhile, in many other parishes Democrats proceeded to carry the election by fraud and ballot-stuffing.[19] All in all, these means worked well to induce blacks to vote Democratic. In Natchitoches, the Democratic party carried the parish by a vote of 2,811 to 0, while in Tensas, Concordia and Madison the large Republican majorities of 1876 simply evaporated.[20]

Violence did not prevent Republicans from maintaining a strong grasp on offices in Iberia and as a matter of fact in all of southern Louisiana. The Republican hold on local offices in that region was overwhelming and lasted into the 1880s. Indeed, Republicans in Iberia held the offices of district judge, district attorney, and parish judge from 1868 to 1884. The offices of clerk of court and sheriff were in the hands of Republicans during the years of 1868 to 1870 and 1872 to 1884. The state representative was also Republican between 1868 and 1870, and 1872 to 1884. Moreover, Republicans had majorities on the board of education until 1877 and on the police jury until 1880. Finally, the city council was the only governmental body in which Iberia Democrats held a majority during the period. Indeed, of the 22 people seated on the city council in Iberia Parish between 1868 to 1884, only five were Republicans.[21]

By 1884 the only remaining Republican stronghold in Louisiana was to be found in the southern parishes. This can be explained by the fact that, even if the planters and freedmen disagreed about wages and work conditions, they generally agreed politically. Not only were many plantations owned by white Republicans and Northern businessmen, but many Democratic planters opposed their party's platform on the tariff question and were asking the federal administration to protect them against foreign sugar imports.[22] As a consequence, the sugar belt was the only region of Louisiana where blacks were not generally coerced after Reconstruction into voting Democratic. However, this situation began to change by 1882 as the Republicans lost control of the police juries.[23]

Members of the police juries, the governing bodies of the parishes, had been elected both before and after the Civil War,[24] but Act 92, adopted in 1882, changed that state of affairs. Under the new law, the governor received the power of appointment of the police jurors.[25] Since police juror was one of the most important parochial offices, the new law, by making the police jury a tool of the state administration, represented an important change in the role and influence of the local authorities. Moreover, the Republicans lost part of their influence in local politics as Governor [Samuel D.] McEnery appointed as members of the police jury only strong Democrats who supported the state administration. Indeed, the *St. Landry Democrat* reported that the new law was "a party measure enacted for the purpose of putting the police juries in those parishes where the negroes [*sic*] predominated beyond their control." Finally, since police jurors were until then responsible for selecting the polling location and had the power to appoint the commissioners of election, the new law meant also that the Republicans were losing their "*droit de regard*" on the way the commissioners of election were appointed, the way they counted the ballots, and signed the official returns.[26]

Even this was not enough. In order to insure to the state administration a total control over the electoral processes, the Democratic legislature adopted in 1882 a new election law. Act 101 took from the police juries the exclusive power of chosing the polling places and commissioners of elections and gave it to a parish supervisor appointed by the governor following a recommendation of the police jury.[27] The new law which had been personally sponsored by Governor McEnery, allowed the state authorities to subvert the democratic character of all local and state elections and to reverse the public choice. Therefore, the Democrats could hope to control all local and state elections and even to carry any parish by resorting, if necessary, to widespread fraud, bribery, and ballot stuffing.[28] Consequently, the new law installed a system of political fraud that made a mockery of elections in late nineteenth-century Louisiana. Fraud had already occurred in the 1882 congressional election as demonstrated by the fact that in many polling places there were more votes cast than names on the poll lists.[29] As the election of April 1884 showed, the new police jury law and the law on election of 1882 had important consequences for the survival of Republican rule at the local level in Louisiana.[30]

In late 1883 and throughout the early spring of 1884, Democrats in Iberia, as well as in many other South Louisiana parishes, launched a bitter campaign against the Republican officeholders of the parish, hoping to capture from them several offices in the coming election of April 1884. Their attacks and recriminations were particularly directed against Judge Theodore Fontelieu, who had held the judgeship in Iberia for the Republican party for the last eight years.[31] A great prejudice against Judge Fontelieu had sprung up in the 1870s, when many whites regarded him as being too close to the black population and too ready to defend their rights.[32] Still, Fontelieu was popular among some whites for his handling of the patronage in the parish.[33]   This brought the complaints by Democrats that Republican officials in Iberia were plundering the white population.[34] They accused Judge Fontelieu of "criminal neglect of the administration of the law both civil and criminal amounting as it does to a denial of justice."[35]

In March 1884, the Democratic Conservative Committee in Iberia and in several other parishes in South Louisiana proposed a plan by which Democrats and Republicans would present a common ticket at the coming election to be held on April 22.[36] Under the Democratic plan, the parish offices in Iberia would be divided between the two parties with the Democrats selecting the candidates for the house of representatives, for district judge and coroner, and the Republicans keeping the offices of clerk of court and sheriff. The Democrats justified their plan on the grounds that a deplorable condition of affairs prevailed in Iberia Parish and that there was a pressing need for better administration of justice and for decreasing parish spending.[37] This plan was not unique to Iberia as similar proposals were presented in almost all the parishes of southern Louisiana. The plan was discussed by the Republican Executive Committee at the state level and rejected although it had been endorsed by William P. Kellogg, a former Republican governor. For the local offices, the committee decided to let each parish adopt or reject the Democratic proposal.[38] Republicans in some parishes, such as Iberville and St. John the Baptist, endorsed the idea of a mixed ticket for local offices, but Iberia Republicans opposed the Democratic plan and both parties presented a separate ticket.[39]

Except for Théogène Viator, the main participants in the Loreauville riot of November 1884 had been candidates for local offices in the election of April 1884. Their involvement in the controversy which resulted in the Loreauville riot was rooted in the role they played during Reconstruction. As a matter of fact, they were all small property owners who gained prominence in local politics only after the war. During and after Reconstruction, they all competed for local offices and the control of the local patronage.

Theodore Fontelieu, who had been the main Republican leader in Iberia for almost twenty years, was again a candidate in April 1884 for the office of district judge. He had held that office for the last eight years after having been parish judge of Iberia during Reconstruction. Judge Fontelieu was born in Louisiana in 1838. He was a small farmer whose property in 1870 was valued at $1300. A member of the Whig party before the war, he came to public office in 1861 when he was elected justice of the peace. Governor Wells appointed him to that same office in 1865. Between 1868 and 1884, he served several times on the city council of New Iberia. Finally, he regularly represented Iberia Parish in the state Republican convention and served several times on the Republican State Executive Committee.[40]

Fred L. Gates emerged after Reconstruction as the main Democratic leader in Iberia. Born in New York in 1829, he encountered his first experience in Louisiana politics as a member of the Whig party during the early 1850s. After serving in the Confederate army as an officer for the duration of the war, he emerged as a confirmed Democrat in 1865. He was appointed by Governor Wells to the office of district judge during the summer of

1865 and was elected to the state general assembly as representative for the parish of St. Mary in November 1865. He served most of the Reconstruction period on the police jury of St. Mary and was closely linked to the political turmoil that affected the parish during the early 1870s. He became a leader of the White League in St. Mary in 1874. He removed to New Iberia in 1878 and became the owner of an oil mill. Judge Gates emerged quickly as a major Democratic leader of Iberia Parish and served regularly on the police jury of the parish. He was closely involved in the Democratic proposal for a common ticket in March 1884 before becoming the Democratic candidate for the office of district judge the following month.[41]

P. A. Veazey, born in 1843, was a retail merchant. He might be considered the chameleon of Iberia Parish politics during that troubled period. Veazey, who was the Democratic candidate for sheriff in 1884, had been a staunch Democrat until 1870. In 1872, however, he became a moderate Republican after obtaining the office of collector of internal revenue in Iberia. Then, in 1873, he became a Radical Republican and served on the police jury until 1876. He sat as a Republican in the state's general assembly in 1878 and 1879. However, as the fortunes of the Republican party in Louisiana began to fade, he again joined the Democratic party in the early 1880s.[42]

Jules Mestayer and Théogène Viator, both Republicans, are the two remaining players in the Loreauville riot. Born in 1845, Mestayer owned a small plantation. During the war, he served in the Confederate army. After the war, he became a Republican but did not hold office before he became that party's candidate for the office of sheriff in 1884.[43] Viator, born in 1823, also owned a small sugar plantation. A friend and supporter of Fontelieu, Viator held the office of sheriff in Iberia between 1876 and 1884.[44]

By early April, the hotly contested campaign had become bitter. Meanwhile, the police jury of Iberia Parish chose only Democrats as commissioners of election. By doing so it paved the way for an overwhelming victory of the Democratic ticket despite a large black vote. It seems clear that the commissioners were guilty of the charge of stuffing the ballot boxes.[45] Because of the subsequent state of excitement in the parish, James L. Burke, the Democratic mayor of New Iberia, appointed fifty extra police officers to preserve the peace on election day.[46] In short, everything was done to insure a Democratic victory and for the first time since its establishment Iberia returned a large Democratic vote of 2,233 and 1,262 votes for the Republicans. The Democratic ticket not only carried the parish for the state offices but also won all local offices.[47]

Judge Fontelieu and his Republican associates asserted that the results were quite different and that the Republican ticket had carried the parish by a vote of 1,406 to 830.[48] The Republicans charged the Democrats with gross fraud as 1,259 fraudulent votes were reported to have been stuffed in boxes in polling places that did not exist.[49] Furthermore, the Republicans announced their determination to contest the election returns in court and to maintain their control of the local offices by force if necessary.[50]

The Iberia Democrats appealed to the governor and the state general assembly which quickly responded by impeaching Judge Fontelieu and suspending him from office.[51]

Meanwhile, Gov. Samuel D. McEnery issued a commission to Frederick L. Gates, the Democratic candidate for the judgeship.[52] Moreover, the governor was determined to settle the whole matter immediately and by the bayonet if necessary. He ordered the state militia to New Iberia to preserve the peace and to install Judge Gates in office.[53]

While the judgeship question was thus being addressed, a new controversy arose around the election of the sheriff. In early June 1884, Jules Mestayer, the Republican candidate for sheriff, asked the courts to determine who was the duly elected sheriff and this in spite of the fact that P. A. Veazey, the Democratic candidate, had been declared duly elected by the governor.[54]

Republican leaders not only rejected the election of the Democrats but also declared their intention to resist.[55] By late June and early July, Fontelieu and other Republican leaders organized a black militia and proceeded, under the leadership of ex-sheriff Théogène Viator, to place the courthouse under guard.[56] Sheriff Veazey reacted swiftly and proceeded to storm and capture the courthouse on July 23; the black guard, taken by surprise, offered no resistance.[57] Sheriff Veazey decided to withdraw from the courthouse, which was immediately reoccupied by blacks. Judge Gates thereupon referred the whole matter to the governor and awaited further orders.[58]

In late July and early August, political strife for offices was revived when Judge Fontelieu contested in court the authority of Judge Gates to appoint new officers and commissioners of the court.[59] Violence seemed unavoidable as the community became committed to one side or the other. The *New Orleans Daily Picayune* reported that "threats of assassination and incendiary" had become a daily occurrence and that "lawless bands of men have paraded the streets at night defying the civil authority."[60] The *Picayune* also reported that dwellings had been fired into and many other riotous acts committed. The inevitable result was that the white property holders of New Iberia began organizing themselves into a citizens' protective association.[61]

As the situation in Iberia deteriorated, Governor McEnery ordered Col. T. A. Fairies, who held the office of assistant adjutant general of the state militia, to go to Iberia and to investigate the conditions that prevailed in the parish. The colonel was also empowered to use the local militia if necessary for maintaining order.[62] A day after his arrival in New Iberia, Colonel Fairies reported to the governor that the community was so excited and the animosity of the opposing factions was so great that he believed an outbreak of violence to be imminent,[63] unless it was prevented by the presence of a large military body.[64]

Following the report of Colonel Fairies, Governor McEnery reacted swiftly. He ordered two hundred militiamen from New Orleans, members of the famous Washington Artillery Battalion, to proceed to New Iberia under the command of General Perry.[65] Upon arriving at New Iberia on the morning of August 14, the militia, supported by local troops, were posted before the courthouse. Only two or three hours after their arrival, General Perry's troops prevented the outbreak of a serious disturbance. As Sheriff Veazey was passing in the vicinity of the courthouse at about 11 o'clock in the morning of the fourteenth, he was met by a large party led by Jules Mestayer, his Republican opponent in the sheriff's election. Words were exchanged and a row followed which was broken up by the militia.[66] On the night of the fourteenth, General Perry's troops proceeded to capture and occupy the courthouse without bloodshed while the Republicans withdrew without offering resistance. Moreover, the militia proceeded to arrest and jail ex-Sheriff Viator and several of his followers.[67]

The militia thus appears to have saved New Iberia from a violent riot. Still, the state troops were forced to remain on duty in the town for another two weeks as the situation remained tense. Since the two factions seemed unready to disengage, it was generally believed that if the troops were to withdraw, the Republican recapture of the courthouse would immediately follow. The troops were asked to patrol the town, as rumors were circulating that a Republican force of 500 men was coming from Jeanerette and St. Martinville to rescue the prisoners by night.[68]

Meanwhile, the threats of incendiarism appeared to be carried into effect as several fires occurred.[69] On the night of August 18, the sawmill of Capt. E. A. Pharr, a leading Democrat who had been largely involved in the local skirmishes, was destroyed by fire. Fires broke out again on the nights of August 23 and August 25. Jules Mestayer, the Republican candidate for sheriff, was arrested on a charge of inciting incendiarism and his bond fixed at $1,000.[70] The Democratic Citizens' Protective Association, established in early August and composed mainly of local merchants, was organized on a permanent basis. More than one hundred men were mustered and began to patrol the streets of the town regularly in order to protect the shopping district from any future acts of incendiarism.[71] The militia, which had been relieved from regular duty on August 25, was finally ordered back to New Orleans on August 29.[72]

The presidential and congressional campaigns of the fall of 1884 only served to renew tensions as the Democrats were determined to prevent the re-election of William P. Kellogg, the Republican candidate for Congress. Both parties conducted a bitter campaign and charged the other with making inflammatory and rancorous speeches.[73] During a torchlight parade in New Iberia on October 22, an attempt was made to assassinate Sheriff Veazey and Capt. Pharr, two leading Democrats who had been involved in the summer feuds. This event created great excitement and was later seen as the germ of the riot that erupted in Loreauville.[74]

As the election campaign reached its closing stage, the Republican leaders planned to hold a political meeting in favor of Kellogg on Saturday, November 1, 1884. Judge Fontelieu, the leading Republican in the parish, and several other Republicans left New Iberia that morning to attend the meeting in Loreauville. Meanwhile, Democrats were determined to use any means to prevent the Republican meeting from taking place. Several Republican leaders were privately advised not to go to the meeting because of possible violence. At the same time whites were heard in saloons to assert openly their intention to stop the meeting.[75]

Around 1 o'clock on Saturday afternoon, November 1, 1884, two hundred Republicans, mainly blacks, entered Loreauville headed by a brass band and led by ex-sheriff Viator, former judge Fontelieu, and Jules Mestayer.[76] As the Republican meeting was about to be called to order, disturbances were created by some ten to fifteen white people who were supporting Edward J. Gay, the Democratic candidate for Congress. Hearing the noise of the disturbance, Joe Guilfoux, a leading Democrat of Iberia, rushed to the scene of the trouble and fired the first shot, only to be shot dead by someone from the black crowd.[77] This was followed by a general row between the blacks who attended the meeting and the whites who attempted to break it up.[78]

As the disturbance grew into a major riot, several whites departed from the scene of the trouble for their headquarters and returned with rifles and shotguns.[79] Armed white men proceeded to surround the Republican crowd. The blacks were really not prepared for such a battle, and the whites began to shoot blacks indiscriminately. The blacks began to run in all directions. Their panic was terrible. They ran wildly, trying to escape, only to be followed and shot down if found.[80] It was reported that some fifty or sixty blacks jumped into the bayou to escape their pursuers and that many of them were afterwards found drowned.[81] In the confusion that followed the engagement, blacks were seen to leave everything behind them including horses, shoes, boots, and clothes.[82] The *New Orleans Daily Picayune* stated that although the engagement had lasted only a few minutes, the houses close to the scene of the riot bore the marks of more than a thousand shots. It was even reported that some twelve horses were killed.[83]

It is difficult to assess the exact number of people who were killed or wounded during the riot. The Democratic press at first put the number of killed at six blacks and two whites, only to increase it to sixteen blacks a few days later. The two whites killed, Joe Guilfoux and Capt. William Bell, were two leading Democrats. But the number of blacks killed must have been much higher than sixteen, if we take into account the report about the excitement that prevailed and the intensity of the riot. Many blacks may have received fatal shots on the battlefield and run a long distance before falling dead somewhere along the roads, in the fields and in the woods. Days later, bodies were still found as far as five miles from the site of the riot.[84] The number of wounded was estimated by the Democratic press to be twenty, but it also must have been much higher as many blacks who were wounded at the riot were not eager to report it and no official investigation was ever conducted.[85] Among the wounded were several white Republicans, but the fact that none of them was killed shows the racial tone of the disturbance.

As the news of the riot reached New Iberia, Judge Gates ordered fifty men from the state militia stationed at New Iberia, and under the orders of Sheriff Veazey, to proceed to Loreauville armed with rifles and shotguns and also with a cannon. The judge furthermore ordered that calm be restored and that all suspected Republican leaders arrested. Although the riot was already over when the militia arrived in Loreauville, they nevertheless proceeded to arrest the Republican leaders.[86]

When the militia returned to New Iberia on the night of the riot, bringing twelve prisoners under heavy escort, the wildest excitement persisted in the town. Among the Republican leaders arrested were former judge Fontelieu, Jules Mestayer, and ex-sheriff Viator. The prisoners were placed in the parish jail located in New Iberia and were protected by a heavy guard because many whites of the town wanted to lynch the arrested parties.[87]

The report of November 2, the day after the riot, to the effect that fifty heavily armed blacks had crossed the bayou some four miles below New Iberia and had disappeared into the woods after firing a few shots, was enough to start the wildest rumors. Whites in New Iberia prepared themselves for all contingencies, as the rumor spread that blacks were gathering in the countryside and intended to come to town to release their leaders.[88] Meanwhile, the district attorney, in agreement with Judge Gates, decided that the arrested Republican leaders could not post bail until after the election and would have to remain in jail until then.[89]

The riot and the arrest of the leading Republicans of the parish produced beneficial results for the Democrats and insured them an easy victory in both the presidential and congressional elections. The Republican party came out of the riot disorganized and without leaders. On November 2, more than 300 blacks who had previously supported Kellogg's candidacy went to a Democratic party meeting to show their support for Gay.[90] The election day passed quietly and the Democratic candidate won by a landslide. Thus ended Radical rule in Iberia Parish.[91]

The Loreauville riot of 1884 had its origins in the refusal of Iberia Republicans to acquiesce in the Democrats' proposal to form a common ticket for the election of April 1884, and thereby to share the benefits of local offices. Still, a close study of the causes underlying this tragic event shows that there were more than simple local skirmishes over offices. The roots of the incident lay in the Democrats' wish to insure their permanent domination of state politics by a strict control of elections at the local level.

In 1882, the legislature voted two new laws which granted the state administration the power of appointing police jurors and of chosing the commissioners of election. It is in these that one finds the roots of the events that led up to the Loreauville riot. Indeed, the police jurors had been until then the only people responsible for selecting polling sites and for appointing the commissioners of elections. Consequently, a Democratic administration would appoint only Democrats as police jurors, who would in turn recommend only Democrats as commissioners of elections; the ultimate result was widespread fraud, bribery and ballot-stuffing.[92] The dreadful consequences of those two laws were apparent during the election of April 1884 when fraud and ballot-stuffing occurred not only in Iberia but all over the state. Dead men whose names were registered were reported to have voted in several parishes and allowed the administration candidates to carry the election.[93] Consequently, the repeal of the election law of 1882 and return to the process of electing the police jury were advocated by many as the only reasonable solution; newspapers from all parts of the state raised that question during the summer of 1884.[94]

In its analysis of the Iberia election, the *Weekly Truth,* a Democratic Baton Rouge paper, rejected the policy of silence that many were advocating and asserted that previous Republican fraud could not justify the use of such means by the Democratic party.[95] The use of such tactics and practices could not continue without impunity and was threatening the basis of the democratic system in Louisiana. "The purity of the ballot box must be sustained, or civil government is a failure."[96] The stern criticism of the press in reporting the frauds did not prevent the governor from supporting his own candidates.

As Iberia Republican leaders contested the election returns of April 1884 before the courts, the Democratic candidates were installed in office by orders of the governor. This arbitrary action did not calm matters as troubles erupted several times in Iberia and the state militia was called upon to restore order. Still, the governor's policy seemed to have triumphed by the end of the summer. But many observers foresaw further troubles. Moreover, not everyone praised the governor's decision to call up the state militia to solve the contested elections.

The press was generally quite critical of the state administrations policy in dealing with the Iberia situation. Many papers agreed with the *Donaldsonville Chief* in asserting that "there was no real necessity or adequate excuse of recalling out the militia" and added that "the threatening state of affairs which existed in Iberia was due to the rascally conspiracy—countenanced and abetted by the State Administration—to steal the election and foist a set of beaten and obnoxious officials upon the people regardless of the consequences."[97] Other papers charged the state administration with having "combined with local politicians in Iberia to defeat the popular suffrage," of having "defeated it by fraud," of having "incited an illegal impeachment proceeding against a Judge," of having "appointed as Provisional Judge the candidate who had resigned all pretensions to the office," of having given "judicial powers to a man who was personally interested in the determining of a grave political controversy," of having ordered "a pretorian guard from New Orleans to impose the orders of this irregular functionary," and finally of having "followed a precedent, set by Kellogg, by violating the democratic principle of home government by importing forces into a parish to overawe its principles."[98] Finally, the press generally agreed in charging the state administration with the responsibility for the troubles that affected Iberia.

> If it was made so by the unwise and shuffling policy of the administration; it grew out of a determining effort on the part of Gov. McEnery or his advisers to circumvent the law and to accomplish by devising ways a settlement that an upright and honorable course would have speedily secured.[99]

Louisiana had already earned an unenviable reputation for its Byzantine politics during Reconstruction and even before the war. As the Loreauville riot shows, Louisiana politics had sunk even deeper into corruption under the Bourbons. Although the governor's policy was triumphant by force of arms, the troubles that occurred in Iberia during the summer and fall of 1884 show that politics under the Bourbons had degenerated into a moral cancer as political corruption, bribery, stuffing the ballot-box, gross fraud and intimidation became a means of governing and a part of the political culture of the state.

Notes for "Politics and Violence in Bourbon Louisiana:
The Loreauville Riot of 1884 as a Case Study"

[1]Numerous and serious disturbances and riots in the parishes of Madison, Tensas, Natchitoches and Caddo in 1878.

[2]Most of the historians who studied that period or the history of Iberia Parish did not make any mention of this riot. Maurine Bergerie, "Economic and Social History of Iberia Parish, 1868-1900" (M.A. thesis, Louisiana State University, 1956); William Ivy Hair, *Bourbonism and Agrarian Protest: Louisiana Politics, 1877-1900* (Baton Rouge, 1969); James K. Owen, "A Study in Local Government: The History of Iberia Parish" (M.A. thesis, Louisiana State University, 1940); Philip D. Uzee, "Republican Politics in Louisiana, 1877-1900" (Ph. D. dissertation, Louisiana State University, 1950); C. Vann Woodward, *Origins of the New South, 1877-1913* (Baton Rouge, 1951). Only Glenn R. Conrad, comp., *New Iberia: Essays on the Town and Its People* (Lafayette, La., 1979), 101; and Alice Bayne Webb, "A History of Negro Voting in Louisiana" (Ph. D. dissertation, Louisiana State University, 1962), briefly cover the subject.

[3]*Bossier Banner,* November 6, 1884; *New Orleans Daily Picayune,* November 3, 4, 1884; *New Orleans Times-Democrat,* November 2, 3, 1884; *Opelousas St. Landry Democrat,* November 8, 1884; Napoleonville *Pioneer of Assumption,* November 8, 1884.

[4]U. S. House Report, no. 261, 43rd Congress, 2nd session, 606-611; Conrad, *New Iberia,* 68-69, 124.

[5]U. S. House Report, no. 261, 43rd Congress, 2nd session, 617; New Iberia *Louisiana Sugar Bowl,* November 24, 1870, February 2, 1871; August 12, 29, 1872; March 3, 13, April 3, May 18, July 3, August 7, 14, 21, 1873; August 8, 1874; April 8, 1875; January 15, May 11, July 6, August 15, 1876; *Lafayette Advertiser,* June 21, July 12, 1873.

[6]*Times-Democrat,* November 12, 1883.

[7]Several congressional reports, and particularly U. S. House Report no. 261, 43rd Congress, 2nd session, treated with conditions that prevailed in Iberia during the Reconstruction period. Moreover, a thorough investigation through several local newspapers, such as the *Louisiana Sugar Bowl, Lafayette Cotton Boll, Franklin Planter's Banner,* and *Lafayette Advertiser,*was most useful.

[8]Our data on Iberia is drawn from a larger set of data covering all Louisiana. Our data set rests on a thorough investigation of 32 congressional reports and documents concerning Louisiana and some fifty local and state newspapers. Information is collected on 4787 cases of killings that occurred in Louisiana during that period, with 3402 during Reconstruction and the 1385 between 1877 and 1884. Our data for Iberia was corroborated by the testimony of Dr. Colgin who held the office of coroner in Iberia between 1870-1873. Dr. Colgin investigated 32 killings that occurred in the parish during those three years. See U. S. House Report, no. 261, 43rd Congress, 2nd session, 333.

[9]We related to political causes all killings that were related to the electoral process, to the holding of offices, or that occurred during a political meeting.

[10]U. S. House Report, no. 261, 43rd Congress, 2nd session, 333; Conrad, *New Iberia,* p. 123; Henry C. Dethloff and Robert R. Jones, "Race Relations in Louisiana, 1877-1898," *Louisiana History,* 9 (1968): 307.

[11]U. S. House Report, no. 261, 43rd Congress, 2nd session, 607; U. S. Senate Exec. Doc. no. 2, 44th Congress, 2nd session, 178-185; *Report of the Secretary of State for Louisiana for the Year 1879* (New Orleans, 1879), 6-8; *Pioneer of Assumption,* November 8, 1884; Opelousas *St. Landry Democrat,* November 8, 1884; Conrad, *New Iberia,* 100, 123.

[12]U. S. House Report, no. 261, 43rd Congress, 2nd session, 613, 786; U. S. House Exec. Doc., no. 30, 44th Congress, 2nd session, 307, 358; *Cotton Boll,* July 8, 1874; *Picayune,* August 13, 1874; *Louisiana Sugar Bowl,* July 19, 29, 1874; Conrad, *New Iberia,* 100; Joe Gray Taylor, *Louisiana Reconstructed, 1863-1877* (Baton Rouge, 1974), 274-75, 283.

[13]U. S. House Report, no. 261, 43rd Congress, 2nd session, 333-337, 607, 613-615, 786; *Picayune,* October 20, 1874; *New Orleans Times,* January 29, 1875; *Louisiana Sugar Bowl,* August 13, 1874; Taylor, *Louisiana Reconstructed,* 284-85.

[14]*New Orleans Bee,* June 24, 1874; *Picayune,* December 27, 1874; *New Orleans Times,* January 29, 1875; Taylor, *Louisiana Reconstructed,* 284-85, 300.

[15]*New Orleans Times,* January 29,1 875.

[16]Hair, *Bourbonism and Agrarian Protest,* 4-5; Otis A. Singletary, "The Reassertion of White Supremacy in Louisiana" (M.A. thesis, Louisiana State University, 1949), 29-52; Taylor, *Louisiana Reconstructed,* 484-85; Ted B. Tunnell, Jr., "The Negro, the Republicans, and the Election of 1876 in Louisiana," *Louisiana History,* 7 (1966): 113; Webb, "A History of Negro Voting in Louisiana," 25-95.

[17]U. S. Senate Report, no. 855, 45th Congress, 3rd session, VI-X; *Bossier Banner,* September 26, 1878; *Bee,* October 22, 25, 1878; *Natchitoches Peoples Vindicator,* September 28, October 12, 1878; Monroe *Ouachita Telegraph,* October 11, 1878; *Shreveport Times,* December 29, 1878; Hair, *Bourbonism and Agrarian Protest,* 77; Garnie W. McGinty, *Louisiana Redeemed: The Overthrow of Carpetbag Rule, 1876-1880* (New Orleans, 1941), 220-21; Webb, "A History of Negro Voting in Louisiana," 25-94.

[18]*Picayune,* October 22, 25, 1878; *Shreveport Times,* January 15, 1879; Hair, *Bourbonism and Agrarian Protest,* 77-79; Uzee, "Republican Politics," 43; Woodward, *Origins of the New South,* 57.

[19]Dethloff and Jones, "Race Relations in Louisiana," 308, 320; Hair, *Bourbonism and Agrarian Protest,* 70; Singletary, "The Reassertion of White Supremacy in Louisiana," 27; Uzee, "Republican Politics," 130.

[20]Hair, *Bourbonism and Agrarian Protest,* 80-81.

[21]Commission Books, Louisiana State University Archives, Reel 2.2, March 1868-March 1877; Reel 2.3, November 1876-May 1884; *Louisiana Sugar Bowl, Cotton Boll,* and *Advertiser,* 1868 to 1884; U. S. House Report, no. 261, 43rd Congress, 2nd session, 336; Webb, "A History of Negro Voting in Louisiana," 129.

[22]*Baton Rouge Capitolian Advocate,* August 2, 1884; *Donaldsonville Chief,* July 19, 1884; *Picayune,* March 13, 1884; *Shreveport Times,* January 19, 1884; Hair, *Bourbonism and Agrarian Protest,* 75-76, 78, 99; Roger W. Shugg, *Origins of Class Struggle in Louisiana: A Social History of White Farmers and Laborers during Slavery and After, 1840-1875* (Baton Rouge, 1939), 152-57; Taylor, *Louisiana Reconstructed,* 360; Uzee, "Republican Politics," 77-78.

[23]*Picayune,* June 5, 1884; *Times-Democrat,* September 15, 1882; *Opelousas Courier,* October 28, 1882; Alexandria *Rapides Democrat,* August 30, 1882; *Baton Rouge Weekly Truth,* January 18, 1884; Webb, "A History of Negro Voting in Louisiana," 129.

[24]U. S. House Report, no. 261, 43rd Congress, 2nd session, 336.

[25]*Courier,* February 28, March 6, 20, 27, 1880; Rayville *Richland Beacon,* February 28, 1880; *St. Landry Democrat,* September 2, 1882; Covington *St. Tammany Farmer,* February 7, 1880; *Weekly Truth,* September 21, 1883, June 20, 1884; Hair, *Bourbonism and Agrarian Protest,* 61, 118; Shugg, *Origins of Class Struggle,* 232-33; Woodward, *Origins of the New South,* 54-55.

[26]*Chief,* June 12, 1884; *Picayune,* May 25, July 25, 1884; *Courier,* February 28, March 6, 20, 27, 1880; *Rapides Democrat,* September 2, 1882, May 24, August 9, 1884; *Weekly Truth,* September 21, 1883, January 11, March 14, May 6, 16, 23, June 20, 1884; Hair, *Bourbonism and Agrarian Protest,* 61, 118-19; Uzee, "Republican Politics," 130; Woodward, *Origins of the New South,* 56-57.

[27]U. S. House Report, no. 261, 43rd Congress, 2nd session, 336; Conrad, *New Iberia,* 126; Webb, "A History of Negro Voting in Louisiana," 129.

[28]U. S. House Report, no. 261, 43rd Congress, 2nd session, 336; *Courier,* March 20, 27, 1880; *Rapides Democrat,* August 30, 1882; *Richland Beacon,* February 28, 1880; *St. Landry Democrat,* September 2, 1882, August 9, 1884; *Weekly Truth,* September 21, 1883, March 14, June 20, 1884; Hair, *Bourbonism and Agrarian*

Protest, 61, 118-19; Conrad, *New Iberia,* 126; Uzee, "Republican Politics," 130; Woodward, *Origins of the New South,* 56-57.

[29]*Picayune,* May 5, 1884.

[30]Ibid., June 5, 1884; *Courier,* October 28, 1882; *Rapides Democrat,* August 30, 1882; *Times-Democrat,* September 15, 1882; *Weekly Truth,* January 18, 1884; Uzee, "Republican Politics," 130; Webb, "A History of Negro Voting in Louisiana," 129.

[31]*Capitolian Advocate,* August 23, 1884; Plaquemine *Iberville South,* November 17, 1883; *Thibodaux Sentinel,* March 8, 1884; Conrad, *New Iberia,* 124.

[32]U. S. House Report, no. 261, 43rd Congress, 2nd session, 611; *Picayune,* August 16, 1884; Conrad, *New Iberia,* 100, 122-24.

[33]Conrad, *New Iberia,* 124.

[34]U. S. House Report, no. 261, 43rd Congress, 2nd session, 607, 613.

[35]*Capitolian Advocate,* August 23, 1884; *Sentinel,* March 8, 1884.

[36]*Chief,* July 7, 1883, January 12, April 12, 26, 1884; *Iberville South,* March 1, 15, 29, 1884; *Picayune,* March 7, 1884; *Shreveport Times,* January 19, 1884; *Sentinel,* March 8, 1884; Uzee, "Republican Politics," 75-76.

[37]*Capitolian Advocate,* August 23, 1884; *Sentinel,* March 8, 1884.

[38]*Picayune,* March 7, April 28, 1884; Uzee, "Republican Politics," 75-77, 137; Webb, "A History of Negro Voting in Louisiana," 141.

[39]*Chief,* July 7, 1883, January 12, April 12, 26, 1884; *Iberville South,* March 1, 15, 29, 1884; *Picayune,* March 7, 1884; *Shreveport Times,* January 19, 1884; *Sentinel,* March 8, 1884; Uzee, "Republican Politics," 75-76; Webb, "A History of Negro Voting in Louisiana," 137, 140-41.

[40]Federal Census, 1870, section 593, reel no. 513; Federal Census, 1880, section 19, reel 453, National Archives, Washington, D. C.; Commission Book, Reel 2.1 (1846 to 1869), Reel 2.2 (1868 to 1877), Reel 2.3 (1876 to 1884); Andrew B. Booth, comp., *Records of Louisiana Confederate Soldiers and Louisiana Confederate Commands,* 3 vols. in 4 parts (New Orleans, 1920); U. S. House Report, no. 261, 43rd Congress, 2nd session, 6-7, 617; *Picayune,* May 25, 1884; *Times-Democrat,* August 23, October 9, 1882; March 6, 1884; *Ouachita Telegraph,* March 28, 1879; *Louisiana Sugar Bowl,* June 3, 1880; Conrad, *New Iberia,* 100, 124, 126.

[41]Federal Census, 1870, section 593, reel no. 513; Federal Census, 1880, section 19, reel 453; Commission Book, Reel 2.1 (1846 to 1869), Reel 2.2 (1868 to 1877), Reel 2.3 (1876 to 1884); Booth, *Records of Louisiana Confederate Soldiers;* Conrad, *New Iberia,* 100, 126, 129.

[42]Federal Census, 1870, section 593, reel no. 513; Federal Census, 1880, section 19, reel 453; Commission Book, Reel 2.1 (1846 to 1869), Reel 2.2 (1868 to 1877), Reel 2.3 (1876 to 1884); Booth, *Records of Louisiana Confederate Soldiers;* U. S. House Report, no. 261, 43rd Congress, 2nd session, 333-37; *Louisiana Sugar Bowl,* July 29, 1874; May 18, 1876; Conrad, *New Iberia,* 100.

[43]Federal Census, 1870, section 593, reel no. 513; Federal Census, 1880, section 19, reel 453; Commission Book, Reel 2.1 (1846 to 1869), Reel 2.2 (1868 to 1877), Reel 2.3 (1876 to 1884).

[44]Federal Census, 1870, section 593, reel no. 513; Federal Census, 1880, section 19, reel 453; Commission Book, Reel 2.1 (1846 to 1869), Reel 2.2 (1868 to 1877), Reel 2.3 (1876 to 1884); Booth, *Records of Louisiana Confederate Soldiers.*

[45]*Capitolian Advocate,* July 25, 1884; Conrad, *New Iberia,* 101.

[46]*Capitolian Advocate,* July 25, 1884; *Times-Democrat,* April 20, 1884.

[47]*Chief,* May 24, 1884; Tallulah *Madison Times,* August 9, 1884.

[48]*Picayune,* June 16, 1884.

[49]Ibid., May 5, 1884.

[50]*Capitolian Advocate,* July 25, 1884; *Picayune,* May 25, 26, June 3, July 25, 1884.

[51]*Capitolian Advocate,* July 25, August 23, 1884; *Times-Democrat,* August 19, 1884; *Picayune,* May 25, 1884.

[52]*Capitolian Advocate,* August 23, 1884; *Times-Democrat,* August 19, 1884.

[53]*Picayune,* May 25, 26, June 3, July 25, 1884; *Times-Democrat,* June 11, 16, 1884.

[54]*Picayune,* July 25, 1884; *Capitolian Advocate,* August 23, 1884; *Times-Democrat,* August 15, 1884.

[55]*Capitolian Advocate,* August 23, 1884; *Picayune,* August 12, 1884.

[56]*Capitolian Advocate,* August 23, 1884; *Picayune,* August 12, 1884.

[57]*Capitolian Advocate,* July 25, August 23, 1884; *Picayune,* August 12, 1884; *Courier,* August 9, 1884.

[58]*Opelousas Journal,* August 9, 1884.

[59]*Picayune,* July 25, August 12, 1884.

[60]Ibid., August 16, 1884.

[61]Ibid., August 16, 1884; Conrad, *New Iberia,* 101.

[62]*Picayune,* August 18, 1884; *Times-Democrat,* August 19, 1884.

[63]*Capitolian Advocate,* August 23, 1884; *Louisiana Sugar Bowl,* August 7, 1884; *St. Landry Democrat,* August 16, 1884; *Picayune,* August 16, 1884.

[64]*St. Landry Democrat,* August 16, 1884.

[65]*Picayune,* August 15, 1884; *Times-Democrat,* August 15, 1884.

[66]*Picayune,* August 15,1 6, 1884.

[67]Ibid., August 16, 21, 1884.

[68]Ibid., August 16, 21, 1884; *Courier,* August 23, 1884.

[69]*Courier,* August 23, 1884.

[70]*Picayune,* August 21, 22, 1884; *Times-Democrat,* August 18, 1884; *Courier,* August 23, 1884.

[71]*Picayune,* August 26, 27, 30, 1884; Conrad, *New Iberia,* 101.

[72]*Picayune,* August 26, 27, 30, 1884.

[73]*Picayune,* November 3, 1884; *Pioneer of Assumption,* November 8, 1884; Webb, "A History of Negro Voting in Louisiana," 152-54.

[74]*Picayune,* November 3, 1884; Conrad, *New Iberia,* 101.

[75]*Picayune,* November 3, 1884; *Weekly Truth,* November 7, 1884.

[76]*Picayune,* November 3, 1884; *Weekly Truth,* November 7, 1884; Conrad, *New Iberia,* 101.

[77]*Times-Democrat,* November 2, 1884; *Weekly Truth,* November 7, 1884; Conrad, *New Iberia,* 101; Webb, "A History of Negro Voting in Louisiana," 155.

[78]*Weekly Truth,* November 7, 1884.

[79]*Picayune,* November 3, 1884; *Weekly Truth,* November 7, 1884.

[80]*Picayune,* November 3, 1884; Webb, "A History of Negro Voting in Louisiana," 155.

[81]*Bossier Banner,* November 6, 1884; *Picayune,* November 3, 1884; *St. Landry Democrat,* November 8, 1884.

[82]*Picayune,* November 3, 1884.

[83]*St. Landry Democrat,* November 8, 1884; *Baton Rouge Daily Advocate,* November 4, 1884.

[84]*Picayune,* November 3, 1884; *Times-Democrat,* November 3, 1884; False River *Pointe Coupée Democrat,* November 8, 1884; *St. Landry Democrat,* November 8, 1884; Webb, "A History of Negro Voting in Louisiana," 155; Woodward, *Origins of the New South,* 57.

[85]*Bossier Banner,* November 6, 1884.

[86]*Times-Democrat,* November 2, 1884; *Weekly Truth,* November 7, 1884.

[87]*Picayune,* November 3, 1884; *Times-Democrat,* November 2, 1884; *Pointe Coupée Democrat,* November 8, 1884; Conrad, *New Iberia,* 101.

[88]*Picayune,* November 4, 1884; *Pointe Coupée Democrat,* November 8, 1884.

[89]*Bossier Banner,* November 6, 1884.

[90]*Picayune,* November 3, 1884; Conrad, *New Iberia,* 101.

[91]Owen, "A Study in Local Government in Louisiana," 75; Conrad, *New Iberia,* 101.

[92]*St. Landry Democrat,* August 9, 1884; *Weekly Truth,* September 21, 1883; June 20, 1884; Hair, *Bourbonism and Agrarian Protest,* 61, 118; Uzee, "Republican Politics," 130; Webb, "A History of Negro Voting in Louisiana," 129-30, 138-40; Woodward, *Origins of the New South,* 54-55.

[93]*Chief,* June 12, 1884; *Picayune,* May 25, July 25, 1884; *St. Landry Democrat,* May 24, 1884; *Shreveport Times,* October 16, 1884; *Weekly Truth,* May 6, 16, 23, June 20, 1884; Hair, *Bourbonism and Agrarian Protest,* 113-14.

[94]*St. Landry Democrat,* May 24, August 9, 1884; *Weekly Truth,* May 6, 16, 23, June 20, 1884.

[95]*Weekly Truth,* May 6, 1884.

[96]*St. Landry Democrat,* May 24, 1884.

[97]*Donaldsonville Chief,* August 30, 1884.

[98]*Weekly Truth,* August 22, 1884.

[99]*Picayune,* August 16, 1884.

BLACK PROTEST AND WHITE POWER*

William Ivy Hair

Why was it, wondered a Bourbon leader of Opelousas that Negroes kept on trying to rise above their station in life. He knew of some who were "scared to death" of visits from white vigilantes and yet, paradoxically, even the most frightened of them persisted in taking an interest in politics and other matters which did not concern them. This was odd behavior for a sub-human species. All he could surmise was that "niggers are strange animals any way you take them.[1]

This view of the black caste as something outside the pale of humanity was heard all too frequently in post-Reconstruction Louisiana. The fierce Negrophobia of Hearsey's *New Orleans Daily States* became the standard response of a predominant portion of the political and journalistic elite; and the supposed horrors of "rapine and robbery" of Reconstruction's "negro rule" were constantly recalled,[2] although the state had never at any time been under the control of blacks.[3] During the 1880s and 1890s individual instances of paternalism toward the Negro were still discoverable, but the ruling classes' public attitude, being one of contempt and cruelty, militated against the humane instincts of *noblesse oblige*. Sometimes even acts of presumed kindness revealed racial discrimination in its shabbiest forms. In a typical example, the *Shreveport Times,* in offering to give away mutilated coins to local children, thought it necessary to add: "the white babies can have the large pieces and the colored ones the nickels."[4]

Not many Louisiana Negroes of the time were able to leave written evidence of their reaction to the increasingly hostile environment in which they lived. There was, to be sure, an articulate and relatively well-to-do black minority in and near New Orleans; their recorded opinions show a grim cognizance of what was happening and a helpless rage against Bourbonism.[5] While on occasion, the actions of the poverty-stricken black majority spoke as loudly as words. The "Kansas Fever" of 1879 gave strong proof of

*First published as Chapter 8 in William Ivy Hair, *Bourbonism and Agrarian Protest: Louisiana Politics, 1877-1900* (Baton Rouge, La.: Louisiana State University Press, © 1969), 170-97.

their discontent. In the decade which followed, although few attempted emigration, mass black protests against conditions within the state by no means ceased.

In 1880 and again in 1887, Negro wage earners in the sugar parishes engaged in strikes which brought down upon them the wrath of their employers and the state government. Upstate, the blacks appeared more docile. The sharecropping system prevalent in the cotton parishes held out less hope for economic advancement than did the meager wages paid cane field workers, but the decentralized nature of cotton plantations limited the possibility of unified protests by Negro families. In the sugar country, on the other hand, the gang labor system and the existence of an active (though white-run) Republican party encouraged cohesion among Negroes; they were allowed a modicum of choice in politics as well as in place of employment. Blacks in the cotton parishes generally had little free will in anything.

The 1880 sugar strikes commenced in the fields of St. Charles Parish on March 17. Plantation owners immediately accused the Negro ringleaders of trespassing upon private property "and inciting the laborers to stop work in the fields." According to the parish judge, the instigators were armed with weapons and had been "forcing workers to join their band by assaults and threats." Judge James D'Augustin admitted, however, that most of the black population of St. Charles was in sympathy with the "rioters." For that reason, D'Augustin claimed that local authorities could not handle the disturbance, and so he called upon the state for militia[6]

Richard Gooseberry, spokesman for the St. Charles strikers, denied the allegation of violence. The colored people, he said, "had simply struck for one dollar a day, as they could no longer work for seventy-five cents." Nevertheless, the planters maintained that Gooseberry's followers threatened to kill white people, burn down dwellings, and seize control of the entire parish. As it turned out, there were no specific acts of violence against the white minority of St. Charles.[7] It must also be said that the strikers displayed remarkable forbearance when they gathered, on March 19, to listen to speeches by Judge D'Augustin and others who "expounded the law to them." One official passed this compliment on to the black audience: "The great arm of the great wheel of agriculture is the nigger. Next is the mule."[8]

A battalion of state militia presently arrived in St. Charles. No resistance was met. Twelve strikers were arrested, sent to New Orleans, and sentenced to jail terms. Ostensibly they were guilty of trespass; but more to the point, they had run afoul of the Bourbon position that "all strikes are wrong, criminally wrong, both in theory and act."[9] The trouble in St. Charles appeared to be over, and as yet there had been no outbreaks reported elsewhere.

But labor discontent soon extended to other parishes along the lower delta. By March 29, the situation in St. John the Baptist Parish looked more serious than had the previous disturbance in neighboring St. Charles. The same demand was voiced: daily wages must be raised from the present level of seventy-five cents. But the St. John Negroes struck a more militant pose. They proclaimed that "the colored people are a nation and must stand together." Indeed, the ringleaders set up a governing council, complete with a constitution. All strikers in the parish took an oath to obey this constitution, which stated that none would work for less than one dollar a day, and any who violated the oath "shall be punished with a severe thrashing." A correspondent for the *Daily Picayune,* though hostile to the strike, was impressed by the earnestness of the blacks. "Strange to say," he wrote, "they have kept sober."[10]

Governor [Louis A.] Wiltz responded to the pleas of the St. John landowners with a warning to "these evil doers and mischievous persons to desist from their evil doings." He also sent in state troops. The militia, it was explained, was being used to "protect the laborers" from harm. Despite a number of arrests, the disturbance in St. John continued for several days. Blacks paraded along the dusty parish roads, carrying banners which read: "A DOLLAR A DAY OR KANSAS," and "PEACE—ONE DOLLAR A DAY." But no violence, outside of the whipping of Negroes by Negroes, was reported. One of the instigators of the strike, when arrested, remarked that he was "glad to go to jail," for at least there he would get "enough to eat."[11]

It was not entirely a coincidence that the St. John strike occurred during the same week that ex-President Ulysses S. Grant paid a visit to Louisiana. The strike leaders knew of it, and apparently timed their activities accordingly. Grant arrived in New Orleans at the peak of the trouble in nearby St. John. "The deluded laborers," one report noted, anticipate that "Grant will come up and make the planters pay extra wages."[12] As the *Weekly Louisianian* rather sadly put it, the unlettered black masses view Grant as a kind of superman.[13] At the opposite extreme, his visit touched off a predictable editorial tirade in the *Daily States.*[14]

The hero of Appomattox was, in one sense, concerned with Negro affairs in Louisiana. During his stay in New Orleans, he attended a reception at the home of P. B. S. Pinchback, where he met "the cream of Negro society."[15] Pinchback and a number of his guests were scheduled to be delegates to the upcoming Republican national convention. And Grant hoped to return to the White House in 1881. Other than that, he demonstrated no interest in local matters except when he said that "I think the South is better suited [for the black man] than any other place. . . . I want him to have the right to stay where the climate suits him."[16]

Shortly after Grant's departure from New Orleans, the strike in St. John was broken. Later in the month of April, however, sporadic strikes by cane field laborers were reported in Ascension, St. James, St. Bernard, Jefferson, and Plaquemines parishes. But in these instances the presence of the militia was not required. Local authorities broke up the disturbances by summary arrests of the ringleaders. Thus the strikes of 1880 had totally failed. During the next few years, wages generally remained at seventy to seventy-five cents a day for "first class" adult males. Only in the busy harvest and grinding season (from around late October to the end of the year) was there a wage raise, usually to ninety cents or one dollar.[17]

Localized labor disturbances, poorly organized and barren of results, sprang up at intervals in the sugar country during the years from 1881 through 1886. Until the latter year, black workers were not affiliated with any recognizable labor organization. Even in the relatively serious strikes of 1880, there seems to have been no effort to unify the laborers of the several parishes. Those in one locality may have taken their cue from events elsewhere, but no attempt at interparish coordination was observed by correspondents on the scene.

In New Orleans, meanwhile, a degree of cooperation among laboring groups was slowly being achieved—including some unity between black and white—but as yet there were no tangible benefits from it. Late in 1880 a vague "Association" of thirteen city unions was formed, embracing whites and Negroes, skilled and unskilled.[18] In September of the following year the various orders within the Association all threatened to strike for higher wages; and the more than ten thousand dock workers, of whom 30 percent were Negro, carried the threat into action. Negro strikebreakers were hired and brought in from as far away as Savannah, but for once the local dock workers of both colors stood together in demonstrations and attacks against the "scabs."[19] The strike eventually subsided without significant concessions to the laborers, but even so an unprecedented degree of biracial harmony had been revealed. When a black demonstrator was killed by police, "it was a source of satisfaction" to the Negro press to see great numbers of white workers march in his funeral procession.[20]

In 1883 the Knights of Labor entered Louisiana. One of the most ambitious and visionary associations in American labor history, the Knights advocated a uniting of all working people, of whatever skill, color, or sex, into one gigantic order. At the same time, however, the Knights shunned the Marxist and anarchistic radicalism of the time; their national leaders did not seek the extinction of capitalism[21] But the very fact that the Knights promoted class consciousness and organized Negroes along with whites made the order, in the eyes of Southern Bourbons, a dangerous disturber of the status quo.

At first confined to New Orleans, and inconsequential there, the Knights drew little attention in the Pelican State until 1886. Nationally, the order reached its peak membership that year, then began to decline. Yet contrary to the trend elsewhere, the Knights developed new strength in the rural South; losses in Northern cities during the late 1880s were partially offset by fresh adherents from the Southern towns and countryside. Particularly was it growing in North Carolina and Louisiana.[22] New Orleans provided most of the leadership for the Knights' plan of expansion in the Pelican State. At least five thousand urbanites joined it by mid 1887 and a Knights newspaper, *Southern Industry,* had commenced weekly publication.[23]

It was from the city that Knights organizers fanned out into the lower delta parishes in 1886, to impress upon cane field Negroes the need for unity in obtaining concessions from the landlord-employers. Higher wages and payment in regular currency "instead of commissary paste board" were the prime rallying points. The Knights simultaneously recruited artisans of both races in South Louisiana's towns. Early in 1887 the Knights were potent enough in Morgan City to run a slate of candidates in the municipal election, and every man on the labor ticket won office. Conservative planters and businessmen were beginning to take alarm.[24]

Louisiana's sugar growers, after experiencing a bad crop in 1886, reduced wages for the following year to sixty-five cents per day, without rations. Most workers averaged twenty days out of every month in the fields. The larger planters paid wages in commissary script, redeemable only at the plantation stores. Actually, a Negro family with one employed member would receive what amounted to six or seven dollars in real wages per month during the ten-month growing season. Workers without rations had to feed and cloth their families out of this small amount, although usually no rent was charged for the cramped living quarters. Pay for the grinding season of 1887 was set at rates varying from seventy-five cents to $1.15 per day for "first class" adult males; and for six hours of overtime night work, called a "watch," the planters offered fifty cents.[25]

During August of 1887, ten weeks before harvest, the Knights leadership requested a conference with local branches of the Louisiana Sugar Planters' Association. They wanted to discuss wages for the approaching busy season. Association officials sent no reply. Later, on October 24, the Knights District Assembly 194 addressed a circular letter to planters in Iberia, Lafourche, St. Martin, St. Mary, and Terrebonne parishes, insisting that wages be raised for the November-December months of harvesting and grinding. The scale drawn up by the Knights proposed $1.25 per day without rations, or $1.00 per day with rations. For a night watch, no less than sixty cents would be accepted. Further-more, instead of monthly payments, the Knights demanded that wages for day work be received every two weeks, and "watch" money each week. The District Assembly of the Knights comprised about forty locals in the five parishes. Planters were informed that they must meet the terms by November 1, or face a general strike.[26]

An estimated six thousand to ten thousand laborers went on strike when the deadline date arrived with no sign of acquiescence from the planters. Nine-tenths of the strikers were Negroes. All were said to be members of the Knights of Labor. The planters, although refusing to negotiate, were visibly disturbed; the growing season of 1887 had been one of near-perfect weather, and a large crop yield was in prospect.[27] Conservative newspapers depicted the strikers' demands as "unreasonable" and "reprehensible," and insisted that the current market price of sugar precluded any increase in wages.[28] As for biweekly or weekly paydays, the planters claimed that this "would demoralize labor." because it was "a well known fact that as long as the average laborer has money he will not work."[29]

The local officials of the Knights, who were white men and literate blacks, received the brunt of landowner wrath. Special bitterness was expressed toward J. R. H. Foote and D. Monnier, white laborers of the town of Thibodaux, in Lafourche Parish. Other leaders among the Lafourche Knights included Henry Cox, George Cox, and P. O. Rousseau. The Cox brothers were Negro artisans. Rousseau, a white man, had once been a planter but "times [had] changed" for him.[30] In Terrebonne Parish, a light-skinned Negro named

Jim Brown led the strike, while in St. Mary, black men took the lead in labor agitation among the sugar workers. They, together with Negroes who urged the strike in other parishes, were categorized by Major [Edward A.] Burke's *New Orleans Times-Democrat* as "bad and dangerous . . . relic[s] of Radical days.[31]

Planter spokesmen also vented anger upon the New Orleans Knights who had first organized the lower sugar country. These urban "communists," as the *Daily States* termed them, were blamed for arousing "passions" among the usually tractable Negroes.[32] Concerning the attitude of rank-and-file laborers, it was obvious that they placed great faith in the Knights of Labor. One wealthy planter, W. W. Pugh, used the word "veneration" to describe Negro attitudes toward the labor society. When directives came down from Knights headquarters, said Pugh, the workers "generally obey at whatever sacrifice it may prove to their own welfare."[33] A leader of the strike remarked, when the trouble began, that the white employers "had never met the negroes united before," and he predicted that every one of the four hundred laborers in his group would lay down their lives before giving in to the planters.[34]

On the morning of the first day of the strike a battery of state militia arrived in Lafourche Parish. Members of the Sugar Planters' Association—not the local government—had asked for the troops. For the landowners perceived that "serious trouble" would result from their announcement that all laborers who refused to work must vacate the plantation cabins. By November 10, Governor [Samuel D.] McEnery had ordered ten companies and two batteries of state militia into the troubled parishes. At least one unit brought along a Gatling gun.[35] These militiamen were assigned the work of eviction.

Some critics of Governor McEnery asserted that he "had acted hastily" in sending out the militia; the *New Orleans Mascot* suggested that His Excellency's action "was caused by his eagerness to curry favor with the . . . wealthy sugar planters in the hopes that he can transfer their allegiance from Nicholls to himself."[36] Major Burke's newspaper, on the other hand, dwelt upon McEnery's alleged knowledge "of the negro [*sic*] character," which allowed the governor "to appreciate the danger." The trouble in the sugar country, philo-sophized this administration organ, was not a mere labor dispute. It was a racial matter.[37]

The first report of bloodshed came on November 2, from Terrebonne Parish. According to pro-planter sources, the blacks shot down four of their race who refused to join the strike. More severe was the disturbance which followed in St. Mary Parish: near the town of Berwick, on the night of November 4, Negroes fired upon and wounded four unidentified white men; the next day, militiamen killed "four or five" strikers outside of Pattersonville community.[38] Each side had its own version of the St. Mary shootings. Spokesmen for the Knights claimed the militia shot without provocation; other reports said the troops were forced to act in self-defense.[39] A St. Mary newspaper accused "leading colored men" in the Pattersonville area of making "incendiary speeches . . . that would put the Chicago anarchists to shame," and it quoted one Negro Knight as saying that "if the planters do not come to our terms we will burn the damn sugar houses."[40] Elsewhere, by November 20, at least one black laborer was killed and several wounded in Lafourche Parish.[41]

The sugar strike reached its violent climax during the last week of November. As some had feared, the town of Thibodaux then was the scene of a bloody riot. For Thibodaux had become a refugee center for the strikers; hundreds of Negro families, evicted from the plantations where they refused to work, were crowding into its dingy backstreets. A *Daily Picayune* correspondent described the spectacle: "Every vacant room in town tonight is filled with penniless and ragged negroes. All day long a stream of black humanity poured in, some on foot and others in wagons, bringing in all their earthly possessions which never amounted to more than a front yard full of babies, dogs and ragged bed clothing. . . . On many of the plantations old gray-headed negroes [*sic*], who were born and have lived continually upon them, left today."[42]

Residents of Thibodaux who were members of the Knights of Labor attempted to provide food and shelter for the homeless blacks. One observer, sympathetic to the refugees, said they behaved peaceably and tried to avoid incidents with local whites. But an opponent of the strike wrote that a number of the incoming male Negroes were armed and that the women "made threats to burn the town down."[43] By late November the atmosphere was growing more tense each day.

Judge Taylor Beattie, who had once been a defender of Negro rights—at least voting rights—when he ran for governor on the Republican ticket in 1879, took the lead in setting up a committee of local planters and Thibodaux property owners for the purpose of keeping the town's new residents under control. Beattie described the black refugees as "ignorant and degraded barbarians."[44] He said flatly that "the question of the supremacy of the whites over the blacks" had become the paramount issue.[45]

Actually, from the planters' point of view the situation was becoming desperate, but for another reason. The entire sugar crop was in immediate danger of ruin. On November 21, the first ice of season formed in the puddles and ponds around Thibodaux; cane in the fields showed considerable damage and it was feared that the remainder of the crop would soon "be lost through the senseless . . . strike of laborers."[46] The day of the freeze Judge Beattie declared martial law in the town. The militia had recently been withdrawn. In place of the troops were armed bands of white vigilantes, composed of local "organized citizens" plus a number of grim-visaged strangers to the community. These newly arrived men were alleged to be "Shreveport guerrillas, well versed in killing niggers."[47]

Reports of the gruesome events that followed are conflicting. All dispatches agreed that the shooting began on the night of November 22. But the planters' and the Knights' versions of who commenced it were, as might be expected, quite different. Each blamed the other.[48] For what it may be worth, the conservative *Iberville South,* which sided with the planters, in later years accused Judge Beattie of having "instigated" the riot "which resulted in the death of so many sons of Africa."[49] There is no question that many were killed.

When the firing ceased at noon the next day at least thirty Negroes lay dead or dying in Thibodaux. The injured list ran into the hundreds, of which only two people were white.[50] One planter journal stated that "quite a number of darkies" were unaccounted for and might also have been killed.[51] The *Daily Picayune*'s reporter told of additional bodies being found in nearby swamps, and related an ugly story about a large, dark canine which one vigilante supposedly shot by mistake, because it "looked like a negro [*sic*] lying down."[52] A member of one prominent planter family, Lavina Gay, cryptically wrote in a letter that "they say the half has not been published."[53]

The massacre at Thibodaux virtually ended the sugar strike of 1887. As a sequel, the two Cox brothers were taken from jail a day or so later and they "disappeared." By the beginning of December, most Negroes were back at work, harvesting and grinding the cane at wages previously set by the planters. Yet the violent repression of the strike appeared to stimulate a shortlived revival of Exodus talk among Louisiana's black population. One group did leave the state to seek, they said, more humane surroundings. Their destination was the state of Mississippi.[54]

Having dealt with the strike, planter interests now gave attention to what was considered the root of the trouble, the Knights of Labor. During the subsequent year a determined effort was made to eradicate the order from the sugar region. As the Jeanerette *Teche Pilot* made plain: "The darkey who steers clear of that organization will always find himself better off in this section." Those who persisted in holding membership in the Knights were likely to find their household goods unceremoniously dumped on the levees and themselves blacklisted.[55] In 1888 minor strikes broke out in four sugar parishes, but were quickly put down. Whites there and elsewhere in the state had meantime put into motion a new "Regulating Movement" aimed at discouraging economic or political assertiveness on the part of Negroes. And so failed the attempt to unionize the field hands of rural South Louisiana. By 1891, state membership in the Knights of Labor was not of any size outside of its original base in New Orleans.[56]

Viewed in perspective, the Thibodaux bloodletting was simply a deadlier-than-usual example of a much broader phenomenon. The lot of the Louisiana Negro, although never good, was growing harder. Indeed, throughout the South, during the late 1880s and the 1890s, repression and discrimination against the black race was on the rise.[57] Nor was this unlovely trend confined to the states of the late Confederacy. As the American nation took up imperialistic adventures in the Pacific and the Caribbean, the Northern public came increasingly to accept the doctrine of the natural superiority of Anglo-Saxons over dark-skinned peoples. Doubtless the expatriate Louisianian George W. Cable was grieved to discover that his pleadings on behalf of the black man, which had fallen upon deaf ears in his native state, now received little better attention in the North.[58]

But it is unlikely that Negroes in any other state suffered more than those in Louisiana. That they received less in the way of education has already been demonstrated. Available evidence also points to the conclusion that Pelican State blacks were subjected to a greater degree of violence than Negroes in other parts of the South during the late nineteenth century. Why was this so? The answer lies partially hidden in the labyrinthine social history of antebellum and colonial Louisiana. Somehow, the commingling of English-speaking and Creole-Cajun cultures had resulted in a milieu of political instability and unusual insensitivity to human rights. Long before the Civil War, the state had been notorious for its lawlessness and for its maltreatment of slaves.[59] When Harriet Beecher Stowe tried to portray the cruelest side of slavery in *Uncle Tom's Cabin,* it was not by chance that she located Simon Legree's plantation up the Red River, near Shreveport.

Upper class conservatives in the post-Reconstruction South have been regarded as being, relatively speaking, the black man's best friends among the white population. Presumably they believed that he was due some protection; that though an inferior, he should not be deliberately hurt or degraded.[60] This generalization, whatever its worth elsewhere, was hardly valid for Louisiana. The ruling class of the Pelican State continued, as in the days of slavery, to hold an extraordinarily circumscribed view of Negro "rights." The most rabid Negrophobes in the state were as consistently vehement in defense of upper class white privileges. Some of the white elite did, to be sure, sincerely try to uphold the ideals of *noblesse oblige.* But, as Daniel Dennett once remarked about honest politicians in the state, "they [were] lonesome."[61]

Editorial diatribes and mob outrages against the black people grew to such proportions by 1890, that at least a few whites thought the time for a moratorium had arrived. "Heavens," exclaimed the *Welsh Crescent,* "how we would enjoy a rest on the 'nigger' question! It seems that four-fifths of the State [newspapers] can't come out without a long-winded article . . . with the negro [*sic*] as their target; and what's more, they have been at it for the Lord only knows how long."[62] Many Negroes, however, bore the brunt of something more hurtful than mere words.

Lynchings not only occurred with growing frequency, but those who died at the hands of mobs might consider themselves fortunate if they expired quickly by a bullet or the rope. For some reason, 1881 marked a turning point toward extreme cruelty; several of the sixteen reported lynchings in the state that year involved brutal tortures. One of the dead had been accused of only stealing a chicken. Another victim, a Negro woman of Claiborne Parish named Jane Campbell, was burned at the stake.[63] At the same time a mob in Morehouse Parish was congratulated for discovering a "new and original mode" of punishment for a black man guilty of cattle theft. He was trussed up inside the carcass of a cow, "leaving only his head sticking out," so that buzzards and crows would pick out his eyes. The *Rayville Beacon* joked that this amounted to "COW-PITAL punishment," but added that "a great many worse things are . . . being done in our vicinity."[64]

Between 1882 and 1903, according to a *Chicago Tribune* survey, Louisiana lynchings accounted for 285 deaths. Of this number, 232 victims were black.[65] Records kept by Tuskegee Institute corroborate the *Tribune* figures.[66] Not included are the numerous deaths resulting from the sugar country riot of 1887, but even without these Louisiana ranked third in the nation in total lynchings for the period. The two states with higher totals had larger populations. Also, the above statistics failed to include many cases reported by the local press. For example, the Tuskegee records for 1888 list seven lynchings for the state, but a contemporary account from just one parish, Iberia, told of no less than ten blacks murdered by vigilantes. The Negroes were described as "vagrant and lewd."[67] Some instances were probably not reported anywhere. The *Monroe Bulletin* refused to print any stories about lynchings in Ouachita Parish because white citizens in the area regarded such matters "not only with indifference but with levity."[68]

Blacks were usually, but not always, the victims of lynch law. Notable among the white sufferers were the eleven Italians murdered by a mob in downtown New Orleans in 1891; the event was praised by much of the leadership of the state, including the editor of the *St. Mary Banner,* who hailed "the killing of the Dagoes" as "the greatest event of the year."[69] Three others of that nationality were strung up in Hahnville in 1896. In reply to the protests of the Italian government over these murders, the *Times-Democrat* thought it well to point out that residence in the Pelican State entailed, for anybody, a certain amount of danger, and that "foreigners who come to this country must take the same risk with natives."[70]

More often than not, serious acts of violence against Negroes in Louisiana were committed by men of some substance in the white community. Contemporary sources make it clear that the poorer whites were not involved in a majority of cases reported. To cite one of the more notorious instances of persecution, a reign of terror was conducted in 1890 against "industrious, reliable" Negroes near Baton Rouge by certain white landowners; only those blacks who had managed to accumulate property were shot, whipped, or otherwise molested. The black farmers were told to sell their property cheaply or be killed. The Bourbon *Daily Advocate* strongly condemned the whites responsible.[71] But almost never did conservatives publicly criticize the many lynchings in which the black victims had been accused of some crime. Often they praised such events, and demurred only if a trivial offense had been involved. "Lynch law," said a prudent gentleman of the town of Arcadia, "should not be resorted to except in very aggravated cases."[72]

"A crowd of the most worthy citizens of our parish . . . took charge of the prisoner, and in a short time he was launched into eternity."[73] This report from Abbeville in the summer of 1881 would be repeated, like a dreary refrain, by other localities in the years which followed. As one example among many, in 1898 "hundreds of the most prominent citizens in Bossier Parish" conducted a dual lynching near the town of Benton.[74] A Tangipahoa Parish group known as the "Phantom Riders" molested Negro families without fear of the law because, it was stated, "good" citizens rode with the band.[75] And upper class participation was most obvious in the lynching which attracted the greatest notice outside Louisiana: the killing of the eleven Italians in New Orleans in 1891. Included among the prominent citizens who headed that mob was none other than the district attorney. The *Nation* was forced to conclude that New Orleans was unique among

American cities in that "even the more respectable and sober-minded portion of the community are in a constant state of readiness for remedial violence."[76]

At least one Bourbon spokesman seemed to fear that the murder of the Italians had momentarily diverted attention away from the more pressing need for lynching Negroes. The *Morehouse Clarion*, which posed as an aristocratic journal, advised its readers shortly after the New Orleans massacre that more "little 'neck tie' parties" would "do a lot of good" among the black population of Bastrop. Years earlier it had similarly urged an increase in "swingings."[77] But it took a Shreveport newspaper to describe a lynching as "beautiful." This was "the right way," the *Evening Judge* decided, "to deal with every such black brute. Before the war they kept their places like the other beasts of the field."[78]

Shreveport advertised itself as a city of New South "energy, push, and vim."[79] Yet at the same time its businessman elite, together with the planters around the town, supported or condoned the most pitiless forms of social injustice to be found anywhere in the state. The "Shreveport Plan" of 1889 was a representative specimen. Conceived by a local publication, the *Daily Caucasian,* the proposal revolved around the old concept that the Negro was a sub-human species and should be treated accordingly. Specifically, Negroes were not to hold "easy jobs." Under this heading were listed the occupations of bootblacks, waiters, porters, cooks, clerks, and teachers. But the plan also implied intimidation of whites. For "no white man" was to "be permitted to employ a colored man . . . in any other manner than at the hardest and most degrading tasks." Apparently an exception could be made for the staff of Shreveport's Negro newspaper, *Bailey's Free South,* because they were supposed to be conservative Democrats.[80]

One New Orleans Negro leader, hearing of the plan, described it as "an old mummy" exhumed from "the Shreveport pyramids." He added: "The pernicious idea must be limited to the mean locality in which it had its origin. It would not live in more generous soil, and there are few places in this wide world so sterile in noble sentiments as that which immediately surrounds the publication office of the *Caucasian.*"[81]

The extent to which the "Shreveport Plan" was actually practiced in the area is problematical. Almost certainly, many residents of the city continued to hire blacks for tasks which were proscribed by the *Daily Caucasian.* But that "white supremacy" was "always . . . the motto" of Shreveport there was never any doubt.[82] Of course "we are kindly disposed to the negro [sic] race," said one prominent citizen in 1896, "wherever and whenever they properly demean themselves."[83] The indications are that the city's gentry often acted in a barbarous fashion toward the less fortunate of both races. This must have been the impression of two white men who once appeared in municipal court on a charge of vagrancy. Both were one-legged. The judge, who was also the mayor of Shreveport, enjoyed a grotesque sense of humor. He gave the crippled derelicts a sporting chance. If they could hop outside the city limits within twenty-five minutes, they would not have to serve one hundred days in jail.[84]

In other parts of Louisiana, well-to-do conservatives such as Howard G. Goodwyn of Colfax, occasionally complained that Negroes "were shamefully and needlessly bulldozed, and could hope for no legal redress."[85] But the most explicit plea for racial justice was voiced by a man who represented lower class whites. He was Aurel Arnaud, a legislator from St. Landry Parish. Arnaud was a political independent and of poor Cajun ancestry.

One day in 1886, Representative Arnaud stood up in the state house to speak on the unfairness of the method by which Louisiana maintained her public roads. His opening remarks were aimed at a statute of 1880 which instructed parish officials to impose twelve days of "road work," or a stipulated cash assessment, upon all adult males. He pointed out that this law worked a special hardship upon Negro tenants and laborers, since most black families seldom had as much as forty dollars a year to spend on clothes, medicine, and fresh meat. Arnaud expanded on his theme with blunt language: "Can you not see that this amount is not sufficient to support the laborer? And every day you divest him from a chance of earning something is a robbery of his daily bread? Should any one familiar with these facts be surprised to hear that the negroes [*sic*] steal? *I am only surprised that they do not steal more.*"[86]

Arnaud raised the possibility of another, more serious, Kansas Exodus of the state's black population, if their sufferings continued. He hastened to add that he was not a "leveller"; he offered no socialistic proposals. He merely believed that Negroes "must be treated with as much consideration as we treat our mules." That, he indicated, would be a vast improvement over present conditions. Finally, in what must stand as among the most candid words ever uttered by a white Louisiana official, Arnaud said:

> I have treated the subject entirely as from a . . . negro [*sic*] standpoint. But are there only negroes involved . . . ? And if there were only negroes involved, would I be here defending their cause? That is a question I have often asked myself, but I have never dared to probe my heart sufficiently to answer it, for fear I would perhaps find myself selfish enough to answer: no, because they are negroes [*sic*]. . . . But in what way is the white laborer treated with more consideration? Does the law give him any more protection? Is he paid better wages? Does he get more or better goods for his money? Do his children get more schooling? Yes, there is an immense difference between the two classes; but this difference exists only in the fancy of unscrupulous and rascally politicians: in every respect the white laborer stands exactly on the same footing with the negro. . . .[87]

Not quite so frank, but to the same point, were statements made by leaders of the more liberal element in the Louisiana Farmers' Union. Especially, John A. Tetts and Thomas J. Guice spoke up for the Negro. "What we want distributed to all men, 'regardless of race, color, or previous condition of servitude,'" Tetts wrote, "is the opportunity for the pursuit of happiness." Tetts believed that the Alliance movement was doing what "the sword, the press and the pulpit" had failed to do: it was forcing the "half Ku Klux and half desperado" white cotton farmer of the South out of his provincial shell, and into an awareness of class interest which transcended racial or regional boundaries. In his typically quaint style, Tetts optimistically reported that "the horns of the Ku Klux were knocked off . . . and the [bloody] shirt that has been waved so faithfully has been torn up . . . and cast into the Mississippi, and by this time no doubt [is] in the maw of some catfish, or making a nest for some mud-turtle of a politician who will have to crawl into his shell when he sees the result of the next election."[88]

Guice, the state Lecturer of the Farmers' Union, agreed with Tetts on the need for biracial unity and joint protest. According to Guice, the "spirit of fairness," if nothing else required that white agrarians include poor blacks in their drive to ameliorate economic and political evils. He believed that working people, "be they white or black," must act together because the "liberties and happiness" of both were at stake.[89] The old agrarian activist from Winn and Grant parishes, the Reverend Benjamin Brian, who was now prominent in the Farmers' Union, had been proposing the same thing since the latter days of Reconstruction.

The Louisiana Farmers' Union was, however, exclusively a white organization. Neither were Negroes admitted to the interstate Alliance proper. But there was a subsidiary association, the Colored Farmers' Alliance, which existed as a means of bringing the South's black agriculturists into the movement. It was founded in Houston County, Texas, in 1886. Spreading across the South with the white alliance, the Negro order claimed 1,200,000 members by 1890. Though separate, the white and colored Alliances pledged "fraternal regard" for each other. Both orders held their annual national conventions at the same date and in the same city, beginning at St. Louis in December of 1889. The following December, both met at Ocala, Florida.[90]

Fifty thousand Louisiana Negroes were reported on the membership rolls of the Colored Farmers' Alliance by the time of the Ocala convention. In 1891, at the peak of activity, the state's Negro Alliance claimed to be organized in twenty-seven parishes.[91] Detailed information regarding it is lacking, but the alleged fifty thousand membership was probably far above the actual number. The Colored Alliance may have entered the state as early as 1887; but the first report discoverable tells of a Grant Parish lodge which was set up in October of 1889.[92] Black Alliancemen were most numerous in the cotton parishes along the Red River. Apparently, few if any Negroes in the Mississippi River delta joined the order.[93] Neither was there much activity in the sugar country; the recent suppression of the Knights of Labor, and the weakness of even the white Alliance there, must have negated organizational efforts among the Negroes. Below the Red River, the Colored Farmers' Alliance was strongest in St. Landry Parish, where it did not take root until 1891.[94]

L. D. Laurent, an Alexandria Negro, was the first superintendent of the state's Colored Alliance. He held the post until succeeded by Isaac Keys of Catahoula Parish in 1891. Another significant black Allianceman was state secretary J. B. Lafargue. These men were rather circumspect in their activities; conservative whites seldom noticed anything they said or did. The mass of Louisiana Negroes, in or out of the alliance, tended toward caution in their dealings with local whites, and Laurent, Keys, and Lafargue were probably no exceptions. Certainly, the rising racial bitterness of the late 1880s hampered attempts at biracial agrarian protest. White Alliancemen who came to offer advice at Negro farmers' meetings were said to be received "with great courtesy," but were likely received with suspicion as well. Many blacks in St. Landry Parish refused to join the Colored Alliance because they believed that the white Farmers' Union included men who were anti-Negro "regulators."[95]

Race relations within the alliance movement were not helped by the fact that the Farmers' Union president, Thomas S. Adams, in 1889, selected the *Shreveport Weekly Caucasian* as the official state organ of the white agrarians.[96] From the Negroes' standpoint, a more insulting choice could scarcely have been made. Equally inauspicious was the fact that in 1890, most of the Democratic state legislators who happened to be members of the Farmers' Union (including ex-president John M. Stallings and G. L. P. Wren) voted for a bill which made racial segregation compulsory on all railroad coaches within the state. Upper class Bourbons were, as a Negro legislator point out, the prime movers behind this bill; but the Farmers' Union solons had, with few exceptions, quietly supported it.[97]

Even so, the possibility of white and Negro agrarian unity was still alive. During the year 1890, a third-party revolt against the conservative leadership of both the Democratic party and the Farmers' Union began to reverberate among the hills of North Louisiana, and the white farmers who led the protest immediately sought the support of the Colored Alliance.[98] The Negro Alliancemen were more than willing to help. At the Ocala gathering of the alliances in December, three of the seven Louisianians present signed a call for a national third-party convention, scheduled to meet the next year at Cincinnati: they were L. D. Laurent, J. B. Lafargue, and I. Miller. All three were Negroes. The state's white delegation at Ocala, dominated by Thomas S. Adams, refused to sign this birth certificate of the Populist Party.[99]

Notes for "Black Protest and White Power"

[1]Opelousas *St. Landry Clarion,* April 4, 1896.

[2]For prime, but not unusual, examples of this continuing theme, see St. Joseph *North Louisiana Journal,* October 30, 1880; Plaquemine *Iberville South,* April 18, 1896.

[3]William E. Highsmith, "Louisiana During Reconstruction" (Ph. D. dissertation, Louisiana State University, 1953), 188.

[4]*Shreveport Times,* quoted in Natchitoches *People's Vindicator,* October 22, 1881.

[5]Based on the files of Louisiana's two leading post-Reconstruction Negro newspapers, the New Orleans *Weekly Louisianian* and the *New Orleans Weekly Pelican.*

[6]*New Orleans Democrat,* March 19, 1880; *New Orleans Daily Picayune,* March 19, 1880.

[7]*New Orleans Democrat,* March 18-21-1880.

[8]*New Orleans Daily Picayune,* March 20, 1880.

[9]*St. Landry Democrat,* September 24, 1881.

[10]*Daily Picayune,* March 29, 31, 1880.

[11]*New Orleans Democrat,* March 27-April 2, 1880; *Daily Picayune,* March 31, 1880.

[12]*Daily Picayune,* April 1, 1880.

[13]*Weekly Louisianian,* April 3, 1880.

[14]*New Orleans Daily States,* quoted in Bastrop *Morehouse Clarion,* April 16, 1880.

[15]Philip Uzee, "Republican Politics in Louisiana: 1877-1900" (Ph. D. dissertation, Louisiana State University, 1950), 97.

[16]*Weekly Louisianian,* April 10, 1880. When James Garfield, rather than Grant, was nominated by the Republicans in 1880, Louisiana's Negroes expressed marked disappointment. Uneducated blacks had never heard of Garfield and asked "who 'Garfish' was." Uzee, "Republican Politics in Louisiana," 100.

[17]Andrew H. Gay, Jr., to Andrew H. Gay, Sr., January 19, 1889, in Gay Family Papers, Department of Archives, Louisiana State University, Baton Rouge; J. Carlyle Sitterson, *Sugar Country: The Cane Sugar Industry in the South, 1753-1950* (Lexington, Ky., 1953), 248, 319.

[18]Arthur Raymond Pearce, "The Rise and Decline of Labor in New Orleans" (M.A. thesis, Tulane University, 1938), 25.

[19]*Daily Picayune,* August 26, September 1-13, 1881; *Weekly Louisianian,* August 13, September 17, 1881.

[20]*Weekly Louisianian,* September 17, 1881.

[21]Frederick Meyers, "The Knights of Labor in the South," *Southern Economic Journal,* 6 (1940): 483; Foster Rhea Dulles, *Labor in America,* 2nd ed. (New York, 1960), 126-27.

[22]*Daily Picayune,* March 26, 1886; Meyers, "The Knights of Labor in the South," 6:485-86; Richard J. Hinton, "Organizations of the Discontented," *Forum,* 7 (1889): 550.

[23]*New Orleans Southern Industry* was edited by William J. O'Donnell. It was one of twenty-one Knights newspapers published at that time in the United States. *Philadelphia Journal of United Labor,* April 9, 1887; *New Orleans Weekly Pelican,* July 9, 1887.

[24]Covington Hall, "Labor Struggles in the Deep South" (MS, undated, in Tulane University Library), 31; *Daily Picayune*, January 4, 1887; Letter from "W. W. F.," Springfield, La., in *Philadelphia Journal of United Labor*, August 27, 1887.

[25]Cf. *Philadelphia Journal of United Labor*, September 17, 1887; *Times-Democrat*, November 6, 1887; *Weekly Pelican*, November 19, 1887; Sitterson, *Sugar Country*, 319-20.

[26]*Daily Picayune*, October 29, 1887; *Weekly Pelican*, November 5, 1887; *Philadelphia Journal of United Labor*, November 26, 1887.

[27]Hall, "Labor Struggles in the Deep South," 32; *Weekly Pelican*, November 5, 1887; William C. Stubbs, *Sugar Cane: A Treatise on the History, Botany and Agriculture of Sugar Cane and the Chemistry and Manufacture of Its Juices Into Sugar, and Other Products* (Baton Rouge, 1897), 1:37-38.

[28]*Thibodaux Sentinel*, November 12, 1887; *Baton Rouge Daily Capitolian-Advocate*, November 4, 1887; *Times-Democrat*, November 3-6, 1887.

[29]*Daily Picayune*, October 29, 1887.

[30]Ibid., November 9, 1887. See also, *New Orleans Weekly Pelican*, November 26, 1887; *Biographical and Historical Memoirs of Louisiana* (Chicago, 1892), 1:133.

[31]Hall, "Labor Sruggles in the Deep South," 32; *New Orleans Times-Democrat*, November 6, 1887.

[32]*Daily States*, quoted in *Baton Rouge Daily Capitolian-Advocate*, November 24, 1887.

[33]Letter from W. W. Pugh, in *Daily Picayune*, November 20, 1887.

[34]*Daily Picayune*, November 2, 1887.

[35]*Senate Journal*, 1888, 22; *New Orleans Mascot*, quoted in *Weekly Pelican*, November 12, 1887; *Philadelphia Journal of United Labor*, November 19, 1887.

[36]*Mascot*, quoted in *Weekly Pelican*, November 12, 1887.

[37]*Times-Democrat*, November 6, 1887.

[38]Ibid., November 3, 1887; *Daily Picayune*, November 3, 1887; *Philadelphia Journal of United Labor*, December 3, 1887.

[39]Cf. *New Orleans Daily News*, quoted in *Weekly Pelican*, November 19, 1887; *Times-Democrat*, November 7-8, 1887.

[40]Morgan City *Free Press*, quoted in *Daily Capitolian-Advocate*, November 12, 1887.

[41]*Daily Picayune*, November 21, 1887.

[42]Ibid., November 3, 1887.

[43]Cf. *Thibodaux Sentinel*, November 12, 1887; *Weekly Pelican*, November 26, 1887; *Daily Picayune*, November 25, 1887.

[44]Letter from Judge Taylor Beattie, in *Daily Picayune*, December 3, 1887.

[45]*Opelousas Courier*, November 26, 1887.

[46]*Sentinel*, November 26, 1887.

[47]*Daily Picayune*, November 25, 1887; *Weekly Pelican*, November 26, 1887.

[48]Cf. New Roads *Pointe Coupée Banner*, November 26, 1887; Thibodaux *Sentinel*, November 26, 1887; *New Orleans Weekly Pelican*, November 26, 1887; *Philadelphia Journal of United Labor*, December 3, 1887.

[49]Plaquemine *Iberville South,* April 18, 1896.

[50]*Times-Democrat,* November 24-26, 1887; *Daily Capitolian-Advocate,* November 24, 1887; Hall, "Labor Struggles in the Deep South," 40.

[51]*Opelousas Courier,* November 26, 1887.

[52]*Daily Picayune,* November 24-26, 1887.

[53]Lavina Gay to Edward J. Gay, December 10, 1887, in Gay Family Papers.

[54]*Courier,* November 26, 1887.

[55]*Jeanerette Teche Pilot,* May 5, 1888; New Roads *Pointe Coupée Banner,* quoted in ibid.

[56]*New Orleans Weekly Pelican,* May 11, 1889; Sitterson, *Sugar Country,* 321-22; *Daily Picayune,* August 7, 1891.

[57]C. Vann Woodward, *The Strange Career of Jim Crow,* 2nd ed. (New York, 1957), 51-56; Arthur S. Link, *American Epoch: A History of the United States Since the 1890s,* 3rd ed. (New York, 1967), 1:30-31.

[58]For Cable's liberal views on race, see especially George Washington Cable, *The Negro Question* (New York, 1890), passim.

[59]Clement Eaton, *The Growth of Southern Civilization: 1790-1860* (New York, 1961), 125-33; Ulrich Bonnell Phillips, *Life and Labor in the Old South* (Boston, 1929), 151-53; John Hope Franklin, *From Slavery to Freedom,* 2nd ed. (New York, 1956), 191; Alfred H. Conrad and John R. Meyer, "The Economics of Slavery in the Ante-Bellum South," *Journal of Political Economy,* 66 (1958): 92-122.

[60]Woodward, *The Strange Career of Jim Crow,* 20; Simkins, *A History of the South,* 509-11; E. Merton Coulter, *The South During Reconstruction: 1865-1877* (Baton Rouge, 1947), 162-64.

[61]*Daily Picayune,* February 19, 1881.

[62]*Welsh Crescent,* quoted in *Baton Rouge Daily Advocate,* March 4, 1890.

[63]*Daily Picayune,* September 19, 1881; *New Iberia Sugar Bowl,* quoted in ibid., October 8, 1881.

[64]*Bastrop Morehouse Clarion,* September 2, 1881;l *Rayville Richland Beacon,* October 1, 1881.

[65]James Elbert Cutler, *Lynch Law: An Investigation Into the History of Lynching in the United States* (New York, 1905), 179, 183.

[66]The Tuskegee records begin with 1885, but bear out the *Tribune* figures quoted in ibid. for 1885-1902. Monroe N. Word, ed., *Negro Yearbook: An Annual Encyclopedia of the Negro, 1918-1919* (Tuskegee, Ala., 1919), 374-75.

[67]*Lake Providence Carroll Democrat,* August 25, 1888.

[68]*Monroe Bulletin,* quoted in *Daily Picayune,* September 28, 1886.

[69]Franklin *St. Mary Banner,* March 23, 1891.

[70]*Times-Democrat,* quoted in *Chautauquan,* 24 (1896): 92.

[71]*Baton Rouge Daily Advocate,* November 26-27, 1890; letter from Anna M. Harris, in Opelousas *St. Landry Clarion,* February 14, 1891.

[72]Arcadia *Louisiana Advance,* May 31, 1889.

[73]*Abbeville Meridional,* August 20, 1881.

[74]*Natchitoches Enterprise,* December 8, 1898.

[75]*Weekly Pelican,* July 16, 1887.

[76]"The New Orleans Massacre," *Nation,* 52 (March 19, 1891), 232. See also, *Philadelphia Journal of the Knights of Labor,* March 14, 1891.

[77]*Morehouse Clarion,* quoted in *Daily Picayune,* August 10, 1891. See also, *Morehouse Clarion,* February 5, 1881.

[78]*Shreveport Evening Judge,* March 23, 1896.

[79]*Shreveport Times,* quoted in *Daily Picayune,* March 21, 1887.

[80]*Shreveport Daily Caucasian,* quoted in *Weekly Pelican,* July 27, August 17, 1889; *Daily Advocate,* February 24, 1896.

[81]*Weekly Pelican,* July 27, 1889.

[82]*Shreveport Evening Judge,* February 24, 1896.

[83]Ibid., March 25, 1896.

[84]Ibid., March 4, 1896.

[85]*Colfax Chronicle,* January 9, 1892.

[86]*Baton Rouge Weekly Truth,* May 28, 1886 (author's italics).

[87]Ibid. Rep. Arnaud's outspokenness naturally irritate the defenders of the status quo. According to a conservative paper in his home parish, Arnaud belonged in either "prison garb" or "a straight jacket." *Washington* (La.) *Argus,* quoted in *Shreveport Times,* May 29, 1887.

[88]J. A. Tetts, "The Good the Alliance Has Done," *National Economist,* 3 (April 12, 1890), 64.

[89]Letter for Thomas J. Guice, in *Daily Picayune,* October 3, 1891.

[90]Frank M. Drew, "The Present Farmers' Movement," *Political Science Quarterly,* 6 (1891): 287-89; Nelson A. Dunning, *The Farmers' Alliance History and Agriculture Digest* (Washington, 1891), 289, 291-92.

[91]*Western Rural and American Stockman,* 28 (December 13, 1890), 789, quoted in Theodore Saloutos, *Farmer Movement in the South: 1865-1933* (Berkeley and Los Angeles, 1960), 81; Opelousas *St Landry Clarion,* October 10 1891.

[92]*Biographical and Historical Memoirs of Northwest Louisiana* (Nashville, 1890), 503.

[93]The two leading journals of the northeastern delta parishes, the *Lake Providence Carroll Democrat* and the *St. Joseph Tensas Gazette,* reported no Negro Alliance activity between 1888 and 1892. Neither paper was in the habit of ignoring signs of unrest or organization among local blacks.

[94]*St. Landry Clarion,* June 27, 1891.

[95]Ibid., June 27, August 8, 15, October 10, 1891.

[96]*Weekly Caucasian,* January 24, 1890.

[97]*Official Journal of the Proceedings of the House of Representatives of the State of Louisiana,* 1890, 200-204.

[98]*Daily Advocate,* October 5, November 18, 1890; *Daily Picayune,* November 8, 1890.

[99]*Alexandria Farmers' Vidette,* quoted in *Colfax Chronicle,* January 10, 1891.

ANY PLACE BUT HERE:
KANSAS FEVER IN NORTHEAST LOUISIANA*

Joe Louis Caldwell

Kansas fever swept across North Louisiana like a wind-driven prairie fire, sucking up discontented black peasants from Caddo Parish in the extreme northwestern part of the state to the Northeast Louisiana Delta parishes along the Mississippi River. Starting from smoldering embers of discontent in 1873, it reached wild-fire proportions by 1879. Kansas Exodusters, as they have been called, have captured the imagination of serious and casual students of Southern history for nearly a hundred years.[1]

Scholars have tended to focus on the Southwide implications of this mass migration. Of course, they have also centered much attention on the impact of the movement on certain states. Kansas fever was confined to the Northern cotton parishes. Probably because of a different political climate and because the planters in the sugar parishes implemented a wage scale that enabled day laborers to earn substantially more than tenant farmers and sharecroppers in North Louisiana, the Exodus movement never reached the epidemic level there that was witnessed in the North Louisiana parishes.[2]

The following key questions will be addressed in this article: Who were the regional and local leaders of the Exodus Movement? What did blacks themselves see as the root cause or causes of the Migration Movement? How did the planter-merchant class react to this threat to their continued economic hegemony? What were the long and short term effects of this socio-economic movement on the black community in the Louisiana Delta specifically and in the state generally? Answers to these and other questions will be framed within the context of the experiences of black people in the Delta parishes.

The first trickle of penniless, ragged blacks appeared at Wyandotte, Kansas, in 1873.[3] By 1880 an estimated sixty thousand black peasants had fled the cotton fields of the South seeking a new definition of freedom on the plains of Kansas and in other Northern states. Based on the available contemporary evidence, it is impossible to determine the number

*First published in the North Louisiana Historical Association *Journal*, 21 (1990): 51-70. Reprinted with the kind permission of the author and publisher.

of blacks who left each state. But an informed estimate of the average number of persons who migrated from each state is possible. If the above mentioned Southwide estimation is used (sixty thousand), and if it is agreed that the vast majority of the migrants were supplied by eight states,[4] one can safely say that Louisiana lost approximately seventy-five hundred blacks between 1873-1880. The bulk of this loss was sustained by the four Delta parishes. Tantamount to the threat of a general strike in an industrial sector, this movement, which began as a mere drip in the early seventies, had become a huge tidal wave by 1879-1880.[5]

Benjamin "Pap" Singleton is credited with organizing the movement on the regional level. While his presence certainly was inspirational, a more fundamental aspect occurs in the story of the movement's organic beginnings in Louisiana. Unquestionably, it had its beginning in the cotton fields of Caddo Parish in Northwest Louisiana; it was the brainchild of Henry Adams, a former slave and an ex-soldier who returned home from the army around 1869 to find the conditions of his people little better than during the days of slavery. Adams took hold of the Exodus idea with evangelical zeal, spreading it throughout North Louisiana. He stated, under oath before a Senate Select Committee investigating the Exodus, that in conjunction with other black men, he formed a committee to look into the conditions of black agricultural workers throughout the South. Members of this committee were sent into most of the Southern states and urged to work among their people in order to gather information on wages and the general way blacks were treated by their employers.[6]

This information was forwarded to the committee in Caddo Parish where the letters were read in meetings attended only by members. The original purpose of this committee was to determine if it were possible for blacks to live and work in the midst of their former masters. Its affairs were conducted as a secret society. The committee continued gathering information until 1874. Reports on the general treatment of blacks throughout the South filtered back to the committee. Most of the reports emphasized charges of high rents, brutal landlords, and workers being cheated out of their yearly earnings.[7] In August, 1874, the committee entered into the second stage of its development. Spurred on by the terrorist tactics of the White League and other kindred organizations, members of the committee formed the Colonization Council.[8] The Colonization Council formulated a plan aimed at ameliorating the conditions of the black race in the southern United States. It consisted of the following proposals: (1) To appeal to the president and congress to protect the rights and privileges of black Southerners; (2) If that failed, to appeal to the president and congress to set aside a territory within the United States to be used exclusively by blacks; (3) This failing, to ask for an appropriation of money to send blacks to Liberia, in West Africa; and (4) as a final resort, to seek asylum under a government outside the United States. Theoretically, Adams plan had a strong flavor of black nationalism.[9]

The affairs of the Colonization Council, like those of the committee, were conducted in the utmost secrecy. Meetings were closed to everyone except members, and no politicians were allowed in either organization. Only laboring people were admitted as organization members. Members were advised not to use their names at meetings, adding another level of security as well as secrecy. This cautious attitude stemmed from a fear of reprisal from the planter-merchant class, and their henchmen, as well as a fear that the inclusion of black politicians would cause disunity within the movement. The migration question created tension between the black masses and the traditional black political leadership elite within the black community of the Louisiana Delta. The pleas of the Colonization Council did not produce a positive response from the national government. Still, the Council took no decisive action until 1877. When the national government, in the hands of the Republican party, abdicated its responsibility to protect black citizens in the southern United States (a fact that was driven home by the symbolic withdrawal of the remnants of federal troops scattered throughout the South in 1877), Adams and his cohorts lost all hope. Seeing the reins of state and local governments placed in the hands of the same class of men who had held power during the days of slavery, they concluded that any place was better than where they were presently situated.[10]

As a result of the return of home rule to the South, many blacks lost all hope of making a better life for themselves and their families in the land of their birth. A profusion of emigration societies sprang up in Louisiana and other Southern states, and mass meetings were held to discuss emigration. In 1877 meetings of this type were held in Caddo, Madison, and Bossier parishes. Adams estimated that over ninety-eight thousand blacks above the age of twelve, from across the South, enrolled their names with the Colonization Council. These actions were certainly indicative of their discontent and an expression of their willingness to consider emigration.[11]

Rev. Alfred Fairfax was one of the most influential and controversial migration leaders. Working closely with laboring people of Tensas Parish undoubtedly gave him great insight into the problems confronting them on a day to day basis. His involvement does raise a question about the validity of Adams's assertion that politicians were barred from membership in the committee as well as the Colonization Council. Either an exception was made in the case of Reverend Fairfax, or he assumed a leadership role without being a member of the organized cells. During the latter part of 1879, he led several black families from their Tensas Parish homes to Chautauqua, Kansas. The possibility also exists that he was singled out and designated a leader by the hostile Democratic-controlled press, therby giving the opponents of the movement a target upon whom to focus. Whatever the case may have been, he loomed on the scene in the turbulent last years of the 1870s.[12]

Local leadership generally was in the hands of Baptist ministers and working men. In Madison Parish, the Rev. Curtis Pollard and a laborer known only as Mr. Shelby were in the vanguard of the movement in its early stage. Pollard was a minister and politician who won the hearts of laboring people in Madison Parish by his willingness to support the Exodus. Of course, some ministers and politicians were opposed to the movement. Their opposition was thought to have been selfishly motivated by some, in view of the fact that their professional success was dependent upon a large local black constituency. Adams claims aside, several politicians attended the State Convention of Colored Men when it met at New Orleans Common Street Baptist Church, April 17, 1879—to consider the migration question. Such participants as David Young of Concordia Parish, and William Murrell, Jr., of Madison Parish, had all held elective positions in state and local government. The Tensas Parish delegation was composed of the following individuals: Frank Watson, Cea[sor] Ray, Duncan Smith, Charlie Harris, and Washington Duncan. It is not clear what role they played in organizing the movement on the local level. The fact that they were sent, or came on their own, does indicate more than a passing flirtation with the Exodus Movement in Tensas Parish.[13]

Many different factors have been cited as having contributed to the large out-migration of black laborers from the Louisiana Delta Parishes. Among these factors the following were paramount: the overflow of 1874-76, outside agitators, propaganda circulated by Northern Republicans and railroad agents, the Compromise of 1877, the counterrevolution of 1878-79, and a ruinous credit system, coupled with high rents and dishonest landlords. The Conservative Democratic press left no stone unturned in its constant campaign to belittle the movement, to defame its leaders, and exonerate the planters from any capability. One of the most frivolous charges was the assertion, made in the *North Louisiana Journal*, that the Exodus was caused by the overflow of 1874-76. This account becomes even more ludicrous when one considers the fact that hardly a spring had passed since 1865 without the inundation of some portion of the Louisiana Delta.[14]

That ubiquitous outside agitator (who has allegedly caused so much disharmony between the races in the South) was suspected of being at it again. In truth, P.B.S. Pinchback was probably one of the few "outside agitators" in the area at that time. He was in Madison Parish in 1879 seeking election as a delegate to the upcoming state constitutional convention. He spoke to black gatherings at Delta and Millikens Bend in Madison Parish and urged them to remain in the state.[15] Northern Republicans and western railroad agents received their share of blame. Northern and mid-western Republicans were charged with luring gullible blacks to their sections to insure continual Republican dominance in those regions. Railroad companies were accused of sending agents into the parishes who promised blacks they would be given land and farming implements in Kansas. The tragic irony of these accusations does not lie in the fact that they had little if anything to do with the movement. It lies in the fact that the white planter-merchant class held a deep seated belief that blacks did not have the ability to recognize their own problems and take corrective actions.

Three main factors caused the Exodus Movement in the Louisiana Delta. They were (1) the unbridled violence unleashed against blacks during the counterrevolution of 1878-1879; (2) the Compromise of 1877 which signaled the demise of the Republican party in the state and local politics (although pockets of Republicanism survived beyond 1877); and (3) a ruinous credit system, coupled with high rents and dishonest landlords, which combined to reduce some blacks to a level of peonage.[16]   But the bloody violence generated by the counterrevolution of 1878-1879 was, by far, the most important single factor which caused the mass flight of black laboring people from the Louisiana Delta.

According to William Murrell, Jr., George Washington, a wealthy Madison Parish farmer, was one of the first black men to leave the Louisiana Delta and settle in Kansas. He sold his land, livestock, and farming equipment at a great loss and moved to Kansas in March, 1879. After settling in Wyandotte, Kansas, he wrote Adolphus Prince, an agricultural laborer residing in Madison Parish, advising him to leave Louisiana and come to Kansas. At about the same time, a Mr. Shelby and the Reverend Curtis Pollard led six or seven hundred blacks from Delta, Louisiana (in Madison Parish), to the state of Kansas. Both P. B. S. Pinchback and William Murrell, Jr., two black politicians who were well known on the local and state level, addressed the crowd of blacks at Delta. Each man attempted to persuade them to remain in Louisiana, but to no avail. Apparently, a substantial number left Milliken's Bend that same day, because, Pinchback reportedly spoke to another large crowd on the river bank at that village without weakening their resolve to leave the state.[17]

Blacks continued to leave the Louisiana Delta throughout the spring and summer of 1879, on the heels of the anti-black politically motivated violence witnessed by them during the fall of 1878.   In a letter of resignation submitted to Green B. Raum, Commissioner of Internal Revenue, Washington, D. C., P. B. S. Pinchback gave an interesting account of just how they left. He stated:

> On a recent visit to my domicile in Madison Parish, I found the colored people in the greatest excitement about the migration question. Hundreds were upon the banks of the Mississippi River awaiting transportation. Streams of them were pouring into Delta by every road and a general stampede . . . threatened. A glance at the situation convinced me that a panic prevailed. Horses, mules, cows, wagons, plows, and every species of property on which means for flight could be raised were being sacrificed.[18]

The Exodus Movement threatened to bring commercial agriculture production to a standstill in the affected area. Because of this devastating possibility, it produced positive results for blacks in the Lower Mississippi Valley from both a short and long term point of view.   An immediate result was the forcing of the white planter-merchant elite (throughout the Lower Mississippi Valley) to admit that their high-handed treatment of black workers was causing a large scale out-migration of the laboring class of that region. Faced with the potential loss of their laboring forces, these men called a meeting of the white planter-merchant elite and carefully selected black guests to be held in Vicksburg, Mississippi, May 10, 1879.[19]

Prior to the convening of the Vicksburg meeting, Louisiana Delta blacks called a few local gatherings to further explore the pros and cons of the migration question.[20] Alluding to the calling of the Vicksburg Convention, one black newspaper editor stressed the economic undercurrents of the Exodus Movement in the following words:

the American is only moved and thoroughly quickened to the core when his pocket is touched. Other people may consider money trash, the American regards the almighty dollar as the chief end of the man, and for such he will sacrifice all other interests. The Negro's cry of distress for years had never been able to stir the conscience of the South until of late when the despised 'man and brother' concluded he would make the last appeal to the dearest right of those who profit by his labor—the pocket.[21]

Gen. W. R. Miles of Yazoo, Mississippi was elected as the convention's president, along with four black vice-presidents: F. E. Cassell of Memphis, Tennessee, James Hill of Holly Springs, Mississippi, H. M. Robinson of Helena, Arkansas, and David Young of Concordia Parish, Louisiana.[22] Some typical paternalistic opening remarks by the president set the tone for the convention. This is an excerpt from those remarks: "The God of Nature had made the colored man a tropical plant; the South was his home according to divine dispensation, but if any desired to emigrate to Kansas or elsewhere, no human power could prevent them. They have the same right to go that I have."[23]

He implored the white landlord to be honest in his dealings with black laborers. A committee on resolutions identified several factors as the basic causes of the movement. The convention passed a series of conciliatory resolutions intended to counteract the popular enthusiasm for Kansas. More than anything else, the Vicksburg meeting demonstrated the important role that blacks played in the economy of the Lower Mississippi Valley.[24] Despite the optimism which accompanied the calling of this convention, the resolutions and promises endorsed by the delegates did nothing to alter the equation of economic power in that area. Nevertheless, by the fall of 1879 the 'Kansas fever" had seemingly subsided in the Louisiana Delta. However, after heinous atrocities were committed in Madison Parish during the election campaign of 1879, many blacks in this area began making plans to follow the trails of their Kansas-bound brethren. The events of November clearly demonstrate the inability of the regional leadership of the Lower Mississippi Valley, the landlords and merchants who attended the labor convention in Vicksburg May 10, 1879, to effectively impose their will on the planter-merchant elite on the local level.[25]

On February 16, 1880, a Colored Exodus Convention met in Dallas, Texas. In the midst of its sessions the convention delegates decided to transform their group into the Texas Farmers' Association. Afterwards, the association voted to establish a colony in the Texas panhandle with a stock capitalization of one hundred thousand dollars. Shares were to sell at twenty-five dollars each. One hundred and fifty black families from Louisiana were expected to take part in the venture.[26]

Due to mild weather in the early months of 1880, the migration of black laborers from the Louisiana Delta continued. Among the migrants were found some of the most respected and prosperous members of the black community. A Madison Parish correspondent to the New Orleans *Weekly Louisianian* reported thusly:

the people do not leave in the squads as they did last year; yet those that are leaving are the very best of our people, and they all carry some money with them—enough to live on until something turns up. Among the many who have recently left are ex-Sheriff Peck and family, Hons. W. H. Hayward, J. B. Brooks, and other prominent leaders. You may expect a large number to leave this spring.[27]

Informed contemporary observers, regardless of race or politics, agreed that a large number of blacks were leaving the northeast Louisiana parishes in early 1880. Since most public officials in those states losing and receiving migrants did not keep adequate records on the movement, it is impossible to ascertain just how many blacks left the three Louisiana Delta Parishes during the peak years of the movement. In 1870, Kansas had a black population of 17,108 and ten years later it had increased to 43,107. One source estimated that twenty thousand Southern blacks came to Kansas within a four year period, from 1878 to 1882. John P. St. John, governor of Kansas, 1877-1881, estimated that sixty thousand blacks entered Kansas between 1877-1880. He believed that forty thousand remained in Kansas while twenty thousand moved on to other midwestern and Northern states. George T. Ruby, a black newpaper editor who was residing in New Orleans at the time he appeared before the Senate Select Committee investigating the Exodus, estimated that about two or three thousand blacks left Louisiana en-route to Kansas. This is a very conservative estimate in view of the fact that Murrell and Pinchback reported seeing a crowd of six or seven-hundred Kansas bound blacks on the levee at Delta, Louisiana in March, 1879. On that same day they observed another group of similar size at Milliken's Bend, Louisiana. In April, 1879 some observers reported seeing about three thousand blacks strung out along the levee between Vidalia and St. Joseph, seeking transportation North. As was previously stated, it is possible that seventy-five hundred blacks left Louisiana between 1873-1880. At least five thousand of that number probably came from the Louisiana Delta.[28] Whatever the exact number might have been, one thing is certain, planters from the Louisiana Delta peered into many empty cabins each spring.

Once planters and businessmen had an opportunity to assess the Exodus, and its implications, it had a most sobering impact on them. Of course, a few took a cavalier attitude at the outset, crying "let them go."[29] More in keeping with the widespread belief that the black man s labor was theirs to exploit, numerous white planters attempted to force black migrants off the levee at Milliken's Bend and elsewhere. Others proposed to import Chinese or European labor. Whatever the response, this movement caused grave concern throughout the Lower Mississippi Valley.[30]

A number of prominent blacks voiced opposition to this grassroots inspired out-migration of blacks. Frederick Douglass, that venerable veteran of the abolition wars, was ambivalent toward the movement. Blanche K. Bruce, the black senator from Mississippi who was also a planter,[31] gave his view on the Exodus in a lengthy letter published in the New Orleans *Weekly Louisianian*. He stated,

> I hold and have ever held, that the interest of the two races at the South are so blended that one cannot suffer without in some sort, materially affecting the other, and that there is no necessary conflict of interest between them which should render an exodus of the laboring classes expedient or desirable. . . .[32]

P.B.S. Pinchback, a nationally known black politician who served as governor of Louisiana for a short time, voiced serious misgivings about the wisdom of the movement. David Young, a black Baptist minister and former state senator, also opposed the movement. Young was a merchant and landowner from Concordia Parish. He credited himself with stemming the tide of migrants from his parish.[33] He commented on the subject with his typical bravado:

> I feel prouder of that than anything I can do in the convention. [The upcoming State Constitutional Convention of 1879]. If I hadn't gone up there, there would not have been 400 blacks left out of a population of 13,000 and in fact, the parish would have been depopulated.[34]

William Murrell, Jr., a newpaper editor and former state representative from Madison Parish, opposed the movement until the "bulldozers" threatened his life, causing him to flee from his home. He then did an about-face and at least paid lip service to the cause.[35] These men who opposed the movement received high praise from the conservative Democratic press which had formerly denounced them as radicals, scoundrels, and drawers of the color line. Indeed they were now held up as the "leading men of the colored race."[36]

In truth, these so-called black leaders found themselves sadly out of step with the rural masses for whom they proposed to speak. Certain economic and demographic factors caused this misunderstanding. Pinchback and Douglass were urban-based cosmopolitan black politicians who moved in a world that was quite remote from the cabins and cotton rows of the Lower Mississippi Valley. They spoke in abstract and theoretical terms to a people all too familiar with the harsh concrete realities of life on the lowest rung of the socio-economic ladder. Because of their vested economic interest, Bruce and Young unconsciously spoke in the same conservative tones as did the white planters and merchants in their sections. In a flash of brilliant insight, William Murrell, Jr., saw the dilemma of black leaders who were incapable of leading the same black masses who had voted them into office time and time again during Reconstruction.[37] He said, in his testimony before the Teller Committee:

> I went out and made speeches against their going and tried to reason with them. And then I found out one thing that was very peculiar—one thing that I would not have believed if I had not seen it—those who had been leading these colored people in political matters could not lead them any more when it came to this matter; the colored people would not pay any attention to them whatever.[38]

Murrell had stumbled upon an important truth; the effective leader must voice the concerns of his followers.

Emboldened by the conciliatory attitude of the white planter-merchant class, black tenants and sharecroppers in the Louisiana Delta began negotiating with their landlords for lower rents and cheaper rates at the gins. A reduction of from one to two dollars per acre was granted by landlords in Madison Parish. A number of black sharecroppers and renters, who agreed to remain, were given new contracts with better terms. In Concordia and other areas, plantation stores canceled all debts. However, the overall half-hearted nature of the planter-merchant reaction was not enough to stem the migration tide.[39] Still, these concessions were significant—all things considered—and serve as a testament to the latent economic power of rural blacks.

The labor unrest brought on by the Exodus Movement, as well as the strained relations between the races in the Louisiana Delta following the election of 1878, caused forty-two of the leading citizens of Tensas Parish to petition Wade H. Hough, judge of the Thirteenth District Court, requesting that he postpone the special term of the District Court scheduled to meet in that parish, June 23, 1879. A few of the signees were H. F. Shaifer, [Dr.] D.P. January, J.H. Bondurant, [Dr.] J.E. Slicer, [Dr.] J.R. Weatherly, and T. C. Saches. The petitioners were some of the most prominent merchants, planters, and physicians in Tensas Parish. They feared that the conviction of a large number of black defendants would add fuel to the Exodus fires. Additionally, on August 2, 1879, the planters of East Carroll Parish held a meeting in Lake Providence, Louisiana, for the purpose of assuaging the fears of black laborers who might have been considering joining their brethren in Kansas.[40]

Two important long term results of the Exodus Movement are rooted in the background of the political dispute that led to the anti-black violence associated with the counterrevolution of 1878-1879. A direct result of the politically motivated violence was the establishment of a solid political working relationship between disaffected white Democrats and disenchanted black Republicans. This symbiotic relationship allowed blacks at least some indirect representation in local affairs, and more that superficial contact with certain white officials on the state level.

The nucleus of that black-white coalition, which had created the independent ticket in Tensas Parish during the election campaign of November 1878, was thrown together on March 6, 1879. On that day a citizen's meeting, attended by blacks and whites, was held in the Grangers Hall in Newellton, a small village in Tensas Parish. The purpose of this meeting was to establish the People's Party as a new political party in Tensas Parish. Obviously the white independents were sending a message to the Democrats, informing them that they refused to be driven from the political field by their terror tactics. Bi-racial in composition, the assemblage did not hesitate to involve blacks in the business of forming the party. Robert J. Walker was elected temporary secretary. William Coolidge, P.E. Tyler, William Price, E.C. Routh, and Noel N. Neely (all black) were placed on a committee of nine that was given the responsibility of recommending individuals to serve on the party's executive committee. Among those placed on the executive committee were William Coolidge, B.C. Routh, Spencer Ross, P.E. Tyler, and Robert J. Walker. Several white men who were actively involved with the formation of the People's Party— Lucien Bland, James D. McGill, J.R. Weatherly, Jim P. Douglass, and Jim Gillespie had played leading roles in the Bland-Douglass fusion effort in Tensas Parish. Each of these men was placed on the executive committee. J.M. Gillespie was selected as the party president and J.D. Douglass was chosen party treasurer. Both he and Douglass were placed on the party's finance committee.[41]

In order to insure that the Democrats understood their position on some key issues expected to be brought before the upcoming state constitutional convention, the People's Party published this digest of its views in the parish newspaper:

1st We are in favor of a competent and incorruptible judiciary, to be appointed by the Governor of the State.

2nd We are in favor of a reduction of public officers and official fees.

3rd We are in favor of a just effort to rid the State of her onerous indebtedness.

4th We are opposed to any attempt to tamper with the right of suffrage, and believe that every male should be permitted to vote as he may see fit, without let or hindrance.

5th Knowing that the welfare of any country depends on the education of its citizens, we are in favor of an impartial distribution of the school funds for the education of both white and colored children.

6th We believe that the election of officers of the General Government, State and Parochial should be held on one and the same day.[42]

The 1879 Tensas Parish People's Party is an historical enigma. It was called into being nearly eleven years before the Populist fever began to sweep over the South and Northwest. Furthermore, it cropped up in the Louisiana Delta (in the Cotton Parishes) an area that was basically free of Populists—according to most experts. Yet its position on eradiction of the State's debt, a reduction of public office holders, and a willingness to work with blacks, was similar to the Populist principles. However, it must be noted that the People's Party of Tensas Parish focused almost exclusively on political reform, while the Populists showed an overwhelming concern for economic issues. Still, it was a legitimate local third party. Evidently the necessary ingredients needed to produce a third party movement grew to maturity with greater rapidity in the troubled soil of Tensas Parish.[43]

The 1878-1879 fusionist movement, which split the re-emerging Democratic party in some areas in Louisiana, robbed white supremacist elements of the solidarity needed to carry through a planned move aimed at disfranchising blacks in the upcoming state constitutional convention in 1879. When the citizens of Tensas Parish called a mass meeting at St. Joseph on Monday, March, 10, 1879, the division was evident. E.D.

Newell was elected president and empowered by the body with the authority to appoint a committee of thirty for the purpose of selecting three men as delegates to the convention. In what was probably designed as a conciliatory move, he appointed ten blacks, ten white independents, and ten white Democrats. They in turn appointed Lewis V. Reeves, a Democrat, Andrew J. Bryant, a black, and Jim Gillespie, a member of the People's Party, as delegates from Tensas Parish and the Tensas-Concordia senatorial district. It is important to keep in mind that this bi-racial meeting of Tensas citizens took place only five months after that parish had been the scene of one of the bloodiest politically motivated pogroms ever initiated against blacks in strife-torn Louisiana. Even though it is clear that black representation is far less than their proportion of the parish's population (blacks made up ninety-one percent of the parish's population in 1880), their inclusion is significant. Although the black involvement in this meeting was certainly proscribed, it was a radical reversal for white men—such as Lewis V. Reeves, T. C. Sachse, Charlie C. Cordill, and G. C. Goldman—to work with black men such as William Coolidge, Noel N. Neely, W. G. Blackburn, and Spencer Ross. Furthermore, the inclusion of A. Bland, James D. McGill, Jim Gillespie and George Ralston,[44] all of whom had supported the Bland-Douglass fusion ticket in November, 1879—is even more reason to conclude that at least a temporary mood of interracial cooperation, guided by the paternalistic hands of the planter-merchant elite, had set in.

The Exodus Movement was the most independent and revolutionary action taken by Southern blacks in the post-emancipation of the South. The threat of a mass withdrawal of their labor forced white Southerners to make some important economic concessions, as well as a public conciliatory gesture (half-hearted though it was) toward black Southerners for the first time in the history of the South. Terribly frightened by the possibility of losing their source of cheap labor, some planters patrolled the Mississippi levees with rifles and shotguns in an attempt to stem the tide of fleeing Exodusters. The climate of interracial cooperation which developed during the 1878-1879 Fusionist Movements, coupled with the planter-merchant's fear of losing their cheap source of black labor, took the cutting edge off the Democrat victories in 1878-1879. Social, political, and economic in nature, this movement was unparalleled in the annals of Southern history. Viewed from its original ideological perspective, the Exodus was a black nationalist movement aimed at finding a permanent home for the dispossessed and despised black masses of the Lower Mississippi Valley. On the grassroots level, Louisiana Delta blacks spoke with a collective voice, through real or vicarious participation in the Exodus Movement, and said, any place but here.[45]

Notes for "Any Place But Here: Kansas Fever in Northeast Louisiana"

[1]The Emigration Question, New Orleans *Weekly Louisianian*, June 14, 1879; ibid., December 25, 1880: Henry Adams, *Report and Testimony of the Select Committee of the United States to Investigate the Causes of the Northern States,* 46th Cong., 3rd Sess. (Ser. Set 1900)(Washington, 1880), 2:107-9. (Hereafter referred to as Senate Report 693). George T. Ruby, ibid., 63; C. K. Marshall, *The Exodus: It Effects Upon the People of the South* (Washington, 1880), passim; Nell Irvin Painter, *Exodusters: Black Migration to Kansas after Reconstruction* (New York, 1977), passim.

[2]See Billy D. Higgins, "Negro Thought and the Exodus of 1879," *Phylon* 32 (1971); Morgan D. Peoples, "Kansas Fever in North Louisiana," *Louisiana History,* 9 (1970); Morgan D. Peoples, "Negro Migration on the Lower Mississippi Valley to Kansas" (M. A. thesis, Louisiana State University, 1950); Walter L. Fleming, "Pap Singleton: The Moses of the Colored Exodus," *American Journal of Sociology,* 15 (1909); John C.Van Deusen, "The Exodus of 1879," *Journal of Negro History,* 21 (1936); Roger W. Shugg, "Survivial of the Plantation System in Louisiana," *The Journal of Southern History,* 3 (1937): 324; J. Carlyle Sitterson, *Sugar Country: The Cane Sugar Industry in the South 1753-1950* (Louisville, 1953), 219-26; *New Orleans Democrat,* September 1, 1880; George T. Ruby, Senate Report 693, 2:62; Richard J. Amundson, "Oakley Plantation: A Post Civil War Venture in Louisiana Sugar," *Louisiana History,* 9 (1968): 26.

[3]New Orleans *Weekly Louisianian,* December 25, 1880.

[4]While the majority of the migrants who made their way to Kansas, and the other Northern states, probably came from three states in the Lower Mississippi Valley—Arkansas, Louisiana, and Mississippi—there were reports of a substantial black migration from such states as North Carolina, Tennessee, Georgia, Kentucky and Texas. Louisiana migrants came from four Delta parishes in the northeastern portion of the state and from Caddo Parish in the northwestern portion of the state. See Henry Adams, *Senate Report 693*: 1 & 2.

[5]New Orleans *Weekly Louisianian,* December 25, 1880; Marshall, *The Exodus,* 4; Alexander Noguez, a black delegate to the 1879 constitutional convention from Avoyelles Parish, estimated that 21,600 blacks left Louisiana in 1879. However, he offers no supporting evidence for this assertion. See New Orleans *Weekly Louisianian,* July 26, 1879. The Rev. C. K. Marshall of Vicksburg, Mississippi, in an address delivered in Washington, D. C. before the American Colonization Society on January 21, 1880, predicted that the Exodus was preliminary to a much larger out-migration of Southern blacks. Harold C. Evans, ed. *Kansas: A Guide to the Sunflower State* (New York, 1939), 210-11.

[6]Fleming, "Pap" Singleton; The Moses of the Colored Exodus," 61; Morgan Peoples, "Seeking a Promised Land for Freemen: A Decade of Secret Actions By A Shreveport "Moses, 1870-1880," *North Louisiana Historical Association Journal,* 9 (1980); Henry Adams, *Senate Report 693,* 2:101; Benjamin Singleton, ibid., Henry Adams, ibid., 101-4; "Address of the Colonization Convention," New Orleans *Weekly Louisianian,* April 26, 1879.

[7]Henry Adams, *Senate Report 693,* 2:101-4.

[8]Ibid.

[9]"The Address of the Colonization Convention," New Orleans *Weekly Louisianian,* April 26, 1879. Ideologically Henry Adams was in the mainstream of African American black nationalist thought. Black Nationalists of varying stripes have taken nearly identical positions before and since the Exodus. Paul Cuffee, Martin R. Delaney, Edward Wilmot Blyden, Alexander Crummell, Chief Alfred Sam, Bishop Henry McNeal Turner, Marcus Garvey, and Elijah Muhammad all took a position similar to the posture assumed by Henry Adams. See the following: Edwin S. Redkey, *Black Exodus: Nationalism and Back-to-Africa Movements, 1890-1919* (New Haven, 1969); William Bittle and Gilbert Geis, "Alfred Charles Sam and an African Return: A Case Study in Despair," *Phylon,* 23 (1972); Kathleen O Mara Whale, "Alexander Crummell: Black Evangelist and Pan-Negro Nationalist," *Phylon,* 29 (1978). Elijah Muhammad voiced similiar sentiments in this statement: "We want our people to be allowed to establish a separate state or territory of their own—either on this continent or elsewhere. . . ." See Elijah Muhammad, *Message to the Blackman in America* (Chicago: Muhammad Mosque of Islam, No. 2, 1965), 161.

[10]Henry Adams, *Senate Report 693,* 2:105-9.

[11]Ibid., 109.

[12]Painter, *The Exodusters*, 163.

[13]William Murrell, Senate Report 693, 2:512; ibid., 528; Affidavits of Refugees, *Senate Report 693*, 3:47-48; Henry Adams, *Senate Report 693*, 2:109, 110; "The Colored Convention," *Weekly Louisianian*, April 26, 1879. The delegates from Tensas Parish, like many of the delegates to the above mentioned convention, were refugees who had fled from their homes in the wake of the bloody anti-black politically motivated violence which swept through North Louisiana in the last months of 1878 and the first part of 1879. Whether they considered migration previous to the political troubles of 1878-1879 is not known. However, their attendance at the conventions shows some 66 interested (on their part) in migration as an alternative to returning to the hell from whence they fled.

[14]"Communicated," *North Louisiana Journal*, August 28, 1880; "Levees and Labor," ibid., October 30, 1880; Van Deusen, "The Exodus of 1879," 111-12.

[15]P.B.S. Pinchback to the Hon. Green B. Raum, April 21, 1879, in the *Weekly Louisianian*, April 26, 1879.

[16]The idea that attractive railroad advertisement and other propaganda (sponsored by western railroads and northern Republicans) was an underlying cause of the Exodus, misses the point entirely. This approach is insensitive and inconsistent with the testimony of the victims who witnessed the bloody violence which prompted the large wave of migration in 1879. Attractive railroad propaganda in and of itself played a minuscule role in motivating blacks to leave their homes in the cotton belt of the Lower Mississippi Valley. Peonage like conditions, augmented by extra-legal politically motivated violence, drove blacks from their southern homes in the closing years of the 1870s. All other interpretations represent a misreading of the historical evidence of blacks in Louisiana and the rest of the Lower Mississippi Valley. Two important questions should be asked about the role of railroad advertisement and other propaganda: (1) Could the Exodus conceivably have occurred without it?; (2) And, could railroad advertisement and other propaganda, independent of any other factors, have caused the Exodus? Obviously, a migration movement would have developed without railroad advertisement and other propaganda. It is equally as apparent that the above factors alone would not have caused the Exodus. See J. W. Hinton, "Von Holst's Constitutional History," *The Quarterly Review of the Episcopal Church South*, 1 (1979): 733; "Vicksburg Labor Convention," the New Orleans *Weekly Louisianian*, May 10, 1879; James B. Runnion, "The Negro Exodus," *Atlantic Monthly*, 54 (1879): 223; *North Louisiana Journal*, March 6, 1879; the *Lake Providence Carroll Conservative*, November 22, 1879; John C. Van Deusen, "The Exodus of 1879," 111-12. This very fine article by Van Deusen completely ignores the impact of legally sanctioned anti-black politically motivated violence and looks instead to attractive railroad propaganda as one of the three causal factors behind the movement. Most contemporary black observers disclaimed the influence of advertising and propaganda on the development of the movement. See the following: Frederick Douglass, "The Negro Exodus From the Gulf States," *Journal of Social Science*, 11 (1880): 5; Richard T. Greener, "The Emigration of Colored Citizens from the Southern States," ibid., 34; Henry Adams, *Report 693*, 2:111, 140; William Murrell, ibid., were generally in agreement on the issue of what caused the Exodus. See for example, "Letter from Hon. B.K. Bruce on the Subject of Negro Immigration to the State of Kansas," New Orleans April 26, 1879; *Proceedings of the National Conference of the United States, Held in the State Capital of Nashville*, May 6-9, 1879, extracts reprinted in John H. Bracey, Jr. et al., eds., *The Afro-American: Selected Documents* (Boston, 1972), 314-18; "The Reason Why," New Orleans *Weekly Louisianian*, May 21, 1879, "The Exodus," ibid., April 5, 1879; George T. Ruby, *Senate Report 693*, 2:39-54.

[17]William Murrell, Report 693, 2:512-13, 528; ibid., 512. Affidavits of Refugees, Senate Report 693, 3:47-48; William Murrell, Senate Report 2: 512-13; P. B. S. Pinchback to Hon. Green B. Raum, April 21, 1879, in the *Weekly Louisianian*, April 26, 1879.

[18]Pinchback to Raum, April 24, 1879, the *Weekly Louisianian*, April 26, 1879.

[19]P. B. S. Pinchback letter to the editor of *Weekly Louisianian* quoted in ibid., November 15, 1879.

[20]"Vicksburg Labor Convention," ibid., May 10, 1879; "The Exodus," ibid., March 6, 1880.

[21]Ibid.

[22]Vicksburg Labor Convention," ibid., May 10, 1879.

[23]Ibid. General Miles dished up an old pro-slavery argument, modified to meet the exigency of the moment.

[24]"Vicksburg Labor Convention," ibid., May 10, 1879; Philip S. Foner, ed. *The Life and Writings of Frederick Douglass: Reconstruction and After* (New York, 1955), 4:325.

[25]William Murrell, *Senate Report 693*, 2: ibid., 518-20.

[26]"Telegraphic Summary," *Weekly Louisianian*, February 21, 1880; *North Louisiana Journal,* February, 1880.

[27]"The Exodus," *Weekly Louisianaian,* January 31, 1880; Madison, ibid., March 6, 1880.

[28]William Frank Zornow, *Kansas: A History of the Jayhawk State* (Norman, 1954), 186; Evans, *Kansas,* 57, 210; ibid., 372; *Weekly Louisianian,* December 25, 1880; George T. Ruby, Senate Report 693, 2:63; William Murrell, ibid., 512; P.B.S. Pinchback to the Hon. Green B. Raum; Earl Howard Aiken, "Kansas Fever" (M.A. Thesis, Louisiana State University, 1939), 10. For a much lower figure, see Painter, *Exodusters,* 147.

[29]"Let Them Go," *Weekly Louisianian,* December 13, 1879.

[30]"Chinese Emigration," *North Louisiana Journal,* April 12, 1879; ibid., May 3, 1879; "State Immigration Agent," ibid., July 24, 1880.

[31]Leslie H. Fishel and Benjamin Quarles, *The Negro American: A Documentary History* (Glenview, Illinois, 1967), 28; Foner, *Frederick Douglass,* 4:324-28, 334-38; "Frederick Douglass's Views on the Negro Exodus," New Orleans *Weekly Louisianian,* May 10, 1879; Vernon L. Wharton, *The Negro in Mississippi, 1865-1890* (Chapel Hill, 1947), 161.

[32]"Letter from Hon. B. K. Bruce on the Subject of Negro Immigration to the State of Kansas," *Weekly Louisianian,* May 10, 1879.

[33]P. B. S. Pinchback to the Hon. Green B. Raum; "The Colored Convention," *Weekly Louisianian,* April 26, 1879. In this article, some very caustic criticisms were leveled at those persons involved in the meeting at New Orleans Common Street Baptist Church that was called for the purpose of considering the Exodus question. The leaders were called "small fry politicians." In view of the fact that this appeared in a newspaper controlled by Pinchback, it is safe to assume his concurrence in this matter. He attended the convention and made a speech calling for moderation and thoughtfulness on the migration question. *New Orleans Picayune,* April 17, 1879.

[34]Ibid.

[35]*North Louisiana Journal,* March 8, 1879; William Murrell, *Senate Report 693,* 2:528, 526.

[36]*North Louisiana Journal,* Fegruary 22, 1879; ibid., December 20, 1579; Painter, *Exodusters,* 26-27. When the leaders of the African Methodist Episcopal Church, meeting in convention in Washington D.C., passed a resolution opposing the Exodus, their action was lauded. See the *North Louisiana Journal,* May 17, 1879.

[37]William Murrell, *Senate Report 693,* 2:528; James Haskin, *Pickney Benton Stewart Pinchback* (New York, 1973), 100-105; Benjamin Quarles, ed., Frederick Douglass (Englewood Cliffs, N.J., 1968), 139-40; Painter, *Exodusters,* 27, 142; "Local Item," Vidalia *Concordia Eagle,* October 2, 1875; *Concordia Parish Tax Roll,* 1880. In the joint custody of the Clerk of Court and Parish Assessor, Vidalia Louisiana; William Murrell, *Senate Report 693,* 2:528.

[38]William Murrell, ibid.

[39]P. B. S. Pinchback letter to the editor of the *Weekly Louisianian*, November 15, 1879; *North Louisiana Journal,* March 8, 1879; ibid., April 26, 1879; Affidavits of Refugees, 693, 3:45-47; William Ivy Hair, *Bourbonism and Agrarian Protest: Louisiana Politics, 1878-1900* (Baton Rouge, 1969), 97; *Vicksburg Herald,* February 28, 1879, quoted in the *North Louisiana Journal*, March 8, 1879; "Stampede of the Blacks," *Weekly Louisianian*, March 9, 1879.

[40]Ibid., November 15, 1879; *North Louisiana Journal*, November 8, 1879; James M. McGill, *Report of the United States Committee to Inquire into Alleged Frauds and Violence in the Election of 1878*, 45th Cong., 33rd Sess. (Ser. Set. 1840) (Washington, D.C., 1879) 1:215 (Hereafter referred to as *Senate Report 855*). William H. Anderson, ibid., 260-61; C.E. Ruth, ibid., 248-49; *North Louisiana Journal*, June 21, 1879.

[41]"Meeting of Citizens at Newellton," ibid., March 15, 1879. For a racial breakdown of local Tensas Parish leaders, see "Proceedings of Citizens Mass Meeting," *North Louisiana Journal*, March 15, 1879. For information relating to the Tensas fusion movement of 1878 see Tensas Parish . . . *Setate Report 855*, 1:169-351.

[42]"Meeting of Citizens at Newellton," *North Louisiana Journal*, March 15, 1879.

[43]C. Vann Woodward, *Origins of the New South, 1877-1913* (Baton Rouge, 1971), 246-47; Melvin J. White, "Populism in Louisiana During the Nineties," *The Mississippi Valley Historical Review,* 5 (1915-19): 15; Lucia Elizabeth Daniel, "The Louisiana People's Party," *Louisiana Historical Quarterly,* 26 (1943): 1055-1149.

[44]Hair, *Bourbonism*, 97-98; "Proceeding of Citizens Mass Meeting," *North Louisiana Journal*, March 15, 1879.

[45]"Vicksburg Labor Convention," *Weekly Louisianian*, May 10, 1879; Affidavits of Refugees, Senate Report 693, 2:149; "The Exodus," *Weekly Louisianian*, April 5, 1879; Arna Bontemps and Jack Conroy, *Any Place But Here* (New York, 1966; originally published as *They Seek a City*, 1945).

1208 SARATOGA STREET*

William Ivy Hair

Throughout the rioting, and while the frantic manhunt for him continued, Robert Charles quietly remained inside his refuge at 1208 Saratoga Street, within the square block bounded on its other sides by Clio, South Rampart, and Erato streets. It was not an ideal hiding place, since many blacks and at least one white man had noticed him going in and out of the residence on numerous occasions during the past three years. But he was wounded and had nowhere else to go. NOPD [New Orleans Police Department] detectives were convinced that Charles was still somewhere inside the city, probably being protected by some black family; yet they feared that unless they obtained a definite lead on his whereabouts he might remain hidden long enough for his leg to heal and then manage an escape.[1]

Robert was in the rear annex of dwelling 1208. Both the front and rear buildings were frail wooden structures, and each was part of a duplex arrangement. The left half of both the front and rear structures constituted dwelling 1210. Both buildings were two-story affairs painted a light shade of green; the front structure, which abutted Saratoga Street, was larger than the annex and had two rooms upstairs and two downstairs in both its 1208 and 1210 residences. The annex, however, had only one room upstairs and one downstairs for each half of the duplex. Between the front building and the annex was a little yard, twenty feet wide—actually two tiny yards, since a flimsy partition divided it in the familiar duplex style.[2]

The rear building, where Charles was hidden, was almost back-to-back with a one-story duplex which faced South Rampart Street. Little space existed between any of the dwellings on that square and the only entrances to the yards between the annex and the main building of duplex 1208-1210 were two narrow alleys—one on the Clio Street (residence 1208) side, and the other on the Erato Street (residence 1210) side. As a place

*First appeared as Chapter 9 in William Ivy Hair, *Carnival of Fury: Robert Charles and the New Orleans Race Riot of 1900* (Baton Rouge: Louisiana State University Press, 1976), 156-82. Reprinted with the kind permission of the publisher.

of defense, the rear building had certain advantages. The upper windows looked down upon the alleys and yard through which any attackers would have to come.[3]

Both buildings within the duplex arrangement were owned by a white man, John Joyce. An electrician by trade, Joyce lived with his family in the four rooms of the front building of 1210, and used one of the ground floor rooms of the annex as a kitchen; but Joyce rented out 1208, as well as the upper annex portion of 1210, to a black laborer named Silas Jackson. Silas and Martha Jackson, and their two children, used as their living quarters only the upper rooms of the annex; Mr. and Mrs. Jackson slept in the upstairs room of the 1208 annex and their children in the upstairs room of the 1210 annex. As was the practice of many black renters in New Orleans of that day, Silas Jackson subrented to other blacks. In the downstairs room of the 1208 side of the annex lived his cousin Burke Jackson, and Silas rented to several people in the 1208 side of the larger main building: Annie Gant and her common-law husband Albert Jackson (no relation to Silas) lived in the downstairs front room; Boss Nixon and his wife Imogene had the downstairs back room; upstairs, the front room was, rented to Silas's cousin Isaac Jackson and the rear room to Silas's brother Charles Jackson. Silas had resided here for about eight years and some of his subtenants had lived in their rooms for almost that long.[4]

Robert Charles had known the Jacksons for at least three years and probably longer. The white salesman of the Poydras Street store, Hyman Levy, had seen him coming and going from 1208 Saratoga on many occasions since 1897, and some of Robert's books and other belongings were stored there. Silas Jackson was from Pike County, Mississippi, but his wife Martha, a tall and angular woman, appears to have been from Copiah County. Three of her sisters were still living there in 1900. Indeed, all of the black renters at the 1208 address were former Mississippians, and at least two of them, Boss and Imogene Nixon, were from the Crystal Springs vicinity of northern Copiah County.[5] It is more than probable that Robert either was related to some of these people or had known them years before in Mississippi. Certainly he trusted them above any other residents of New Orleans, since it was there he sought refuge. And they at great peril granted it to him.

There must have been a number of other New Orleans blacks who knew that 1208 Saratoga was Robert Charles's most likely hiding place in the city. But for the police that piece of information proved hard to get. In addition to the reward posted by the city and state, the NOPD also offered money for any leads on where Charles's associates or relatives might be living in New Orleans. Yet the blacks, complained the *Picayune,* were holding what information they had, and price could not tempt them.[6] There was, however, one exception.

Fred Clark lived at 1129 South Rampart Street, about three blocks from Silas Jackson's residence. Clark was considered by whites "a good negro [*sic*], ready to help the police at all times." He had furnished valuable leads in the past, and on late Friday morning, July 27, he did again. Superintendent of Police Gaster's office at that time received word from Clark that Robert Charles had a relative or relatives (Clark thought a brother) named Jackson, who lived somewhere near the intersection of Saratoga and Erato streets. Clark also related that the person in the Jackson household most likely to harbor Charles was a woman named Martha.[7] Superintendent Gaster had received many tips during the past three days, and so far all had proven worthless. But all possibilities were being checked out. Shortly before 3 P.M. Gaster sent two memos to the commanding sergeant of the second precinct, Gabriel Porteous. The superintendent had learned from an unnamed source (later revealed to be Clark) not only about the possible relationship between Charles and the Jacksons, but also that Lenard Pierce's mother was now living at an address on Freret Street, and it was thought Charles might be hiding there. Porteous, receiving the memos, decided to check out the Jackson possibility first. To assist him he selected the three best available men at the second precinct: Corporal John F., Lally, Patrolman Andrew Zeigel, and Supernumerary Patrolman Rudolph Esser.[8]

There was no better man in the NOPD than Sgt. Gabriel Porteous. He was one of the few policemen who treated whites and blacks alike and was considered, a local black publication reported, "a liberal-minded high-toned gentleman [who] was esteemed by the colored people of this city who knew him." His reputation for bravery was equally well established; Porteous had received complimentary mention in the Board of Police Commissioner's *Annual Report* many times. Forty-seven, he had lived in New Orleans all his life and had been on the force since 1889. At one time or the other he had served in every precinct in the city.[9]

Sergeant Porteous and his three men took a patrol wagon up Erato Street. Arriving at the corner of Erato and Saratoga, they began to ask passersby about a black woman named Martha. They were first directed to the residence of a Martha Williams, one block away from the Jacksons, at 1305 Saratoga. Mrs. Williams, quite old, was ironing when Porteous came to her door. When interviewed later she said that she told the "white folks" to come on in and search her house if they wanted to. Porteous wanted to. "They went through every place," even the garret, Mrs. Williams recalled, "and then [one of them] asked me if I knew a Si Jackson or Martha Jackson and I said yes, they live down there in that green house near the corner of Clio." A few minutes later she heard some shooting and she knew that Robert Charles had been found.[10]

Robert had been told or had seen that a patrol wagon was in the neighborhood and he had hidden himself in a closet on the bottom floor of the 1208 annex, in Burke Jackson's room. The closet, beneath a rickety staircase, was rather large and Robert had obviously spent much time in it during the past three days. Inside was a chair, about eight pounds of lead pipe from which he had been making bullets, and a miniature charcoal furnace, in which some of the lead pipe was already melted down. (Martha Jackson later testified that the little furnace had been left there some time earlier "by a girl" whom she did not know.) Two pieces of steel pipe lay near the furnace; the diameter of this was the same as the calibre of Robert's Winchester, so he had been using it to mold his homemade bullets. The closet, with its door slightly ajar, gave the man inside a direct view of the front doorway of the 1208 side of the annex. Burke Jackson was away; there was nobody in the room when Robert seated himself in the closet, with the Winchester across his lap.[11]

Silas Jackson, weary from his day's work at the Illinois Central Roundhouse, had come home about 3 P.M., gone to his upstairs room in the annex, and immediately fallen asleep. About 3:20 he was awakened by the shouting of Imogene Nixon, from her downstairs rear room in the main building. Sergeant Porteous and Corporal Lally were standing in the alley next to her window, and they had wanted to know where Si and Martha Jackson lived. She told Porteous that Silas Jackson was upstairs in the annex and the sergeant asked her to call him out. Imogene had to yell twice before Silas woke up. Looking down from his window, Jackson saw the policemen and quickly he descended the stairway above the closet where Robert Charles sat hidden. Porteous and Lally were the only officers in the yard, for the sergeant had stationed Zeigel and Esser on Saratoga Street.[12]

In the middle of the little yard Jackson and the two officers met. Porteous asked Silas "where his brother Robert Charles was." Silas replied that he "had a brother named Charles Jackson, but Robert Charles was no relation of his." Porteous and Lally insisted that the killer was his brother; then, placing Silas Jackson under arrest, they told him to lead them through the rear building. Porteous and Lally, following Jackson, entered the doorway of the 1208 side of the annex. Directly across the room was the closet where Robert Charles waited, absolutely still.

Seeing a water bucket and a dipper atop a little stand next to the closet, Sergeant Porteous remarked that he was thirsty and walked toward it. Now Robert Charles thrust the barrel of his Winchester out the crack in the closet door and fired. First he shot at Porteous and then at Lally. Like Captain Day, Porteous was struck in the heart and died almost immediately. Lally, hit in the abdomen, would die at Charity Hospital the next day.[13]

Frantically, Silas Jackson bolted from the room, ran through the yard and narrow alleyway and into Saratoga Street. "Oh, Lordy," he began to shout. "Oh, Lordy. Oh, Lordy." Then, not knowing what else to do, he dashed back into the yard of 1208 Saratoga. He was still standing there when Officer Peter Fenney, who lived at the corner of Saratoga and Erato and had been awakened by the shooting, came into the yard and arrested him. Officer Fenney then learned about Porteous and Lally and went into the room to see about them.[14]

Officers Zeigel and Esser were meanwhile busy catching a black man named John Willis who upon hearing the shots went running down Saratoga Street. Willis lived at 1204 Saratoga, and, as he was of a nervous, fearful disposition (he probably knew of Charles's presence and thus realized what those shots meant), his only thought was to flee the neighborhood at once. "There he goes! There he goes over the fence!" several white men shouted at Zeigel and Esser; and the two patrolmen, thinking Willis was Robert Charles, ran him down a few blocks away on Clio Street. But they quickly realized by his demeanor that he could not be the wanted man. Described as being "insane from fright," Willis literally groveled at the feet of his captors. "Boss," he sobbed, "I'm an innocent nigger."[15]

By the time Officer Fenney discovered Porteous and Lally, Robert Charles was gone from the bottom floor of the annex. Taking his Winchester and Colt pistol, along with most of the ammunition he had been making during the past three days, Robert had run up the stairs to Silas and Martha Jackson's room, immediately above where Porteous and Lally had been shot. Hastily he went to the wall separating this room from the other half of the duplex arrangement; on the other side was the Jackson children's room. Using his feet, Robert began pounding a large hole through the plaster and timber. Soon he was able to pass to and fro in the two upstairs rooms, and the windows on the 1210 side gave him added visibility on the yards and alleyways below, Neither of the Jackson children was home. Outside, Silas and Martha were being led away to police headquarters, and white people were beginning to gather along Saratoga Street.[16]

With the exception of Robert Charles, everybody inside residences 1208 and 1210 fled the buildings at some time or another after the shooting commenced; and with the exception of John Joyce, the white landlord, those away at the time decided not to go home when news of what was happening there reached them. Inside the main building, fronting Saratoga Street, John Joyce's wife grabbed up her two baby daughters as soon as the gunfire began and ran across the street to a neighbor's house; Mrs. Joyce's sister and elderly mother, who were in 1210 at the time, also wasted no time in getting out.[17] Since they were the only white occupants in the two buildings, the Joyces were thus the only residents assumed by the police not to have known of Charles's presence.

Charles Jackson, Silas's brother, was upstairs in the main building when he heard the shots, and he immediately fled to a nearby house; Burke Jackson was coming home from work when two white women stopped him and warned him that a mob was gathering in his neighborhood and he, thinking the trouble probably involved Robert Charles, departed that day for his parents' home in Mississippi. Isaac Jackson, another cousin of Silas, was out of town at the time and was therefore the only one of the black residents of 1208 not arrested later. Boss Nixon, who had a job with a New Orleans veterinarian, was nursing some sick horses that afternoon and remained at the stable overnight. His wife Imogene took flight at the first shots and hid in or under a nearby grocery store that night; the following day Nixon's employer gave him some money along with advice to get himself and his wife out of town. The Nixon couple on the morning of Saturday, the twenty-eighth, took the train to Crystal Springs. Albert Jackson, who lived with Annie Gant, sat on the front steps for a minute or so after the first shots, considering what to do; presently he crawled under the annex building where Robert was located and remained there most of the time from Friday afternoon until the following Wednesday night, August 1, when he emerged to seek water and was arrested. Annie Gant stayed in her room for over an hour after the shooting started, Eventually some white men burst into her room and one of them told her: "You better get out of here you damned old fool." She then ran into the street, where the police placed her under arrest.[18]

Most bizarre of all the stories told by the blacks who were in the duplex when Charles shot Porteous and Lally was that of George Ford. He was visiting Boss Nixon's wife Imogene. They both fled upon hearing the gunfire, but Ford was confused by the excitement and remained too long in the little yard. Someone in the crowd of men now gathering on nearby streets and rooftops shot at Ford, the bullet grazing his back. Although the wound was superficial, it convinced Ford that he had best not remain where he was, so he ran into the 1210 portion of the annex, going upstairs into the room of the Jackson children. Robert Charles must have been in the other upper room at the time, or at least Ford insisted later on that he had not seen him. Ford then hid under a bed, pulling the mattress and sheets down so that he was totally concealed. He remained there during the siege that followed and was not discovered until 8:30 that evening, when some police officers pulled him out by his legs.[19]

When Patrolman Fenney entered the lower right room of the annex, he saw that Sergeant Porteous was already dead but Corporal Lally was sitting up in the midst of a spreading pool of blood, which kept flowing from the wound in his stomach. Lally spoke first: "I am fatally wounded. I'd like to see a priest. Please go and get me one, quick." A priest was already on the way, attracted like hundreds of other people by the shooting. Father Fitzgerald of St. John's Church was stopped by Fenney on Clio Street and told that he was needed to administer the Last Sacrament to a dying policeman. The priest was shown the way to the room behind the little yard.[20]

As yet Robert Charles had given no indication of his continued presence in the building, and for a time it was assumed by the police and the growing crowd outside that he had fled. White spectators were now coming through the alleys and into the partitioned yard of the duplex, unaware of danger. A policeman went to the door of the room where Porteous and Lally were, then came out and told those in the yard not to make any noise as Father Fitzgerald was giving the Last Sacrament. At this point—it was now close to 3:45 P.M. Robert Charles, upstairs, decided it was time to clear the yard below. He selected as a target a nineteen-year-old white youth named Arthur Brumfield. Oddly, Brumfield only two weeks earlier had been arrested for "unlawful retailing" of whiskey in Copiah County, Mississippi.[21]

An eyewitness to Brumfield's death said he heard the unmistakable crack of a Winchester and looked up to see a rifle, held in black arms, jutting out of an upstairs window. Brumfield, hit in the hip, struggled to the outside stairway of the front building and attempted to climb it. The young man moaned, "Oh, God," then looked up at the window from which the shot came and cried out, "For God's sake, do not shoot!" Charles fired once more, and Brumfield fell dead with a bullet through his lung and heart. Some accounts had it that Brumfield was only a child, and that he had been assisting Father Fitzgerald when Charles shot him ("BLACK FIEND DELIBERATELY MURDERED A PRAYING BOY," headlined the *New York Times*).[22] Neither statement about Brumfield was true, but he was the first unarmed man, and the first civilian, that Charles had put a bullet into. The black man from Mississippi obviously realized that his own death was now inevitable and had decided to take as many whites with him as possible. About the same moment that Brumfield fell, the telephone in Superintendent Gaster's office transmitted the news that "a policeman had been wounded at the corner of Clio and Saratoga Streets." Gaster sent a patrol wagon from the first precinct, but within fifteen minutes he was informed again by telephone that more than one person had been shot and that firing was still going on. As yet no one was absolutely certain the trouble involved Robert Charles, but every minute the shooting continued the more likely it seemed that he had indeed been cornered. Mayor Capdevielle was enjoying a Turkish bath at the St. Charles Hotel when a telephone message reached him a minute or so after 4 P.M. "that Charles' hideout had been discovered." The mayor, knowing the mood of the city and fearing that some massive butchery of the black population might take place, called upon the state militia units, which had been mobilized since Thursday, to go to the scene with—and he made a special point of this—their two Gatling guns. Capdevielle declared that if things got completely out of hand, the Gatling guns should be fired into the white mob.[23]

Special police headquarters got the news from Mayor Capdevielle about 4:05 P.M. Since most of the citizen volunteers were not supposed to go on duty for another hour, less than fifty men were in the armory at Camp and Lafayette streets, about twelve blocks from Charles's refuge on Saratoga. W. L. Hughes, in charge of operations at the armory, reported later, "I didn't feel that it was a time when red tape should be insisted upon, and I armed whoever presented himself as a special officer with a Winchester and placed the squad under the leadership of Captain [Charles] O'Connor." One member of O'Connor's command, hurrying to Saratoga Street, was a young medical student at Tulane, Charles A. Noiret.[24]

Before the day was over vicious, degrading things would transpire on and around the 1200 block of Saratoga Street, but there was also one act of genuine heroism. About 4 P.M., not long after Father Fitzgerald had administered Extreme Unction to Corporal Lally, a man named Vic Mauberret and a *New Orleans Times-Democrat* reporter, "Billy" Ball, decided that Lally, Porteous, and Brumfield—it was not certain any of them were actually dead—must be rescued. Father Fitzgerald and the officers who had gone in and out of the lower room had dashed for safety soon after Charles shot Brumfield, leaving Porteous and Lally where they were. Billy Ball had earlier distinguished himself, during the Wednesday night rioting, by saving the life of a black man on Canal Street. Announcing their decision to the crowd of white men now encircling the square, Ball and Mauberret asked those who had weapons and were in a good position to direct a covering fire into the windows of the upper room of the annex, while they attempted to get the fallen men out. For five minutes or so the fusillade into Charles's rooms continued while first Lally's, then Porteous's, and finally Brumfield's bodies were carried out to Saratoga Street by Ball and Mauberret. Robert Charles made no effort to fire while this was going on, but several bullets from the crowd came close to the rescuers. Porteous and Brumfield were sent to the morgue; Lally was taken to Charity Hospital, where he died the following afternoon.[25]

The news that police officers had been shot and that Charles's hideout was discovered traveled across town with amazing rapidity. Throngs of white men and boys, many of them armed with rifles, shotguns, or pistols, came running from distances twenty or thirty blocks away. Streetcars of the St. Charles and other lines which passed close to the area became absolutely jammed. By 4 P.M. at least five thousand people were gathered on the streets of the square surrounding Charles's refuge; Saratoga was the most densely packed, but Clio, Erato, and South Rampart were filling up fast. An hour later, with the siege still going on, somewhere between ten and twenty thousand whites had crowded around the block. Thousands more were assembled in front of the *Times-Democrat* building along Camp Street where bulletins on an enormous blackboard were posted at five-minute intervals as to the progress of the siege.[26]

An estimated thousand of the men who surrounded the square block had firearms of some description. The crowd included regular policemen, the special police under Captain O'Connor, and state militiamen; but most of those present had no authority to do any shooting, or even to carry weapons. But shoot they did. And with the forces available it would probably have been impossible to stop them even if anyone had cared to; the police and militia were clearly not planning to act against their fellow whites unless a wholesale massacre of blacks in the neighborhood commenced. Bullets from police, militia, and citizens continued to pepper the upper rooms of the annex. Those standing on the streets were not in a position to do effective shooting and were in little danger of being hit by one of Charles's bullets. The partitioned yard between the two buildings of 1208-1210 had been empty since the rescue work of Ball and Mauberret. But over a hundred men climbed to sheds and housetops on the square block, and lying on the protected sides of the slopes, were able, to shoot into Charles's windows from there. Cartridges of all sorts and sizes were passed up to the rooftops, along with buckets of water to cool the heated rifle and pistol barrels. At intervals of a minute or so, Charles would appear for an instant at one of the windows and fire at his attackers.[27]

Trenchard, the humiliated survivor of the yellow house encounter, made an appearance on South Rampart Street, near the siege, and was immediately recognized by his unforgettably Gallic face and Kaiser Wilhelm II moustache. First came individual shouts and then the crowd began chanting: "Trenchard! Trenchard! Trenchard!" Someone in a booming voice, heard above the chanting, roared out: "Now redeem your reputation—let him through!" Corporal Trenchard, carrying a shotgun, seemed to want nothing more than redemption at that moment; rushing through the narrow space between two of the houses back of Charles's hideout, he approached a side of the green annex and fired two barrels of buckshot upward into the room Charles was presently in, but the loads went through the wrong window. After firing again without effect, Trenchard withdrew to seek a better angle. The corporal's progress, however, was impeded by constant advice and recriminations from dozens of amateur strategists.[28]

The one-sided siege continued until a few minutes past 5 P.M. During the almost two hours since he had killed Porteous and fatally wounded Lally, Robert Charles remained in the two upper rooms of the annex, becoming the target of eventually a thousand guns. Observers the next day estimated that the structure was marked by at least five thousand bullet holes, and bullets from the high-powered rifles had torn through the cheap planking. How Robert had survived so long in that place defies logical explanation. He must have been hit several times. But until the end he continued to appear for an instant every minute or so at one of the upstairs windows and get off a shot at his besiegers. Apparently he was never aware of the presence of the hapless George Ford, who all the while lay quietly under the Jackson children's bed.[29]

Under the circumstances, Robert's aim was as remarkable as his hold on life in those little rooms. Not having an unlimited supply of ammunition, and lacking the time to fire repeatedly in any one position, he carefully hoarded his bullets; counting the shots he fired into Porteous and Lally, it was estimated that he pulled the trigger of his Winchester about fifty times between 3:20 and 5 P.M. that Friday afternoon of July 27. Apparently he did not use his Colt revolver. Of the fifty bullets from Charles's Winchester, twenty-four hit human flesh. For in addition to Porteous, Lally, and Brumfield, he fatally wounded two other men and injured nineteen more. The two others who died from his bullets were Andrew Van Kuren, an employee of the city jail, and a civilian from Mississippi named Howell H. Batte. Seven were seriously wounded, but recovered: Patrolman J. W. Bofill, Patrolman F. H. Evans, and five civilians—G. J. Lyons, John Banville, Frank Bertucci, A. S. Leclerc, and Henry David. A dozen other besiegers sustained grazing or superficial wounds from Charles's Winchester and required emergency treatment only. "Not a time was there a flash from his rifle," wrote one eyewitness, "that some besieger was not either hit or had the ball come so close that he knew he was the target."[30]

Counting the deaths of Captain Day and Officer Lamb and the wounding of Officer Mora Monday night, Charles had now left seven dead (four of whom were police officers), eight seriously wounded (three of whom were police officers), and twelve slightly wounded who were not identified by name or occupation.[31] Robert Charles had shot twenty-seven white people since Monday night. But now at 5 P.M. Friday afternoon he was about to die.

Early in the siege the thought of setting fire to Charles's lair had occurred to many in the crowd. A detachment of firemen with chemicals and hoses had arrived, but the firemen expressed strong doubts about such an undertaking, since all residences in the area were closely packed wooden structures. And many of the areas's residents were white. The danger of a general conflagration was obvious. Also there were rumors—un-founded—that more wounded police officers were upstairs in the rooms Charles now occupied. Mayor Capdevielle, who had rushed from his Turkish bath to City Hall, listened to various suggestions during the next hour and a half as to how Charles's resistance might be ended. (Tear gas had not yet been developed.) The fire chief proposed that the structure be blown up, which he insisted would be safer for the neighborhood than starting a fire. One of the state militia officers suggested that the two Gatling guns, already hauled to the area as a means of intimidating the crowd, now be turned upon the two upper rooms of the annex and fired. But Capdevielle cautioned the military against this, pointing out that the spraying effect of these machine guns would "spread destruction far and wide." While the mayor's office debated these and other alternatives, word came to Capdevielle that a fire had already been started, and Charles was smoked out.[32]

Capt. William King of the Julia Street Fire Patrol, along with several citizens, had managed to sneak into the bottom floor of the 1208 annex just before 5 P.M. Charles could be heard walking about upstairs. An old horsehair mattress in Burke Jackson's room, where Porteous and Lally had been shot, was carried to the foot of the staircase. Kerosene was poured upon it, and William Porteous, Gabriel's brother, was allowed to strike the match. As soon as the mattress began to blaze, King expertly dribbled water upon it so that the fire would smoulder and produce clouds of black smoke. Carefully, the mattress was positioned so that most of the choking cloud would be drawn upstairs. Then King, William Porteous, and the other men hastily left the room.[33]

For the next five minutes the expectant thousands outside watched the black smoke pour out of the little two-story structure. Yet Robert Charles continued, as he had now for almost two hours, to move suddenly or strike a shutter from one window so as to attract gunfire, and then shoot at his besiegers from another window. Somehow, he was able to endure the smoke. But the heat could not much longer be tolerated, for the mattress had caught the staircase on fire, and from there the flames were spreading. Robert came down the stairs on the 1210 side of the annex, since the other stairway was now completely ablaze. Some of the snipers on the rooftops caught glimpses of him through one of the downstairs windows, and then his form was obscured by the smoke and flames.[34]

It began to seem that Robert Charles would be burned alive inside the annex building. Flames were now breaking through the roof. But at last he appeared at the 1210 front door of the annex, holding his Winchester at shoulder level; he was still wearing his brown derby hat, pulled low in front. Before anyone on the rooftops could take aim, he dashed the twenty feet to the rear entrance of the 1210 section of the main building, the downstairs back room of the Joyce residence. Some protection was afforded him by the heavy vines which hung over the pathway between the two buildings.[35]

Just before Robert reached the door, a man in the room he was approaching fired a rifle. Robert stopped momentarily and, reported an eyewitness, "his arms seemed to sink with the weight of his gun." But a second later he had lifted the Winchester again and was at the door. Eight whites were in the little room, three of them city detectives. But the man who killed Robert Charles was Charles A. Noiret, a medical student and a member of the special police. Noiret may not have fired the shot that struck Robert outside, but it was he who fired when the black man entered the door. Robert fell just inside the room, not two feet from where Noiret was standing; he dropped face first, but continued to clutch his rifle as he fell. Upon hitting the floor, Robert made an attempt to turn over, and Noiret sent three more bullets into him.[36]

Now a wild shooting into the body commenced. First the eight men who had been in the room, and then the dozen or so more who were able to pack themselves into it during the next minute, fired at the corpse, many of them cursing while others gave wordless victory howls. When the ammunition of those in the room ran out, someone suggested that the body be dragged outside. Immediately those nearest lifted Robert up and carried him, dripping, through the Joyce house, to be dumped at the front entrance on Saratoga Street. The crowd outside was quiet for a second or two and then broke into cheers. Men ran up and dragged the body from the doorway into the muddy street. More shots were pumped into the corpse. Then room was made for Corporal Trenchard, who came running up with his double-barreled shotgun. Trenchard placed the muzzle directly against the torso and in a loud, triumphant voice exclaimed: "Now who says I am a coward?" Then he fired both barrels.[37]

Those who possessed no guns cursed at or kicked the corpse, which soon became almost indistinguishable from the trodden mud of Saratoga Street. One woman in a sunbonnet pushed her way forward and tried to do some kicking, but she was led away. A son of one of the dead police officers came up and, with the crowd's permission, stomped upon the face. Shouts of "burn him! burn him!" began to grow louder, and someone brought up a small container of kerosene. (The next day, one of the local papers excused this conduct by pointing out that "the satisfaction of his capture and death was in a measure embittered by the knowledge that he had suffered less than any of the men he had slain . . . death had come altogether too swiftly and easily to the fiend.")[38]

Police did not attempt to discourage the shooting or kicking of the corpse, but were able to prevent its burning. A patrol wagon had been brought up and, related someone who was there, "The police raised the body of the heavy black from the ground and literally chucked it into the space on the floor of the wagon between the seats. When Charles's body landed on the wagon it fell in such a position that the mutilated head hung over the end. Now, as the wagon prepared to move off toward the morgue, people in the crowd began to protest, demanding that the body remain there and be burned, while others ran up with sticks and poked at or stuck the battered head. As soon as the wagon wheels began to turn, hundreds ran after the vehicle; then as it picked up speed on Clio Street, headed toward Baronne Street and the morgue, the crowd chasing it swelled to as many as five thousand for several blocks. But as the wagon moved further away most of the men and boys returned to watch the firemen extinguish the blaze in the duplex on Saratoga, and to look for Negroes within the square block where the shootout had occurred.[39]

The bulletin board of the *Times-Democrat* had informed the other big crowd, on Camp Street, that the body was being carried to the deadhouse, and many who had been watching the bulletins rushed away in that direction. What they saw should have satisfied even the most morbid. The patrol wagon, clattering through the rough streets as rapidly as possible, caused the corpse to sway and bounce, and the head, looking by this time something like a mud-splattered black skillet, swung and jerked over the end of the wagon. Outside the morgue another large crowd was gathered, and the police had difficulty preventing the utter destruction of the corpse before it could be taken inside. Afterward the mob outside grew larger and broke the glass on the morgue doors. Some wanted merely to view the cadavers of Charles and the men he had killed, whereas others were still anxious for further vengeance on the body of the black man who had shot almost thirty whites.[40]

The unsated desire for revenge, the feeling on the part of many whites that it was grossly unfair for a black to have died so quickly after having shot so many whites, was to have fatal consequences for two other black men that afternoon. While the siege on Saratoga Street was coming to an end, a roving mob of about a hundred white men saw a black laborer, about thirty years old, passing through the French Market. They began to chase him and the man ran into a residence on Gallatin Street. Climbing the stairs of the house, with some of his pursuers immediately behind him, the Negro leaped from a second-story gallery and upon landing on the sidewalk tried to get up and run, but the mob surrounded him and shot him to death.[41] Not long afterward another innocent person would die, thought at first to be Burke Jackson.

The man police assumed was Burke Jackson was murdered by someone in the crowd along Clio Street only minutes after Charles's body had left the scene. As soon as the patrol wagon with the corpse disappeared down the street, dozens of white men frantically began searching all houses on the block for "accomplices," but at first they found no blacks (most Negroes in the area at the beginning of the shootout had either fled or been taken away by the police). Toward the end of the siege Annie Gant and three other black women still on the block had been placed in a patrol wagon, and reporters present believed that these women would have been dragged out and killed, except for the determination of a Winchester-carrying city councilman who took charge of their transportation to Parish Prison. By 5:45 P.M. the police and volunteer forces were beginning to show some success in persuading the mob to cease their ransacking of houses and disperse, when little Arthur Baumgarden, a white child who lived at 1205 Saratoga, ran into the street and began shrieking that he had seen two Negroes upstairs in house 1203. Several policemen were able to outrace the mob to the second floor of that residence and they discovered only one black man, about thirty-five years old. The police led him down Clio Street toward a patrol wagon, with the mob tearing at the officers and their prisoner at every step; he was almost safely aboard when one man in the crowd leaned forward and fired a pistol bullet into the back of the Negro's head. The dead man was listed as Burke Jackson, until that individual—who had fled New Orleans—was arrested in Mississippi a few days later.[42] The real name of this victim would never be known to the authorities.

Rumors of racial incidents and reports of arson in black neighborhoods continued throughout the night of July 27. But only one report proved true. The best Negro schoolhouse in Louisiana, named for Thomy Lafon—a philanthropic Creole of color who when he died in 1893 left a fortune for both white and black education and charities in

New Orleans—was burned at about midnight. The burning of Lafon school was actually a lesser atrocity than had been planned by the mob which set the fire; earlier, around 10:30 P.M., a crowd of about fifty white men got off the trolley at South Rampart and Fourth, under the leadership of a fierce-looking, one-legged man who carried a shotgun, and this man announced that they were going to set fire to an entire block of Negro homes, then shoot all the inhabitants when they ran out. The proposal was cheered, but much to the man's disgust it was found that his followers were not carrying a sufficient number of guns to accomplish the sort of massacre he had in mind. Then somebody suggested they go to Seventh Street and burn Thomy Lafon school instead. Their leader indignantly demurred, saying that he "was willing to go 'coon hunting,' but would not stand for burning public property." But several mob members went ahead with the idea, especially after someone pointed out that the body of Sergeant Porteous was supposed to be arriving in the neighborhood for a wake about this time; the Negro school, it was declared, would make an appropriate "bonfire in his honor." Soon flames from the three-story wooden structure were visible over much of New Orleans. The firemen arrived too late. A witness insisted that four or five policemen in the vicinity saw the arsonists go to the building, but had made no effort to stop them.[43]

Fortunately, by the next morning, Saturday, July 28, the furious mob spirit among so many New Orleans whites appeared to be ebbing. The 1,500 special police volunteers who had saved the city from total anarchy earlier in the week remained on duty until Sunday morning; but after Friday night there was little for them to do. Property owners among the black and Creole of color population were said to be more gratified at Charles's death than were the whites, since their fear of racial retaliation had grown with each day he remained at large. Poorer blacks, on the other hand, were reportedly regretful only that he had not taken more policemen with him when he died. Among lower class blacks he became an immediate folk hero and "the Robert Charles song," praising his exploits, would occasionally be played at all-black gatherings for years to come. But "that song never did get very far," according to Jelly Roll Morton. "I once knew the Robert Charles song," Morton told Alan Lomax, "but I found out it was best for me to forget it and that I did in order to go along with the world on the peaceful side."[44]

The white daily newspapers of New Orleans, powerful shapers of public opinion, were rather at a loss to explain a black man who had acted with the kind of courageous defiance which it was assumed only white men could display. Charles was not enough of a mulatto to prompt even Major [Henry James] Hearsey to say that his bravery had come from Caucasian blood. The relatively liberal *New Orleans Item* believed Robert's courage was born of despair and, like some of the other papers, implied that cocaine may have influenced his seeming disregard of death. The *Times-Democrat* had to admit its bewilderment at his marksmanship and his coolness under great stress, but was convinced that his simple Negro mind would never have thought of resistance toward the superior race unless inspired by Northern propaganda. "He steeped his little brain in the poison," explained the *Times-Democrat,* "until his lawless lower centres were raw and inflamed."

Of course, this paper hastily added, Charles "knew nothing of grievances or oppression until it was drummed into his head by the exaggerated and sentimental writers on the wrongs of the negroes [*sic*]." The *New Orleans Daily Picayune,* on the other hand, conceded that Charles was an extraordinarily brave and ferociously determined man, but suggested that his deeds were simply the exception which proved the rule that virtually all Negroes were cowards who could never match the fighting abilities of the white race. The *Picayune* insisted that "Robert Charles was the boldest, most desperate and dangerous negro [*sic*] ever known in Louisiana," and assured itself and its readers that "there is not another negro [*sic*] in the State who can perform such acts under like circumstances."[45]

Major Hearsey's observations in the *New Orleans Daily States* on the personality of Robert Charles may have surprised some people. As an extreme Negrophobe of long-standing, Hearsey might have been expected to attribute Robert's courage to cocaine, or insanity, or anything except manly qualities. Yet the image of anyone—even a black person—battling so resolutely against such hopeless odds irresistibly appealed to the major's strong romantic and medieval instincts. The day after Robert died, Hearsey confessed to his readers that even though Charles was colored, and despite the fact that he had killed and wounded so many white citizens and police, "[I] cannot help feeling for him a sort of admiration prompted by his wild and ferocious courage. In fact, wrote Major Hearsey, he could think of no instance in history where one person had resisted so many for so long. "Never before," the *States* informed its readers, "was such a display of desperate courage on the part of one man witnessed." Yet, as if suddenly remembering that Charles was not white, Hearsey added that the bravery he was saluting was not that of true manhood but "the courage of the brute the lion or the tiger."[46]

Robert Charles remained at the morgue from late Friday afternoon until shortly before daybreak on Sunday morning. His autopsy report listed thirty-four bullet holes in the torso alone, plus "three large openings undoubtedly due to volleys." Numerous other wounds were found in the arms and legs; the skull had been fractured and shattered "and almost beat to a pulp," wrote the coroner. His penis had been shot. Shortly after Robert's body arrived at the deadhouse (as many New Orleanians still called the morgue) one of the attendants attempted to mold the battered face back into some semblance of humanity, but with no great success. Various black people who had known Charles, including Lenard Pierce, were brought in to identify the body; and because of the clothing and personal effects all made a positive identification except Annie Gant. Miss Gant's assertion that the body was that of Robert's "brother, Si[las] Jackson," was not, however, taken seriously; for she was visibly terror stricken and seemed to have the idea that if she identified the corpse as that of Charles the police would turn her over to the mob outside. All the other identifications were positive; his size and teeth matched descriptions, and the papers and clippings he had about him were concerned with racial wrongs and African emigration. A small-caliber wound about three or four days old was found on his leg, wrapped in green gauze. Some of the black people brought in told authorities that the dead man was also known as "Curtis Robertson."[47]

Friday evening and all day Saturday hundreds of curious white New Orleanians were admitted inside the morgue to view the body of the notorious "black fiend." One of those who filed by was in for quite a shock. Hyman Levy, after the clothing store on Poydras Street closed Friday night, went by the morgue "to take a look," he said, "at the desperate negro [*sic*]." Either Levy had not seen Robert's picture in the paper or—more likely—none of the drawings reproduced in the dailies were close likenesses. As soon as he looked at the corpse Levy thought of his friend Curtis Robertson. The salesman then went to one of the morgue attendants and asked to see the clothing the murderer had been wearing. "I immediately recognized a blue serge double-breasted coat that I had sold him last February," Levy related. Talking to a reporter the next day, he said, "You could imagine my surprise when I [realized] it was Robertson, as I never for an instant thought that he was such a desperate scoundrel."[48]

Notes for "1208 Saratoga Street"

[1]*New Orleans Times-Democrat*, July 28-29, 1900; Parkash Kaur Hams, "The New Orleans Race Riot of 1900" (M. A. thesis, Louisiana State University in New Orleans, 1970), 34.

[2]See the diagram of 1208 and 1210 Saratoga Street in *New Orleans Times-Democrat*, July 30, 1900. But this needs supplementation with the statement of John Joyce, who described exactly where the various black occupants lived, in *New Orleans Daily Picayune*, May 15, 1901.

[3]*New York Times*, July 28, 1900; *New Orleans Daily States*, July 28, 1900; *New Orleans Times-Democrat*, July 28-30, 1900.

[4]"Testimony of John Joyce," in *New Orleans Daily Picayune*, May 15, 1901. See also *New Orleans Times-Democrat*, July 28, 30, August 4, 1900.

[5]Levy interview, *New Orleans Sunday States*, July 29, 1900; Crawford and others to Handlin, December 2, 1900, in Case No. 30,086 file in Criminal District Court, Parish of Orleans, Louisiana; *New Orleans Times-Democrat*, August 1, 4, 1900.

[6]*New Orleans Daily Picayune*, July 28, 1900.

[7]Ibid., September 3, 1900; "Report of Superintendent D. S. Gaster," in *New Orleans Times-Democrat*, August 1, 4, 1900.

[8]*New Orleans Daily Item*, July 28, 1900; "Report of Superintendent D. S. Gaster," in *New Orleans Times-Democrat*, August 31, 1900.

[9]*New Orleans Southwestern Christian Advocate*, August 2, 1900; "Record of Inquests," Coroner's Office, Parish of Orleans, July 27, 1900, 317-18, in City Archives Department, New Orleans Public Library; *Annual Report of Board of Police Commissioners, Superintendent of Police and Police Surgeon of the City of New Orleans, 1900*, 28; *New Orleans Daily States*, July 28, 1900.

[10]*New Orleans Daily States*, August 4, 1900. Mrs. Williams knew Robert Charles and believed, as did several other people, that Silas Jackson was his brother. However, several white residents of Pike County, Mississippi, positively stated that Silas and Charles Jackson had lived there all their lives, before coming to New Orleans. Robert may have been distantly related to Silas and Charles Jackson, but it is more likely he was a nephew or cousin of Silas's wife Martha, who was from Copiah.

[11]Ibid., July 28, 1900; *New Orleans Daily Picayune*, July 28-29, 1900.

[12]*State of Louisiana* v. *Silas Jackson et al.*, Case No. 30,085, Criminal District Court, Parish of Orleans, Louisiana; "Testimony of Imogene Nixon," in *Daily Picayune*, May 16, 1901.

[13]"Testimony of Silas Jackson," in *Daily Picayune,* May 15, 1901; *Louisiana* v. *Silas Jackson et al.,* No. 30,085; "Record of Inquests," Coroner's Office, July 27, 1900, 317-18, and July 28, 1900, 313-14.

[14]*Louisiana* v. *Silas Jackson et al.,* No. 30,085; "Testimony of Officer Fenney," in *Daily Picayune,* May 15, 1901.

[15]*Daily Picayune*, July 28, 1900; "Testimony of Officer Esser," ibid., May 15, 1901.

[16]*Times-Democrat*, July 28-29, 1900; *New York Times*, July 28, 1900.

[17]*Daily States*, July 28, 1900.

[18]*Times-Democrat*, July 28, 29, August 1, 4, 1900; *Daily Picayune*, August 1, 3, 1900; *Daily Item*, July 28, 1900.

[19]*Daily Picayune,* July 28, 1900; *Times-Democrat,* July 28, August 1, 1900.

[20]*Times-Democrat,* July 28, 1900; "Testimony of Rev. Father Fitzgerald," in *Daily Picayune,* May 15, 1901,

[21]"Testimony of Rev. Father Fitzgerald," in *Daily Picayune,* May 15, 1901; *Hazlehurst Courier,* quoted in *Brookhaven Leader,* August 8, 1900. Brumfield had been a candy and soft-drink salesman on the Illinois Central line, and was caught selling whiskey when the train passed through the dry county of Copiah.

[22]Interview with C. A. Kent, in *Daily Picayune,* July 29, 1900; *Atlanta Constitution,* July 28, 1900; *Boston Morning Journal,* July 28, 1900; "Record of Inquests." Coroner's Office, July 27, 1900, 315; *New York Times,* July 28, 1900.

[23]"Report of Superintendent D. S. Gaster," in *New Orleans Times-Democrat*, August 31, 1900; *Daily Picayune,* July 28, 1900.

[24]W. L. Hughes to Elmer E. Wood, August 2, 1900, in Mayor's Office Correspondence.

[25]*Times-Democrat*, July 28, 1900.

[26]Ibid.; John Smith Kendall, *History of New Orleans*, 3 vols. (Chicago, 1922), 2:540; letter from the Rev. D. A. Graham, in *Indianapolis Freeman*, August 18, 1900.

[27]*Richmond Planet*, August 4, 1900; *Daily Item*, July 28, 1900; *Times-Democrat*, July 28-29, 1900.

[28]*Times-Democrat,* July 28, 1900.

[29]*Chicago Tribune,* July 28, 1900; *Daily States,* July 28, 1900; *New Orleans Sunday States,* July 29, 1900.

[30]Bains, "The New Orleans Race Riot of 1900," 60; *Annual Report of Board of Police* Commissioners, 1900, 10-11; *Rolling Fork Deer Creek Pilot,* August 3, 1900; *Times-Democrat,* July 28, 1900.

[31]*Daily Picayune,* July 28-29, 1900; *Boston Morning Journal,* July 28, 1900; *New Orleans Sunday States,* July 29, 1900.

[32]*Daily Picayune,* July 28, 1900.

[33]*Times-Democrat,* July 28-29, 1900; *Daily States,* July 28, 1900.

[34]*Times-Democrat*, July 28, 1900.

[35]*Daily Picayune*, July 28, 1900; *Times-Democrat*, July 28, 1900.

[36]*Times-Democrat,* July 28, October 10, 1900. There were three claimants for the "dead or alive" reward money on Charles, but the more reliable witnesses agreed that Noiret was the man who fired the fatal shots.

[37]*Natchez Daily Democrat,* July 28, 1900; *New Orleans Daily Item,* July 28, 1900; *Daily Picayune,* July 28, 1900.

[38]*Times-Democrat,* July 28, 1900.

[39]Ibid.; Bonnet Carre *Le Meschacebe,* August 4, 1900; *Natchez Daily Demoocrat,* July 28, 1900; *Atlanta Constitution,* July 28, 1900.

[40]*Times-Democrat,* July 28, 1900; *Vicksburg Daily Herald,* July 28, 1900.

[41]*Boston Morning* Journal, July 28, 1900; "Record of Inquests," Coroner Office, July 27, 1900, 320-21.

[42]*Times-Democrat,* July 28, 1900; *Daily Picayune,* July 28, August 7, 1900.

[43]Letter from the Rev. D. A. Graham, in *Indianapolis Freeman,* August 18, 1900; Kendall, *History of New Orleans,* 2:540; *Daily Picayune,* July 28, August 10, 1900.

[44]"Report of the Operations of the Special Police Force," in Mayor's Office Correspondence; *Times-Democrat,* July 29-31, 1900; *Brookhaven Lincoln County Times,* August 2, 1900; Alan Lomax, *Mister Jelly Roll* (New York, 1950), 57.

[45]*Daily Item,* July 25-28, 1900; *Times-Democrat,* July 26, 30, 1900; *Daily Picayune,* July 28, 1900.

[46]*Daily States,* July 28, 1900.

[47]"Record of Inquests," Coroner's Office, July 27, 1900, 322; *New York Times,* July 28, 1900; *Times-Democrat,* July 28-29, 1900; *Daily Picayune,* July 28, 30, 1900. The *Daily Picayune,* on July 30, claimed to have found a Caroline Robertson living in New Orleans who said she was the mother of a "Curt" Robertson, who was presently in Mississippi and had no connection with Robert Charles. If so, it was simply a case of the alias used by Robert Charles being similar to the real name of another black man, for this Caroline Robertson was not Robert Charles's mother, and evidence from both white and black sources point to the fact that Robert Charles used the Curtis Robertson alias both in Mississippi and in New Orleans, when he first came to the city. Hyman Levy knew him as Curtis Robertson, and several of the black people arrested at the Saratoga Street neighborhood knew he had used that alias. Also, the old Storyville-era black musician Frank Amacker, who in 1974 was still living, recalled in an interview done for Tulane University, that Robert Charles had used the alias of Robertson. Interview with Frank Amacker, July 1, 1965, in Wlliam Ransom Hogan Jazz Archive, Tulane University.

[48]Levy interview, *New Orleans Sunday States,* July 29, 1900.

TURNING POINTS: BIRACIAL UNIONS IN THE AGE OF SEGREGATION, 1893-1901*

Eric Arnesen

At the end of the 1880s, hundreds of black cotton screwmen and their families gathered to lay cornerstone of a two-story union hall. The ceremony was an occasion for reflection as well as celebration. Following musical entertainment and opening prayers, several speakers assessed the progress of New Orleans's black workers and their prospects for the future. Despite "the fact that there has been much opposition and prejudice to be encountered," observed James Madison Vance, the union's attorney and Republican party activist, the black screwmen had made steady progress and now stood "at the head of the colored associations." Similarly, R. W. Gould found that although a strictly drawn "line between the races" had endured from the antebellum era to the present moment, the "condition of affairs has gradually been improved and better things are looked for by the colored race."[1] Infused with holiday oratory appropriate to such occasions, their portraits did not ignore the persistence of racism, but preferred to emphasize black labor's real accomplishments.

The optimism toward the future expressed by Vance and Gould drew upon black workers' experiences during the 1880s. Many no doubt believed that their associations might ultimately remove the color line in employment. The peculiar conditions of waterfront work—the largely unskilled labor, the potential of overcrowded labor markets, and the multiplicity of connected trades—had made biracial and inter-trade collaboration both possible and necessary for the advancement of all dock workers. Even though the Cotton Men's Executive Council was no longer the vehicle for sustained interracial and inter-trade cooperation after 1887, blacks and whites continued to labor in close proximity without overt hostility and dock unions maintained wage rates and work rules for the next

*From *Waterfront Workers of New Orleans: Race, Class, and Politics, 1863-1923* by Eric Arnesen. Copyright © 1991 by Eric Arnesen. Used by permission of Oxford University Press, Inc.

seven years. And the New Orleans general strike of 1892 would demonstrate that the biracial impulse was not confined solely to the docks and cotton yards.

But if black workers' experiences in the 1880s underscored the New Orleans celebrants' portrayal of achievement, subsequent events would make a mockery of their predictions of future progress, at least in the short team. In the interrelated realms of economics, politics, and race relations, blacks suffered severely. The century's worst economic crisis, from 1893 through 1897, produced high unemployment and deep wage cuts for blacks and whites alike. corporate employers delivered staggering blows to the labor movement, sparing neither white nor black union members. By the end of the century, the political and social status of Southern blacks had deteriorated further. The fleeting interracialism of the Populist movement had collapsed under severe governmental repression and internal strains. Throughout the South, state after state had disfranchised its black voters as Democratic politicians consolidated a politics of white supremacy. Widespread segregation had found full legal sanction, and white violence against blacks increased. At the same time, white Northerners had abandoned what little interest they had retained after Reconstruction in the plight of Southern blacks, embarking on their own imperial ventures and subjugating "colored peoples" around the globe. The Mississippi Plan, as C. Vann Woodward once noted of that state's efforts to subordinate its black citizens, had become the American Way.[2]

New Orleans and its waterfront were deeply affected by the twin threats of heightened racism and employer aggression. By 1893 the relative commercial prosperity and earlier flexible racial codes had given way to a harsher reality of economic distress and racial antagonism. Over the next two years, the complex network of alliances sustaining the interracial and inter-trade cooperation of the 1880s disintegrated; in late 1894 and early 1895, the New Orleans waterfront exploded in crisis. White screwmen and longshoremen, seeking the total exclusion of black workers from their trades, utilized strikes and violence to achieve their goals. Their repudiation of the interracial alliance led to a rapid decline of all union power, complete loss of control over the labor supply, widespread elimination of work rules, and severe wage reductions. By early 1895, the golden age of union power and the "era of good feeling" between black and white dock workers had come to an end. "Looked at from every standpoint," the black *Indianapolis Freeman* observed after the New Orleans waterfront riots in 1895, "the condition of the Negro in America is most deplorable and discouraging. It may well be asked, in what direction shall we bend our vision to find the signs that promise release and freedom from the NEW BONDAGE that has come to him within the years since he was declared a free man and citizen?"[3]

Obituaries for New Orleans' biracial waterfront movement, however, were premature. Their experiences after 1894 taught blacks and whites along the docks that race relations, working conditions, and union influence were bound inextricably together. But before dock workers could recoup their losses, they would have to relearn the lessons of solidarity across trade and racial lines. With the return of commercial prosperity at the turn of the century, the alliance of black and white waterfront unions rose, phoenix-like, from the ashes of the 1890s violence. Determined black unions, an improved political environment for labor, the legacy of past collaboration and power, and the specific character of dock work—all made possible the formation of the new Dock and Cotton Council in 1901. The changes it effected were indeed dramatic. Although "professional white politicians" sought "to make it understood that the races find it difficult to get along together in the South," the *New York Age*, a black newspaper, reported in 1913, "the best of feeling exists between the colored and white longshoremen [of New Orleans] . . . and a working agreement is in force between them which guarantees all a square deal."[4] Much the same could be said for other riverfront workers as well. While race and class dynamics on the New Orleans docks continued to defy any simple formula, the waterfront alliance challenged the strictures of white supremacy at the dawn of the Jim Crow era.

I

The collapse of the national economy in 1893 set the stage for the crisis on the New Orleans docks. The depression of 1893-97 produced business failures, massive wage cuts, and increased poverty across the nation; up to a fifth of the country's industrial labor force may have been unemployed in the winter of 1893-94. The depression hit the labor movement particularly hard. The craft unions that made up the young American Federation of Labor lost considerable ground, as employers successfully took the offensive against union work rules and wages. The Pullman Boycott, which had pitted the American Railway Union against both the nation's rail lines and the federal government, resulted in a major setback for the advocates of industrial unionism. In New Orleans, commerce suffered tremendously from "diminished trade and unsettled confidence," reported the Young Men's Business League in 1894. Statistics in "nearly every branch of trade reflect the depression and dullness which have prevailed." Although the city experienced relatively few business failures, shippers complained of low cotton prices, small crops, and non-existent profits.[5]

The depression of the 1890s, while of critical importance, was not alone responsible for New Orleans' waterfront crisis. Practices specific to the world of the city's docks also contributed to the breakdown of work-sharing agreements and interracial union structures. At the center of the controversy stood the so-called aristocrats of the levee, the cotton screwmen. White screwmen occupied the top of the port's employment hierarchy. As the most skilled laborers on the docks, they formed the port's strongest union, commanded the highest wages, and exercised the greatest control over the conditions of their labor. By the mid-1880s, they also received steady criticism from employers. Steamship agents and owners identified high labor costs in general, and the cost of the screwmen's services in particular, as "the backbone of all the excessive charges" facing the port. While few challenged the screwmen's wages of $6 a day for regular men and $7 a day for foremen, many singled out for attack the screwmen's 75-bale rule, adopted in 1878, which limited the amount of work performed. While nine hours ostensibly constituted a day's work, gangs of screwmen frequently quit early after loading their 75 bales.[6]

By the 1890s, the screwmen's work rules no longer affected all employers in the same way. Some ship operators remained highly dependent on the screwmen's skills. The careful, balanced storage of screwed cotton enabled smaller ships to sail more safely with far greater quantities of cotton than if the bales had been loaded loosely into their holds. "So closely do they pack the bales together," the *New Orleans Daily Picayune* remarked, "that when a ship is properly loaded, the cotton seems to be a solid mass, as if it were a part of the vessel, and so buoyant that a ship so loaded could scarcely be made to sink. . . ." Many tramp ships often arrived with the sole purpose of carrying away as much cotton as possible. With no strict sailing schedule, these vessels remained in port for as long as it took the screwmen to load them properly.[7]

Other employers were considerably less dependent upon the screwmen's services. New technological and economic imperatives drove them to search for alternatives to union power. Unlike smaller tramp ships, large transatlantic steamers followed specified sailing schedules. The screwmen's rule, one steamship manager complained, "gave ship owners very little opportunity to figure on a definite time for the departure of their vessels." More important, for many large steamships the careful screwing of cotton was far less important than speedy stowage and quick turn-around time in port. By 1894, the royal mail steamers of the West India and Pacific Line and the ships of Charles Stoddart relied little upon the screwmen's skills; similarly, the Cromwell Steamship Line carried only unscrewed cotton. Yet the screwmen's union required these companies to employ union men, observe union work rules, and pay union wages. The 75-bale limit "operates very unfairly . . . against the regular lines that make their living out of this port and come here regularly . . . [and whose] time is very valuable," complained agent Sanders of the West India and Pacific Line in 1886. By the early 1890s, a growing number of powerful, foreign-owned companies were objecting to the slow and expensive loading process that the screwmen's monopoly and work rules imposed upon them.[8]

Shipping agents' need to circumscribe the screwmen's work rules might have gone unaddressed had it not been for the rise of assertive black opposition to the white screwmen and the subsequent collapse of the unequal biracial agreements in that trade. The black critique of white labor focused on the general behavior of the national labor movement as well as the specific practices of New Orleans white screwmen. The case against the larger movement was articulated in the pages of the *Southwestern Christian Advocate*. The black weekly newspaper had always taken a tentative stance toward unions—praising local bodies that encouraged black and white cooperation, condemning those whose activities fostered violence or excluded blacks from membership. Though apprehensive at the unrest surrounding the Homestead strike in 1892, for example, it could still anticipate a better day when the labor movement welcomed "every honest loyal son of toil whether he be as black as ebony or as white as the parian marble" into its

ranks. But by the summer of 1894, the *Advocate* had little good to say about organized
labor. Surveying the outbreak of widespread class conflict across the nation, the paper
concluded that "unions have failed, miserably failed thus far, in successfully dictating the
terms by which our great interests have been managed." Strike-related violence and the
considerable paralysis of the country's business during the nation-wide Pullman Boycott
signified that unionized workers represented an "irresponsible and unreasonable class of
citizens." And not least was the indictment of national unions' racial practices. To the
Advocate, the "existence of the color line in nearly all of the unions" and numerous
strikes by whites against the employment of black labor had "impressed the colored
laborer that he may expect but little sympathy" from white workers.[9]

But exclusionary practices, the *Advocate* suggested, were not an "unmixed evil."
Systematic racial exclusion meant that few black wage earners participated in the violent
strikes that obstructed the country's economic progress. "The Negro for the most part is a
disinterested spectator," the paper observed during the May 1886 strikes for the eight-hour
day, being "so situated that he cannot be seriously hurt or helped by any issue of the
conflict."[10] If the *Advocate* called on white unions to admit blacks during the 1880s and
early 1890s, its tone had changed sharply by 1894. "The well-known reliability of the
colored man as wage worker," it now argued,

> should favorably commend him to every department of mechanical and industrial
> activity. He is thoroughly American; is not an anarchist or socialist; loves American
> institutions, and, with proper encouragement and protection, could be made a most
> efficient and valuable acquisition to our vast commercial, mechanical and industrial
> interests.
>
> We believe that the non-affiliation of the colored man into the labor unions of
> the day, places him in the forefront, among the most reliable wageworkers of the
> land, and will the more effectually solve some of the problems which are vexing the
> American capitalist.[11]

This prescription for black advancement resembled Booker T. Washington's philosophy
on capital and labor. In his many speeches and writing, the Wizard of Tuskegee analyzed
the situation of black Americans largely in economic terms, decrying their "agitation of
questions of social equality" as extreme folly and cautioning blacks to abandon their interest in political and social rights. The development of a firm economic foundation took
precedence over all else: "When it comes to business, pure and simple," Washington
argued, "it is in the South that the Negro is given a man's chance in the commercial
world." His hostility to organized labor led him to advise black workers to eschew strikes
and unions and to stand by the better class of Southern whites who offered their only hope
of redemption. As anthropologist John Brown Childs has argued, Washington believed
that "the cold unsentimental calculations of the capitalist would exert a tremendous
corrosive power on the irrational racial sentiments of the agrarian South."[12] Black unionists in New Orleans, of course, hardly followed this advice to abandon their organizations.
But as the relations between black and white workers deteriorated, black workers on the

city's riverfront found it necessary to enter into uneasy and often unpleasant alliances with port employers in order to address long-standing and new problems.

If the *Advocate* framed its critique of white labor in broad terms, black dock workers had more specific objections to waterfront union practices, particularly the white domination of the screwmen's trade. Unlike longshoremen and yardmen, screwmen had no equitable work-sharing agreement. Rather, the white association imposed a strict twenty-gang, or 100 men, limit on their black counterparts. The black union's membership, however, exceeded that number (in 1889, it boasted 500 members). In late 1892, the issue of the racial quota system split the black screwmen's ranks. A smaller group of roughly 100 men (which became the Screwmen's Benevolent Association No. 1) sought to preserve the status quo; a larger group (which became the Screwmen's Benevolent Association No. 2) rejected the twenty-gang limit altogether, announcing its intention to pursue an independent course.[13]

Black opposition to racial restrictions coincided with the shipping agents' efforts to circumscribe the screwmen's limit. During the early depression years, black screwmen of Association No. 2 secured work by undercutting union wages and dissolving long-standing union work rules. Utilizing their own black stevedore, they found a receptive agent in Charles Stoddart, who long had denounced high labor costs and the 75-bale limit. Stoddart found the Association's offer quite attractive: it charged 35 cents per bale of cotton, 15 cents per bale lower than the other white and black unions, and abolished the 75-bale limit. Unable to secure a promise of future labor peace from the white union, Stoddart turned permanently to the black union as "a guarantee against trouble" and of "peace and uninterrupted industry." The establishment of a low-wage black labor enclave had raised a serious challenge to white union power even before the depression began.[14]

The Cotton Men's Executive Council responded to these racial divisions not by addressing legitimate black complaints but by modifying slightly the status quo. Meeting in mid-January 1893, shortly after the split in the black screwmen's ranks, the Cotton Men's Executive Council expelled Association No. 2 for jeopardizing the screwmen's interests by working below the tariff rate. Agreeing to abide by the old twenty-gang limit, the black screwmen's Association No. 1 applied for—and eventually received—admission to the Council. Although both the white and smaller black screwmen's unions worked together in "harmony" under the old rules for the next year and a half, the earlier cooperative spirit had disappeared.[15]

By the opening years of the depression, black efforts to undermine onerous racial restrictions and white screwmen's resistance to those efforts had produced a bifurcated labor market on New Orleans docks. The events of 1893 through 1895 represented a variation on the model of ethnic antagonism outlined by sociologist Edna Bonacich. A key source of antagonism between ethnic (in this case, racial) groups, Bonacich contends, lies in the emergence of a split labor market, in which different groups receive different wages for the same work. Historian George Frederickson, who has applied this analysis to industrialization in South Africa and the American South, has argued similarly that

Racial or ethnic antagonism is thus aroused by a three-cornered struggle between capitalists desiring the cheapest possible labor, workers of the dominant ethnic group who resist being undercut or displaced by cheaper labor from a minority group or subordinate group, and the alien newcomers who are struggling to find a niche in the economy. The outcome of the conflict depends in theory on the extent to which the higher-priced workers can bring pressure to bear on the capitalist class to entrench their advantage either by excluding the lower-priced workers or by establishing some kind of industrial caste system which will allow them to monopolize the best jobs.[16]

New Orleans' black screwmen, of course, were by no means newcomers to the city or their trade, and at least a small group of blacks initially adhered to the restrictive union clauses. But the efforts of some black workers to shatter the industrial caste system and find a niche in New Orleans' commercial economy, as well as white resistance to those efforts, inaugurated a new era in labor and race relations on the waterfront—one that contrasted sharply with the experiences of the 1880s.

Two particular developments in the slow summer season of 1894 contributed to growing tensions between white and black screwmen. First, the press reported that shipping agents were searching for ways to eliminate the white screwmen's 75-bale limit. In July, one journalist alleged that at least one, and possibly both, associations of black screwmen were plotting to work for large shipping agents at a reduced tariff with no limit on the number of bales stowed. The consequences for white unionists would be severe: they would be "shut out from those ships or would have to work for the same [low] rate. They would make a hard fight against it, and a bitter factional and race contest might result." There is no evidence to confirm this particular rumor. But given the lack of coordination and communication between white and black unions, many whites probably believed it was true. The second development was the emergence of a black stevedoring firm, headed by Alcide Bessant. Black screwmen who had long complained that white stevedores discriminated against them now could turn to a black middleman for employment. Although Bessant failed to win any contracts outside of Stoddart's low-wage enclave, many white workers undoubtedly grew alarmed at the prospect of increased black competition.[17]

That alarm found expression in the increasingly harsh criticism white screwmen leveled at black screwmen during the late summer and early fall of 1894. While black Association No. 2 admittedly charged 15 cents a bale less than the white union, white screwmen falsely accused all blacks of tariff cutting. Whites also denounced alleged violations of the work-sharing agreement, renegotiated in January 1893, that allocated 20 gangs per day to members of the black Association No. 1. The whites charged the black Association No. 1 with dispatching up to 24 gangs per day—it had "insidiously started in to bolster itself up and reach out for more men and work than they had agreed to"—and admitting into its ranks green hands, unskilled men who had not served the two-year apprenticeship required by the white union. Underlying the white concern was a general fear that increased black competition would lead to the further degradation of their trade and higher white unemployment.[18]

White workers might have found a barely plausible basis for their fears in demographic trends. The city's population, which had grown at the rate of 13 percent in the decade of the 1870s and 12 percent in the 1880s jumped by 19 percent in the 1890s. While blacks continued to constitute roughly a quarter of the city's population (27 percent) in 1900, the actual black growth rate rose from 12 percent from 1880 to 1900. Economic hardship and escalating white political violence drove many Louisiana and Mississippi blacks to New Orleans, a city with a reputation for relative racial liberalism and available work. Large numbers of blacks frequently were lured to New Orleans with the "promise of steady work, high wages and a good time," the *Southwestern Christian Advocate* warned in mid-1893. But these promises were "a mere subterfuge," and black migrants were compelled to return home or work for wages "which will barely give them support."[19]

White workers contended that the influx of blacks only exacerbated the unemployment and economic hardship experienced by whites. Blacks, one white worker complained in 1894, "had already all the steamboat and coal business. They got all the work on building street railroads and did all the carpenter work. . . . The result was that the white men must either keep their work on the levee or leave the city."[20] James Shaw, president of the white Screwmen's Benevolent Association (SBA), concurred. It had come to "such a condition in this city that you could go nowhere but the negroes [*sic*] were doing the work. On the streets, on the railroads and everywhere one is in darkest Africa," he complained that December. Plantation hands coming to the city "were constantly being used as a menace to labor." As for black screwmen, he denounced them for "gradually usurping the rights of whites."[21]

Black workers, of course, interpreted the situation very differently. L. J. Olbert, president of the Colored Screwmen's Benevolent Association No. 1, acknowledged working over twenty gangs, but denied that blacks displaced whites. "The negroes [*sic*] were never given a job," he explained, "until all the white men were at work and there remained yet ships to be loaded." He also rejected other charges of bad faith. His members had always complied with the rules of their compact, had never worked below the regular tariff, nor loaded over 75 bales of cotton per gang per day. All members of Association No. 1 were residents of New Orleans, and were skilled, not incompetent, workers who had served a regular two-year apprenticeship; most of them were "sons of screwmen, who had been employed steadily since the war." Moreover, Association No. 1 men had stood steadfastly by the whites for two years and had "in no way aided or recognized the Colored Screwmen No. 2, parting from them on a question of principle, and remaining loyal to that principle." It was unjust, Olbert concluded, for the white screwmen "to throw them overboard now, because of some fancied or real in jury sustained by other colored screwmen."[22] Olbert's choice of words—"throw them overboard"—soon would serve as a description of reality, not merely as a figure of speech.

Tensions flared into the open by mid-October 1894. The SBA notified stevedores that, beginning on October 15, white union men would no longer work for any employer who hired black screwmen. In exchange for the total discharge of blacks, the white union promised to provide all necessary labor to handle every bale of cotton put on the docks. Agents and stevedores, fearing that a major strike in the early cotton season would cripple business, reluctantly complied with the whites' demand. Only agent Charles Stoddart continued to employ Association No. 2 blacks at the lower wage rate.[23]

The white screwmen's ultimatum marked the passing of an era. At the request of the black cotton teamsters and loaders, the Cotton Men's Executive Council—composed of only the white screwmen, the black screwmen of Association No. 1, and the cotton teamsters—met on October 17 for the last time. The expulsion of the black screwmen gave effective control of the organization to the whites, and the teamsters saw "no use in belonging to a council which was only maintained for the benefit of the white men." The resolution to dissolve the organization found approval almost without discussion. Council president James F. Breen, an employee in the city engineer's office and brother John Breen, a former president of the white screwmen and now waterfront saloon operator, supported the measure. The council's disbanding was hardly "a matter of any great importance," he noted. Since the "retirement of the Colored Screwmen No. 2 it had been merely a formality, the white screwmen having the entire control of everything." Breen was keenly aware that the black teamsters could do little "in the present difficulty . . . [I]f the [white] screwmen withdrew their support from them and agreed to work with other men as teamsters and loaders, the boss draymen could then reduce the wages or employ the other men." Almost a decade and a half after its formation, the Cotton Men's Executive Council finally crumbled; whatever remained of the initial spirit of interracial cooperation died with it.[24]

A period of conflict and violence quickly followed the Council's demise. Black workers attempted to regain their jobs, whites sought to preserve their dominant position, and stevedores and shipping agents used the crisis to manipulate racial tensions to their own advantage. Black screwmen met with stevedores and shipping agents to negotiate the conditions of their return to the levee. Toward the end of October, their efforts met with some success. Charles K. Lincoln, the stevedore for the firm of Ross, Howe and Merrow, had traditionally employed only white labor. The recent racial conflict, however, had eliminated black screwmen and increased the overall demand for white screwmen. As a result, he was unable to secure a sufficient number of whites to load his ships adequately. Under pressure from his firm, Lincoln broke ranks with his fellow stevedores on October 26 and hired a large number of black screwmen. This violation of the status quo raised the stakes dramatically. White screwmen immediately struck all ships in port, while the white longshoremen supported them by striking all of Ross, Howe and Merrow's ships. Their strike backfired, as some thirty-three gangs of black longshoremen and screwmen found immediate employment loading the cotton the whites refused to touch.[25]

White workers responded with unprecedented violence. That evening around nine o'clock, some 150 to 200 armed men, wearing false beards, handkerchiefs, and masks, gathered in the "shadow of the buildings" on Front Street. Their targets were six ships being unloaded by black screwmen. Creeping forward toward the river, they quickly occupied the levee from Second to Seventh streets, where four English ships being loaded by the firm of Ross, Howe and Merrow and two ships being loaded by the black stevedore Alcide Bessant for Stoddart and Company were docked. Posting sentinels, the crowd easily overpowered seven private watchmen. They first attacked the steamship *Constance*. "Swarming over the side of the vessel and overflowing the deck," the crowd broke open the hatches, seized the black screwmen's tools stored in the ship's hold, and threw them into the river. When the white men had completed their task, they moved on to the next ship. By one a.m., the raiders had boarded six ships and destroyed the black screwmen's equipment on each. "The crowd didn't do any damage to any of the freight and behaved all right so far as we were concerned," one ship captain told the police, "except they made prisoners of us."[26] And, he might have added, they destroyed roughly $4000 worth of the black screwmen's property.

White strikers renewed their attack the following day, Saturday, October 28. As many as fifty black screwmen and longshoremen were at work on several of Stoddart's steamships under the protection of a small number of police. At 2:30 that afternoon, at least one hundred whites rushed the docks from all directions. For the next two hours, the *New Orleans Times-Democrat* reported, "the levee was in full charge of the white screwmen and their sympathizers, who terrorized every one there into submission." Whites fired pistols and Winchester rifles at the black workers who attempted to escape by jumping into the river, seeking refuge beneath the wharves, or fleeing down streets. As smaller crowds of armed whites pursued their black prey down the streets from the levee, others boarded ship after ship and, using steam derricks or sheer strength, hoisted the black screwmen's jackscrews and logs out of the ships' holds and into the river. By the end of the attack, two hundred shots had been fired; at least five people were shot and one black screwman, J. Gordon Taylor, drowned. The following day, white workers mistook the arrival of black screwmen to collect their pay as an effort to resume work. Immediately the whites mobilized, seized their weapons, and greeted the blacks with racial epithets and gunfire. "Upon the countenances of each one" of the white men, a reporter observed, "was an expression clearly indicative of their anger and hatred toward the negro."[27]

White longshoremen soon followed the white screwmen's example of black exclusion. On October 29, black longshoremen arrived for the evening shift only to learn that white longshoremen had voted to terminate the half-and-half arrangement and now refused to work with the blacks. With police patrolling in large numbers as the white longshoremen went to work, the levee from Jackson Avenue to Sixth Street resembled and "entrenchment behind cotton bales for the purpose of defending the city against some foreign foe."[28] The whites' action apparently took black longshoremen by surprise. "The colored longshoremen have been unjustly dealt with. It is an outrage the way they have been treated—without cause or provocation," black union leader Lafayette Tharpe complained.

> The colored and white longshoremen had no grievance. . . . Fourteen hundred colored longshoremen have been denied work to-day on the levee by the foremen, who claim that they received their instructions from their association to hire nothing but white men. We are sorry of this race issue, more especially when it comes unprovoked—without the slightest cause or provocation. We have a conference committee, twelve white men and twelve colored men, and we have worked on each and every ship, whether cargo or cotton, half and half. What induced them to break the conference rules and refuse to work with the colored longshoremen who have violated no rules no regulations, we are at a loss to know.[29]

Another black longshoreman, Henry Crittenden, concurred: "White and colored have worked side by side for months and there have been no manifestations of enmity between the races," the *Times-Democrat* reported his saying. While it appeared that 1400 black longshoremen had been "driven off the levee for good," some now joined the black screwmen in Association No. 2, working on Stoddart's ships under the protection of fifty policemen. Barred from union work at union rates, the black longshoremen took refuge in the low wage, all-black enclave.[30]

In the short run, white crowd violence appeared effective. While the white SBA officially repudiated the riotous activities and insisted that no white screwmen were involved, its members clearly reaped the benefits of the disorder. Although the Cotton Exchange promised to protect black labor, its members capitulated to the white screwmen's demands, reaffirming the pre-riot but post-ultimatum situation. Following this agreement, for example, stevedore Charles Lincoln discharged his entire black labor force. Only Charles Stoddart continued to employ members of the black screwmen's Association No. 2, at the lower wage rate, through a black stevedore.[31]

But the pronounced racial tensions that produced a split labor market also gave steamship agents the opportunity to address their long-standing complaints about waterfront labor costs and the organization of work. The "whole thing in a nutshell," one prominent cotton businessman summarized, "is will the others who are employing white labor be able to stand around and see the ships loaded and unloaded at a less cost by negro labor while they are paying the regular rates to the whites?"[32] The temptation proved too great for M. J. Sanders, agent for the West India and Pacific line. With ships that followed a regular sailing schedule between the United States, Liverpool, and the West Indies and that required less care in the loading of cotton, Sanders seized the opportunity to reduce loading time by hiring black labor unencumbered by restrictive work rules. Denying that he had agreed to the original Cotton Exchange compromise, Sanders terminated his firm's twenty-year relationship with the white screwmen. The terms "dictated by the white screwmen were unfair and improper," Sanders complained, and the union's inability to provide him with a sufficient number of experienced men made the employment of the "other labor" imperative. Asserting his right to hire any man he chose, he contracted with the new black stevedoring firm of Carey, Allen and Company to load his company's ships with the black screwmen of Association No. 1.

Individual efforts did not get agent Sanders very far. On November 4, a large cotton fire swept through the West India line wharves and freight sheds between St. James and Felicity streets, destroying an estimated 4000 bales of cotton, and large quantities of oil cake, cotton seed meal, staves, molasses, and other goods. Although the white screwmen's union denied any connection to the suspicious blaze, it maintained its vigilance against black competition. In response to false rumors that black workers upriver at Southport were attacking the white men's tools, an armed white force immediately mobilized. The "entire levee filled with [white] men, all armed and patrolling the levee in regular soldierly fashion," noted one journalist. The following day, November 6, an unknown attacker shot and wounded the black stevedore Carey near Southport.[33]

Neither arson nor armed patrols by white workers had the desired impact. Within days, the West India line and Charles Stoddart and Company put their black dock laborers—in Associations No. 1 and 2 respectively—back to work under the protection of a small army of police, both committing themselves to employing black labor on a permanent basis. Unsatisfied by guarantees of protection by city and state troops in the event of renewed violence, representatives of the West India and Pacific company discovered a powerful new weapon in the battle against white labor: the injunction. At the West India and Pacific company's request, a U. S. circuit court issued a restraining order barring members of the white screwmen's and longshoremen's associations from interfering in any way with black workers. The temporary order was made permanent in early December, and white workers reluctantly abided by its provisions. The violence temporarily subsided.[34]

Agents and stevedores sought an ally in the courts because municipal authorities and police offered them less than complete cooperation. Numerous witnesses testified that city policemen had stood idly by while armed whites seized the tools of the black union and assaulted its members. Police officers, black workers observed, "were like spectators upon a theatrical performance"; not only were the police in active sympathy with the whites, but many policemen also maintained membership in the white screwmen's union, owing "more allegiance to that association than they do to their oaths and the protection of life and property." The *Times-Democrat* concurred in a strong denunciation of municipal complicity in the riot: "All these riotous acts . . . were perpetrated in full view of a police force which not only did nothing to interfere with them, but actually seemed to sympathize with the rioters."[35]

Not surprisingly, the strongest voices against the riots came from New Orleans' black community. On November 8, some 1500 people, including sixty preachers, gathered for a religious service and protest meeting at the Wesleyan chapel. The protesters adopted a series of resolutions condemning the behavior of the civil authorities and calling for greater Christian forbearance and faith. "At a time when the peace, prosperity, and even the very life, commercially speaking, of a great city like New Orleans, is endangered by the ruthless hand of the murderer, outlaw, assassin, and incendiary torch," they argued,

> when the blood of half a score of defenseless law-abiding citizens . . . [has] been slaughtered in cold blood, or wounded nigh unto death, by mob violence, in open day and in the presence of those whose duty it is to protect the defenseless and preserve the peace of the city; when the blood of these men is calling aloud for redress at the hands of injured justice and outraged law; when the only plea thus far given or hinted, by these insurgent violators of the peace and perpetrators of these deviltries, is the fact that those against whom these greatest of outrages are perpetrated are negroes [*sic*] and are incapable of resentment or redress; when the representatives of civil government, municipal and gubernatorial, seem to act with a measure of indifference to such condition of affairs, may it not well be said, as in the day of primitive Christian experience: 'Lord, unto whom shall we go?'

Promising a firmer reliance upon God than ever before, the black protesters ended by appealing

> to all true Christians of every creed and faith to unite with us in asking God to turn and overturn, as in the days of old, until the arm of the oppressor shall be broken and the right of the people of every race and hue shall be respected and protected on every foot of American soil from east to west, and from north to south.[36]

If breaking the arm of the oppressor was God's work, black unions had the more difficult task of devising some strategy to cope with the new state of affairs. Sharp divisions immediately arose. A small number of black screwmen in Association No. 1 expressed their willingness to turn back the clock and accept the pre-ultimatum limit of 20 to 26 gangs, in exchange for racial peace. A majority of union members objected at a special meeting called to denounce the unauthorized offer by advocates of the racial quota system. "We deplore said unmanly actions," members declared in a public statement, and "can only characterize their actions as being menial and of the lowest and basest design, calculated to destroy both the veracity and stability of any organized body." The violence had destroyed the old foundation permanently. Some black unionists maintained:

> They had been driven off the levee and prevented from working and they would not now make any settlement that would not give all of them a chance to go to work again. They would not agree to any contract which would give 100 work and leave 200 or more without it.[37]

H. J. Randle, vice president of Association No. 1, exclaimed that black workers would rather "go off the levee than make any such compromise." Principle and pride aside, black workers had a more pragmatic ground for opposing the restoration of the modified prior arrangement: they currently enjoyed more employment. A compromise move, one group of black screwmen observed, "would savor a great deal of imbecility, as they have all the work they can get now, whereas, under such an agreement as the one reported, they would have to turn three-fourths of their number adrift." For a majority of black workers, however, the situation was far more bleak. While black screwmen found work under Stoddart and Sanders, a far larger number of black longshoremen remained unemployed.[38]

The collapse of the Cotton Men's Executive Council, the demise of work-sharing agreements, and the refusal of white riverfront men to work with blacks, forced black workers to seek new allies in the struggle to secure employment. The thoughts of one union leader suggested both the indignation felt by black workers and the new directions that blacks might be forced to look. "We have been deprived of our implements of labor," he told the press in early November 1894,

> our wives, some of them, have been made widows; our children orphans, and our right to live denied. We can only rely upon those who seek to establish New Orleans as a great port of entry, who by their industry, their expenditure of time and money, have brought her to the height of her personal competition with other ports, who by years of toil and great loss have stood the ravages of time and the . . . sting of strikes, we ask them to aid us in the pursuit of a livelihood. . . .
>
> The strike is now settled. We are still unemployed. We have received no pay for our losses. . . . Of the Cotton Exchange and all other exchanges we now implore assistance in the reinstatement of affairs as they were prior to the strike. All we ask is a showing to make our living and to keep away the wolf from the doors. . . .
>
> To the charge made against us, that of "wage cutters," we simply say that prostitution of rights, threatening the continuance of our cotton trade and other trades, the denial of work and the assassination of our brothers, will force us to seek the arms of protection in the nearest way and under the most available terms.[39]

Led by former black union president E. S. Swann, a committee from the black longshoremen's association made one last appeal to the white union men in mid-December. When that move failed, black workers finally turned to their employers and the city's elite for assistance.

Black longshoremen resolved to break the deadlock and recapture their lost jobs. As "a matter of salvation for their very existence," they proposed to undercut the white longshoremen by reducing their tariff from 50 to 40 cents an hour for day work, from 75 to 60 cents for night work, and from $1 to 80 cents for Sunday work—in effect, restoring the pre-1885 wage standard. "We have done everything in our power," labor veteran Swann explained to his fellow longshoremen,

> but it was all in vain. . . . We did not like to reduce our rates without first trying to get them to divide the work with us, as has been done before, but as they would not, we are obliged to do something to get bread and butter. We have been trying to get them to come to some agreement with us for the past forty-eight days, but they have driven us off without cause or provocation, although we have always been loyal to them.
>
> We don't think it is right that we should have our men shot and killed on the levee like they were dogs, as they did with J. Gordon Taylor. . . . Now there are six white men working on the levee to every one colored man, and we have about 900 or

1000 who are on the eve of starvation. The only work we have is the little that is given to us by Messrs. M. J. Sanders and Chas. Stoddart. The colored Longshoremen's Association sincerely thanks these gentlemen for what they have done for us.[40]

Swann found a receptive audience among many individual stevedores. Immediately seizing the opportunity to slash wages for the first time since the depression of the 1870s, employers announced that they would employ any man, "irrespective of color," who agreed to work for 40 cents an hour, signaling, in the words of the *New Orleans Times-Democrat*, that "none but colored union or white non-union longshoremen need apply for work . . . for no one expected the white longshoremen to meet the cut as a means of maintaining their monopoly." Anticipating a serious conflict, the contracting stevedores called on Mayor John Fitzpatrick to provide adequate protection along the entire riverfront.[41]

This time, white riverfront workers did not resort to violence. Nonetheless, they managed to halt most levee work as soon as stevedores cut wages. Although the white screwmen's union took no official action and disavowed responsibility for its members' actions, the white screwmen's tactics proved central. The men, one screwmen stated, had "come to the conclusion not to handle the cotton from negroes [*sic*]." Half of the white screwmen stayed home on account of "illness;" a few said they had to purchase Christmas turkeys; the rest claimed that there was simply no one (i.e. union white longshoremen) to bring cotton to the ships. Although the stevedores had plenty of black longshoremen on hand, there were too few experienced black screwmen available to carry on the work. Without the full number of white screwmen, there was little stevedores could do.[42]

The unsettled state of affairs troubled all parties involved. Whites feared wage cuts and loss of work; blacks dreaded renewed racial violence and sustained unemployment; employers faced financial losses due to the periodic cessation of work at the height of the cotton loading season. The first stage of the labor and race crisis ended on December 20, the second day of "absolute idleness" on the levee. A conference of black and white workers and cotton merchants agreed to return to the old state of affairs. Both black and white longshore workers would reestablish the pre-October arrangement, dividing existing work equally on all ships—except those of Stoddard and Sanders, who refused to participate—and restoring the 1885 wage rates and the old conference rules. As much as the stevedores desired a 20 percent wage reduction, they recognized that the old rules provided a basis for labor stability and rescinded the wage cut.[43]

The December 1894 compromise revealed both the precarious position of blacks in the depression-era New Orleans economy and the tensions within black labor's ranks regarding the new arrangements on the docks. While black and white longshoremen returned to an equal division of work, white screwmen reimposed the restrictive quota system on black screwmen in Association No. 1. But one fact had changed since the summer: two agents—Stoddart and Sanders of the West India and Pacific line—now fell completely outside these arrangements and employed only black workers. Tempted by stronger managerial control, lower wages, and fewer work rules, Stoddart and Sanders offered blacks a refuge in an increasingly hostile economic world. For their part, unemployed blacks and those union men bitter at the screwmen's racial quota system welcomed these employers' offer. But the new relationship being forged hardly represented employer paternalism and benevolence, on the one hand, or black acquiescence and passivity on the other. The bottom line for Stoddart and Sanders was economic; both kept their wage rates significantly below those of other agents and stevedores. Black workers' expressions of gratitude toward these companies during the fall (and later spring) crisis implied neither a wholesale adoption of Booker T. Washington's philosophy nor an abandonment of the principles of unionism. When Stoddart and Sanders refused to follow the port's other employers' example in restoring the wage cut in late December, the black longshoremen's union forbade its members still employed to work below the old association rate. And when black union longshoremen struck on December 27, Stoddart and Sanders quickly, and without interruption, filled their places temporarily with black non-union men.[44]

The end-of-the-year pact represented more of a truce than a solution to long-standing problems on the docks. It resolved neither the fundamental differences between black and white workers nor those between employers and unions. Many agents remained hostile to the white screwmen's union; labor solidarity across racial lines was all but dead on the waterfront; white screwmen still refused to share work equally with blacks; and the black screwmen's resentment of racial restrictions remained strong. Moreover, the December agreement contained the seeds of its own destruction, for it left intact—and indeed, legitimated—a racially split labor market on the docks. In the highly competitive world of transatlantic shipping, New Orleans employers constrained by union work rules and wage rates felt compelled to adopt measures enabling them to match the advantages of the all-black, low-wage waterfront enclave. In such a highly unstable and volatile environment, it did not take long for race and labor relations to deteriorate dramatically.

II

"This is an opportune moment to draw the attention of our great shipowners in England carrying on a large and regular trade with New Orleans," a British Consulate official remarked in a 1895 report, "to the fact that the fight against the exorbitant and ruinous charges of the screwmen and longshoremen must be met by concerted action on their part." By the start of the new year, shipping agents in New Orleans did not need to be convinced that the time for action was ripe. Their counterparts in Great Britain had already demonstrated that riverside and dock unions could be challenged successfully. Not only had the union upsurge on British docks, beginning with the London general waterside strike of 1889, been contained, but the Shipping Board and other employer associations had delivered a crippling blow to the young waterfront labor movement.[45] Much closer to home, the events of the fall of 1894 demonstrated clearly to the New

Orleans agents of British shipping lines that the screwmen's control of the waterfront could be broken at last. They seized the initiative early in the new year.

The low-wage enclave of black labor proved too attractive a model for employers to resist. In February 1895, the Harrison Steamship Line of Liverpool ordered its agent, Alfred LeBlanc, to follow the example of competitors Stoddart and Sanders and cut the wage rates of the screwmen and longshoremen. Discharging his all-white labor force, LeBlanc contracted with a new black stevedore, George Geddes, and began loading his ships under heavy police protection with some 300 non-union black workers at 40 cents an hour.[46] In March, after experiencing lengthy delays in obtaining necessary labor, the Elder-Demster line also abandoned its long-standing preference for white workers. Rejecting demands by the newly organized Jefferson Association, composed of white unemployed Gretna men, to hire only local white Gretna residents, Elder-Demster's stevedores imported non-union black workers by tugboat. An attack on these new black workers by whites led the Elder-Demster line to obtain an injunction restraining white longshoremen from interfering with their employees. Each time a shipping firm switched to lower paid, all-black labor, stevedores and agents relied heavily on their allies in the judiciary. "In every instance the United States Court has been appealed to for protection by the agents of our regular liners," the British consular official noted approvingly, "and the loading continued in the presence of United States marshals." Backed by court injunctions, federal marshals, and occasionally squads of police, the agents and stevedores successfully rolled back waterfront wages.[47]

But New Orleans' men of commerce denied that their actions were motivated by "a question of wages or compensation"; instead, they asserted that managerial rights lay at the heart of the matter. In a statement adopted in March by representatives of fifteen businessmen's associations, many of which were not directly involved in river transportation, it was declared that the central issue was "simply and solely one of whether the merchants of New Orleans shall conduct their own business in their own way, or whether they shall be dictated to by a handful of employees." The only way to protect the commerce of the city, it was insisted, was to permit every man who wanted to perform "honest labor" to do so,

> regardless of race, color or previous condition: no man shall be interfered with in the pursuance of his daily avocation, and we insist on the right of every employer to hire whom he may choose, to have his work performed in such a manner as he may direct. We do not deny the right of working men to combine together for mutual protection, or to stop work when they choose, but we deny their right to prevent others from working.[48]

Arguing that all labor should be "free and untrammeled" and that employers should retain non-union stevedores and foremen to direct the loading on their ships and ensure that laborers were performing a "commensurate amount of work," agents savored the opportunity to place the cotton screwmen at last "in the position of all other labor along the levee front," abolishing "anything like limitations" on the number of bales stowed per day. Given the high unemployment levels generated by the current depression, they believed that market forces would accomplish this task. "So many colored men were being employed and so many others were being brought in to the front," agent Ross told Governor Foster, that "the natural result will be the cutting of the prices of labor, and the questions will then settle themselves without interference."[49]

A managerial triumph on the docks, white longshoremen and screwmen countered, would have devastating consequences for their trades and their lives. Placing the agents' degradation of the screwmen's craft at the center of their analysis, president James Shaw and recording secretary John Davilla of the white SBA offered one interpretation of the recent crisis in a public notice:

> We saw an honorable occupation, which by dint of intelligent exercise had risen above the grade of mere physical force onto the plane of intelligence and skill, about to be dragged back down to the level of pure muscular exertion, where brawn without brains, and muscle without skill, would be all that were required.[50]

Longshoremen, with fewer skills to protect, emphasized less the preservation of their "honorable occupation" than the impact of job competition between rural and resident workers. Whites were "opposed to the employment of tramp labor secured from the plantations of other states," explained Henry O. Hassinger, general inspector of the white longshoremen's association and himself a foreman.

> The white men could not work for the prices paid these tramp negroes [*sic*], for the season is a short one, and taking into consideration the many rainy days when it is impossible to work, the men do not make the large amounts they are supposed to earn. Then, too, they have to secure enough money to tide them over a long and dull summer.[51]

The employment of non-union labor meant that a class of unskilled, mostly black men would soon dominate the levee, Hassinger predicted. "They are unreliable and can be safely called a floating population."[52] Shaw and Davilla concurred, further warning that "it is . . . a folly for the merchants of New Orleans not to realize . . . that an irresponsible spendthrift labor population, impotent to perform its task, while temporarily and apparently a blessing, is eventually and really a curse."[53]

Were white screwmen and longshoremen protesting the increase in the number of inexperienced rural workers, black dock workers, or both? If the issue of race figured prominently in their discussions, they framed it in ambivalent ways. In practice, white strikers and rioters exhibited an intense hatred for their black counterparts, destroying their property, attacking and sometimes killing them. But in their public appeals, white union leaders were often unwilling to resort to the racist conventions of the day. According to Shaw and Davilla, it is folly for the public to remain under the impression that the problem on the levee involves social rights or race antipathies. There is no question of social equality nor any of race prejudice involved in the controversy. Any organization of skilled labor, finding themselves dragged down to be eventually classed as unskilled labor, would have made the issue thus thrust upon us.

Walking a very fine line, Shaw and Davilla justified their stance toward black workers not on the basis of their race—that is, not because they were *black* workers—but on the basis of their behavior. Black screwmen, they argued, had

> proved the truth of the assertion that he was not, and has never been worthy of trust. Every agreement we made with him, or compact to which he is a party with us, to adhere to rules which had been adopted, not for our individual, but for the aggregate, good, he violated. We declined and refused to further harbor him among us or to hold any contractual relations with him. He was an enemy to be feared, because he degraded the calling which he had adopted. He was and is the parasite of skilled labor.

Despite these disparaging remarks, white union leaders refused to acknowledge an explicitly *racial* foundation of their criticism. "If his skin had been such as would excite the envy of the fairest Caucasian," Shaw and Davilla said of the black worker,

> and his ancestry such as to fit him for association with the most exclusive circles, he would have received the same treatment at our hands. It is not a question of wealth, nor a question of color, nor a question of social rights. It is a question of preserving an honorable calling against the corruption to inevitably follow from dishonorable methods. We know the master and we know the puppet.[54]

Similarly, longshoreman Hassinger stressed that the current fight was "not a struggle of races, for the resident negroes are equally interested in seeing the work done by local men."[55] However true that latter claim was, white labor's behavior and its failure to appreciate the divisions within black labor's ranks belied its rhetoric.

Blacks could hardly ignore the racial dimension of the crisis as easily as whites. Yet differences of opinion existed as to how black workers should respond to the challenges or opportunities before them. Black Screwmen's Benevolent Association No. 2, the break-away group that sought greater employment for its members, offered one approach. Reiterating their hostility to the white unions, its members declared at a mass meeting that black screwmen and longshoremen

> do not intend to hurt the interests of the port by fooling with white screwmen. You have seen what they have done in the past. They make their application at reduced rates to get the colored screwmen off the levee, and just as soon as they get the colored screwmen and longshoremen off the levee, then they will find that the reduced rate is too low.

Moreover, they made clear their intention to "stand firm to the firms that stood by us in the time of trouble"—those of Ross (of Ross, Howe and Merrow), LeBlanc (Harrison line), and Sanders (Leyland line)—which now provided them with secure employment in the face of white threats.[56] Undoubtedly, it was this group's behavior, inspired by the white screwmen's racially exclusive practices, that most white workers found objectionable.

But since the crisis began the previous year, black workers had not acted as a unified group. In late December, the black longshoremen's association struck when agents Sanders and Stoddart refused to rescind their wage cut (white workers apparently ignored the short-lived and unsuccessful walkout). The following year saw continued tension between the two black screwmen's unions. If the Screwmen's Benevolent Association No. 2 accepted lower wages and undermined standards in exchange for a greater number of jobs and security, black screwmen in Association No. 1 attempted to maintain wages, work rules, and an alliance with whites, however distasteful they found the racial quota system imposed upon them. When the Harrison line reduced its employees' wages in early 1895, Association No. 1 rejected the company's job offer and forbade its members from accepting employment outside the West India and Pacific Steamship Company. Following the wage reduction, only Association No. 2 and black non-union men would work under Sanders, Stoddart, and the Harrison line.[57] The different approaches adopted by the two black screwmen's associations mattered little to whites. White workers' failure to recognize the important divisions in black labor's ranks demonstrated that, their denials notwithstanding, they viewed the crisis primarily through a racial lens.

As they confronted an expanding low-wage black enclave, white workers adopted a two-prong strategy. First, they declared that the widespread wage cuts constituted a lockout, and, accordingly, withdrew their labor from all ships in mid-February. Second, white screwmen offered a comprehensive plan that they hoped might "completely revolutionize the manner of conducting business along the river front." They targeted the contracting stevedores, "purely ornamental and unnecessary individuals," who made enormous profits but performed no useful work. The fee paid to stevedores, they declared, was "money practically thrown away," adding unnecessarily to already high port charges. Refusing to work any longer for middleman, white screwmen announced that they would contract directly with steamship agents. To make their proposal attractive, they appointed a business agent, established an office, and, most important, reduced substantially their rates for stowing cotton. White longshoremen quickly following the screwmen's lead. (Cutting their charges on all articles of freight, they claimed that their rates "could not be met even by the negroes.")[58] In retaliation, black Association No. 2 screwmen lowered their wages even further—to 30 cents a bale on steamships and 35 cents on sailing vessels, five cents below the SBA's new rates. The "war in prices" kept relations between blacks and whites tense. While white screwmen and longshoremen found work on a few vessels, non-union and union blacks employed by stevedores and agents continued to receive most jobs.[59]

Furiously denying the charges of profiteering and angry at white union efforts to bypass them, stevedores precipitated yet another crisis by taking steps to replace permanently white longshoremen and screwmen who refused to work for them. They contracted with Norris Cuney, a black stevedore of Galveston, Texas, to provide them immediately with approximately 65 additional black workers. Since the Galveston shipping season was nearly over, as many as 500 black dock workers were potentially available. Mayor John Fitzpatrick denounced the importation of outside laborers as a breach of good faith that would foment "the ill-feeling and discord" which existed in the community. More important, he refused to provide additional police protection for the imported men. Nonetheless, on March 9, the Galveston crews arrived in the city on the Southern Pacific Railroad. Placed on a barge, they were kept away from local workmen and transferred directly to the ships of two stevedoring firms, A. K. Miller, Meletta and Company and Ross, Howe and Merrow. The arrival of the black Galveston workers, the *Picayune* observed, was "in self enough to increase the already bitter feelings of the whites against the negro [*sic*] laborers."[60]

Importing outside blacks hardly solved the stevedores' problems. No sooner had they arrived than the new men demanded higher wages. Stevedores reluctantly agreed to pay them the white screwmen's old daily rate of $5. In addition, Galveston blacks claimed that New Orleans stevedores had misrepresented the local situation to them. Once aware of the real situation, one black Galveston foreman ordered his men to quit work while he negotiated with white screwman. At a waterfront barroom on Jackson Avenue, white labor leaders James Shaw and John Breen related the history of recent events to the Galveston men, warning them of dire consequences if they continued to work. Convinced that the white men of New Orleans were "even worse than they were thought to be," many of the Galveston blacks accepted the white union's offer of a free return trip to Texas. Those that remained also quit work, adopting a wait-and-see attitude.[61]

Outright force soon replaced coercive persuasion. On the evening of March 9, between 300 and 500 armed white men forced their way into the Morris Public Bathhouse at the head of St. Andrew Street, where the West India and Pacific Steamship Company stored the equipment of its black screwmen. Seizing 45 out of 90 sets of tools, the men threw them into the river. Two days later, on March 11, approximately 150 whites shifted the target of their anger from property to people, attacking black workers on the docks near Breen's saloon and the West India and Pacific Company wharves. In the five-minute assault, whites fired at least twenty-five shots, hit two black men, and chased another group of black workers down the levee.[62]

A more deadly outbreak of violence occurred the following morning, when whites coordinated two armed attacks against blacks working on the levee. The first took place opposite the French Market between St. Anne and Dumaine streets. At 7 o'clock, several hundred whites made their way through a dense fog, taking cover behind Louisville and Nashville Railroad freight cars and piles of tarpaulin-covered cotton bales on the wharf. When a gang of twenty to thirty black workers began removing the covers from the forward hatches on the Harrison line steamer *Engineer*, the crowd of whites rushed the ship. "Bullets sang and whistled round the wharf like hail," as whites fired hundreds of shots at unarmed blacks dashing for cover. Not content with merely scaring off workers, one group of whites angrily boarded the ship and "emptied their pistols and guns at the unfortunate negroes," while another group "pursued with relentless pertinacity" blacks who sought escape on the wharves. Black workers "were given no quarter and were shot down like dogs," the *States* observed, and "[b]lood flowed like water." Another journalist noted that "shots seemed to come from doorways, windows, galleries, and street. Look where they would, the negroes [*sic*] saw pistols." Victims included black workers as well as blacks who happened to be working or passing through the area; by the end of the assault, three blacks had died. The handful of city police guarding the black workers stood by, taking no action.[63]

A second assault took place four miles uptown, where black longshoremen and screwmen worked on the ships of Ross, Howe and Merrow and the Elder-Demster line. At 7:30 a.m., between 200 and 500 men, hiding behind cotton bales and freight cars, "rose up out of the heavy mist like grim death spectres," the *Times-Democrat* reported, and attacked blacks working on the steamships *Merrimac* and *Niagara*. For more than an hour, one reporter observed, the whites "held a bloody carnival on the wharf." After killing one black and wounding another, the mob raced up and down the wharf, "terrorizing everyone and holding absolute sway" until the police drove them back. The two attacks left six dead and many more wounded.[64]

Military intervention followed the riverfront massacre, putting and end to the violence. Vowing to use the state's entire police power to uphold the law, Gov. Murphy Foster on March 13 denounced the riots, barred assemblages near the riverfront, and placed the state militia on alert.[65] The following day, some black workers resumed their labors under police and state military protection. The initial procession of militiamen from the armory to the waterfront assumed theatrical proportions. As the soldiers left the Washington Artillery, they were "met along the line by enthusiastic and admiring crowds." The St. Charles Street route—an upper-class area—took on "almost a Carnival appearance" as "bevies of fair girls . . . applauded them extravagantly." The "Cotton Exchange and other commercial bodies always received them with enthusiastic cheers." Yet as the soldiers moved into the working-class neighborhoods near the docks—"the district of saloons and tenement houses, the dark neighborhoods of alleyways and squalid houses and gutter-reveling children"—the contrast in reception could not have been more extreme:

> This was the land of the [white] screwmen and their sympathizers, of the longshoremen and their affiliates, and the women and children no sooner caught sight of the serried columns of militia than they made up their minds that woe unspeakable had come into their midst. . . .
>
> In the neighborhood of Rousseau and Jackson streets, a ragged, nondescript crowd of people, in which women largely predominated, jeered and hooted the troops

as they marched by. A woman in a greasy, torn wrapper, cried out in a shrill voice: "Shame, shame! Ye're not statisfied wid takin' de bread outen our mouths. Ye want to shoot it out. Oh march away, and shame go wid ye." The men were silent. With set, dogged faces, they looked on and never said a word.

Troops cleared the docks of the crowds that had gathered; mounted police patrolled the wharves; a battalion from the Washington Artillery trained its howitzers on the screwmen's headquarters; and troops guarded black workers. With the riverfront under military control, union and non-union black screwmen and longshoremen gradually returned to work.[66]

Although an armed peace prevailed, the outcome of the "military protectorate" remained uncertain. After all, the militia could not occupy the levee indefinitely, and many businessmen believed that the "bloody business of breaking the law" would resume the moment the troops were withdrawn. While the commercial exchanges initially contributed $6000 for the maintenance of the soldiers, they expected the state government to assume the financial burden of keeping the militia on guard to protect their right to hire whomever they desired at the wages they set, for as long as necessary. Reluctant to draw too heavily upon the state's finances to support New Orleans' commercial elite, Governor Foster did not view military repression as a long-term solution designed to promote peace and prosperity. As the state's leading Democratic politician, he walked a fine line in trying to reconcile the opposing sides. "In the problem submitted for our solution," he explained in an interview with the *Times-Democrat*, "are two elements more difficult to handle than any that have ever tested political wisdom, to wit, the antagonism of race, and the conflicts of labor with the capital. . ...." Claiming that his own power was "purely negative and preventative . . . with no legislative function," Foster declared himself "impotent to impose on any of the parties to the conflict any specific scheme of settlement." That task fell to the representatives of the city's organized commercial bodies and the white levee laborers. The presence of the troops served to preserve peace, to protect commerce, and to "allow the parties immediately involved in the labor difficulties an opportunity to come to some satisfactory adjustment." Given the passage of ample time in which the parties could have negotiated, and given the screwmen's assurances that they had no intention of indulging in additional violence, Foster withdrew most militiamen on March 25, ending their twelve-day occupation. The governor maintained some companies on alert, however, and local police continued to stand guard over the black workers.[67]

The March violence and subsequent military occupation of the waterfront dealt a severe blow to the white screwmen and longshoremen. In the riots' aftermath, white screwmen resolved to go it alone, promising to attend strictly to their own affairs. Some turned to other sources of employment, as they did every summer, journeying to the cod fisheries of Newfoundland or finding work in the lumber business in Scranton or Canada. But the majority who remained in New Orleans faced new challenges. Union leaders ordered their members to keep away from the waterfront, permitting only the union agency, the Excelsior Co-operative Association, to dispatch union men. At the same time, screwmen reiterated their earlier proposal to steamship agents to eliminate the "useless luxury" of the stevedore, and offered to sacrifice their 75-bale a day limit and traditional wage rate in exchange for work. A small number of white union dock workers found employment on the Hammond line ships through their hiring agent, and the screwmen's union sent recording secretary John Davilla on an unsuccessful business trip to Europe to bargain directly with ship owners. But in general, the white screwmen found little work. Most agents and stevedores continued to load their ships with black labor.[68]

White longshoremen were hit even harder. "It is a fact that white laborers have been almost entirely driven from the levee, and negroes [*sic*] employed in their places," the *Picayune* observed in May. In mid-April, a small but growing number of white longshoremen broke from the union and applied to stevedores and agents for employment at 40 cents an hour—10 cents below the union tariff. The union expelled one hundred such "scabs"—including longshore leader H. O. Hassinger, who stated with regret that it "may be a virtual confession of defeat to go back to work at the reduced rates, but what can we do? Starvation faces us." By October, the press noted that white labor presented "a pitiful picture of the suffering which has come to a once prosperous class of workmen through the demand for cheaper labor."[69]

Wracked by internal dissent, white screwmen admitted defeat. Union members held their leaders responsible for the Association's hard-line stance against working for stevedores. In late October, they disbanded their powerful executive committee of twenty-one—initially formed in 1882 and composed of the union's top five officers, five delegates to the now-dissolved Cotton Men's Executive Council, and eleven other members of the Association. Two weeks later, the SBA rescinded its order barring members from working for anyone except the Excelsior Co-operative Association and announced that any member could work for any stevedore. This action, the *Picayune* observed "amounts to a complete abandonment of the contest on the part of the Screwmen's Association, and is the end of the long labor controversy over the loading of ships along the levee."[70]

If everyone recognized that the waterfront crisis of 1894-95 had brought to an end almost a decade and a half of union power in New Orleans, there was no consensus on the deeper meaning of the riots. All observers had witnessed the disintegration of the interracial alliance, increased white hostility toward blacks, and employer efforts to reduce wages and eliminate work rules. But opinion divided on the relative importance of racial versus class issues. Throughout the crisis, white screwmen denied an explicitly racial foundation to their attacks against blacks. Instead, they framed the matter around standards and prior pacts, holding blacks responsible for violating traditional rules (concerning wages, the bale restriction, and the quota system) and degrading a once honorable craft. Their employers adopted an economic interpretation that implicitly denied the claim that they were manipulating racial tensions to their own advantage. By enlarging the low-wage enclave of black labor, stevedores and agents were merely responding to market forces, which alone determined wage rates and conditions of employment. Race, color, or previous condition should play no role in the allocation of work, they held.

Many prominent white Southern newspapers supported the contention that the waterfront crisis reflected fundamental economic issues. "The affair will be heralded as a race war [by a certain class of newspapers], and as a proof of the barbarity of the southern whites to the southern blacks," the *Florida Times-Union* contended following the March riots:

> Of course, thoughtful men know it was nothing of the kind. It was not a race war, but a war between strikers and men who had been employed to take their places. If these men had been white, the result would have been the same. Color had nothing to do with it. Just such riots have occurred at Pittsburgh, at Homestead, at Chicago, at Brooklyn, and in almost every northern city. . . .[71]

Less sympathetic to white workers though similarly stressing an economic analysis was the *Baltimore Sun*. The substitution of blacks for whites "may possibly have slightly intensified the bitterness of the strikers," its editors conceded. But

> the trouble was essentially industrial in character and did not originate in race prejudice. Many colored laborers regularly employed in New Orleans and other Southern cities along the water front and in the loading of vessels, and white men work amicably side by side with them all the year round. [The] riot was due to the same general causes that produced the labor disturbances in Chicago last year and in Brooklyn this year.[72]

The problem, according to the *Mobile Daily Register*, was rooted in economics—the "ability and willingness of the negroes [*sic*] to work for lower wages than the white laborers." Even if New Orleans whites killed or drove off the "first batch of cheap [black] laborers . . . there are more to come and come they will until they have absorbed all in New Orleans that is worth having." The law of economy, like the law of gravity, was irresistible, the *Register* lectured. "The side which acts according to that law will win. The opposition must lose." Only a commitment by white dock workers to lower their wages could secure their survival.[73] Of course, in denying the racial origins of the riots, Southern white editors sought to shield their region from national criticism. After all, they implied, however unfortunate and unjust the waterfront riots, New Orleans workers were simply acting out a scenario first scripted in the industrial North.

Blacks, the riots' victims, were the one group of Southerners who failed to dismiss the racial dimensions of the crisis. Deep racial animosity, reflected in the epithets hurled at them by union white workers—whatever the underlying cause—could hardly elude black riverfront union members. White screwmen denounced their Association No. 1 black allies—without cause—as rate busters and rule breakers, and lumped them with the

Association No. 2 men. Drawing their own color line, white longshoremen ostracized and denied work to black longshoremen, for no other reason than to express solidarity with the powerful white screwmen. And for those blacks who had been shot, chased, or beaten by white rioters in October and November 1894 and March 1895, the reality of their attackers' racist anger was particularly poignant.

The national black press concurred. The *Washington Bee* blamed a number of white screwmen for letting their "race prejudice get the better of them" and "inaugurating a crusade against the colored brother" to drive him from the field of employment. The *Southwestern Christian Advocate* concluded that New Orleans' white laboring men discriminated against their fellow laborers for the "sole reason that they are colored."[74] The purpose of the white violence was clear:

> From observation and investigation we are of the opinion that there is a disposition and a determination on the part of the white laborers, skilled or unskilled to supplant Negro labor. . . . There is a combination of forces against the colored man that is very suggestive. Almost every other nationality enters into the alliance which threatens the utter elimination of the Afro American labor as a part of the industrial system of the Crescent City.[75]

The *Indianapolis Freeman* saw the New Orleans experience not merely as an example of Southern racial injustice but as a problem endemic to the nation. "Just now it is the white organized law-breakers and murderers of New Orleans we have to deal with," it noted. But "tomorrow the same condition of bloodshed and outrage is possible, and would be probable, in Indianapolis, Boston and Chicago, at the slightest encroachment of Negro labor on what are held the sacred rights of the province of white labor."[76]

In reality, it is impossible to separate the labor and race issues. Taken alone, neither can account fully for the violent drama of the early depression years. Undoubtedly, by the early 1890s New Orleans white screwmen and longshoremen had fused their long-standing consciousness of the rights of laboring men to a renewed belief in the superior rights of white men. For their part, black workers logically linked notions of laboring men's rights to the right to labor—that is, access to equal employment. The city's biracial union structure once had been predicated upon the assumption that all workers, black and white, gained more from unity than division; white workers eventually rejected that assumption. By the mid-1890s, white longshoremen and screwmen had come to privilege the "sacred rights of the province of white labor" over the rights of all labor. In doing so, they destroyed the entire foundation upon which the waterfront workers' power had rested.

III

From different perspectives, New Orleans businessmen and black residents saw in the Fitzpatrick administration's response to the 1894-95 riots the dangers of Ring rule in New

Orleans. Long hostile to the labor movement and the pro-white labor machine, members of the commercial elite again focused their attention on the political arena, eventually taking control of the city government in 1896. Not surprisingly, their success severely circumscribed the political influence of white dock workers. Defeated by military occupation of the New Orleans waterfront, white levee laborers now suffered the depression's effects with few allies indeed. The change in municipal administrations did with the approval of some black workers, who blamed Mayor John Fitzpatrick for complicity in the racial violence. Attacked at the workplace in the early depression years, blacks now sought political solace in alliance with elite whites. But while they welcomed the elite's victory, they quickly learned that black support paid no political dividends in an age of white supremacy. By the end of the century, the position of blacks had deteriorated to a new low. Sharply at odds, black and white workers remained powerless to meet the economic and political challenges that confronted them.

While New Orleans's commercial elite often had denounced machine-controlled municipal politics, the Fitzpatrick administration's handling of both the 1892 general strike and the riverfront violence of 1894-95 gave it new cause for complaint. In each case, employers had turned to the state government and the courts for assistance when local officials failed to act. Following the screwmen's raid in March 1895, representatives of the city's commercial exchanges denounced what they saw as the white screwmen's "tyranny" and censured Fitzpatrick for failing to protect their property. Addressing fellow businessmen, reformer John M. Parker condemned Fitzpatrick's record on labor affairs. When the police proved "unable to prevent the lawlessness which then prevailed" during a streetcarmen's strike that preceded the 1892 general strike, the mayor had done "all he could to demoralize the community." In 1895, Parker held Fitzpatrick responsible for the riots, arguing that he had "encouraged the strikers to every act of violence by his apparent lack of sympathy with the class of men, employers and employees, who were engaged in the controversy with the screwmen." Shipping agent H. Meletta also condemned the "futile efforts of the police to curb the fury of the mobs, and the seeming disposition of Mayor Fitzpatrick to remain in an apathetic state while all this was going on." The only way Parker argued, "to stop this business"—that is, the Ring's tolerance of labor's lawlessness—"was to go to the fountain head, which was in the city hall, and wipe that out of power."[77]

The commercial elite had not been politically inactive during the first half of the 1890s. In 1890, urban elite opponents of Louisiana's powerful Lottery formed an Anti-Lottery League, temporarily allying with rural Populists and, in one of the state's most bitter elections in years, defeated the multi-million dollar business at the polls in 1892. Critics of the Ring carried out thorough investigations of municipal corruption during Fitzpatrick's terms as mayor and pressed for his impeachment. When the Fitzpatrick administration awarded a franchise to the Illinois Central Railroad, permitting it to lay tracks through the upper-class Garden District, residents of that neighborhood protested by forming an uptown Citizens' Protective Association in May 1894. Successful in their efforts to stop the tracks, many of the Association's members went on to form a larger and more powerful Citizens' League in January 1896.[78]

The Citizens' League represented only the latest incarnation of the commercial elite's ongoing reform efforts. Like its predecessor, the Young Men's Democratic Association, it developed a well-organized and disciplined structure. Ostensibly non-partisan, the League denounced the "official venality and incapacity" which "have fretted public endurance almost to the point of revolution." Its platform, resembling earlier reform documents, called for a reduction in the size of the city council, clean voter registration laws, a secret ballot, efficient administration of municipal affairs, an enlargement of the police force, and the elimination of "political loafers" from the city payrolls. Its mayoral candidate, Walter Flower, was a wealthy lawyer, cotton merchant, and former president of the Cotton Exchange. For the business elite, the campaign assumed a crusade-like quality. For black Republican leaders who endorsed the League, the campaign signaled their resentment of Fitzpatrick's support of white dock workers the previous year. Copying the tactics of its 1888 predecessor, the League dispatched some 1500 armed citizens to guard polling places and to protect voters and their ballots. Their efforts proved successful. The April 1896 municipal elections swept the League into power, delivering a decisive, if not mortal, blow to the Democratic machine.[79]

The Citizens' League worked quickly to implement structural reforms that would consolidate its hold over municipal affairs. Securing a new city charter from the state legislature, the Flower administration reorganized the municipal government to reduce the influence of the regular Democrats and enhance the reformers' position. The new charter attacked sources of Ring strength by drastically reducing the size of the city council (whose members, elected by ward, tended to be dependent on the Ring), eliminating elective administrative offices within the executive branch, and granting board appointive powers over city departments to the mayor. Finally, it created a board of civil service commissioners, appointed by the mayor, with overlapping terms to prevent political manipulation. However, while some of the changes enhanced business power in the long run, these reformers failed to solidify their newly won power. In 1897, defeated machine politicians reconstituted themselves as the Choctaw Club, rebuilt their ward organizations, endorsed state Democratic efforts to disfranchise black voters, and accepted state patronage from Democratic Governor Foster. In 1900, they staged a municipal comeback, putting their mayoral candidate, businessman Paul Capdevielle, in office. With the assistance of state officials, Ring politicians softened civil-service regulations that restricted their patronage powers.[80]

Black voters, who backed the Citizens' League against the Ring, once more learned that elite reformers could be as hostile toward black interests as machine officials were.[81] While their political experiences in the 1880s had driven that point home earlier, the consequences proved far more severe in the 1890s. In the aftermath of the 1896 statewide election, in which regular Democrats violently crushed the rural Populist insurgency, Governor Foster proposed to disfranchise the poor and uneducated of both races. By the end of the century, Louisiana's Democratic leaders had largely accomplished that task, ending an important source of potential political revolt. The elite Citizens' League, ignoring its black supporters, joined machine Democrats in endorsing these moves. (The "celerity with which the upper-class elements of that defunct coalition turned on their erstwhile allies and voted to disfranchise them," historian J. Morgan Kousser notes, "underlines the complete opportunism with which they solicited Populist and Republican votes. . . . [T]he New Orleans businessmen-reformers' claim to favor 'honest elections' " was nothing more than "pure cant.") The consequences for blacks—and poor whites— were severe. In 1896, the state legislature "reformed" the election laws by barring officials from helping illiterate voters, requiring voters to re-register after January 1, 1897, and empowering registrars and representatives of political parties to purge the voting lists. According to Kousser, the registration act reduced the white electorate by more than one-half and the black electorate by 90 percent. The subsequent 1898 Constitutional Convention further restricted political participation, requiring eligible voters to demonstrate literacy in their native tongue or to own property worth at least $300, and after 1900 to pay a poll tax. Although few Louisiana blacks could meet these stringent and discriminatory requirements, whites could take advantage of important loopholes. A grandfather clause permitted poor whites whose relatives had voted before 1867, when a constitution enfranchising blacks had been adopted, to register within four months of the 1898 convention's ending.[82]

Disfranchisement was but one, albeit very important, manifestation of blacks' deteriorating status in both New Orleans and Louisiana at the end of the nineteenth century. If the new constitution removed most black voters from the registration roles, it hardly removed the issue of race from the political agenda. In June 1900 the New Orleans City Council rejected efforts to revive the "star car" system of segregated streetcar seating. But only two years later, the white Louisiana state legislature overrode local officials, voting to require that streetcar companies either set aside separate cars or install screens to cordon off black riders from whites.[83] Politics affected blacks in other ways as well. Despite disfranchisement, the *Southwestern Christian Advocate* observed in October 1899, "there are few speeches being made during the present [city] campaign in which some one is not crying out to beware of the Negro." Choctaw Club Democrats promised, if elected, to employ only local white labor on municipal public work projects. While "reform" mayor Flower advocated "home labor without regard to color," his administration's record on black employment inspired little confidence. The "great city of New Orleans gives nothing, absolute nothing [to the black community] except a very few Negro policemen," complained the black press.[84] This effort to

> shut the Negro out, even from the most ordinary labor, seems to indicate a result, not to say one of the purposes of disfranchisement. He has no redress, his ballot is not feared. Disregard him if you wish, starve him, or strike him down, he is too weak to defend himself either by force or with the ballot.[85]

Over the two decades after Reconstruction's demise, blacks had voted regularly in municipal elections, a fact that Ring politicians and reformers alike had to take into electoral consideration. By the end of the century, disfranchisement had eliminated the need to make even a gesture toward accommodating black voters.

Another index of New Orleans blacks' deteriorating position was the increase in racially motivated violence. "There are few places in this country where the life of a Negro is held in less [sic] contempt than here," the *Southwestern Christian Advocate* concluded in July 1895, months after the waterfront riots. "In most of the instances the murders have been brutal and cold-blooded, the victims going to the death only because they were Negroes. . . . [T]he Negro of New Orleans has surely fallen upon evil times."[86] Racial violence, not merely a product of economic hardship and fierce competition for employment, survived the depression's end. In the first year of the new century, as historian Joel Williamson has written, white mobs in New Orleans unleashed "one of the most serious outbreaks of racial violence since Reconstruction." The focus of the upheaval was Robert Charles. Born and raised in rural Mississippi, Charles was one of thousands of rural, unskilled blacks to migrate to New Orleans during the 1890s and was a supporter of black nationalist Bishop Henry Turner. When white policemen harassed him one evening in late July 1900, he shot one of his assailants before escaping. For several days, Charles eluded vast numbers of police and white vigilantes. Once cornered, he remained defiant, fatally shooting seven whites who were firing at him, before being shot and killed himself. Seizing the opportunity this "outrage" presented white mobs terrorized black neighborhoods, killing at least a dozen people.[87]

There was nothing new about racial or ethnic violence in New Orleans; whites had targeted blacks regularly during Reconstruction and the depression years in the 1870s and 1890s, and an elite-led mob had lynched several Italians in 1891. Given its severity, what did this particular explosion of white violence mean for New Orleans? William Ivy Hair, in his outstanding book on the episode, concludes that "white reaction to Charles vividly illustrated the hardening of racial attitudes which occurred around that time." Dale Somers, writing in the early 1970s, contended similarly that, by the end of the century, "blacks in the city knew Jim Crow and racial intimidation as intimately as blacks in the countryside." The Charles riot "established the pattern for Negro-white relations for the next half century."[88]

Undoubtedly, the Charles riot served as an important symbol of the changes under way in the Crescent City's racial codes and sensibilities. Racial hatred, discrimination, segregation, disfranchisement, and violence all worked to secure black subordination in the new racial order. But despite the rise of a virulent white supremacy and a general consolidation of a segregationist order across the South, the dynamics of race in New Orleans reserved something of the complexity that had marked the earlier era of the 1880s. Once again, that complexity was best reflected in the attitudes and behavior of the city's labor movement.

While the labor movement was by no means free from anti-black hostility during the 1880s and early 1890s, its racial codes revealed a remarkable flexibility. Often resistant to employers' efforts to separate black and white workers, the Cotton Men's Executive Council, the Central Trades and Labor Assembly, and the Workingmen's Amalgamated Council provided structured forums for mediating trade and racial issues. The interracial cooperation that marked the 1892 general strike, however, had been strained by the strike's defeat, and had vanished by the onset of the economic depression. Heightened white supremacy in politics and the rapid growth of white craft unions at the end of the century codified the change. Yet even in the age of Jim Crow, the parameters of action were not completely rigid. Different groups of workers drew different lessons from the economic crisis and the racial tensions that flourished in its wake.

IV

The great depression severely weakened, but did not destroy, the city's labor movement. "It is awful to think that in New Orleans, which once was one of the best organized labor cities, should now have but three live unions," AFL president Samuel Gompers wrote to organizer James Leonard in 1899. While Gompers underestimated the number of functioning unions, his general assessment of the labor movement's decline was accurate. In its review of the 1897 commercial year, the *Picayune* observed that ever since the waterfront riots the labor movement had been in "a sadly demoralized condition as far as the wages of the laborer was concerned, as well as the demand for their services." The business depression, low cotton prices, and a relatively small harvest due to a severe drought, had produced a great many more applicants for work than there was work to do." As a result, even the "most industrious and careful man virtually lived from hand to mouth." Lower wages, irregular work, and a flooded labor market often forced dock workers—whose "savings and earning proved inadequate"—to seek employment in other lines of work.[89]

The labor movement limped through the depression years. A short-lived United Labor Council succeeded the defunct Workingmen's Amalgamated Council and advocated "arbitration in all differences which may arise between employers and employees. . . . [S]trikes should only be resorted to after all other means of mutually satisfactory settlement have failed." The Council's Directory and Index of Unions in 1895 listed 54 locals affiliated either with the American Federation of Labor or the Knights of Labor Directory of the *Southern Economist and Trade Unionist*, a new weekly labor journal, listed 56 locals. In its first editorial, the journal predicted optimistically that in the near future, "trade unionism is certain to be bound forward with tremendous strides, its future was never brighter than it is to-day, and it is our heart's desire to place this, our native city, not only in line with sister cities . . . but to make it in due time the brightest jewel in the glorious diadem of the American Federation of Labor." While excessive in its rhetoric, the *Southern Economist* was not far off the mark. As the depression gave way to renewed commercial prosperity in the late 1890s, the national labor movement, under the AFL's banner, expanded tremendously. Between 1897 and 1904, the AFL grew by over 360 percent, adding over one and a half million new members to its ranks. While much of that growth occurred outside the South, union membership in New Orleans followed the national pattern, as city workers rebuilt and extended the organizational structure of the pre-depression era. By 1903 the *Union Advocate*, a local labor paper, could boast that "there has sprung into existence so many new unions with such an overpowering membership . . . as to place New Orleans in the very front ranks of the cities where organized labor is in the majority."[90]

Union organizing in the South, national AFL leaders believed, offered unique difficulties. Slavery, the " 'peculiar institution' which, until the commencement of the present generation, dominated the social and industrial life of the Southern States," the AFL's official journal, the *American Federationist*, argued, "has hitherto prevented any great expansion of the voluntary organization of labor, and has thereby imposed upon the American Federation of Labor today an immense and most difficult task, a task unparalleled in the history of the world." To take on this "herculean yet delicate mission," the AFL modestly appointed three general organizers—all "well acquainted with Southern conditions." William H. Winn, of the International Typographical Union and a general organizer; Prince W. Greene, president of the National Textile Workers' Union; and L. F. McGruder of the Iron Molders, journeyed across the South preaching their gospel of unionism, organizing new locals, and breathing new life into old ones. "Thus, step by step," one official explained, "do we plant outposts in the enemy's country."[91]

Organizer Winn found more friends than enemies in New Orleans, making his task far less difficult than anticipated. Throughout the summer and fall of 1899, Winn and AFL organizer James Leonard, one of the leaders of the 1892 general strike and subsequent member of the state's labor arbitration board, organized locals of boiler makers, carriage makers, broom makers, tobacco workers, freight handlers, and other workers. In June 1899, they announced plans to form a new Central Trades and Labor Council.[92] In the wake of the 1890s depression, labor's accumulated defeats, and the sharp rise in racial tension, the new federation heralded a spirit of harmony and conciliation between labor and capital. Addressing nearly thirty-five member unions in August 1899, Leonard declared that it was "time to do away with old methods which engendered violence, strife, dissatisfaction, bitterness and poverty, and which clog the wheels of industry and commerce." He called for the

> establishment of the reign of cooperation and good will and amicable discussion between labor and capital. . . . We will not resort to strikes or to any such violent measures. We will not countenance going into sympathetic strikes, but will invoke calm discussion with employers.

The Central Trades and Labor Council, which went into permanent organization on September 10, 1899, differed from the Central Trades and Labor Assembly of the 1880s, the Workingmen's Amalgamated Council of 1892, and a short-lived Union Labor Council of the mid-1890s in another crucial respect. In an era of growing racial hostility, the new Council admitted into membership only white AFL-affiliated unions. Racial segregation, which increasingly permeated the city's political and social life, finally had infected its principal labor body.[93]

For James Leonard and the white craft unionists in the Central Trades and Labor Council, the crisis of the 1890s demonstrated that labor's success required abandoning interracial cooperation and adopting a white prosegregationist stance. Indeed, it appears that Leonard's earlier, outspoken defense of a somewhat militant interracial alliance did little to win him support. For example, although he was president of the Workingmen's Amalgamated Council and a member of the Committee of Five that directed the 1892 general strike, a significant faction within his own Typographical Union Local 17 adopted a craft-first stance and strongly opposed any sympathetic action in that strike. Elected president of the local in December 1892, Leonard encountered growing criticism. In March 1893, union members refused to send him as a delegate to the International's convention, and when he resigned the presidency in May, the Typographical Union withdrew from the Amalgamated Council.[94]

A year and a half later, Leonard turned his energies toward the electoral sphere, spearheading an Independent Workingmen's Political Club. The Club denounced monopolies and trusts and called on working people to "purify the political atmosphere by electing good men to office" and "to place principle above party, patriotism above politics." An interracial movement, the Independent Workingmen offered an alternative to the increasing racism of white dock workers. While white screwmen and longshoremen were renouncing all interracial collaboration, some 25 blacks—including waterfront labor leaders Alexander Paul and Lafayette Tharpe—joined 225 whites at the Club's organizational meeting in September 1894. The black and white delegates nominated Leonard as their congressional candidate. Local machine politicians however, denied the Workingmen physical representation at the polls, and Leonard lost overwhelmingly to the Democratic party candidate. After their defeat, white Independent Workingmen placed some of the blame on the "race question," which they believed had divided the white electorate unnecessarily; they seriously suggested that the elimination of black voters would enable the working class to further its—and blacks'—aims. The next year, an all-white Workingmen's Democratic Club of the Eleventh Ward advocated the employment of white labor in all city and state contracts. "Good government and white supremacy," the *Picayune* observed, "are the summing up of their tenets." As Southern white workers exhibited a more strident racism, Leonard followed the path parallel to one trod by many white Populists during the same years, abandoning an earlier interracialism for a whites-only craft unionism.[95]

This was consistent with the AFL's official position toward black workers at the turn of the century. Federation leaders were, of course, aware of the dangers that a large, unorganized pool of black workers posed to their movement. The "wage workers ought to bear in mind that unless they organize the colored men, they will of necessity compete with the workmen and be antagonistic to them and their interests," Samuel Gompers wrote to John Callahan, a waterfront union leader and New Orleans AFL organizer in 1892. "The employers will certainly take advantage of this condition and do all they can to even stimulate the race prejudice."[96] At the same time, the AFL championed the craft union, whose exclusive structure aimed at restricting membership in the trade, as labor's most effective organizational building block. Adherence to a belief in craft union autonomy limited the AFL's ability to interfere in its affiliates' affairs. Over the course of the 1890s, earlier proclamations on the need to organize workers regardless of their race, creed, or sex, and the Federation's denial of membership to any international union which constitutionally excluded black workers from its ranks, had given way to a policy of tolerating all white unions. Accepting the intractability of white workers' racism, the organizers of the AFL's Southern drive did little to challenge the hardening racial lines. Discrimination and racism, one Northern writer observed in 1898, had "entered into the very soul of the workday world, and infected even those workmen who are not organized . . . [W]herever the union develops effective strength the black workmen must put down the trowel and take up the tray."[97]

New Orleans black workers, however, neither took up the tray nor abandoned their unions when interracial cooperation fell victim to the white racism of the depression years. Nor did many heed the advice of religious leaders who counseled the pro-business perspective advocated by Booker T. Washington. In the aftermath of the Charles riot, for example, the *Southwestern Christian Advocate* reiterated its belief that the black worker's "only hope is to keep close to the best white citizens of the city. He has learned that these recognize his worth as a laborer and a well behaved citizen and will stand by him in the time of need."[98] Yet there is no evidence that black riverfront workers shifted their allegiance from their unions to employers in appreciation of the commercial elite's defense of its right to employ whomever it wished. Black waterfront unions survived the depression and attacks by whites, although they were in no position to challenge managerial authority. "[N]otwithstanding the many obstacles encountered," secretary James Porter reported at his union's anniversary celebration at Union Chapel in 1899, the longshoremen were in "splendid financial shape." Of the "many strong Negro trade unions in Louisiana." W. E. B. DuBois' 1902 study *The Negro Artisan* singled out black longshoremen, screwmen, cotton yardmen, teamsters and loaders, round freight teamsters, and Excelsior Freight Handlers. Paralleling the tremendous national growth of the AFL, black membership in New Orleans unions grew substantially after 1899. The DuBois study estimated that New Orleans had some 4000 black trade unionists in 1902; following a year of substantial growth, the Central Labor Union boasted that between 10,000 and 12,000 black members in some twenty unions had marched in its 1903 Labor Day parade.

The *United Mine Workers' Journal* put the city's membership in some nineteen black union at 11,000 in 1904.[99]

Working tirelessly, James Porter deserved much credit for the strength of New Orleans' black unions. As secretary of the black longshoremen's association, he attended the annual conventions of the International Longshoremen's Association (ILA), with which his union had affiliated. Delegates to the International's 1901 meeting in Toledo, Ohio, elected Porter to the post of ninth vice president. Upon his return to New Orleans, he began an ambitious unionization drive "with the purpose in view of bringing about a complete organization of all Water Front Workers of New Orleans and vicinity." Between the 1901 and 1902 conventions, Porter sent nine charter applications to the ILA and established several federal labor unions. Such "wonderful progress" had been made in the Crescent City that the ILA's eleventh annual convention acknowledged that it was "every much indebted" to Porter for the successes in that city.[100]

Porter and other black riverfront workers remained committed not only to their unions but to the national labor movement as well. Many black dock unions affiliated with the newly formed ILA early in the new century, often before their white counterparts.[101] Porter's commitment to the AFL also put him at odds with organizer James Leonard, a man with whom Porter had served on the Committee of Five that directed the 1892 general strike. When Leonard and white craft unionists barred blacks from the new Central Trades and Labor Council (CTLC), Porter spearheaded a new solution to the problems created by racial exclusion in the labor movement. If white locals refused to admit blacks into city-wide organizations composed of AFL-affiliated unions, then black AFL unions would form their own city-wide organizations. Shortly after the creation of the white CTLC in 1899, New Orleans black unionists pressed the AFL for official recognition of an all-black Central Labor Union.[102]

Porter's plan to confederate black unions encountered strong objections from white labor leaders. "The feeling here against a project of this kind is so great that I am afraid it would cause a great deal of trouble at this particular time," James Leonard wrote to Gompers.

> It is a very delicate question to handle, considering the prejudice that exists here against the negro. I thought at one time it could be accomplished, but I am very much afraid that the chances are growing worse every day. . . . I am in hopes that some kind of agreement may be reached whereby both races will act harmoniously together, but as I said before the chances are very poor at present.[103]

That was precisely the problem. If white workers were unwilling to work harmoniously with blacks, then blacks would have to go it alone. Writing to Gompers in early summer of 1900, Porter complained:

> My members are very impatient and I cannot understand the remark you made in your letter . . . to me that there is no use kicking against the pricks, and we cannot

overcome prejudice in a day. I did not understand that there is prejudice where the wages and interest are the same, and can only be upheld by concert[ed] action.[104]

The American Federation of Labor's own rules presented obstacles to Porter's demand for a dual central body. While the Central Trades and Labor Council was free to exclude blacks, the national Federation had no power to recognize an alternative city central. At the AFL's 1900 convention, however, Gompers successfully advocated that the Federation issue certificates of affiliation to central bodies composed solely of black unions. New Orleans' black Central Labor Union finally received an official AFL charter in June 1901.[105]

By themselves, black unions could do little to secure employment for black workers in clerical jobs or in the new, mechanized trades, but they did provide substantial protection to members in at least two important industries—the building trades and waterfront commerce. The 1902 DuBois study suggested that New Orleans black artisans, many of whom were property holders, had grown in number since the Civil War; they were "either gaining or at least not losing" ground. One respondent noted that New Orleans black artisans who "receive recognition in their respective trades, are widely employed and paid remunerative wages."[106] A number of studies in the first decade of the twentieth century found that where blacks and whites performed the same work, they received the same wages. While the unions could claim some credit, they were only partially responsible for these blacks' success. In its 1911 survey of American cities, the British Board of Trade suggested that the types of industries found in New Orleans also contributed. "It is probable that in New Orleans there is a larger number of white and negro [*sic*] people in very much the same economic position than in any other American city, or anywhere else in the world," the British investigators noted, because New Orleans' industries "are of a kind which employ many unskilled or semi-skilled labour, with the result that both white men and negroes [*sic*] are found doing the same kind of work and earning the same rates of pay."[107]

Yet such interracial tolerance—if it can be called that—in unskilled and semi-skilled work had clear limits. "It must not be supposed," the Board of Trade report concluded,

> that social equality of the two races is recognized, even amongst the unskilled labouring population, for on the whole the "colour line" is drawn with all the strictness common to the Southern States. The two races will work side by side, but they will not play together, go to the same schools, or sit together in tramway cars.[108]

Disfranchisement, legalized segregation, and increased racial violence were certainly the hallmarks of the new racial order; in crucial ways, racism infused and shaped the twentieth-century labor movement. Most whites repudiated "social equality," adhered to a strict color line, and refused to identify with blacks in any way (especially outside of the workplace). Their actions weakened the overall strength of the working class in the post-depression era.

While the white craft unions of the Central Trades and Labor Council institutionalized segregation and white supremacy within the local labor movement, a very different dynamic operated on the riverfront. The important challenge to Jim Crow in the city came from the ranks of organized dock workers. Repudiating the violence of 1894-95, they built an interracial labor movement that stood alone as an example of black and white solidarity. One black longshoremen reported to W. E. B. DuBois in 1902 that "in New Orleans, we have been the means of unity of action among the longshoremen of that port, both in regards to work, wages, and meeting" together. The secretary of the black Central Labor Union argued similarly that "by amalgamation of organization and through international connections we expect to have the color line in work removed." Although the color line would remain a permanent fixture on the docks, there was indeed cause for optimism. In 1908, a commission investigating labor conflicts and port charges concluded that from the perspective of waterfront employers, "one of the greatest drawbacks to New Orleans is the working of the white and negro [*sic*] races on terms of equality."[109] Clearly, the dock workers by 1908 had traveled a tremendous distance since the crisis of the mid-1890s.

Two incidents that preceded the formation of the new biracial alliance—the 1900 Charles riot and the 1901 longshoremen's and trimmers' strike—cast some light on the process of reconstitution. In the first, white riverfront workers apparently took little part in the widespread violence aimed at blacks in July 1900, in sharp contrast to their role in the 1894-95 riots. The *Times-Democrat* reported only one incident implicating riverfront workers in anti-black violence. On July 27, a group of whites, whom the paper presumed to be longshoremen or screwmen, pursued and wounded a black man along the levee in the French Quarter; shortly thereafter, a group of Italians, who had no affiliation to the dock unions, killed the victim. Other "hoodlums"—not dock workers—also seriously wounded two black riverfront workers on the levee near Jackson Avenue. During the height of the crisis, two white longshore labor leaders accompanied the Commissioner of Police and Public Buildings on a tour of the riverfront, where they found the men "busy and thinking little of mingling with the mobs"; according to the *Picayune*, dock union leaders assured the mayor that no union had participated in the ongoing "lawlessness."[110]

White longshoremen, demonstrating opposition to the mob violence, also quit work. At least half of all black dock workers remained at home during the worst rioting; those who went to work remained apprehensive, and eventually stopped work early. Although the white longshoremen "do not feel kindly towards the negroes [*sic*]," reported the *Picayune*,

> but for their own self-respect they assured the negroes [*sic*] working near them that they should not be molested. There has always been more or less feeling toward the negro [*sic*] on labor questions which have arisen between them, but the dominant spirits among the white longshoremen were busy yesterday impressing them with the fact that it would greatly damage their cause if they allowed the labor questions to

influence them into any action with the disorderly hoodlum element making itself so obnoxious to all the good people by its outrageously wanton conduct.[111]

Based as it was on pragmatic, strategic reasoning, such behavior did not signify a renewed commitment to interracial collaboration or solidarity. It was, however, a first step, and perhaps laid some groundwork for subsequent negotiations. At the very least, it indicated that all white workers did not fully embrace the ethos of the new, increasingly hostile racial order.

The second step in the reconstruction of the waterfront alliance took place a little more than a year later. An improved economic climate after the turn of the century provided the context for this experiment in renewed cooperation.[112] In September 1901, white longshoremen struck to increase the wages of the approximately 250 grain trimmers in their union and to reestablish the position of the union foreman. The fact that trimmers' work was "very trying on the health of the men," the union explained, ought to be a factor in wage determinations. Moreover, trimmers

> frequently had to wait for five hours in idleness before getting a couple hours of work. At times, the men had to go from one point to another to load one vessel, and the time lost in going and coming was quite an item, involving considerable cost. Often the trimmers would start on a vessel at Chalmette, continue on it as Stuyvesant Docks and finish at Southport. [Thus] a week would be consumed in getting out three days' work. For the times lost, there was no compensation.[113]

The white longshoremen announced that they would handle no cargo of any stevedore or shipping agent who had not signed the new contract by September 12. Alfred LeBlanc, the Harrison line's agent, objected most strongly to the union foreman issue, insisting on his right to hire whomever he wanted, union or non-union. Leyland line agent Sanders protested the wage question, arguing that his firm, with a regular sailing schedule, could not afford to pay the same rates that ships coming irregularly did. In general, stevedores and agents feared that the trimmers' wage demand would trigger new demands by other longshoremen. Most rejected the union's ultimatum.[114]

Reminiscent of the 1880s, white longshoremen pledged to get "every class of laboring people into the Federation of Labor and [prevent] them from taking the places of the strikers." Establishing a close working relationship with black longshoremen was their first priority. When the black union agreed to participate fully in the strike, a joint committee assumed control over its direction and established its headquarters in the office of the all-black Central Labor Union. On September 12, some 1700 black and white longshoremen and 250 grain trimmers struck all employers who refused to sign the new wage scale. Longshoremen secured the support of other waterfront workers as well. Fearful that employers might utilize black roustabouts to load and unload ships, an interracial committee of longshoremen presented its case to the riverboat hands, who promised not to break the trimmers' strike. Both the black Central Labor Union and the white Central Trades and Labor Council endorsed the strike; president Robert E. Lee of the white CTLC promised the strikers moral and financial support, declaring that all of organized labor "would help to win this battle for the men." Union ship carpenters backed the strikers by withdrawing from the ships of two key companies, the Harrison and Leyland lines. While meeting in separate halls, both black and white screwmen also agreed to perform none of the longshoremen's work. By September 17, all of the port's small firms had signed the new contract.[115]

But the revival of interracial and inter-trade collaboration threatened to reverse the victories won by large employers during the 1890s, and several of the largest steamship companies—the Harrison and Leyland West Indian and Pacific Lines—remained adamant. Agent Sanders resorted to strikebreakers to implement a new, innovative scheme to by-pass the longshore unions. Promising no discrimination against blacks or even union men, Sanders proposed to hire 250 men, and pay them between 30 cents and 40 cents an hour (well below union rates), but to guarantee them $50 a month—in place of the existing system of irregular longshore work. But getting men and getting them to work during a strike, Sanders discovered, were two different matters. Some 150 union strikers were on hand to greet twenty new laborers hired by Sanders, persuading them, as well as forty to fifty Harrison line strikebreakers, to abandon work and join the union. This "intimidation," as Sanders called it, continued unabated.[116]

Unconvinced by the agents' case, machine Mayor Paul Capdevielle refused to involve himself seriously in the matter. Indeed, his sympathies appeared to lay with union workers. From what he had seen and heard, he noted striking laborers "were trying to do just what was right." LeBlanc and Sanders, deserted by fellow employers and unable to hold onto their strikebreakers or secure adequate police protection, surrendered on September 22. The contract, signed before the joint executive committee of the black and white longshoremen, represented a complete union victory.[117]

Between 1000 and 2000 union men resumed work on the docks. "The conditions on the levee are now in the most peaceable condition that they have been for a long time," one labor leader observed.

> White and colored laborers are working in harmony. They realize that opposition to each other destroyed their power at the first big strike previous to the recent . . . trimmers' walkout, and they have recently been combining their efforts. Every important action is indorsed by the coordinated organizations on both sides, and there are plans being formulated for an equitable distribution of the work, so that neither side shall have any complaint.[118]

A collaborative spirit extended even to the ranks of the cotton screwmen. Ever since the winter of 1895, black screwmen had performed most of the work for the Harrison line, monopolizing the work on the forward hatches of its ships. Toward the end of the 1901 strike, Harrison agent LeBlanc attempted to manipulate racial divisions once again by offering work on forward hatches to the white screwmen. Despite deep animosity between the two unions, the white workers rejected the company's offer, declaring that black screwmen were entitled to retain their positions. At a subsequent meeting, white screwmen agreed unanimously that "there would be nothing done that would cause bad feeling between the two races working on the levee." Had there not been "cool judgement," the press noted, "the incident might have opened up an avenue to trouble."[119]

Waterfront unions cemented their informal working alliance with the founding of the Dock and Cotton Council in early October 1901. Eight unions—the black and white cotton screwmen, black and white longshoremen, black teamsters and loaders, the black and white cotton yardmen, and the black coal wheelers—joined the new organization. With the exception of the coal wheelers, all of the Dock and Cotton Council's members had participated in the Cotton Men's Executive Council of the 1880s and early 1890s. As its first president, Dock and Cotton Council delegates elected Judge James Hughes of the white longshoremen; as first vice president, Isom G. Wynn of the black yardmen; and as secretary, veteran black labor leader James Porter. Under the Council's rules, six delegates from each constituent union attended council meetings, and each union had equal vote in all decisions. While white workers always held the Council's presidency, blacks occupied important roles. It was not uncommon, for example, for a black officer to chair a Council meeting in the absence of the white president.[120]

Conditions unique to the world of waterfront labor help to explain the reconstruction of the biracial alliance in the age of Jim Crow.[121] The largely unskilled nature of the work made this recovery of the legacy of interracial collaboration imperative. While, in theory, familiarity with the techniques of loading, unloading, coaling, rolling, or carting cotton or round freight gave experienced workers important advantages over green hands, employers could easily replace these workers in practice. Most individual unions, representing specific groups of workers in a wide array of waterfront occupations, possessed insufficient power to control the labor supply or prevent unilateral employer actions (the white screwmen being an obvious exception). However, alliances among unions and, most important, between black and white unions, could reduce job competition, dramatically increase a union's resources, and tip the scale toward the labor. The experience of the 1880s had illustrated this plainly. Pacts between black and white branches of the yardmen, longshoremen, and to a lesser degree screwmen, had mediated racial tensions; work-sharing agreements and joint rules had reduced the ability of employers to exploit racial tensions. The Cotton Men's Executive Council had institutionalized a solidarity linking all cotton waterfront workers in a powerful circuit. From 1800 to 1887, and to a lesser extent, to 1894, formal and informal alliances among groups of waterfront workers kept wages high and union work rules strong. The collapse of the inter-trade and interracial alliance after 1894 presaged the collapse of union power.

The strength of New Orleans black waterfront unions also appreciably narrowed the options available to white waterfront unions. White screwmen and longshoremen realized that, unlike whites in the skilled crafts, they were powerless to enforce a whites-only policy on their employers. The economic depression and the upheavals of 1894 and 1895 had underscored their vulnerability. Neither black unions nor aggressive employers had any intention of permitting whites to drive black workers from the riverfront. Moreover, from 1896 to 1900, the Flower administration was sympathetic to business interests and would not turn a blind eye to such attempts, as the earlier Fitzpatrick administration had done. Had whites again sought to eliminate black waterfront workers, they would have found the task impossible.

Dock leaders came to appreciate the real difference that the alliance made with regard to conditions and wage rates. As the rise of union power in the 1880s had depended in large part upon inter-trade and interracial alliances, the fall of waterfront union power in the 1890s had resulted from the collapse of those alliances. Shipping agents and contracting stevedores would later look back on the late 1890s as a golden age of high productivity and profits; black and white workers recalled it as a dark age of fierce competition, degraded working conditions, and low wages. In the early twentieth century, union leaders of both races pointed to the riots of 1894-95 as a turning point for the worse for all longshore laborers. The lessons of division were evident enough. With the return of commercial prosperity and the election of a machine mayor more sympathetic to white working-class voters, longshoremen initiated a process that quickly led to the reestablishment of joint work rules, unified wage rates, and interracial and inter-trade collaboration. At the start of the new century, waterfront workers would relearn the lessons of solidarity.

"In its heyday" in the early twentieth century, radical Covington Hall recalled to researcher Abram Harris in 1929, the Dock and Cotton Council was "one of the most powerful and efficient Labor Organizations I have ever known."[122] Its formation in 1901 resurrected biracial and inter-trade alliances in the age of segregation. Under its auspices in the ensuing years, riverfront workers eliminated the dangers of a racially segmented labor market and successfully met many new challenges posed by changing technologies and renewed employer assaults. More than ever, the issue of work rules and job control assumed a central place in the conflicts between workers and their employers. During the first decade of the new century, the docks of New Orleans constituted a battleground not between blacks and whites but between social classes with very different visions of the economic order and the role of unions and workers within it.

Notes for "Turning Points: Biracial Unions in the Age of Segregation, 1893-1901"

[1]*New Orleans Weekly Pelican*, June 8, 1889; *New Orleans Times-Democrat*, June 3, 1889. On Gould's activities in Galveston as president of the Independent Colored Organization in the twentieth century, see speech by R. W. Gould, *Proceedings of the Seventeenth Convention of the International Longshoremen's Association, Galveston, Texas, July 12th to 17th inclusive, 1909* (Detroit, 1909), 105.

[2]C. Vann Woodward, *Origins of the New South, 1877-1913* (1951; reprint ed., Baton Rouge, 1971), 321-49.

[3]*Indianapolis Freeman*, March 23, 1895.

[4]"Longshoremen Draw No Line," *New York Age*, August 14, 1913.

[5]Young Men's Business League, *New Orleans of 1894: Its Advantages, Its Prospects, Its Conditions, as shown by a Résumé of a Year's Record, 1893-1894* (New Orleans, 1894), 4, 21-23. "Almost every department of our vast commercial and industrial interests have felt the effects of the unusual commotion in our great financial system," complained one black paper. *Southwestern Christian Advocate*, August 17, 1893. On the depression, see Nell Irvin Painter, *Standing at Armageddon: The United States, 1877-1919* (New York, 1987), 116-26; Alexander Keyssar, *Out of Work: The First Century of Unemployment in Massachusetts* (New York, 1986), 47; Michael Katz, *In the Shadow of the Poorhouse: A Social History of Welfare in America* (New York, 1986), 147; Carlos A. Schwantes, *Coxey's Army: An American Odyssey* (Lincoln, 1985), 13-17; David Montgomery, *The Fall of the House of Labor: The Workplace, the State and American Labor Activism* (New York, 1987), 171-74.

[6]*New Orleans Times-Democrat*, November 20, 1886; November 2, 1894; *Mobile Daily Register*, November 4, 1894; *New Orleans Daily Picayune*, July 22, August 6, 1894.

[7]*New Orleans Daily Picayune*, October 28, 1894.

[8]*New Orleans Daily Picayune*, July 22, August 6, October 28, November 11, 1894; *New Orleans Times-Democrat*, December 4, 1886; November 2, 20, 1894; John Lovell, "Sail, Steam and Emergent Dockers' Unionism in Britain, 1850-1914," *International Review of Social History*, 32 (1987): 237-42. See Chapter 5 for a detailed discussion of the technological changes in the maritime industry.

[9]*Southwestern Christian Advocate*, August 4, 1892; July 12, 1894. On the *Advocate's* stance toward unions and strikes, also see *Southwestern Christian Advocate*, September 15, 1881.

[10]*Southwestern Christian Advocate*, May 20, 1886. The paper continued: "If he united with the strikers they would drop him as soon as they carried their point, and should he united with the capitalist he would go down when the troubles were over. Choosing either horn of the dilemma the benefits would be given him only by necessity, and denied him so soon as it became convenient to do so. Therefore . . . the Negro remains passive spectators of this far-reaching revolution."

[11]*Southwestern Christian Advocate*, July 12, 1894.

[12]Booker T. Washington, *Up from Slavery: An Autobiography* (1901; reprint ed., New York, 1977), 157, 155; Booker T. Washington, "The Negro and the Labor Unions," *Atlantic Monthly*, 3 (1913): 756-67; Louis R. Harlan, *Booker T. Washington: The Making of a Black Leader, 1865-1901* (New York, 1972); August Meier, *Negro Thought in America 1880-1915: Racial Ideologies in the Age of Booker T. Washington* (Ann Arbor, 1963), 100-18; John Brown Childs, "Concepts of Culture in Afro-American Political Thought, 1890-1920," *Social Text*, 4 (1981): 29.

[13]*New Orleans Daily Picayune*, January 14, 1893; *Birmingham Age-Herald*, January 16, 1893; *New Orleans Times-Democrat*, October 14, 1894. On membership figures, see *New Orleans Weekly Pelican*, June 8, 1889. Black resentment over racial restrictions and practices first emerged publicly more than a decade before when black and white unions struck briefly on behalf of white screwmen against employers of black screwmen, demanding that the black wage rate be raised to match that of the whites. During the 1881 strike, two groups of black workers broke ranks with the Cotton Men's Executive Council and independently contracted with employers. The Cotton Men's Executive Council forced the longshoremen's groups to merge with the larger Longshoremen's Protective Union Benevolent Association in 1886. If the black screwmen chafed at the enduring restrictions on the number of members who could work, they nonetheless sided with the more powerful whites against the largely black, old Cotton Men's Executive Council during the Cotton

Councils war in 1886-87. Race, craft identification, considerations of power, and the dynamics of group politics produced complicated alliances in this era. See Chapter 3.

[14]"Until last year," Stoddart explained in October 1894 "I always employed white labor, but when I was offered considerably reduced rates I thought it only fair to give the other people a trial." *Daily Picayune*, October 10, 14, 1894; *New York Times*, October 28, 1894.

[15]*Daily Picayune*, January 14, 1893; July 22, 1894; *Galveston Daily News*, October 27, 1894. The black and white screwmen, the Galveston paper explained, "some years ago were on terms of the utmost harmony, working together and parading together and belonged to the same council. Trouble has been brewing between them for some time . . . The appearance along the river front of firms of negro [*sic*] stevedores hiring negro [*sic*] screwmen has served to accentuate the trouble, and the white screwmen have been charging that negroes [*sic*] have been cutting rates and that the whites are losing ground [due to the] influx of negro [*sic*] labor."

[16]Edna Bonacich, "A Theory of Ethnic Antagonism: The Split Labor Market," *American Sociological Review*, 37 (1972): 547; George Frederickson, *White Supremacy: A Comparative Study in American and South African History* (New York, 1981), 212.

[17]*Daily Picayune*, July 22, August 7, 10, 15, 1894; *Galveston Daily News*, October 27, 1894.

[18]*Daily Picayune*, October 14, 15, 1894; *Times-Democrat*, October 14, 1894; *Sunday States*, October 14, 1894; *Southwestern Christian Advocate*, November 29, 1894.

[19]*Southwestern Christian Advocate*, June 29, 1893.

[20]*Times-Democrat*, October 14, 1894; *Daily Picayune*, October 14, 15, 16, November 4, 1894; also see William Ivy Hair, *Carnival of Fury: Robert Charles and the New Orleans Race Riot of 1900* (Baton Rouge, 1976), 94; *Galveston Daily News*, October 27, 1894; *New York Times*, October 27, 1894.

[21]*Daily Picayune*, December 20, 1894; *Sunday States*, October 14, 1894.

[22]*Times-Democrat*, October 14, 1894; *Daily Picayune*, October 14, 15, 1894.

[23]*Times-Democrat*, October 14, 15, 1892; *Daily Picayune*, October 15, 16, 1894; *Sunday States*, October 14, 1894; John Smith Kendall, *History of New Orleans*, 2 vols. (New York, 1922), 2:515.

[24]*Daily Picayune*, October 17, 18, 1894.

[25]*Times-Democrat*, October 27, 1894; *Daily Picayune*, October 27, 28, 1894; *Birmingham Age-Herald*, October 27, 1894; *Appletons' Annual Cyclopaedia and Register of Important Events of the Year 1894*, New Series, 19 (New York, 1895), 443; F. Ray Marshal, *Labor in the South* (Cambridge, 1967), 63; Carroll George Miller, "A Study of the New Orleans Longshoremen's Union from 1850 to 1962" (M.A. thesis, Louisiana State University and Agriculture and Mechanical College, 1962), 17-19.

[26]*Times-Democrat*, October 27, 1894; *Daily Picayune*, October 27, 1894; *New Orleans Daily States*, October 27, 1894; *Galveston Daily News*, October 27, 1894; *Washington Bee*, November 10, 1894; *New York Times*, October 27, 1894; British Foreign Office, *Diplomatic and Consular Reports on Trade and Finance. United States. Report for the Year 1894 of the Trade of the Consular District of New Orleans*, Annual Series No. 1551, May 1895, 15. For general accounts or mention of the 1894-95 riots, see Woodward, *Origins of the New South*, 267; Joy J. Jackson, *New Orleans in the Gilded Age: Politics and Urban Progress, 1880-1896* (Baton Rouge, 1969), 230-31; Raymond Arthur Perch, "The Rise and Decline of Labor in New Orleans" (M. A. thesis, Toulon University, 1938), 31-37; *Appellation's Annual Cyclopaedia . . . 1894*, 443; Kendall, *History of New Orleans*, 2:515.

[27]*Times-Democrat*, October 28, 29, 1894; *Daily Picayune*, October 28, 29, 1894; March 20, 1908; *Baton Rouge Daily States*, October 28, 29, 1894; *Southwestern Christian Advocate*, November 1, 1894; *Washington Bee*, November 10, 1894.

[28]*Daily Picayune*, October 30, 1894; *Times-Democrat*, October 30, 1894.

[29]*Times-Democrat*, October 30, 1894.

[30]*Times-Democrat*, October 28, 30, 31, November 1, 1894; *Daily Picayune*, October 30, 31, November 1, 4, 1894; Meeting of Board of Directors, November 1, 1894, New Orleans Cotton Exchange Minute Book, H (Manuscripts, Rare Books and University Archives, Howard-Tilton Memorial Library, Tulane University), 81.

[31]*Times-Democrat*, October 28, 1894; *Daily Picayune*, October 28, 1894; *Baton Rouge Daily States*, October 27, 28, 1894; Meeting of Board of Directors, October 29, 1894, New Orleans Cotton Exchange Minute Book, H, 72.

[32]*Daily Picayune*, November 3, 1894. "Neither race conflicts nor any other sort of conflicts must be allowed to destroy a great shipping industry," the *Picayune* editorialized. "The labor of both whites and blacks is needed. Laborers of all classes and both races have their rights, and the protection of these laborers in their rights must be maintained without any failure or default." *Daily Picayune*, October 30, 1894.

[33]*Times-Democrat*, November 5, 1894; *Daily Picayune*, November 4-7, 11, 1894; *Baton Rouge Daily States*, November 5, 1894; Minutes of Meeting of Board of Directors, November 7, 1894, New Orleans Cotton Exchange Minute Book, H, 83.

[34]Following the blaze at the West India and Pacific Steamship wharves, black workers threatened to seek their own injunction and to demand federal intervention to prevent further harassment by whites. If the president of the United States "did not allow them the troops," they noted, "he would have to apologize for the action he took in the late railroad strike, headed by Mr. Debs." Federal troops, however, were unnecessary, as white longshoremen and screwmen abided by the terms of the injunction received by the West India line. *Times-Democrat*, November 9, 11, 1894; *Daily Picayune*, December 2, 9, 10, 1894; *Daily States*, November 9, 11, 1894; *Birmingham Age-Herald*, November 9, 18, 1894.

[35]*Times-Democrat*, October 28, 29, 31, 1894; *Daily Picayune*, October 28, 29, November 1, 2, 5, 1894; *Southwestern Christian Advocate*, November 1, 8, 1894. The *Times-Democrat* declared: "It may as well be understood now as later that if the force furnished to-day shall prove inadequate that then the Governor of the State will be called upon for troops, and that if the State should unfortunately prove not to have sufficient men at command to enforce the law and disperse the rioters, then the Federal government will be asked to take a hand in the affair." *Times-Democrat*, November 13, 1894.

[36]*Daily Picayune*, November 9, 1894; *Southwestern Christian Advocate*, November 15, 1894; *Birmingham Age-Herald*, November 9, 1894.

[37]*Daily Picayune*, November 7, 1894.

[38]*Times-Democrat*, November 8, 1894; *Daily Picayune*, November 7, 11, December 17, 1894; *Daily States*, November 7, 1894.

[39]*Daily Picayune*, November 2, 1894.

[40]The demise of the interracial alliance and the return to the pre-1885 rates must have been particularly difficult for Swann, one of the architects of the alliance. "I have been doing all I could to help the white laboring men ever since the formation of the union," he recalled to his members, "and I can say that I have done all I could for the white men, as well as the colored men." *Daily Picayune*, December 16, 1894. Not all black union officials felt this way, however. Black screwmen always had had a far more problematic relationship than black longshoremen to the federation of riverfront labor. One leader of the black screwmen's Association No. 1 reflected in November 1894:

> I lay the cause of this trouble to a much older strife, and date its origin to the very establishment of a labor council in this city. As colored men, when the council was first organized, bowing in humble submission to the dictates of the white screwmen, and acting under the advice of some colored men, who were members of other laboring organizations, even though we feared our chances for justice, blindfolded to self, we became members of said council, then known as the Cotton Men's Executive Council. We upheld the price . . . and in order to preserve what was then called the union, we made the best out of a bad bargain.

Daily Picayune, November 2, 1894.

[41]*Daily Picayune*, December 17-19, 1894; *Times-Democrat*, December 21, 1894; *Daily States*, December 17, 18, 1894; Minutes of Meeting of Board of Directors, December 19, 1894, New Orleans Cotton Exchange Minute Book, H, 115-16.

[42]*Daily Picayune*, December 20, 1894; *Daily States*, December 19, 20, 1894; *Birmingham Age-Herald*, December 21, 1894.

[43]*Times-Democrat*, December 21, 1894; *Daily Picayune*, December 21, 1894; *Baton Rouge Daily States*, December 20, 1894.

[44]*Daily Picayune*, December 28, 1894.

[45]British Foreign Office, *Diplomatic and Consular Reports . . . 1894*, 16-17. For accounts of waterside unionism in Great Britain during this period, see E. L. Taplin, *Liverpool Dockers and Seamen, 1870-1890* (York, 1974); Raymond Brown, *Waterfront Organization in Hull, 1870-1900* (Hull, 1972); Philip J. Leng, *The Welsh Dockers* (Lancashire, 1981); E. J. Hobsbawm, "National Unions on the Waterside," in *Labouring Men: Studies in the History of Labour* (London, 1964), 204-30; John Lovell, *Stevedores and Dockers: A Study of Trade Unionism in the Port of London, 1870-1914* (London, 1969); Jonathan Schneer, *Ben Tillett: Portrait of a Labour Leader* (London, 1982).

[46]*Daily Picayune*, February 1, 5, 7, 8, March 3, 1895; *New Orleans States*, February 5, 1895; British Foreign Office, *Diplomatic and Consular Reports*, 7. Also see: *Daily Picayune*, February 24, 1886.

[47]The unemployed Gretna whites, the *New Orleans Picayune* noted, "thought it a little hard that a crowd of unskilled negroes should be allowed to cross the river and literally take away their means of making a living. All the mills had closed, and the men employed there had nothing to do, and were forced to work on the levee or seek employment on this side of the river." *Daily Picayune*, March 3, 5-8, 1895. On the use of injunctions, see British Foreign Office, *Diplomatic and Consular Reports*, 17; *Sunday States*, February 10, 1895; *Daily Picayune*, March 6, 1895.

[48]*Daily Picayune*, March 13, 1895.

[49]*Times-Democrat*, March 22, 24, 26, 1895.

[50]*Times-Democrat*, February 11, 1895; *Daily States*, February 11, 1895.

[51]*Daily Picayune*, February 9, 1895.

[52]Ibid., January 25, 1895.

[53]*Times-Democrat*, February 11, 1895; *Daily Picayune*, February 11, 1895; *Daily States*, February 11, 1895.

[54]Ibid.

[55]*Daily Picayune*, February 9, 1895. The *New Orleans States* agreed with this interpretation: when the Harrison line agent Alfred LeBlanc dismissed his white labor force and instead contracted with black stevedore George Geddes for some 300 black screwmen and longshoremen, the paper predicted trouble, "for it is more than flesh and blood can stand to see work taken out of the mouth of a man by another who is affecting his purpose by a dead 'cut' in the rate of wages that prevailed." *Daily States*, February 5, 1895.

[56]*Daily Picayune*, March 3, 1895.

[57]Ibid., February 5, 8, 9, 1895.

[58]Ibid., January 24, 25, February 11-14, March 1, 3, 7, 1895; *Times-Democrat*, March 12, 1895. A third approach that never materialized was the reconstitution of a Cotton Men's Executive Council. Although the details are sketchy, accounts suggest that four organizations—the black and white yardmen and the black and white longshoremen—formed a new cotton council at some point in January, electing on a temporary basis white longshoreman H. O. Hassinger president and black longshoreman James Porter vice president. In February, the *New Orleans Picayune* reported rumors that "a union of the cotton organization"—although in a "crude state"—would "be brought about [soon] and a general strike would follow." Although teamsters allied with the new organization, the white screwmen remained apart. The move toward unification, however, abruptly ended on February 12. "The stumbling block seemed to be Sanders' men [—black screwmen and longshoremen hired by stevedores Geddes—] and as they could not be induced to join the council, the matter was for the time dropped." See *Daily Picayune*, February 1, 8, 11-13, 1895; *Twentieth Century*, 14 (1893): 4.

[59]*Daily Picayune*, March 3, 5, 7, 14, 1895.

[60]*Times-Democrat*, March 9, 1895; *Daily Picayune*, March 9, 10, 1895; *Mobile Daily Register*, March 10, 1895; *Savannah Morning News*, March 10, 1895. For a discussion of Cuney's role as a contracting stevedore in Galveston and for a history of Galveston dock workers, see Maud Cuney Hare, *Norris Wright Cuney: A Tribune of the Black People* (New York, 1913); Virginia Neal Hine, "Norris Wright Cuney" (M. A. thesis, Rice University, 1965); Lawrence D. Rice, *The Negro in Texas* (Baton Rouge, 1971); Ruth Allen, *Chapters in the History of Organized Labor in Texas* (Austin, 1941); James V. Reese, "The Evolution of an Early Texas Union: The Screwmen's Benevolent Association of Galveston, 1866-1891," *Southwestern Historical Quarterly*, 85 (1971): 158-85; Allen Clayton Taylor, "A History of the Screwmen's Benevolent Association from 1866 to 1924" (M. A. thesis, University of Texas, 1968); Kenneth Kann, "The Knights of Labor and the Southern Black Worker," *Labor History*, 18 (1977): 47-70.

[61]*Daily Picayune*, March 10, 11, 1895; *New Orleans States*, March 10, 1895; *Times-Democrat*, March 10, 1895; *Birmingham Age-Herald*, March 10, 1895; *Atlanta Constitution*, March 11, 1895; *Mobile Daily Register*, March 12, 1895; *Savannah Morning News*, March 11, 1895. George A. Patrick, a black Galveston screwman, explained upon his return that he and his fellow men had been misled by stevedore Lincoln, who told them that New Orleans suffered from a serious scarcity of labor. *Galveston Daily News*, March 12, 1895.

[62]*Times-Democrat*, March 10-12, 1895; *Daily Picayune*, March 10-12, 1895; *Daily States*, March 11, 1895; *Mobile Daily Register*, March 10, 12, 1895; *Galveston Daily News*, March 12, 1895; *Appletons' Annual Cyclopaedia and Register of Important Events of the Year 1895*, New Series 10 (New York, 1896), 427-28; *Southwestern Christian Advocate*, March 14, 1895; *St. Louis Post-Dispatch*, March 12, 1895; *Louisville Courier-Journal*, March 12, 1895; Benjamin Brawley, *A Social History of the American Negro* (New York, 1921), 321. For a collection of articles on the 1895 riots, also see Charles C. Titcomb Collection, 1895-1900 (Newspaper Clippings: Labor and Levee Riots, March, May, June 1895), Louisiana State University, Baton Rouge.

[63]Ibid., March 13, 1895; Ibid., March 13, 1895; Ibid., March 12, 1895; Ibid., March 13, 1895; *New York Times*, March 13, 1895; *Chicago Daily Inter-Ocean*, March 13, 1895; *Galveston Daily News*, March 13, 1895; *Jacksonville Florida Times-Union*, March 13, 1895; *Southwestern Christian Advocate*, March 14, 21, 1895; *Boston Evening Transcript*, March 13, 1895; *The Nation*, March 21, 1895; *Harper's Weekly*, 29 (1895): 295; Minutes of Meeting of Board of Directors, March 12, 1895, Cotton Exchange Minute Books, H, 144.

[64]*Daily Picayune*, March 12, 1895; *Daily States*, March 12, 1895; *Times-Democrat*, March 12, 1895; *Southwestern Christian Advocate*, March 21, 1895; *Galveston Daily News*, March 12, 1895; *Mobile Daily Register*, March 12, 13, 1895; *Boston Evening Transcript*, March 12, 1895; *Baltimore Sun*, March 13, 1895; *Appletons' Annual Cyclopaedia . . . 1895*, 427-28.

[65]The federal government's role in crushing the recent American Railway Union strike stood as a powerful example for employers, who petitioned Governor Murphy Foster to request federal troops to quell the disturbances. Refusing to work without ample protection, black union leaders also announced that they "did not care to risk the protection of the police again, but wanted State militia or Federal soldiers." Promising to cooperate with city merchants to end the lawlessness, Governor Foster rejected the demand for federal troops and instead issued a proclamation barring crowds from assembling and ordered the state militia to the waterfront. On the military occupation, see *Times-Democrat*, March 14, 1895; *Daily Picayune*, March 13, 1895; *Daily States*, March 13, 1895; *Southwestern Christian Advocate*, March 21, 1895; *New York Times*, March 14, 1895; *Galveston Daily News*, March 14, 1895; *Mobile Daily Register*, March 14, 1895; *Baltimore Sun*, March 14, 1895.

[66]*Times-Democrat*, March 15-17, 20, 21, 1895; *Daily States*, March 14, 1895; *Daily Picayune*, March 14, 15, 16, 17, 19, 21, 1895; *Chicago Inter-Ocean*, March 15, 16, 1895; *Florida Times-Union*, March 15, 16, 1895; *Savannah Morning News*, March 15, 16, 1895; *Galveston Daily News*, March 15, 1895; *Mobile Daily Register*, March 14, 16, 1895; *New York Times*, March 15, 1895; *Baltimore Sun*, March 15, 1895; *Baltimore American*, March 15, 1895; *Birmingham Age-Herald*, March 15, 16, 1895.

[67]*Times-Democrat*, March 22-26, 29, 1895; *Daily Picayune*, March 22, 23, 25, 26, 1895; *Sunday States*, March 17, 1895; *New York Times*, March 21, 22, 26, 27, 1895; *Mobile Daily Register*, March 21, 1895; *Birmingham Age-Herald*, March 22, 23, 26, 27, 1895. Although peace reigned on the New Orleans side of the river, there were several incidents of racial harassment and violence in Gretna. Unemployed Gretna whites—who were not members of the New Orleans longshore unions—carried out a small-scale "labor riot" in mid-May against black workers employed by stevedore Geddes on a West India and Pacific steamship. The "riot" was not a white effort to drive all blacks off the docks; whites demanded half of the available work. The violence began when the stevedore attempted to work a number of white men under the supervision of a black foreman. See *Daily Picayune*, May 17, 22, 1895; *Southwestern Christian Advocate*, May 23, 1895; *New York Times*, May 17, 1895; *Birmingham Age-Herald*, May 17, 1895.

[68] *Times-Democrat*, March 23, 26, 29, 1895; *Daily Picayune*, March 17, 26, 29, April 9, 1895.

[69] *Daily Picayune*, April 9, 11, 18, May 17, 22, 29, July 27, October 12, 15, 1895; *New York Times*, May 17, 1895; *Southwestern Christian Advocate*, May 23, 1895.

[70] Ibid., October 15, 29, November 15, December 6, 1895; *Birmingham Age-Herald*, November 15, December 11, 1895.

[71] *Florida Times-Union*, March 14, 1895. Northern newspapers saw the matter differently. The riots were not born of "a short-lived fit of popular madness," the *Boston Evening Transcript* noted. The origins lay in the simple fact that the screwmen had decided that cotton screwing was "exclusively a white man's business, and that the colored men must leave it." *Boston Evening Transcript*, March 14, 1895. The *New York Tribune* saw the source of the riot in labor competition and in the heritage of violence that marked the state:

> The New Orleans riot is a labor conspiracy rather than a race outbreak. The negroes [*sic*] were shot down on the wharves not because they were blacks, but because they were substitutes for strikers. . . . The white mobs of longshoremen are profiting by the education in lawlessness which they have received in the politics of Louisiana. There were white leagues riding roughshod over political rights guaranteed by the Constitution, and there were negroes [*sic*] coerced, intimidated and shot down in order to secure the establishment of Democratic ascendancy in the State. . . . There is nothing which the longshoremen have done in the way of intimidation, murder and massacre which was not anticipated during the political period immediately following reconstruction times. With a population trained in the use of bowie-knife and revolver, and with police and militia in sympathy with 'nigger-hunting,' New Orleans is to-day the most turbulent and lawless city in the South.

New York Tribune, March 14, 1895. Days later, the *Tribune* expressed approval of the city's commercial elite for standing up for the rights of blacks to work:

> The declaration of New-Orleans business men and leading citizens that they will henceforth uphold and defend, with armed force if necessary, the right of men to work if they wish, without regard to race, color or previous condition, is only astonishing because it is the first time the controlling influences in the State have been enlisted to defend the rights of negroes [*sic*] formerly enslaved. Self-interest in this case opens the eyes blinded so long and so completely by race prejudice, and by the habits of the 'peculiar institution.'

New York Tribune, March 16, 1895. Also see *Twentieth Century*, 14 (1895): 2.

[72] *Baltimore Sun*, March 13, 1895. Both the *Florida Times-Union* and the *Baltimore Sun* were referring to the Chicago-centered 1894 American Railway Union strike on behalf of Pullman Car Company workers and the January 1895 strike of trolley car workers in Brooklyn. See Nick Salvatore, *Eugene V. Debs: Citizen and Socialist* (Urbana, 1982), 126-38; Joshua B. Freeman, *In Transit: The Transport Workers Union in New York City, 1933-1966* (New York, 1989), 16.

[73] *Mobile Daily Register*, March 13, 1895.

[74] *Washington Bee*, November 10, 1894; *Southwestern Christian Advocate*, March 14, 1895.

[75] *Southwestern Christian Advocate*, November 29, 1894.

[76] *Indianapolis Freeman*, March 23, 1895.

[77] *Daily Picayune*, March 12, 1895; *Times-Democrat*, March 13, 1895; *Birmingham Labor Advocate*, November 19, 1892. For further discussion of Parker's views of labor, see Matthew J. Schott, "John M. Parker of Louisiana and the Varieties of American Progressivism" (Ph.D. dissertation, Vanderbilt University, 1969), 64-67. Fitzpatrick received widespread press condemnation as well. See *Savannah Morning News*, March 14, 15, 1895; *Charleston News and Courier*, March 14, 1895; *Baltimore Sun*, March 13, 1895; *Daily Picayune*, March 18, 1895; *Chicago InterOcean*, March 14, 1895; *Atlanta Constitution*, March 14, 16, 1895. Also see statements of Produce Exchange President E. S. Stoddard and Cotton Exchange secretary Henry Hester on poor government and business prospects, in Young Men's Business League, *New Orleans of 1894*, 4-5.

[78] Schott, "John M. Parker of Louisiana," 57; George E. Cunningham, "The Italians, A Hindrance to White Solidarity in Louisiana, 1890-1898," *Journal of Negro History*, 50 (1965): 25-28; Henry C. Dethloff, "The

Alliance and the Lottery: Farmers Try for the Sweepstakes," *Louisiana History*, 6 (1965): 141-59; Kendall, *History of New Orleans*, 2:483-501, 509-11.

[79]*Southwestern Christian Advocate*, September 19, 1895; Edward F. Haas, *Political Leadership in a Southern City: New Orleans in the Progressive Era 1896-1902* (Ruston, 1988), 39-55; Kendall, *History of New Orleans*, 2:517-23; Raymond O. Nussbaum, " 'The Ring is Smashed!': The New Orleans Municipal Election of 1896," *Louisiana History*, 17 (1976): 283-97; Philip D. Uzee, "The Republican Party in the Louisiana Election of 1896," *Louisiana History*, 2 (1961): 332-44; George M. Reynolds, *Machine Politics in New Orleans, 1897-1926*, (1936; reprint ed., New York, 1968), 26-27; Schott, "John M. Parker of Louisiana," 70-77; Matthew J. Schott, "Progressives Against Democracy: Electoral Reform in Louisiana, 1894-1921," *Louisiana History*, 20 (1979): 253-54; Lucia Elizabeth Daniel, "The Louisiana People's Party," *Louisiana Historical Quarterly*, 26 (1943): 1109. On black attitudes toward the machine and the reformers, also see the *Crusader*, no date, *Crusader* Clipping File, Folder P58, Xavier University; The *Crusader* clipping fill n.d., 1895, Folder P101, Xavier University; *Southwestern Christian Advocate*, May 16, 1895.

[80]Reynolds, *Machine Politics in New Orleans*, 32-34; Kendall, *History of New Orleans*, 2:517-31; Edward F. Haas, "John Fitzpartrick and Political Continuity in New Orleans, 1869-1899," *Louisiana History*, 21 (1981): 7-29.

[81]William Ivy Hair, *Bourbonism and Agrarian Protest: Louisiana Politics, 1877-1900* (Baton Rouge, 1969), 234-67; Uzee, "The Republican Party," 332-44; Reynolds, *Machine Politics in New Orleans*, 27-30; Daniel, "The Louisiana People's Party," 1107-11. By mid-decade, Louisiana politics had reached a crisis point. Incumbent Democrats faced a twin threat: the Populist upheaval (always a rural phenomenon in Louisiana) and the emergence of "sugar republicans" (pro-sugar tariff planters who bolted the anti-tariff Democratic party to form a faction within the Republican party). When an alliance between Populists and the sugar Republicans threatened to unseat Governor Foster in 1896 state election, Democrats crushed the insurgency through widespread intimidation and violence.

[82]J. Morgan Kousser, *The Shaping of Southern Politics: Suffrage Restriction and the Establishment of the One-Party South, 1880-1910* (New Haven, 1974), 152-65; Hair, *Bourbonism and Agrarian Protest*, 268-79; Reynolds, *Machine Politics in New Orleans*, 26-30; Charles Barthelemy Rousseve, *The Negro in Louisiana: Aspects of his History and his Literature* (New Orleans, 1937), 132. On black reactions to disfranchisement, see *Southwestern Christian Advocate*, April 2, 1896; December 16, 1897; February 24, 1898.

[83]*The Harlequin*, June 23, 1900; *Southwestern Christian Advocate*, July 19, November 1, 1900; June 5, 26, November 6, 1902; February 26, March 26, April 23, 1903; A. R. Holcombe, "The Separate Street-Car Law in New Orleans," *The Outlook*, 72 (1902); *Times-Democrat*, November 4, 1902; *Daily Picayune*, July 31, 1902; *Galveston Daily News*, August 7, 1903.

[84]*Southwestern Christian Advocate*, September 21, 1899.

[85]Ibid., October 19, 1899.

[86]Ibid., July 25, 1895.

[87]Hair, *Carnival of Fury*; Joel Williamson, *The Crucible of Race: Black-White Relations in the American South Since Emancipation* (New York, 1984), 201-9; Ida B. Wells-Barnett, *Mob Rule in New Orleans. Robert Charles and His Fight to the Death* (1900), reprinted in Wells-Barnett, *On Lynchings* (New York, 1969); *The Harlequin*, July 28, August 4, 18, 1900; *Southwestern Christian Advocate*, August 2, 9, 16, 1900; Herbert Shapiro, *White Violence and Black Response: From Reconstruction to Montgomery* (Amherst, 1988), 61-63; "The New Orleans Mob," *The Outlook*, 65 (1900): 760-61.

[88]Hair, *Carnival of Fury*, xiv; Dale A. Somers, "Black and White in New Orleans: A Study in Urban Race Relations, 1865-1900," *Journal of Southern History*, 40 (1974): 42; Williamson, *The Crucible of Race*, 201.

[89]Gompers to Leonard, March 18, 1899, Samuel Gompers Letterbooks, Volume 27 (January 27 to April 12, 1899), Reel 18, Frame 633, Library of Congress; *Daily Picayune*, September fl, 1897.

[90]*United Labor Council Directory of New Orleans, Louisiana* (New Orleans, 1895), in Louisiana Collection, Howard-Tilton Memorial Library, Toulon University; *Southern Economist and Trade Unionist*, 1 (1897); *Union Advocate*, April 27, 1903. On the growth of the AFL, see Leo Wolman, *The Growth of American Trade Unions 1880-1923* (New York, 1924), 33-34.

[91]"The New South," *American Federationist*, 6 (1899): 57-58; Gompers to Leonard, March 18, 1899, Samuel Gompers Letterbooks, Volume 27 (January 27 to April 12, 1899), Reel 18, Frame 633. Correspondence from Winn, Greene, and McGruder can be found in the Gompers letterbooks for 1899.

[92]*American Federationist*, 6 (1899); *Daily Picayune*, June 28, 1899. From the Samuel Gompers Letterbooks, Reel 20 (July 22-September 26, 1899), see Gompers to Winn, August 3, 1899, frames 120-21; Gompers to Leonard, August 9, 1899, frame 267; Gompers to Leonard, August 17, 1899, frame 4457; Gompers to Leonard, August 25, 1899, Frame 538; Gompers to Winn, September 1, 1899, frame 691.

[93]*Daily Picayune*, August 14, September 11, 1899; *Times Democrat*, August 14, September 11, 1899. Also see Minutes of the Central Trades and Labor Council, October 8, 1899-April 26, 1901, in Stoddard Labor Collection, Archives and Special Collections, University of New Orleans.

[94]Bernard Cook, "The Typographical Union and the New Orleans General Strike of 1892," *Louisiana History*, 24 (1983): 382-88.

[95]*Daily Picayune*, September 21, 28, 30, October 19, November 1, 2, 30, 1894; October 23, 1894; *Daily States*, October 29, 1894; *Crusader*, January 10, 1895 (date unclear), Folder P23, in *Crusader* Clipping File, Xavier University; Minutes of Special Meetings on November 1, 4, 5, 7, 9, December 11, 1892, in Records of the New Orleans Typographical Union No. 17, in Archives and Special Collections, University of New Orleans. On some Populists' repudiation of interracialism and adoption of white supremacy, see Woodward, *Origins of the New South*, 323.

[96]Gompers to John Callahan, May 17, 1892, in Samuel Gompers Letterbooks, Reel 6 (Vol. 7), frame 419; also cited in Philip Taft, *The A. F. of L. in the Time of Gompers* (New York, 1957), 311. Gompers maintained this line of reasoning, arguing that white New Orleans workers accept the formation of a separate black city union council at the end of the century: "I have always insisted on the right to organize being accorded to colored men. And if we do not give them this opportunity and thus make friends of them, they would of necessity be our enemies and utilized by our opponents in every struggle and whenever opportunity presents itself." Gompers to Leonard, May 23, 1900, Samuel Gompers Letterbooks, Reel 24 (Vol. 34), frame 344.

[97]Philip S. Foner, *History of the Labor Movement*, Vol. 2, in Foner and Ronald L. Lewis, eds., *The Black Worker: A Documentary History from Colonial Times to the Present* (Philadelphia, 1980), 350; John Stephens Durham, "The Labor Unions and the Negro," *The Atlantic Monthly*, 81 (1898): 226; Taft, *The A. F. of L. in the Time of Gompers*, 308-13.

[98]*Southwestern Christian Advocate*, August 2, 1900.

[99]*New Orleans Republican Courier*, December 2, 1899; W. E. B. DuBois, ed., *The Negro Artisan: Report of a Social Study Made Under the Direction of Atlanta University; Together with the Proceedings of the Seventh Conference for the Study of the Negro Problems, Held at Atlanta University, on May 27th, 1902* (Atlanta, 1902), 127-28; *Daily Picayune*, September 8, 1903; *United Mine Workers Journal*, June 9, 1904.

[100]"Report of Vice President James E. Porter," *Proceedings of the Eleventh Annual Convention of the International Longshoremen, Marine and Transportworkers' Association held at Chicago, Illinois, July 14-19, 1902*, 73-74; *American Federationist*, 8, No. 6 (1901): 224; *American Federationist*, 8, No. 10 (1901): 438; *American Federationist*, 8, No. 11 (1901): 489. On Porter, other black longshore leaders, and the International Longshoremen's Association, see *New York Age*, July 13, August 7, 1913.

[101]The National Longshoremen's Association of the United States was founded in 1892 by representatives of ten lumber handlers unions from the Great Lakes. It joined the AFL the following year, eventually changing its name to the International Longshoremen's Association. By 1901, the organization claimed as many as 250 locals with 40,000 members in its ranks. The International's strength centered on the Great Lakes, though by the 1910s, a Southern Gulf District of the ILA joined together Galveston, New Orleans, Mobile, and a number of smaller ports. From the ILA's formation through 1911, some New Orleans longshore workers valued their institutional independence, maintaining a rocky relationship with the ILA. Some years locals affiliated with the ILA, other years they broke with it. Not until the First World War did membership in the larger organization have much direct bearing on the struggles of the New Orleans men. On the ILA's early history, see: John R. Commons, "The Longshoremen of the Great Lakes," *Labor and Administration* (New York, 1913), 267-68; Maud Russell, *Men Along the Shore: The I. L. A. and Its History* (New York, 1966), 62-74; Lloyd G. Reynolds and Charles C. Killingsworth, *Trade Union Publications: The Official Journals, Convention Proceedings and Constitutions of International Unions and Federations, 1850-1941*, Vol. 1, *Description and Bibliography* (Baltimore, 1944), 95-100; "International Longshoremen's Association," *Report of the Industrial*

Commission on Labor Organizations, Labor Disputes, and Arbitration, and on Railway Labor (Washington, 1901), 17:264-65.

[102]In the Samuel Gompers Letterbooks, see Gompers to Leonard, March 9, 1900 (Reel 22, Vol. 32), frame 908; Gompers to Porter, March 9, 1900 (Reel 24, Vol. 34), frame 907; Gompers to Porter, April 25, 1900 (Reel 24, Vol. 34), frame 754; Gompers to Leonard, May 23, 1900 (Reel 24, Vol. 34), frame 344.

[103]Leonard to Gompers, June 29, 1900, cited in Philip S. Foner and Ronald L. Lewis, eds., *The Black Worker: A Documentary History from Colonial Times to the Present*, Vol. 5: *The Black Worker from 1900 to 1919* (Philadelphia, 1980), 121; also see Foner, *History of the Labor Movement*, 2:351-52; Morrison to L. B. Lauwdry, March 16, 1901, in Central Trades and Labor Council, New Orleans, Louisiana, Correspondence, in Stoddard Labor Collection, Archives and Special Collections, University of New Orleans.

[104]Porter to Gompers, June 14, 1900, cited in Foner and Lewis, *The Black Worker: A Documentary History*, 5:120.

[105]American Federation of Labor, *Report of Proceedings of the Twentieth Annual Convention held at Louisville, Kentucky, December 6th to 15th, inclusive, 1900*, 12-13. "Separate charters may be issued to Central Labor Unions, Local Unions, or Federal Labor Unions, composed exclusively of colored members, where, in the judgement of the Executive Council, it appears advisable and to the best interest of the Trade Union movement to do so," read the amended article to the Federations' constitution. AFL, *Report of Proceedings of the Twentieth Annual Convention*, xiii. For short documents on the CLU, see Porter to Gompers, May 20, 1901; and Application for Certificate of Affiliation to the American Federation of Labor, May 20, 1901, in Charter File, The George Meany Memorial Archives, Silver Spring, Md. Also see *American Federationist*, 8 (1901): 224; *American Federationist*, 8 (1901): 438; *American Federationist*, 8 (1901): 489; *American Federationist*, 8 (1901): 562; David Paul Bennetts, "Black and White Workers: New Orleans, 1880-1900" (Ph.D. dissertation, University of Illinois at Urbana-Champaign, 1972), 527-30; *Official Roster of the Central Labor Union of New Orleans* (New Orleans, 1907), in Vertical File (Trade Unions), Louisiana Collection, Tilton Memorial Library, Toulon University.

[106]"There is no apparent discrimination in wages in this city and the trade unions are open to Negroes in most cases," the DuBois study noted. "On the whole the Negro artisans seem better organized and more aggressive in this state than in any other." DuBois, ed., *The Negro Artisan*, 127-28.

[107]Board of Trade, *Cost of Living in American Towns, Report of an Enquiry by the Board of Trade into Working Class Rents, Housing and Retail Prices, Together with the Rates of Wages in Certain Occupations in the Principal Industrial Towns of the United States of America* (London, 1911).

[108]Board of Trade, *Cost of Living in American Towns*, 290, 292.

[109]DuBois, ed., *The Negro Artisan*, 160, 128; "Report of the Joint Committee of the Senate and House of Representatives of the State of Louisiana, Appointed to Investigate the Port of New Orleans," *Official Journal of the Proceedings of House of Representatives of the State of Louisiana at the First Regular Session of the Third General Assembly*, May 28, 1908, 200.

[110]*Times-Democrat*, July 28, 1900; *Daily Picayune*, July 27, 1900.

[111]*Daily Picayune*, June 27, 1900.

[112]*Harlequin*, May 12, 19, July 28, October 13, 1900; November 28, 1901; *Daily Picayune*, November 17, 1901; *Baltimore Sun*, September 26, 1900.

[113]*Times-Democrat*, September 11, 12, 1901; *Daily Picayune*, September 11, 1901; Perch, "The Rise and Decline of Labor," 43; Daniel Rosenberg, *New Orleans Dockworkers: Race, Labor, and Unionism 1891-1923* (Albany, 1988), 72-73.

[114]*Daily Picayune*, September 19, 1901.

[115]*Daily Picayune*, September 11-14, 17, 19, 22, 1901; *Times-Democrat*, September 13, 1901; *Tribune*, September 13, 1901; *First Annual Report of the Bureau of Labor Statistics for the State of Louisiana, 1901*, Thomas Harrison, Commissioner (Baton Rouge, 1902), 191. Labor's widespread backing for the port's grain trimmers extended beyond the city's limits. Unable to unload in New Orleans because of the strike, the German ship *Pointers* sailed for Galveston. Texas union screwmen, in support of the New Orleans

longshoremen, refused to handle the cargo, forcing the ship to return to the Crescent City. Its agent reluctantly signed the trimmers' tariff. This action, the *Picayune* observed, "effectively stopped any attempt that the railroads or anyone else might have made to divert commerce to that port." *Daily Picayune*, September 19, 23, 1901.

[116]*Daily Picayune*, September 19, 1901.

[117]*Daily Picayune*, September 20-24, 1901; *Times-Democrat*, September 23, 1901; Gompers to Porter, September 13, 1901, Samuel Gompers Letterbooks, Reel 33 (vol. 46), frame 199.

[118]*Daily Picayune*, September 26, 1901.

[119]Ibid.

[120]*Daily Picayune*, October 6, 8, November 30, 1901; September 21, 1903; April 20, 1904; Perch, "The Rise and Decline of Labor," 49.

[121]On the other examples of late nineteenth- and early twentieth-century interracial labor collaboration that qualify the earlier historiographical portrait of total black exclusion from trade unions, see: Paul B. Worthman, "Black Workers and Labor Unions in Birmingham, Alabama, 1894-1904," *Labor History*, 10 (1969): 375-407; Herbert Gutman, "The Negro and the United Mine Workers of America: The Career and Letters of Richard L. Davis and Something of Their Meaning," *Work, Culture and Society in Industrializing America: Essays in American Working Class and Social History* (New York, 1977), 121-208; James Green, *Grassroots Socialism: Radical Movements in the Southwest, 1895-1943* (Baton Rouge, 1978), 176-227; Karin A. Shapiro, "The Convicts Must Go! The East Tennessee Coal Miners' Rebellion of 1891-2" (M. A. thesis, Yale University, 1983); Paul B. Worthman and James Green, "Black Workers in the New South," in *Key Issues in the Afro-American Experience*, Vol. 2, eds. Nathan Huggins, Martin Kilson, and Daniel Fox (New York, 1971), 47-69.

[122]Covington Hall to Abram L. Harris, August 27, 1929, in Abram L. Harris Papers, Collection 43-1, Moorland-Spingarn Research Center, Howard University.

RACE RELATIONS IN LOUISIANA, 1877-98*

Henry C. Dethloff and Robert R. Jones

"There is no State in the Union, hardly any spot of like size on the globe, where the man of color has lived so intensely, made so much progress, been of such historical importance and yet about whom so comparatively little is known."[1] Unlike the pioneering Alice Dunbar-Nelson and Charles B. Roussève few scholars today recognize the active and significant role played by the Negro in the history of Louisiana. In particular, historians have failed to examine adequately the political, civil, and social relationships between the races in Louisiana in the post-Reconstruction period, or to explain how Jim Crow legislation markedly altered those relationships. Thus the study of race relations in Louisiana in the period 1877-1898 constitutes a critical void in Negro historiography.

There is no question that one of the most important recent contributions to Negro historiography is C. Vann Woodward's provocative and path-breaking *The Strange Career of Jim Crow* (1955). Woodward, seeking to explode the Southern argument of the mid-1950s that the Jim Crow system was dictated by the "immutable 'folkways' of the South" and thus could not be altered by legislation or judicial decision, maintains that systematic segregation, whether legal or extralegal, has not in fact been a permanent feature of Southern life. In the period between 1877 and 1900, for instance, "three alternative philosophies of race relations were put forward to compete for the region's adherence and support." Redeemer paternalism, Populist and radical "realism," and the liberalism of a few Southerners such as George Washington Cable and Lewis H. Blair constituted Southern alternatives to extreme racism. It was not, Woodward concludes, until the last years of the 1890s that white Southerners rejected these alternatives and imposed a system of "consistent, thorough, and legally sanctioned segregation."[2]

Until then the "race policies accepted and pursued in the South were sometimes milder than they became later." During the experimental years between 1877 and 1900,

*First published in *Louisiana History*, 9 (1968): 301-23. Reprinted with the kind permission of the authors and the Louisiana Historical Association.

Negroes in the South voted in large numbers; held numerous minor offices; rode side by side with whites on trains, streetcars, and common carriers; served on juries with whites; and even occasionally used the facilities of dining rooms, restaurants, saloons, and waiting rooms. The birth of Jim Crow had to await the 1890s when Northern liberalism, Southern conservatism, and Southern radicalism failed in effectively opposing the "elements of fear, jealousy, proscription, hatred, and fanaticism."[3]

Because his was a pioneer study in an inadequately researched area, Woodward invited further exploration of his thesis. Thus far, two studies of individual Southern states have explicitly tested the "Woodward thesis" for the period between Reconstruction and the turn of the century. Both Charles E. Wynes in *Race Relations in Virginia, 1870-1902* (1961) and Frenise A. Logan in *The Negro in North Carolina, 1876-1894* (1964) conclude that the Woodward thesis is essentially sound for those states, although they maintain that the segregation of Negroes in public carriers, waiting rooms, hotels, and restaurants was more effective and pronounced in Virginia and North Carolina than Woodward suggests. The Wynes and Logan studies differ, however, on the coming of Jim Crow. In Virginia, maintains Wynes, the chief impetus to disfranchisement and segregation came from the Conservative and Democratic political leaders. In North Carolina, according to Logan, the ultimate subordination of the Negro reflected the "illiberal spirit of a large majority of the white citizens" of the state.[4]

Two other state studies of the Negro, published before the appearance of *The Strange Career of Jim Crow,* are pertinent to a consideration of the Woodward thesis. In *The Negro in Mississippi, 1865-1901* (1947), Vernon Lane Wharton's evaluation of the post-war era in that state varies markedly from that of Woodward for the South as a whole. According to Wharton the period from 1865 to 1890 was one of "violent flux and change" during which the Negro came "to recognize and to comply with a code . . . stronger than the law," a code which "marked the completion of the transition from slavery to caste as a method of social control." By 1890, and before the advent of Jim Crow legislation, the Negro in Mississippi was "in his place."[5]

Similarly, George B. Tindall in *South Carolina Negroes, 1877-1900* (1952) concludes that the general trend of race relations in South Carolina after 1877 was in a "reactionary direction." Yet he point out that before 1890 Negroes were "freely admitted to theaters, exhibitions, and lectures" and were served at bars and soda fountains in cities like Columbia and Charleston. This did not apply, however, to rural areas and small towns. Nevertheless, as early as the 1880s South Carolina began to abandon the Hampton tradition of tolerance, moderation, and cooperation in a clearly discernible movement toward disfranchisement and segregation. In a word, Wharton and Tindall suggest that Jim Crow legislation largely finalized and legalized what custom and social pressures had earlier effected.[6] Woodward, on the other hand, contends that Jim Crow legislation marked a new departure in Southern race relations.

Up to this point, there has been no systematic effort to test the Woodward thesis for Louisiana between 1877 and 1898.[7] As in the other Southern states the period between

1877 and 1898 in Louisiana was a time of flux and experimentation. That the place of the Negro had not been settled by the 1890s is suggested by the newspapers' habitual use of phrases like "The Negro Question" or "The Negro Problem" to headline comments on race and race relations.[8] One native Louisianian, writing in the *Lafayette Advertiser* early in 1889, observed that the "race Question" was "as far from settlement": as it had been on its "natal day" at Appomattox.[9] The period of flux and change was no golden era for the Negro in Louisiana; he enjoyed neither social nor political equality with whites, and he was subject to violence, discrimination, economic coercion, and political trickery. Nevertheless, he possessed greater political, social, and civil rights before 1898 than at any time thereafter until the 1950s.

Until 1898 Negroes exercised considerable political influence by voting, holding state and local offices, receiving federal and state patronage, and participating in party conventions and councils. The Negro also possessed greater civil rights in this period; he served on juries and often exercised his rights of assembly, speech, and press freely and with considerable effect. While his social movements encountered strong restraints he was subject to fewer restrictions and less discrimination before the enactment of Jim Crow legislation than after.

The degree to which the Negro could exercise his political, social, and civil rights depended upon a wide range of circumstances, as did the degree of discrimination to which he was subjected. Perhaps the most striking aspect of race relations in Louisiana from 1877 to 1898 was the absence of system. There existed no consistent, thorough, and effective system of social control, legal or extralegal, governing relations between the races. The place of the Negro and his relationship to the white man had yet to be carefully defined.

The proportion of Negroes to whites in Louisiana was much greater before 1900 than it is today. Negroes actually outnumbered whites by a small margin. Sixty percent of Louisiana's Negro population lived in the so-called "black belt," the area composed of the alluvial parishes along the Mississippi River. Less than 15 percent lived in New Orleans, and the remaining 25 percent lived in the upland, hill parishes. Negroes substantially outnumbered whites in the alluvial parishes, were themselves greatly out-numbered by whites in New Orleans, and formed less than half of the population in the upland and southwestern prairie parishes.[10]

In general, Negroes in Louisiana occupied a socially and economically depressed position. In 1895 three-fourths of Louisiana's Negro farmers were farming less than fifty acres, as compared to three-tenths of the white farmers, and there were almost three times as many Negro tenant farmers as white. White farm owners outnumbered their Negro counterparts by more than six to one, and the valuation of property owned by whites far exceeded that of property held by Negroes. The same disparity between the races held true in the matter of literacy. As late as 1896 more than two-thirds of the state's Negroes were unable to read or write as compared to approximately one-third of the white population.[11]

A marked exception to the generally depressed condition of Louisiana Negroes was the status of the descendants of the New Orleans "Free People of Color." These Negroes had accumulated substantial propertied interests by 1860, and their wealth, social standing, and education set them apart from most rural Negroes.[12] Nevertheless, in nearly every category of activity—jobs, property holdings, education—Louisiana Negroes generally lagged far behind the average white.

A factor which was a major deterrent to the complete fastening of second-class citizenship on the Negro was his political influence in 1867 when some 83,000 Negroes, as compared to approximately 45,000 whites, qualified to vote under the provisions of the Reconstruction Acts.[13] Republicans and Negroes dominated the state Constitutional Convention of 1868, which produced a constitution guaranteeing Negroes equal political and public rights, including the right to utilize all public places and conveyances on an equal basis with whites. Throughout the Reconstruction period Negroes exercised considerable political power, at times comprising a near majority of the state House of Representatives and holding numerous local and state offices, up to and including the office of governor.[14] Although the number of Negro officeholders declined thereafter, the number of registered Negro voters increased until 1898.

Indeed, the redemption of Louisiana from Radical rule in 1877 brought little change in the politics of Louisiana or in the political status of the Negro. According to historian Garnie W. McGinty, "the most significant factor in the transition from Radical to Redeemer rule was the absence of outstanding change."[15] Contrary to common historical opinion, a basic continuity existed between Radical and Redeemer rule, particularly in the significant role played by the Negro in politics.

One reason for the continuing importance of the Negro in politics was the strength which the Republican party in Louisiana retained until the turn of the century.[16] Despite internal dissension Republicans were able to present a unified front between 1880 and 1892, electing an average of sixteen Republicans to each legislature and winning no less than one-third of the popular vote cast in state gubernatorial elections. Republicans, however, failed to utilize fully their numerical strength because of traditional factionalism within the party. A Pure Radical faction championed the cause of Negro rights while the Liberal Republican faction favored compromise with Southerners in matters of race and consistently opposed any independent display of Negro power within the state party.[17] Negro political strength, already buffeted by persistent Democratic hostility and by threats of violence and economic coercion from whites, was seriously undermined by this division in Republican ranks. By 1894 the Liberal Republican faction had seized control of Republican machinery, and the party now looked to white rather than to Negro support and counsel. But had it not been for the Republican party's influence before 1894, nationally and locally, the Negro might well have been politically and socially ostracized long before 1900.

Despite its image as the Negro party, the Republican party rarely received over 50 percent of the potential Negro vote. In 1880, for example, the Republican candidate for governor received a total of 42,555 votes, yet there were 88,024 registered Negro voters, In 1884 and 1888 the proportion of Negro votes won by Republican candidates was even less.[18] Ironically the party of white supremacy attracted many Negro voters; some were attracted by the Democratic party's paternalistic racial policies, other by the promise of personal gain. Still others succumbed to Democratic coercion and violence. In any event, the Democracy could claim, in the words of the *Gretna Courier,* "'lots' of colored Democratic voters all through the state."[19]

Under the "Ouachita Plan," allegedly devised by Democratic Gov. Samuel D. McEnery (1881-1888), Negroes in the northern alluvial parishes were not allowed to vote, but were carried on the registration rolls and simply counted for the Democratic ticket.[20] In addition, the Negro population was counted in apportioning delegates to the Democratic nominating conventions, thus also giving the alluvial parishes disproportionate strength in choosing the party's candidates. Clearly Louisiana conformed to V. O. Key's conclusion that the black-belt dominated Southern politics.[21]

Despite such limitations upon his exercise of political power, the Negro continued to exert an important influence as an independent factor in Louisiana politics. Until 1890 registered Negro voters outnumbered whites. In 1880 there were 88,024 registered Negro voters as compared to 85,451 white voters; in 1884 the numbers were 105,631 Negro and 100,945 white voters; in 1888 registration lists showed 127,923 Negroes and 126,884 whites; and as late as 1896 Negro voters constituted 44 percent of the total number registered.[22]

A minor politician of St. Landry Parish noted in his reminiscences (1876-1902) that in almost every election "Everybody wanted" the Negro's vote "and everybody was soliciting it."[23] The Negro often capitalized on this situation and won election to state and local office—both as Republican and Democrat. Republican Henry Demas, the remarkable Negro politician from St. John the Baptist Parish, remained in the state senate from 1868-1892 and was a power in the state.[24] A Negro sheriff and deputies served in St. James Parish, in Demas's district, as late as 1896.[25] In an adjoining district the "independent" Negro vote appeared decisive in the election of state Senator Albert A. Batchelor, a Democrat, in 1896.[26] Four years earlier three Negroes had won election to the legislature on the Democratic ticket.[27] In 1894 a Negro won election to the legislature from St. Landry Parish, and three other Negro Republicans won seats in 1896.[28] As late as 1888 Negroes campaigned for state executive offices on the Republican ticket.[29]

Even in the "controlled" Democratic parishes, Democrats made substantial concessions to the Negro. Democrats in East Carroll Parish, a Bourbon stronghold, ran Negro sheriff W. H. Hunter for re-election in 1896.[30] In the adjoining parish of Madison two Negroes were elected to the state legislature on the Democratic ticket in 1886.[31] Democratic governors as a matter of course appointed Negroes to minor public offices, such as parish and state school boards.[32] Negroes sat in Democratic caucuses and conventions and voted in Democratic primaries.[33] In Opelousas Negroes traditionally served on the town Board of Police.[34] In New Orleans a Negro newspaper, the *Progress,* solidly supported the

Democracy. It opposed the "bloody shirt" tactics of the Negro leader Frederick A. Douglass and praised the "peaceful relations between the two races."[35]

As a further reflection of his political influence the Negro in Louisiana continued to receive federal patronage through 1900. For example, Henry Demas received an appointment as naval Officer for the Port of New Orleans in 1898, and in the same year Raeford Blount of Natchitoches declined an appointment as register of the parish land office.[36] Negro Walter L. Cohen held the latter office in New Orleans.[37] Although the Negro was unable to achieve political equality with the white man except in certain parishes, he enjoyed far more political opportunities and influence throughout the state before 1898 than after.

In civil, as in political life, Negroes encountered substantially fewer restraints before the advent of Jim Crow legislation than afterwards. Thus, the Negro did exercise the duty and right to serve on juries.[38] An unidentified Louisianian, replying to charges of Negrophile George Washington Cable, maintained that in Cable's "native city and State the number of colored jurors are one-third in the former and one-half in the latter."[39] Such a conclusion is exaggerated, but evidence indicates that the Negro frequently, but not invariably, sat on juries. He also competed in bidding on state building and work contracts. One Negro contractor noted that he had completed $35,000 worth of state levee work, using "white superintendents and colored superintendents, white laborers and colored laborers, working side by side for the same wages."[40]

The Negro often used his rights of assembly, speech, and press with considerable effect. Sometimes Negroes worked in conjunction with whites to further a cause or reform. In New Orleans in early 1896 mass public meetings of Negroes pledged support to the reform Citizens' League organization.[41] Several years earlier Negroes in Rayville campaigned vigorously with whites for prohibition.[42] The Negro journal, the *New Orleans Daily Crusader,* "attacked unjust laws, denounced the state legislature, flayed the Southern view of white superiority," and defended Negro interests against church, state, and mob injustices.[43] Other Negro newspapers published in New Orleans included the *Weekly Louisiana,* the *Standard,* and the *Progress.*[44] And in New Orleans descendants of the "Free People of Color" organized the *Comité des Citoyens* specifically to protect Negro rights.[45]

Negroes were also active in the organized labor movement. Negro laborers, some of them members of the "integrated" packers union, participated along with whites in the New Orleans general strike of 1892.[46] Other laborers worked through all-Negro unions to win substantial improvements for their race. For example, in the mid-1890s Negro longshoremen, discriminated against since 1885 in wages for jobs, forced the New Orleans Cotton Exchange and shippers to equalize wages and job opportunities for both races.[47] Many white unions all over the country were meeting with considerably less success. In another labor case in 1887 Negro laborers on sugar plantations in South Louisiana struck in protest against the lowering of their wages, although without much success.[48]

Thus, in both the political and civil realm Negroes retained considerable freedom, and many opportunities remained opened to them. By 1876 the Louisiana Negro had become, insofar as state and federal statute could effect it, the civil equal of the white man, and until 1890 no change in race relations occurred that could be measured in terms of statutory law.[49] Nor were there in this period any perceptible changes in race relations engendered by changing social habits or customs.

Nevertheless, from the beginning of Reconstruction until 1898 the Negro was far more circumscribed in the social realm than in the civic. The rather limited evidence available indicates that he was generally segregated in hotels, restaurants, theaters, schools, and libraries.[50] Yet there was social contact between the races, particularly in New Orleans. There Negroes and whites competed against each other in a variety of sports, and Negroes and whites used the same bathhouses, picnic ground, and beaches along Lake Pontchartrain. One "first-class" saloon at Spanish Fort served refreshments to both races, and at the World's Cotton Exposition in New Orleans Negroes and whites frequented a restaurant operated by Negro James Lewis.[51] Clearly the Negro encountered fewer social restraints before 1898 than after. The oft-cited case of the ejection of a white planter and his Negro companion, legislator T. T. Allain, from a fashionable Baton Rouge bar, serves to illustrate further this point.[52] One looks in vain for examples of white men who would even consider socializing with Negroes in polite society after the advent of Jim Crow.

In the field of education racial segregation was the practice long before it was recognized by law. Despite a constitutional provision against racial discrimination, integrated schools had operated only in New Orleans even during Reconstruction.[53] After 1877, when educational opportunities for both races were extremely meager, the Negro school system was even more deficient than the white because of widespread public sentiment opposed to spending much for the education of Negroes.[54] Nevertheless, the walls of segregation were not so firm nor tall as they later came to be. Lines of communication between the races remained more open by virtue of common administrators, white teachers in Negro schools, and the absence of any clearly defined laws maintaining segregation. Seven of the twelve Negro public institutions of higher learning were staffed with white faculties, and one parochial school, Leland University, had a mixed faculty.[55] The first separate Negro institution in Louisiana, Southern University, organized in 1880, allowed qualified white students to attend, although there is no record that any did so. However, many white students enrolled in the law courses at predominantly Negro Straight University in New Orleans.[56]

The first legal provision for separate public schools was made in 1898. No laws required racial segregation in other state institutions until 1900, although women were separated by race in the charity hospitals and the insane asylum by 1884.[57] Separation of the races was less thorough among male inmates of the State Insane Asylum at Jackson. According to the *Baton Rouge Advocate,* here were "thrown together . . . idiots, incurables, old and young, [and] black and white." The *Advocate* noted approvingly, however, that at least the races were separated "as far as possible"; Negro and white inmates ate at different tables and slept in different wards although they were housed in the same building.[58] As late as 1894 charity hospital patients of both races in Shreveport were reported using the same bathrooms.[59]

It was in the area of public transportation that the lack of uniformity in race relations was most clearly evident to observers like George Washington Cable. The treatment accorded to Negroes, wrote Cable, was not uniform in all the Southern states, nor even in all parts of the same state: "In Louisiana certain railway trains and steamboats run side by side, within a mile of one another, where in the trains a Negro or mulatto may sit where he will, and on the boats he must confine himself to a separate quarter called the 'Freedman's bureau.'"[60] On some Louisiana steamers, however, Negro passengers mingled with whites on the deck,[61] and on streetcars Negroes could sit where they wished. The treatment accorded Negroes on the railroads varied greatly. In some instances they rode alongside whites in first-class accommodations and used the same waiting rooms and restrooms.[62] Some degree of integration seems to have been the rule rather than the exception on most Louisiana railroads, and newspapers complained about "the indiscriminate commingling of races in travel."[63] On the other hand, Jim Crow coaches for Negroes had come into general use on many lines by the late 1880s, although Negroes were not forced to use them and whites sometimes rode in them.[64]

Contact between the races also extended into other areas of social life. A number of cases appeared in current newspapers indicating that the social ban on racial intermarriage failed to prevent fully permanent-type marital unions between Negroes and whites[65] In addition, many Negroes continued to practice their religion in association with white.

Most of the 75,000 Negro Catholics in Louisiana continued to go to church with whites, although seating was segregated and sacraments administered to Negroes last. Catholic schools and charitable institutions had long been segregated, but not until 1895 did Archbishop Francis Janssens authorize the establishment of a "national church" for Negroes on an experimental basis. This action, however, provoked opposition from archdiocesan officials, most members of the clergy, and Negro Catholics, and not until 1920 did the Jim Crow church become accepted as the Catholic Church's permanent solution to the racial problem. Although separate churches developed much earlier among Protestant faiths, George Washington Cable observed in 1881 that Negroes sometimes sat in the galleries of white Protestant churches in New Orleans and received the sacraments after whites. Another observer reported seeing in 1885 "a colored clergyman in his surplice, seated in the chancel of the most important white Episcopal Church in New Orleans, assisting the service."[66]

Thus, the Negro held a social and political position before 1890 which, although of a second-class order, kept him from the literal "mudsills" of society and promised his advancement. The loss of this status came through a revolutionary change, effected largely by Jim Crow legislation.

Jim Crow legislation, which in the post-Reconstruction era first appeared in Tennessee in 1881, was not enacted in Louisiana until 1890.[67] In that year a separate car law required railroads to seat Negroes and whites in accommodations which were separate and equal.[68] In 1894 Jim Crowism expanded with the passage of an anti-miscegenation law which had failed to passed in 1880 and in 1888.[69] In 1894 a law was passed requiring separate accommodations in railroad depots.[70]

But the white "counter-revolution" did not climax until the Constitutional Convention in 1898, which disfranchised the Negro through educational and property qualifications. Disfranchisement was the product of two direct political interests: (1) Reform elements wanted to reduce Bourbon power; (2) Bourbons wanted to prevent the reformers from getting the Negro vote, which would be worse than losing that vote. In effect, disfranchisement, aside from its racial implications, was a political compromise. Disfranchisement resulted in a substantial political restructuring in Louisiana. A glance at registration figures will show what happened.

Between 1890 and 1900 the number of registered Negro voters dropped from 127,923 to 5,320.[71] The total number of registered white voters dropped from 126,884 to 125,437.[72] The six alluvial and Democratically controlled parishes of East Carroll, Madison, Tensas, Concordia, Caddo, and Red River now had a total of only 5,453 registered voters, as opposed to the 28,598 which they had in 1896. The Populist parishes which had 27,702 voters registered in 1896 had 16,043 registered in 1900.[73]

The Populist parishes had almost 13,000 fewer voters but now could outvote the alluvial parishes by 3-1 whereas in 1896 the alluvial parishes had been able to outvote them. New Orleans lost about 6,000 votes as a result of the new election laws, but relatively the political strength of New Orleans and the upland hill parishes was substantially increased. Disfranchisement tended to shift power away from the alluvial parishes to the upland, white parishes of North Louisiana, and to the city.[74]

The Bourbons were down but they were not out. They still held advantages because representation in the legislature and in the nominating conventions was based upon total population. The Negro still counted toward Bourbon political strength. Although Louisiana Populists approved Negro disfranchisement in 1898, they angrily denounced his being counted toward representation.

> Verily the 'nigger' is to remain an important factor in Louisiana politics. He is to be disfranchised but his white neighbors will now make use of him in naming candidates of every political party, instead of using them in the election. The black belt can control the policy of every political party in this state and therefore cannot be much interested as to which party wins.[75]

But the fact was that disfranchisement substantially undermined black-belt strength. Simply being able to name party candidates was not an absolute guarantee that they would get the vote. In 1906 even this advantage was lost when the legislature introduced the party primary law and in effect abolished the convention and made nominations contingent upon popular votes. It was this political restructuring in the nineties and in 1906 which made it possible for a governor of Louisiana to come from Winn Parish, and more recently from Caldwell Parish. It also facilitated the rising progressive spirit which brought about dramatic improvements in schools, roads, prisons, levees, and labor and business conditions between 1900 and 1924. Contrary to the view held by William Ivy Hair, V. O. Key, and others, Boubonism failed to emerge triumphant from the 1890s. The fate of the Negro was far worse.[76]

The Constitution of 1898 also established the first legally separated school systems for white and Negroes.[77] Legal and enforced separation, segregation, and subordination did what custom and habit had failed to do. It thoroughly prevented the Negro from sharing in the white man's civilization after 1898.[78]

The rest was mere aftermath. In 1900 laws effected the separation of the races in public institutions, excluding jails.[79] In 1902 a separate street car bill passed the state legislature against the combined protests of the New Orleans press, who regarded the act as economically unfeasible.[80] Finally, in 1918, Jim Crow legislation included even the jails.[81] Jim Crow laws, unlike custom and tradition, did not presume merely to keep the Negro "in his place," but constantly pushed the Negro farther down.

Louisiana Negroes had no effective means of protest. The attitude of many is reflected by that of the stalwart Negro Radical leader, Raeford Blount. Ending a long career of protest and agitation, Blount denied in 1896 that he was "organizing Negroes against whites." "I am an old man," he said, "and desire to pass the remainder of my days in peace and good will to all men."[82] Similarly, some affluent Negroes and the editors of such Negro newspapers as the *Standard* and the *Progress* consistently counseled moderation and caution.[83]

Others protested. Two of the most important Supreme Court cases of the late nineteenth century involving civil rights were initiated by Louisiana Negroes—*Hall v. Decuir* (1878) and *Plessy v. Ferguson* (1896).[84] The Jim Crow car law of 1890 drew sharp criticism from a Negro organization centered in New Orleans, the American Citizens' Equal Rights Association, and from Negro legislators. Other Negroes deliberately violated the law as a form of protest.[85] A special delegation of Negroes formally objected to disfranchisement in the Constitutional Convention of 1898. And in the era of religious conservatism Negro Catholics criticized their archbishop for establishing a Jim Crow church, and they boycotted services. In Henry Demas's district Negroes in 1896 actually, and with some success, sought by force of arms to protect the ballot boxes from Democratic "regulators" who threatened to turn traditionally Republican boxes Democratic.[86]

But the vast majority of Louisiana Negroes were apathetic or inarticulate, or both, and there was never any mass or popular movement among Negroes in opposition to Jim Crowism. Moreover, by 1894, the Negro's one effective instrument of mass resistance, the Republican party, had been usurped by the white man and the Negro had been ousted from party councils.[87]

In the meantime, because of growing factionalism among Democrats, the Negro was becoming an increasingly significant factor in the outcome of elections. Anti-Lottery Democrats, Populists, New Republicans, and Citizens' Leaguers charged that regular Democrats used the Negro vote to forestall popular white rule, but at the same time these "independents" made every effort to capture the Negro vote for themselves.[88] This led the regulars or "Bourbons" to have second thoughts about their chances of retaining Negro support. The possibility that the Negro might contribute to the success of the opposition prompted both "independents" and regular Democrats to advocate Negro disfranchisement.[89] More and more whites came to believe that the "doctrines of Louisiana" should be decided by white, not Negro votes.[90] In 1889, reflecting this popular opinion the *Shreveport Democrat* changed its name to *The Caucasian* and took up the cry that "this government should be controlled by white men."[91]

Another factor which contributed to the advent of Jim Crowism was increasing lawlessness, violence, and corruption. Between 1882 and 1903, 285 known lynchings occurred in Louisiana, most of them after 1890, and every election was marked by corruption and intimidation. Many white Louisianians blamed the Negro for this state of affairs, although a good part of the lawlessness, particularly that involving feuds and duels, had no racial orientation whatsoever; nevertheless, the Negro became the scapegoat for the iniquities of the white man.[92]

It was no accident that violence, corruption, and lawlessness increased in the 1880s and 1890s. Unlike the older generation of the Redeemers, whose youth had been spent in a stable society, the generation reaching its maturity in the eighties and nineties had been schooled in resistance and hostility to law, order, and government. The leaders of the later period had never known a system of race relations as stable as slavery. Thus it is not surprising that George Washington Cable found the moderation of his "Silent South" only in the older generation.[93]

Yet another factor contributing to the stiffening racial attitude in Louisiana was the resurrection of the "bloody shirt" and the threat from pseudo-Radicals in the North of a "force bill" to protect Negro voting rights with federal troops.[94] Just as the debate over the Elections bill alarmed the South, so its defeat convinced Southerners that the friends of the Negro in the North had now deserted him. Moreover, in the South the popular policies of Booker T. Washington seemed conducive to the fastening of a segregated, non-voting status upon the Negro.[95]

Last but not least, the great majority of white Louisianians believed in white supremacy and had never accepted as a means of racial adjustment a life on "terms of equality" with the Negro. Most white believed that the Negro desired social equality and racial intimacy. Consequently, while many white Louisianians expressed a willingness to grant the Negro his legal and political rights," those rights were very reluctantly conceded for fear that they would be used by the Negro to gain social equality. Admittedly there were more tolerant expressions from some whites in Louisiana. In George Washington Cable, Louisiana could boast one of the South's few champions of

Negro rights. Whites in the Pure Radical faction also advocated equalitarianism. In addition, there were articulate Louisianians who would educate and protect the Negro as a freedman, just as they had as a slave, in order to prepare him to exercise his political and civil rights prudently and maturely. Nevertheless, whatever their views, most white Louisianians were "race" conscious.[96]

In light of the foregoing evidence, the Woodward thesis is basically sound for Louisiana between 1877 and 1898. As Charles Wynes points out, Woodward himself qualified his thesis, couching it in moderate and reserved language and disclaiming the existence in the post-Reconstruction era of ideal race relations. Clearly, segregation in Louisiana did not exist before 1898 as a permanent and thorough system of race relations. Clearly the "place" of the Negro in Louisiana had not been fixed before 1890 and before the advent of Jim Crow legislation, as in Mississippi, nor was the general trend of relations between the races after 1877 so decidedly reactionary as in South Carolina. The history of race relations in Louisiana is similar to that of North Carolina in that it is difficult to detect in either state any systematic movement before 1890 to achieve rigid segregation. Moreover, when Jim Crowism came, it came with the approval of a large majority of white citizens of the state, as in North Carolina.

Woodward's suggestion that the movement toward Jim Crowism came earlier to the new states of the old Southwest should be qualified in the case of Louisiana. The "political regression" of Virginia, for instance, was not characteristic of Louisiana, and the Negro retained great political power well into the 1890s. Moreover, segregation in restaurants, bars, waiting rooms, and public places of amusement was probably less general in Louisiana than in the much older Old Dominion.

Just as slavery, according to U. B. Phillips, was primarily designed as a social system to maintain white supremacy, so Jim Crowism was devised to maintain a white man's civilization. But it is likely that the latent, and sometimes overt, racism in Louisiana could not alone have clamped the Negro in a rigid and thoroughgoing caste system. There is little evidence that by 1890 it had. Just as slavery was effected and maintained by legalistic and mechanistic bonds, so Jim Crowism came about because of man-made, rather than natural laws.

Notes for "Race Relations in Louisiana, 1877-98"

[1] Alice Dunbar-Nelson, "People of Color in Louisiana," Part II, *Journal of Negro History,* 2 (1917): 78, quoted in Charles B. Roussève, *The Negro in Louisiana: Aspects of His History and Literature* (New Orleans, 1937), 1.

[2] C. Vann Woodward, *The Strange Career of Jim Crow,* 2nd rev. ed., (New York, 1966), xv-xvi, 13-30, 41-47, 88-91.

[3] Ibid., 13-26, 47-52.

[4] Charles E. Wynes, *Race Relations in Virginia, 1870-1902* (Charlottesville, 1961), 147-48, 150; Frenise A. Logan, *The Negro in North Carolina, 1876-1894* (Chapel Hill, 1964), vii-viii, 215-19.

[5] Vernon L. Wharton, *The Negro in Mississippi, 1865-1890* (Chapel Hill, 1947). 274-76.

[6] George B. Tindall, *South Carolina Negroes, 1877-1900* (Columbia, S. C., 1952), 291-308.

[7] There have been studies of certain aspects of Negro history in post-Reconstruction Louisiana; in addition to those cited hereafter, some of the more useful are P. A. Kunkel, "Modifications in Louisiana Negroes' Legal Status Under Louisiana Constitutions, 1812-1957," *Journal of Negro History,* 44 (1959); Betty Porter, "The History of Negro Education in Louisiana," *Louisiana Historical Quarterly,* 25 (1942); A. B. W. Webb, "A History of Negro Voting in Louisiana, 1877-1906" (Ph.D. dissertation, Louisiana State University, 1962), Millard W. Warren, Jr., "A Study of Racial Views, Attitudes, and Relations in Louisiana, 1877-1902" (M.A. thesis, Louisiana State University, 1965)

[8] See, for example, *Opelousas Courier,* December 29, 1888, June 29, 1889; *New Orleans Times-Democrat,* May 17, 1886.

[9] Unsigned letter in *Lafayette Advertiser,* January 5, 1889

[10] E. W. Hilgard, "Report on the Cotton Production of the State of Louisiana, with a Discussion of the General Agricultural Features of the State," *U. S. Census, 1800,* I, *Report on Cotton Production* (Washington, D. C., 1884), 111-41; see also *U. S. Census, 1900,* I, *Population,* xiv.

[11] Ibid.; *New Orleans Daily Picayune,* October 30, 1895; *U. S. Census, 1900,* V, *Agriculture,* 2-3.

[12] Robert C. Reinders, "The Free Negro in the New Orleans Economy, 1850-1860," *Louisiana History,* 6 (1965): 273-85; *Daily Picayune,* October 30, 1895, January 2, 1896.

[13] John Rose Ficklen, *The History of Reconstruction in Louisiana* (Boston, 1910), 187-93.

[14] Agnes Smith Grosz, "The Political Career of Pinckney Benton Stewart Pinchback," *Louisiana Historical Quarterly,* 27 (1944): 527-612.

[15] Garnie W. McGinty, *Louisiana Redeemed: The Overthrow of Carpet-Bag Rule, 1876-1880* (New Orleans, 1941), 248.

[16] For the continuing significance of Southern Republicanism, see Vincent P. DeSantis, *Republicans Face the Southern Question: The New Departure Years, 1877-1898* (Baltimore, 1959); Dewey W. Granthan, Jr., *The Democratic South* (Athens, Ga., 1963); 1 and Stanley P. Hirshson, *Farewell to the Bloody Shirt: Northern Republicans and the Southern Negro, 1877-1893* (Bloomington, Ind., 1962).

[17] Henry Clay Warmoth, *War, Politics, and Reconstruction: Stormy Days in Louisiana* (New York, 1930), 114-86, 197-201; *Daily Picayune,* March 29, 1892.

[18] *Biennial Reports of the Secretary of State of the State of Louisiana,* 1902 (Baton Rouge, 1902), 552-58.

[19] Quoted in *Opelousas Courier,* February 11, 1888.

[20]Warmoth, *War, Politics and Reconstruction,* 254-59.

[21]V. O. Key, *Southern Politics in State and Nation* (New York, 1949), 5.

[22]*Biennial Reports of the Secretary of State of the State of Louisiana, 1902,* 552-58.

[23]Gilbert L. Dupre, *Political Reminiscences, 1876-1902* ([Baton Rouge], 1917?]), 20, 27, 36, 58, 84-89.

[24]*Lafayette Advertiser,* January 12, 1889; see also *Biennial Reports of the Secretary of State of the State of Louisiana,1868-1900;Official Journals of the House and Senate of Louisiana, 1876-1900.*

[25]*Daily Picayune,* April 22, 24, 28, 1896.

[26]Oliver O. Provosty to Albert A. Batchelor, April 29, 1896, Albert A Batchelor Papers, Department of Archives and Manuscripts, Louisiana State University, Baton Rouge.

[27]*Official Journal of the House of Representatives of the State of Louisiana, 1892* (Baton Rouge, 1892), 3-4.

[28]*Opelousas Courier,* April 4, 1896; *Daily Picayune,* February 22, 27, March 18, April 5, 20, 1896.

[29]Warmoth, *War, Politics, and Reconstruction,* 251.

[30]*Daily Picayune,* December 1, 1895.

[31]*Opelousas Courier,* October 29, 1887.

[32]Ibid., November 26, 1887.

[33]Ibid., October 29, 1887, January 7, 1888.

[34]Ibid., April 5, 12, 1890.

[35]Ibid., March 24, April 14, June 30, 1888.

[36]*Daily Picayune,* January 9, 1898; *Natchitoches Enterprise,* February 2, 1898.

[37]Roussève, *The Negro in Louisiana,* 130.

[38]*Times-Democrat,* September 29, October 15, 1886.

[39]Anonymous "Mr. Cable, 'The Negrophilist'," in Thomas M'Caleb, ed., *The Louisiana Book* (New Orleans, 1894), 203-5.

[40]*Times-Democrat,* December 30, 1888.

[41]*Daily Picayune,* April 3, 1896.

[42]Ibid., September 21, 1894, November 3, 21, 1895.

[43]Roussève, *The Negro in Louisiana,* 157-60.

[44]*Opelousas Courier,* October 8, 1887, March 10, June 30, 1888.

[45]Roussève, *The Negro in Louisiana,* 129-39, 156-59.

[46]C. Vann Woodward, *Origins of the New South, 1877-1913* (Baton Rouge, 1951), 231-32.

[47]*Daily Picayune,* December 16, 18, 20, 21, 1894.

[48]*Opelousas Courier,* November 12, 1887, citing *New Orleans City Item,* undated.

[49]Germaine A. Memelo, "The Development of State Laws Concerning the Negro in Louisiana, 1864-1900" (M. A. thesis, Louisiana State University, 1956), 102, 107.

[50]Roussève, *The Negro in Louisiana,* 128-29; Warmoth, *War, Politics, and Reconstruction* 93; Henry M. Field, *Bright Skies and Dark Shadows* (New York, 1890), 151; George Washington Cable, "The Silent South," in Arlin Turner, ed., *The Negro Question: A Selection of Writings on Civil Rights in the South* (Garden City, N.Y., 1958), 102-8.

[51]An observer at the International Exposition in New Orleans in 1885 noted that Negroes "took their full share of the parade and the honors. Their societies marched with the others, and the races mingled in the grounds in unconscious equality of privileges." Woodward, *The Strange Career of Jim Crow,* 24. Roger A. Fischer, "The Segregation Struggle in Louisiana, 1850-1890" (Ph.D. dissertation, Tulane University, 1967), 175-77, 183; Dorothy Rose Eagleson, "Some Aspects of the Social Life of the New Orleans Negro in the 1880s" (M.A. thesis, Tulane University, 1961), 57, 60, 101-6.

[52]Fischer, "The Segregation Struggle in Louisiana," 176-77.

[53]Memelo, "State Laws Concerning the Negro in Louisiana," 108; Fischer, "The Segregation Struggle in Louisiana," 165-69.

[54]Thomas H. Harris, "The Negro School System, 1916," unpublished manuscript, Thomas H. Harris Papers, Southwestern Archives and Manuscripts, University of Southwestern Louisiana, Lafayette.

[55]*Daily Picayune,* September 29, 1892.

[56]Memelo, "State Laws Concerning the Negro in Louisiana," 110; Eagleson, "The Social Life of the New Orleans Negro," 57-60.

[57]Memelo, "State Laws Concerning the Negro in Louisiana," 112-16.

[58]Quoted in *Opelousas Courier,* April 19, 1890.

[59]Memelo, "State Laws Concerning the Negro in Louisiana," 117.

[60]George Washington Cable, "The Negro Question," in Turner, ed., *The Negro Question,* 129. For a contrary view on the treatment of Negroes on common carriers, see John Webre to R. A. Hitchcock, August 22, 1884, George Washington Cable Papers, Tulane University Archives, New Orleans.

[61]George C. Benham, *A Year of Wreck, A true Story by a Victim* (New Orelans, 1880), 84-86.

[62]George Washington Cable, "My Politics," in Turner, ed., *The Negro Question,* 12, 14-20; *Daily Picayune,* December 16, 1895; *Opelousas Courier,* April 23, May 7, 1892, May 17, 1890.

[63]Clipping from the *New Orleans New Delta,* September 5, 1890, in the Debaillon Family Papers, Southwestern Archives and Manuscripts, Universty of Southwestern Louisiana, Lafayette.

[64]Ibid.

[65]*Times-Democrat,* September 9, 15, 16, 1886; *Daily Picayune,* January 13, 14, 1896.

[66]Dolores Egger, "Jim Crow Comes to Church: The Establishment of Segregated Catholic Parishes in South Louisiana" (M.A. thesis, University of Southwestern Louisiana, 1965), 34-36, 43-45, 54-61; Roussève, *The Negro in Louisiana,* 138-40, 158-59; George Washington Cable, "The Good Samaritan," in Turner, ed., *The Negro Question,* 35-36; Woodward, *The Strange Career of Jim Crow,* 24.

[67]Maurice S. Evans, *Black and White in the Southern States: A Study of the Race Problems in the United States from a South African Point of View* (London, 1915), 140; Woodward, *The Strange Career of Jim Crow,* xv-xvi.

[68]*Acts of Louisiana, 1890,* 5.

[69]*Daily Picayune,* July 28, 1894.

[70]Memelo, "State Laws Concerning the Negro in Louisiana," 137.

[71]Negro registration had risen to 130,344 in 1897.

[72]*Biennial Report of the Secretary of State, 1900-1902,* 552-58.

[73]Ibid., 556-57.

[74]It cannot be substantiated that 25 percent of the white voters were disfranchised by the convention of 1898. It is true that almost 40,000 fewer whites registered in 1900 than in 1896, but they were not disfranchised. The grandfather clause, and another part of section 5, allowed every previous white voter to register if he so desired. See *Proceedings of the Constitutional Convention, 1898,* 142-46, 379; *Senate Journal, 1898,* 33-35; and confirmed by the *Louisiana Popoulist* (Natchitoches, La.), June 3, 1898, August 12, 1898.

[75]*Louisiana Populist,* April 22, 1898.

[76]The view that the nineties produced substantive changes in the political structure and in race relations in Louisiana is not fully in accord with the views of Perry H. Howard, *Political Tendencies in Louisiana, 1812-1952* (Baton Rouge, 1957); Roger Wallace Shugg, *Origins of Class Struggle in Louisiana: A Social History of White Farmers and Laborers During Slavery and After, 1840-1875* (Baton Rouge, 1939); Allan P. Sindler, *Huey Long's Louisiana: State Politics 1920-1952* (Baltimore, 1956); V. O. Key, *Southern Politics in State and Nation;* and William Ivy Hair, "The Agrarian Protest in Louisiana, 1877-1900" (Ph.D. dissertation, Louisiana State University, 1962).

[77]Memelo, "State Laws Concerning Negroes in Louisiana," 112.

[78]The authors are in agreement with C. Vann Woodward that law, while not the whole story, has a special importance in the history of segregation. This is clearly evident in the case of Louisiana. See Woodward, *The Strange Career of Jim Crow*, 2nd rev. ed. (New York, 1966), ix.

[79]Memelo, "State laws Concerning the Negro in Louisiana," 112.

[80]Ibid., 141.

[81]Ibid., 112; Germaine A. Reed, "Race Legislation in Louisiana, 1864-1920," *Louisiana History,* 6 (1965): 379-92.

[82]*Louisiana Populist,* March 13, 1896.

[83]*Opelousas Courier,* October 8, December 3, 1887, March 24, April 14, June 30, 1888.

[84]See Louis H. Pollak, "Emancipation and Law: A Century of Process," in Robert A. Goldwin, ed., *100 Years of Emancipation* (Chicago, 1964), 166-69; *Hall v. Decuir,* 93 *United States Reports* (1978), 485.

[85]Memelo, "State Laws Concerning the Negro in Louisiana," 129-32; *Opelousas Courier,* July 1, 1892; *Lafayette Advertister,* September 12, 1891.

[86]Egger, "Jim Crow Comes to Church," 43-45, 54-61; Roussève, *The Negro in Louisiana,* 138-40, 158-59; *Daily Picayune,* April 23, 1895; *Official Journal of the Proceedings of the Constitutional Convention of the State of Louisiana, Held in New Orleans, Tuesday, February 8, 1898* (New Orleans, 1898), 142-46.

[87]*Lafayette Advertiser,* January 20, 1894; *Daily Picayune,* September 5, 13, 1894; Philip D. Uzee, "The Republican Party in the Louisiana Election of 1896," *Louisiana History,* 2 (1961): 332-44.

[88]Henry C. Dethloff, "The Alliance and the Lottery: Farmers Try For the Sweepstakes," *Louisiana History,* 6 (1965): 141-60; *Opelousas Courier,* December 20, 1890, August 15, 1891, October 27, 1894; *Daily Picayune,* October 20, 1892, May 5, July 21, September 5, 6, 7, 1894, March 13, April 2, 22, 1896.

[89]*Tensas Gazette* (St. Joseph, La.), March 16, June 8, 1894.

[90]See footnote 8.

[91]*Opelousas Courier,* June 22, 1889.

[92]Walter White, *Rope and Faggot: A Biography of Judge Lynch* (New York, 1929), 255; *Daily Picayune,* May 3, 1894.

[93]McGinty, *Louisiana Redeemed,* 245-48; C. Vann Woodward, *Origins of the New South,* 352-53; George Washington Cable, "The Freedman's Case in Equity," in Turner, ed., *The Negro Question,* 61.

[94]*Opelousas Courier,* May 24, November 8, 1890.

[95]Turner, ed., *The Negro Question,* 212; Richard E. Welch, Jr., "The Federal Elections Bill of 1890; Postcripts and Prelude," *Journal of American History,* 52 (1965): 525-26.

[96]*Daily Picayune,* January 15, October 15, 1895; *Opelousas Courier,* March 7, 1891; *Louisiana Populist,* August 24, 31, October 19, 1894, October 25, 1895, February 21, 1896; George Washington Cable, "Freedman's Case in Equity," *Century Magazine,* 29 (1885): 413, 425-18; Charles Gayarré, "Mr. Cable's Freedman's Case in Equity," and Anonymous, "Mr. Cable, 'The Negrophilist'," in M'Caleb, ed., *The Louisiana Book,* 198-202, 203-5; George Washington Cable, *The Negro Question* (New York, 1890), 12, 14-20, 74.

BLACK AND WHITE IN NEW ORLEANS: A STUDY IN URBAN RACE RELATIONS, 1865-1900*

Dale A. Somers**

Cities have played a major role in establishing racial practices in the South since the Civil War, but scholars generally have ignored their importance. In pursuit of the strange and elusive career of Jim Crow, historians either made no distinction between urban and rural racial policies, thereby implying that racial mores varied little between country and city, or they focused on racial segregation in antebellum cities. This approach produced two unfortunate results. It left unanswered the question of the city's influence on race relations in the South after the war, and it resulted in a tendency by some to dismiss the subject with the statement that racial practices established by municipal ordinances and social custom in antebellum cities remained intact after 1865 and provided models for Jim Crow laws passed in all Southern states after 1890.[1] Historians seeking to discredit the notion that formal segregation practices appeared in the South only in the late nineteenth century eagerly accepted this hypothesis without a thorough investigation of postwar Southern cities.[2] An examination of race relations in New Orleans after 1865 suggests that the color line drawn in antebellum cities did not survive as a permanent or inflexible divider of the races. Furthermore, the key to understanding the complexity of racial practices in the postbellum as well as the antebellum South may lie in the region's cities.

A relatively small percentage of nineteenth-century Southerners lived in cities even after 1865 when urbanization accelerated, but urban communities exerted an influence far out of proportion to the number of their inhabitants. Serving as hubs of trade and manufacturing in an agricultural region and as centers of culture and education in a section notorious for its lack of letters, cities offered ethnic, religious, and economic diversity, contrasting sharply with the general homogeneity of the countryside. They were crucibles of change in the seemingly unchanging South and as such exerted an important influence on racial practices especially after emancipation. The large concentration of blacks, the

*First published in the *Journal of Southern History*, 40 (1974): 19-42. Copyright 1974 by the Southern Historical Association. Reprinted by permission of the Managing Editor.

proximity of the two races, and the accessibility of public accommodations and conveyances gave an urgency and immediacy to questions of equal political and civil rights.

In the rural South such conditions did not exist. Racial violence and various forms of agricultural peonage before and after the Civil War kept rural Negroes in a condition of economic and physical subordination and built up well-defined social barriers that prevented challenges to the caste system. Intimidated by the ever-present threat of force, they reluctantly accepted and tried to make the best of a miserable existence. Their spokesman, Booker T. Washington, represented perhaps as well as anyone could the interests of rural blacks. Vocational training and acquiescence in segregation, a program developed out of Washington's experiences in the rural South, offered a realistic alternative to the increased violence that would certainly have accompanied any overt challenge to white supremacy.[3]

City life, on the other hand, blurred social distinctions and undermined the rigid controls of the South's paternalistic, agrarian society by fostering a spirit of tolerance which, however grudgingly yielded, seldom appeared in the rural South. Although municipal ordinances created a system of racial segregation in antebellum cities, frequent violations indicated a flexibility which plantation slavery and, later, agricultural peonage and Jim Crow laws lacked. Urban and rural white Southerners usually shared a belief in Anglo-Saxon superiority, but since urban whites were less inclined to insist upon complete Negro subordination, blacks in Southern cities enjoyed a freedom of movement and association unknown in the countryside.

New Orleans, the metropolis of the lower South, provides an excellent example of this pattern of race relations. A thriving port city whose resilient economy recovered quickly from the war, New Orleans' multiracial and polyglot population mix dated back to the early eighteenth century. In the nineteenth century its residents included large numbers of blacks and mulattos, thousands of foreign-born, migrants from all over the rural and urban South, and a fair sprinkling of Northerners. Between 1860 and 1870, while the white population declined from 144,601 to 140,923, blacks more than doubled in numbers, from 24,074 to 50,456. This Negro infusion, which began when the city fell to Federal forces in 1862, brought increasing pressure for housing and jobs, exacerbating tensions of the Reconstruction period. Although the rate of the black increase declined after 1870, it never fell below 11.9 percent in any decade before 1900. By the turn of the century 77,714 blacks accounted for 27.1 percent of the city's population of 287,104. The presence of this proportionately large black enclave in the midst of the white population produced racial tensions. However, the city's tradition of polyglot living helped create a façade of racial harmony that enabled blacks and whites to reside in the same community with a minimum of friction, although fear, distrust, and hatred existed, and periodic outbursts of hostility and violence occurred. Nevertheless, for nearly a quarter of a century after the Civil War white New Orleanians only infrequently displayed the extreme virulence that characterized racist thought and action after 1890.[4]

This essay, in focusing on two major aspects of postbellum New Orleans race relations—black protest and the wavering color line—seeks to establish that, whatever the case in the rural South, racial policies and attitudes in this key Southern city remained far from rigid before the 1890s.

New Orleans Negroes began their struggle for equal rights when the city surrendered to the Union in 1862 and continued their crusade until repressive policies at the end of the century left them powerless. Leadership fell mainly to the city's freeborn Negroes, sometimes referred to as colored Creoles, a talented, educated, and well-to-do group that included merchants, men of property, lawyers, doctors, journalists, musicians, and artists, and skilled workmen. In the antebellum period their style of life had set the pace for the entire black community, whose behavior towards whites, in the words of one scholar, "was singularly free of that deference and circumspection which might have been expected in a slave community."[5] On several occasions they challenged the color line in antebellum New Orleans,[6] but these episodes were merely preludes to the massive assault of racial barriers after the Civil War. Although white Republicans, mostly Northern-born, supported the movement, Louisiana blacks clearly had capable, native-born leaders of their own. Whatever the case in other Southern states, the demand for legal equality in New Orleans and Louisiana was not an imported product.

Blacks began their drive for full legal equality against severe opposition. For several years after the war the color line drawn in the antebellum period remained basically intact. Negroes possessed no political rights; black and white children attended separate schools; common carriers assigned black passengers to special cars; black theater and opera patrons occupied galleries set aside for them; and hotels, restaurants, and saloons generally denied service to blacks.[7] Believing that Negroes no less than whites deserved all the rights that usually accompanied citizenship, blacks endorsed civil rights legislation, "not so much because we specially coveted the privilege of attending theaters and operas and saloons," said a black newspaper, "not even because we desired the still more important privilege of freely using public conveyances and hotels" but rather because "under the present order of things, our *manhood is sacrificed.* The broad stamp of inferiority is put on us." Another newspaper, the *Louisianian,* echoed this theme in language which made it evident that Sambo was dead if indeed he had ever lived in New Orleans:

> A condition of bondage, making one race dependent upon the will of another for not only the necessities but even the amenities of life, is well-calculated to make the subordinated people servile—but our white friends over-rate the demoralizing influence of our servitude, when they suppose that we attach such value to their personal intimacy, as will make us seek it, by either improper legislation or a personal humiliation. We are not slaves now, and have no slavish instincts. With our freedom, came back our self-respect and largely to meet the social wants of our own people, do we seek the legislation which, by giving us equal prerogatives as citizens, and removing the reproach, that customs springing out of a dead civilization have imposed upon us, will enable us to grow as a race in all the true, good and beautiful things that adorn a people.[8]

Blacks in postwar New Orleans moved toward equality in stages, seeking first to win basic political rights, especially the vote.[9] Once that victory appeared secure, they began emphasizing the right of equal access to all public facilities. The quest for full citizenship made little progress until Radical Republicans cleared the way for Congressional Reconstruction in March 1867. Blacks then moved rapidly toward legal equality. The Louisiana Constitution of 1868, written by black and white Radicals, granted full rights to all citizens, including the vote, prohibited segregation in public schools, and opened public facilities "to the accommodation and patronage of all persons, without distinction or discrimination on account of race or color." Before the end of Reconstruction several legislative enactments supplemented constitutional guarantees. By 1867 various public-accommodations acts outlawed discrimination on all common carriers and by businesses and other places of public resort licensed by state or municipal authorities. By 1870 bills had been passed establishing racially integrated public schools throughout the state. Between 1868 and 1876 legislators outlawed discrimination in other state institutions as well and legalized interracial marriages. Federal action, including the Fourteenth and Fifteenth amendments and the Civil Rights Act of 1875, reinforced state measures.[10]

Black New Orleanians soon found that the quest for equality involved more than the passage of legislation. Some racial barriers still remained untouched. Yet the achievements of the Reconstruction period stand out in brilliant contrast to the Jim Crow policies implemented after 1890. In 1867, after several years of sporadic complaints, a sustained protest against racial discrimination on the streetcars brought an end to segregation. Despite complaints like the *Picayune*'s, that integration of public conveyances was "simply the introductory step to more radical innovations, which must materially alter our whole social fabric," the streetcars remained legally integrated until 1902.[11] Public schools also yielded to pressures for racial justice. By January 1871, a little more than two years after the Constitution of 1868 called for mixed schools, black children entered several of New Orleans's formerly white institutions. Before this experiment in duochromatic education ended in 1877, a third of the city's schools opened their doors to both black and white youngsters. White students at first objected to the practice, reported the state superintendent of education, but soon "the children of both races who, on the school question, seemed like deadly enemies, were, many of them, joined in a circle, playing on the green, under the shade of the wide-spreading live oak." Opposition continued as long as the schools remained integrated, but according to a careful student of the subject, white resistance "was fruitless, sporadic, separated by long period of tacit acceptance, and successful in the end only because Reconstruction itself failed."[12]

Other public facilities proved more impervious to black demands for equal treatment. White-owned theaters, hotels, restaurants, railways, steamboats, saloons, and other accommodations assigned black customers to separate sections or refused service altogether. If "we venture into a theater or an opera house," said a black journalist in February 1869, "we are seized by the officers of *justice*, and rudely hustled out amid the jeers of the vulgar." This situation changed little despite constitutional and legal guarantees. Whites remained determined to resist racial integration, and relatively few blacks took up the challenge.[13]

Despite white intransigence, the enactment of civil rights laws encouraged some New Orleans blacks to test their legal privileges. Negroes [*sic*] on several occasions during Recon-struction attempted to enter white saloons, coffeehouses, theaters, railroads, and other public facilities. The reception varied, but nearly every case involved open hostility.[14] Proprietors of coffeehouses and saloons either turned them away or served unpalatable drinks. In one Canal Street saloon when blacks complained about distasteful beverages, white customers threw them out. "The irate negroes," said a *Picayune* reporter, "concluded evidently that this sort of treatment was more than they had bargained for, and hurriedly left the scene foiled and disappointed. Next."[15] Theater audiences reacted only a little less intemperately. When two Negro politicians took seats in the dress circle at the St. Charles Theater, white patrons withdrew from the area, leaving the blacks "in the quiet enjoyment of the entire wing . . . during the whole performance."[16] Surprisingly, during Reconstruction black residents of New Orleans actually lost the right to attend some places of amusement on an equal basis. In April 1871, probably to demonstrate opposition to Radical civil rights policies, racial segregation began for horse-racing fans at the Metairie Racecourse, a gathering place for the city's social elite. "For the first time," announced the *Louisianian,* "there has been erected a separate stand on the ground, to prevent the mingling of whey faces, and *sang melées. . . .* The managers of the [Metairie] course have pandered to the ignoble passions and prejudices of those who possess no other claim to superiority, than the external shading of a skin." The editor urged the "many well to do men of our race . . . , [who] annually spend money liberally at the course," to boycott all institutions" which take your money, and give the value of it to others." Economic pressure evidently brought satisfaction elsewhere if not at the Metairie Course. The Louisiana Jockey Club admitted Negroes to the public stand at the Fair Grounds Course in 1874 while barring them from the quarter stretch, a stand at the finish line.[17] The French Opera House, which once admitted Negroes to all parts of the theater without discrimination, also curtailed Negro rights in the winter season of 1874-1875, allegedly in response to "the clamor of the White League and its foolish prejudices." The loss "of many thousands of dollars" resulting from the exclusion of this "wealthy and appreciative class" of black patrons had little effect on the opera's managers. Although stars of the French Opera House subsequently appeared for a benefit performance at Economy Hall sponsored by "our cultured and refined colored citizens," this concession failed to dispel the rage of the Negro press.[18]

Seeking legal redress from such practices brought little satisfaction. Of several suits brought in state and federal courts to win protection of their civil rights only one produced a favorable ruling. In January 1871, C. S. Sauvinet, black civil sheriff of Orleans Parish, charged the proprietor of the Bank Saloon on Royal Street with violating his rights under the Louisiana constitution and the state's Civil Rights Act of 1869 by refusing service. Republican Judge Henry C. Dibble of the Eighth District Court of Orleans Parish agreed with Sauvinet and awarded exemplary damages of a thousand dollars.[19] Another case involving the law of 1869 ended less happily. When Mrs. Josephine DeCuir initiated a suit against an upriver New Orleans steamboat that barred her from "the cabin specially set apart for white persons," the Eighth District Court and the Louisiana Supreme Court ruled in her favor. The Supreme Court of the United States reversed the decision on the ground that Louisiana had no power to regulate common carriers engaged in interstate commerce. Although the Louisiana law still applied to common carriers operating within the state, the Supreme Court had begun the legal journey toward the *Civil Rights Cases* of 1883, in which it ruled that Congress lacked the power to prohibit discrimination by individuals. Next, the Court permitted states to require interstate railroads to furnish separate accommodations for black passengers; and finally, in *Plessy* v. *Ferguson*, the Court formally endorsed "separate but equal" facilities.[20] For black residents of New Orleans, *Hall* v. *DeCuir* (1878) as well as the withdrawal of federal troops in 1877 signaled the end of Reconstruction.

With the collapse of the state's Reconstruction government, the adoption of the Redeemer constitution in 1879 (which repealed the equal-rights provisions of the Constitution of 1868), and the handing down of various unfavorable decisions by the United States Supreme Court, Negroes were left with few legal or political weapons, but they continued to press for the creation of a society based on the free exercise of all rights by every citizen. While many despaired of persuading whites to accept this principle, others remained optimistic throughout the 1880s. And indeed, some modest accomplishments followed.[21] Renewed efforts to win equal rights in public facilities or simply to preserve the gains already made yielded varying results. Streetcars continued to serve both races without separation, and railroads grudgingly granted equal accommodations. When black passengers on an excursion to Mobile in May 1880 were assigned special cars, the practice apparently lacked the rigidity that racial segregation on railroads later assumed, for the *Louisianian* noted that: "Of course decent colored people will leave these special cars alone." The implication that Negroes could sit where they chose was confirmed by an *Atlantic Monthly* reporter who traveled through the South in 1882. Throughout most of the 1880s New Orleans Negroes evidently rode in first-class cars if they wished to do so. Similarly, when the Louisville and Nashville Railroad attempted in 1882 to provide a separate waiting room for blacks in its new depot the *Louisianian* complained until the local superintendent explained "that it was not the intention of the R. R. Company, in affixing the obnoxious sign to make it obligatory upon colored persons as a class to use exclusively the apartment thus designated. As a proof of the fact the sign—'Colored People's Sitting Room' has been removed."[22]

Blacks also succeeded in weakening the color line at such Lake Pontchartrain resorts at Spanish Fort and New Lake End. "The most respected colored citizens of our community are deprived of the pleasures and benefits of these resorts by the glaring insults offered them, by bluntly refusing to accommodate them to refreshments in common with others," the *Louisianian* angrily declared, "while the most despicable, or depraved white man or woman, can enjoy the hospitalities as bountifully as our most respected white citizens." By June 1880 such complaints brought temporary relief. The *Louisianian*'s "warning relative to the ostracism of colored people at Spanish Fort" had been heeded. "Mr. J. A. Brett has opened a fine saloon and restaurant, called the 'Sea Breeze,' where all can be entertained in first-class style, without distinction of color. The bath houses and picnic grounds are delightful and convenient for pleasure seekers. Mr. Brett should be liberally patronized." The following summer racial segregation returned to Spanish Fort bars and restaurants. However, "upon the cars, in the gardens, and along the walks," reported the *Louisianian,* "there is no distinction whatever."[23]

While qualified access to some public facilities and conveyances was possible, insurmountable barriers arose in others. Public school officials abandoned integrated education soon after the end of Reconstruction. Hotels and restaurants generally denied service to blacks, inspiring Negroes to open the Planter's House on Baronne Street, which, a black journalist observed, filled a genuine need for top-quality hotel service. Nevertheless, "colored travelers, opera, minstrel, other troupes and excursionists are often in the papers with a tale of grievances about the hardships of travel because of caste distinctions by which they are kept out of the first-class hotels and public comforts." Theaters, steamboats, and other facilities admitted blacks but assigned them to separate sections. As George Washington Cable observed in the mid-1880s, "the adherent of the old régime stands in the way of every public privilege and place—steamer landing, railway platform, theater, concert-hall, art display, public library, public school, courthouse, church, everything—flourishing the hot branding-iron of ignominious distinctions." Blacks protested to no avail. "The color line in the theaters here is an outrage on civilization and a serious loss to lessees," the *Louisianian* complained in January 1881, but segregation continued. Even "a person having a few drops of African blood in his veins, no matter how white he may be is considered a nigger and has to be cooped in the cockloft of a theater or stay at home," a Negro wrote anonymously to Cable in February 1877. "I think that man has a right to choose for himself, weather [*sic*] he will be a white man or a nigger. So it is, the moral suffering of a man having a little negro [*sic*] blood in his veins is something terrible—for he is always in hot water."[24]

The persistence of racial discrimination in many public facilities was an important gauge of racial sentiment, but it tells only part of the story of race relations in New Orleans in the late nineteenth century. During this period many ordinary citizens, black and white, ignored or paid scant attention to the issues raised by the civil rights crusade and instead formulated personal codes of racial conduct, flexible codes based not on laws and abstract rights but on day-to-day needs and demands. Toward the end of the century these individual racial practices lost much of their flexibility as more and more whites demanded racial segregation. But for at least two decades after the war many residents from the rank and file of both races played and worked together on amicable, harmonious, even equalitarian terms.

The relations between black and white workers, bitter competitors in antebellum New Orleans, provided an especially significant indication of racial cooperation. Forgetting the struggles that had once divided them, laborers of both races collaborated regularly after the Civil War. In December 1865 the longshoremen struck for higher wages. According to May Hugh Kennedy, "They marched up the levee in a long procession, white and black together. I gave orders that they should not be interfered with as long as their interfered with nobody else; but when they undertook by force to prevent other laborers from working, the police promptly put a stop to their proceedings." Several years later waterfront workers tried to eliminate interracial competition by organizing affiliated unions to equalize wages and divide jobs. Following the pattern set by whites, who organized Screwmen's Benevolent Association Number One in 1850, blacks in 1870 founded Screwmen's Benevolent Association Number Two. Other Negroes formed the Longshoremen's Protective Union in 1872, which divided jobs with white dock workers. Before further action could be taken, the Panic of 1873 temporarily arrested this spirit of cooperation, and the ensuing lean years brought renewed bitter competition between the races. Merchants and shipowners exploited the situation and exacerbated racial tension by hiring black workers as strikebreakers and paying them starvation wages. A riot occurred in the midst of the depression when black longshoremen attempted to drive whites from the levee.[25]

Cooperation resumed with the return of prosperity and continued until the 1890s. Periodically, employers attempted to exploit racial hostility, but the recognition of common economic problems encouraged both races to work together. Negro and white longshoremen and screwmen continued their arrangements for sharing work on the docks, and in 1880 black workers founded Cotton Yardmen's Association Number Two to divided jobs with Cotton Yardmen's Association Number One, a white group formed in 1879. Some unions, such as the Teamsters, enlisted members of both races. In 1881, led by the Typographical Union, New Orleans labor formed the Central Trades and Labor Assembly, which by 1883 embraced more than thirty black and white organizations with fifteen thousand members. Its vice-president the following year was a Negro. According to a nineteenth-century labor historian, who was also a former abolitionist, "The formation of this association of trades and labor unions . . . [helped] break the color line in New Orleans [more] than any other thing . . . since the emancipation of the slaves; and to-day the white and colored laborers of that city are as fraternal in their relations as they are in any part of the country. . . ." Whether the Central Trades and Labor Assembly had such a far-reaching effect may be debated, but it certainly contributed to interracial cooperation among the city's workers. The Knights of Labor, which admitted all workers regardless of race, recruited actively in New Orleans in the mid-1880s and on occasion conducted strikes in which Negroes and whites participated. In the summer of 1881 dockworkers "banded themselves together, white and colored, to conduct a strike for higher wages and other demands." When police killed a black striker, two thousand union men of both races marched in the funeral procession, a display of racial harmony and solidarity which the *Loiuisianian* regarded as "a source of satisfaction." Four years later several white unions joined a sympathy strike to help Negro draymen win union recognition. The most notable example of interracial cooperation was the general strike of 1892, which involved twenty thousand men and was, in the words of one scholar, "The first general strike in American history to enlist both skilled and unskilled labor, black and white, and to paralyze the life of a great city. . . ." According to Roger Wallace Shugg, a meticulous student of the subject, "trades unionism in New Orleans was remarkable not only for its early origin, strength, persistence, and rapid development after the Civil War, but also for its racial accommodations. . . ."[26]

Casual contact between the races, particularly in leisure-time activities, furnished additional evidence of harmony. In the antebellum period blacks and whites occasionally met socially in the relative privacy of grogshops, gambling dens, and Negro dance halls, but mainly on white terms.[27] After 1865 the number of activities involving both blacks and whites increased, and a new openness and objectivity in reporting interracial events appeared. During the celebration of Mardi Gras, said the *Louisianian* in February 1871, "every shade of complexion, natural, political and Religious, all mixed in one indiscriminate procession and paraded New Orleans from early morn till long after the shades of night had closed over us." Freedom also gave Negro musicians opportunities to play in places formerly closed to them. In August 1865 the *Tribune* announced that black musicians would perform at the white Orleans Theater and play several musical pieces, including a "great symphony" composed by "our well-known fellow citizens" Edmond Dédé, which had been "enthusiastically received on the French stage." Negroes subsequently performed in other facilities formerly closed to them, such as Lyceum Hall, Mechanics' Institute, and Masonic Hall, but usually before racially segregated audiences.[28]

While New Orleans residents listened to black musicians in segregated halls, they often came into direct contact in other leisure activities. From the World's Industrial and Cotton Centennial Exposition, held in New Orleans in 1884 and 1885, reports indicated strongly that as late as the mid-1880s the color line had not yet become rigid and inviolable in the Crescent City. Blanch Kelso Bruce, chief commissioner of the colored people's exhibit, told a Washington audience that "there is no color line, and that is a great feature of the Exposition. The colored people are treated like the whites, and there certainly can be no complaint that discrimination is shown." James Lewis opened the Experimental Restaurant at the exposition to ensure that "the colored visitors here were certain of accommodations . . . but everybody eats there now regardless of color." On Louisiana Day the Reverend Aristides Elphonso Peter Albert, a Negro, told exposition visitors that the condition of blacks had steadily improved since emancipation. "Louisiana leads the Southern rank of States in the recognition of the right to 'life, liberty and the pursuit of happiness.'" Charles Dudley Warner, who visited the fair the same day, reported that "white and colored people mingled freely, talking and looking at what was of common interest. . . . On 'Louisiana Day' . . . the colored citizens took their full share of the parade and the honors. Their societies marched with the others, and the races mingled on the ground in unconscious equality of privileges." Similarly, when black residents held a Colored State Fair in November 1887 with the aim of "turning the attention of the public to the many and varied improvements made by the Negro in the last two decades," the *Pelican,* a Negro newspaper which had begun publication the previous December, reported that "immense crowds gather, both white and colored, to do honor to the occasion."[29]

Blacks and whites also cavorted together in less respectable amusements, often gambling and drinking together in the same saloons. White and black prostitutes served an interracial clientele, sometimes in the same brothels. A local tabloid observed a "surprising amount of co-habitation of white men with Negro women." Another paper complained a short time later that "white girls becoming enamored of Negroes is becoming rather too common." According to one writer the city in 1890 also had a house of assignation which kept boys for male degenerates. "Balls were frequently given at the house, to which both white and Negro men were invited."[30]

Sporting events, perhaps more than other pastimes, provided opportunities for residents to lower racial barriers. Black and white sports enthusiasts generally pursued their pastimes separately, but on many occasions after the Civil War they joined in common pursuits. Crowds and handlers at cockfights and dogfights, both popular activities in New Orleans until the Society for the Prevention of Cruelty to Animals attacked them, included men of both races.[31] Horses at local racecourses ran under black and white jockeys, who competed without providing racial antagonism. "The darkies and whites mingle fraternally together," reported the *New Orleans Times* in December 1873, "charmed into mutual happy sympathies by the inspiring influence of horse talk." The city's outstanding jockey during Reconstruction, a former slave named Abe Hawkins, rode on tracks throughout the country. Black jockeys continued to ride on local tracks in the 1880s and 1890s and often dominated the winner's circle. Negroes gained the right to attend races on equal footing with whites in the 1880s after professional sportsmen assumed control of local racing from the city's socially exclusive jockey clubs.[32] Negro and white baseball teams played frequently during and after Reconstruction, often before mixed crowds. When the black Pinchbacks defeated a white nine in May 1887 the *Pelican* reported that "The playing of the colored club was far above the average . . . and elicited hearty and generous applause from the large crowd in attendance, which was about evenly divided between white and colored." Another example of the camaraderie obtaining among ballplayers was a game played between two black teams in February 1878 for the benefit of William F. Tracy, a white sportsman.[33] Blacks and whites also met in the prize ring, battling each other before mixed audiences throughout the 1880s. In June 1884, for example, a fight between "two colored sluggers," one of them seconded by a white man, attracted a crowd described as "a strange mixture, every element being represented." A few days later a "very orderly [crowd] . . . mainly composed of a good class of people," watched a mulatto defeat a white fighter. The *Picayune,* later a staunch opponent of mixed bouts, reported that the winner was "very clever with his hands."[34]

Although race relations in New Orleans began to deteriorate rapidly between the late 1880s and the turn of the century, it is perhaps remarkable that blacks and whites lived in relative harmony for so long after the war. Certainly, most of the explanation lies in New Orleans's urban setting. Racial tranquility prevailed primarily because the urban environment gave New Orleans blacks opportunities unavailable to Louisiana's rural Negroes. Urban blacks could safely refuse to acquiesce in a social system that denied political and civil equality. In this urban setting effective Negro leadership could develop. Although handicapped at times by divisive tendencies within the black society, Negro leadership played a decisive role in retarding the progress of racial discrimination. While the city's freeborn Negroes failed to create a permanent alliance with freedmen and other blacks in the rest of the state,[35] an active Negro press and the talented, often well-to-do black community, drawing on an antebellum tradition of resistance to encroaching subservience, could seek to restrain the tide of racism through the use of organized protests, legal action, and the ballot box. Furthermore, in an urban environment many black and white residents, mainly from the lower ranks of society, were willing to engage in some formal and a number of casual and amicable interracial activities especially during leisure hours. Although the color line never broke down completely in postwar New Orleans, blacks and white between the late 1860s and 1880s sometimes came together under circumstances suggesting that racial prejudice was not part of the "immutable folkways" of the South.

The conventional explanation that whites hesitated to deprive blacks of their rights as long as the threat of federal intervention existed is also important and is particularly applicable to race relations in an urban setting. During Reconstruction federal laws and policies absolutely prevented whites from creating a legal color line, and after Reconstruction Southern white politicians were reluctant to invite a return to federal control by depriving blacks of their political and civil rights. When the Redeemers took office in Louisiana in 1877 the state senate promised "acceptance in good faith of the Thirteenth, Fourteenth, and Fifteenth amendments, equal protection of the laws and education for black and white, the promotion of kindly feeling between the two races . . . ." Although Gov. Francis T. Nicholls and his Bourbon successors quietly encouraged the local officials and private citizens who separated the races in schools, hospitals, and other public institutions and facilities, they refrained from passing discriminatory legislation until the 1890s, when it became clear that the federal government and the courts had abandoned the civil rights movement.[36]

While federal power checked the impulses of many New Orleans white until the late 1880s, black ballots also offered a formidable obstacle to racial segregation. During Reconstruction black suffrage protected by federal troops enabled Negroes to demand and sometimes to exercise equal rights in the use of public institutions. Black voting strength also accounted for the willingness of some whites to acquiesce in civil rights. Louisiana's black majority kept the Republicans in power and seemingly held the balance in any attempt to drive them from office. Accordingly, in 1873 white business and professional leaders in New Orleans approached black spokesmen with an offer to form a new party pledged to full support of black voting and officeholding, racially integrated schools, and equal access to public accommodations and conveyances. If whites could win the Negro vote by such a ploy, they hoped to replace what they regarded as a corrupt and unstable government with an honest and tranquil administration. To that end they were willing to grant blacks full political and civil rights. "I am not afraid that they will in any considerable degree, abuse their privileges," one businessman remarked, "and, for ourselves, we want nothing but peaceful government." This plan, known as the Unification Movement, failed, but its existence underscored the power black voters wielded during Reconstruction.[37]

Even after the withdrawal of federal troops in 1877, blacks in New Orleans remained a powerful voting bloc. Although Bourbons in the country parishes systematically counted out or controlled Negro voters, municipal politicians, according to a recent study, actively sought black ballots: "Both the Democratic-Conservative Right and its reformer opposition vied for their votes until Negroes were disfranchised by the state constitutional convention of 1898."[38] Since blacks represented only a fourth of the city's population, they lacked the power to command racial integration in all public facilities, but as the balance of power between reformers and the Ring they avoided complete subordination and on occasion breached the color line during the 1880s.

If federal power, the suffrage, and effective Negro leadership operating in an urban setting delayed full-scale segregation, the color line became increasingly visible and rigid after the late 1880s, primarily because a majority of the whites in New Orleans and elsewhere became committed to white supremacy and a caste system identified with the Southern way of life. By the end of the century racial segregation had become the established policy of the white population; black citizens, deprived of the vote, intimidated by violence, and often betrayed by white allies, had little choice but to submit. Evidence of this change in the city's racial practices abounded. Separation of the races in public institutions and accommodations, widespread throughout the postwar period, became complete toward the end of the century. Railroads in the late 1880s ignored the complaints of Negroes and insisted that black passengers occupy separate cars and waiting rooms. Court appeals, of course, availed nothing. A state law in 1890 requiring separate coaches and another in 1894 ordering separate waiting rooms merely ratified existing conditions, although these practices had become rigid only in the late 1880s. Shortly after the turn of the century a rural legislator from a parish which had no streetcars introduced a bill calling for segregation on public conveyances in New Orleans. White and black residents resisted the law for a time, but in 1902 Jim Crow boarded the city's streetcars. The legislature subsequently passed other acts that either required or encouraged segregation in saloons, circuses and other tent shows, in jails and prisons, and in residential areas.[39]

Interracial cooperation among workingmen also ended in the 1890s. Although earlier competition had periodically exposed signs of racial discord, blacks and white had usually managed to suppress their differences in pursuit of mutual improvement. But the scarcity of jobs and the threat of wage reductions during the depression of the 1890s revived racial animosity and destroyed the amity that had produced interracial collaboration. When British shippers in 1894 tried to violate the job-distribution agreement between the two screwmen's associations by replacing whites with Negroes, violence flared along the waterfront. Rioting, killing, and the burning of cotton sheds and warehouses punctuated the fall and winter months of 1894-1895 before the governor called out troops to restore order and to protect black screwmen. A degree of harmony returned after the depression, but the racial climate of New Orleans and the South prevented a complete resumption of the conditions that had characterized the city's labor movement for nearly thirty years after the war.[40]

While workingmen divided along racial lines, pleasure-seekers also parted company. Municipal authorities in the late 1890s extended the color line to one of the city's best-known leisure activities—prostitution. When the city council created the famous "Storyville" district in 1897, white and black ladies of pleasure could not occupy the same houses, although they might inhabit adjoining buildings. Similarly, whites became increasingly sensitive on the subject of miscegenation. The *Picayune* in February 1887 reported "a vigorous movement" in the state's northern parishes "for the preservation of race purity." The idea, said the *Picayune*, deserved "the attention of the statesman and political philosopher, as well as the moralist." The *Times-Democrat* in 1892 expressed the belief "that the law ought to step in and forever forbid the idea of equality by making marriages between them [blacks and whites] illegal." The same paper later argued that it might be "unpleasant" to sit by Negroes in public places, but "it is more than unpleasant—it is dangerous—to tolerate miscegenation. To do so is to encourage it, and to encourage it is to threaten Louisiana with mulattoism and the social equality of the races." The legislature responded to such logic by prohibiting interracial marriages in 1894 and outlawing concubinage in 1908.[41]

Black and white sports enthusiasts also experienced racial division toward the end of the century. Two white baseball teams, protesting a Negro-white game in July 1885, threatened to ostracize white players who crossed the color line. Any white nine competing with a black team, warned the approving *Picayune*, "will have to brave considerable opposition on the part of the other clubs." Under this threat, other teams gradually restricted themselves to lily-white competition. In the late 1880s the city's professional Southern League team, the Pelicans, played black nines, and the Ben Threads, the "champion amateur white club," engaged in a few contests with the Pinchbacks, the "colored champions," before crowds "composed of the best elements of both colors," but by 1890 interracial competition had ceased.[42]

Bicycling, a highly popular pastime, also suffered from racial hostility. In the summer of 1892, the head of the Louisiana Division of the League of American Wheelmen (L.A.W.) sent his national president a vigorous protest against "forcing obnoxious company upon southern wheelmen" by admitting black cyclists. He threatened to dissolve the state association unless the L.A.W. changed it membership policies. H. E. Raymond, chairman of the league's racing board and "a thorough Northerner," appreciated and shared "the feelings of southern wheelmen on the negro question" but thought it was "more or less unfair to ask us to cut out the negro [*sic*] up here, where he is not so obnoxious and does not rub up against us as frequently as he does in the south." When Southern cyclists began to resign, the L.A.W. responded at its national convention in February 1894 and inserted the word "white" in the section of its constitution outlining qualifications for membership.[43]

Jim Crow also entered the prize ring. When the black featherweight champion George Dixon soundly defeated a white fighter in New Orleans in September 1892 whites concluded that interracial contests must end. Many white fans "winced every time Dixon landed on Skelly," observed a reporter for the *Chicago Tribune*. "the sight was repugnant to some of the men from the South. A darky is all right in his place here, but the idea of sitting quietly by and seeing a colored boy pommel a white lad grates on Southerners." reflecting on the white man's outrage, the *Times-Democrat* declared it "a mistake to match a negro [*sic*] and a white man, a mistake to bring the races together on any terms of equality, even in the prize ring." Such warnings produced the desired result. Most promoters aban-doned interracial bouts, and those who violated the color line did so at their peril. During a fight in 1897 between Joe Green, a Negro, and a white pugilist known as "the Swede," Henry Long, "a loyal Southerner," jumped into the ring and stopped the contest. "The idea of niggers fighting white men," he declared. "Why, if that darned scoundrel would beat that white boy the niggers would never stop gloating over it, and, as it is, we have enough trouble with them."[44]

As the darkening color line established social distance between the races all contact except between master and servant ended. Meanwhile, blacks received constant reminders of their lower station in life. "It is true that the white people of the South do object to contact with the negro [*sic*] upon terms of equality in public places, and it is also true that they do not object to the negro's [*sic*] presence when the negro occupies the position of a servant," the *Picayune* declared in March 1888. "There are differences between the colored man and the white man which neither education nor law can abrogate. . . . To sit by a negro's side at a hotel table or a concert hall would be, in the opinion of the white people, to ignore the truth." A few native whites spoke out against discriminatory practices, but most accepted without question the idea that blacks should occupy a subordinate and servile position. Even in the midst of the Unification Movement few of the city's white residents developed an authentic commitment to the cause of equal rights. Whites supported unification because they wanted stability in government and control of the black vote. Only a few individuals, such as the prominent businessman Isaac N. Marks, expressed genuine hostility to racial discrimination. "It is my determination to continue to battle against these abstract, absurd and stupid prejudices, and to bring to bear the whole force of my character . . . to break them down," Marks declared.[45] It seems doubtful, however, that Marks convinced many other whites of the justice of his views.

In the mid-1880s, when the city produced a more famous and outspoken critic of racial practices in George Washington Cable, few whites ventured support for his position.

As segregation practices increased, any violation of the color line seemed like a threat to the system of racial control. So long as blacks enjoyed equal access to any facilities and associated with whites in some leisure pursuits the social structure would be imperfect. White supremacists demanded the complete and absolute separation of the races in all public institutions and in all activities that encouraged interracial social intercourse. State laws and municipal ordinances accomplished part of the task; unrelenting public pressure and periodic outbursts of violence complete it. After a race riot in the black community of Freetown, Louisiana (near New Iberia), in August 1888, R. C. Hitchcock, white president of Straight University, overheard a white New Orleanian declare that "For the first time since the war we've got the nigger where we want him." The *Times-Democrat* endorsed similar sentiments in September 1892: "We of the South who know the fallacy and danger of race equality, who are opposed to placing the negro [*sic*] on any terms of equality, who have insisted on a separation of the races in church, hotel, car, saloon, and theater . . . are heartily opposed to any arrangement encouraging this equality, which gives negroes [*sic*] false ideas and dangerous beliefs." No one could doubt that the writer spoke for the city's white community.

By the turn of the century blacks in the city knew Jim Crow and racial intimidation as intimately as blacks in the countryside. In 1900 the city experienced a race riot that in effect established the pattern for Negro-white relations for the next half century. For two days in late July, after Robert Charles, a black man, killed two policemen and wounded another, white mobs roamed the city killing and beating blacks. In the midst of the upheaval the *Picayune* observed: "The city has not seen such an utter disregard of the law since the days of 1868 [1866], when the revolution against negro [*sic*] domination occurred, and the streets of the city ran with blood. . . . As it was, there seemed to be no leader, and the mobs moved first one way and then another. The supreme sentiment was to kill negroes [*sic*]." Although such was the tenor of the new era in race relations in the metropolis of the lower South, New Orleans's urban and cosmopolitan environment had for a time, at least, provided a degree of freedom seldom enjoyed by Negroes elsewhere in Louisiana, enabling them to elude temporarily the worst aspects of white supremacy.[46]

Notes for "Black and White in New Orleans:
A Study in Urban Race Relations, 1865-1900"

[**]Mr. Somers was formerly professor of history at Georgia State University. He was unable to finish reworking the article prior to his death on March 27, 1972. Additional revising and editing have been done by Professor Merl E. Reed of Georgia State University with aid and suggestions from Mrs. Sally Ann Somers of Atlanta, Georgia, and William E. Sims of the University of Texas at Austin.

[1]Richard C. Wade, *Slavery in the Cities: The South 1820-1860* (New York, 1964), 266-77; Roger A. Fischer, "Racial Segregation in Antebellum New Orleans," *American Historical Review,* 74 (1969): 926-37. For additional statements by these authors see Wade, "An Agenda for Urban History," in Herbert J. Bass, ed., *The State of American History* (Chicago, 1970), 61; and Fischer, "The Segregation Struggle in Louisiana, 1850-1890" (Ph.D. dissertation, Tulane University, 1967), 24, 190. Most of the important literature on the origins of segregation is discussed by C. Vann Woodward in "The Strange Career of a Historical Controversy, in Woodward, *American Counterpoint: Slavery and Racism in the North-South Dialogue* (Boston and Toronto, 1971), 234-60.

[2]See for example Lawrence J. Friedman, *The White Savage: Racial Fantasies in the Postbellum South* (Englewood Cliffs, N. J., 1970), vi.

[3]Louis R. Harlan, "Booker T. Washington in Biographical Perspective," *American Historical Review,* 75 (1970), 1581-99; see also Harlan, "The Secret Life of Booker T. Washington," *Journal of Southern History,* 37 (1971): 393-416; and Pete Daniel, "Up from Slavery and Down to Peonage: The Alonzo Bailey Case, *Journal of American History,* 57 (1970): 654-70.

[4]Population figures are taken from the published census reports for 1860, 1870, 1880, and 1890, and from U. S. Bureau of the Census, *Negro Population, 1790-1915* (Washington, 1918), 93, 782. The best account of the riot of 1866 is Donald E. Reynolds, "The New Orleans Riot of 1866, Reconsidered," *Louisiana History,* 5 (1964): 2-27.

[5]Joseph G. Tregle, Jr., "Early New Orleans Society: A Reappraisal," *Journal of Southern History,* 18 (1952): 33; see also Donald E. Everett, "Free Persons of Color in New Orleans, 1803-1865" (Ph.D. dissertation, Tulane University, 1952), especially 203-25, for a discussion of the achievements of this anomalous class; and Robert C. Reinders, "The Free Negro in the New Orleans Economy, 1850-1860," *Louisiana History,* 6 (1965): 273-85. Rodolphe L. Desdunes, *Nos hommes et notre histoire . . .* (Montreal, 1911); and Charles B. Rousséve, *The Negro in Louisiana: Aspects of His History and His Literature* (New Orleans, 1937) are also useful.

[6]*New Orleans Argus,* August 1, 1833, quoted in *Niles' Weekly Register,* 554 (August 24, 1833): 423; *New Orleans Daily Crescent,* September 24, 1861, quoted in Everett, "Free Persons of Color," 243-44.

[7]*New Orleans Tribune,* February 4, 1869; Greville J. Chester, *Transatlantic Sketches in the West Indies, South America, Canada, and the United States* (London, 1869), 217-18; George Rose, *The Great Country; or, Impressions of America* (London, 1868), 196; J. E. Hilary Skinner, *After the Storm; or, Jonathan and His Neighbours in 1865-6,* 2 vols. (London, 1866), 2:73, 75, 77; David Macrae, *The Americans at Home: Pen-and-Ink Sketches of American Men, Manners and Institutions,* 2 vols. (Edinburgh, 1870), 2:219.

[8]*Tribune,* February 7, 1869; New Orleans *Louisianian,* March 14, 1874.

[9]For examples of this early emphasis on voting see *Tribune,* July 28, 1864; January 18, 19, 1865; November 25, 1866; see also Donald E. Everett, "Demands of the New Orleans Free Colored Population for Political Equality, 1862-1865," *Louisiana Historical Quarterly,* 38 (1955): 43-64. In writing this essay I have relied heavily on four newspapers published by blacks in New Orleans in this period: *L'Union* (1862-1864), the *Tribune* (1864-1870), the *Louisianian* (1870-1882), and the *Pelican* (1886-1889), but few copies of these papers have survived.

[10]*Constitution Adopted by the State Constitutional Convention of the State of Louisiana, March 7, 1868* (New Orleans, 1868), passim, especially 3-4, 17; Germaine A. Memelo [Reed], "The Development of State Laws Concerning the Negro in Louisiana, 1864-1900" (M.A. thesis, Louisiana State University, 1956), 57-58, 63-67, 72-78, 84-87; Germaine A. Reed, "Race Legislation in Louisiana, 1864-1920," *Louisiana History,* 6 (1965): 382; Fischer, "Segregation Struggle in Louisiana," 25-98.

[11]Roger A. Fischer, "A Pioneer Protest: The New Orleans Street-Car Controversy of 1867," *Journal of Negro History,* 52 (1968): 219-33 (quotation on page 230); August Meier and Elliott Rudwick, "A Strange Chapter in

the Career of Jim Crow," in Meier and Rudwick, eds., *The Making of Black America: Essays in Negro Life and History*, 2 vols. (New York, 1969), 2:14-19.

[12]Louis R. Harlan, "Desegregation in New Orleans Public Schools During Reconstruction," *American Historical Review*, 67 (1962): 603-75; quotations on page 664.

[13]*Tribune*, February 4, 1869; Henry C. Warmoth, *War, Politics and Reconstruction: Stormy Days in Louisiana* (New York, 1930), 92; *Louisianian*, April 14, 1872; Memelo [Reed] "Development of State Laws," 84, 92; Fischer, "Segregation Struggle in Louisiana," 79.

[14]*New Orleans Daily Picayune*, January 28, April 28, 1871; March 6, 10, 18, 23, 1875; *Louisianian*, July 9, 1871; March 3, 1872; *New Orleans Bulletin* October 21, 1875; Fischer, "Segregation Struggle in Louisiana," 90-92.

[15]*Daily Picayune*, March 23, 1875.

[16]Ibid., March 10, 1875; see also ibid., March 11, 1875, for the editorial reaction of the *Picayune* and other local newspapers; and Fisher, "Segregation Struggle in Louisiana," 77, 90-92.

[17]*Louisianian*, April 9, 1871; May 2, 1874.

[18]Ibid., May 15, 1875.

[19]*Daily Picayune*, January 28, 1871; Fischer, "Segregation Struggle in Louisiana," 77-78.

[20]*Hall* v. *DeCuir*, 95 U. S. 485 (1878); *Civil Rights Cases*, 109 U. S. 3 (1883); *Louisville, New Orleans and Texas Railway Company* v. *Mississippi*, 133 U. S. 587 (1890); *Plessy* v. *Ferguson*, 163 U. S. 537 (1896); Memelo [Reed}, "Development of State Laws," 155-75; Millard J. Warren, "A Study of Racial Views, Attitudes, and Relations in Louisiana, 1877-1902" (M.A. thesis, Louisiana State University, 1965), 120; Fischer, "Segregation Struggle in Louisiana," 89, 175-76, see also Rayford W. Logan, *The Betrayal of the Negro from Rutherford B. Hayes to Woodrow Wilson* (New York, 1965), 105-24.

[21]*Louisianian*, May 27, 1882; January 15, 1881; *New Orleans Weekly Pelican*, June 8, 1889.

[22]"Studies in the South," *Atlantic Monthly*, 50 (1882): 626; quotations in the paragraph of the text are from the New Orleans *Louisianian*, May 1, 1880; March 25, 1882; see also *Louisianian*, February 25, March 4, 1882; Charles D. Warner, *Studies in the South and West, with Comments on Canada* (New York, 1889), 13.

[23]Quotations in this paragraph, in the order cited, are from the *Louisianian*, June 18, 1881; June 19, 1880; July 23, 1881; see also ibid., May 1, 1880; June 25, July 30, 1881.

[24]*New Orleans Southwestern Christian Advocate*, March 24, 1887; George W. Cable, *The Silent South, Together with the Freedman's Case in Equity and the Convict Lease System* (New York, 1885), 20; *Louisianian*, January 15, 1881; "Justice" to Cable, February 24, 1887, George Washington Cable Papers (Special Collections, Howard-Tilton Memorial Library, Tulane University, New Orleans, La.).

[25]John T. Trowbridge, *The South: A Tour of Its Battle-Fields and Ruined Cities, a Journey through the Desolated States, and Talks with the People* (Hartford, 1866), 405 (quotation); Roger W. Shugg, *Origins of Class Struggle in Louisiana: A Social History of White Farmers and Laborers During Slavery and After, 1840-1875* ([Baton Rouge], 1939), 301-4; Shugg, "The New Orleans General Strike of 1892," *Louisiana Historical Quarterly*, 21 (1938): 548-50; Joy J. Jackson, *New Orleans in the Gilded Age: Politics and Urban Progress, 1880-1896* ([Baton Rouge], 1969), 227; Arthur R. Pearce, "The Rise and Decline of Labor in New Orleans" (M. A. thesis, Tulane University, 1938), 15-18.

[26]Quotations in this paragraph, in the order cited, are from George E. McNeill, ed., *The Labor Movement: The Problem of To-Day* (Boston and New York, 1887), 158; *Louisianian*, September 17, 1881; Shugg, "New Orleans General Strike," 547, 559; see also the *Daily Picayune*, November 26, 1884; John R. Commons et al., *History of Labour in the United States*, 4 vols. (New York, 1918), 2:310-12; McNeill, ed., *Labor Movement*, 167-68, 611-12; Charles H. Wesley, *Negro Labor in the United States, 1850-1925: A Study in American Economic History* (New York, 1927), 255; Pearce, "Rise and Decline of Labor in New Orleans," 18-37; Shugg, "New Orleans General Strike," 550-59; Jackson, *New Orleans in the Gilded Age*, 223-31; and William Ivy Hair, *Bourbonism and Agrarian Protest: Louisiana Politics, 1877-1900* (Baton Rouge, 1969), 175-77.

[27]Wade, *Slavery in the Cities,* 258-62; Fischer, "Racial Segregation in Ante Bellum New Orleans," 933-35; Henry A. Kmen, *Music in New Orleans: The Formative Years, 1791-1841* (Baton Rouge, 1966), 30, 42-55, 119, 229-30; Everett, "Free Persons of Color in New Orleans," 232-40, 256, 262-66.

[28]*Louisianian,* February 23, 1871; *Tribune,* August 22, 1865; see also *Louisianian,* February 12, 16, May 18, June 18, August 13, October 12, November 12, 1871; November 1, 1879; Everett, "Free Persons of Color in New Orleans," 221-22.

[29]*Daily Picayune,* January 19, 1885; *Southwestern Christian Advocate,* March 26, 1885; Herbert S. Fairall, *The World's Industrial and Cotton Centennial Exposition, New Orleans, 1884-1885* (Iowa City, 1885), 165; Warner, *Studies in the South and West,* 13, 15; *New Orleans Weekly Pelican,* November 12, 19, 1887; Dorothy Rose Eagleson [Henson], "Some Aspects of the Social Life of the New Orleans Negro in the 1880's" (M. A. thesis, Tulane University, 1961), 105-106.

[30]*New Orleans Lantern,* May 22, 1888, and *New Orleans Mascot,* November 30, 1889, quoted in Herbert Asbury, *The French Quarter: An Informal History of the New Orleans Underworld* (New York and London, 1936), 388; see also ibid, 387-93.

[31]*Daily Picayune,* April 28, 1873; December 21, 1874; *Harper's Weekly,* 10 (July 21, 1866): 452; *Every Saturday,* N. S., 3 (July 15, 1871): 68, 70; Mark Twain, *Life on the Mississippi* (New York, 1883), 457.

[32]*New Orleans Times,* April 12, 1866; April 13, December 14, 1873; *Daily Picayune,* December 24, 1871; April 19, 1879; January 22, 1884; January 21, 1885; *New Orleans Daily Crescent,* April 12, 1866; *Wilkes' Spirit of the Times,* 16 (May 11, 1867): 173; *Spirit of the Times,* 117 (March 16, 1889): 289; (March 30, 1889), 382; 125 (April 1, 1893), 418.

[33]*Daily Picayune,* December 12, 21, 1869; February 10, 1878; March 1, 1880; August 29, September 12, 1881; September 18, 1882; May 29, July 20, 1885; May 23, 1887; *New Orleans Times,* December 21, 1869; *New Orleans Bulletin,* June 18, 1876; *Louisianian,* May 7, 1881; *Weekly Pelican,* May 28, 1887.

[34]*Daily Picayune,* June 7, 8, 16, 1884; *Times-Democrat,* August 3, 1890.

[35]Before the Civil War came to an end New Orleans's freeborn Negroes, despite reluctance to identify their interests with the freedmen formed an alliance with rural blacks that lasted through Reconstruction. For material relevant to this alliance see *Tribune,* quoted in Everett, "Demands of the New Orleans Free Colored Population for Political Equality," 55-56; *Tribune* March 5, 1865; Jean-Charles Houzeau, "Le journal noir aux Etats-Unis, de 1863 à 1870," *Revue de Belgique,* 7 (1872): 11-12, quoted in Finnian P. Leavens, "*L'Union* and the *Tribune* and Louisiana Reconstruction" (M. A. thesis, Louisiana State University, 1966), 28; see also *Tribune,* December 27, 1864; January 3, 11, 12, 13, March 18, 1865; Everett, "Demands of the New Orleans Free Colored Population," 55-64; Harlan, "Desegregation in New Orleans Public Schools," 672-75; Meier and Rudwick, "A strange Chapter in the Career of 'Jim Crow,'" 14-19; Shugg, *Origins of Class Struggle in Louisiana,* 243-44; *Louisianian,* April 5, 26, May 10, 1879.

[36]*Nation,* 24 (April 19, 1877): 227; Desdunes, *Nos hommes et notre histoire,* 179-181; Allen J. Going, "The South and the Blair Education Bill," *Mississippi Valley Historical Review,* 44 (1957): 290; Richard E. Welch, Jr., "The Federal Elections Bill of 1890: Postscripts and Prelude," *Journal of American History,* 52 (1965): 511, 525; Dabuek W. Crofts, "The Black Response to the Blair Education Bill," *Journal of Southern History,* 37 (1971): 41-65; Crofts, "The Blair Bill and the Elections Bill: The Congressional Aftermath to Reconstruction" (Ph.D. dissertation, Yale University, 1968), especially 344-55.

[37]T. Harry Williams, "The Louisiana Unification Movement of 1873," *Journal of Southern History,* 11 (1945), 349-69 (quotation on page 354); Williams, *Romance and Realism in Southern Politics* (Athens, Ga., 1961), 17-43; Desdunes, *Nos hommes et notre histoire,* 181-82.

[38]Jackson, *New Orleans in the Gilded Age,* 20; see also Hair, *Bourbonism and Agrarian Protest,* 234-79; Henry C. Dethloff and Robert R. Jones, "Race Relations in Louisiana, 1877-98," *Louisiana History,* 9 (1968): 306-10.

[39]*Weekly Pelican,* July 6, 1889; *New Orleans Daily Crusader,* July 10, 1894. For information regarding the color line in public accommodations see Memelo [Reed], "Development of State Laws," 102-49; Fischer, "Segregation Struggle in Louisiana," 177-90; A. R. Holcombe, "The Separate Street Car Law in New Orleans," *Outlook,* 72 (November 29, 1902): 746-47; Dethloff and Jones, "Race Relations in Louisiana," 315-16.

[40]Pearce, "Rise and Decline of Labor in New Orleans," 31-37; Jackson, *New Orleans in the Gilded Age,* 229-31.

[41]Twenty years after the "Storyville" district was established the city created a separate area for black prostitutes, but before the ordinance took effect the federal government compelled New Orleans to abolish Storyville. *Daily Picayune,* February 10, 1887; *Times-Democrat,* September 8, 1892; *Times-Democrat,* n. d., quoted in *Shreveport Weekly Caucasian,* June 7, 1894, quoted in Memelo [Reed], "Development of State Laws," 123-24; see also Asbury, *French Quarter,* 436, 451-52, 455.

[42]*Daily Picayune,* July 4, 1885; November 5, 1888; July 8, 1889; *Weekly Pelican,* July 6, 13, September 21, 1889.

[43]*Daily Picayune,* August 16, 1892; February 21, 1894.

[44]*Chicago Tribune,* September 7, 1892; *Times-Democrat,* September 8, 1892; *Daily Picayune,* January 25, 1897.

[45]*Daily Picayune,* March 13, 1888, quoted in Eagleson [Henson], "Some Aspects," 103n; *New Orleans Times,* July 23, 1873; quoted in Williams "Louisiana Unification Movement," 362.

[46]Hitchcock to George Washington Cable, September 1, 1888, Cable Papers; *Times-Democrat,* September 8, 1892; *Daily Picayune,* August 17-19, 1888; July 24-30, 1900 (quotation in issue of July 26).

A SELECTIVE LIST FOR FURTHER READING

Baker, Riley E., "Negro Voter Registration in Louisiana, 1879-1964," *Louisiana Studies*, 4 (1965): 332-50.

Bell, Caryn Cossé, *Revolution, Romanticism, and the Afro-Creole Protest Tradition in Louisiana, 1718-1868* (Baton Rouge, 1997).

Bergeron, Arthur, "Free Men of Color in Grey," *Civil War History*, 32 (1986): 247-55.

Berlin, Ira, *Freedom: A Documentary History of Emancipation, 1861-1867: Series 1, Vol. III: The Wartime Genesis of Free Labor: The Lower South* (New York, 1990).

Carleton, Mark T., *Politics and Punishment: A History of the Louisiana State Penal System* (Baton Rouge, 1971).

DeLatte, Carolyn E., "The St. Landry Riot: A Forgotten Incident of Reconstruction Violence," *Louisiana History*, 17 (1976): 41-50.

Everett, Donald Edward, "Demands of the New Orleans Free Colored Population for Political Equality, 1862-1865," *Louisiana Historical Quarterly*, 37 (1955): 43-64.

Haskins, James, *Pickney Benton Stewart Pinchback* (New York, 1973).

Hewitt, Lawrence Lee, *Port Hudson Confederate Bastion on the Mississippi* (Baton Rouge, 1987).

_____, "Incompetence, Disorganization, and Lack of Determination: The Federal Assault on Port Hudson, May 27, 1863," *Gulf Coast Historical Review*, 3 (1987): 63-83.

Hirsch, Arnold and Joseph Logsdon, eds., *Creole New Orleans: Race and Americanization* (Baton Rouge, 1992).

Highsmith, William E., "Some Aspects of Reconstruction in the Heart of Louisiana," *Journal of Southern History*, 13 (1947): 460-91.

Jones, Howard J., "An Analysis of the Deposit Records of the Shreveport, Louisiana Freedman's Bank," *Journal of North Louisiana Historical Association*, 23 (1992): 85-91.

Joshi, Manoi K. and Joseph P. Reidy, "'To Come Forward and Aid in Putting Down This Unholy Rebellion': The Officers of Louisiana's Free Black Native Guard During the Civil War," *Southern Studies*, 21 (1982): 326-47.

Lanza, Michael, "Getting Down to Business: The Public Land Offices in Louisiana During Reconstruction," *Louisiana History*, 29 (1988): 177-82.

McFreely, William, *Yankee Stepfather: General O. O. Howard and the Freedmen* (New York, 1968).

McTigue, Geraldine, "Patterns of Residence: Housing Distribution by Color in Two Louisiana Towns, 1860-1880," *Louisiana Studies*, 15 (1976): 345-88.

Painter, Nell Irvin, *Exodusters: Black Migration to Kansas after Reconstruction* (New York, 1976).

Peoples, Morgan, "'Kansas Fever' in North Louisiana," *Louisiana History*, 9 (1970): 121-36.

Powell, Lawrence N., "Reinventing Tradition: Liberty Place, Historical Memory, and Silk-Stocking Vigilantism in New Orleans Politics," *Slavery and Abolition*, 19 (1998): 127-49.

Rankin, David, "The Impact of the Civil War on Free Color Community of New Orleans," *Perspectives in American History*, 2 (1977-78): 377-416.

Reed, Germaine A., "Race Legislation in Louisiana, 1864-1920," *Louisiana History*, 6 (1965): 379-92.

Reynolds, Donald E., "The New Orleans Riot of 1886: Reconsidered," *Louisiana History*, 5 (1964): 5-27.

Richardson, Joe M., "The American Missionary Association and Blacks on the Gulf Coast during Reconstruction," *Gulf Coast Historical Review*, 4 (1989): 152-61.

Roland, Charles P., "Difficulties of Civil War Sugar Planting in Louisiana," *Louisiana Historical Quarterly*, 38 (1955): 40-62.

Sanson, Jerry P., "White Man's Failure: The Rapides Parish 1874 Election," *Louisiana History*, 31 (1990): 39-58.

Sitterson, Joseph Carlyle, "The Transition from Slave to Free Economy on the William J. Minor Plantation," *Agricultural History*, 17 (1942): 216-24.

Shugg, Roger W., *Origins of Class Struggle in Louisiana: A Social History of White Farmers and Laborers during Slavery and After, 1840-1875* (Baton Rouge, 1939).

Trelease, Allen, *White Terror: The Ku Klux Klan Conspiracy and Southern Reconstruction* (Baton Rouge, 1971).

Tunnell, Ted, "Free Negroes and the Freedmen: Black Politics in New Orleans During the Civil War," *Southern Studies*, 19 (1980): 5-28.

Vandal, Gilles, "Black Violence in Post-Civil War Louisiana," *Journal of Interdisciplinary History*, 25 (1994): 45-64.

Vincent, Charles, *Black Legislators in Louisiana During Reconstruction* (Baton Rouge, 1976).

_____, "Louisiana's Black Legislators and their Efforts to Pass a Blue Law During Reconstruction," *Journal of Black Studies*, 7 (1976): 47-56.

Westwood, Howard, "Benjamin Butler's Enlistment of Black Troops in New Orleans, 1862," *Louisiana History*, 26 (1985): 5-22.

Williams, T. Harry, "The Louisiana Unification Movement of 1873," *Journal of Southern History*, 11 (1945): 349-69.

Winters, John, *The Civil War in Louisiana* (Baton Rouge, 1963).

Wilson, Keith, "Education as a Vehicle of Radical Control: Major General N. P. Banks in Louisiana, 1863-64," *Journal of Negro Education*, 50 (1981): 156-70.

Woodward, C. Vann, *The Strange Career of Jim Crow* (New York, 1955).

_____, *Origins of the New South, 1877-1913* (Baton Rouge, 1951).

Index